Force and Contention in Contemporary China

Why is contemporary China such a politically contentious place? Relying on the memories of the survivors of the worst catastrophe of Maoist rule and documenting the rise of resistance and protest at the grass-roots level, this book explains how the terror, hunger, and loss of the socialist past influences the way in which people in the deep countryside see and resist state power in the reform era up to the present-day repression of the People's Republic of China Central government. Ralph A. Thaxton, Jr. provides us with a worm's-eye view of an "unknown China" – a China that cannot easily or fully be understood through made-in-the-academy theories and frameworks of why and how rural people have engaged in contentious politics. This book is a truly unique and disturbing look at how rural people relate to an authoritarian political system in a country that aspires to become a stable world power.

RALPH A. THAXTON, JR. is Professor of Politics at Brandeis University and a Research Affiliate at the Harvard University John King Fairbank Center for Chinese Studies. He is the author of *Catastrophe and Contention in Rural China* (2008) and the winner of multiple international fellowships, including grants from the National Endowment for the Humanities, the Harry Frank Guggenheim Foundation, the Chiang Ching-kuo Foundation, and the United States Institute for Peace. Professor Thaxton has been a fellow at the Dartmouth College John Sloan Dickey Center for International Understanding and a distinguished Croxton Lecturer in the Amherst College Department of Political Science.

Advance Praise for *Force and Contention in Contemporary China*

"This book is the culmination of a trilogy that will stand as the most important documentary study of rural China under communism. The singular message of this installment is that the reform era, for all its material advance, has done nothing to redress the legitimacy crisis produced by Maoism. Thaxton shows convincingly that China's rural people have never accepted authoritarianism."

Bruce Gilley,
Associate Professor of Political Science,
Director of Graduate Programs in Public Policy,
Portland State University

"This work provides new insight into the mentality and actions of villagers for whom the post-Mao reforms have brought more injustice and hardship. While others have exposed the problems of reform, no other presents so clearly the peasant perspective of when and why things went wrong and who is to blame – often the central rather than just local authorities. Arguing that memories of the Great Leap Forward catastrophe played a powerful role in shaping resistance in the reform period, Ralph Thaxton will surely spark debate about the role of memory in political action and thus advance our understanding of the complexity of the Chinese countryside and the challenges that the CCP faces."

Jean C. Oi,
William Haas Professor in Chinese Politics,
Department of Political Science, and Senior Fellow,
the Freeman Spogli Institute for International Studies,
Stanford University

Cambridge Studies in Contentious Politics

Editors

Mark Beissinger   *Princeton University*
Jack A. Goldstone   *George Mason University*
Michael Hanagan   *Vassar College*
Doug McAdam   *Stanford University and Center for Advanced Study in the Behavioral Sciences*
Suzanne Staggenborg   *University of Pittsburgh*
Sidney Tarrow   *Cornell University*
Charles Tilly (d. 2008)   *Columbia University*
Elisabeth J. Wood   *Yale University*
Deborah Yashar   *Princeton University*

(continued after Index)

Force and Contention
in Contemporary China

Memory and Resistance in the Long Shadow
of the Catastrophic Past

RALPH A. THAXTON, JR.
Brandeis University

CAMBRIDGE
UNIVERSITY PRESS

One Liberty Plaza, New York, NY 10006, USA

Cambridge University Press is part of the University of Cambridge.

It furthers the University's mission by disseminating knowledge in the pursuit of education, learning, and research at the highest international levels of excellence.

www.cambridge.org
Information on this title: www.cambridge.org/9781107539822

© Ralph A. Thaxton, Jr. 2016

First published 2016

Printed in the United States of America by Sheridan Books, Inc.

A catalog record for this publication is available from the British Library.

Library of Congress Cataloguing in Publication data
Thaxton, Ralph A., 1944–
Force and contention in contemporary China : memory and resistance in the long shadow of the catastrophic past / Ralph A. Thaxton, Jr.
    pages cm. – (Cambridge studies in contentious politics)
Includes bibliographical references and index.
ISBN 978-1-107-11719-8 (Hardback) – ISBN 978-1-107-53982-2 (Paperback)
    1. Dafo Cun (Henan Sheng, China)–Politics and government.   2. Political corruption–China–Dafo Cun (Henan Sheng)   3. Government, Resistance to–China–Dafo Cun (Henan Sheng)
4. Collective memory–China–Dafo Cun (Henan Sheng)   5. Zhongguo gong chan dang–China–Dafo Cun (Henan Sheng)   6. Communism– China–Dafo Cun (Henan Sheng).   7. China–Politics and government–2002–   8. China–Politics and government–1976–2002.   9. Legitimacy of governments–China. I. Title.
JS7365.D28T53 2015
951.05–dc23   2015023283

ISBN 978-1-107-11719-8 Hardback
ISBN 978-1-107-53982-2 Paperback

For my grandparents – especially for Pearl, who was always there for me when I was a boy – and for Sarah, whose enterprising genius lifted us out of the coal mines and off the farm lands, giving me the chance to find my way to the University of Wisconsin and its great scholars.

Contents

Illustrations

Acknowledgments

This book owes its inspiration to four intellectual giants, each of whom taught and/or mentored me at one point in my career. Charles Tilly was kind enough to invite me to a graduate student conference at Johns Hopkins University in Baltimore many years ago and to take a long-term interest in my work. Ultimately, this book was inspired by his commentaries on the importance of individual acts and testimonies in understanding history and contention, some of which he related in 2008 as an outside press reader of my previous book manuscript, *Catastrophe and Contention in Rural China*. Edward Friedman, my generous mentor at the University of Wisconsin, encouraged me to pay attention to the importance of the extraordinary human beings whom we often refer to as "ordinary people" in seemingly hopeless struggles for social justice. Ed's brilliant teaching, scholarship, and wise advice inspired me to dig deeper into how those without power see power, and so he too has pointed me toward a social science that begins with individual suffering under state power. This book, it is hoped, is a testimony to his wisdom. James C. Scott, my other wonderful mentor at Wisconsin, long ago taught me the importance of under-standing the arts of individual resistance to misrule. In some ways, this book is really about how individuals have forged what Jim and our colleague Benedict J. Kerkvliet would call everyday forms of resistance. The book is influenced greatly by what Jim has taught us, showing that these forms have a link back to a state-induced catastrophe about which we still do not know very much. I only hope that it begins to add to what Jim Scott has taught us. Last, but not least, I am indebted to Susanne Weigelin-Schwiedrzik, Professor of Sinology and East Asian Studies and Vice-Rector at the University of Vienna. Susanne's work on trauma and memory in twentieth-century China inspired me to pursue system-atic study of the Great Leap Forward Famine, especially how its survivors remember this political and social disaster. Our discussions in Berlin and Heidelberg, in Waltham and Boston, and in Chicago and Philadelphia were important stepping-stones to this project. In many ways, these discussions motivated me to investigate how individual memories of encounters with power during the first decade of the People's Republic of China shaped the way in which rural people saw power in the aftermath of the greatest catastrophe of Chinese Communist Party rule.

I do not know how to sufficiently thank the many colleagues who put so much effort into reading the manuscript, offering critical suggestions for improvement, and encouraging me to think harder about how to present the case and the argument. Jonathan Unger, Bruce Gilley, Steven I. Levine, Michael Szonyi, Alfred Chan, Paul Cohen, and James C. Scott – all exceptionally generous colleagues – read the entire manuscript at different stages of its development. I am especially grateful for their critical insights, many of which I have relied on to improve this book. Jonathan Unger, Bruce Gilley, and Steven I. Levine went the extra mile, saving me from many errors and helping me place the case study in theoretical perspective. I hope this study lives up to their high standards.

I also have benefited greatly from the comments of Antonius C.G.M. Robben, Bruce Dickson, and Zhou Xun on the Introduction; Harold M. Tanner and Fei-ling Wang on Chapter 1; Thomas P. Bernstein on Chapter 2; Kay Ann Johnson, Susan Greenhalgh, and Kimberley Ens Manning on Chapter 3; Michael Szonyi on Chapter 5; Edward Friedman on Chapter 6; Christianne Hardy Wohlforth and Edward Friedman on Chapter 7; Neil J. Diamant and Edward Friedman on Chapter 8; Martin King Whyte, Dorothy J. Soligner, Sarah Swider, and Denise Walsh and Mary Elizabeth Gallagher on Chapter 9; and Peter Lorge and Edward Friedman on Chapter 10.

Additionally, I have benefited from personal (mostly written) exchanges with Harold M. Tanner, Mark R. Beissinger, Alexander Pantsov, Liu Woyu, Lu Huilin, Han Dongping, Susan Greenhalgh, Kay Ann Johnson, Murray Scot Tanner, Edward Friedman, Thomas P. Bernstein, Dorothy Solinger, Perry Link, Glen Peterson, Steven I. Levine, Neil J. Diamant, Anthony Garnaut, Cormac O'Grada, Sarah Swider, Marta Baziuk, Kevin J. O'Brien, Mary Elizabeth Gallagher, James C. Scott, Andrew Wedeman, Bruce Gilley, and Robert P. Weller. All of these exchanges have enriched this book. My verbal exchanges with Minxin Pei during my tenure at the Dartmouth College John Sloan Dickey Center for International Understanding and with Jean C. Oi, Kevin J. O'Brien, and Lianjiang Li during a National Association for Asian Studies panel in Honolulu helped me refine its argument. My last minute correspondences with Mary Elizabeth Gallagher reassured me of the importance of placing the present in the Great Leap past, and also helped me sharpen the analysis in Chapter 9.

I also want to thank several institutions for inviting me to make presentations on some of this book's themes over the past fifteen years. A pivotal development in my career occurred when I joined the Harry Frank Guggenheim Workshop on Trauma and Memory, held in two sessions, first in Portugal in December 1997 and then in New York City in February 1999. My engagements with Allen Feldman, Antonius Robben, Paul Stoller, Valentine Daniel, Eric Santner, Rene

Devisch, and other workshop participants engendered a sea-change in my thinking about both the nature of the modern Chinese revolution and the meaning of the evidence I was gathering through interview work in the Chinese countryside. I also learned a great deal from interacting with colleagues in a seminar on political corruption during my tenure at the Princeton-based Institute for Advanced Study, from exchanges with colleagues while I was a visiting fellow at the Dartmouth College John Sloan Dickey Center for International Understanding, from a presentation to the Yale University Agrarian Studies Colloquium and later to the James C. Scott–Peter Perdue course on Agrarian Societies, and from lectures (and follow-up discussions) on "China's Dangerous Future" given at the Dickey Center at Dartmouth College, in a Scott Hawkins Lecture sponsored by the Dedham College of Humanities and Sciences at Southern Methodist University, and at Amherst College during my tenure as Croxton Lecturer in Political Science. Additionally, I want to thank Arthur Kleinman, Elizabeth J. Perry, and Lili Feng for inviting me to participate in workshops convened at the Harvard-Yenching Institute. My interaction with these three top-rank scholars and their colleagues was most rewarding. My engagement with participants in the Brown University Mini-Symposia on The Social Lives of Dead Bodies helped me further improve this work. This book also owes some of its insights to knowledge gained from exchanges with colleagues at the Conference on Communism and Hunger, sponsored by the Holodomor Research and Education Consortium and held at the University of Toronto.

This study was facilitated in part by grants from the Chiang Ching-kuo Foundation and from the United States Institute of Peace. I am grateful to both institutions for their support. I also am grateful for the support of librarians at Dartmouth College, Amherst College, Brown University, Brandeis University, and Harvard University.

Yet my greatest heartfelt thank you goes to *the one with the stars in her eyes.* This book could never have been completed without her support, encouragement, and patience.

Waltham, MA
March 1, 2016

Cast of Characters for Da Fo Village and Several Other Villages in the Hebei-Shandong-Henan Border Area, 1945–2013

Bao Chengling. Head cook of the public dining hall in the commune period and the dictatorial, corrupt, and immoral principal of the Da Fo school in the Mao era and early reform period. Target of struggle led by Bao Sheping and the Da Fo teachers.

Bao Chuanxi. Poor and timid farmer. Bullied by Bao Wenxing. Forced to plead for right to use electricity and water his crops.

Bao Haizhen. Arbitrary Chinese Communist Party (CCP) leader in Da Fo. Received more than his share of land in the 1982 land division. Target of arson.

Bao Hongwen. Da Fo farmer. Feared and disliked Bao Yinbao and his friends. Saw Bao Yinbao-led mafia as criminal and in league with corrupt CCP officials.

Bao Junling. Da Fo farmer who mounted a physical challenge to "electricity tiger" Bao Wenxing in the reform period, stirring memories of resistance to party leaders and their brutal cronies in the Great Leap era. Champion of more timid farmers.

Bao Junwei. Da Fo farmer and migrant worker. Said all Chinese officials are corrupt, and gave up on CCP-guided democracy.

Bao Nianxi. Eight years old at the start of the Great Leap Forward. Dropped out of school in 1960 because of hunger. Survived the great famine by secretly eating raw grain, sweet potato, and pumpkin crops in the collective fields. Thirty-two year-old farmer in 1983. Victim of Strike Hard campaign. Arrested and treated as a petty criminal for taking off government-monopolized chemical fertilizer from state trucks.

Bao Ruimin. Suffered a ten-year prison ordeal because of *yanda*, missing his chance to mentor his young sons. Petition writer for fellow prisoners falsely accused and arrested in the throes of the Strike Hard campaign. Unpaid Da Fo migrant worker who joined with other migrant workers to wage sit-ins at homes of unscrupulous subcontractors in villages and towns in between Beijing and Da Fo. Leader of New Year's Eve dumpling rebellion.

Bao Sheping. Teacher and principal of Da Fo school in the reform era. Leader of protest against corrupt Mao-era principal and of movement to democratize the school administration. Driven by Confucian ethics imparted by his father to improve the school and serve the students.

Bao Shunhe. The corrupt, do-nothing reform-era Da Fo CCP secretary groomed by Mao-era party boss Bao Zhilong and nominated and placed in power by Liangmen township leaders fearful of democratic electoral process. Unaccountable to villagers and unavailable for consultation on important village issues.

Bao Timing. Co-leader of refusal tax resistance in Da Fo. Write-in candidate who actually won the election for Da Fo party secretary against CCP favorite Bao Shunhe. Denied office by Liangmen township CCP leaders who nominated Bao Shunhe and put the latter in power.

Bao Wenxing. Son of pre-1949 pauper, vagabond, and hustler Bao Zhigen. Appointed electrician by the Da Fo reform-era party leadership. Fierce beneficiary of the extension of the Li Peng–led electricity monopoly into Dongle county and Liangmen township. Known as the "electricity tiger." Bullied both villagers and township leaders.

Bao Xuejing. Progressive Da Fo party secretary who first succeeded and turned against Bao Zhilong. Falsely accused and persecuted for attempting to democratize and make fair the process of land division in the early 1990s. Dismissed as party secretary.

Bao Yibin. Vice-party secretary of Da Fo brigade in the Great Leap Forward. Helped party secretary Bao Zhilong impose the Great Leap famine. At odds with Bao Zhilong in the run-up to the Cultural Revolution. Responsible for his mother's starvation in the Great Leap famine. Hated by many villagers, who held him responsible for his mother's death in 1960, for the moral decline of village leadership in the Mao era, for the corruption of the taxation process in the post-Mao period. Target of villagers' anger and contention in the 1990s.

Bao Yinbao. The post–Great Leap leader of martial artists in Da Fo village and Hebei-Shandong-Henan border area. Took up study of martial arts after the Great Leap in order to defend his family against CCP bullies. Co-leader of early reform-era tax resistance in Da Fo. Important player in the formation of parallel system of martial artist counterforce, power, and influence in Da Fo area, and kingpin and beneficiary of mafia operations in the wider border area. Saw himself as a modern-day Song Jiang.

Bao Zhanghe. Born in 1948. Mother died of hunger during the Great Leap. Reform-era Da Fo village public security chief and secret informant who ratted out pregnant couples to the Special Task Force. Target of villagers' silent contention and shaming. Turned to periodic migrant work to survive.

Exploited for many years in the Mao and post-Mao periods by subcontractors in the construction industry.

Bao Zhifa. Abandoned by his mother in the Great Leap famine. Joined the People's Liberation Army (PLA) in 1967 at age of nineteen in order to escape hunger in Da Fo. "Volunteer" to help the PRC build the Pakistan National Defense Highway. Important player in Da Fo area petitionist movement of PLA veterans looking for compensation for sacrifices in Pakistan.

Bao Zhigen. Local Da Fo area hustler and thug. Toady of Great Leap–era party boss Bao Zhilong, and pistol-toting rapist in the Leap period. Beneficiary of the extension of the Li Peng–supervised electricity monopoly into Dongle county in the early reform era.

Bao Zhilong. Leader of underground Da Fo CCP and militia force prior to 1949. Early CCP secretary in Da Fo. Vice-director of Liangmen People's Commune and corrupt enforcer of the Great Leap Forward. Target of villagers' anger during the Cultural Revolution. Beneficiary of reform-era economic change. Hoarded tax grain in his private home in reform period. Target of arson for Great Leap–era wrongdoings and for reform-era corruption and greed.

Du Yufeng. Pingyuandi village marital artist. Hired by businessmen to beat up competitors. Owner of three-story house, fierce Tibetan dog, and Land Rover. Operated mafia business under cover of a legitimate "Green Tea Shop" business establishment.

Huang Xiangjun. Director of the Dongle county Education Bureau in the reform period. Cunning and corrupt hustler who turned teacher reform into a racket to line his own pockets. Object of teacher exasperation and indignation.

Li Changquan. Corrupt Liangmen township leader who benefited from birth planning campaigns by issuing "second-child certificates" for a fee to farmers.

Lin Zhiyan. Liangmen village birth planning activist who was shocked by brutality of Special Task Force sent to enforce the one-child policy in the 1980s. Hated the government for such brutal enforcement.

Pang Lianggui. Da Fo teacher, farmer, and bread peddler. Ate tree leaves and stole from the public dining hall to survive the Great Leap famine. Feared the government escalation of the grain tax in the mid-1990s would lead to another great disaster, and possibly to a rebellion.

Pang Siyin. Member of pre-1949 Da Fo militia and later vice-secretary of Da Fo CCP. Astute and fairly objective critic of Deng Xiaoping reform policies and their implementation. Opposed Liangmen township officials' attempt to usurp Da Fo's old periodic market.

Ruan Jingwei. Da Fo migrant worker. Victim of nonpayment of wages by greedy subcontractors with "dark hearts."

Wu Shunchang. CCP chief of Liangmen township in early 1990s and sworn brother of corrupt party secretaries in different villages. Fought with Yan Zedong over the spoils of reform in front of villagers.

Yan Zedong. Head of Liangmen township government in the early 1990s. Target of physical assault by CCP party secretary Wu Shunchang, who challenged Yan's authority.

Yang Faxian. Dongle county martial artist who built a powerful army and fascist regime in the Hebei-Shandong-Henan border by recruiting orphans, small-time criminals, and ex-Kuomintang soldiers in the late 1930s. Leader of ultrarepressive Japanese Puppet Army in 1939–1945. Headquartered in Da Fo, this popular force fought CCP and killed 300 Eighth Route Army soldiers. Hero of Bao Yinbao and many of the reform-era marital artists.

Zhao Junjie. Leader of petitioning PLA veterans in Puyang county–Dongle county area. In touch with Jiangsu- and Henan-based veterans and important figure in the multiprovincial petition movement of veterans looking for just compensation for sacrifices in constructing the Pakistan National Defense Highway.

Zheng Huiqing. Da Fo farmer and nonparty member. Survived the Great Leap famine by eating unripened green crops in the collective fields. Expressed contempt for the reform-era police. Declared farmers could live without the police officers and government officials.

Zheng Yunxiang. Member of Da Fo brigade militia in the late 1950s. Maverick leader of an armed raid on collective fields of another brigade during the Great Leap famine. Punished by Da Fo party secretary Bao Zhilong. Fed up with the reform-era village and township leaders and with the Central government.

Zhou Chunxue. Poor, illiterate, and unskilled Da Fo farmer. Family reduced to ruin in the Great Leap Forward. Fled from unscrupulous subcontractors in Henan. Begged his way to Yongji city, Shanxi. Sued a subcontractor for inhuman treatment. Could not get procedural justice from CCP-controlled Yongji city court. Embittered by the cruelty and disappointment of reform.

Zhou Jian. Liangmenpo farmer. Questioned the motives of Central government leaders in abolishing the agricultural tax in 2006. Said Beijing did it out of fear of a ramified rebellion rather than out of benevolence. Later gained firsthand knowledge of corruption at the very top of the Central government. Disgusted with CCP leaders, both locally and nationally.

Maps

MAP 01. Provinces of China, neighboring countries, and area of study.
Map by Kate Blackmer

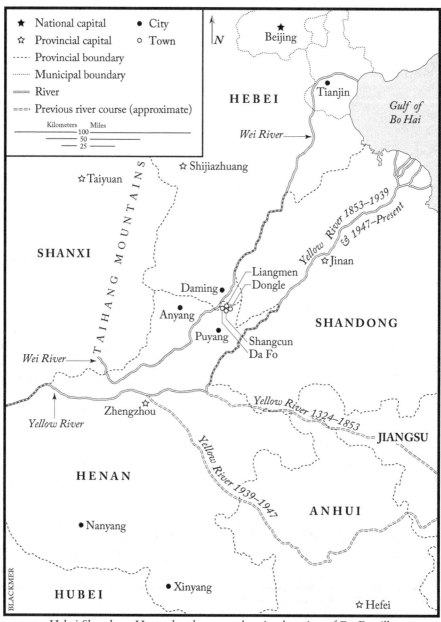

MAP 02. Hebei-Shandong-Henan border area, showing location of Da Fo village.
Map by Kate Blackmer

Introduction

This book is about the troubled relationship between the Chinese Communist Party (CCP) and village dwellers in a rural border area of China. These villagers hold durable memories of the most traumatic episode of the Maoist past, known as the Great Leap Forward, a state-driven campaign to regiment and collectivize every aspect of human life in the years 1958–1961. Imposed by Communist Party activists loyal to Mao at the county, township, and village level, this campaign produced the most catastrophic famine in modern world history,[1] killing at least 40–45 million rural dwellers in one way or another.[2] The scale of death from this campaign is mind boggling. Almost twice as many people died in the Great Leap famine as in the Taiping Rebellion – the world's most devastating civil war. Actually, Mao and his political base wiped out three times more people during this episode of war communism than were exterminated by Stalin's and Hitler's cadres, armies, and death squads in Eastern Europe between 1933 and 1945.[3]

In the throes of the great famine, many of China's rural people came to believe that the Mao-led Communist Party had deliberately starved them to death.[4] Their instincts were right. As early as March 1959, Mao Zedong knew about the famine unfolding in the countryside, yet he and his party still

---

[1] Yang, *Calamity and Reform*, 1.

[2] The figure of 45 million is from Dikotter, *Mao's Great Famine*, x. Mao Yushi has calculated that 36 million people starved to death. Mao Yushi, "Lessons from China's Great Famine," 484–486. Mao's estimate is in line with the research of Yang Jisheng, *Tombstone*, 430. Nonetheless, Yang Jisheng also has noted that the estimate of 36 million "is still too low," in part because the reports by different localities, frequently amassed or screened by local officials, were inaccurate. Yang, *Tombstone*, 430. I agree. Moreover, it is important to note that the official reports on the death rate rarely include the number of people who died from forced hard labor, from famine-related diseases, from industrial accidents, from cadre brutality, and from politically induced suicide.

[3] See Snyder, *Bloodlands*.   [4] "Gansu Shengwei."

relentlessly pushed for higher levels of grain procurement, thereby delivering millions on millions of villagers into the arms of death.[5]

People in Tianxia village, Qin'an county, Gansu province, suffered this fate. Here commune party leaders and their brigade-level accomplices seized all of the harvest for the state, leaving villagers to starve on a grain ration of only two *liang* per day – a far cry from the officially promised ration of one pound per day.[6] Qin Ruisheng, one of Tianxia's survivors, lost her father and four siblings to the sharp hunger of late 1958. At age fourteen, Qin managed to survive by scavenging wild grass and plant stems from the stark landscapes of various brigades (villages). In the course of her desperate travels, Qin found that brigade-level cadres routinely tossed dozens of starved bodies into nearby ditches. Qin also discovered that both young and old Gansu villagers spread this satirical verse about Mao and the performance of his regime: "Mao Zhuxi xiang taiyang, Yi tian zhi gei chi er liang," which translates "Chairman Mao is like the Sun. He gives us two *liang* a day."[7] Historically, the imperial order had earned the Mandate of Heaven by keeping taxes fair and flexible and storing grain to prevent famine. In the Great Leap, Mao and his party failed on both counts. Although Liu Shaoqi and Deng Xiaoping, the "enlightened" leaders of the Central government, subsequently scurried to convince rural people that the CCP was a benevolent institution and that Mao and the Communist Party still had the interest of rural people at heart, farmers who had experienced the famine first-hand did not buy into this propaganda. They felt betrayed by both Mao and his party.[8]

In wide swaths of China's deep interior, the Mao-led Communist Party induced a catastrophe in 1958–1961 and completely shredded the legitimacy of the one-party state. Following the Great Leap, the Communist Party strived to erase popular memory of the devastating famine in the countryside. But in the bleak twenty-year aftermath of the Great Leap famine, China's rural people waged a silent day-by-day, inch-by-inch struggle to climb out of the submarginal existence to which Mao's cadres had assigned them in the famine, and

---

[5] For the seminal scholarship on Mao's fanatical push and Mao's role in accelerating the Leap and its famine, see MacFarquhar, *Origins of the Cultural Revolution*, 333; Bernstein, "Mao Zedong and the Famine," 422–445; Yang, *Tombstone*, 17–18, 352–353, 363–366, 384–389, 483–484; Dikotter, *Mao's Great Famine*, xiii, 70, 84–89, 134; and Zhou Xun, *The Great Famine in China*, xiii, 23.

[6] Qin Ruisheng, interview, August 4, 2014.

[7] Ibid. Cf. Eva Song, *Xunzhao Dajihuang Xingcunzhe*, 104. For a similar anti-Mao satirical verse, see Wemheuer, "The Grain Problem Is an Ideological Problem," 114.

[8] See "Gansu Shengwei." Cf. the interviews of farmers conducted by Eva Song, especially the one from Gansu's Ji Chuanjen, in Eva Song, *Xunzhao Dajihuang Xingcunzhe*, 254–255, 261. On this point, also see Thaxton, *Catastrophe and Contention*, 117, and conclusion, and Thaxton, unpublished Anhui interviews of 2010. This is implicit in Wemheuer, "Dealing with Responsibility for the Great Leap Famine," 176, 186, 188–190, and it is strongly implicit in Yang, *Tombstone*, 466–473, 484, especially on the riots and rebellions in Yunnan, Gansu, Sichuan, Guizhou, and Hebei provinces.

there was little if any institutional support for this struggle.[9] Their memories of the famine and the struggle that followed were ungovernable, and they played a role in constructing the monstrous and troubling visions, dreams, and nightmares of famine survivors. To many of them, the Mao-led Communist Party had lost the right to rule.

Scholars of politics in the People's Republic of China (PRC) have argued that the post-Mao Central government implemented a reform process that redressed the material devastation caused by the failings of the Mao era, lifting several hundred million rural dwellers up from a submarginal existence to a plane of subsistence.[10] They are correct. The post-1978 Deng Xiaoping reform did just that, initially reviving the hope of the rural poor for a better, adequate life, free from predatory state interference. Nonetheless, the life stories of the survivors of the catastrophe of the Great Leap Forward offer little evidence that the post-Mao reforms *actually* restored the legitimacy of the Communist Party in the villages of the deep agricultural interior. In the eyes of many villagers, the legitimacy crisis engendered by the failed performance of the Mao-led CCP in the Great Leap Forward Famine persisted into the so-called reform era. The political habits originally responsible for the Great Leap disaster – habits of party rule that persisted over many decades – were not reformed. True, some local CCP leaders had one foot in the new world of reform, but these same political actors often had the other foot in old ways of ruling.[11]

In China's unreformed authoritarian political context, the old habits of rule sometimes stirred up agonizing memories of the Great Leap episode. In the deep countryside, the institutionalized propensity to dominate increasingly gave rise to contentious encounters with power holders, and rural people drew on such memories to defend themselves against the possibility of another round of suffering and loss. This book is about these memories and about how they have informed resistance in a North China border region with a population and territory the size of France. It is about how the catastrophic Maoist past has infused the present, about how memories of this past have been pricked by

---

[9] For an understanding of how rural people initially escaped the great famine largely by their own efforts, see Thaxton, "How the Great Leap Forward Famine Ended," 251–271, esp. 259–270; on the continuous struggle to thwart Maoist attempts to eliminate household farming and independent marketing after 1961, see Thaxton, *Catastrophe and Contention*, chapter 8.

[10] On this uplifting, see Lin, "Rural Reforms and Agricultural Growth," 35–40; Friedman, Pickowicz, and Selden, *Revolution, Resistance, and Reform*; Qian, "China's Market Transition," 232–235; Dittmer, "China's Global Rise," 496; Naughton, *Chinese Economy*, 212–215, 219, 251, 263–265; Whyte, *One Country, Two Societies*; and Xiang, "Bo Xilai Affair," 60.

[11] In other words, the local party leaders who were stuck in old ways of ruling were unprepared to give them up. This brings to mind Fan Yuan's 1994 film *The Accused Uncle Shanggang*, in which a village party secretary who was in power in both the Mao and Deng eras means well and wants to keep order, but he addresses wrongdoing in the village by pillorying and subjecting villagers to public criticism. Therefore, the authoritarian habits by which he ruled the village in the Mao era carried over to the Deng era.

corrupt, force-addicted local party leaders who were implicated in the Great Leap famine, and about how rural people, in some instances, have resisted these leaders in the reform period. The evidence in parts of the book suggests that resistance to the CCP and its reform-era policies would have formed without the Great Leap being a factor, and this might be true in some instances. Nevertheless, my purpose here is to show that resistance at the village level occasionally was linked to memories of the Great Leap's harm and that such memories influenced, and sometimes inflamed, acts of resistance and opposition. By focusing on this latter, more complex genre of contention we can better understand that resistance from below does not necessarily bode well for Central government leaders, whom some villagers hold responsible for a failed political reform and renewed suffering.

POCKETS OF CONTENTION IN "DEEP CHINA"

This book is focused on the rise of contention in Da Fo village, located in Dongle county, Henan province, and within the Hebei-Shandong-Henan border area.[12] My earlier book, *Catastrophe and Contention in Rural China*, focused mainly on political conflict in this small market village during the Great Leap Forward Famine and brought the story up to the start of reform in 1978, by which time Da Fo had approximately 2,800 people.[13] This book continues the story of Da Fo's fate under CCP rule in the 1978–2013 period. However, it also relies extensively on interview data from twelve other villages in this same border area: Liangmen, Liangmenpo, Shangcunji, Dingcun, Daweicun, Weicaicun, Wangguocun, Hongwucun, and Yuanchao in Henan province and Pengdi, Pingyuandi, and Yuezhuang in Hebei province. Most of these villages share marriage and often market ties, and also a common political history.

This North China tri-provincial border area has more than a thousand-year history of political turbulence. Challengers to imperial rule historically recruited the foot soldiers for their rebel armies from the villages of this yellow-earth region. During the Republican period, Mao Zedong took advantage of the rebellious political culture of this area by sending the 129th Division of the CCP's Eighth Route Army, led by Liu Bocheng and Deng Xiaoping, into

---

[12] The term "deep China" is from Arthur Kleinman, who associates it with the often hidden, underlying moral values that are at work in the quest of people in China to achieve a good life in the shadow of Mao-era attacks on individuals and communities. I accept this definition, but by "deep China" I also mean the remote places of the countryside and the hidden, indelible memories of rural people whose lives were upended by the CCP exercising power on them in the Great Leap Forward. I also use this term to refer to the tendency of such individuals to draw on such memories to negotiate survival and resistance to intrusive, corrupt authoritarian rule in the present. This latter use is in keeping with Kleniman's use of the term, too. Cf. Kleinman, *Deep China*, 8–16, 261–290, esp. 286–288, in which we find fantastic revelations and analyses of the reform era party-state corruption of morals important for individual honesty and integrity.

[13] Thaxton, *Catastrophe and Contention*.

this border area, and underground CCP leaders were able to draw the independent farmers who had suffered mistreatment at the hands of warlord, Kuomintang, and Japanese Puppet Army forces to their cause, building local support for the military strikes of the People's Liberation Army (PLA) against Chiang Kai-shek's armies in the 1946–1949 civil war. Village people in this border area provided the rear service support for these strikes, including movement of artillery to the front lines and transportation of wounded PLA soldiers to rear area CCP hospitals, and some of their fathers, brothers, and sons gave their lives to help upend the Nationalist government and bring the Mao-led CCP to power. This border area is still a place with a resistive political culture, discernible in part by the return of statues of Guangong, the War God whose legends inspired and justified resistance to state oppressors, to the household shrines and neighborhood temples of villagers in the post-1978 reform period.[14]

On the other hand, this border region is also a place where the Communist Party has not yet fully recovered from the legitimacy crisis engendered by the Great Leap Forward Famine. Though the Central government may well have reclaimed legitimacy among China's urban, more highly educated population, and also may have repaired the damage of the Great Leap famine in parts of the agricultural interior, we must keep in mind that China is a vast country and that many of the remote, poor, provincial border regions in which the pre-1949 CCP persuaded villagers that it stood for their interests were neglected, and sometimes abused, by the Mao-led Central government after the revolutionary victory. In fact, until recently these regions were still barely on the radar of Beijing-based reformers. Hence, in the case of the border region under study, it seems, following the scholarship of Heike Holbig and Bruce Gilley, that China is a complex country that "has *both* high overall legitimacy *and* serious legitimacy fissures if only because of its size and complexity."[15] This book taps the memories of individuals who survived the state-inflicted disaster that gave rise to one of these fissures. It focuses on the political and psychological damage stemming from the disaster of 1958–1961 in the villages of this one border area. It constitutes an effort to understand the extent to which, in the words of Holbig and Gilley, the reform-era policies and practices of CCP rulers have addressed the issues that made for a "pocket of legitimation failure" in this border area,[16] and to examine the consequences of the party's effort to preserve its power without undertaking genuine political reform.

---

[14] I witnessed the return of this deity in the post-Mao period, all through the 1980s and 1990s. See Thaxton, *Catastrophe and Contention in Rural China*, and Duara, *Culture, Power, and the State*; Duara's work first brought our attention to the importance of the War God in popular culture.

[15] Holbig and Gilley, "Reclaiming Legitimacy in China," 399.   [16] Ibid.

THE CHALLENGE OF STUDYING CONTENTION THROUGH
MEMORY IN AUTHORITARIAN CHINA

Understanding popular contention in micro-level settings patrolled by authoritarian Chinese rulers who have manufactured a recent catastrophe poses a daunting challenge. Few, if any, survivors of the Great Leap famine will talk with outsiders about state power, let alone voice judgments about the institutionally appointed agents of that calamity. In the PRC, where there has been no meaningful political reform, rural people often still live side by side with the perpetrators of Mao-era suffering. In this situation, many are fearful of expressing their genuine political emotions to anyone. Speaking truth about power, especially the truth about a topic tabooed by the Communist Party, is dangerous. Here the Communist Party–directed state and its local agents periodically warn village leaders against providing testimony about specific experiences of suffering in the Great Leap Forward and its famine. In this political context, few villagers will discuss internalized memories of this disaster, let alone talk openly about the link between this past disaster and personal suffering in the present.[17]

In June 1987, while interviewing in Qiliu village, in Hua county, Henan province, I had an experience that underscores this point. At the time, I was studying Republican-era political history. The Great Leap famine was not on my research agenda. I had befriended the young village party secretary, and I usually would drop by his home to chat right before I departed the village around 6 PM. One day I decided to break away early from my interview work routine to visit him. As I approached the front gate to his courtyard, I heard one of my academic hosts, a university-based Communist Party historian who was one of my minders, yelling loudly at the village secretary: "You can tell him [me] anything he wants to know about pre-1949 history, but do not tell him one damn thing about what happened here after 1949."[18] The secretary did not tell me anything about the Great Leap episode that summer, and so I left the issue alone. However, when I returned to Qiliu the following summer he invited me to come with him to meet a small group of villagers who were in their sixties and seventies in a yard enclosed by four high walls. The villagers wanted me to know, and were eager to explain, that one-ninth of the village's

---

[17] Arthur and Joan Kleinman remind us that the top-down mass movements that defined Mao era politics created a "culture of terror" and fear that worked against speaking candidly in the presence of power. Kleinman and Kleinman, "The Appeal of Experience," 16–17. Surely the cadre violence of land reform, experienced by kin and neighbors, warned ordinary villagers of the potential for future violence and repression. Additionally, Neil J. Diamant has discovered that people in China experienced the CCP writing of the draft 1954 constitution through fears of what the Mao-led party might do to *further* harm them, so that a fear of power already had crept into party relations with ordinary people even before the disasters of the Great Leap and the Cultural Revolution. Neil Diamant, "Talking about the Revolution, " and personal correspondence with Neil J. Diamant, May 5, 2013. This is my understanding of Diamant's insightful work.

[18] Thaxton, *Catastrophe and Contention.*

inhabitants, roughly 200 people, had died in the famine of the Great Leap Forward. This meeting took place when my academic hosts – and minders – were away from the village and well out of earshot; that is, within a space that was free of state agency.

In 1991, I had a similar experience in Da Fo village, also in Henan province. When I asked villagers to detail their experiences in the Henan Famine of 1942, some of them explained how they survived the famine by ageless strategies of self-help, including migrating to better-off agricultural places and begging in lively markets. But some of them also started to talk about their experiences in the great famine of 1958–1961, and their revelations began to eclipse their interest in relaying information about their fate in the Henan Famine, which had occurred under Kuomintang rule. Many wanted me to know that during the Great Leap Forward the CCP had prevented them from migrating out of Da Fo to find succor in towns and cities and, further, that the party had shut down market activity and then tabooed begging as a shameful act. Such political closure, I learned, contributed to starvation and death in the years 1958–1961, and the Great Leap famine proved far more lethal than the Henan Famine,[19] which, in contrast to the Leap famine, was the result of prolonged drought, war, and poor transport networks – not to mention the warlord infighting that impeded Nationalist government relief efforts.[20] Increasingly, when I returned to Da Fo between 1991 and 1995, many interviewees unexpectedly steered me toward the devastating impact of the Great Leap famine years; by the late 1990s I was learning more and more about the famine from these incremental, often unplanned outpourings, which took place in guarded local spaces.

The agents of the Communist Party–led state are determined to inhibit access to such spaces and to the deep *independent* judgments rural people hold of power. Scholars who do not repeatedly visit local settings or interact with villagers in such settings, who do not find ways to win trust with villagers, and who do not learn how to conduct research in small, nonstate spaces will be challenged to understand how the episodic memory of the Great Leap past influences responses to inhumane treatment by power holders since 1978. Without this understanding, we cannot get at the hidden core of contention in contemporary China.[21]

---

[19] Ibid.

[20] In 2012, the Central government approved the dissemination of Feng Xiaogang's film *Back to 1942*, which portrays the 1942 famine as the result of the politically dark forces soon to be ousted by the CCP-led October 1, 1949, revolution, part of an attempt to legitimize party rule. The film did not question the usual estimate of 3 million deaths, when probably no more than 1.5 million died in the 1942 famine; Clarissa Sebag-Montefiore is correct to argue that the release of this film is part of an effort to deflect attention from the growing popular demand that the party-state openly confront the history of Mao's great famine. See Sebag-Montefiore, "Great Silence," and Mackinnon, "Is China Finally Confronting?"

[21] I am not suggesting that the Great Leap episode can provide a "magic lantern" for seeing and comprehending every aspect of political life and political contention in contemporary China. Instead, my purpose is to show, by studying memory and contention in one rural place, that the

ORAL HISTORY METHODOLOGY

Of course we cannot sustain the commitment of villagers to actively participate in remembering without building trust. The methodology of oral history interviewing used for this book was aimed explicitly at cultivating such trust. The approach was grounded in a number of complementary strategies of interview work. First, only the villagers who wanted to tell their life stories were interviewed. They could refuse to participate in interviews or withdraw from the interview process if they felt inconvenienced or uncomfortable with questions. Second, most villagers were interviewed in the privacy of their homes, and they were guaranteed anonymity. Hence this book uses pseudonyms for all important persons and places in its narrative. I have invoked this procedure to protect all of the informants in the study.

Third, the interview questions were rarely about "grand official political history and events" – the Great Leap Forward itself, the Cultural Revolution, or the Deng Xiaoping Reform. Instead, open-ended questions focused on the quotidian life experiences of individuals over long periods of time.[22] The goal was to grasp encounters with power only when villagers chose to speak of how power holders intervened in, and sometimes disrupted, everyday routines of survival and efforts to preserve earned household entitlements. The questionnaires were designed to ascertain how individual villagers remembered the ways in which such encounters jeopardized survival in the Great Leap and its famine, but they also were drawn up to guard against being skewed by the interviewer's interest in the link between the Great Leap and post-Mao-era injustice. That is, the focus was on ascertaining the link between injustice in these two eras through open-ended interviewing rather than through directly introducing or emphasizing the subject of the Great Leap itself. In this way, the interviews aimed to arrive at an objective understanding of whether some of the contentious performances in the post-Mao period reflected memories of suffering engendered by the Great Leap episode.

Much like the book *Catastrophe and Contention in Rural China*, this book is based on interactive interviews and face-to-face discussions with ordinary villagers who, in spite of suffering, managed to survive the Great Leap and its famine. To a lesser extent, the work is founded on interviews of village and township Communist Party leaders, some of whom were directly implicated in imposing the policies engendering the Leap famine. My previous book was based on 400 in-depth interviews with villagers aged 21–85. This work is based on the original oral history data set plus an additional 130 interviews. For the most part, the additional interviews were undertaken with individual

---

assumption that the Great Leap disaster exerts little influence on politics in the present is questionable.

[22] This approach finds its origins in Braudel, *On History*, 11–12, 35–38, 45, 78–79, and in Tomich, "The Order of Historical Time"; also see Bourdieu, "To the Reader."

villagers in the privacy of their homes and courtyards and in strict internal confidentiality, which is to say no other people living within the PRC were allowed to access any of the interviews. The age range for this additional group was 17–90, and the great majority of interviewees were between the ages 45 and 75.

In attempting to reconstruct the long-term episodic memory of the catastrophe of Mao-era rule, and to get villagers to play a central role in this retrieval process, the preframed, easily exploitable format of survey research was abandoned. Instead, individuals were engaged in iterated and intimate verbal exchanges in order to explore their past and present relationships with power. This fourth strategy was pursued with mindfulness of Uradyn E. Bulag's warning that oral history, as practiced in the Mao-era PRC, was a party-organized practice designed to discipline its subjects and, above all else, "to contain subversion from within and without the Party."[23] To dissociate the interview process from the Maoist attempt to produce "correct remembrance" of suffering through dictation, interviewees were free to take the reins in guiding the motif of discourse.[24] Villagers were allowed not only to question the usefulness of the questions but also to instinctually and instantaneously introduce their own ways of refining, or transforming, the questions into questions that seemed more worthwhile *to them*. This procedure sometimes led to unimagined paths, introducing new kaleidoscopes of political, social, and cultural knowledge that, to say the least, could not have been discovered through a preformulated way of asking questions.[25]

The lessons learned in viewing these different kaleidoscopes of local knowledge were used to rewrite questionnaires for the next round of interviews, leading to a deeper insight into what the previous round of interview work had taught. This method offered a bridge for building trust with key informants in different villages, especially in Da Fo, the village on which field work was most sharply focused. As a result, the research was continued over time, even in the face of regime efforts at the township level to scuttle it. In the early summer of 1998, a small contingent of police came to Da Fo village to question some of the interviewees. The police wanted to know what the villagers were being interviewed about. The interviewees, now trusted allies, refused to tell the police anything. They protected the research project while protecting themselves. Had research been initiated with pointed, blatantly political questions about the official transcript of hegemonic state power holders in Beijing,

---

[23] Bulag, "Can the Subalterns Not Speak?," 105, also 97–99.

[24] As Jun Jing has pointed out, Maoist controls on memory were pervasive, and people whose memories were at odds with regime narratives were at risk, so it was important to reassure villagers that they could relate the unabridged personal stories of *their* lives. Cf. Jing, *Temple of Memories*, 8.

[25] Scott has implicitly talked about the importance of such a process. Scott, "James Scott on Agriculture as Politics."

Zhengzhou, or Dongle county, in the collective or post-collective eras, this would have alarmed villagers and perhaps alienated them. They, in turn, more than likely would have been inclined to expose the project to the police, whom, we will discover in this work, they despise. Recognizing individuals, getting to know and respect them for *who they are*, listening to *their stories* of how they have survived the trials of single party rule, is vital to winning trust and getting to the core of human suffering and political contestation in village China.

Following Earl R. Babbie, the research also made use of the "snowball sampling" technique, relying on each individual interviewee to help locate yet another individual to interview, thereby building up a substantial network of individual villagers with local knowledge of survival and suffering in the Great Leap era and beyond.[26] This technique made it possible to interview villagers from all walks of life and villagers with varying degrees of loyalty to the party-state. Occasionally, individual informants were engaged in small group discussions, but snowballing was used mainly to identify people who had knowledge of the topic and to differentiate between those with party-state connections and those without such ties, so that Communist Party–structured sampling would not skew the results. This also made it possible to avoid mixing powerless villagers with party-connected leaders and clients in shared interview spaces and formats.

Finally, the interviewing strategy targeted clusters of ten, fifteen, and thirty individual villagers who had stories to tell about a well-defined issue that was entangled with suffering in the Great Leap and in the post-1978 path to contention. Individual interviewees were patiently nudged to think and talk about how the past was connected to a common stream of reform-era contention over treatment from the powerful.[27] When, for instance, it came to light that more than a few Da Fo villagers turned migrant workers were agitated by urban labor contractors who refused to pay them a promised wage for construction work, in-depth interviews with thirty-three migrant workers were conducted targeting this issue. By gathering more and more information about each individual migrant worker's attempt to cope with the ordeal of survival in the construction industry, it was possible to locate the particulars of each interview within a comparative individual qua individual framework of claims making and identify the common causes of contention within this issue area. An attempt was then made to follow the story of group contention in the present back to memories of similar threats to survival in the Great Leap era. This was difficult and sometimes led down dead-end alleys. But it sometimes connected persistent individual memories of past injustices to shared indignation in the present, thereby yielding a representation of contention with a lineage to the Great Leap's injustice.

[26] Babbie, *Practice of Social Research*, 114–115.
[27] Tilly and Tarrow, *Contentious Politics*, 188.

HORIZONS OF TIME

Most social science research on contemporary China operates on "high state time," that is, a construct of time informed by approaches that locate popular evaluations of state authority and legitimacy in policy changes initiated by Communist Party leaders in Beijing. This approach has enhanced our understanding of how rural China has changed in the post-Mao period, making it possible to grasp variations in popular attitudes toward powerful high and low state actors and the effects of policy locally. To be sure, China's rural people see politics mainly in the present. By the same token, however, most older villagers and some of the middle-aged villagers approach political life through two other kinds of time: the deep historical time of the dynastic past and the deep political time of the collective era, with its episodes of trouble and terror.

This book takes seriously Paul Pierson's reminder that time horizons matter greatly in analyses of how power holders, and the institutions they control, are experienced by society.[28] To Pierson, temporal considerations are important in creating the "grounding for theoretical claims about how things happen in the social world."[29] In short, tapping into local knowledge of the past is essential if we are to grasp how rural people see state power in the present. Yet most renditions of how rural people see the Communist Party take the post-1978 reform period as a starting point, thereby divorcing contemporary contention from events and episodes that stretch back to the Mao period and beyond. The resulting "snapshots of reform" slight the ways in which the troublesome past often shapes the dynamics of resistance, protest, and contention in the post-Mao countryside.

For many rural dwellers, the promise of the post-1978 reform has been compromised by the lingering moral divide of the most traumatic episode of Mao-era rule. In Da Fo village, whose inhabitants are well aware of Beijing's policies, the majority of farmers still refer to the reform-era Liangmen township government as *the commune* – the lowest tier of state power in the collective era – and most farmers in the villages surrounding Da Fo more or less presume that the Communist Party leaders who rule from the township level operate with the same style of commune-era leaders, a style implicated in the Great Leap disaster. Yet Kevin J. O'Brien and Lianjiang Li's innovative and insightful work, *Rightful Resistance in Rural China*, does not even mention the episode of the Great Leap Forward or address the way in which this Mao-era catastrophe has conditioned popular emotions about CCP rule in the contemporary period. Starting the story line with the Deng Xiaoping-led reform in 1978, O'Brien and Li have argued that Central government leaders have introduced policies and laws that provide rural dwellers with the right to resist the wrongdoings of local party leaders. In this paradigm, the rural poor supposedly were institutionally

---

[28] Pierson, *Politics in Time*, 2.   [29] Ibid., 4.

encouraged to assert and defend their interests through policy-sanctioned channels, and thus embraced a new process of contention to justify their claims by
aligning with the center's beneficial policies and supportive rhetoric.[30]

Whereas China's rural people might credit the post-Mao center for
providing them with a policy-based tool for resisting bad cadre behavior,
Beijing's policy reforms did not give them a cause for holding local party
leaders accountable for misconduct. This book argues that contention
often has links back to the collective era, when villagers did whatever they
could to hold on to earned household entitlements threatened by the Mao-led
center's mission of rapid, aggressive collectivization – a mission that engendered the Great Leap catastrophe. The cause of such contention, therefore,
cannot be found simply – or only – in the shrewd efforts of villagers to
exploit the post-Mao center's policies, norms, and promised reforms for their
own purpose.[31] The small, often hidden everyday struggles of individuals
and households to regain these entitlements, which were violently usurped
by Beijing rulers and their rural cadre base in the Great Leap Forward,
continued on into the late Mao and early post-Mao periods. This study helps
us understand that rural people *who had been struggling all along* found
in the Deng-crafted reform policies the chance, and sometimes the means,
to more openly and effectively contest long-standing grievances against
party-state aggrandizement.

INDIVIDUAL ENCOUNTERS WITH POWER

Social science work on contentious politics by and large emphasizes collective
action at the expense of the individual, who often appears as a nameless
member of a "social movement." Yet challenges to state domination almost
always begin with the attempts of courageous individuals whose elementary
social rights have been violated, sometimes brazenly, by the agents of government organizations whose main purpose is to serve their own interest, usually
in the name of public good or public order.[32] Collective political contention
often grows out of the decisions of individuals to avoid or challenge the reach of
such organizations, if only by small acts of resistance. As F. G. Bailey has
pointed out, such resistance often entails a struggle against "organizational
trespassing" into the treasured kingdom of individual space,[33] and the individuals who take up this resistance do so at great risk. If we trace the long fuse to
collective-based contention back to its origins, therefore, we frequently discover
that its roots lay in the efforts of individuals to prevent government officials,
or those in their employ, from intruding into spaces and routines essential for
survival, dignity, and self-respect.[34]

---

[30] O'Brien and Li, *Rightful Resistance*, 2–3.   [31] Ibid.   [32] Bailey, *Kingdom of Individuals*.
[33] Ibid., 9.   [34] Ibid., 16.

This book is based on individual recollections of encounters with power. The methodological starting point for grasping collective action is not the social group involved in such action, but rather the individual human beings who act to defend themselves and the groups to which they are attached: families, friends, lineages, neighborhoods, villages, and market communities. In short, this study takes inspiration from the methodological individualism of Max Weber, who, as Stephen E. Hanson points out, saw "collective social outcomes as generated by the actions of individuals who are motivated by their diverse subjective interpretations of their positions in the social world."[35] Following Weber, this work has its origins in interview techniques that recognize individuals as independent causal agents of struggles for existence with dignity. I assume, and attempt to demonstrate, that virtually all collective forms of contention, and almost all group-based modes of resistance, are closely linked to "the particular acts of particular persons, since these alone can be treated as agents in a course of subjectively understandable action."[36]

In this study, individual contestants have lives, norms, interests, and pursuits of their own. Their resistance to authority is dependent neither on the protective support of leaders in Beijing nor on the opportunistic exploitation of the collapse of elite mechanisms of control pure and simple. Rather, they frequently turn to contention out of "longstanding interests."[37] The premise of this work is that many of them interpret such interests in light of what they remember about the humiliation and harm delivered in the catastrophe of the Great Leap Forward.[38]

In taking societies and states as the units of strategic political action, scholars of contentious politics have by and large slighted the importance of individuals in challenging institutional authority and domination. The Weberian paradigm, however, would argue that collective forms of contention are nothing more or less than the aggregated resistance of individuals and that individuals who suffer from state domination and oppression, and who find the courage to resist, are the key actors who galvanize the social groups whose claims, demands, and protests represent a contentious expression of collectivity.[39] Just as we cannot understand why authoritarian regimes, like the one in Beijing, decay and crumble without understanding why the individuals who make up the local staffs of such regimes lose faith in their superiors at the apex of state power, so we cannot understand why governments either are compelled to change policies or are overthrown without

---

[35] Hanson, *Post-Imperial Democracies*, 11.   [36] Weber cited in ibid., 14, n32.

[37] Cf. Goodwin, Jasper, and Polletta, "Return of the Repressed," 69–70, 73.

[38] In this respect, the individual activism I am speaking of is not the product of the methodological individualism of "rational choice" theory, for the contention it engages is dependent on interpretation, and not solely or mainly objective incentives and constraints. This cautionary note has been inspired by Bruce Gilley, personal correspondence, October 4, 2012.

[39] Cf. Hanson, *Post-Imperial Democracies*, 19, 25.

examining why state-abused individuals have been able to express their indignation and resistance in ways that magnetize scores of other victims of political injustice to their cause.

PERSISTENT MEMORIES: A SOURCE OF ENERGY AGAINST PRESENT-DAY INJUSTICE

In *The Seven Sins of Memory*, Daniel L. Schacter has informed us that persistent memories often originate in traumatic experiences with accidents, life-threatening illnesses, bullying, brutal official mistreatment, or insurgencies and wars. "The intrusive memories that result from such experiences," writes Schacter, "usually take the form of vivid perceptual images, sometimes preserving in minute detail the very features of trauma which survivors would most like to forget."[40]

The testimony of fifty-six-year-old (in 2010) Chen Zhigao of Jidan village, in Xuanzhi county, Anhui province, suggests one of many ways in which such memories were transferred to the next generation. Born in 1954, Chen Zhigao was only six when his first and second elder sisters starved to death in the great famine. They died in part because his mother was an honest person and hesitated to pilfer the crops of the collective and in part because his father was taken away from the village to build a huge reservoir, and hence did not know what was going on back at home. After his second elder sister died, Chen's mother also succumbed to starvation. At the height of the Leap, the CCP leaders of Jidan village gave food only to those who worked and, according to Chen Zhigao, "allowed the younger children who could not work to starve." Thus, like Zhang Ying, whose story we will take up later, Chen remembers the scene of dead children strewn across the village as very scary. But the most intrusive, disturbing memory of all is that of the fate of his father. Trapped in the commune's reservoir work camp and panicked over the possibility of losing his remaining two children, his father, Chen Zhiming, stole grain from the public dining hall, for which he was tortured to death by the CCP reservoir team leaders in a public criticism session. "The leaders," Chen tells us, "tied my father's thumbs to his back, and then tied his back to a bamboo pole. Then they hung him over the main beams of the house. After that, they forced him to kneel down on a bench with broken glass under his knees. They broke my father's back in the process. My father was unable to work after the torture. He was kicked out of the reservoir team, and he could not find enough food to eat in the village. He died after two months. *Before he died, my father told me everything that had happened to him. I have not forgotten any of this, and I will not forget it as long as I live.*"[41]

---

[40] Schacter, *Seven Sins of Memory*, 174.   [41] Chen Zhigao, interview.

Zhang Ying also was speaking through a persistent, troubling memory in the summer of 2007, when she related her Great Leap experience as a six-year-old child in Shilu village, in Shandong's Ji Qing county:

I was only six years old at the time of the Great Leap Forward. I remember I was hungry all the time. But the hardest thing for me was that my playmate died. Chunying was the same age as me, and I played with Chunying every day. At the time, we were not in school. Children in our neighborhood all played together. We played simple games. We jumped rope together. We played marbles together. We played with other kids, but we were the closest of friends. She came to my household a couple of times a day, and I went to hers. When she came to my home my mother would offer her some food, and when I went to her home her mother would offer me whatever food they had.

One day I went to look for Chunying to play. But her mother said she was not at home. I asked her where Chunying was. She said that she was in the big ditch outside the village. Therefore I went to the big ditch to look for her. I did not expect that anything was wrong with her at the time. But when I arrived there, I discovered Chunying's body. She had died the night before [from malnutrition and diphtheria–RT], and her parents had left her there for the dogs. Her hair was messed up in the wind, and I was frightened by the sight of her, and so I ran home to tell my mother that Chunying had died.

But what frightened me the most was that Chunying's mother did not show any sign of sadness about her daughter's death. Maybe she did not want to scare me. The way she related Chunying's fate was as if her daughter was away on a journey and would come back someday.

For many years afterwards, I was not able to go that ditch, and I have had many nightmares over the death of my childhood friend. Her death posed many troubling questions for me. Did she have someone to play with in the other world? What was it like to die? What if I had to die someday? I could not sleep at night for thinking about these questions.[42]

Zhang Ying and her mother survived Mao's great famine, partly by plying the black markets on the outskirts of Qingdao and partly by jumping onto freight trains headed for the rural villages north of Ji Qing, where they traded family valuables for small bags of wheat, corn, and soybeans.[43] Though her trauma was real, Zhang Ying's Great Leap experience seems to have strengthened her will to survive, lift herself out of the dystopia of the famine and its aftermath, and confront subsequent life crises head-on.[44] One of these crises occurred in 1988, when the Deng-led reformers were starting to push for privatizing the state-owned factories. At the time, Zhang Ying rented forty *mu* of Shilu village land to start a textile factory, and within a few years her fortunes took off. Unbeknownst to Zhang Ying, however, the village party secretary, whom she had trusted, secretly sold the land supporting her factory to a developer with powerful county-level connections, and shortly thereafter the local court ordered bulldozers to clear the land and ship all of her plant machinery to a

---

[42] Zhang Ying, interview.   [43] Ibid.

[44] As the work of Laurence Gonzales would anticipate. *Deep Survival*, 218–225.

storage lot. For the next twenty years, Zhang Ying fought to reverse this decision, successfully blocking the developer's effort to develop the land. According to Zhang Ying, "the developer underestimated my perseverance, and was never able to develop the land because of my continuous efforts to fight the case."[45]

Until recently, global China scholars were by and large skeptical about the political salience of the memories of such Great Leap survivors. Endel Tulving's research on *episodic memory* would argue for salience, however. According to Tulving, episodic memory, "the only memory system that allows people to consciously re-experience past experiences," factors importantly in human efforts to gain mastery over the present.[46] Building on this insight, and on the sagacity of Zhou Xun, the author of *The Great Famine in China*, this book is based on the premise that memories of the episode of the Great Leap and its famine are indelible, that they persist, and that they play an energetic role in the dynamics of present-day contention. The argument here is that such memories mitigate the way in which power is exercised on individuals and, further, that individuals occasionally act on the basis of such memories to galvanize collective support for contention.[47] Under the right circumstances, these persistent memories have the capacity to flood the present with the past. Such durable, receptive memories can affect the way in which people see the natural or human agents responsible for a traumatic experience in the first place. The literature on post-traumatic stress disorder tells us little about how survivors of traumatic encounters with absolute power have mobilized such memories to prevent a repeat of past harm and suffering in unsafe political environments. Relying on oral testimonies, this book shows how the survivors of Mao-era traumas have harnessed memory to build inner strengths and wage long-term struggles for survival and renewal under authoritarian rule.

In authoritarian China, rural villagers, damaged by the trauma of the Great Leap and its famine, cannot find psychic relief from safely positioned apolitical priests, grief counselors, or professional therapists. Nor can they easily escape the places in which the party-based networks implicated in the Great Leap still operate – they have little in common with Jung Chang, whose well-known book *Wild Swans* was enabled, and informed by, such a privileged escape. In this situation, memories of the Leap's trauma remain powerful. They have the potential to significantly influence the attempts of individuals to prevent reform-era rulers from inflicting yet another round of suffering and loss. Following Arthur Kleinman[48] and Steven M. Southwick and Dennis

---

[45] Zhang Ying, interview.   [46] See Tulving, "Episodic Memory," 1–5 and esp. 6.

[47] As Zhou Xun has argued, "there's a lot we can see in what happened then [the Great Leap era] in what happens now." Cf. Zhou Xun, *The Great Famine in China*; the quote is from Tatlow, "The Enduring Legacy of China's Great Famine."

[48] Kleinman, *Deep China*, 8–16, 269–272, 286–288; Kleinman et al., *Social Suffering*; and Kleinman, "How Bodies Remember."

S. Charney,[49] this book provides us with an understanding of how survivors of the Great Leap's disorder and suffering have relied on such memories to mobilize resistance to Communist Party misrule in the present, and invites us to conceive of resistance as a way of carrying on with everyday life and, in the process, freeing themselves from the disordered past.

HOT COGNITION VERSUS COLD COGNITION

In attempting to ascertain whether China is a stable or unstable country, social scientists have relied on survey questionnaires to record the political attitudes, opinions, and beliefs of the subjects of China's authoritarian political system, finding relatively high levels of popular support for the Central government.[50] Nevertheless, as Murray Edelman has pointed out,[51] attitudinal correlates of regime support constitute a dubious predictor of the conditions under which people will acquiesce to or actively challenge the schemes of official power. In actuality, political arousal is often situation specific and more or less influenced by memory-derived lessons of how to limit the impact of government threat and harm. The survey approach is informed by Cartesian logic, which holds that political consciousness is separate from emotional states affiliated with deep survival instincts. It is based on a model of politics conceived in isolation from memory-informed political emotions that ordinary Chinese villagers are reluctant to reveal to outsiders. Inviting respondents to answer questions that have little bearing on the engagement of the brain with everyday survival, this approach more or less skips across discrete and deep-seated memories of efforts to survive a distant episode of political damage, such as China's Great Leap disaster.

The model of information processing in survey research assumes that human beings operate through "cold cognition," articulating political dispositions by a retrospective, deliberative process structured by intellectual reasoning. In this empirical approach, human perception is based on quick, observational thinking, and such thinking is rarely processed by the body, including the brain and the emotion it can access. If rural Chinese villagers hold an emotionally conceived strategy for countering state power and force, therefore, we are not likely to discern the way in which this strategy plays out in their interaction with local Communist Party leaders by accessing "cold cognition." The latter has little to do with how villagers access emotional markers associated with memories of past state-inflicted suffering in order to hold such leaders at bay.

[49] Southwick and Charney, *Resilience*, 1, 5–6, 53–55.
[50] Nathan, "Political Culture and Diffuse Regime Support"; Gilley, *The Right to Rule*, 22, 25, 186–187; and Saich, "Chinese Governance," 2. Cf. Shi, "Cultural Values and Political Trust," 401–419.
[51] Edelman, *Public Policy and Political Violence*, 1–12.

Instead, this study attempts to discern how such a strategy plays out in the real world of contentious China by accessing "hot cognition," for in this world heated emotions are sometimes closely associated with long-term memories that, under the right circumstance, come to mind in a millisecond. As James P. Morris and his associates have pointed out, "everyday thinking about social and political objects will tend to unitize our beliefs, feelings and behavioral intentions in long term memory. When they are 'contingently activated,' as they frequently will be, beliefs, feelings, and intentions become linked in memory, perhaps so strongly that the mere exposure to a 'triggering event' will bring them automatically to mind."[52] The book investigates the way in which Chinese villagers locate the claims placed on them by present-day local, provincial, and national Communist Party rulers within the episode of the Great Leap Forward, why such claims tend to become emotionally charged, and why and how specific individuals have mobilized long-term memories to protect themselves from the implicit danger in being exposed to such claims.[53]

Following Joseph LeDoux, I am interested in the moments when villagers under attack from the agents of China's reform-era authoritarian single-party system rely on deeply positioned markers, located in memories of past threats, to activate the networks of the brain that demand quick improvisation for survival.[54] Precisely because the CCP ultimately rules the countryside by force and fear, villagers who are the targets of its fear-based politics are constantly challenged to use the power of counteremotions to survive and maintain self-respect.[55] For villagers, everyday politics is permeated by emotional encounters with powerful local party leaders. But because these encounters are oral, physical, short lived, and unrecorded in official records and archives, it is not easy to document them, let alone gather enough evidence to explain them from the standpoint of "hot cognition." Still, this book gives us a glimpse into the hot zone of everyday contention at the ground level, capturing some of the moments when specific individuals, many of whom were born prior to the Great Leap, have accessed what Laurence Gonzales has termed a system of "emotional bookmarks"[56] to challenge an aggressive mode of domination that crystallized in the Great Leap and its famine. In several of this book's chapters, we will see how this process has triggered bad, fearful memories of the brutes who enforced Mao's Leap policies, and how it has charged villagers to stand up for their rights to survival and self-respect.

---

[52] See Morris, Squires, Taber, and Lodge, "Automatic Activation of Political Attitudes," 3.

[53] This section has benefited from ibid., 3–4, and it is consistent with Jing, *Temple of Memories*.

[54] LeDoux, *Emotional Brain*; also see *Synaptic Self*; Gonzales, *Deep Survival*, 37, 51–55, 122–123, 197–198.

[55] For the logic here, see Gonzales, *Deep Survival*, 197–198.   [56] Ibid., 51, 55.

ENGAGEMENT WITH REFORM IN DEEP CHINA

Ever since the nominal end of the Great Leap famine (i.e., the winter of 1961 to the spring of 1962), rural people in the zones of its carnage have lived in a state of emergency, due largely to the Leap's damage to the material security of the household. Few China scholars have acknowledged the persistence of this emergency or the difficulty of escaping it by merely putting trust in Communist Party–led governance.[57] There has been no significant political reform in the deep countryside. Villagers in deep China have had to find ways to enable their families to survive and achieve a good life outside of, and often in spite of, the Central government and its sprawling party-state network at the provincial and subprovincial levels. This book derives its narrative from their stories, drawing on them to help us understand that individual villagers have been able to survive only through daily struggles purposefully aimed at carving out free space previously usurped by the Communist Party in the peak years of collectivization and that they have utilized this space to simply "make do" under the otherwise suffocating oversight of party-state networks in the reform period. It shows that "making do"[58] cannot be equated with "accepting authoritarianism."[59]

Beijing's highest officials, and the plethora of academics, cultural workers, and party cadres with ties to the national state, want us to believe that the individuals who have led these struggles have succeeded by compromising with a CCP-led national revival of safe, integrated local communities, but the oral history evidence from Da Fo and scores of surrounding villages calls this claim into question. Based on the stories of individual villagers who have persisted in showing up each day to wage the struggle for their households to operate without interference from Communist Party–based networks, this book introduces us to people who have challenged the notion of the party as a community-enhancing political institution. It focuses on how the memories of the Great Leap have influenced these struggles, reminding us that rural people who hold these memories can at any minute become the targets of violent state intrusions involving arrests, tortures, and brutal imprisonment at the hands of public security forces. It asks us to think harder about whether such targeted people interact with local Communist Party officials in order to improve the policies governing their lives. Its narrative suggests that such an assumption reflects the CCP-orchestrated illusion that policy making is a mutually interactive process through which the ruling group bolsters legitimacy.[60]

---

[57] Friedman, however, does this. Friedman, "Persistent Invisibility of Rural Suffering."

[58] De Certeau, *The Practice of Everyday Life*, chapter 3.

[59] Compare the premise and approach here with Wright, *Accepting Authoritarianism*.

[60] This illusion is advanced in the scholarship of Xu Wang, *Mutual Empowerment of State and Peasantry*. In constructing this argument, I have benefited from Allen Feldman, "Punition, Retaliation and the Shifting Crises of Social Memory and Legitimacy in Northern Ireland."

The voices of Da Fo's inhabitants, and of people in other border area villages, seem to tell a different story. They suggest that the party-led state hardly interacts with anyone – it mainly dictates, and rural people therefore have little choice but to respond through contention. These voices also offer a different way of thinking about policy. Contrary to the master narrative of CCP-framed historical memory, which represents policy as a benign prescription for improving the human condition, people in Da Fo and surrounding villages have long equated "policy" with magnum force aimed at compelling them to instantly serve the interest of Beijing, whose local party agents redirect the center's policy bullet to produce largess almost exclusively for their own networks – a process that brought on the catastrophe of the Great Leap. This book is about how individual rural people remember, narrate, and inflect this force and how they interpret CCP-framed policies and propaganda in light of the party's long-standing use of force to achieve its agenda.

Of course the official narrative of Central government leaders naturally promises reward from reform. Rural people welcome this promise. But they interpret the promise through deeply stored, encoded memories that caution engagement with reform policy and that warn its delivery can be a potential threat. Even as Da Fo's farmers endorsed the end of the commune and pressed for household farming and market entry, they were reluctant to embrace the Deng-led center's version of modernity, which, as Daniel Kelliher has taught us, was to be realized by radically increasing grain harvests in order to promote state-managed industry and generate foreign exchange.[61] They shared the concern of their counterparts in Xianning county, Hubei province, who, on catching wind of the center's plan to quadruple grain output, expressed fear that this "new" version of progress would mirror the Great Leap Forward, which "was pushed to the point where there was no food to eat."[62]

As the preceding example suggests, the reform-era developmental agenda of the CCP has been superimposed on such alternative memories, which constitute an endless dense forest of local knowledge that competes with the thin edge of dominant institutional memory and the external identities, training, and experiences of China scholars whose efforts to understand political contention in rural China are undertaken on the outer edge of this forest. Once we enter the forest through individuals and their personal life stories, we meet up with memories that come shooting out of the terrible Maoist past. These memories, in combination with the injuries and injustices of reform, structure polychromatic discourses that compete with the CCP's monochromatic claim on the sole, sovereign right to use force to promote development and crush any challenge to its hold on power.

This book draws on these oral discourses with individuals to show that the official, monochromatic narrative of the Communist Party has crumbled under

[61] Kelliher, *Peasant Power in China*, 40–42, 46–49.   [62] Ibid., 45.

reform. People in Da Fo and other border area villages increasingly see the attempt to maintain it as discredited folly. Their counternarratives emerge from the forest of long-term memory to challenge the party's attempt to confiscate their understanding of the past, posing an obstacle to the party's efforts to create a civilization in which rural people are not individuals with memories of a state system that has repeatedly attempted to take ownership of personal and private life, to take away the cultural resources necessary for individual remembering of its violence, and to build deniability into the process whereby its agents endanger those who rely on what has previously been learned to challenge inhumane methods of rule.

A RECOVERY OF RIGHTS

In attempting to explain the proliferation of mass protest incidents in the PRC under reform, some China scholars have pointed to the phenomenon of a growing "rights consciousness" movement, attributing this movement to the desire of would-be citizens to freely establish the right to participate in governance in order to reform the exclusive and harmful politics hitherto practiced by the CCP-captured state.[63] Whether the rise of rights-focused contention has occurred independent of the influence of CCP rule is an important question. To Elizabeth J. Perry, the reform-era assertion of popular claims through protest and resistance reflects a long-standing commitment of the Mao-led CCP to guarantee the livelihood of the rural poor and the Maoist embrace of Confucian norms supportive of the state obligation to care for the basic social rights of its subjects.[64] Such resistance, understood as a "state-conferred privilege" rather than an inviolable right, and representing a quest for social justice rather than a challenge to regime authority, allegedly has supported, rather than subverted, China's authoritarian political system.[65] Starting with a somewhat different premise, O'Brien and Li have asserted that the rural people who have turned to "rightful resistance" have justified their claims in the participatory language, statutes, and policies of the regime itself, a process that sometimes has enlisted leaders in Beijing in their cause, so that such resistance most likely has bolstered the legitimacy of the party-state.[66]

By way of contrast, this book conceives everyday contention in the Chinese countryside as an attempt by villagers to exercise long-standing indubitable rights – rights that historically were acquired through household-based struggles to keep the state at bay. Such rights were indeed enshrined in Mencian-Confucian philosophy and passed on locally through practice.

---

[63] See Goldman, *From Comrade to Citizen*, 71–74, and O'Brien and Li, *Rightful Resistance in Rural China*, 126–127.

[64] Perry, "Chinese Conceptions of 'Rights,'" 38–40, 42.   [65] Ibid., 45–46.

[66] O'Brien and Li, *Rightful Resistance*, 123–128. For a review that concurs with this reading of O'Brien and Li, see Froissart, "Book review," 2.

Following Perry Link, this book questions the notion that Mao and the CCP ever stood for such rights. It argues that the Mao-led CCP actually was against the codes of humane political conduct demanded by Mencian-Confucian teachings[67] and that the Communist Party attempted to destroy the core of this philosophical system, especially in the campaign of the Great Leap Forward, when Mao, operating on the assumption that this philosophical system had trapped the countryside in poverty, declared socialism superior to Confucianism.[68]

All through the Great Leap, local party leaders were busy suppressing the right of the former independent tillers who opposed the transcript of socialist collectivization, and during the Leap famine Mao himself subverted the core principle of Mencian-Confucian thought – the right to remonstrate with imperial power and, if necessary, to remove tyrannical rulers through rebellion.[69] In reality, therefore, Chinese villagers have resisted state intrusions into life-sustaining routines and struggled for individual and family dignity for centuries, but the tight repressive controls of the Mao era made such resistance exceedingly difficult, if not impossible. Thus it should not occasion surprise that the upsurge of contention in present-day rural China has resonance with popular Confucian norms and that such contention has a root in the failures of Mao-era governance.[70]

The post-Mao CCP leaders in Zhongnanhai could not convince the survivors of the Great Leap episode in this rural North China border region that they stood for popular Mencian-Confucian norms, for several reasons. For one thing, the institutional density of the Communist Party's hegemonic institutions – schools, credit cooperatives, health clinics, and media outlets – was never impressive in the remote villages, so that pro-Confucian individuals, groups, and networks were not constantly subjected to the canon of party ideology and, in any event, were not the beneficiaries of a competent party-led performance that could make a case for supplanting common-sense notions of right and wrong, empowerment and disempowerment. In reality, illiterate,

---

[67] Link, "China's Core Problem." Further support for Mao being anti-Confucian can be found in Pantsov, whose work argues that the moral teachings of Confucius played no role in shaping Mao's character or soul. Pantsov, *Mao*, 173, 193, 195. According to Hans Steinmueller, conflict in contemporary China often reflects tensions that were intensified by the CCP-guided process of early state formation, which drew on "a Maoist discourse that violently denigrated Confucian-sim." Steinmuller, "Communities of Complicity," 547. Also see Wenguang Huang, whose book, *The Little Red Guard*, shows how commitments to honor pre-1949 Confucican family obligations persisted, even within the households of lower party leaders, in spite of the Maoist attack on such. Huang, *The Little Red Guard*, esp. 67, 77, 125–127, 162.

[68] See Lemos, *End of the Chinese Dream*, 32–33, 36–37, 104–105, 129–130; Xiang, "Bo Xilai Affair," 60–61; and Zhou Xun, *The Great Famine in China*, 91.

[69] See Yu and Pei, "Seeking Justice: Is China's Petition System Broken?"; Link, "Popular Chinese Views," 9–10; Thaxton, *Catastrophe and Contention*, introduction; and Zhou Xun, *The Great Famine in China*, 142–143.

[70] On this point, I draw especially on Link, "Popular Chinese Views."

often ignorant local party leaders were pressed to compete with the Confucian messages passed on through memory-structured oration and story telling, and so the old mnemonic systems of folk norms continued to compete, more or less effectively, with the party's institutional propaganda.[71] For another thing, because the Maoists shut down rural schools in the Great Leap Forward, and did further damage to rural education in the Cultural Revolution, the CCP was never able to use the school system to bring popular everyday Confucian teaching and thinking to an end at the grass-roots level. As a result, even though the Confucian discourses came under attack in Mao-era campaigns, Confucian values continued to infuse, as Columbia University historian W. Theodore De Bary has put it, "forms more subtle yet still palpable in the popular imagination" – proverbs, songs, doggerels, and poems reflecting the tenacity of this alternative to socialist ideology and community.[72]

In reality, many of the Da Fo villagers born prior to 1978, and especially before the Great Leap Forward, had imbibed key precepts from the *Four Books* and learned from the *Analects*. Consequently, they knew, and still know, what Everett Zhang has discovered in his brilliant scholarship: from Mao Zedong to Deng Xiaoping to Xi Jinping, the CCP has been, and is, more interested in maintaining the "power of death" over rural people than in ensuring their basic social rights.[73] Faced with the legitimacy crisis inherited from the Great Leap episode of state building, reform-era Central Party leaders attempted to appropriate Confucian language and concepts to elicit personal sacrifice from individuals and families in order to promote and defend the party's own interest. However, the anti-Confucian Mao-era campaigns not only had failed to wipe out popular Confucian norms but also discredited the CCP. In this situation, therefore, the survivors of the Leap disaster understood that the Communist Party's unreformed modality of rule was anything but Confucian, and, by extension, they could not put faith in insincere center promises to support struggles to recover basic rights surrendered to Great Leap–era savageries.

RECONCILIATION VERSUS REVENGE

To fully understand the problem with the Communist Party strategy of ritualizing the Great Leap into oblivion, we first need to turn to the work of Jose

---

[71] This is why the Mao-led CCP had to shut down oral dissent through the Hundred Flowers Campaign on the eve of the Great Leap Forward. In constructing this section, I have benefited from Thompson, *Voice of the Past*; Yates, *Art of Memory*, xvii, xi, chapters 1 and 2, esp. 4, 38–47; and Foer, *Moonwalking with Einstein*, 10, 18–19.

[72] De Bary and Tu, *Confucianism and Human Rights*, 22.

[73] Zhang, "The Truth about the Death Toll in the Great Leap Famine in Sichuan," in Zhang, Kleinman, and Tu, eds., *Governance of Life*, 72; also see Watson, "Feeding the Revolution," in Zhang, Kleinman, and Tu, eds., *Governance of Life*, 35.

Maria Naharro-Calderon, a scholar of the place of memory in the aftermath of the Franco-era brutality in Spain. Naharro-Calderon asks us to consider three different types of memory:

1. *Inframemoria* : memories of a harmful direct personal encounter with power, stored in individual victims
2. *Intramemoria*: memories formed when individual encounters with power are given meaning by a community
3. *Supramemorias*: collective memories appropriated by power and used to legitimate the dominance and advantage of those who rule.[74]

Using this conception of memory, we can see that the CCP-originated *yiku sitian* ritual, designed to encourage villagers to recall the bitterness of the pre-1949 Kuomintang period and to savor the sweetness of the good life delivered by the CCP-led revolution, was highly problematic. This ritual, used by the Mao-era CCP to recast the Great Leap disaster as a minuscule sacrifice in the party's long-term struggle to improve popular livelihood and save the nation, failed to revive the legitimacy of the party-state in pre-1978 rural China, as it did not address the personal suffering inflicted on individuals by party activists during the Great Leap and the ensuing famine. The CCP had invoked this ritual to evacuate the kingdom of *inframemoria*, but in reality the antihuman track record of fanatical local party leaders who did the dirty work of the center was seared into the memories of individual survivors.[75] Through these memories, people made sense of their efforts to endure the Great Leap's ruin, so few wanted to give them up.[76] *Yiku sitian,* which was designed to laud the advantage of CCP rule, did not resonate with individual memories of Mao's harm, and so the post-Mao Central government faced an enormous challenge when it came to persuading famine survivors that they could trust the party to perform in ways that would serve their basic interests. In reality, the CCP was not up to this challenge, for the experience of the Great Leap and the ensuing famine inoculated villagers against the post-Mao CCP scheme to reshape consciousness, and the party-state effort to force-feed a bowdlerized version of the ghastly past floundered on the overreach of the *yiku sitian* ritual.[77]

This legitimacy dilemma more or less compelled the Deng Xiaoping–led center to come up with a plan to take the "heat" out of the explosive issue of the Great Leap famine, and so in 1981 *People's Daily* published *A Resolution on Certain Questions in Our Party's History since the Founding of the PRC.* As Susanne Weigelin-Schwiedrzik has pointed out, in this resolution the CCP

---

[74] For a summary of this, see Faber, "The Price of Peace: Historical Memory in Post-Franco Spain," 215.

[75] On this point, see Thaxton, *Catastrophe and Contention*, 292–324.

[76] Cf. Kleinman, *Deep China*, 27–271.

[77] I am indebted to Steven I. Levine for helping me sharpen this point; personal correspondence, spring 2014.

leadership assumed responsibility for the Great Leap disaster and also for the antirightist movements of the Mao era. But the Deng-led reformers also relied on this same resolution to establish institutional domination of public discourse on this topic, making it clear that publicly expressed individual counternarratives of this episode were unwelcome.[78] If the Deng-led center sanctioned a discourse of reconciliation with the Maoist past, this discourse was primarily a nation-building propaganda effort to persuade alienated rural subjects that they had best follow the Communist Party in addressing the past. The purpose was to create a shared memory of the turbulent Maoist past and to convince wounded individuals they could join in a national process of healing wounds incurred in the Mao era. Precisely because the Deng-led transition did not end the authoritarian state system, and in reality was aimed at shoring up that system, there remained a yawning gap between the center's supra-representation of the past and the *inframemoria* of the individual survivors of the Great Leap famine. In failing to create an institutional framework and mechanisms supportive of a reconciliation process attentive to individual discussion about who had harmed whom and who had taken the lives of loved ones, the Communist Party left each living victim of Mao's willed famine[79] to carry the burden of hurt, grief, and resentment within a hidden, silent interior self and to address the wrongdoings of the party's Leap disaster *outside* the channels of the reform-era political system.[80]

Precisely because there was not enough regime change after Mao and because reform-era Central government leaders did not carry out a deep reform of the political work style of party leaders at all levels, the survivors of the Great Leap found it difficult to exit the past and, further, to take up contention that was not linked with active memories of the Leap's injustice. By retaining its village-level political base, the Communist Party granted a silent amnesty to the perpetrators of the Great Leap famine, relieving them of institutional pressure to face up to the criminal violence inducing the famine's damage. By coddling these unapologetic accomplices of a distant, state-orchestrated atrocity, the Deng-led center reassured local party leaders, for whom the CCP was the extension of a robust political identity. Rooted in an understanding that their positions of power and privilege were significantly dependent on a narrative prescribed from higher-ups in Beijing, this identity put the cause of the party above the worth of individual villagers and stressed building state power at any cost to civil society.

In the early 1980s, these local party leaders not only were stuck in the time warp of Mao-era war communism, they also were fearful the angry survivors of the Great Leap might seize on reform to dislodge them and destroy their families. This explains why, in the case of Da Fo village, the old-guard Maoists

---

[78] Cf. Weigeliln-Schwiedzik, "Taking the Heat Out of a Problem," 11–12, 18–19.
[79] On Mao's willful politics, see Bernstein, "Mao Zedong and the Famine."
[80] Cf. Hamber and Wilson, "Symbolic Closure."

who still ruled the roost in the Mao-Deng transition frequently responded to popular complaints and claims in a defensive, arrogant, and vulgar manner, thereby exciting memories of unrepentant evil. Their persistent justification of the ruthless means of Mao-era rule, coupled with the continuing rewards for obeying the orders of superiors, poisoned the soil of reform, transforming it into a garden in which the hostile memories of Great Leap–era injustice and loss could grow like weeds. As we will see in Chapters 3, 5, 6, 7, and 10, in the Da Fo area these memories infused contention in the reform period, and contention took the form of ostracism, beatings, arsons, and threats of extinction against local party leaders and their clients.

I began to understand the importance of these politically charged memories toward the end of my first decade of field work in Da Fo. In previous field work, I had avoided interviewing Bao Yibin, the vice-party secretary who was seriously implicated in the moral descent of the Great Leap and its famine, in the presence of other villagers. In August 1997, I asked several of the individual survivors of the famine to join me in an interview with Bao in his courtyard. I had interviewed them on many occasions, so I knew them well. On their arrival I could tell something was wrong. After a few minutes of silence, they implored me not to speak with Bao Yibin, and they let me know *they* did not want to speak with him. I discovered that they, and scores of other villagers, including Bao Yibin's brother, who was deeply angered by Bao's Leap-era refusal to assist their starving mother in 1960, had not spoken with Bao for nearly four decades. Bao was being ostracized for his Great Leap sins. The village had mounted a silent challenge to Bao's cold-hearted work style, and the challenge included avoiding Bao and occasionally stoning his house to keep him from roaming the village freely. These acts, much as the beatings and arsons targeting other Da Fo party leaders in the reform era, were small ways of punishing local party leaders who were members of a political system that was not about to allow the institutionalized involvement of rural people in any healing and reconciliation process.

Furthermore, although Deng Xiaoping should be credited with dismantling the vigilante institutions of Mao-era killing, the Deng-led center did not go far enough. The so-called reformers failed to provide any forum for desensitizing the local party leaders who had inflicted the terrible acts of the Great Leap's politics. Worse, in some villages they allowed the perpetrators of such acts to operate with impunity across the early decades of reform. The unimaginable cruelty of the Great Leap episode, and its seepage into the post-Mao era, is lost in mainstream academic writings on the so-called great reform of the Deng-led center. By way of contrast, the visceral nature of the Communist Party was not lost on the villagers who, like their counterparts in the USSR in the post-Stalin period, or those in post–Pol Pot Cambodia, had to live in uneasy coexistence with the perpetrators of mass killing and cataclysm. I conducted field work in the Hebei-Shandong-Henan border area villages for many years before I began to grasp the importance of this phenomenon to apprehensive village dwellers.

It first came to me in 1991, when I was conducting an interview of a local party leader who played an important role in helping bring the Communist Party to power in this border area. This particular leader, Yu Weirong, was from Jinglu village, in Neihuang county. In the reform era, Yu had moved out of the border area to Zhengzhou, the capital of Henan province. Villagers helped me find him in Zhengzhou, where I interviewed him on a cloudy day in June. In the course of explaining to me how he had strangled an opponent to death with his bare hands during the pre-1949 revolution, Yu Weirong started to embellish and praise his murderous accomplishments. What struck me was Yu's insistence that the killing of his individual opponents was a necessary, fully justified engagement with Mao's Communist Revolution. Killing was, he said, what the politics of the epoch was all about; that is, killing was central to the normal order of the revolutionary process.

Later, in an August 1997 interview in Da Fo, I discovered that Bao Zhilong, the Da Fo party secretary before and after Mao, also took his identity significantly from being a member of a group of killers and that killing opponents was, to Bao, necessary for keeping the Communist Party in power. I began to develop an understanding that the core identity of many of the key local party leaders in Da Fo had formed in the years of pre-1949 insurgency and crystallized in the war communism of the Great Leap.

The post-1978 Deng-orchestrated reform did not instantly, or systematically, disband this group of killers in rural China – it only dismantled the mechanisms they had relied on to make villagers comply with the routine tasks of Mao-era rule. At the village level, many of these killers were still around, either in power or lurking in the shadows of power. Villagers still feared them. Their presence was a warning that the "normalcy" of Mao era might return, and this presence served as a constant reminder of the pain and loss suffered in the Great Leap upheaval, when the center and its accomplices swiftly imposed a violent normalcy on the countryside. That these local party leaders by and large still ruled with impunity was not lost on villagers, who in the turbulent years of the Mao-Deng transition were still fearful of the aggressive self-serving acts of these leaders. The threat of a return to this past normalcy, coupled with the ability of local party leaders to use their privileged positions and networks in the struggle for the rewards and spoils of reform, made it impossible for villagers to move toward a reconciliation based on forgetting, a politics that infused contention within and beyond the village.

APARTHEID CHINA AND THE STRUGGLE FOR SURVIVAL

The question of why flammable memories of loss in the Great Leap persist, and from time to time foment contention in the countryside, whether it be an individual or community clash with the agents of the party-state, cannot be fully understood without reference to the perpetuation of the Mao-era system of partitioning city and countryside. This state-designed rural-urban divide system – in essence an *apartheid* system – was institutionalized in the run-up to the Great Leap Forward, and it gave urbanites, as opposed to rural villagers, better food security and hence a better chance of surviving the Leap famine. At the village level, the rising social tensions over CCP rule in the present swirl around the failure of Beijing to muster the will and courage to resolve half a century of discrimination against rural dwellers. This book suggests that the harm delivered by such discrimination in the present has reminded individuals, and the small groups of which they are a part, of the fundamental nature of the politics underlying the CCP-dominated political system: in this system, policy is prioritized to serve the material interest of powerful urban-based aristocrats at the apex of the party-state hierarchy. In the reform era, the Communist Party apparently has focused mainly on priming this *apartheid* system, thereby stranding the rural poor in a state of poverty that, to a greater or lesser extent, recalls the damaging inequality and material deprivation of the Great Leap episode.

It is important to emphasize that the reform-era Communist Party has accomplished little if anything by way of effectively altering the core policy–structured *apartheid* practices engendering traumatic loss in the Great Leap Forward, all of which planted angry memories of the "fake rights" of participation in the developmental schemes of socialist dictatorship and seriously damaged the credibility of the party-state. Chapters 4 and 9, which deal with rural education and rural-to-urban migration, suggest that the post-1978 center has continued this pattern of Mao-era *apartheid*, which has become entwined with the fraudulent ad hoc developmental projects of corrupt local power. After listening to villagers express resentment of this entwinement, it seems they live with the specter of a repeat of the deceptive politics in which local party leaders engaged to push the developmental agenda of the Great Leap. To be sure, the CCP-led Central government has attempted to reform the system of rural education and to recognize the importance of labor mobility in lifting rural people out of poverty. But the data on Da Fo show that local power not only has falsified reports pertaining the center's universal goal of nine years of schooling for each rural child but has also designed a "new" education system that mainly puts money into the pockets of corrupt leaders whose local clients were implicated in stunting the development of an empowering school system in the Great Leap. In a similar vein, the reform-era fate of Da Fo's migrant workers has underscored Beijing's failure to put an end to one of the most exploitative labor scams of the Great Leap era: the false promise of a living wage paid to villagers who were pressed, or fled, to work in rural and industrial construction projects. In each of these issue areas, the center has tolerated a pattern of politics that recalls the injustice of the commune era and hinders the amiable and civil pursuit of livelihood.

Chapters 4 and 9 make it clear that whether we are talking about the delivery of a public good (education) or the development of a quasi-public industry (construction), the CCP is first and foremost an organizational empire of rent collectors, and its powerful local operatives do little more than collect rents from the rural poor, while leaving the targets of their plunder to fall behind urbanites. Thus, by complicating villagers' chances to move ahead to a decent life, to move beyond the despair and discontent of the Great Leap episode, the CCP has unwittingly increased the possibility that increasingly mobile villagers will consult such memories in mounting resistance to a state system that specializes in promoting disparities in basic public services and basic social rights.

The testimonies given in this book make clear that the Great Leap, among other CCP-powered failures, had laid bare the lie that the party knew how to make the world a better place for individual villagers and their families. As Barry Naughton has pointed out, in the early years of reform Deng Xiaoping actually did not have a clear plan for the economic development of rural China.[81] Rural individuals, working in myriads of villages like Da Fo, seized on the indecision of Central government rulers, and on the power vacuum created by the collapse of Mao-era controls, to enact their own plans for creating wealth.[82] Invariably, such transcripts called for the revival of ageless household strategies of cereal cultivation, animal husbandry, and petty trade. Rational, benevolent national policy did not direct this revival. Instead, as Fang Lizhi has argued, farmers across China (including those in Da Fo) embraced a slow-moving, day-by-day, year-by-year struggle to lift their families to subsistence, above the poverty into which the unprecedented famine of 1958–1961 had plunged them.[83]

Of course Deng Xiaoping and his allies took credit for this internal, rural ascent even though the December 1978 Third Plenum of the Eleventh CCP Central Committee, which proclaimed Deng to be the paramount ruler of China, forbade many of the reforms that rural people wanted. In the final analysis, therefore, Deng and his allies facilitated the ascent by reluctantly and slowly relaxing Mao-era controls on market participation and by allowing villagers to practice family efficiencies in agriculture and to put creative energies into household-based enterprises.[84] In the meantime, their policy efforts were focused mainly on getting rich from embracing globalization, and in any event they used "reform" internally to benefit their own privileged families and keep power in the hands of their local political networks.[85]

In short, the quest for recovery from the painful material damage of the Mao era did not take place within, and was not driven by, some post-1978 imaginary moral community of reform. Villagers, including those in Da Fo, welcomed reform in order to sustain a long-running, low-profile struggle to regain the

---

[81] Naughton, *Chinese Economy*, 81.
[82] See Zhou, *How the Farmers Changed China*, and Thaxton, *Catastrophe and Contention*.
[83] See Fang, "The Real Deng."
[84] See Friedman, Pickowicz, and Selden, *Revolution, Resistance, and Reform*, 254–255.
[85] For this continuity, see ibid., 279.

economic freedom of the household, including the freedom to till and trade outside the sphere of state rent. If the fabric of everyday material life had been ripped apart in the Mao era, the major concern of Da Fo's farmers in the post-Mao years was how to reconstitute the material basis of a secure, normal life. The evolving site of popular memory of the material deprivation resulting from the great famine, therefore, shifted to two alternative economic spaces in the first decade of reform: the first site was the land, the second the market. The act of tilling a small plot in the solitude of a protected self was vital, for this particular alternative economic activity reflected a household qua household rejection of the state-colonized agricultural system of the collective period, and the act of trading and acquiring material goods in the market constituted a rejection of the Mao era's stifling controls on individual creativity, sense of worth, and material security.

Social science literature tells us that the Deng-led center supported a state-framed version of household agriculture, known as *baochan daohu*. But it does not tell us why. By advancing support for this system the Deng-led reformers attempted to leap ahead of poor farmers who were determined to go it alone, to take credit for alleviating the pain associated with material loss in the famine and its grinding twenty year aftermath, and thus draw villagers into a social contract with the center. In reality, however, people in Da Fo and countless other villages opened this breathing space through everyday struggles, for which the Deng-led center took credit. In reality, Deng and his men were slow to keep up with such everyday struggles to detach the household economy from the state-planned economic system.[86] This book shows how these struggles became entwined with contention, especially when local party leaders threatened their progress with demands that reminded villagers of the Great Leap's harm, and how the counterforce they have mustered against this threat has changed rural power relations.

OVERVIEW

The book's chapters are divided into roughly five parts. The opening chapter transports us into Da Fo village at the dawn of reform, when millions upon millions of rural dwellers still lived a submarginal existence and the Deng-led Central government had to do something to address rural poverty and prevent the rural poor from storming the cities en masse in search of food security.[87] The chapter relates how Deng and his men instituted reform by imposing a violent Strike Hard Campaign known as *yanda*, which was enforced by local public security forces targeting poor farmers who could not afford to pay the rents demanded by state monopoly. It looks into the impact of this campaign

---

[86] Naughton implicitly recognizes this; *Chinese Economy*, 95–96.

[87] See Yang, *Calamity and Reform*, and Fewsmith, *Elite Politics in Contemporary China*, 41.

on Da Fo's desperate farmers, and asks whether this campaign resolved the legitimacy crisis that originated in the Great Leap disaster.

The next three chapters focus on the way in which reform-era Central government policy was received at the township and village level, by both local party leaders and villagers. Chapter 2 is about the way in which villagers responded to state appropriation. It focuses on how Da Fo's farmers saw the reform-era attempt of Communist Party rulers to impose taxes on the countryside and on why taxation stoked fears of another episode of state-delivered famine. It describes what people in Da Fo and other villages did to resist the renewed burden of taxation.

Chapter 3 explores the process whereby villagers, particularly females with the support of their patriarchal families, attempted to reclaim the rights to their bodies, especially the right to produce children as they saw fit. This chapter focuses on the one-child policy and the renewed state invasion of child bearing in a village where the production of children was seen as essential to overcome Great Leap–era ruin of customary social insurance arrangements. It introduces us to the agents of this invasion, to why their unprincipled acts stoked bad memories of the Great Leap, and to how villagers attempted to resist the one-child policy.

Chapter 4 is about villagers' efforts to reinstate a historic entitlement that was all but destroyed by poorly educated, ignorant Mao-era local party leaders: the entitlement of education and enlightenment. This chapter sheds light on the impact of the Great Leap famine on schools and teaching in Da Fo, on the importance of education to poor farmers as well as teachers, and on why and how teacher grievances with roots in the Great Leap era informed resistance in the reform period.

The third part of the book is organized around the theme of corruption. Chapter 5 provides a worm's-eye view of the dangerous wave of corruption that has spilled over Da Fo and the surrounding countryside under reform. This chapter focuses mainly on corruption within Da Fo village and Liangmen township, enabling us to see that this phenomenon has links to the Mao period. It explores how corrupt reform-era party leaders continued to violate popular Confucian ethical codes of conduct that were forsaken in the Great Leap, and how such behavior spurred everyday challenges to party misconduct. Finally, this chapter sheds light on the corruption enveloping the reform-era police force and helps us grasp how rural people saw the police and their version of protective order.

Chapter 6 investigates the way in which Central government leaders have prospered from the state monopoly of a vital public good: electricity. It traces this monopoly all the way down to the village level and focuses on the process whereby the same local party leaders who benefited from the inequities and injustices of the Great Leap Forward took charge of the monopolistic delivery of electric utility services, thereby repositioning themselves and their families to get rich at the expense of farmers. This chapter reveals why the post-Mao

CCP's artificial reform of a state monopoly fueled villagers' confrontations with its ground-level operatives in Da Fo, whose family reputations for venality extended back to the Great Leap calamity.

Chapter 7 focuses on the attempt of villagers to remove corrupt Communist Party rulers by embracing electoral democracy. This chapter shows how the township-level party leaders undermined the democratic project, leaving in place a *nomenklatura* system of power that has changed little since the Maoist era. In Da Fo, the CCP subversion of villagers' quest for democracy was of no small consequence, for this quest was driven by villagers' fears of corrupt and incompetent party leaders engendering another famine. Focusing mainly on Da Fo but on other villages as well, Chapter 7 documents the political weapons frustrated villagers used after the CCP usurped the electoral process, providing us with a hint of why this part of rural China is such a turbulent place.

Constituting the fourth part of the book, Chapter 8 is concerned with an ageless form of contention: deferential petitioning of the powerful. With the CCP capture of the democratic experiment in Da Fo, petitioning became the order of the day – it was one of the few ways villagers could express grievances and present claims to powerful officials. In this chapter, we meet an individual petitioner whose contention was influenced by an incessant yearning to make sense of life in the aftermath of the Great Leap famine. His fate became linked with a transvillage, transcounty, and transprovincial protest movement of ex-PLA soldiers whose efforts to survive and escape village-level dearth in the post-Leap famine period led them to the frozen mountainous terrain of Pakistan. This chapter traces their long struggle for compensation for a distant, secretive sacrifice for the nation, and shows how it was thwarted by higher-ups, including powerful CCP-controlled military hierarchies in Beijing and in Zhongnanhai. Pointing out that Mao also had suppressed petitioners who called attention to the pain of the Great Leap, this chapter invites us to reflect on whether the reform-era repeat of this pattern pricked memories of Mao-era neglect, repression, and betrayal.

Chapters 9 and 10 comprise the fifth part of the book. Each focuses on the rise of counterforce in the reform-era countryside. Chapter 9 documents the engagement of Da Fo's migrant workers, many of whom hailed from households ruined by the Great Leap, with the construction industry in far-flung cities, where they suffered terms of work life that in some ways resembled those of the militaristic labor regime of the late 1950s. This chapter is about the *apartheid* system engendering this suffering, about its unstudied link back to the Great Leap era, and about the forms of everyday resistance to which migrant workers turned to defend themselves from the abuse and injustice of this system. This chapter examines migrant worker–crafted forms of contention in rural places spatially separated from the native villages of migrants and their urban job sites, some of which unfolded outside the formal channels of the Central government.

Chapter 10 is about the rise of the so-called rural mafia in Da Fo and scores of sister villages during the reform period, considering "mafia" from the vantage point of the rural people who became its foot soldiers. This chapter traces the group's origins in a network of friends sporting martial art skills. Focusing on why the key leaders of this network took up martial arts training in the decades following the Great Leap famine, it helps us understand why they were attracted to *Water Margin* legends of marginalized desperados. It explicates the complex link between the need of villagers for protection against local party leaders who were fond of using force in the Great Leap and the attempt of villagers to rely on martial skills to fulfill this need in the late Mao to early Deng period. In asking whether it was the local mafia system or the system of CCP rule that posed the greatest threat to villagers and their preferred way of life, this chapter digs into the complex nature of the Da Fo area martial brotherhood, revealing that its leaders were connected with powerful trans-village and trans-county party leaders and police operatives but also with village social forces opposed to CCP rule. This chapter scrutinizes how Da Fo area "mafia" leaders saw the party-state they occasionally colluded with and, on the other hand, examines why they were attracted to notions of political justice that historically shaped rebellions against imperial tyranny.

In all of these chapters, the book shows how the Great Leap Forward, including the famine it produced, has influenced the way rural people think about life and politics. It also shows that the missing variable of memory is critical to understanding why and how ground-level contention has unfolded in the countryside. This book is about individuals in rural China, about their memories, and about the ways in which those memories affect how they go about life and resist authoritarian rulers who attempt to exercise power on them.

I

The Violent Dawn of Reform

When Mao died in September 1976, China's rural people were still suffering from the impact of his party's great famine. In much of the countryside per capita total daily consumption was below the poverty line, and material deprivation was shocking. In some villages of the Hebei-Shandong-Henan border area, where I interviewed in the following decade, dollar-poverty measures actually rivaled those of poverty-stricken Malawi, Niger, and Sierra Leone. Mao-era disasters, especially the Great Leap famine, had set rural China's economy back to the level of development that obtained in 1928. As Elizabeth Gooch has demonstrated, even with the post-1978 economic improvement, the imprint of the great famine's intensity seriously hindered the recovery of social well-being.[1] With Mao gone, Beijing-centered reformers started to move rural China out of this predicament, or so it seemed.

Convened during late December 1978 in Beijing, the Third Plenum of the Central Committee of the Chinese Communist Party (CCP) solidified the triumph of Deng Xiaoping and his reform agenda, which called for market-driven economic growth and political stability aimed at setting China on a pragmatic course of modern national development. When it came to restructuring the rural economy, this new course would be free of damaging party-state interventions in the habitual survival routines of the rural poor – or so it seemed.[2] Assuming this was the case, Harry Harding proclaimed that the Central government was engineering a "Second Revolution" under Deng.[3] And indeed, the post-Mao center's policy-making process raised the hopes of rural dwellers: the reformers apparently intended to enable farm people to abandon

---

[1] Gooch, "Estimating the Long Term Impact of the Great Famine," 1–21.
[2] Meisner, *Mao's China and After*, 434–435.   [3] Harding, *China's Second Revolution*.

monocropping of grain for a diversified pattern of agriculture, to sell their crops to the state at higher prices, to garner off-farm income through petty trade in reinvigorated local markets, and to break away from the bondage of the collective by pursuing jobs in rural township-based factories and in urban-centered construction work.[4]

Da Fo's farmers by and large welcomed this liberation from the Maoist collective. After all, as I demonstrated in *Catastrophe and Contention in Rural China*, in the two decades following Mao's Great Leap famine, many of them had waged day-by-day, year-by-year struggles to escape state control of their attempts to scratch out a living. Even as Deng Xiaoping proclaimed his reform agenda, they were still cultivating small, private strips of sweet potato land into which they invested most of their energy and organic fertilizer; stuffing their skinny bodies with grain that the state would otherwise procure from them at a low price; and conducting petty trade in small markets off the radar of the Liangmen People's Commune leaders – and not one of these endeavors was authorized by the Maoist collective.[5] For most Chinese villagers, the dramatic policy shift of the 1978 Third Plenum did promise a better world. But people in Da Fo had already envisioned this world through decades of resistance. By embracing the general thrust of the Deng-conceived policies, farmers in Da Fo hoped to improve productivity and sustain the inch-by-inch ascent they had engineered in the last years of the collective. As matters unfolded, however, the state violence that accompanied reform made this climb problematic.

In the early years of China's opening to the world, when *Time* magazine was proclaiming Deng Xiaoping "Man of the Year" and John Denver's popular song "Shanghai Breezes" connected Americans with the image of a warm, gentle, and exotic China, a handful of American scholars were permitted to commence field work in the Chinese countryside. One of the privileged few, I was granted rare access to villages in the remote Hebei-Shandong-Henan border area in the mid-1980s, and this access eventually led me to Da Fo. Little did I realize the extent to which my access was arranged in ways that walled me off from a wave of police state violence that was rolling over the countryside. Only later, after twenty trips to the rural interior, did I begin to detect a bone-deep enmity among Da Fo's farmers, a hatred that stemmed in part from unjust treatment at the hands of an emerging Deng Xiaoping–led police state at the violent dawn of reform.

---

[4] For this intended and happy outcome, see the excellent studies by Harding, *China's Second Revolution*, 101–107; Zhou, *How the Farmers Changed China*, 137, 144–145, 146–147; Zweig, *Freeing China's Farmers*, 70–73, 139, 189–193; and Friedman, Pickowicz, and Selden, *Revolution, Resistance, and Reform*, 242–243. A great strength of Friedman et al. is that they show reform was difficult and that local power holders in the thrall of Maoist ideology were recalcitrant and slow to move.

[5] Thaxton, *Catastrophe and Contention*, chapter 8.

THE RESUMPTION OF WAR COMMUNISM

In 1983, Deng Xiaoping officially conceived and then pushed for a centralized national anticrime movement known as *yanda*, the Strike Hard Campaign. Ostensibly designed to halt the rise of lawless gang activity engendered by the Cultural Revolution – a phenomenon the Third Plenary Session did not address – the Strike Hard Campaign stemmed in reality from the desire of Beijing's post-Mao leadership to address a crisis in public security resulting from decollectivization and to prevent the rural poor from entering cities en masse in search of food security.

The first five years of decollectivization (1978–1983) had dismantled Mao-era militia controls on rural villages, thereby weakening the Communist Party's ability to colonize and directly rule the countryside. With the disintegration of the commune, local Public Security forces that had previously been subordinate to commune and county-level governments increasingly lost control of rural communities and suffered a power deflation, due in part to the decay and apprehensiveness of local party branches and in part to a shortage of professionally trained police.[6] A rise in economic crime in the countryside was accompanied by the mushrooming of large groups of criminals in cities, including Beijing, Tianjian, and Qingdao. Urban Public Security forces were pressed to effectively patrol and suppress this "criminal uprising," which threatened the privileged networks, neighborhoods, and kin of the key leaders of the CCP. Many of the so-called criminal bands were composed of poor drifting ruralites who wanted a better life in urban China. Some had been released from prison labor reform sites; others were just rootless unemployed villagers. Upper-level Communist Party leaders' great fear of these desperate floaters, who roamed cities in search of jobs and food security, combined with the center's fear that they would accost global diplomats, business folk, and tourists to drive the nationwide *yanda* campaign.[7]

The Cultural Revolution had indeed unleashed waves of hooliganism, vigilantism, and criminality across China. In the early years of reform, public order proved a major headache for the Chinese police. In 1980, there were 750,000 cases of police-logged crime. The figure shot up to 890,000 in 1981, dropped to 740,000 in 1982, and then spiked again in the first quarter of 1983. The crime rate went up dramatically in the peak summer tourist season, magnifying the need to establish order for city residents and global travelers. Determined to arrest the spread of urban crime, in the summer of 1983 Deng Xiaoping convened a series of meetings with Liu Fuzhi, Peng Zhen, and Zhang Jieqing. According to Liu Fuzhi's memoir, Deng criticized a published Public Security report as not being radical enough, urging Public Security forces to arrest and strictly punish criminals and to improve public education about the CCP's anticrime policies. He insisted on organizing multiple three-year-long "battles"

---

[6] Cf. Xu, *Mutual Empowerment*, 13, 43–44, 46–47.   [7] Liu, "Yanda Jiu Shi Zhuanzheng," 1–3.

that would exterminate criminality in large cities. "We should arduously arrest, penalize, and reform criminals, including assassins, robbers, gangsters, and human traffickers," Deng declared. He went on to insist: "We should not leave criminals fearless. This is a people's dictatorship, and here we protect the safety of the majority. This is humanitarianism." The first *yanda* campaign, targeting 70,000 criminals – with its primary focus on hooligans, kidnappers, rapists, and murderers in key state-developed cities – exploded in August–December 1983.[8]

Deng Xiaoping's battle plan for the Strike Hard Campaign had its roots in his historical engagement with internal public security in the People's Republic of China (PRC). During the Anti-Japanese War of Resistance, Deng had served as the secretary of the party's antiespionage bureau in the Shanxi-Hebei-Shandong-Henan area. When the CCP won the civil war and the PRC was established, Mao Zedong called on Deng to host a series of meetings on public security, and Deng subsequently influenced PRC guidelines on internal public security, crime, and law. He played a key role in carrying out the ruthless antirightist campaigns against those who spoke up against the Great Leap Forward. He also endorsed Mao's 1959 decision to promote Xie Fuzhi to head of Public Security, knowing full well that Xie had served as Yunnan CCP provincial secretary when thousands of villagers lost their lives to the famine and that Xie was to take charge of suppressing the social unrest stemming from the intensifying famine.[9] With his triumph in the Eleventh Plenum, Deng Xiaoping instinctively seized leadership of public security work. According to Liu Fuzhi, Deng's decision to launch the 1983 Strike Hard Campaign resonated with the practical wisdom of Marxism-Leninism-Maoism, for Deng reasoned that historical experience had taught the CCP that "an iron hand is essential in implementing the people's democratic dictatorship."[10] Not surprisingly, therefore, the template for the Strike Hard Campaign was remarkably similar to that of the tempestuous war communism campaigns utilized by Mao and Deng in the 1950s: it was a party-orchestrated outburst of the sort of political militancy that had driven rural people to ruin in the Great Leap Forward and its famine.[11]

Yanda shared at least two important features with the monstrous campaigns of the Mao era. Throughout 1983, city dwellers were detained on the basis of unproven, sometimes false accusations supported by party-state propaganda. In a number of cases, *yanda* was employed to target people who posed cultural threats. A movie star named Chi Zhiqiang was one victim. *China Youth Daily*

---

[8] Ibid. and Tanner, *Strike Hard!*, 87–94.
[9] This information comes from two sources: Guo, *China's Security State*, 16, 205–206, and Zhou Xun, *Forgotten Voices of Mao's Great Famine*, 7–8.
[10] Liu, "Yanda Jiu Shi Zhuanzheng," 1–3.
[11] See Bernstein, "Mao Zedong and the Famine"; Thaxton, *Catastrophe and Contention*; and Wemheuer, *Famine Politics*, Part 2, "Politicization of Hunger."

accused Chi of being a criminal "black sheep" for dancing, watching movies, and engaging in one-night stands with relatives of high party cadres, and Nanjing Pubic Security forces sentenced Chi to four years in prison just as his career was taking off. Deng Lijun, whose love songs had begun to spread among young people through private cassette reproduction, was defined as a "spiritual polluter." During the Strike Hard Campaign, Sichuan Public Security pressed the courts to sentence Zhou Shifeng, a staff member of a Chengdu guest house and a fan of Deng Lijun's songs, to seven years in prison for illegally producing "obscene" music tapes. If the early 1980s saw an expansion of the private sphere in urban China, *yanda* placed limits on that expansion.[12]

Strike Hard also replicated Mao-era repression. In city after city, top CCP leaders and Public Security personnel stoked public indignation toward accused criminals, often issuing calls for quick, violent revenge against the accused. In the last quarter of 1983, tens of thousands of "criminals" were detained, arrested, and rapidly executed. In this period, the Ministry of Public Security revved up the same chilling theatrical performances of the Maoist past: people were sentenced and shamed in mass public meetings, and alleged wrongdoers were paraded through the streets with derogatory signs around their necks while scores of police cars, sirens screaming, were dispatched to seize "criminals" reported by "the masses." Presenting *yanda* as a military campaign, the CCP's Propaganda Department did everything in its power to persuade urban dwellers that such repressive violence was necessary and effective.

Whether the first Strike Hard Campaign enabled the CCP to swiftly regain the trust and loyalty of its urban constituency is unclear, but it seems that this campaign did relegitimate the Communist Party. Although urban people realized that many wrongful prosecutions had taken place and that Deng's violent policy trumped the rule of law, the majority reportedly supported the campaign. According to one report, "A lot of people paid visits to the Public Security Bureaus to thank them for their work."[13] Apparently, they felt safer because the crackdown had reestablished clear boundaries that could not be crossed without penalty.

At the same time that Deng and his reform team were carrying out Strike Hard, moreover, they were also dismantling some of the terrifying mechanisms of Maoist rule, including the public criticism session. This process allowed people in state-favored cities and towns to recover space in which they were increasingly free to reactivate the arts of family and neighborhood discourse, as well as family-based entrepreneurship and small trade. To be sure, Deng was reconfiguring a single-party-led police state, but the reformers could promise there would be more privacy and personal freedom, and they were able to

---

[12] See Li Jun, "1983 'Yanda' de Beilun" and "Cong Zhong Cong Kuai: 1983 Nian 'Yanda' De Beilun."

[13] Ibid.

justify the Strike Hard Campaign as a measure for restoring political and social order so that economic development could progress unhindered by crime.[14] Still other subtle changes offered reassurance that the party-state operated differently in the era of reform. In the first Strike Hard Campaign, a few privileged, high-ranking Communist Party officials were targeted and summarily punished, cuing urbanites that the Central government would not tolerate the crimes of party-based "princelings." Additionally, some of the harshest sentences against wrongly accused celebrities were reduced, signaling the urban public that expressions of disbelief over false accusations would be heard.

The lawless politics of the Mao years had created a great fear of chaos and crime among urban dwellers, and the center was able to take advantage of this fear to override popular distrust of the emergent police state and elicit sympathy for Public Security forces portrayed as working overtime and sacrificing to protect urbanites from imagined enemies of prosperity and progress.[15] Apparently, therefore, the "right-wing populism" of the Deng-led reformers that is underscored in the writings of Jonathan Unger and Edward Friedman had a lineage going all the way back to the first Strike Hard Campaign, which appealed to educated, career-aspiring urbanites who were predisposed to support an antidemocratic police state in return for the center's retreat from constant direct interventions in daily personal life.[16]

If those with urban residence permits (*hukou*) and connections to the CCP-structured apartheid order were the principal beneficiaries of the Strike Hard Campaign, the impact of *yanda* on people in distant rural villages was more problematic. In late 1983, Public Security forces spread the Strike Hard Campaign to the Hebei-Shandong-Henan border area. Here, the campaign was designed to maintain the discriminatory city-based polity of the Communist Party as well as address crime, and so it was even more punitive. Scores of Da Fo's farmers experienced *yanda* as forceful exclusion from the promise of reform, and some still equate *yanda* with suffering and loss. We do not have any studies of *yanda* in rural China. What follows is a small step toward understanding how it was implemented, who gained and lost from it, and its political consequences in the Henan village of Da Fo.

RURAL SURPLUS LABOR AND PETTY CRIME

Da Fo's farmers hold deeply layered historical memories of the "Second Revolution" wrought by the Deng reform. These memories undercut the dominant representation of reform – one that villagers would argue was based on a distant Central government transcript that paid scant attention to local

---

[14] I am indebted to Harold M. Tanner for this insight. Personal correspondence, May 20, 2009.
[15] Tanner, personal correspondence, May 30, 2009.
[16] Cf. Unger, "China's Conservative Middle Class," 27–31, and Friedman, "Post-Deng China's Right Wing Populist Authoritarian Foreign Policy," 21–24.

knowledge of the politics delivering Deng's economic policy, and one whose adherents evaluated reform policy by using an abbreviated time scale that obscured the party-state violence infusing the early years of reform.[17] The initial impact of reform on the existing condition of rural surplus labor – which in the Da Fo area meant young farmers without the means to effectively practice household agriculture, engage the market, or pursue city-based jobs – has not been fully appreciated.

The Great Leap famine and the twenty years of dearth that followed had ruined Da Fo's small farmers, and the small, infertile strips of land provided in the 1982 land redistribution severely tested their efforts to immediately boost the protein component of their food supply. In the early phase of reform, therefore, the first generation of reform-era farmers, whose fathers had barely survived Mao's assault on agriculture, faced two serious challenges. Lacking sufficient food, they were often undernourished and weak and thus unable to find the physical strength required to clear the fields for planting, to dig and maintain individual wells, and to harvest crops in a timely fashion. They were also bereft of capital and hence rarely had the ready cash to obtain seeds, chemical fertilizers, and pesticides for their fields. The Deng "reform" did not automatically resolve these problems.[18] The official image of reform as an overnight miracle in which tillers could snap their fingers and suddenly bolster grain crop yields, increase per capita income, and fully recover earned household entitlements was not consistent with everyday reality for Da Fo's poorest farmers.

The transition to household-based agriculture was a period of vulnerability. Precisely because the Central government reenacted the pre-1949 practice of investing mainly in agricultural zones with superior crop lands and with comparatively developed transport links to the cities, where its high-grade cadres resided, the poor interior villages with infertile lands and primitive links to faraway Beijing, Tianjin, and coastal magnets of global commerce were neglected. The late-Qing/early-Republican-era pattern of disinvestment in marginal agricultural regions reappeared.[19] Da Fo's farmers suffered from this state neglect. Even when the Central government began to import phosphate-based fertilizer from the United States and Japan, Beijing and its Henan provincial clients maintained a monopoly on chemical fertilizer, selling it through state agents at artificial, dictated prices beyond the reach of Da Fo's ordinary farmers.[20]

The challenge of transitioning to household-based farming was even more daunting in Da Fo because many of the village's poor eighteen- to

---

[17] I am indebted to Pierson for helping me grasp this point. Cf. *Politics in Time*, 45.

[18] To his credit, Harding found that villagers were not investing capital in farming in the early reform period, though he did not locate the dearth of capital in the enduring impact of Great Leap deprivation. Cf. *China's Second Revolution*, 105.

[19] On this pattern, see Pomeranz, *Making of a Hinterland*.

[20] On the state monopoly of chemical fertilizer, see Friedman, "Deng versus the Peasantry," 39.

twenty-five-year-old farmers hailed from families whose labor force had been decimated in the Great Leap famine. At the dawn of reform, they were farming alone. They had to use primitive tools to plow, plant, and harvest their fields individually, and they often worked those fields with their bare hands (instead of using farm tools). For some, the longer, harder work days of the Great Leap years were coming back.

Da Fo's half-starved farmers had managed to escape Mao's great famine in part by planting sweet potatoes in small household plots in 1961–1962, and they survived over the ensuing decades by relying on this durable, high-yield, fallback tuber crop. Bao Chaoxiang describes how Da Fo's farmers came to rely on sweet potatoes: "During the collective time, we did not have chemical fertilizer. We had to plant more sweet potatoes. Other crops, like wheat and corn, demanded more fertilizer, but sweet potatoes could produce high yields without fertilizer. As a result, we had a lot of sweet potatoes at home, and we had to eat them all the time."[21] The cost to farmers' health was tremendous.[22] Long-term reliance on this starchy tuber caused serious gastrointestinal disorders, including bleeding ulcers, so that sweet potatoes were associated with the woefully poor food regime of Maoist disorder. After Deng came to power, Bao and his peers were desperate to abandon sweet potato production, not just because it was unhealthy but also because they needed a high-protein diet to perform labor-intensive family-based farming, ply local markets, and occasionally search for jobs in distant towns and cities. They could not do this, however, because they were cash poor and could not afford chemical fertilizer, the price of which, again, was dictated by the state.[23]

They faced, moreover, the perennial scourge of tillers: the tax burden. To be sure, early-Deng tax claims provided relief from collective-era procurement, but in Da Fo the per-household grain tax spiraled upward, reaching 20 percent of total income in the first decade of reform. Da Fo's farmers could have coped with these difficulties if the Deng-led reformers had funded vocational training programs supportive of family-based farming as an enterprise, but the center failed them, leaving them with no way of developing the skills they needed to produce specialized products for the market or to acquire the knowledge necessary to engage in legal, quickly profitable sideline production.

Finally, we must include a much neglected factor in this counternarrative of the politics of the early years of the Deng-led reform. In places such as Da Fo, farmers remained powerless to effect reform on their terms or to openly challenge local CCP leaders who either opposed or reworked reform to enrich mainly themselves, their families, and their cronies. For the center, power still grew out the barrel of a gun, and the center's local cadres hustled to make certain that guns did not fall into the hands of farmers when decollectivization

---

[21] Bao Chaoxiang, interview.   [22] Thaxton, *Catastrophe and Contention*, chapter 9.
[23] Bao Chaoxiang, interview.

triggered the disbandment of the militias. In Da Fo, the years 1978–1983 witnessed an upsurge in the attempts of farmers to acquire primitive hunting rifles. Fearing its rural cadre base would be hunted, the center responded by issuing an order for local party activists to seize all such weapons, which is precisely what they did. Though it is unlikely that rural people would have used such weapons to directly challenge the center, the important point is that they were left without the resources to enforce the promise of reform against local power holders who twisted reform to serve their own ends.

Whereas the early 1980s saw *People's Daily* churning out columns on the dangers of an emergent class of self-serving, ostentatious, rich peasants, this was hardly an issue in Da Fo village. The more salient problem was that few of its poorest inhabitants, whose households had yet to recover from loss in the Great Leap famine years, were able to achieve a stable livelihood through family-based farming. To be sure, with reform, life was getting better. For nine months a year, there was more food, but farmers still lacked the capital and the chemical fertilizer needed to improve food quality and provide for their households across an entire year. Many recall that they remained handcuffed by the inherited poverty of the collective era, and they remember the challenge of making up the cost of government disinvestment, improving soil fertility, and keeping up with tax claims as overwhelming. Coupled with local party corruption, the center's policy of rushing the transition to household-based agriculture left Da Fo's poorest tillers in the lurch. Many, therefore, had to engage in high-risk behavior in order to survive.

Desperate young males frequently turned to petty theft in order to compete in the political economy of the reform era. The Hebei-Shandong-Henan border area was convulsed by a wave of economic crime in the early 1980s. By 1983–1985, Da Fo's poor farmers had joined this rat race, pilfering both private and public goods in order to make ends meet. Many of the petty thieves were the young adult orphans of Mao's war communism, protected from police investigators by kin who had themselves suffered from the debilitating consequences of Mao-era malfunctions. They most often targeted the state-monopolized good that was absolutely essential for any chance of success in farming the fields: chemical-based fertilizer. This black gold was not only a requirement for boosting productivity in Da Fo's nitrogen-deficient fields, it was associated in the popular imagination with party-state domination and was inextricably connected to popular memories of the debilitating food regime of Mao's Great Leap famine and its long-term damage to the body.

Bao Nianxi, who was thirty-two years old and a father of three when Da Fo's collective broke up, recalls how he became a petty criminal and target of the *yanda* campaign:

After the land was divided to my household, I was in a dilemma. I did not have any chemical fertilizer. Chemical fertilizer was very hard to find at the time.... Since we did not have any chemical fertilizer in Da Fo, a few young people in Da Fo discussed what to do. Someone suggested that we should try to steal some chemical fertilizer bags from the passing government trucks. We thought this was a good idea. Therefore, a few of us went to the roadside to take the bags from the trucks. We dug some holes in the highway, which slowed down the passing trucks. As the trucks slowed, we mounted them and threw down bags of the chemical fertilizer. The drivers ... did not dare stop us, because there were quite a few people doing this. They were afraid we would beat them up.[24]

Scores of Da Fo's young farmers secretly boarded government trucks passing along Dongle county's poor roads in the midnight hours and threw huge bags of fertilizer onto the ground. Villagers escalated this struggle to rectify the exclusive party-state domination of chemical fertilizer with abandon until local Public Security forces began replacing the fertilizer truck drivers with nonuniformed agents and then, increasingly, engineering surprise arrests of the culprits. The official crackdown on such petty crime became entwined with the politics of the Strike Hard Campaign. Thus, in late 1983, the Deng-led center initiated a police onslaught against a rising tide of rural petty crime that its own flawed developmental policies had exacerbated and to some extent produced. As Scot Tanner has noted, the *yanda* campaign was characterized by "frenetic overtime police activity."[25] In the vicinity of Da Fo, this activity was characterized by injustice in the identification and selection of "criminals" for arrest, the classification of crimes, the treatment of prisoners, and the severity of sentencing. To some extent, therefore, this campaign replicated the Great Leap model of policing, for between 1958 and 1961 the tensions between rural people and the CCP were, according to Xiezhi Guo, the result of the public security's harsh treatment of villagers who had turned to small crime out of desperation as well as the pain of acute hunger.[26]

THE INJUSTICE OF *YANDA* IN DA FO

In the name of *yanda*, Public Security forces throughout the Hebei-Shandong-Henan border area subjected poor farmers to everything from arbitrary arrest, frame-ups, and false accusations of group crime to kangaroo trials with laughable procedural protections to cruel sentences and punishments, including, according to Scot Tanner, "the use of execution on a tremendous numerical scale."[27] Public Security relied on local party leaders and their minions to implement the Strike Hard Campaign at the village level.[28] This practice, coupled with the poor training of the police, gave rise to discretionary arrests involving arbitrary decisions by village party leaders implicated in the unjust punishments of the Mao era. Describing the theft of electrical wire – the sort of petty crime common in the early years of reform – Tang Wensheng offers one

---

[24] Bao Nianxi, interview.   [25] Tanner, "Campaign-Style Policing," 171.
[26] Guo, *China's Security State*, 205–206.   [27] Tanner, "Campaign-Style Policing," 171.
[28] Cf. ibid., 177.

glimpse of how Da Fo's party leaders protected themselves and their families from the harsh punishments of the *yanda* campaign. He mentions both party secretary Bao Zhilong, who had held power in Da Fo almost continuously since the CCP took power, and Bao Wanqing, who was tapped to succeed him: "Bao Zhilong was still the party secretary, and Bao Wanqing was the deputy party secretary. At the time, Bao Wanqing's young brother was stealing electricity wire from the village. My father caught him. But instead of admitting fault, he beat up my father. My father was very angry with Bao Wanqing's younger brother. He wanted to sue him in court. But Bao Zhilong said it would not be a good thing if my father brought a lawsuit.... Secretary Bao persuaded Bao Wanqing and his younger brother to apologize to my father. My father had to listen to Bao Zhilong, and so in the end he agreed not to sue."[29]

By contrast, Da Fo farmers without connections to party leaders rarely got away with small economic transgressions. Da Fo's party leaders sold these people down the river, collaborating with the police to apprehend and jail fellow villagers for stealing farm animals, motor carts, and electrical wires and transformers. In speaking of the arrest of his two brothers during the 1983 Strike Hard Campaign for stealing a goat, Tang Wensheng makes this point: "Theirs was not a serious crime by any standard. But it took place at the same time when the government was cracking down hard on criminals. Deng Xiaoping started this campaign to severely punish criminals and criminal gangs. His word was the law of the land. Because he wanted it this way, millions of Chinese families were negatively affected. Two of my brothers were ruined in this campaign. As a result, my family also acquired a very bad reputation in Da Fo. My fourth brother lost his wife, and my fifth brother was unable to marry. He is still single at the age of thirty-six. I did not like Deng Xiaoping's policy."[30]

The discretionary policing of the first *yanda* campaign also gave rise to a culture of frame-ups, the result of which was a massive transfer of spontaneous, haphazardly planned individual petty crimes into the category of premeditated and serious group robbery – a process the police embraced to convince superiors they were fulfilling Deng Xiaoping's mandate to get tough with "criminal gangs." Bao Nianxi recalls how the process worked in his own case:

I personally took five bags of chemical fertilizer that one time.... All together, we stole about one thousand yuan worth of this good. According to the law of the state, as individuals we had not committed a crime serious enough to be arrested and sentenced to prison. However, at this time Deng Xiaoping started a Strike Hard Campaign to severely punish criminal activities.... In order to punish us severely, the police put us in the category of a criminal gang. Actually, we were not a gang. We did not have any organization, and we did not do anything except take chemical fertilizer this one time, individually and in small groups. The police also added up the total value of *all* the stolen

[29] Tang Wensheng, interview. On Bao Zhilong's rise and Mao-era actions, see Thaxton, *Catastrophe and Contention*.
[30] Ibid.

fertilizer bags, which came to over one thousand yuan. According to the law, any theft involving over one thousand yuan could be prosecuted. They arrested more than a dozen people from our village for theft of chemical fertilizer. My case involved seven people. . . . I received the most severe sentence, which was four years in prison, in part because Bao Zhilong, the Da Fo party secretary, was biased against my family. Secretary Bao was upset with me, and he said something bad about me to the Dongle county police when they talked with him about our case.[31]

Politics colored the criminal justice system, giving the police a pretext to create artificial "gang crime" where it did not exist and giving small-fry Communist Party leaders the chance to hurt personal enemies.

The practice of the police frame-up was facilitated by a culture of snitching. Fostered by local Public Security, snitching made it more difficult for Da Fo's farmers to treat family and fellow villagers compassionately, and it often gave rise to vendettas, imagined and real. Take the case of Ruan Sheping. In the first *yanda* campaign, Ruan's nephew, Ruan Yongqiang, was involved in a case of dog theft. Out of compassion, Ruan had allowed his nephew, a poor orphan, to sleep in his home. When the police came to arrest the nephew, however, they also arrested and detained Ruan Sheping for forty-eight days. To be sure, Ruan Sheping knew that his nephew was wanted by the police, "but," Ruan tells us, "I could not kick him out of my house, or report him to the police. If I had done that . . . villagers would have thought I had betrayed my relative, and I would not have had the face to appear in the village." How, then, did local Public Security locate Ruan's nephew? According to Ruan, "Somebody in Da Fo reported me and him to the police. I do not know who did it. Without someone to inform the police, they would never have known that my nephew was sleeping in my house. They would not have known where my house was located. The police gave the informant a sum of money. . . . I do not believe that I had an enemy in Da Fo who would want to sell me out to the police. So the person who reported us to the police must have done so because of money."[32]

Ruan Sheping was framed and sent to prison. His family had to spend 8,000 yuan to get him out, and his nephew put another 20,000 yuan into police pockets to secure his release, "because," says Ruan, "he felt guilty that I had been implicated by him."[33] There were three other young Da Fo villagers involved with his nephew's case, however, and because they had unintentionally killed the dog's owner during the theft, the case lingered on after Ruan Sheping secured his freedom. One of the other thieves was sentenced to life in prison; the remaining two got fifteen years, lesser sentences purchased by payoffs to the police. In the course of making the payments, one of the relatives of Da Fo's young dog thieves learned the identity of the police informant, and this discovery triggered great anger and set the families of the imprisoned thieves against those of the snitch and his kin.

---

[31] Bao Nianxi, interview. [32] Ruan Sheping, interview. [33] Ibid.

The story of the snitch, who turned out to be a thief himself, sheds light on the way local Public Security operated in the first Strike Hard Campaign and why villagers found it so unsettling. The police informant was named Yi Ding, the son-in-law of Da Fo's Ruan Xiantang, a poor farmer with two sons and one daughter. Normally in Da Fo, someone with two sons would not permit his son-in-law to live in his house, but Ruan Xiantang allowed Yi Ding to live with him. Only later did villagers come to understand the reason: Yi Ding was a skilled professional thief, and Yuan had arranged for his daughter to marry Yi Ding in order to enrich the family. Revealed to be the snitch, Yi Ding fled the village. Ruan Xiantang and his family had to continue living in Da Fo, however, and they had to pay for their failed scheme – and for Yi Ding's role in it. Ruan Sheping explains that the four families of the sentenced thieves had "made life miserable for Ruan Xiantang and his family" ever since.[34] In this case and many others, Deng's emergent police state pitted the poor against the poor, using big thieves to catch small thieves whose thievery was largely the product of state policy. Drawn into the drama of other revenge-seeking families, Ruan Sheping's life was turned upside down by the policing of reform. A small act of compassion had become entwined with damage to individual honor and, moreover, had thrown the social harmony that so many of Ruan's counterparts hoped for out the window.

Police trickery and cruelty degraded the individual worth of the accused offenders. In Dongle county, small thieves were put in jails, where they were beaten. Speaking of the time he spent in prison, Ruan Sheping recalls: "We were locked up in a small room, a space of about thirty square meters. There were over twenty prisoners in this one room. It was terribly overcrowded. The police chose the criminal with the worst criminal record and the fiercest demeanor to be the head of this detention room. He was the one who beat the other criminals under his command. He beat the people whom the police indicated needed to be beaten. He also beat people for his personal reasons. If he did not like someone, he would beat him up. He asked other criminals to do things for him, and if they did not obey he would beat them up."

Ruan's testimony also helps up grasp why Public Security teamed up with such criminals in the early phase of the reform. According to Ruan, "The police did not beat the detainees themselves. If they wanted us beaten, they asked the criminals to beat us. In this way, the police would not be held responsible for the beatings."[35] Apparently, this practice was widespread, occurring in other county jails of the border area. Recalling the time when his two brothers were arrested by Daming county police for a goat theft, Tang Wenshen says that "hardened criminals" beat up prisoners who had not yet been sentenced "with police encouragement" in Daming county.[36]

---

[34] Ibid.   [35] Ibid.   [36] Tang Wensheng, interview.

Oral testimonies also indicate that during the period of custody Da Fo's farmers were not given enough food to meet the needs of daily consumption, and they were compelled to perform unpaid labor to generate revenue for the state. Bao Guihang, imprisoned for five months, describes such an experience:

This five months was the hardest time in my life. I was treated worse than a dog. The police . . . made us work hard every day. We were told to make paper and cloth flowers. They gave each person a quota. If you did not finish this job on time, you were beaten by the leader of the prisoners. We had to wake up at six a.m. and start work right away without breakfast. . . . People who were slow workers had to continue working until midnight. You were not permitted to go to sleep until you finished your day's quota. If you did not finish, the next morning the leaders of the prisoners would beat you.

The prison leader was the cruelest person I had ever encountered. He beat other prisoners very hard. He kicked them with his leather shoe. He broke the tailbones of many prisoners. Deprived of food, sleep, and rest, many of the prisoners were easily cowed into submission. The conditions were so terrible that people in good health were broken in a few months.[37]

This pattern of harsh treatment was right out of the Great Leap, when party-backed brigade and company leaders relied on brute force to make villagers comply with the rules of the commune, which were imposed in ways that were demeaning. Reflecting on reform-era prison labor, Bao remarked: "Those paper and cloth flowers were produced for export. It seemed that they were to be used at funerals in some foreign country. Making them was very delicate work, and not the right job for men. But the police forced the male prisoners to do it, and they saw this as a means of making the prisoners suffer."[38]

For many prisoners, this suffering was protracted by sentences far too harsh to fit their crimes. In some of the Da Fo cases, people who were accused of stealing goats caught while grazing the wheat fields were given sentences comparable to those who were charged with manslaughter or murder. Da Fo's Tang Dianpu was sentenced to ten years in Shijiazhuang Prison for stealing one goat, and Pang Xinghai, implicated in this same act of theft, was sentenced to thirteen years. In each case, the culprit served the full sentence. The families of these small thieves did not have the money to hire lawyers to defend them nor did they understand the actual penalties that were to be applied under the law, so they were at a loss when it came to contesting this outcome of the Deng policy of relying on tough police measures to deter crime.[39]

The harsh sentences culminated in an escalation of executions. According to Scot Tanner, at least 30,000 were executed in the first Strike Hard Campaign.[40] Actually, we have little information on just how many were put to death nationally or regionally. At least two *yanda* victims were from Da Fo village.

---

[37] Bao Guihang, interview.   [38] Ibid.

[39] Tang Wensheng, interview. On the excessive punishments of *yanda*, see Tanner, "Campaign-Style Policing," 174–176.

[40] Tanner, "State Coercion," 175.

Both Bao Guofa and Ruan Liangwang were executed in the first *yanda*.[41] From this point on, fear gripped the Da Fo area. The fathers of young farmers, terrified that their sons would be accused or apprehended for this or that alleged petty theft, constantly preached the importance of staying out of trouble with Public Security – a point that comes up in countless oral history testimonies. The wisest feared that petty theft charges would become entwined with criminal gang activity and result in a death sentence. Public Security meanwhile changed the location of public executions and kept it a secret from the public, mainly because, recalls Bao Ruimin, "They worried that some people would come to rescue the criminal from the death penalty."[42] The verdicts in Da Fo's two death penalty cases were announced in Daweicun, not in Da Fo, and after the announcement the prisoners were put on a truck and swiftly driven to the execution grounds to be shot without public fanfare.

All of the horrible details on the Strike Hard Campaign in the vicinity of Da Fo raise an important question: why did the post-Mao Central government leaders impose such harsh and punitive measures on the countryside through this campaign? Could it be that Deng and his men worried that accumulated Mao-era grievances might produce a tidal wave of revenge killings against local party officials and their minions, and thus used Strike Hard to suppress this impulse? Even if we cannot answer definitively, it is clear that Deng Xiaoping sought to teach the rural poor that Public Security was prepared to deal with crime by deadly force if necessary, and perhaps the upsurge in death penalty sentences provided the shock that deterred people from engaging in small crime or from taking revenge on local party leaders responsible for Mao-era injustices. But Da Fo's poor farmers had their own understanding of Strike Hard and its violence. They tell us that when Ruan Liangwang was executed, he did not show any sign of fear. Instead, Ruan walked straight to the execution ground with his head lifted high to show the police he was a strong person. The police feared this display of courage might be contagious, and they worried it would invite a raid on the execution grounds borne of public reaction to "unjust death." From this point on, villagers say, the Dongle county police lost confidence in the Strike Hard policy: police officers involved in the executions wore masks and dark glasses to conceal their identities for fear of retaliation by local people, and Public Security increasingly had to call in police from other places in order to safely carry out executions. Strike Hard shocked, but it angered more than it awed.[43]

PUBLIC SECURITY AND THE *YANDA* RACKET

How can we understand the violation of basic human and civil rights by Public Security forces in village China during the initial burst of reform? Apparently, the Deng-led center extended Strike Hard to the countryside on the assumption

[41] Bao Juntang, interview.   [42] Bao Ruimin, interview.   [43] Ibid.

that this policy was the fastest and potentially most effective way of deterring crime and stabilizing rural society. To Central government reformers, *yanda* was a means of resolving a struggle between imagined rural enemies and the party-state, and this struggle was predicated on the notion that "politics should be the leading consideration, *and politics and the law were one and the same.*"[44] The problem was that the policy did not spell out a process of implementation, so that as Strike Hard spread downward its local implementers interpreted it to serve their own interests. In this political context, the most powerful armed local group in rural China, Public Security, stepped up to take charge of implementation – and addressed its own concerns in doing so. At the county level, local Public Security embraced Deng's Strike Hard policy out of a desire for gain and an equally strong fear of loss. These two concerns were not incompatible, and they came together to intensify the severity of *yanda* in the Da Fo area, transforming the campaign into a "war without mercy."[45]

In an important sense, local Public Security forces in Dongle county and much of the Hebei-Shandong-Henan border region saw Deng's economic reform as a threat to the rewards they derived from everyday police work. When the termination of the commune and the move toward a market economy set off a wave of popular crime aimed at garnering resources over which the party-state had previously established monopolistic controls, this challenge to exclusionary Communist Party privilege and order created a serious dilemma for local Public Security leaders: if they were unable to contain the rise of petty crime against the institutions of state monopoly, they stood to be criticized by their superiors, and their salaries, which were based on yearly achievements, would be docked. Frightened by the potential loss of salaries on which their families depended, many town-based Public Security leaders were also concerned that loss of income would compel them to give up their urban residence permits and hence necessitate a return to a hard, uncertain life on the land. These fears, combined with concern about the growth of popular antigovernment consciousness engendered by the brazenly corrupt acts of commune and brigade party leaders in the 1978–1983 period, most likely predisposed the agents of Public Security to welcome Strike Hard as a means of resecuring the gains of everyday police work.

At the outset of the campaign, the Central government and its provincial clients offered monetary rewards to push *yanda* in the countryside, and the Henan party leaders set quotas for the number of "criminals" to be apprehended. From this point forward, promotion and higher pay within the local Public Security bureaucracy was directly tied to surpassing the quotas – a prescription for increasing the scale of arrests and harsh sentences. Prior to this time, local Public Security had more or less ignored petty theft and small

[44] Zhou, "Boyi Chengben Yu Zhidu Anpai," 1–4 (emphasis added).
[45] The phrase is from John Dower, *War without Mercy*.

criminals in much of the border area. With money to be made from apprehend-
ing small-time thieves, however, they ramped up operations to seize and incar-
cerate even the smallest fish. Understaffed for this mission and under pressure
from Beijing to implement the Strike Hard policy and rapidly demonstrate
results – strong residuals of the work style of Mao-era war communism – local
Public Security forces secretly approached and absorbed criminal black gangs
(*hei bang*) to carry out their version of Strike Hard.

Public Security forces allied themselves with organized criminal gangs
because their key actors were sufficiently familiar with the local terrain and
knowledgeable about local crime to assist with surveillance, reporting, and
arrests. Their collaboration also was rooted in corruption, which the *yanda*
policy encouraged. Potential gain from *yanda* prompted local police to intentionally ignore organized criminal episodes in order to devote more time and
energy to arresting poorly organized, less dangerous, small-fry criminals. At the
same time, Public Security protected organized criminal networks in order to
gain their support in carrying out random sweeps and arrests of rural people
and in concocting false reports of achievement. Conveniently, if these false
reports to superiors were discovered, then local Public Security leaders could
blame the misinformation on their unreliable local collaborators – a practice
that would continue to color this aspect of reform.

Frank Dikotter has written of the prison as a "cathedral of modernity" – a
place where the modern state attempted to exercise benevolent care of its worst
citizens. In the Republican period, he explains, Central government penologists
attempted to apply this principle in developing penal institutions.[46] While
paying lip service to this principle, the Deng-led reformers allowed Public
Security forces to operate locally in accordance with the official slogan of
reform, which proclaimed, "Material accumulation is glorious."[47] When this
concept was wedded to Deng's mandate to crack down on crime, it gave rise
to a headlong, callous police rush to get rich by fleecing the rural poor. In the
Da Fo area, the process of arrest, custody, and incarceration became a finely
tuned police racket.

One aspect of the racket involved the proliferation of fines imposed on
persons held in pre-trial Public Security detention facilities. Increasingly, it
became possible for accused offenders to purchase their way out of police
custody by paying fines. Initially, the Dongle county police came up with a
plan to sell a quota of expedited "exit passes," thereby providing an incentive
for individual detainees to exhibit the good behavior qualifying them for such
passes. But in the heat of *yanda*, the officials started selling the passes to anyone
who had enough money to buy his way out of jail. Captured Da Fo villagers
recall paying fines ranging as high as 20,000–30,000 yuan – the equivalent of

---

[46] Dikotter, "Penology and Reformation," 29–36, 58–59.
[47] Dutton and Xu, "A Question of Difference," 106–107.

US$2,500 to $3,000, well over a year's income for most Da Fo households – in order to reduce or overturn sentences for minor offenses like animal or motor cart theft.[48]

Bao Guihang explains how the terrible conditions in Public Security and/or local police facilities encouraged the payment of these fines. He describes being incarcerated in Dongle county jail and sharing a room with more than thirty other people, all of whom slept on the floor in spaces "about one foot wide." Bao says: "People who have never been locked up in such a confined space cannot understand what it is like – what it means to lose your freedom. You lose your mind easily when confined to such a small space. I discovered that you could easily lose control of yourself. Your pent-up emotions start to burn inside your body. You feel a need to immediately release them. Otherwise, you feel you will explode." Many prisoners fought one another in order "to vent their emotions." Bao Nianxi, who also spent time in Dongle county jail, remembers frequent jail brawls involving prisoner gangs from different counties.[49] Bao Guihang spoke of the desperation of imprisonment in such conditions: "I do not know how I survived the first few days in that environment. I did not ever want to go back to that jail – ever. I would rather die than be locked up in that small space. Like everybody else who was there, I felt as though my lungs were going to burst inside me. I felt as though a fire was raging inside me, and I felt that I had no control over myself. It is simply inhuman to put anybody in such an environment."[50] The kin of Da Fo's incarcerated farmers paid the police as much money as they could possibly get their hands on to facilitate their relatives' exit from the hell of pretrial custody.[51] Indeed, the Dongle county security forces discovered that fear of a quickly delivered long sentence could secure payment of a higher fine, and of course this only encouraged unfair sentences.

Some Da Fo farmers suspected that the availability of fines was an important reason why local Public Security leaders embraced reform. The racket was so lucrative that prospective police force applicants had to bribe the Dongle county police chief with 300,000 yuan to secure a position – or so it was rumored. In speaking of this rumor, Tang Wensheng spoke for many of his counterparts when he quipped: "This is how much the post of police office is worth. It must mean that a police officer will be able to make that much money from his job very quickly once he gets the position."[52]

Public Security forces' desire for gain was, in the early years of reform, fueled by a corresponding fear of loss that went beyond even concerns about lost salaries and urban residence permits. With the disappearance of the commune, the local Public Security forces lost control over public food supply, a change that made it difficult to subsidize local spies and local workers to serve their

---

[48] Ruan Sheping, interview.   [49] Bao Nianxi, interview.   [50] Bao Guihang, interview.
[51] Bao Nianxi, interview.   [52] Tang Wensheng, interview.

ends. At the same time, in 1983, the center decided to transfer the administration of the prison system from Pubic Security to the Ministry of Justice, a change that portended a loss of profit originating from products created by prison labor.[53] In this situation, local Public Security leaders seized on the 1983 Strike Hard Campaign to accelerate arrests and then establish their own additional labor reform prison camps, where they compelled inmates to work overtime at digging up minerals, making cement, and producing plastic flower arrangements for global export. As far as I can determine, during the first *yanda* campaign, the proceeds from this prison labor went to Public Security units.

But more than money was at stake: the first Strike Hard Campaign contained an imperceptible struggle for control of the "cathedral of modernity." In the hands of local security forces, Strike Hard itself swelled the number of people serving time in police jails, labor camps, and makeshift prisons, providing Public Security with a pretext for justifying requests for state revenue to grow its local forces, build modern security facilities, and expand the number of prisons under its control. The importance of this phenomenon, which remains to be researched in detail, cannot be overstated: in this period, a massive, sprawling rural prison complex was beginning to replace the commune as a holding device for troublesome rural surplus labor in Henan province, and scores of Da Fo's poorest younger farmers ended up in this *gulag*, which for the time being gave local Public Security forces a greater stake in reform.

The administration of everyday prison life also became a money-making endeavor from which Public Security reaped benefits. Da Fo's farmers recall that Public Security forces came up with new ways to exploit captured farmers over time. After the second Strike Hard Campaign, Ruan Gaiwang remembers, the chief of the Dongle jail detention center purchased a telephone and began charging prisoners fifty yuan to make calls to the outside, all the while denying them any opportunity to use any other device to make calls. Dongle county jail officials set up a few special "Love Rooms" inside the detention center walls. Although they declared that these rooms were designed to allow model prisoners to spend a few nights with their wives (for a price), in reality some of the prisoners without wives were able to pay for prostitutes to visit them in the rooms – which were, according to Da Fo's farmers, very expensive. In the wake of the third *yanda* campaign, the Dongle county Public Security forces became even more bold and started to sell jail buy-out passes to the highest bidders, a practice that spread to Anyang prison, which was under the jurisdiction of the provincial-level penal system. "In all of these ways," says Ruan Gaiwang, "money corrupted our state machinery very quickly."[54]

The data on Da Fo suggest another, more powerful fear at work in inspiring the storm of the Strike Hard Campaign in the deep countryside, a fear that

[53] Personal discussion with Murray Scot Tanner, Harvard University, October 26, 2009.
[54] Ruan Gaiwang, interview.

was explicitly political. The Communist Party historically used policy rather than law to rule China, and in the end the Strike Hard Campaign reflected this practice, which seemed to be threatened at the dawn of reform. In 1982, just prior to the first *yanda* movement, Central government politicians and some provincial and county leaders attempted to revive an important legal institution in the countryside: the *shenpan weiyuanhui*, or Adjudication Decision Committee. Originally established in 1952, this committee theoretically held the power of "final judgment" on criminal cases. Strictly speaking, no punishment could proceed without permission of its members. With the passage of a 1982 law on legal process, Beijing called for the members of the *shenpan weiyuanhui* to be recruited from local procurator organs, court offices, and law-related agencies as well as from local Public Security. In essence, this proposed legal reform was designed to create an institutional space in which different agencies could engage in competitive discourse on issues of law and order. The local Public Security leaders in Dongle county and much of Henan province proved reluctant to welcome this officially sanctioned pluralism, however. Feeling threatened, they frequently attempted to subvert the revival of the Adjudication Decision Committee by increasing their participation in it, and the 1983 Strike Hard Campaign provided them with a rationale for seizing leadership of the committee locally.

According to Zhou Changjun, local Public Security forces often broke the law in pursuing the goals of the Strike Hard Campaign. "Moreover," declares Zhou, "during the Strike Hard movement the Public Security Bureau, the procuratorate, and the courts came under the control of the leading team of *yanda*, and this team's office was located in the Public Security Bureau itself. Both the procuratorate and the court surrendered to the guidance of this team. The power of the court, therefore, was seriously weakened. It could no longer counterbalance the power of Public Security and the procuratorate." Nor could it guarantee the legal rights of suspects and the accused. Operating unrestricted by courts and judicial staff, Public Security investigators were inclined to exercise power without consultation. Their actions were determined not by the law but rather by political goals.[55] This helps explain why violations of due process, beatings of prisoners, forced confessions, and interminable prison detainments became the order of the day in the first Strike Hard Campaign, as well as why so many innocent rural people were executed between 1983 and 1987.[56]

In the Da Fo area, the Public Security takeover of the *yanda* adjudication process was facilitated by a judicial culture weakened in the Mao era. In the early years of reform, independent judicial action was so much frowned on that many judges believed the unwise decisions of three people were better than a

[55] Zhou, "Boyi Chengben Yu Zhidu Anpai," 1–3.
[56] Cf. Xia, *Zhouxiang Quanli de Shidai*, 529–538.

wise decision by one judge. A culture that valued connections reinforced this fear of courageously standing up for what was right. In the throes of the Strike Hard Campaign, therefore, individual judges were fearful of writing out and submitting detailed trial reports that included facts and accusations from all parties; fairness and compassion for the accused were not compatible with the Public Security desire for simple, quick trials.[57] The campaign undercut intermediate legal arrangements for mediating conflicts between Public Security forces and marginalized rural people, and it made official political violence the first rather than the last choice of state security in dealings with desperate innocents.

Powerless to counter the stern vigilance of Public Security forces, Da Fo's farmers lived in fear of arrest in the first Strike Hard Campaign. This fear was aggravated by the second and third Strike Hard Campaigns of 1996 and 2001, respectively. By 2005, *yanda* had taken its toll on Da Fo. More than two hundred people from Da Fo village were serving time in police jails, labor camps, and prisons. Ninety percent of them were in prison, and scores of other villagers were on the run from the police for a range of alleged crimes. Those who were incarcerated made up slightly more than 6.5 percent of Da Fo's population. The incarceration rate for this one Henan village, therefore, was six times that of the national average for the United States, which in 2008 was reportedly the world leader in percentage of its residents incarcerated.[58] The center's message was clear: failure in agriculture was no excuse for crime, and even the smallest offense could result in a new, postcommunal type of confinement and ruin. Increasingly, it seemed better to migrate out of Da Fo and search for work in towns and cities than to be trapped on poor-yielding lands or in the prison system of a single-party police state.

RESPONSES TO THE INJUSTICE OF *YANDA*

Those who were apprehended in the first Strike Hard Campaign could not emigrate, of course. They had to find ways to survive and struggle for justice within the prison system formed to cope with the fruits of *yanda*. As far as I can determine, life inside the impromptu, early-reform-era Henan provincial prison system, though miserable, was better and far more orderly than life in the pretrial detention centers where alleged criminals were still in the custody of county-level police and security forces. Within the prison system, there were two major complaints. One was that the food was insufficient. The other was that prisoners felt they had been given harsh and unjust sentences. Some of

---

[57] See Gao, "Zhongguo Shenpan Weiyuanwei Zhidu Gaixing Hechu," 2–7.

[58] According to the Pew Center, the U.S. rate was one in every hundred, or 1 percent of the population. See N. C. Aizenman, "New High in U.S. Prison Numbers," *Washington Post*, February 29, 2008.

them were able to launch challenges to these sentences from within the prison, often with the help of fellow prisoners who wrote petitions for them.

Bao Ruimin was one of these "petition writers." During his stay in Qi county prison, Bao secretly helped many prisoners appeal their sentences. Most of them were young and had received extremely harsh sentences for small crimes without adequate investigation or sufficient evidence. Bao Ruimin describes one of his successful cases, that of Zhou Angang, who was arrested in Jinglu, in the vicinity of Zhengzhou, at age twenty-one, "for picking pockets and resisting arrest" and received a ten-year sentence. Bao Ruimin petitioned for Zhou "on the grounds that he was not resisting arrest," because his pursuers were nonuniformed police, "and he had no way of knowing that the people who were pursuing him were the regular Public Security forces." At the same time, Zhou's father, a middle-school teacher, used his influence and that of his former students who worked in the Public Security Bureau to put pressure on the authorities to release Zhou. His family connections to the Public Security Bureau no doubt helped his petition to receive a favorable hearing; Zhou was ultimately released after serving a few years of his sentence.[59]

The second person Bao helped was twenty-two-year-old Liu Dongtian from Xihua county, who was sentenced to thirteen years on charges of rape and, according to Bao, was "a victim of the Deng campaign to severely punish criminals." Bao argued that Liu had not in fact raped the girl, whom he met while watching a movie in the open on the village grounds. Bao recalls: "He touched the girl first. She did not refuse his advance. He then fondled the girl, and she responded positively. Eventually, they had a sexual relationship, and they engaged in sexual intercourse on several occasions." Later, "the girl accused him of raping her because their sexual relationship was discovered by her parents," who compelled her to make the accusation. "This kind of case was very common among the young people in rural China," Bao explains. The parents felt their daughter would not have had sex with Liu if she had not been "lured." Imprisonment for consensual sex with a young woman was "not uncommon" in the early reform period. Bao's appeal succeeded, however, and Liu was released after five years.[60]

Bao also attempted to help Zhao Yanyun from Queshan county. At the age of twenty-eight, Zhao had been charged with rape and theft and was sentenced to twelve years in prison. To be sure, Zhao had some kind of relationship with the woman he was accused of raping, but he adamantly insisted he had never had sexual intercourse with her. On the other hand, Zhao did not deny that he had stolen grain from the public threshing ground. Bao Ruimin's petition spelled out the nuances of the case and argued that Zhao should not be sentenced so harshly for the latter transgression. The court denied this petition, however.[61] Finally, Bao defended Lan Yushan, a young Muslim from Sanchang

[59] Bao Ruimin, interview.   [60] Ibid.   [61] Ibid.

township in Xihua county. The young man was in prison for petty theft but was sentenced to seven years in prison for gang crime. Bao petitioned for him on the ground that he had committed the theft by himself and, according to PRC law, should have been given a sentence of only three years. The petition was denied, and Bao's client wasted seven years of his youth in prison. "He was punished too severely for this crime," recalls Bao.[62]

Most victims of the Strike Hard Campaign were reluctant to stand up and wage a legal fight for their rights, however. The experience of Bao Nianxi, arrested in the Da Fo area for petty theft during the first Strike Hard movement, sheds light on the politics engendering such reluctance. In 1981, Bao, aged thirty-one, began to steal chemical fertilizer. "I could not find any other way to find money and food to feed my family," he says. After successfully stealing and selling fertilizer a dozen times, Bao and five of his accomplices were arrested and imprisoned in Dongle County jail for eleven months, where they were beaten. Sentenced to four and a half years' imprisonment, Bao was sent to a labor farm. The severity of the punishment, Bao explains, was the result of his being "classified as the principal leader of a criminal group." The lightest sentence received by anyone in Bao's group was two months; Bao suspects that this prisoner's family paid the police. Four of the fertilizer thieves were involved in more serious crimes. Two of them were executed, and the other two received lengthy prison terms.

"None of us appealed our sentence," Bao says. This was not because they felt the sentences were fair. Indeed, Bao Nianxi explains that he did not consider stealing fertilizer to be a crime: "To me, chemical fertilizer belonged to everybody. I thought it would be all right to take something from the public." Rather, Bao decided not to appeal because he was concerned that an appeal would result in an even harsher sentence: "I felt that if I appealed my case it would indicate that I was not convinced I was wrong and that I would be seen as opposed to the court system and the government. I was convinced at the time that whoever opposed the government in any way would not end well." This impression was reinforced by the fate of several of the men arrested alongside Bao who did appeal:

The two people who were executed originally were sentenced to nineteen and thirteen years in prison, respectively.... At the time of their appeal, Deng Xiaoping and his family were vacationing in Beidaihe. It was rumored that one of Deng's grandchildren was harassed by hooligans. Apparently, Deng Xiaoping was shocked to see that his own family was not safe. So Deng ordered the Chinese police and courts to severely punish any gangster and any group-based criminals. His order was to execute the top two or three leaders of any gangs, and the government was given some kind of quota to execute so many criminals. The four people involved in my case therefore were facing Deng's new order. In the end, two of them were executed, and the other two got even heavier

---

[62] Ibid.

sentences. I worried about what might happen to me if I were to appeal my case. That was the first time that Deng Xiaoping issued an order to render severe punishments to criminals. He did this several times later on, and each time the normal sentencing was put aside and a more harsh punishment was applied. In this situation, many criminals who should have gotten only a few years could end up being executed. The number of people executed in this manner remains a national secret.[63]

Da Fo's besieged farmers did not trust the emergent Communist Party-led police state or its poorly regulated, corrupted courts and prisons – with good reason. An honest attempt to admit to a criminal misdemeanor and petition for a lighter "just sentence" was potentially dangerous, for during any *yanda* campaign that decision could be interpreted as a challenge to the official representation of reform as the pursuit of a peaceful, harmonious, and civilized polity. The reluctance of small, desperate thieves such as Bao Nianxi to engage in petitionist appeals was rooted in a fear that politics since Mao had not changed that much. In reality, for many poor, young Da Fo farmers, the first *yanda* campaign was nearly as destructive as the life-threatening antirightist campaigns of the Mao era.[64]

THE SOCIAL COST OF *YANDA* IN THE COUNTRYSIDE

Zhang Wenjun, aged thirty, received a sentence of twelve years' imprisonment for stealing a goat and fighting with its owner. Bao Guifa, thirty-six, and Ruan Lianwang, thirty-four, were executed for stealing from a People's Liberation Army (PLA) storehouse. Ruan Xianwen, thirty-five, received a twenty-year sentence for stealing electrical wire. Bao Yanling, thirty-five, arrested for petty theft, spent thirteen years in prison. The list of young Da Fo men arrested and imprisoned during the first *yanda* campaign is a long and repetitive one. The fate of petition writer Bao Ruimin provides a microcosm of the suffering countless young farmers endured under the 1983–1987 *yanda* campaign, and it helps us grasp why the Deng Xiaoping–led state engendered deep resentment among the hundreds of young Da Fo farmers who were caught in the web of *yanda*.

Born in 1949, the victory year of the Communist Revolution, Bao Ruimin was ten years old when the Great Leap famine crashed down on Da Fo village. His father, Bao Fuxian, a smallholding "middle peasant" and a commodities trader, died on the collective road to the Great Leap. When the 1978 reform began, Bao Ruimin was penniless and propertyless, and he found it difficult to make the transition to household-based agriculture. Desperate to make a good life for himself and his family, in late 1982 he pilfered grain from the Da Fo public granary – a mode of survival dating back to the Great Leap, when theft of grain from collective granaries was common – and he took chemical fertilizer

---

[63] Bao Nianxi, interview.   [64] Thaxton, *Catastrophe and Contention*.

from state trucks passing along the highway. When local Public Security forces began to arrest Da Fo's suspected fertilizer thieves in the 1983 *yanda* campaign, Bao Ruimin was frightened. By this point, he had given up stealing, and he was beginning to find a niche in farming. His brothers, fearful that Bao Ruimin's past would be revealed by a snitch in the Da Fo party network, urged him to confess to Public Security. Bao did so, assuming the police would release him after his confession. He was wrong – he did not, at this critical moment, understand the political dynamic of *yanda*. Instead, he was sentenced on four separate occasions, originally to four years in prison, then to fifteen years, then to ten years in two separate appeals trials.[65] The ten-year prison ordeal punched a hole in Bao Ruimin's heart. His bitter reflection on his losses in this period helps us understand how rural people who went slightly astray but were treated as hardened criminals came to view Deng's system of power and reform. Four of Bao's losses were shared by many petty thieves, and so we will focus on them.

Reform promised a material ascent, but policing reform perpetuated scarcity, taking the major household provider from scores of impoverished farm families. The reason why many of these poor young farmers had risked minor theft in the first place was to help a family member – a spouse or child – cope with an extremely challenging situation. Bao Ruimin had turned to petty theft right after he and his young wife had moved out from under his parents' roof, when the young couple barely had enough food to last them until the fall harvest. At this difficult time, Bao's wife became sick, and Bao sold grain that he stole from the collective in order to buy medicine for her.[66] From Bao Ruimin's perspective, the state bore responsibility for putting him in this position: compelled to sell his own scanty grain harvests to the state at a dictated low price, and bereft of the skills needed to earn a living in the nascent market economy, Bao, like many of his Da Fo counterparts, took grain from the collective to make up for state theft of income, which had continued on at a lesser scale in the aftermath of the Great Leap's unbridled plunder. He resented having to pay for making this choice with ten years of his life.

This long imprisonment not only made it more difficult for Bao's young family to survive, it also separated him from his sons at a time when they most needed his guidance as a father. "I had three sons at the time of my arrest," Bao says. "They all grew up without my presence in their lives."[67] The Strike Hard Campaign dealt a severe blow to the identity of fatherhood, crushing the chances of imprisoned fathers to perform as protective, care-giving patriarchs for their sons. Bao Ruimin, among other imprisoned Da Fo petty thieves, suffered great mental anguish over this state theft of patriarchy. To be sure, Bao Ruimin pulled off a miracle: despite his prison stint, he was able to help several of his sons find respectable employment; he built each of his

---

[65] Bao Ruimin, interview.   [66] Ibid.   [67] Ibid.

sons a house so that they could marry, and he helped to find wives for them. Despite this feat, Bao Ruimin did not necessarily succeed in reclaiming the prerogatives he sought for his sons, for he, like so many of his Da Fo counterparts who suddenly found themselves in Deng's prison system, was gripped by great anxiety about his failure to perform as a responsible father.[68]

This anxiety was stoked by two serious regrets. First, the young sons of *yanda* victims were not mentored by fathers to endure the everyday grind of farm life and meet the unexpected challenges to becoming a successful farmer. It was virtually impossible for their fathers to transmit the knowledge, skills, and instincts that were necessary for them to succeed in agriculture. It should not surprise us, therefore, to learn that this state-ordered patriarchal abandonment, in combination with the state disinvestment in agriculture and the suppression of grain prices, fostered a generation of fatherless young people who, having failed to master the arts of family-based farming, became candidates for jobs that would serve the subsequent reform-era industrial transformation and that, in the end, would pose serious harm to their physical and mental health.

Bao Ruimin and other imprisoned fathers also regretted not having been there, in the home and the village, to teach their sons courage and the arts of self-defense when in harm's way. Robert Bly reminds us that parenting means doing all sorts of mundane daily tasks that run the gamut from putting children in touch with the wonders of nature to teaching them to heed the wisdom of their elders to taking them to school, checking on their school work, and fostering their school-based friendships. These tasks also include helping children fend for themselves when harassed by bullies.[69] Historically, in Da Fo, as in countless other Chinese villages, male patriarchal farmers were active parents, and this is precisely why Da Fo village produced so many successful high-school and college graduates and martial arts champions in the Republican era.[70] In the Mao era, Da Fo's party leaders interrupted this fatherly orchestrated empowerment, in part by making it very difficult for sons to even be with and listen to parents (who were stunned by overwork in collective fields and left speechless by hunger), to acquire school-based practical and ethical knowledge, and to develop their bodies into an agency of athleticism and a weapon for self-defense. Many of Da Fo's farmers yearned to recapture this empowering approach to parenting sons at the outset of reform, but the *yanda* crackdown transferred scores of male parents into a rapidly expanding prison system, leaving their little sons to figure out on their own how they would deal with the continuing party-state effort to keep them ignorant, passive, and unable to act on knowledge of the difference between right and wrong. Not all of them could. Bao Ruimin's "miracle" was less than complete: Bao Jianrong,

---

[68] Some of the conceptual starting points for this argument are in Bly, *Sibling Society*, 34–35.

[69] Cf. Bly, *Iron Man*, 62–63. In developing the rest of this section, I have relied heavily on some of the premises in ibid., 34, 226–227, 233–235.

[70] Cf. Thaxton, *Catastrophe and Contention*, chapters 1 and 2.

one of his sons, who grew from age three to thirteen when his father was serving his ten-year sentence, was arrested after the 2001 Strike Hard Campaign, and he wound up serving a prison sentence in a labor camp about 130 li from Da Fo village.[71] In short, Deng's *yanda* campaign hounded patriarchy, dredging up the existential anxiety of the Great Leap disaster, when so many fathers were denied empowering communion with their young sons, who often were left to live a life of misfortune and trouble. Such experiences call to mind the politically determined plight of young African-American males in the United States, where their residentially segregated, wage-poor inner city fathers are disproportionally imprisoned, often for nonviolent nickel-and-dime drug-related offenses, leaving them without paternal caregivers and everyday heroes, and hence with a high chance of becoming the targets of discriminatory police arrests and court sentencing when they reach early adulthood.[72]

The harsh ten-year prison sentence and Bao Ruimin's status as a criminal also caused his family to lose respectability in Da Fo. This pained Bao greatly. His younger brother, Bao Shizeng, was nineteen years old at the time of Bao's arrest and sentencing. Tall and exceptionally handsome, Bao Shizeng was not able to find a wife, "partly because," says Bao Ruimin, "my prison term affected him." Bao explains that no one wanted to marry his brother because Bao Ruimin was imprisoned.[73] He recalls that around the time when his young brother should have gotten married, "quite a few" of Da Fo's young males had to resort to purchasing wives from outside the village, sometimes through kidnapping rings. It seems plausible, therefore, that the Strike Hard Campaigns damaged other family reputations and compounded the already difficult challenge for poor village males of finding marriage partners – a process that left young "criminals" such as Bao Ruimin with heavy guilt and strained relations among brothers.

Finally, the 1983 *yanda* campaign placed unbearable pressure on the family-based system of fidelity and harmony. At the height of Mao's great famine, militia-based vigilantes pressed Da Fo's families to rat out their closest relatives and friends for stealing food from the collective granary or for collaborating to sustain household-based strategies of survival made taboo by the party-state.[74] The Strike Hard Campaign revived this practice. In Bao Ruimin's family, the question of whether spur-of-the-moment fears of a snitch among them had driven his brothers to unwisely press Bao to give himself over to the police nagged the entire family, occasionally giving rise to unhappy quarrels implicating Bao's brothers in his imprisonment and his disconnection from village-based fatherhood.[75]

---

[71] Bao Ruimin, interview.
[72] I am indebted to Steven I. Levine for encouraging me to consider this comparison. For the evidence supporting it, see Mauer and Huling, "Young Black Americans and the Criminal Justice System," 6–7, 11–17.
[73] Bao Ruimin, interview.   [74] Thaxton, *Catastrophe and Contention*, 190–198.
[75] Bao Ruimin, interview.

THE PARADOX OF *YANDA* AND REFORM IN THE COUNTRYSIDE

The Strike Hard Campaign produced a paradox in the deep countryside that Da Fo's political history illuminates. The oral interview data from this village indicate there was widespread support for the Strike Hard Campaign among frightened, conservative tillers. Two aspects of this support are significant. First, many Da Fo farmers who supported the Deng crackdown were reluctant to publicly voice that support in the years when *yanda* unfolded, because they feared *any* entwinement with Public Security and its local targets. Second, the support they expressed in interviews twenty years after the first *yanda* campaign seems to echo the support registered for the Deng-orchestrated *yanda* in the cities. This echo is found in the memory of Bao Chengdan, the son of a Da Fo farm household.

Da Fo's first middle-school graduate in the 1950s, Bao Chengdan worked as an accountant for the Liangmen People's Commune. In recalling the early years of the reform, he says: "Villagers were not able to sleep peacefully because they worried someone would steal [their] crops. It was very bad. *Yanda* did not affect people like me. Only the criminals were punished. These people were causing a lot of trouble in the village. Villagers did not like them at all. Most villagers were happy that these criminals were taken away by the police." Referring to the continuing taboo against speaking harshly of those who were arrested during the *yanda* campaign, Bao concludes: "I cannot say this publicly in the village. I will tell you that these people deserved to be punished. If the police and the government did not do something to stop them, the criminal activity in Da Fo would have been worse."[76]

The Strike Hard Campaign in village China was violent, but Bao Chengdan's remarks suggest that it was more popular than anti-Deng forces would have us believe. Still, there was a powerful contradiction built into the Strike Hard Campaign, and it gave rise to a frayed legitimacy. Although this campaign temporarily reduced crime in the Da Fo area, the crime rate in rural China reportedly increased at a rate of 40 percent per year between 1985 and 1991,[77] partly because the center maintained the apartheid system of power and economy, treating marginalized village dwellers unequally in the crackdown on crime. In Da Fo, as elsewhere, Deng and his allies ultimately made these marginalized people the main de facto target of *yanda* while discriminating against them when it came to the allocation of government resources for rural economic development and basic social needs (education, medical care, and social welfare). What were these young, marginalized would-be farmers to do if not turn to crime?

Thus, although the Strike Hard Campaign reaffirmed the hold of the Communist party-state locally, it damaged the legitimacy of the center with the poor, desperate young farmers who became its victims. Deeply cynical about

[76] Bao Chengdan, interview. [77] Zhou, "Boyi Chengben Yu Zhidu Anpai," 1–3.

equating local Public Security forces with order and safety, many of them organized their political thinking about the police around the memory of suffering under *yanda* long after Deng himself was gone. Bao Nianxi is speaking through this memory when he asserts: "It seems that the harsher the Central government punishes criminals, the more crime we have in the countryside. Nobody in Da Fo feels safe now. The presence of the police has increased under reform, but crime is still on the rise."[78] Farmers such as Bao – those who had lost under *yanda* – saw the local police, whose numbers had increased from thirty in 1976, when Mao died, to five hundred in 2006, as a swarm of locusts whose efficiency in devouring their household resources had improved under reform. To a significant minority, the police were the agents of a failed, dysfunctional modernity. Many in this minority held Deng and his allies in Beijing, not just local Public Security forces, responsible for the suffering and loss that came with reform.

– – –

The onset of reform left many of Da Fo's poorest young farmers in the lurch. Their households had not yet recovered from material losses suffered in the Great Leap famine, and the discriminatory policies of the center made it difficult for them to make a quick and successful transition to family-based farming and the market. The center defined their pitiful efforts to give themselves a chance in farming by taking hold of collective property as the criminal sabotage of socialist modernity. In reality, however, the disadvantaged tillers of Da Fo's bad, saline earth were only attempting to cope with the rash advance of the center's flawed agrarian reform policy, particularly its monopoly on chemical fertilizer – and after all, rash advance and party monopoly of chemical fertilizer reminded everyone of the institutional dynamics that drove the Great Leap disaster.

In the Mao years, the commune had become a holding colony for surplus labor, but with the collapse of the collective, surplus labor once again became a problem, and Beijing politicians saw the poor farmers who made up this freed, desperate labor force as dangerous.[79] The possibility of poor, restive lumpen elements joining bandit groups, Liangshanpo brotherhoods, and antistate religious sects and societies frightened the center, for, as the history of Da Fo illustrates, poor rural farmers were no longer the friends of the center's local cadre base. While engaging the global democratic community and propagandizing a commitment to a peaceful, harmonious strategy of domestic economic development, Deng Xiaoping conceived the 1983 Strike Hard Campaign to combat this possibility, relying on police force to make the rural poor comply with

[78] Bao Nianxi, interview.
[79] Cf. Thaxton, *Salt of the Earth*; also see Thaxton, *Catastrophe and Contention*.

reform policy. Deng's successors relied on *yanda* in 1996 and again in 2001 to pacify the countryside.

The Strike Hard policy was inseparable from the Deng-led Central government's development strategy: Deng and his allies wanted the poorest of the rural poor to either stay down on the farms and sell their grain to the state at discriminatory prices in order to provision the cities or, with state guidance, to move to the cities and shoulder the cost of urban construction work designed to realize modern industrial growth and national grandeur. The Strike Hard Campaign was, as Susan Trevaskes has pointed out, "the key mechanism" for attaining this goal,[80] and of course Beijing's decision to build industry in state-dominated cities receiving global capital, technology, and knowledge eventually drew surplus labor out of the countryside into urban China.[81]

An authoritarian-conceived modernity, the Deng-led center's urban-centric Strike Hard policy did not automatically resolve the existential dilemma of the rural poor.[82] In the early reform era, rural people in remote villages such as Da Fo continued to suffer in ways that were hidden to outsiders: given the long-term damage of the Great Leap disaster, many Da Fo farm households did not have the means to leave the land, the connections to secure a job in a still-primitive construction industry, or the street smarts to cope with police restrictions on urban *hukou* (household registration). Some worried that a move to the city would result in a fate similar to that of Great Leap–era migrants, who had been seized and deported back to Dongle county by Public Security.[83] In this situation, many of Da Fo's poorest farmers opted to engage in forbidden gray-zone acts of survival – but in the throes of *yanda* these acts were defined as serious crimes. The cost of being caught in the sweeps of *yanda* actually made it more difficult to survive by staying in the village and working the land. No wonder that many of Da Fo's poor farmers say they decided to become migrant workers only after they had unhappy encounters with local Public Security forces in the first Strike Hard Campaign.[84] Surely the officially trumpeted material incentives – that is, the pull factors emphasized in Western economic analyses – helped produce the wave of post-Mao rural-to-urban

---

[80] Trevaskes, "Yanda 2001," 277–278.   [81] Solinger, "China's Floating Population," 225–227.

[82] Building on the work of Barrington Moore Jr., Edward Friedman has illuminated the persistent suffering of rural people in China and reminded us of the capacity of modernizers to impose harm and simply treat rural poverty as if institutional reform has addressed its root cause. Friedman, "Persistent Invisibility of Rural Suffering," 10–17; Cf. Moore, *Social Origins of Dictatorship*.

[83] As Zhao Shukai has argued, the Deng-led reformers *did nothing* to reassure people in remote villages such as Da Fo that they had reformed the Public Security forces assigned to regulate the floating population. The center did not even address this issue until the end of the first decade of reform. Zhao, "Report from the Field," 110. On the process of deportation, see Thaxton, *Catastrophe and Contention*.

[84] I am indebted to Sarah C. Swider for this insight. Personal correspondence, December 29–31, 2008.

migration, but the neoliberal paradigm that equated the Deng-engineered reform with a spontaneous, willing movement of labor from interior villages to coastal cities by and large ignored the violent politics that pushed the rural poor out of the countryside.

The Deng-conceived *yanda* also gave the police a monetary stake in policing, encouraging them to treat the rural victims of Deng's discriminatory pro-urban policies as if they really were criminals. Perhaps, as Scot Tanner has argued,[85] Strike Hard was designed to restore the image of the party-state as the final arbiter of force and to convince villagers the state possessed the awesome power to provide the order and stability needed for a transition to a market-focused economy. The problem was that the Maoist past was not completely dead, and Deng's *yanda* seemed to revive it. In Dongle county, *yanda* followed a template of Mao-era campaign methods that went all the way back to the 1947–1948 land reform, when the enemies of the party were paraded through rural villages, subjected to public criticism, and executed following quick police-influenced trials;[86] in Da Fo, police reliance on local party leaders implicated in the worst disaster of Maoist rule stirred awful memories of the Great Leap's concerted violent attacks, ultimately engendering more anger than awe.

To be sure, *yanda* was the fulcrum for addressing the nagging legitimacy crisis of the party-state in the deep countryside, and the Strike Hard campaign underscores the complexity of legitimacy at the local level. Apparently, the majority of Da Fo's farmers took Strike Hard as necessary for curtailing the vigilantism and harmful anarchy of the Mao era. But this campaign was not based on moral governance, and it hurt scores of young would-be farmers. Strike Hard occurred in a zone of lawless police violence that was the product of a CCP-designed legal framework in which the party-state actually had the power to suspend any rights of the rural poor. The extrajudicial power exercised by public security forces in *yanda* was propagandized as "exceptional," but, as Flora Sapio has shown, in the PRC the exceptional could become a new police-ordered normalcy, and subsequently everyone could become subject to illegal detention, persecution, and killing – all justified by the sovereign power of the party-state and its security forces.[87]

Compared with the catastrophic disruptions of Mao-era rule, especially the damage of the Great Leap, the new Deng-conceived Leviathan most likely was seen as the lesser of two evils by many of Da Fo's farmers. But even villagers who were not seriously hurt by *yanda* understood that the center's mandate was based on force and that *yanda* was meant to teach them a lesson: under this form of sovereign power, individuals and their families could have even their right to exist suspended in any Beijing-defined state of emergency. If there

---

[85] Tanner, "State Coercion," 93–94. Also see Tanner, "Campaign-Style Policing," 172.
[86] Thaxton, *Salt of the Earth*, 21, and *Catastrophe and Contention*, chapters 1–3.
[87] Sapio, *Sovereign Power and the Law*, 3–4, 17.

were feeble legal checks on the sovereign power of the center, Deng and his allies in the Public Security forces were responsible for such weakness. They intentionally predicated *yanda* on the subordination of law to politics, and in the distant countryside they implemented this campaign in a way that preserved the dominant decision-making powers of local security forces in the adjudication of conflicts arising from its ferocity. And after all, the campaign did nothing to break the taboo on speaking truth about the Great Leap and Deng's role in pushing it – nor, for that matter, did it address the deep personal hurt stemming from disappearances and deaths of love ones lost to the fratricidal war communism of Mao, Deng, and their comrades. If anything, the Strike Hard Campaign highlighted the arbitrary and capricious nature of Deng's police-based order and taught caution in seeking justice from it. Intentionally or unintentionally, *yanda* also reminded people in Da Fo that reform was not about healing the damage of the past and that they had no guarantee that the past would not spoil the present.[88]

---

[88] Cf. Hamber and Wilson, "Symbolic Closure."

2

Contemporary Tax Resistance and the Memory of the Great Leap

In Da Fo, as in countless other Chinese villages, the Maoist Leap had ratcheted up pressure on tillers to give up more of their grain harvests to the state, resulting in a "procurement famine" of unprecedented magnitude. A pervasive memory of this state plunder and its attendant starvation persisted over the next four decades. This memory influenced popular thinking about political authority, making it difficult for post-Mao politicians to overcome the deep crisis of legitimacy they inherited. In essence, the failure of the Maoist procurement system was so profound that the Communist Party lost the authority to effectively collect taxes in much of the countryside.

The Central government relied on the mechanism of the household responsibility system (*baochan daohu*) to resolve this legitimacy crisis. Under this system, each farm household was to enter into a contract that gave its members the right to manage their own agricultural production. The household, in turn, was responsible for meeting a state grain quota, after which it was allowed to use the surplus however it chose.[1] In Da Fo and much of Henan province, the obligation to pay a tax of 20 *jin* (0.50 kilograms) per *mu* (hectare) – the equivalent of a fixed land tax – was retained alongside the *baochan daohu* quota. Although designed to re-create Central government legitimacy by returning a degree of freedom to tillers at the same time that it gave them an incentive to increase harvest yields, the household responsibility system was highly contested in Dongle county villages.

Da Fo's farmers refused to accept the system. They harbored two fears, both of which were shaped by memories of suffering in the Great Leap famine. To begin with, they saw the *baochan daohu* system as a watered-down version

---

[1] On this system, see Meisner, *Mao's China and After*, 461–464; Bernstein, "Farmer Discontent," 204–207; and Unger, *Transformation of Rural China*, 75, 100–101.

of procurement, which had not ended with the dismantling of the communes but continued to play a role in the development of the post-Mao tax burden.[2] The *baochan daohu* system required tillers to meet a quota set by the party-state before they could deploy whatever was left for their own needs. But what if the grain harvest was poor and the required quota cut into the portion of the harvest needed for basic consumption? In the absence of any public, democratic controls on party leaders, Da Fo's tillers worried they might be hurled back to the conditions of the Maoist Leap.

In addition, the *baochan daohu* quota was pegged to grain. But at the outset of reform, Da Fo's farmers and many of their counterparts in other Dongle county villages were relying on sweet potato production to pull their households up to subsistence-level consumption, and as we have seen, many could not afford chemical fertilizer to boost grain production in the early years of reform. What if they switched to a greater emphasis on grain in order to comply with *baochan daohu* and after a few years faced a sudden, steep decline in grain harvests?[3] There was no guarantee that state quotas would be relaxed in response to falling harvests or that Communist Party leaders would allow a return to small private sweet potato plots to accommodate a real disaster. The experience of the Leap taught otherwise, for Mao had pressed to abolish such plots and to return them to the grain fields of the collective only a few years after Da Fo's farmers had embraced them to escape famine.[4]

In short, Da Fo's farmers wanted to retire the *baochan daohu* system, to produce without being menaced by any state quota arrangement that, after all, was designed to make them serve the state first and promised no relief in the event of a really poor harvest. In the early years of reform, they repeatedly expressed this desire to local party leaders, and the latter, in turn, complained to township and county leaders about the difficulties of managing this system.

In response to Da Fo farmers' rejection of the household responsibility system, local party leaders, acting with the nod of higher-ups, increasingly came to generate revenue from fixed land taxes. These taxes began to rise sharply in the 1988–1993 period, threatening the subsistence of the poorest farming families and providing a spark for both individual and collective resistance. Resistance with similar roots spread throughout Henan, Hubei, Jiangxi, Hunan, Shaanxi, and Anhui provinces in the 1990s and early 2000s, complicating the government effort to regain legitimacy and ultimately resulting in the 2006 abolition of the agricultural tax.

This chapter sheds light on how the memory of suffering in the Great Leap disaster structured resistance to the tax claims of Da Fo party leaders in the reform era. Tax resistance in reform-era Da Fo started out as defensive

---

[2] See Bernstein and Lu, *Taxation without Representation*, 45.

[3] According to Meisner, this fear proved to be well-founded, for the 1985 drop in grain output in neighboring Hebei province "evoked memories and fears of famine." *Mao's China and After*, 464.

[4] See Yang, *Calamity and Reform*, 151, and Thaxton, *Catastrophe and Contention*.

mobilization,[5] but its leaders soon launched a counteroffensive, ultimately refusing to cooperate with the state effort to tether them to its schemes of appropriation. The propagandists of the central party-state would have us believe that rural people succeeded in this refusal because they found support from within regime-sanctioned channels of protest. To be sure, in parts of rural China reform-era tax protest was prompted by local party leaders who manipulated Central government tax guidelines to their own advantage, leaving villagers to engage in contentious tax resistance cued by state policy.[6] If tax protest in Da Fo occasionally resonated with this paradigm of policy-based contention, however, it also occurred in the context of a memory that constantly warned villagers of the risks of dealing with the remains of the regime that had perpetrated the tax injustice of the Great Leap. Furthermore, villagers' contention against tax abuse succeeded in part because the farmers who embraced it pursued intractable, regime-threatening forms of protest that resonated with their long-term anger over both central and local party efforts to expropriate household and village resources.

In Da Fo, a tradition of protracted "everyday resistance" to the dictatorial rule of Communist Party secretary Bao Zhilong and his power network weakened the ability of the party-state to dominate villagers and make them pay taxes. This resistance, which began with the popular *chi qing* refusal to comply with the "procurement-first" claims of the Maoists in the 1958–1961 famine, continued to undermine the tax powers of the party-state in the late Mao period and beyond and was more important than the reform-era relaxation of political restrictions in influencing the way tax protest unfolded in the village.[7] This point is lost in many analyses of the origins of popular tax resistance under reform because these analyses have not focused on long-term, locally grounded struggles over taxation.[8] In focusing on the *longue durée*, we can see that tax resistance in Da Fo was linked to an embedded historical crisis and, further, that some of its forms originated with popular memory of what had worked in escaping the enormous burden of grain expropriation in the Great Leap era.

---

[5] On defensive mobilization, see Tilly, *From Mobilization to Revolution*, 73. On tax resistance in China as the major historical form of "peasant resistance," see Bernhardt, *Rents, Taxes, and Peasant Resistance*, and Bianco, *Peasants without the Party*, 18–20, chapter 5. For an insightful review of tax resistance as a by and large defensive response to state making, see Wong, *China Transformed*, 235–251. Wong also shows that tax resistance in China could produce popular counteroffensives to take over the processes of state appropriation.

[6] O'Brien and Li, "Politics of Lodging Complaints," 770, and O'Brien and Li, "Villagers and Popular Resistance," 29–30, 41–42, 50–51, 54–55.

[7] For the view that the relaxation of official controls on rural society was the critical factor contributing to the formation of reform era tax resistance, see Bianco, *Peasants without the Party*, 244–246.

[8] See Bianco, in particular, who thinks that villagers were helpless and impotent prior to the Deng-led policy shift ("Tax Protest," 245–246), and O'Brien and Li, "Politics of Lodging Complaints" and "Villagers and Popular Resistance." On the importance of history and long-running conflicts, see Perry and Selden, "Reform and Resistance," 2.

THE GREAT LEAP-ERA ROOTS OF VILLAGERS' OBJECTIONS
TO THE RISING TAX BURDEN

Historically, the people of Da Fo village had demonstrated a high level of tolerance for burdensome taxes. In the Republican period, when they had every reason to rebel against perilous Nationalist government taxes, they went to great lengths to avoid contention. It was only when the Kuomintang salt tax police imposed new taxes on earth salt and resorted to cruel methods of tax collection that villagers turned to revolt. They had also endured heavy taxes under the Japanese Puppet Army without openly rebelling, though the puppet army tax demands, in combination with the 1942 Henan Famine, drove a few villagers to resist taxation vigorously. Whereas Mao-era procurement imposed a new system of super-efficient taxation,[9] Da Fo's farmers did not participate in contentious tax resistance until the Great Leap, when party boss Bao Zhilong and his men drove them to the desperate practice of *chi qing*,[10] a method of refusing to give up the harvest by eating the standing crops in the fields that alarmed party leaders at every level of government. In the reform era, Da Fo's farmers still held traditional beliefs that cautioned against tax resistance. Speaking in the summer of 1998, Zheng Yunxiang put it this way: "We villagers understand our obligation to pay the grain tax. In Da Fo, there is a strong belief that if we have a horse, then we have to do government errands, and if we farm the land, then we have to pay the grain tax. We do not have a problem with this obligation. What we resent is that we have to pay too much in taxes, and this is the problem now."[11]

The amount of grain collected by party leaders in Da Fo and in Liangmen township increased substantially between 1988 and 1993. In 1993 the percentage taken on the total crop alarmed tillers. In that year, the Da Fo party leaders took over 190,000 *jin* of wheat as the cost of managing village affairs – 50,000 *jin* over and above the 140,000 *jin* Da Fo's farmers paid to the township, county, and provincial government. In 1953, the yearly village grain tax had stood at 47,000 *jin*. It increased to 52,000 *jin* in 1955, and then jumped to 80,000 *jin* during the first year of the Great Leap Forward.[12] It remained at this level across the last two decades of collectivization (when it was actually calculated in inferior millet, not superior wheat, which became government practice between 1987 and 1992). In other words, after remaining stagnant for twenty years, the grain tax paid by Da Fo more than doubled between 1978 and 1993, and much of this increase occurred in the five years between 1988 and 1993. When we add in the additional 140,000 *jin* grain tax that went to the central party-state, it appears that the total grain tax claim on Da Fo – 330,000 *jin* in 1993 – *quadrupled* during the first fifteen years of decollectivization, and the sharpest uptick came in the 1988–1995 period.

[9] Kuhn, *Origins of the Modern Chinese State*, 106.   [10] Pang Fang, interview.
[11] Zheng Yunxiang, interview.   [12] Bao Peilian, interviews.

Da Fo's farmers suffered from the upward spiral of grain taxation as their individual tax burdens increased correspondingly. The tax for each *mu* of wheat land was only 40 *jin* per *mu* from 1982 until 1990, but in 1991 it increased to 70 *jin*, and in 1992 it soared to 170 *jin*. A few households were told to pay 200 *jin* per *mu*, which amounted to 20 percent of total income. At this point, some farmers considered giving up agriculture completely. When farmers in nearby Luzhuang, Hebei province, threatened to cease tilling the land and to go to work on construction sites in the cities instead, Da Fo's farmers began threatening to do the same thing.[13] They were not making any money from wheat production, they argued. The major incentive to till the land was the gain from the fall crop, on which they were not taxed.[14]

Villagers were indignant, and not only because of the increase but because party leaders mandated the increase in a way that recalled the runaway state extraction that had engendered the Great Leap disaster. The hidden genesis of popular tax resistance in Da Fo was the memory villagers held of the years when party boss Bao Zhilong had gone along with the exaggerated production reports of upper-level cadres, thereby collaborating in the authorized state plunder that led to Mao's great famine. Pang Lianggui explained in 2000:

During the Great Leap Forward, Da Fo suffered. Bao Zhilong was illiterate. He did not understand the Central government's [tax] policy well. And he was too eager to please the upper government leaders. He boasted about our grain yields. Thinking we had more grain, the Liangmen People's Commune leaders came to Da Fo to take more and more grain from the village. Bao Zhilong could not contradict himself, and so he let the commune leaders take more grain from us. As a result, we suffered more than did people from any of the surrounding villages. Looking back, it seems we were stupid to allow this to happen.

But today's village leaders have begun to boast about village income again. They like to tell the Liangmen township government leaders how much our income has improved over the years, and the township leaders then have reported our income to their superiors as proof they have done an outstanding job. This is the basis for their promotion. But the consequence has been that we farmers have suffered, as we have had to pay more and more in grain taxes and other fees to the government. *I think this tendency of boasting and lying is very dangerous. It could lead to another disaster in our society.*

Everybody in Da Fo feels the government is taking too much grain from farmers, and that we farmers cannot make a living from tilling the land. But the government is constantly increasing the amount of tax imposed on us.... What will happen if the farmers gradually lose confidence in the government's ability to give farmers a fair chance of survival? I am sure that if this situation continues, a peasant rebellion will still be possible in China.[15]

This fear of another Great Leap–era government-induced grain shortage is deeply embedded in the psyche of even some of Da Fo's successful farmers,

[13] Pang Zhenfa, interview.   [14] Bao Shaolin, interview.
[15] Pang Lianggui, interview. Emphasis added.

particularly among those who lost kin to Mao's great famine. Bao Hongwen, whose father died of hunger in 1959, reflected this deep-seated fear when he said that his summer 2011 wheat harvest was good but that he was not willing to follow his peers who were not storing grain for their family needs. "Even though I have to go to the trouble to dry the grain and make sure it does not mold, and to deal with mice who are after it, I am determined to keep enough grain for myself and my family for at least two years," said Bao. "I do not want my family to face grain shortages like the Great Leap Forward, when we were unprepared. When the Great Leap Forward occurred in Da Fo, most people did not have much grain saved up. That was one of the reasons we suffered. This year we did have a good harvest. Many people have begun to think that we are invincible, that we will always have a good harvest. I do not think so. I think we have had a good harvest partly because of irrigation and partly because of luck. If the drought had continued one month longer, we would have been in big trouble. Therefore, I want to be prepared for a bad time."[16] Bao Hongwen knew the good harvest was also subject to tax-reform-era claims, which were pressing against the budgets of his counterparts.

By 1991–1992, the impact of the rising grain tax on family subsistence had alarmed tillers. Nearly half of Da Fo's five hundred households earned off-farm income to help offset grain tax increases. But what about the remaining families, whose living was derived almost entirely from tilling miniature strips of poor, saline land? In the 1991–2001 decade, a six-person household in Da Fo had about 1.1 *mu* of land per production team member. In an abundant harvest year, a family with three production team members and 3.3 *mu* of land could harvest 1,000 *jin* per *mu*, or a total of 3,300 *jin* of grain. Needing 2,400 *jin* for survival and 640 *jin* to cover the 200-*jin*-per-*mu* grain tax, the family would have a surplus of approximately 290 *jin* – or so it seems. But this calculation leaves out two key components of the political economy of Da Fo's poorest land-dependent households. By the early 1990s, the price of farm supplies had skyrocketed: the total cost of sowing 3.3 *mu* of wheat came to 1,320 *jin*, which left scores of households 1,060 *jin* short of their minimum annual subsistence requirement. With globalization and growing Central government purchases of grain on the world market, moreover, the price of grain often fell, leaving poor tillers with a less valuable product. Important, too, the reform witnessed a collapse of the system of collective medical care benefits, and each family had to fend for itself. Da Fo's three private doctors refused to see any patient who failed to pay cash up front. In this situation, the poorest households – who had to pay the government first, thus preempting any chance of paying for medical treatment – had little hope of securing a physician's services. In Da Fo, the heads of many such households were terrified of being plunged into debt

---

[16] Bao Hongwen, interview.

by a serious family illness. By 1993, the fear of family bankruptcy had generated widespread contempt for reform-era grain taxes.

Villagers constantly questioned the rationale for grain tax increases. When
the price of grain fell, the Liangmen township government would demand more
grain in order to produce the same amount of revenue, and administrative costs
were constantly going up. Da Fo's farmers saw no way out of this threatening
dilemma. Between 1998 and 2001, verbal fights often broke out between
farmers and Da Fo party secretary Bao Shunhe. In 1998, after Premier Zhu
Rongji made a speech about falling grain prices, Ruan Shifan and several other
farmers told the Da Fo secretary that he was totally unreasonable in expecting
villagers to make up any government revenue loss.[17] In the summer of 2000,
Da Fo party leaders threatened to call in the Liangmen township police to
collect the *huang liang* – a term villagers used to describe the grain tax collected
historically for China's emperors. At this point, farmer Bao Guoshan confronted Bao Shunhe, insisting on his right to know how much of the grain-
tax increase was going to the Central government, how much to the township,
and how much to the Da Fo party leadership: "I asked the village party
secretary if I had the right to know the answers before I paid my grain tax.
But he did not know the answer to the question. I then asked him why this year
we had to pay so much grain tax. He said that this year the price of wheat was
low and that we had to pay more to make up the price difference. I asked him
if the price of wheat came all the way down to three or four cents a *jin*, and if
we were told to give up everything we produced to the state in order to make
up the difference, then would we still have to do it? He would not answer."[18]

Bao Guoshan's question was inspired by his memory of loss in the Great
Leap, and so he really was asking: "Will you tell us that you will not allow the
government to appropriate all of our grain, as it did in the Great Leap Forward,
and leave us without any food for survival?" We must keep in mind that in
the Maoist Leap, Da Fo's party leaders never said they were going to take away
all the grain by procurement, but in fact they all but did. They could not do this
in the reform period without paying a price – becoming targets of arson or
being beaten severely by villagers. So in this context, Bao's question actually
was a way of reminding the Da Fo party secretary of the serious consequences
of allowing the Liangmen township tax barons to go too far.

As Bao Guoshan's questions imply, villagers were loath to pay taxes not just
because of the absolute burden but also because they often were kept in the
dark about the relationship between Central government tax policy and the
process of local government taxation. Prior to 1990, government taxation
policies were read aloud at village mass meetings, and people were allowed
to ask questions. But as the 1990s wore on, this practice was discontinued.
By 1993, Bao Peiling could proclaim, "Nowadays farmers no longer know

---

[17] Ruan Shifan, interview.   [18] Bao Guoshan, interview.

what the government policies are. It is up to the village leaders to decide how much grain they want to collect from the villagers. There is no place that villagers can express their complaints about village leaders now."[19] Da Fo's farmers suspected that local party leaders had an interest in keeping them ignorant of state tax guidelines. Indeed, they discovered that the total amount of taxes in 1993 was 190,000 *jin* only after village leaders carelessly leaked the information by publicly quarreling over the unequal distribution of the appropriated grain among themselves.[20]

Whereas the major tax squeeze was occurring at the village level, Da Fo's farmers discovered their leaders were under township-level pressure as well. Of the 190,000 *jin* of wheat that Da Fo party leaders collected in 1993, for example, approximately 50,000 *jin* was collected because of a Liangmen township-level order, and this 50,000 *jin* was held in township storage bins until the end of the year. The Liangmen township officials told Da Fo party leaders that if they were to meet the township-level tax demand for 140,000 *jin*, they would receive the escrowed 50,000 *jin* as their salary – a bonus for squeezing the villagers. If they performed poorly, however, they were to receive nothing or only a part of the 50,000 *jin*.[21] Although unhappy with Da Fo leaders, villagers held the Liangmen township officials responsible for this tax gouge.

The fixed harvest claims of the Maoists, along with the party-state attack on household-based food entitlements, had induced the famine of the Great Leap Forward.[22] Although post-Mao Central government leaders had adjusted the terms of procurement,[23] by the second decade of reform the Liangmen township government had once again imposed an inflexible tax claim. When the June harvest was good, as it was throughout much of 1985–1995, the 170- to 200-*jin*-per-*mu* tax claim was not too great an imposition, but when the harvest was poor the township government's rigid grain-tax system threw Da Fo's farmers into a panic. In May 1998, for instance, a stretch of overcast weather, followed by a hail storm, reduced yields from 1,000 to 500 *jin* per *mu*; for some of the poorest households, yields fell to 200–400 *jin* per *mu*.[24] Hoping for a grain-tax reduction, villagers reported the poor yields to the Liangmen township government. In late June, a team of Liangmen township leaders and Dongle county–level cadres arrived in Da Fo to evaluate the harvest. Subsequently, Da Fo party secretary Bao Shunhe accepted a tax increase.[25] "In the past," lamented Bao Wenfang, "when there was a natural disaster ... the government would reduce the grain tax. But now they no longer do this.

[19] Bao Peiling, interview.   [20] Bao Faming, interview.   [21] Bao Guanjun, interview.
[22] Bernstein, "Stalinism, Famine, and Chinese Peasants," and Thaxton, *Catastrophe and Contention*.
[23] See Friedman, Pickowicz, and Selden, *Revolution, Resistance, and Reform*; Meisner, *Mao's China and After*; Yang, *Calamity and Reform*; and Bernstein and Lu, *Taxation without Representation*.
[24] Zheng Jiangyin, interview; Bao Wenfang, interview.   [25] Bao Guoshan, interview.

This year we suffered a big loss because of some bad weather. But instead of reducing the tax, the Liangmen township officials increased the tax burden."[26]

Popular anger over this inflexible claim was intensified because the Liangmen township government had encouraged farmers to plant several new varieties of wheat that proved vulnerable to the violent preharvest weather. Although the Liangmen township government had held a seminar on propagating the seeds, its cadres issued the information to only one party member per village, who in turn broadcast the general information over loudspeakers at his whim. Consequently, the specific warning about seed vulnerability to bad weather was not communicated effectively.[27] When Da Fo's farmers attempted to make this point to Bao Shunhe and to Liangmen township leaders, they were told they had not listened to the loudspeakers. This added distrust to anger and revived memories of losses suffered from the hastily imposed, poorly conceived, pseudoscientific agricultural experiments of the Great Leap past.

The burden of taxation was spread unevenly over the village in the 1990s, moreover, creating yet another source of popular irritation. In the past, Da Fo's production team accountants were paid a few hundred work points for figuring out the team budget. By the early 1990s, they no longer worked for the team, but they still helped figure out how much each household should pay in grain taxes. When the accountants had been in office they paid the tax also, because if they did not pay it, then villagers would not pay either. After the accountants gave up office in 1995, however, they stopped paying the grain tax on the pretext that the village owed them back salaries amounting to several thousand yuan per accountant. The ex-accountants used this "credit" to "pay" their taxes, exempting themselves for several years and shifting the extra burden of taxation to ordinary farmers. "It has been like this for the past few years," noted Bao Wenfang, "and villagers are angry about it."[28]

Villagers were also perturbed by the aggressive methods of tax collection. In the early 1990s, Liangmen township government leaders justified virtually any method of squeezing villagers who, in their eyes, did not grasp the reform project. Beginning in 1995, each summer after the wheat harvest Da Fo's party leaders roamed the neighborhoods with loudspeakers, urging timely payment of the *huang liang* and threatening to arrest those who did not pay.[29] In 1998, Bao Junjie, the head of the village Communist Youth League, organized Da Fo's schoolchildren into small groups to demonstrate on the village streets, shouting encouragement for their parents to pay the grain tax on time – a tactic similar to those used in the Great Leap to urge farmers to work harder in the collective fields and to comply with grain procurement.[30] These methods, though not always effective, called up memories of party-state aggrandizement in the Great Leap, further alienating villagers.

---

[26] Bao Wenfang, interview.   [27] Bao Shunhe, interview.   [28] Bao Wenfang, interview.
[29] Bao Guoshan, interview.   [30] Bao Shunhe, interview.

Starting in July 1998 and continuing through the summer of 2001, Da Fo party leaders went directly to the homes of people who did not pay taxes voluntarily, telling the head of each household that if he refused to pay, they had the authority to seize the grain themselves. Other party branches in Liangmen township soon adopted this tactic, recalling for villagers the anti-concealment campaign and forceful grain seizures of Wu Zhipu and the Henan Maoists in the Great Leap and raising the specter of another lawless regime of search and seizure. This Great Leap pattern of household break-ins prompted farmers in the remote village of Du Zhuhu in rural Anhui province to organize violent resistance against tax collectors in the mid-1990s.[31] Fearing the aggressive tactic would backfire and trigger attacks on party-appointed tax collectors, Da Fo's Bao Shunhe came up with an alternative. Villagers who refused to pay were "invited" to participate in compulsory study sessions in Liangmen township, where township officials made them pay for their daily food and lodging and prevented them from returning to Da Fo until they had agreed to pay the grain tax.[32] Speaking of the Liangmen township officials who organized the tax collection force and of their accomplices in Da Fo, Ruan Shifan declared, "They were no better than the leaders of the Great Leap Forward, and much worse than the leaders of the Cultural Revolution years."[33]

By this point, many Da Fo households were paying 15–20 percent of their total grain harvest in taxes.[34] Angry complaints that the grain tax was taken without any compensation spread across the village. The Mao-era procurement system had been presented to villagers as a system of "unified purchase and sale" (*tonggou tongxiao*) in which the state purchased villagers' surplus grain at a price below the market rate. In the frenzy of the Great Leap Forward, villagers' subsistence requirements and the state purchase price of grain were continually revised downward until Da Fo was turning over more than four-fifths of its grain to the state and receiving nothing in return. Even at this nadir, however, the logic of the procurement system continued to promise compensation (albeit theoretical) for grain surrendered to the state – a feature that reform-era grain taxation lacked. "Right after Liberation and until the abandonment of production teams, the state usually paid farmers for the grain tax they turned over to the state," explained Bao Faming. "However," continued Bao, "now we do not get anything back for the wheat we give to the state, the township government, or the village management."[35] Bao Zhenmin made the point another way: "Under the collective, the state paid a price for the grain purchased from the villagers, and farmers could get money at the end of the year. But now the village managers collect grain from the villagers without distinguishing between taxes and purchase. They do not pay us at all. If we ask them where the grain tax money went, they make up a list of costs to show us

[31] See Yang, "Dark Side."   [32] Bao Shunhe, interview.   [33] Ruan Shifan, interview.
[34] Pang Fang, interview.   [35] Bao Faming, interview.

where it has gone, like teachers' fees, militia training fees, birth planning fees, and so on."[36] Frustrated, and sometimes understating the burden of pre–Great Leap procurement, some villagers compared the "dirty hands" squeezing them in the reform period with the "clean" leaders who, in the early years of Communist rule, reportedly spent their own money on bus fares and bought their own food when attending government meetings in Dongle county town.

In short, if Da Fo's farmers had difficulty understanding the difference between compulsory state grain purchases at low prices and an actual grain tax, they knew that in both systems the state took a treasured asset. The reform-era Chinese Communist Party (CCP) had switched the form of extraction, but farmers saw that both systems involved a squeeze.

An important source of popular frustration over taxation was the way in which party leaders in Da Fo and Liangmen used taxes, an issue that proved inseparable from political corruption. Bao Peiling spoke for the majority when he said: "If the local village leaders had collected the grain tax to do just a few good deeds for the villagers, then it would have been all right. However, the money gotten from the grain tax was not spent on improving irrigation or any other public facility. The Da Fo party leaders used the money for drinking and eating, and they also pocketed a lot of the public money." To Bao, the leaders were "no better than the officials of the old [pre-Communist] society."[37] Bao Fen echoed this judgment: "Chairman Mao tried all his life to educate the leaders to serve the people, but Deng Xiaoping's leaders think only of pocketing the public money."[38] It infuriated villagers that the grain tax was being used to underwrite the corrupt lifestyle of party leaders and government officials from the highest levels in metropolitan China to the lowest rungs of party rule in rural towns and villages. They saw that officials' craving for banquets, foreign cars, nightclubs, and sexual pleasure was insatiable and that village and township leaders squandered their tax payments to enjoy a saucy, rapturous lifestyle – a lifestyle they associated with the political and moral problems that had plagued the countryside since the Great Leap catastrophe.

Knowing that they were paying for the corrupt lifestyle of the same party leaders who engaged in tax gouging, Da Fo's inhabitants often spoke of such leaders as parasites who depended on taxes to support immoral habits. They gave several examples of this parasitic behavior, one of which is especially troubling. In 1993, the Dongle county government entered into a secret joint venture with a Taiwan business group to fund the construction of a huge entertainment complex on the outskirts of Dongle county town. The complex was modeled after the similar Buyecheng nightlife district in Shanghai in the 1920s, complete with glittery upscale restaurants, nightclubs, strip bars, and brothels. Within a few years, this pattern was replicated in other parts of Dongle county and in other towns and villages of the triprovincial border area.

---

[36] Bao Zhenmin, interview.   [37] Bao Peiling, interview.   [38] Bao Fen, interview.

By 1998, government officials, party leaders, and some of the young adult villagers in the Hebei-Shandong-Henan border region had caught "nightclub fever." To Da Fo's farmers, this pattern of "development" was inseparable from the official corruption of tax policy. They were particularly upset because the Liangmen township party leaders became major patrons of these establishments – a habit sustained by the leaders' collection of ever-larger grain taxes. Not only were the Liangmen township leaders spending tax money to pay for automobile travel to these dens of modernity, but many of the village-level Communist Party leaders were rumored to have joined the officials, sometimes paying for visits to brothels with credit that was due on collection of the grain tax.[39]

To some extent, the vices of local Communist Party leaders and officials were seen by poor tillers through the prism of the memory of the giddy, lustful years of the Great Leap, a time when Liangmen People's Commune leaders used the grain and property taken from formerly private farm households to build palatial headquarters and to entice poor, hungry women to engage in sexual intercourse.[40] For poor, land-dependent farmers, often saddled with sons who could not afford to marry, daughters whose school tuition they could not pay, and kin who could not afford medical care, underwriting the vices of local party leaders was unacceptable. Bao Wenfang said: "The Liangmen township leaders' bellies are becoming bigger and bigger, as they are continuously banqueting at our expense and buying imported cars with our tax money. This is why some villagers have refused to pay the grain tax. They said that they did not want to feed the 'pigs' in the government. We farmers understand that we have to pay the tax. But we resent paying money to the township government leaders to support the things they have been doing."[41]

Villagers' contempt translated into foot dragging. Each year after 1995, the process of collecting the grain tax dragged on longer and longer, from two weeks in 1995 to two months in 1999. According to Da Fo deputy party secretary Pang Siyin, it usually took about ten days for most other villages in Liangmen township to collect the grain tax. It took longer in Da Fo because the village was farther away from the township granaries and because villagers resisted efforts to collect the grain tax.[42] By the late 1990s, resistance to tax collection was testing the ability of Da Fo's Communist Party leaders to govern. Leaders had to plead with villagers to pay, and for several years they were unable to collect the grain tax until late October, long past the

---

[39] Bao Xianpu, interview.
[40] On this phenomenon during the Great Leap in the Sun County Irrigation Project, which Dongle and Liangmen party leaders supervised, see Bao Wanxuan, interview, and for documentation of the pattern for the Ji County Tong Tin River Dig Project, see Thaxton, *Catastrophe and Contention*.
[41] Bao Wenfang, interview.   [42] Pang Siyin, interview.

upper-government deadline. They responded by breaking into houses to seize the grain, confirming that the collection of taxes was virtually impossible without resort to force.[43]

FORMS OF TAX RESISTANCE IN THE 1990S

Between 1990 and 2000, increasingly militant collective protests over harsh grain taxes, combined with low grain prices, swept through the rural interior provinces of Jiangxi, Hunan, Hubei, Shaanxi, Anhui, and Henan – the home of Da Fo.[44] The political life of Da Fo farmers during this decade was increasingly devoted to expressing anger over taxation. That anger spawned confrontations with village party leaders. Eventually, Da Fo's farmers carried the fight for just taxes to higher-level government officials, particularly to the Liangmen township leaders, who, although acting without the explicit approval of the Central government, were inclined to rely on repression to put down resistance.

In Da Fo, resistance to taxation took a number of forms that escalated in severity over the course of the 1990s. The first of these was rumor. As Ranajit Guha has noted, the power of rumor in fueling autonomous struggles among preliterate rural people is enormous, serving as an "indispensable vehicle of insurgency," charging passions, and creating a shared identity among the oppressed.[45] Da Fo's farmers relied on rumor to spread antitax sentiment among cohorts, and rumor became a valued instrument of their antitax activities. In the first post-1978 decade of household-based farming, Liangmen township government leaders added twenty-three surtax fees onto the Central government tax claim. Not all villagers were aware of the origins of these extra taxes. Most knew only that they had to pay so much every year, but the whisper mill had it that the center's tax claim was minimal. In the absence of village party leaders who would accurately explain national tax policy, a few villagers took it on themselves to spread rumors that the Central government had proclaimed it unlawful to collect *any* tax at all from villagers, so that all of the taxes taken by local tax agents were said to have been taken illegally.[46] Fueling arguments about the illegitimacy of taxation, this rumor was a source of constant headache for Da Fo's party leaders.

Initially, the most widespread form of reform-era popular tax resistance in Da Fo was evasion. Clearly, it was easier to evade the lax tax controls of the postcollective period than it had been during the Mao years. Several techniques

---

[43] As related by Bao Xuejing, interview; he admitted that the only way to collect taxes during his tenure as party secretary was by break-ins and force. For the social science wisdom on this point, see Pei, "China's Governance Crisis," 107.

[44] The best source on these collective protests and the violence enveloping them is Bernstein, "Unrest in Rural China," 1–12, 17–18. On the issue of falling market prices for agricultural commodities and rising taxes, see also Lu, "Nongmin Zhenku," 2, 5.

[45] Guha, *Elementary Aspects*, 118, 188, 251–258.   [46] Bao Zheng, interview.

of evasion stood out. We have seen that one was foot dragging, not showing up to pay taxes on time. Purportedly, at the beginning of the early 1950s farmers in Da Fo were grateful to Chairman Mao and the Communist Party, and according to Ruan Xiaoxian they expressed their gratitude by voluntarily lining up in front of the village office to pay the grain tax to the state.[47] Bao Peilian, the head of Da Fo village in 1950 and the tax collector from 1950 to 1952, recalled that in this early period of CCP rule the village tax collector needed only to beat the gong once to tell villagers it was time for taxes, and the people would line up promptly to pay. The leaders were able to collect the tax in two days – or so we are told.[48] (All this said, we must keep in mind that people were never happy about procurement, which farmers separate from the formal tax claim of the early 1950s.) After the reform began, however, Da Fo's party leaders had to visit each farm household and urge the family head to pay the grain tax, and some farmers had to be summoned to the village office and given an ultimatum before they would pay.

As the first decade of reform wore on, the ultimatums often fell on deaf ears. As a result, in 1991 Da Fo party leaders began collaborating with Liangmen township officials to establish a Special Task Force for collecting the grain tax from villagers. Frequently accompanied by the police, the Task Force increasingly broke into the homes of defiant farmers to seize grain.[49] In 1991, for example, the Task Force broke into the home of Bao Guobao and took away his wheat by force, adding an extra 70 *jin* fine onto his tax assessment.[50] The direct involvement of Da Fo party leaders in these break-ins diminished in 1993–1994. Afraid to confront Da Fo's farmers directly, they more frequently enlisted local toughs to engineer the break-ins and carry out the grain seizures – and only when farmers were not at home. To more than a few Da Fo farmers, these break-ins recalled the vigilante politics of the Great Leap era, when cadres invaded homes to seize food grain in 1959–1960.[51]

Nearly every household strove to pay in the worst-quality grain available or in cash, keeping their superior grain from the state. Village tax collectors preferred payment in wheat and told farmers to give up superior wheat at a two-cent discount per *jin*. As Nicholas R. Lardy and Kate Zhou have pointed out, in the late Mao era local party leaders more or less compelled tillers to pay taxes in grain, forcing households without grain to purchase it at the highest price in order to pay the taxes – an important factor in the impoverishment of villagers.[52] Freed from this political obligation during the 1990s, Da Fo's farmers more and more frequently opted to sell their wheat to a private flour miller at the going market price and pay the grain tax in cash.[53]

---

[47] Ruan Xiaoxian, interview.   [48] Bao Peilian, interview.
[49] Bao Shaolian, interview; Zhou Jian, interview.   [50] Bao Guobao, interview.
[51] Bao Bingyong, interview.
[52] Lardy, *Agriculture*, and Zhou, *How the Farmers Changed China*, 25–26.
[53] Zhou Weihai, interview; Ruan Fen, interview.

Far more effective than foot dragging or cash substitution was the underreporting of total income. Officially, the amount of grain taken by tax collectors
was not to exceed 5 percent of the total previous year's household income – a
limit established by the Central government and emphasized by CCP general
secretary Jiang Zemin in December 1992. When it came to enforcing this rule,
however, the party's locally appointed tax collectors were severely handicapped,
for though they knew villagers' total land holdings (on which the grain-tax
assessment was based), villagers were not obliged to report to anyone how
much grain they harvested from their land or how much income they took in
from petty trade or side occupations.[54] Da Fo party leaders could not possibly
keep track of off-farm income earnings, so growing numbers of villagers could
get away with underreporting total income. This is precisely what they did,
while warning party leaders of disciplinary action if they made demands in
excess of the 5 percent limit. Some villagers also appealed to local party
leaders for tax relief, citing a poor harvest or a shortfall in family income.
Village leaders found the people who voiced such appeals difficult to deal with
and worried that if they did not accommodate them, the informal appeals
would lead to refusal to pay.

By the mid-1990s, outright refusal to pay taxes was rampant in Da Fo: in the
summer of 1994, following the lead of People's Liberation Army (PLA) veteran
Bao Timing and martial artist Bao Yinbao – both of whom had traveled outside
Da Fo, and both of whom we will get to know in the pages and chapters
ahead – more than half of Da Fo's farmers refused to pay the grain tax to
Liangmen township.[55] By this point, the township leaders invariably had
to come to Da Fo with the police in order to make villagers comply with their
tax demands. They frequently called villagers to a meeting and required them to
view a movie about tax obligation. Afterward, they told villagers how much
they had to pay, and they followed up by threatening those who refused to pay
with jail time.[56] After one standoff between villagers and tax officials, for
instance, the head of Liangmen township came to Da Fo flanked by policemen
brandishing handcuffs. He warned Da Fo's farmers to either pay the grain
tax or be handcuffed and taken to the police station, which, he declared, had
room to house them all.[57]

---

[54] Bao Dongwen, interview.

[55] Bao Timing, interview; Pang Puli, interview; Bao He, interview. Resonating with the scholarship
of Thomas P. Bernstein and Neil J. Diamant, the testimonies of Da Fo's farmers indicate that
disgruntled ex-PLA soldiers played a prominent role in leading tax resistance in the Da Fo area.
Diamant, *Embattled Glory*, and Bernstein, "Unrest in Rural China," 7. These more widely
traveled and worldly wise villagers were the catalytic agents for collective antitax activities
within Da Fo and Liangmen township. Dependent on off-farm income for survival, they
developed close, trustworthy relationships with the tillers they served in other villages and
counties of the triprovincial border area. Hence, they were positioned to coordinate transvillage
antitax actions.

[56] Pang Puli, interview.   [57] Bao Timing, interview.

In 1995–2001, refusal protest evolved into boycotts and eventually became entwined with another, bolder form of contention employed by otherwise conservative farm people: the mode of eviction, that is, of pitching tax authorities out of the space in which taxes were to be collected. In late 1993, farmers in Xinglong village, Xinglong township, collectively refused to pay the grain tax. When the police attempted to assist Xinglong party leaders with tax collection, a crowd drove them out of the village. They subsequently joined farmers in other villages to rush to Xinglong township, where they beat up the head of the township government. Far from being punished, participants in this collective action sued the township leaders for overtaxing them, and they won their lawsuit. The Dongle county government ordered the Xinglong township leaders to return part of the grain tax payment to the village, and the head of Xinglong township was transferred.[58]

Yet another tax refusal incident, this one in Sanlizhuang, only a few li from Da Fo, alerted Da Fo's farmers to the efficacy of collective antitax protest and eviction. In late 1993, Sanlizhuang's farmers collectively refused to pay the grain tax. Village party leaders reported the refusal to the Liangmen township government, and the township leaders went to Sanlizhuang to press for payment. Farmers responded by surrounding them and pummeling them with questions about the righteousness of taxation. Unable to provide satisfactory answers, the township government tax officials were beaten up and driven out of Sanlizhuang; it was rumored they were fortunate to have escaped. There were too many people involved in this concerted action, and the township leaders dared not punish anyone.[59]

Seeing that other villages had achieved success in collectively resisting local taxation, Da Fo's denizens took up their own initiatives to free themselves from payment of unjust taxes. In late 1993, Pang Siyin, the Da Fo deputy party secretary, caught wind of a Liangmen township plan to start up a new market in Liangmenpo on the same periodic market schedule as Da Fo's market: the third, sixth, and ninth days of every ten-day cycle.[60] Responding to popular alarm over this scheme, which threatened to suck trade out of Da Fo, Pang Siyin petitioned township leaders to reconsider, insisting that the new market could not meet on the same days as Da Fo's. Shortly thereafter, Da Fo's party leaders discovered that the Dongle county government had given the Liangmen township leaders 10,000 yuan to jump-start the market development in Liangmenpo. Within six months, people in other villages, including Da Fo, began shifting their market activities to Liangmenpo, and Da Fo began to lose market share. Its party leaders and ordinary residents felt they had been sold down the river. Fear of abandonment turned frustration into anxiety, no doubt magnified by the memory of the hard times associated with the loss of their

---

[58] Bao Peijian, interview; Pang Zhenfa, interview. [59] Pang Zhenfa, interview.
[60] Pang Siyin, interview.

market in the Great Leap years. The villagers insisted that they and they alone had the customary right to operate a market on the third, sixth, and ninth days of the old ten-day cycle, but they lacked the institutional resources to enforce this claim. Called to action by Tang Dafa and Ruan Yunchang, some twenty Da Fo residents who depended on off-farm income joined with small farmers, market brokers, and store merchants to organize a protest against the Liangmen township government. Initially taking the form of a collective refusal to pay any taxes on small business income, this protest quickly escalated: in late 1994, its leaders evicted the Liangmen township tax collectors from Da Fo. From 1995 to 1998, they barred the collectors from the village, their resistance increasingly reflecting a rejection of township rule.[61]

Thomas P. Bernstein and Lu Xiaobo have demonstrated that farmer anger over tax burdens exploded in collective protest organized and orchestrated by informal village leaders in the 1993–2001 period[62] and that extraneous surtaxes were implicated in township- and county-level petitions, marches, clashes, and riots. We also know from Lucien Bianco's scholarship that, historically, tax protest in rural China was not just the product of an increasing state claim on grain crops. It was often triggered by the sudden and unpredictable imposition of a new rigid surcharge on some crucial aspect of peasant household economy.[63] In line with the above logic, antitax protest in Liangmen township during the mid-1990s was also sparked by the proliferation of surcharges on off-farm income – specifically, a surcharge on the use of motor carts.

After the Great Leap famine, farmers in Da Fo and surrounding villages had attempted to find ways to facilitate travel from home to fields and markets and to free their household economic activities from the monitoring of local party leaders, neither of which proved easy in the Mao era. The appearance of small motor carts in Dongle county during the second decade of reform gave them their chance. From 1990 to 1995, farmers in Da Fo and scores of villages operated such motor carts without a license, using them to skip from one household strip of land to another and to travel to and from local periodic markets. In 1997, the Liangmen township government suddenly proclaimed a new sixty-yuan license fee for each motor cart in the villages within its jurisdiction. People in different villages came together to challenge the fee.[64] In Dingcun, where there were more than a hundred motor-cart owners, village leaders told the Liangmen township leaders they had only fifty. Wanxiuzhuang's farmers villagers organized a boycott and refused to pay any motor cart fee. And in

---

[61] This kind of tax resistance seems to be in line with that uncovered by Perry, *Rebels and Revolutionaries*, 163–166, 205, and also with the reasons for resistance stated in the work of Wong, *China Transformed*, 235, 247, 251.

[62] Bernstein and Lu, *Taxation without Representation*, chapter 5.

[63] Bianco, "Tax Protest," 26–32.   [64] Zheng Yunxiang, interview.

Liangmenpo, where township officials attempted to arrest those who sought to avoid the motor-cart surtax, villagers fought back with fists.[65]

When Liangmen township leaders attempted to force the surcharge issue, farmers in Da Fo, Wanxiuzhuang, Liangmenpo, Weicaicun, and several other villages drove their motor carts to township government headquarters to launch a protest complaint. Officials fled in fear as several thousand motor carts sped toward government headquarters. The protesters then drove all the way to Puyang city government, to which Liangmen township reported, where they won official acceptance of their complaint. Waving red flags, they raced their motor carts back to the Dongle county seat to demand the removal of the head of the Liangmen township government. In the end, he was removed.[66] In recalling this struggle to end tax injustice, Zheng Yunxiang characterized it as "a rebellion against the township government."[67]

Perhaps the memory of the mistake of not acting collectively to oppose the takeover of private family lands and the confiscation of instruments of production and transportation in the years winding to the Great Leap disaster was a factor behind the quick formation of this antitax mobilization. Many of Da Fo's farmers recalled that the Mao-led central party-state had imperiled consumption not only by overtaxing production through procurement but also by impeding movement to and from the market. Now they were acting collectively to reaffirm their right to speedy market access without penalty.

TAX PROTEST AND THE STATE

In the early 1990s, the Liangmen township leaders repeatedly twisted government tax policy to serve their own ends. This pattern of "loosely regulated authoritarianism,"[68] wherein township leaders intercepted and distorted national-level tax policy, opened the door to a wave of tax refusals that went far beyond regime-contained resistance. In the very years when the Central government was exhorting rural people to express their discontent over taxation in language supportive of scaled-down state tax claims, Da Fo's farmers did the opposite: in expressing their thoughts about taxation, many Da Fo farmers articulated a contentious invective that resonated more with the painful

---

[65] Bao Guoshan, interview. [66] Bao Guojun, interview. [67] Zheng Yunxiang, interview

[68] When it comes to center-local party interactions, I think "loosely regulated," as opposed to "fragmented authoritarianism," better captures the essence of how rural China is ruled by the reform-era neo-Leninist party-state. "Fragmented" implies broken into pieces whereas "loosely regulated" implies loose control, or serious lapses in control, and yet the possibility of tightening control when absolutely necessary. On the concept of "fragmented authoritarianism," see Lieberthal, "The Fragmented Authoritarianism Model," in Lieberthal and Lampton, eds., *Bureaucracy, Policy, and Decision Making in Post-Mao China*, 1–30; Lieberthal and Oksenberg, *Policy Making in China*, 20–25; and Tong, *Transitions from State Socialism*, 10.

memory of political injustice in the Great Leap era than with the regime-serving discourse of either radical Maoist or conservative post-Maoist reformist eras.[69] Official tax pronouncements aimed at instructing rural bumpkins in how to think about tax policy apparently failed to create a new lens through which villagers saw the political world and experienced citizen identity.[70]

In refusing to pay taxes, Da Fo farmers and those of scores of surrounding villages frequently declared their unwillingness to give up their grain to the "animals" in local government. For three full years, roughly 1992–1995, the inhabitants of Daweicun, a village characterized by greater poverty and weaker Communist Party presence than Da Fo, refused to turn in any grain tax to the Liangmen township government. When tax officials confronted them about the refusal in 1996, villagers declared that they were not willing to provide "animal feed" for the "pigs" who posed as township government leaders.[71] In making this kind of open insult, which had been taboo in the Great Leap, villagers were taking a dissenting stab at the unrighteous system of reform-era appropriation, which, as Patricia Thornton has observed, was in some important respects only a "reclassification of some of the 'hidden burdens' of pre-reform state procurement."[72] By gathering to speak out against the "pig" abuse of tax power, moreover, farmers in Da Fo, Daweicun, and other villages signaled that they would not silently comply with the dominant claims of party tax cadres and that they would not tolerate another Great Leap–style tax disaster.

If the refusal to pay taxes was triggered by the weight, timing, and collection method of reform-era tax policy, it was nonetheless a mode of contention that drew on the lessons of the Maoist era as well as a venerable tradition of tax resistance. In the case of Da Fo, reform-era tax refusal protest drew on the arts of resisting procurement in the worst years of the Great Leap Forward Famine, when half-starved farmers who slaved in collective fields took up the practice of *chi qing*. When Da Fo's citizens took up refusal in the 1990s, therefore, it stirred up old tensions. Villagers knew they could threaten to play the wild card of *chi qing* against excessive taxation – and so did the township-based successors of the people's commune leadership.[73]

The revival of contentious refusal seemed even more threatening than it had been in its previous incarnation, for the acts of tax refusal increasingly

---

[69] For the view that reform-era organization and linguistic repertoires of popular collective protest have their lineage in Mao era radicalism see Perry's seminal writings. See Perry, "'To Rebel Is Justified': Maoist Influences,"; and Perry, "'To Rebel is Justified': Cultural Revolution Influences"; also see Thornton, "Comrades and Collectives in Arms."

[70] This section owes a great debt to Guha, *Elementary Aspects*, 40–53, and to Scott, *Domination*, 148–172.

[71] Bao Xianpu, interview.   [72] Thornton, "Comrades and Collectives in Arms," 5.

[73] I am indebted to Tilly's work for helping me grasp this point (see "Contentious Repertoires," 42) and to Thornton for reminding us of the power of Tilly's conceptual framework and its usefulness in studying tax protest and contention in present-day China ("Comrades and Collectives in Arms," 5).

were associated with open boycotts led by farmers who railed against paying any taxes. At least on the face of it, villagers seemed more keenly aware than ever before of why and how the "pigs" at the lower rungs of the national tax hierarchy preserved their special tax privileges. This awareness seems to have inclined Da Fo's farmers to extend the silent, sequestered mode of contention that characterized *chi qing* to tax-refusal battles conducted openly and collectively in villages, market streets, and sites of township governance. Officials were alarmed that they might lose not just revenue but the power to manage tax extraction from the farmhouses of the hinterland.

An intriguing question arises. Why did Da Fo's party leaders sometimes refrain from enlisting the police to back up their tax claims? And why didn't Da Fo's tax resisters suffer from repeated police arrest? One reason for the lapse in village leadership tax enforcement was the lingering psychological legacy of the Great Leap Forward, for Da Fo's party leaders understood that the long-term debilitating effects of Mao's procurement famine predisposed villagers to find ways to take revenge on agents of menacing tax claims. Da Fo's leaders were reluctant to call on the township police to rigidly enforce taxation, for they feared this might prompt villagers to take revenge on them at a later date, just as nocturnal arsonists had taken revenge on Bao Zhilong and the other party leaders who were implicated in the famine. According to Bao Peilian, one of the most astute inside observers of politics in Da Fo, the fingerprint of the Great Leap famine continued to inhibit the strict enforcement of tax claims by Da Fo's party leaders under reform: "The leaders could not afford to let the police arrest too many people in the village anyway. . . . If you hurt someone in the village, someday they might strike back at you. Think about Bao Zhilong's fate. His household was set on fire on several occasions. There is no doubt that this was done by someone Bao Zhilong had hurt when he was in power during the three years of economic difficulty [the three years of the Great Leap famine]. Now he is a harmless old man. It is easy to get him now. The case of Bao Zhilong offers a lesson to anybody who is in a position of power."[74]

By the time I began interviewing in Da Fo in the 1989–1990 period, its Communist Party leaders had started to pick up stories about farmers in other places who refused to pay their taxes. They learned of villagers beating up village party leaders, of the courts deciding against such leaders, and of the Central government making examples of leaders who pressed for the police arrest of tax resisters.[75] The Da Fo party leaders knew, therefore, that they would face difficulty in obtaining the necessary backing from upper-government agencies to compel villagers to pay. They also feared being punished if something untoward happened in the village on the issue of taxation and higher-ups decided to investigate the case.[76] Consequently, they assumed a low profile when it came to grain tax collection.

---

[74] Bao Peilian, interview.   [75] Bao Jingjian, interview.   [76] Zheng Xutang, interview.

In the early 1990s, Da Fo's farmers also enlisted the helpful tax policy reforms of the Central government in their struggle against excessive local taxation. Ruan Jing explained how Da Fo's farmers were able to employ high-level institutional support to protect them against the tax squeeze of local party leaders:

Of course, village leaders decide how much tax grain we must pay to the state. But it is not within their power to do so. . . .. the state actually does not allow them to add so much onto the tax. In 1993, the State Council published a brochure about the state taxation policy in the countryside. Each farmer was given a copy to use as protection against excessive taxation. It was very useful for villagers. With that small brochure in hand, people knew the state policy on taxation, and the village leaders knew the state policy. The leaders were not deterred completely from overtaxing us, but the idea that some of us could use the state policy to challenge them was in their minds. Thus, the amount of grain they took from us in 1993 was reduced from the amount they took the year before.[77]

Most agreed with Pang Puli when in September 1993 he asserted: "The Central government has not attempted to collect much by way of the grain tax. It is the local government – the village, the township, and the county – that has increased the amount. The villagers are angry, but not because they have to pay a tax. What they really resent is the extra grain they have to pay to the village, township, and county governments."[78] In May 1994, Bao Yibin, who had served briefly as the Da Fo deputy party secretary in 1992, admitted that in the very years when the grain tax was soaring, the Central government's tax was only 5 yuan per *mu* for summer wheat, thus revealing that the burgeoning tax assessment was largely the result of township government fees piled onto a rather meager center tax claim.[79] With this information, Da Fo's farmers more and more frequently attempted to make village and township leaders abide by the center's "legitimate" tax formula.

All of the above underscores the explanatory power of the O'Brien-Li concept of policy cued "rightful resistance." Yet if popular tax protest in rural China under reform had simply unfolded within an institutionalized framework of fairness, contention over taxation would have reflected, to use Kevin J. O'Brien's words, "a degree of accommodation with the structure of domination, the deft use of prevailing culture conventions, and an affirmation – sometimes sincere, sometimes strategic – of existing channels of inclusion."[80] In other words, villagers would have engaged in tax resistance that was not officially out of bounds. Instead, the most widespread form of tax resistance in reform-era Da Fo was refusal – a form of resistance that was explicitly prohibited by the central party-state.

---

[77] Ruan Jiang, interview.   [78] Pang Puli, interview.   [79] Bao Yibin, interview.
[80] O'Brien, "Neither Transgressive nor Contained," 107.

Popular acceptance of the official Deng-era transcript of tax policy – which included the 5 percent tax limit on household income – did not necessarily imply endorsement of the center's tax scheme. Many farmers questioned the legitimacy of central party-state revenue claims. In the case of Da Fo, it seems that refusal protest was driven by deeply engrained distrust of the taxation pledges of Beijing rulers. The same Da Fo farmers who said, for example, that the Liangmen township rulers cared only about getting as much personal benefit as possible from tax collection while meeting the Central government's tax claims also said that the center's unwillingness to check the excessive tax claims of township government was to blame for "most of the bad things" in rural China. Thus, while Da Fo's farmers shifted their resistance to accommodate the tax-framing process of the center, villagers did not see the center's reformed tax policy as a "right" granted by a regime that suddenly had their best interests in mind. The reform-era center's adjustment was appreciated, but it was taken as a small official pocketknife to be used in a larger antitax battle that farmers had been fighting with the sword of refusal for a long time – and they were not about to give up the latter for the former.

Farmers also declared Beijing politicians to be responsible for the tax gouge locally because those politicians pressed the Dongle county and Liangmen township leaders to raise tax revenue to cover the center's unfunded plans for development. In 1994, when the Central government adapted a new tax division formula, Beijing started to regain control over rural-based tax revenue, and so county and township governments were less and less able to retain the taxes garnered from local people. Facing center pressures for impressive developmental performance and yet losing tax revenue at the same time, the Dongle county and Liangmen township leaders placed a host of new claims on villagers. The result was predictable. By 1995, farmers in Da Fo were openly attributing the excessive rural tax burden to unfunded Central government mandates for development, which placed a greater pressure on the Liangmen township government leaders to pursue rent seeking as a way of complying with centrally issued tax regulations. In this respect, the political thinking of Da Fo's "backward" farmers was in line with the most sophisticated of global social science writings on state taxation and rural instability in contemporary China, which linked tax protest to a national policy that placed the burden of developing rural China on local government.[81]

To many farmers, this modality of state appropriation seemed to resonate with the Great Leap past, when the Maoist seizure of more and more grain to fund rural industrial projects and the Maoist failure to institutionalize a merit-based living salary for local party leaders combined to deplete household food supplies and produce deadly political corruption. Hence, they came to see the

---

[81] Liu Mingxing, unpublished paper, 2003, 1–15; Lin et al., "The Problem of Taxing Peasants in China"; Wang and Hu, *The Chinese Economy in Crisis*; Zhan, "Decentralizing China"; and Takeuchi, *Tax Reform in Rural China*, 4.

reform-era system of Central government taxation as something that reflected more than the greed of local autocratic officials with discretionary powers: it was a remnant of the irrational rural public finance system that had helped engender the famine of the Great Leap.[82] This, explained Bao Xianpu, was one reason why villagers were angry with the Central government as well as the township government.[83]

To be sure, Da Fo's antitax activists did not openly express their resistance as a struggle against the Central government, because the center could easily have mobilized force to crush them. To villagers, it made sense to take the center's announced tax policy and use it as a weapon in the struggle against the township and village tax agents.[84] They did this without openly declaring war against the center. Nonetheless, they also judged Central government leaders by the actions of the local officials, who had been appointed by those in the upper reaches of the state. Knowing well that Da Fo, Liangmen township, and Dongle county party rulers were subordinate to a national system of neo-Leninist state power, villagers understood the problem as structural. So much was this the case that Bao Timing and some of the tax resisters intimated that if given the opportunity, they might extend the struggle against greedy and corrupt local tax agents to the upper government in Beijing, although fear precluded them from declaring this openly.[85]

Da Fo's tax resisters, like their counterparts in other villages of this poor-soil part of the north China plain, more or less concluded that the center's attempt to reform its system of rural taxation had failed. They were not alone. In this same period, roughly 1995–2000, Qinghua University scholar Qin Hui reported seeing the early signs of an "irreversibly accumulating disaster" in villages where the Central government had allowed rural tax reform to be taken over by township-level autocrats. The latter enforced "irrational extortion"

---

[82] Just as the scholarship of Thomas P. Bernstein and Lu Xiaobo would suggest. See *Taxation without Representation*, 85–90, esp. 90. Also see Sun, *Corruption and Market*, 160.

[83] Bao Xianpu, interview.   [84] See Scott, *Weapons of the Weak*.

[85] Compare with O'Brien and Li, who argue that policy-based resisters by and large avoid challenging Central government cadres and seek instead to cultivate allies at the center. "Villagers and Popular Resistance," 54–55. Also compare with O'Brien, "Rightful Resistance," 54–55. The O'Brien and Li model, while powerful, does not look at how resisters who prefer to change regimes rather than invigorate reforms in their institutions use policy-based resistance to fight against the local component of such regimes while honing their repertoires of resistance for a possible struggle with the distant center. It is difficult for Western-trained scholars and for Chinese intellectuals to get rural people who have been wounded by the state to tell them what they really think of centrist rulers or to admit that they would like to get rid of such rulers through revolt. Because of state domination, so-called policy-based resisters have no choice but to speak out in nonthreatening ways. How do we know, therefore, whether rural people would keep wearing the hat of deference and the clothes of "loyal dissenters" if the balance of power were altered in favor of a rebel movement with ties to villagers? Given a drastically changed political situation, they might join in revolt or support revolutionary goals in ways that would surprise us.

against tillers, denying them any right to an equal democratic voice in matters of state revenue extraction and recalling the days when Mao's cadres dictated the terms of procurement.[86]

Besieged with growing resistance to the grain tax, and under pressure from the center to alleviate the burden, the Liangmen township government reduced its tax claim in the 2001–2004 period. It was not enough; taxation remained an intractable problem. Responding to this problem, the Central government abolished the centuries-old agricultural tax in 2006,[87] by which time the tax was generating less than 1 percent of total Central government revenue.[88] *People's Daily*, the official newspaper of the CCP, hailed the change as transformative, and so did some of the farmers in Dongle county. Yan Weisheng of Dingcun expresses their sentiments when he said: "There are many people who are not happy with Hu Jintao and Wen Jiabao. They are upset about the corruption and crime. However, I do not care about this. They eliminated the agricultural tax, and have given farmers a subsidy. As long as I can get money from grain, as long as the government officials do not take anything from me, I am happy."[89] Though worried about the future of China, Yan agreed with Wang Guojing (a Liangmen village farmer whose family survived the Great Leap intact), who reasoned that "as long as there is enough food for people to eat, rural people will not rebel against the Central government."[90]

This response must be taken with a grain of salt, however. Dingcun was a model village in the Mao era, and Yan's family, along with the great majority of Dingcun families, did not suffer greatly in the Leap famine. Furthermore, in the early years of decollectivization, farmers in party-favored Dingcun were able to boost yields through privileged access to huge amounts of chemical fertilizer. In less-favored villages, of which Da Fo was more typical, many farmers, especially those aged forty to sixty, evaluated the 2006 tax reform differently. Many perceived that the cost to the Central government of the 2006 tax reform was negligible, partly because the government was experienced at recouping the loss in other ways.[91] Wu Anwen, a farmer from Pingyuandi village, in Wei county, Hebei province, a short distance from Da Fo, emphasized this point: "The greed of the local officials was still there. When they could not get the money from farmers by adding on to the state taxes, they would find new ways to get the money, such as charging us to get some dirt from the fields."[92] Between 2000 and 2008, the price of grain continued to fall, in part because domestic grain production increased and in part because Central government

---

[86] Qin, "Tax and Fee Reform," 6–7.   [87] Perry, "Permanent Rebellion," 214.
[88] Chan, "Beijing Abolishes."   [89] Yan Weisheng, interview.
[90] Ibid.; see Wang Guojing interview.
[91] Compare with Cai, whose work helps us understand that collective protest has a better chance of success when the costs to the regime are minimal and, in any event, prove less than the costs of repression. Cai, *Collective Resistance*, 185–186.
[92] Wu Anwen, interview.

grain purchases from the international market further increased supply. In this same period, the Central government price for chemical fertilizer nearly doubled, and its agents sold seeds to farmers at nearly two times the market price asked by private sellers (1.8 yuan versus 1 yuan per *jin*). Meanwhile, the cost of pesticides, electricity, and gasoline also went up.[93] Da Fo's farmers complained that these charges were transferred back to them.[94] "This was why I did not think the agricultural tax exemption was a big help for farmers," proclaimed forty-year-old Bao Guofa in 2006. "Most farmers did not see it that way."[95] To be sure, the raw hunger of the Mao era was gone. Da Fo's farmers had wheat flour noodles in their diets. But their earnings from working the land were reduced by government charges on inputs; their household incomes were not keeping up with inflation; and they were still far behind most urban dwellers when it came to material consumption.

Evaluation of the 2006 tax reform was also wrapped in dangerous popular thinking about its real political motive. Some of the interviewees saw the center's tax reform as an act compelled by contentious hostility from below, a policy driven by central party-state fears of protest that posed a threat to the use of police force in fleecing the countryside. Sixty-one-year-old Zhou Jian, a Liangmenpo farmer, said of the motives of the central party leaders who fashioned the reform: "Many farmers say Wen Jiabao was a good leader because he canceled taxes for the farmers and gave subsidies to the farmers. Actually, he was only a clever politician. By eliminating taxes and giving a small subsidy, he eliminated the direct confrontation between the people and the government. But he continued to get more money from the people through inflation. The livelihood of people did not improve, even though he talked about this all of the time. Deng Xiaoping, Jiang Zemin, and Zhu Rongji were even worse. They taxed people heavily."[96] The grain tax was canceled, in Huang's judgment, because the central party-state was facing an upsurge in ramified tax rebellion in the countryside.[97] This upsurge resulted from the center's failing performance on the very issue that had most ruined its legitimacy in the Great Leap, and the abolishment of the agricultural tax was an intended – though not so effective – sedative to a popular demand that had its origins in resistance to a prior episode of state tax plunder.

– – –

In both dynastic China and *ancien-régime* France, the growth of state power was predicated substantially on taxation. Historically, this issue generated a lot of deferential protest, which by and large turned into a popular jacquerie only after local gentry, in the case of China, or local nobles, in the case of France,

---

[93] Bao Guofa, interview; Bao Xuejun, interview.
[94] Bao Wenfang, interview; Bao Guofa, interview.   [95] Bao Guofa, interview.
[96] Zhou Jian, interview.   [97] Ibid.

failed to convince high officials to address unjust claims on tiller harvests and bodies – claims that were often contested through established political channels. The evidence from Da Fo village and Dongle county suggests that the Deng Xiaoping–led center did not train and dispatch tax inspectors who could monitor taxation and accommodate the entreaties of burdened tillers. To be sure, Central government officials issued guidelines aimed at keeping grain taxes tolerable, but when it came to enforcement, tillers were more or less left to their own devices. What motivated Deng and post-Deng reformers to make concessions on taxing the grain harvest was a popular challenge rooted in the defiant act of noninstitutionalized refusal protest – not the deferential presentation of claims through official, state-fashioned channels for protest. CCP rulers, both in Beijing and in the Da Fo village–Dongle county area of Henan, had reason to fear this challenge might spawn a rebellion, for it was driven by the harm of the past as well as the hardship of the present. This refusal protest was rooted in memory of Mao-era pain, for Da Fo's farmers associated the tax burden of the reform era with the specter of the unrestrained procurement that produced the Great Leap crisis. As Ethan Michelson has discovered, this same identification produced fear-driven antitax initiatives in other Henan villages, including those in Ru'an county, where nearly half of the population perished in the Leap famine.[98]

In Da Fo, villagers had relied on refusal as a means of contesting and escaping procurement-engendered food insecurity in the Great Leap Forward. They reached back to this strategy of surviving famine to challenge the rising burden of taxation in the first decade of reform, compelling the center to reduce the burden in the 1990s and then, in 2006, to abolish the agricultural tax. What appeared to be a product of institutionally encouraged resistance was therefore the result of a long-embedded, intermittent popular challenge to extraction that could not be contained without risk of a rebellion against the central party-state. Without contentious refusal, which resonated with the popular insistence that officials honor "subsistence-first" principles in harvest appropriation,[99] the center's tax reform policies and prescriptions were impotent – at least in Da Fo. Here, even the abolishment of the agricultural tax did not address the problem of monopolistic state influences on the economic life of farmers. The structural problem, which included not merely taxation without representation but also central and local party-state interference with family procreation and neglect of youth education, would persist and turn Da Fo and much of rural China into a politically volatile place.

---

[98] Michelson, "Climbing the Dispute Pagoda," 480; also see Wemheuer, "Stone Noodles."
[99] On subsistence-first principles in state taxation, see Scott, *Moral Economy*, 15.

3

Birth Planning and Popular Resistance

When Deng Xiaoping and his allies launched the one-child birth planning policy between 1980 and 1983, a step Tyrene White calls "the most extensive, aggressive, and effective attempt ever made to subject child-bearing to direct state control and regulation,"[1] it was received in the countryside with suspicion and resistance by both farmers and some of the Communist Party cadres whose mission it was to implement it. Western scholarship on the policy tends to focus on the process whereby the central party-state overcame this resistance, thereby imposing its policy, or on popular acceptance of a modified version of its virtuous – though violent – demographic scheme.[2] While such approaches certainly help explain some of the pedestrian forms of popular resistance to state attempts to manage child bearing, they slight a fundamental reason for the swift formation of popular resistance to the birth-planning campaign: this campaign threatened to overstep the boundaries of even the one-child policy and to rely on repressive methods that raised the specter of the Great Leap past, in which the perpetrators of Mao's famine had imposed a de facto no-child policy in Chinese villages, preventing villagers from bearing children. Behind the hostility to the one-child limit, in other words, was the memory of the Great Leap's harm, which had all but destroyed the credibility of official interference in family procreation.

This chapter investigates the evolution of resistance to the implementation of the center's birth-control policies in Da Fo village over the course of the 1980s and particularly the 1990s. The evidence from Da Fo suggests that Chinese villagers had kept alive memories of the party-state as the enemy of

---

[1] White, "Domination, Resistance, and Accommodation," 102.
[2] Ibid., 105, 115–117; Greenhalgh, "Evolution of the One-Child Policy"; Greenhalgh, "Controlling Birth and Bodies"; and Greenhalgh, Zhu, and Li, "Restraining Population Growth."

motherhood and child bearing.[3] To many villagers, the regimentation of child bearing in the 1990s suggested a transposition of the Maoist context of the Great Leap to that of reform.[4] What they actually were resisting was not the one-child policy per se but rather the attempt of a powerful central party-state to once again secure control over the entire process of procreation. Furthermore, the memory of the Great Leap famine and villagers' delayed retaliation against Leap-era party leaders affected the willingness of Da Fo's leaders to press the birth-planning policies of Liangmen township, ultimately resulting in the defeat of the most stringent interpretations of the center's policies and their replacement by a conciliatory "bottom-line" local policy that accommodated tillers' unwillingness to accept a one-child limit on their reproduction. The compromise did nothing to assuage villagers' anger at the party-state for imposing on their perceived right to bear children, however.

REPRODUCTION AND SECURITY IN EARLY-REFORM-ERA DA FO

In 1982, the first year of the post-Mao land division, there were 1,800 people in Da Fo, an increase of 330 from the start of the Great Leap Forward. By 1994, there were more than 2,500 village residents. The growth magnified China's ageless problem of too many people on too little land, a dilemma reflected in the changing population-to-land ratios of Da Fo's production teams. Pang Zhenfa's team, for example, had 210 people assigned to work 370 *mu* of land in 1982. Twelve years later, the team had 270 people working the same amount of land, reducing per capita landholding from 1.6 to 1.3 *mu* – and this particular team had the *lowest* population growth rate in Da Fo following the land reform.

In 1994, I conducted a household survey of family demographic trends in Da Fo, interviewing the heads of twenty-two farm households. The average number of children in these households was 4.1, a figure that included those who had lived beyond the age of twenty-one and who were still living at the time of the survey. Further, Da Fo had three hundred unreported *hei haidz*, or "black" (illegal) children, between the ages of one and fifteen, putting its population closer to 2,800 than the official figure of 2,500. Nearly three-quarters of households reporting four children evidently had five, and more than a few families had six. Most of the Da Fo households reporting in the four-child-per-family category had their first through third children in the

---

[3] Feminist scholars have deconstructed the term "motherhood," paying attention to the subordination of women to the household labor duties and state-fostered obligations. My conception here is more or less focused on mothers as individuals with ties and commitments to their children. Using this conception, I have documented the Maoist attack on motherhood in *Catastrophe and Contention*. Compare my conception with that of Gail Hershatter in chapter 7 of her pathbreaking *The Gender of Memory*.

[4] I am indebted to Damousi, "Marriage Wars," for this conception of memory.

1962–1975 period and the fourth (and sometimes fifth) child right after the 1982 land division.

By the end of the 1980s, however, Da Fo's farmers were starting to think twice about producing more than four children, especially because the cost of raising and marrying off sons was rising rapidly. The tendency to try for a fourth (or fifth) child had become most pronounced among families whose first three children were females, and thus it was limited to a small number of households. The available evidence suggests that the fertility rate in this rural Henan village was on the decline by the end of the 1970s and heading toward three to four children per household by the end of the 1980s, thus bringing it roughly in line with the national fertility rate.[5]

Da Fo's enhanced fertility of the 1960s and 1970s reflected a well-established pattern of "compensatory births" that, as Fernand Braudel has reasoned, so often follows in the aftermath of a major catastrophe – in this case, Mao's Great Leap famine.[6] While Mao had equated birth control with a Western bourgeois scheme to impose a "bloodless genocide" on China and had at best paid lip service to a gradualist approach to birth planning, the Maoist leap had created a highly uncongenial environment for pregnancy and brought child bearing among poor farm households to a screeching halt.[7] Nationwide fertility rates fell from 5.6 per female before 1958 to 3.06 in 1961.[8] In 1960, the peak year of the famine, the fertility collapse in Da Fo village was even more dramatic: few, if any, Da Fo women without connections to the dominant party network were able to give birth to children, and only the wives of a small number of local party leaders with special food privileges were able to sustain nutrition levels supportive of full-term pregnancy. In this way, the Maoists had imposed a de facto "no-child policy" on the poor farm couples of Da Fo for nearly two and a half years during the Great Leap Forward, roughly the autumn of 1959 to the spring of 1962. Those few women who were able to avoid starvation and achieve childbirth were challenged to adequately nourish their infants and keep from giving them up to others during the deep

---

[5] Thanks to Kay Ann Johnson for helping me interpret the demographic trend in rural China and in Da Fo in this period. Personal correspondence, March 2, 2010. According to Johnson, the total national fertility rate went from 6 to 2.8 in the decades between the end of the Great Leap famine and the late 1970s to early 1980s. Johnson finds support in the seminal work of Wang, Cai, and Gu, who argue that "most of China's fertility transition was completed during the decade of the 1970s, that is, *before* China's one-child policy was enacted." "Population, Policy, and Politics," 121. See Coale, *Rapid Population Change*, and Greenhalgh, "Controlling Birth and Bodies," 5–6 (citing Coale). Also see Hershatter, "State of the Field," 1005; Chen, "Birth Control Methods"; and Banister, *China's Changing Population*. White estimates a similar trend, in this case 6–3. White, "Policy Case Study," 301.

[6] Braudel, *Civilization and Capitalism*, 71.

[7] On Mao's attitude toward family planning, see Goodspeed, "Fewer Children," and White, *China's Longest Campaign*, 36–39.

[8] Peng, "Demographic Consequences."

subsistence crisis of 1960.[9] "At the time of the Great Leap Forward," remembers Ruan Xiulan, "very few women gave birth to babies. We were so hungry that we could not afford to have sex or have children. Everybody just wanted to get enough to eat and to survive. Things began to improve after we secured our private plots. People began to get pregnant when they again could produce enough good food to eat."[10]

In reform-era Da Fo, four interrelated factors motivated villagers to want to freely produce children. The demographic history of Zheng Xutang's household reflects the first: the desire to add to the family labor force.[11] This factor was paramount in the economic thinking of farm couples. Born in 1940, fifty-four-year-old Zheng and his wife had produced three sons and one daughter by 1994. Their first son was born in 1964, the second in 1971. A third son, born in 1977, died in 1992 at age fifteen. Thus, even though the Zhengs already had three sons at the 1982 land division, they nonetheless had a fourth in 1983. The Zhengs were educated people, and there is little doubt that they were knowledgeable about government birth planning goals and about the political costs of adding to their household. Yet they still decided to try for a fourth child in order to bolster the family labor force. This pattern of family expansion was common in Da Fo over the decade of the 1980s and into the early 1990s.

The economic pressure on tillers was reinforced by their ageless desire to have sons who would take care of them in their old age. During the collective years, a few Da Fo party loyalists had begun to presume that the brigade would take care of them if they did not have a son in the village, but after the onset of household-based farming in 1982, when villagers were informed they would have to rely on their own families to make a living, village-based assistance to aged villagers started to dwindle. "Consequently," says Ruan Jing, "villagers wanted more children to work for them in the fields to support them in old age, especially sons."[12]

China's patriarchal culture, which places great pressure on women to produce a son to continue the family line, further hindered the process of state birth planning.[13] Because Da Fo's male household heads knew there was fierce competition in the local market for marriageable daughters, moreover, the temptation to risk bearing yet another female child in order to gain the immortality that would come with the birth of a son apparently became harder to resist during the early period of reform.

Finally, a fourth, explicitly political, factor that had contributed to family decisions to produce more children in the aftermath of the Great Leap famine was still at work: the desire to have a stable of strong males in one's family to afford protection from the arbitrary and brutal village Communist Party leadership. After 1982, Da Fo had disbanded its militia, so that party boss and

[9] Thaxton, *Catastrophe and Contention*.   [10] Ruan Xiulan, interview.
[11] Zheng Xutang, interview.   [12] Ruan Jing, interview.
[13] Zhou, *How the Farmers Changed China*, 177–181.

militia commando Bao Zhilong and his clients were no longer able to rely on this Mao-era force to promote compliance, order, and security. Most villagers saw Da Fo as a jungle wherein the households with the largest number of strong and tough males could circumvent the normal party channels of politics, mobilizing their strength to challenge the leaders of the collective era and to impose their will in disputes with fellow villagers, including smaller, poorer families. Pang Lianggui makes the point this way: "There is no justice to be found in the village. Might is right. If one has sons, nobody in the village will bully you. Without sons, anybody can bully you."[14]

Villagers' penchant for sons was also related to a desire to take revenge on the Da Fo party leaders who had taken away the chance to procreate during the Great Leap Forward Famine, when those same leaders, by virtue of their strategic position in the communal food supply chain, managed to stay comparatively healthy and beget Mao-blessed sons. Indeed, some of the agents of antiparty arson in Da Fo apparently hailed from households whose families had suffered dearly in the Leap famine and whose fortunes subsequently rose with the birth of three and four males. In the first decade of reform, the latter made up part of an unorganized army of macho male characters who were feared by Da Fo party leaders and villagers alike. In some cases, they openly rejected the orders and demands of party leaders. Some of Da Fo's farmers envied such multiple-son households, which demonstrated that it was possible to participate in village affairs outside party-dominated spheres of order.

THE ESCALATING VIOLENCE OF BIRTH PLANNING IN DA FO

In the late 1983–1988 period, the Deng-led Central government reformers, acting on the unsubstantiated assumption that "peasants" were producing more and more children and that rural population growth was outstripping per capita grain production, thereby posing a threat to economic development, intervened to tighten party-state control over population growth in the countryside.[15] In Henan province, Da Fo became one of the many targets of this crackdown, which, according to White, was carried out through a martial campaign that, as in the Great Leap past, trumpeted the use of force to serve the center's transcript. This scheme, which was based on high state hysteria, placed a strict two-child limit (if the first child was a daughter) on farm households.[16] The scientific rationale for the policy had been formulated by Song Jian, a key central party-state advisor, and was based on narrow-minded empiricism,

---

[14] Pang Lianggui, interview.

[15] On this point, see White, *China's Longest Campaign*, 215–227, 230–231, 258–259. In White's work, the campaign was not put into practice until 1989–1990, but the evidence from Dongle county and Da Fo village suggests that it was felt locally as early as 1983–1984 and 1988. Cf. White, 219.

[16] White, "Policy Case Study," 299–300.

mesmerizing computer modeling, and spurious birth statics,[17] all of which were divorced from the real cause of national impoverishment: the devastation of Maoist rule. Ironically, according to Susan Greenhalgh, Mao-era habits of rule were not completely dead: "wishful Leap thinking" persisted and influenced the institutionalization of the one-child policy.[18] In December of 1979, for example, Liang Zhongtang, a pragmatic instructor affiliated with the Shanxi provincial Party School, warned of the potentially tragic social and political consequences of a one-child birth policy.[19] But Liang was ignored, and Deng and his team put the policy into practice on the premise that "if the party exerted enough effort, every problem could be solved."[20] In Henan province, officials began putting pressure on Liangmen township government leaders to impose a birth-planning scheme on villagers. Township leaders who failed to prevent the birth rate from surpassing government quotas were threatened with dismissal.

In the three decades following the Great Leap, while Da Fo's tillers were attempting to compensate for the disaster by producing large enough families to ensure their security, they had experienced little pressure from village leaders to limit births. "For quite a few years," says Pang Zhenfa, "there was no mention of birth planning."[21] In the 1970s and 1980s, this part of the north China plain had no unified state birth-control policy. Policy was formed locally, mainly by brigade and commune leaders. For most of the 1962–1982 period, Da Fo party leaders, with the knowledge of Liangmen officials, merely attempted to persuade villagers to give birth to no more than three children; there was no penalty for exceeding the ambiguous three-child limit. Bao Dongwen recalls, "In the days before [decollectivization], birth planning was more humane. If a household refused to take any birth planning measure, it would only be labeled as backward, and the government would not impose a fine."[22] Except for a brief spell during the Cultural Revolution, party leaders did not disseminate any contraceptive information, and many households produced five, six, seven, and more children.

When I visited Da Fo in August 1990, party secretary Bao Zhilong, who was charged with implementing Deng Xiaoping's reform agenda in the 1980s, complained that the Central government had not been clear enough or sufficiently vigilant in getting its birth-planning goals across to the village leadership. Without support from Beijing, Bao and other party leaders paid less and less attention to birth planning, and they seldom disciplined families for producing too many children. By 1989–1990, however, the majority of Da Fo's

---

[17] Greenhalgh, *Just One Child*, 281–283, 287.   [18] Ibid., 291.

[19] Yang Min and Xieying, "Birth of the One Child Policy"; Mei Fong, "China's Quiet Two-Child Experiment"; and Whyte, Wang Feng, and Yong Cai, "Challenging Myths About China's One Child Policy," 152–154.

[20] Greenhalgh, Just One Child, 291.   [21] Pang Zhenfa, interview.

[22] Bao Dongwen, interview.

population was under thirty years of age, and several gangs of eight- to eighteen-year-olds roamed the village. This scene resonated with the center's fear that the perceived demographic momentum of 1978–1979, when 65 percent of the population was under the age of thirty, would carry over to foil reform without state intervention.[23]

In the absence of useful guidance from the center, the best predictor of how many children Da Fo's villagers felt they could give birth to was the number of children sired by village leaders. Because many village leaders had four or five children, it was difficult for them to enforce a limit lower than the number of children in their own households. Bao Jianzhuang, the director of family planning in Da Fo from 1992 to 1995, alluded to this dilemma when he described his appointment to the position. "I did not want to do it," he explained. "I did not have a good record on this score myself. I myself have four children. So how can I tell others to have less?"[24]

The Chinese Communist Party (CCP)-directed birth planning went through four phases in Liangmen township. Prior to 1980, women with more than two children were encouraged to have intrauterine rings inserted in order to prevent another pregnancy. In response to Beijing's 1981 call for more energetic birth planning, the Dongle county government started to pressure local party leaders and party members to undergo vasectomies if their wives already had two children. Surprisingly few of Da Fo's farm households objected to this government initiative. By this point, many villagers were looking to find ways to limit child bearing, but few knew how to do this. The reason for this desire, which seems to be at odds with the multiple pressures to produce more children, is to be found in the dilemma of poor middle-age male farmers with many sons. Zheng Tianyuan, only fifty-six years old when interviewed in 1994, had five sons, aged twelve to thirty. Zheng explained: "I am very distressed with my situation. My main worry is that my sons cannot find wives. Of course it is difficult for them to find wives basically because I have too many sons. I have to build a house for each of them. Nowadays, it costs so much money to build a new house and finance a wedding. My sons are not bad boys. They are hardworking and honest. But I feel I am looked down on by other villagers for being poor. My worry over finding wives for my sons is killing me."[25] When the Liangmen township family planning team approached Da Fo with a plan for female sterilization, forty-two male farmers volunteered to participate in a vasectomy program so that women did not have to submit to sterilization procedures rumored to be more harmful to females than males. Many of the men who volunteered for the program were attempting to deal with worries such as Zheng's. In any event, this first campaign was one of nonviolent

---

[23] Milwertz, *Accepting Population Control*, 53, and White, Presentation at the Brandeis University East Asian Studies Colloquium.

[24] Bao Jianzhuang, interview.   [25] Zheng Tianyuan, interview.

persuasion, and many people in Da Fo went along with it because they had faith that the center was conducting it in their interest.

Phase two began when the Dongle county government pressed the village-level Women's Federation leaders to visit families with more than two children, talking with them daily about the importance of having a vasectomy or abortion. The emphasis still was on convincing villagers to voluntarily embrace birth planning. Force rarely was used. Consequently, recalls Lin Zhiyan, the head of Liangmen village's Women's Federation and the Communist Party leader in charge of birth-planning work, more than a few people were able to opt out of the plan for limiting children "simply by refusing to give consent."[26]

The third phase began in the autumn of 1983, when the Central government and the National People's Congress put forth the slogan that birth planning was a basic state "law." According to Lin Zhiyan, "this slogan empowered the Dongle county and Liangmen township leaders. They began to feel that they could use violent force to get people to submit to abortion and vasectomy. They argued it was legal to enforce birth planning because it had become a basic law of the state, and they said this *policy* took precedence over all other state laws."[27] Operating with this mindset, the Liangmen township party leaders proclaimed that everybody, without exception, would be taken to the hospital to undergo an abortion, or vasectomy, after they had two children. Insisting they did not need consent, the township leaders told the Women's Federation leaders in each village that they could break into houses at night to surprise targeted couples, arrest them, and take them to the hospital to perform an abortion or vasectomy on them by force. When Lin Zhiyan expressed reservations about this radicalism, she was told by township leaders that if she did not enforce the state's basic law of birth planning she, and they, would be committing an illegal act.

During this third campaign the Liangmen township government organized a Special Task Force to enforce the birth-planning scheme of the center. This Special Task Force was directed by township and village party leaders and was composed of young hooligans and thugs, many of whom were the unemployed sons of the local party leaders themselves.[28] In some instances, the Task Force went after every pregnant woman in a village. Consequently, in the heat of the third phase, state birth planning became synonymous with malice, and many village women panicked, fearing that they would be the next targets of the campaign.

[26] Lin Zhiyan, interview.   [27] Ibid.

[28] Ibid. Da Fo's Qin Yanrong more or less confirms this point when she says: "The township government had a special birth planning enforcement squad. They were mostly young people hired by the township government from the village party leaders' children. The leader of these squads usually was one of the township officials in charge of birth planning." Qin Yanrong, interview.

Working with crowds of young thugs, Lin Zhiyan recalls that she and the Task Force broke into the homes of families who refused to consent to abortion. They captured twenty pregnant women in one night and then dragged them to the hospital to undergo abortions. There were some women who fled Da Fo and other villages before this surprise attack, but the township Special Task Force had a way of compelling them to give themselves up. According to Chen Suping, the Da Fo Women's Federation leader in charge of birth planning in this militant phase, the Dongle county government empowered this township-level Task Force to arrest the parents of the pregnant couple if they could not catch the fugitive herself. They first would arrest the parents-in-law of the woman and torture them in the Liangmen township jail to make the son feel guilty. If that did not work, they would arrest the parents of the woman and then torture them to make the daughter feel guilty.[29] "When their mothers were arrested," recalls Lin Zhiyan, "these pregnant women would come out to have an abortion. They did not care about their mothers-in-law, but they had to care about the suffering of their mothers."[30] According to Qin Yanrong, the Da Fo successor of Chen Suping, "it was birth planning by any means, and Chen Suping was scared in her heart, but she had to follow the line and do it with others."[31] And so did the health-care workers. The Special Task Force leaders told the doctors and nurses that they would have to kill the babies if the latter survived the abortion procedure. This third campaign seriously damaged the Deng Xiaoping government's relationship with rural dwellers.[32]

In the spring of 1984, the Dongle county and Liangmen township governments launched the fourth campaign of birth planning with the slogan "No Third Child Will Be Allowed to Be Born." In reflecting back on this bloody political time, Lin Zhiyan says: "It was really like we were fighting a war, so we used whatever means we could think of to force people to undergo an abortion. Birth planning was the most important focus of life and work at the time."[33] This forced-abortion work, done by the Communist Party in hundreds upon hundreds of villages beyond the binocular range of global scholars who at best had limited, monitored access to the Chinese countryside, spared few rural women and implanted a great fear of the Deng Xiaoping center's modality of rule long before it presented its real face to the world on June 4, 1989.[34]

---

[29] Qin Yanrong, interview.   [30] Lin Zhiyan, interview.   [31] Qin Yanrong, interview.

[32] The method of relying on social ties to manipulate villagers reflects the kind of "relational repression" documented by Deng Yanhua and Kevin J. O'Brien. In the case of Da Fo, this method, while achieving success in the short term, did little to legitimate the regime's presence or purpose. See Deng and O'Brien, "Relational Repression in China," 533–552.

[33] Lin Zhiyan, interview.

[34] For some limited evidence on these involuntary late-term abortions and their brutal, painful application, see Greenhalgh and Winckler, *Governing China's Population*, 253, 259, 261.

Lin Zhiyan of Liangmen village recalls the pain delivered by the Orwellian surgical strike of 1984:

At that time, I was in charge of enforcing the government's birth planning campaign in Liangmen village. I was pregnant with my third child, and I was in my ninth month. The village party secretary's wife was pregnant with his third child and in her eighth month. There were many other women in the village who also were pregnant, and in their eighth and ninth months. We all were hoping that we would be able to keep our children.

However, the Dongle county government and Liangmen township government all sent representatives to the village to enforce the abortion policy. The government required us to undergo an abortion at the hospital. The leaders told me and the village party secretary that as party members and party leaders we had to take a leadership role in the birth planning campaign. They threatened to kick us out of the party and to remove us from the party branch if we did not act immediately. In the end, I and twenty other pregnant women agreed to have an abortion in the hospital. At the time, there were more than two hundred villages in Dongle county, and each village sent about twenty pregnant women to have an abortion, so there were more than four thousand babies aborted on that one day.

At the time, the Central government imported some lethal injection medication from the United States. [Whether the medication actually came from the U.S. is an open question – RT.] It could induce an abortion quickly. After one shot, the child would die inside the mother's womb. My adopted mother did not want me to have an abortion. She had bound feet, but she walked with me and cried all the way to the hospital. Perhaps the doctors took pity on her. Somehow, my child did not die after the injection. He came out of the womb still alive. I did not know what happened exactly. Anyway, all of the other women from Liangmen village aborted a dead baby that day. They were crying very loudly. But my adopted mother hid my baby in a basket, and she carried him out of the hospital without being detected. He turned out to be the smartest of my three children. He is intelligent and very active.[35]

The 1984 campaign witnessed the suspension of all law. With no legal restraints on the enforcement procedures, the agents of this campaign could engage in unaccountable acts of savagery if a pregnant woman was found to be in violation of the newly concocted birth-planning rules. Such acts evidently involved murder, as Lin Zhiyan reveals: "In 1984, when I was undergoing an abortion in Dongle county, an old grandmother attempted to smuggle out her aborted grandson. But she was stopped at the gate by two guards. One of the guards threw the baby to the ground and killed him. Nothing happened to the guard who murdered the baby. There were numerous such tragedies in rural China because of Deng Xiaoping's one-child policy."[36]

Bao Wending, a fifty-five-year-old resident of Daweicun whose family survived the Great Leap because his father secured a position in the Dongle County

---

[35] Lin Zhiyan, interview. [36] Ibid.

Grain Bureau and secretly funneled grain to his mother, had two daughters whom he had to hide with relatives in Hebei province so that he and his wife could try a third time to produce a son. Bao's analysis of the legal status of the one-child policy reminds us that it was based on the same heartless politics of the Great Leap Forward and that it implicated the *entire* CCP-led government in a visceral lawlessness:

During the height of the birth planning campaign, the government was very strict with people who dared to violate its policy. In carrying out this policy, the government allowed its officials to disregard the normal legal restrictions. The government simply passed a law that said the birth planning policy was the basic law of the nation. All other law was subordinate to the birth planning policy. At the time, most rural people did not understand what it meant to define the birth planning as the basic law. It actually meant that the government officials who were enforcing the birth planning policy were pro- tected by the government, and that they would not be persecuted for violating other laws of the PRC in carrying out the birth planning law. This is why, at the time, some government officials were able to impose abortions on women in late-term pregnancy, and this is why some government personnel were able to murder babies who were born just prior to a scheduled abortion.

Some people tried to sue the government officials for such behavior, but the courts refused to accept their lawsuits. We went through a decade of brutality, mostly during the 1980s and 1990s. The government carried out a birth planning campaign for about three months out of each year. During that three-month period, the entire government was mobilized to carry out birth planning. Every person in the government was a member of a birth planning enforcement team. They went to villages to find out who was pregnant, arrested mothers, and took them to the hospital to undergo an abortion. Consequently, the relationship between the people in the countryside and the govern- ment was completely ruined.[37]

From 1984 to 1988, the Liangmen township government institutionalized this lawlessness by repeatedly empowering thugs in the Special Task Force to rush into homes at midnight to arrest pregnant women. "Many of these pregnant women were sleeping naked on the bed," says Lin Zhiyan, "but the Special Task Force would drag them out of bed and take them to the hospital to undergo an abortion. One injection and the baby was dead. The doctor was not obligated to do anything else. So the hospital staff would leave the women to struggle in pain on their own. I was in charge of birth planning at the time. I lost control of the whole thing." Required to accompany the Special Task Force, Lin Zhiyan was powerless to help the women of her village. Speaking from frustration years later, Lin said the whole campaign was "an exercise in banditry" – that is, a brutal theft of life. "I never thought the Communist government would allow something like this to happen," laments Lin, "but Deng Xiaoping's government was willing to go that far to push through the

---

[37] Bao Wending, interview.

one-child policy. This was worse than anything the Kuomintang ever did to the Chinese people. For this, Deng Xiaoping will not be remembered well."[38]

By the late 1980s, the Deng-led center was insisting that population growth be kept at ten to twenty births per thousand, so that a village with 2,000 people could not exceed the quota of twenty to forty births per year. In parts of the Hebei-Shandong-Henan border area, the year 1988 witnessed a Great Leap–style push for birth planning – impetuosity, compulsory mega-schemes for meeting state quotas, and administrative chaos became the order of the day. In this year, the Dongle county Communist Party secretary, just returned from meetings in Beijing and Zhengzhou, told county, township, and village party leaders that birth planning was to be pursued at the expense of any other agenda, and he said that anyone who failed to wholeheartedly implement birth planning would be dismissed from his or her position.[39] Subsequently, the Dongle county government declared that all extra pregnancies had to be aborted (and it seems that couples without party affiliation were especially targeted). The site for abortion injections was shifted from the small county hospital to Shawochang, a vast open field outside Dongle county town. This Shawochang was a space in which the local Chinese state had long exercised total sovereignty – it had been a military training field in the late Qing period, a sentencing and execution ground in the Republican era, and the location of Mao-era mass meetings, public trials, and mass killings. The 1957 Anti-Rightist Movement against the One Hundred Flowers dissidents had been unleashed here, and this was the field in which alleged criminals were assembled and shot in the Deng Xiaoping–instigated *yanda* campaign, which now was unfolding at the same time as the birth-planning movement.

For month after month, several hundred women from across Dongle county and Liangmen township were taken to this space en masse, forcefully injected for abortion, and left to suffer and cry without any help from health-care givers. They were given nothing to eat, nothing to drink, and nothing to cover their naked bodies. Their plight was compounded by a new Central government target of eight babies per thousand people, which neighboring Shandong provincial leaders took literally. Because of the ensuring official pressure to abort so many babies, the Shandong hospitals could not accommodate the women who were waiting to undergo abortions, and so hundreds of rural Shandong women were trucked to Dongle county hospitals – and then, to cope with the overflow, to the Shawochang abortion injection site, where delirious women from Liangmen township villages were grieving and pleading for salvation. Speaking of one such ghastly scene, Lin Zhiyan remembers, "At that moment, it occurred to me that a human life was worse than a dog's life."[40] Needless to

---

[38] Lin Zhiyan, interview. Greenhalgh and Winckler confirm that many cadres who had to enforce this policy hated it and wanted nothing to do with it, thus giving credence to the validity of Lin Zhiyan's testimony. Greenhalgh and Winckler, *Governing China's Population*, 252.

[39] Lin Zhiyan, interview.   [40] Ibid.

say, the victimized women suffered from short- and long-term health problems stemming from the violent late-term abortions delivered in this killing field.[41]

With the Central government and Henan provincial officials violently pushing for quota goals, villagers equated birth planning with the kind of rash policy advancement of the Great Leap, and they increasingly expressed anger toward Deng Xiaoping and Hu Yaobang, the general secretary of the CCP. In this period, the state media printed many stories claiming that Chinese farmers supported Deng Xiaoping and Hu Yaobang for pushing reform, especially for breaking the "momentum" of a demographic explosion. "In fact," declares Lin Zhiyan, "we hated them for enforcing the birth planning in such a brutal manner. Privately, farmers in this area called Hu Yaobang, the puppet of Deng Xiaoping, 'Hu Laguang' (the Hu who has smashed everything and left us with nothing to live for). Farmers hated Deng and Hu, but they dared not speak out publicly, for if anyone openly denounced them, [that person] could be arrested. Nonetheless, once Deng Xiaoping embarked on the enforcement of birth planning by force, the Communist Party lost the support of people in the countryside."[42] In Liangmen township, the enforcement of this radical center policy eventually gave rise to resistance that occasionally went beyond the pale of officially sanctioned opposition – and Da Fo's farmers joined in this resistance.

FEIGNED COMPLIANCE WITH BIRTH PLANNING, 1992–1995

The most notorious local agent of the new birth-planning initiative was Li Changquan, the CCP head of the Liangmen Township Family Planning Agency. In 1990, Li bought his position for about 20,000 yuan. In the past, the township government had issued birth certificates free of charge. Beginning in 1992, however, Li began to sell certificates of permission to bear a second child at a price of 3 yuan per certificate. Thousands of villagers in Liangmen township purchased the certificates, allowing him to recoup his office fee and make a profit.[43] Village party secretaries were incriminated in this corruption. The night before the moon festival of 1992, for example, Da Fo's secretary, Bao Xuejing, took more than US$500 worth of gifts obtained with village funds to Li Changquan's home, partly to keep Li inclined to issue "second-child certificates" to Da Fo and partly to prevent Li from penalizing Da Fo's birth-planning cadres for poor performance. During this visit, Bao Xuejing was surprised to find scores of other village party secretaries lining up with gifts in front of Li's home gate.

---

[41] On the long-term negative impact of the abortions on women's health, see Greenhalgh and Winckler, *Governing China's Population*, 261.

[42] Lin Zhiyan, interview.

[43] Bao Yibin, interview; Bao Wenfang, interview. This account resonates with Greenhalgh's findings and her statement that "In some places, peasants were treated no better than farm animals." Greenhalgh, in Zhang, Kleinman, and Tu, *Governance of Life*, 153.

When the Henan provincial government began to press the center's birth planning campaign in Dongle county again in the early 1990s, Li, his deputies, and his clients were able to play on the fear of being seized and subjected to an abortion in order to extort more money from villagers. Huang Bingwen, a teacher from Sanlizhuang, reports that when Deng Zhenxi, a deputy head of the Liangmen township government, was in power, Deng worked with Li's clients to stoke this fear. If they could not track down a pregnant woman, Deng Zhenxi and his men would seize her mother-in-law. "They would force the elderly women and the pregnant captives to run around in a circle in the courtyard of the Liangmen township government," says Huang. "One time, just after it had rained, some of the women fell down and crawled in the mud. Deng and his followers made an ugly comment like 'Let them crawl like pigs.' The rumor of this one comment spread, and villagers from seven Liangmen township villages gathered with a banner to protest outside the township government. They were determined to beat up Deng Zhenxi and his colleagues. In the end, the head of Dongle county government, Wu Xigui, had to come to pacify the angry crowd."[44] Later on, when Deng Zhenxi and one of his colleagues were killed in an automobile accident, villagers said it was retribution for the abuse of power.

Still, the march of the Special Task Force continued. If the Task Force was unable to apprehend a targeted pregnant woman, then family members were seized, illegally detained in Liangmen township headquarters, and released only when the pregnant woman gave in to forced abortion.[45] Apparently the Task Force targeted fathers-in-law too. In the spring of 1993, for instance, the Special Task Force seized Bao He, Pang Fang, and several other elderly villagers, took them to government headquarters, and compelled them to shout through a public loudspeaker that they wanted their sons, who were accused of violating birth-planning rules, to come to their rescue by agreeing to comply with the campaign.[46]

The indiscriminate nature of these birth-inhibiting acts especially angered victimized families. The agents of the Liangmen township government frequently proved oblivious to some families' struggles to procreate. Da Fo's Bao Mingxin recalls a telling episode involving the daughter-in-law of Bao Wenfang, a party member:

Bao Wenfang's daughter-in-law could not get pregnant for five years after her marriage. The family spent a lot of money on medical bills to find out the cause of her infertility and to seek medical treatment. Finally, she got pregnant. But during her pregnancy, the birth planning campaign intensified, and the Liangmen township birth planning force came to the village to seize her husband, or her, in order to force an abortion. However, Bao Wenfang's son and daughter-in-law fled. Shortly thereafter, Bao Wenfang himself was taken away to Liangmen township in the early morning hours. He was forced

---

[44] Huang Bingwen, interview.   [45] Ruan Bingyong, interview.   [46] Pang Cunbin, interview.

to kneel on the ground. In the end, the family paid the fine to get him out. Many people were hurt during the birth planning campaigns, and they were angry with the township government for that reason.[47]

The Special Task Force continued to employ troublesome young toughs, some of whom were the sons of discredited and dismissed village-level Communist Party secretaries who had not fared well in the emergent market economy. Between 1995 and 2000, the Liangmen township government relied on these elements to routinely dismantle the houses of poor farmers accused of violating birth-planning policy, and villagers were angered by their rough and ruthless behavior, which left some of their targets without any shelter.[48] "These young people," recalls Ruan Shunhe, "behaved like thugs, and many people hated them."[49] Like the young and ignorant agents of Mao's Great Leap, they showed little compassion. Just as women who fell sick from forced labor were nonetheless pressed to go to work in the collective fields during the Great Leap, so in the birth-planning campaign of the mid-1990s women who did not inform Da Fo leaders of their inability to undergo the compulsory bimonthly pregnancy test were considered to be pregnant and consequently fined for their failure to appear at the test site. Overlooking the fact that the women were sick and receiving medical treatment at home, and hence could not report on time, the young militants in the Special Task Force badgered them in their homes.[50]

By 1995–1996, the cruelty of the Task Force's enforcement methods had reached an extreme. In these two years, the Special Task Force sometimes organized schoolchildren in Da Fo and surrounding villages to demonstrate on the streets and shout slogans that struck fear into villagers. One slogan threatened: "If you are required to have the operation to inhibit fertility but you refuse, we will dismantle your homes. If you are required to undergo an abortion but you refuse, we will take away your oxen and tear down your houses. If you want to commit suicide by ingesting poison, fine, go right ahead, for we will not stop you by taking away your bottle of poison. If you want to commit suicide by hanging yourself, we will not stop you by cutting the rope. We would rather let you have a broken family than let the whole country be ruined by overpopulation."[51]

Official slogans such as this one, coupled with the strong-arm tactics of the young thugs assisting the Special Task Forces, pointed scores of rural women toward suicide in rural China during the 1990s. In 2011, the Thomson Reuters Foundation published a list of the world's most dangerous countries for women, placing Afghanistan, the Democratic Republic of Congo, Pakistan,

---

[47] Bao Mingxin, interview.   [48] Deng Yifeng, interview.   [49] Ruan Shunhe, interview.
[50] Ruan Xufeng, interview.
[51] *Gai sha bu zha, fang dao wu ta; gai liu bu liu, chei wu qian nu; he you bu du ping; shang diao bu duo sheng; ning ke ja po, bu ke guo wang.* Bao Yunshu, interview.

India, and Somalia at the top.[52] Women in each of these countries faced grave threats to personal safety and health, taking the form of rape in the Congo, gender-selective abortion and infanticide in India, and genital mutilation, abduction and sex slavery in Somalia. Whether women in these countries suffered more than their counterparts suffered in the violence of the People's Republic of China (PRC) birth-planning campaigns of the 1980s and 1990s remains to be seen. But in no country on the list was the violence, as illustrated in the case of Da Fo, unleashed by a central government policy that deliberately targeted the female body. The Deng-conceived birth-control policy, along with the CCP exclusion of rural women from national decision making on this matter, turned countless female villagers toward suicide, making reform-era China as dangerous as any country on the Reuters list. By the turn of the twenty-first century, 56 percent of all female suicides worldwide occurred in China – by far the highest rate on the planet. Significantly, 71 percent of all the suicides occurring in the countryside were among rural women living in remote villages such as Da Fo, and the majority of women who took their own lives did so by ingesting poisonous pesticides.[53] Of course, rural women committed suicide for a range of reasons. Nonetheless, in Dongle county there was a definite correlation between forced abortion and suicide, and many young females who were pressed to abort by birth-planning cadres – not merely or mainly by their communities – killed themselves by drinking lethal agricultural pesticides that were stored and supervised by local authorities. Fortunately, women in Da Fo apparently did not surrender to this political poison, which, as in the radical Maoist past, originated in the pursuit of domination by overzealous local officials.

The Liangmen township birth-planning activists also began to use force against offenders of the one-child policy in the mid-1990s.[54] Beginning in 1994, they destroyed the homes of several villagers, often forcing the villagers to flee Da Fo or to live in damaged dwellings.[55] High state officials in Beijing and Zhengzhou did nothing to stop this violence; whether they were aware of it

[52] Thomson Reuters Foundation, *Factsheet on the World's Most Dangerous Countries for Women*. In constructing this section, I also have benefited from Christie, Wagner, and Winter, *Peace, Conflict and Violence*, esp. chapter 11.

[53] On this point, see Phillips, Li, and Zhang, "Suicide Rates in China," 338–339; Shank, "China's Female Suicide Mystery"; Reardon, "Abortion Is Four Times Deadlier"; Liu, "Suicide Rates Called Crisis for Rural Young People"; "Concerns Rise over China's Mental Health Problem"; and Wu Chong, "Doctor in Life-and-Death Struggle." On suicide as resistance, for confirmation that China has 56 percent of all of the globe's suicides by young women, and for evidence that resonates with much of the above argument, also see Lee and Kleinman, "Suicide as Resistance," 221–224.

[54] See Hershatter, "State of the Field," 1006, and White, "Policy Case Study," 301, 303–304. White sees the revival of campaign methods, shock tactics, and coercion coming in the years 1991–1995.

[55] Bao Xiufang, interview.

remains an open question.[56] Whatever the case, the violence undercut the center's quest for legitimacy. In Da Fo, villagers attempted to discredit the party-directed Task Force by calling it the "250th Army," a sarcastic colloquial expression that in folk parlance refers to someone who is unwittingly used by others to perform an act of folly.[57]

Just as refusal protest became a widespread tool of tax resisters in Da Fo, so villagers often relied on this mode of protest to counter state birth planning. Refusal to report to the Liangmen township–sponsored health clinic for periodic pregnancy check-ups was common practice, involving the great majority of women by 1993. Pang Peiyun, the Da Fo Public Security chief, was recruited by the Liangmen township birth-planning unit to stop the disobedience, but, as Pang explains, enforcement was a risky proposition: "If they did not want to go there, there was nothing village leaders could do. You dared not drag them to the hospital clinic. As a village leader, you did not want to offend your neighbors, or make your neighbor angry for the sake of government policy."[58]

A second weapon used to get around birth-control regulations was bribery, which in Da Fo, as elsewhere, took the form of gift giving. To gain the privilege of bearing more than one or two children, villagers offered countless gifts to party leaders. "When one has the protection of the village leaders," says Bao Peilian, "one can violate the birth control measures and gain other benefits at the expense of the village."[59] Da Fo's farmers unanimously agreed that the gift giving was far more common in the 1990s than in the collective era and that the most lavish gifts were given to persuade leaders to turn a blind eye to violations of state birth-control regulations. Bribery and gift giving of this sort were so widespread in Da Fo village, Liangmen township, and Dongle county during the mid-1990s that many people believed that the structure of government birth quotas had been compromised in favor of the freedom to procreate.

Those villagers who used bribes to avoid restrictions on child birth rates did not perceive themselves as "corrupt."[60] They did, however, characterize the Da Fo party leaders who solicited the bribes as corrupt, and some understood such corruption as part of a larger threat to the stability of party rule. According to Bao Peijian, "Village leaders often cheat the township leaders, especially on the birth planning question. They find ways to cover up the fact that some people have gone against birth planning policy. The Liangmen township officials cheat the Dongle county government, and the county government officials in turn cheat their superiors. It is said that when the upper-level inspection team leaders come to investigate birth planning work, the village and township leaders often put the members of the team in separate rooms to bribe each of them separately."[61] "The truth of the matter," explains Pang Zhenfa, "is that the leaders of each level have conspired with their subordinates to cheat the outside

[56] Ruan Guobao, interview.   [57] Bao Jingxian, interview.   [58] Pang Peiyun, interview.
[59] Bao Peilian, interview.   [60] Levy, "Corruption in Popular Culture," 51.
[61] Bao Peijian, interview.

investigators to get away with their poor performances in birth planning. This is a disease that eventually will ruin the government."[62]

There was, however, a limit to this practice. If the birth inspection teams sent down to Dongle county, to Liangmen township, and to Da Fo discovered that the lower units had done a poor job of enforcing policy, then the local party leaders stood to lose their salaries and their positions. From 1993 to 1996, Liangmen birth-planning officials came under tremendous pressure from superiors, and they, along with Da Fo party leaders, had to set limits on favors extended in return for birth rate dispensations. Needless to say, in this situation those villagers with the biggest gifts were most likely to succeed.

Those who could not afford lavish gifts sought other methods of resisting the regulations. One method was feigned sterilization. Once the Central government tightened up on the single-child policy, township leaders began insisting that women who already had one child present themselves for tubal ligation in the township hospital.[63] Many of the village women who submitted to this operation later became pregnant and gave birth to "accidental" second or third children. The high failure rate of the surgical procedure stemmed from discreet connections between farm households and the doctors who performed the operations in Liangmen township hospital. Smaller than Dongle county hospital and off the beaten path of advanced medicine, the township hospital was staffed mainly by doctors who still resided in villages such as Da Fo. Sympathetic to village child-bearing customs, these country physicians often performed "operations" on women without actually tying their tubes. Many of the physicians who carried out such fake operations and issued tubal ligation certificates shared the common folk belief that relieving a woman of the power to bear a son is against the Will of Heaven.[64] Knowledge of which doctors most strongly held this belief was highly sought after.

Without permission from the Liangmen township government to bear a second child and without a tubal ligation certificate, women who petitioned for the right to bear more than one child could not easily persuade the Da Fo birth-planning cadres. Increasingly, in the early 1990s, they imposed penalties on families with unsanctioned second children on the way. Before the second child of Bao Dongwen's son was born, for example, the village birth planning activists confiscated the Baos' motorized cart and informed Bao that it would be returned only if his daughter-in-law agreed to an abortion. Bao Dongwen pleaded his daughter-in-law's case to the Da Fo birth-planning committee, promising that his son would undergo sterilization if they would permit the

---

[62] Pang Zhenfa, interview.
[63] According to White, tubal ligations increased nationally from 1983. White, "Policy Case Study," 303. The big increase in ligations in Dongle county apparently occurred in the early 1990s, however.
[64] Bao Yibin, interview.

child to be born. The leaders refused to approve his petition. To fool the committee, Bao Dongwen resorted to a form of resistance to state birth planning that became widespread in Da Fo village, Dongle county, and much of rural China: he purchased a false abortion certificate for 38 yuan to show the committee leaders that his daughter-in-law had submitted to an abortion. Subsequently, Bao was able to recover his motor cart; the baby was born several months later without the knowledge of township birth-planning cadres.[65] Some couples for whom evading abortion via the purchase of a false abortion certificate proved difficult asked another woman to undergo an abortion, for which they paid. The woman undergoing the abortion turned over the certificate to the couple, who in turn somehow fudged the transfer of names and used it to save their unborn child.

Villagers occasionally also launched direct legal challenges to the arbitrary operationalization of birth guidelines by township leaders. This mode of resistance, which often started out as petitioning, drew Da Fo's farm couples into confrontations with the Special Task Force and clashes with top officials of the Liangmen township Birth Planning Agency. As the case of Bao Jingxian illustrates, this form of resistance was fraught with risk. Like most villagers, Bao was aware that prior to 1992 it was not against Central government policy for rural dwellers to produce a second child if their first was a girl and that Li Changquan, the head of the Liangmen township birth-planning unit, had sold hundreds of child permission certificates even after the single-child policy was enunciated in 1992. Along with a few other villagers, Bao Jingxian went to special lengths to obtain updated, accurate information on state birth policy after the Liangmen township government turned up the heat in early 1993. Bao was motivated by his own family situation. Although he already had a child, he did not yet have a son. "But according to state policy," declares Bao, "people like me who had no sons . . . could have a second child if the first one was a girl."[66]

When Bao Jingxian's family was denied this centrally sanctioned entitlement by overzealous Liangmen township officials during the birth planning campaign of 1993, he went to Liangmen township armed with a copy of the Central government birth regulations, intending to reason with Li Changquan. He was told that his copy of the regulation was outdated and no longer applicable – an outright lie. When Bao persisted with his case, Li dispatched a unit of the Special Task Force to Da Fo to arrest Bao and his entire family, forcing them to flee. When the Da Fo village chief refused to comply with an order from Li to round up some villagers to dismantle Bao Jingxian's house, Li personally led the Special Task Force to destroy the roof of the house and confiscate 2,000 yuan worth of furniture. While the Baos were away from Da Fo, their cotton crop was destroyed by insects, another cost of their challenge. "In the end," says Bao,

[65] Bao Dongwen, interview.   [66] Bao Jingxian, interview.

"I was very angry. But there was nothing I could do to protect my property or seek justice."[67]

In the absence of legal protection, some Da Fo women chose to run away in order to avoid pregnancy tests and abortions.[68] A few couples fled to give birth to babies outside the village, returning to Da Fo only after the birth of their children.[69] Part of the growing rural-to-urban migrant population, some of these couples gave birth to their children in poorly supervised urban spaces in which countless rural women sought freedom from birth-planning agents.[70] This "guerrilla birth practice" gave Da Fo's runaways greater leverage in negotiations with local party-appointed birth-planning leaders back in the village. Few of them were punished when they returned with new babies.

The rigid birth-planning rules of the Central government made it all but impossible for Da Fo's farmers to use legitimate channels of discourse to press for the old, natural right to freely bear children.[71] Given the Central government's birth-planning scheme, local party leaders could not afford to actively sympathize with their decisions to produce children, and indeed, in the context of the single-child policy there was little hope of mobilizing support from the party-state birth-planning hierarchy for producing "out of plan" children.

Many Da Fo farmers consequently held the Central government responsible for their fate under birth planning. Bao Dongwen's story is instructive here. When the wife of Bao's first son was pregnant with his second child, village and township leaders seized all of Bao's valuables and refused to return them unless the child was aborted. Bao purchased a falsified abortion certificate, paid a fine, and gave gifts to Liangmen township leaders to regain his property. When his second son wished to have a second child after his first was a girl, Bao Dongwen had to pay 2,000 yuan to Da Fo and Liangmen leaders, ostensibly for a permit for the second child. In fact, he received only "a promise that they would not come and confiscate our household property"; his daughter-in-law was still made to leave the village when upper-government inspectors arrived. His third son was asked upon his marriage to pay 440 yuan for a permit to have a first child. Bao Dongwen paid the fee, but he did not receive a receipt or a permit. While telling this story, Bao repeatedly expressed the distrust for government that his experiences with birth planning had fostered: "The government officials did not care whether you had more children or not. They just wanted to get money from you," he said. "In this way, over twenty years [since reform], birth planning became a money-making scheme for Chinese officials." Although angry with Liangmen township leaders, Bao Dongwen reserved his

---

[67] Ibid.   [68] Bao Dongwen, interview; Deng Yifeng, interview.

[69] White has documented this pattern in "Domination, Resistance, and Accommodation," 108.

[70] As both Kate Zhou and Tyrene White have pointed out, kin-based networks were crucial in facilitating their success. Zhou, *How the Farmers Changed China*, 191, and White, "Domination, Resistance, and Accommodation," 108.

[71] For this notion, see O'Brien and Li, *Rightful Resistance*, 2–4.

strongest contempt for Central government reformers and laid blame for the birth regulations, which local township leaders manipulated to their advantage, directly at the feet of Deng Xiaoping, whose one-child policy was an affront to the core moral values of village people: "We farmers cannot afford to have only one child. What if our child dies, either from a disease or accident? We still have to rely on farming with our own hands. We expect our children to help us with manual labor in the fields. The logic here is straightforward and simple. So why were Deng Xiaoping and the other Central government leaders unable to see this? Why did they force us farmers to hate the government by imposing such a brutal policy of only one child per family?"[72]

Da Fo's farmers saw the Liangmen township birth-planning unit as the arm of the center, and understood this unit as an extortion racket thinly disguised as the state. They blamed the center for allowing the greedy leaders of this unit to make a mockery of Communist Party rule and for permitting its violent Special Task Force to sow the seeds of angry contempt for the expansive system of central party-state power. Bao Wenfang spoke for the majority of farmers when he remarked, "Birth planning has become an important source of income for Liangmen township government in recent years, but family planning is a farce. As long as you are willing to pay fines, you can have as many children as you want."[73] Bao Dongwen went further, claiming that the process of centrally dictated birth planning had "completely ruined the relationship between the government and the people." The ruin, according to Bao, was deep and irreversible, because birth planning was a fundamental policy of the state and too sensitive an issue for farmers to challenge either within or outside the Communist Party's system of policy and rule. "If we were to organize a collective protest against this state policy," says Bao, "the state would crush us with police force." Da Fo's farmers did not believe that they had any state-bestowed right to resist this birth-planning policy, and they understood they were living under an authoritarian police state that stood ready to enforce it. Speaking of the hidden future consequences of the policy for party rule, Bao said: "The people may appear to be powerless before the squeeze by the officials. But they will remember this squeeze and store it in their minds. Someday, when they have the opportunity, they will let it out, and act on what they remember."[74]

THE DEVELOPMENT OF A BOTTOM-LINE LOCAL POLICY, 1996–2000

In 1996, only a year after Hillary Rodham Clinton pressed for the right of women to govern their reproductive powers at the 1995 UN Women's Conference in Beijing, the Central government again stepped up the pressure to

---

[72] Bao Dongwen, interview.   [73] Bao Wenfang, interview.   [74] Bao Dongwen, interview.

enforce its one-child policy in village China.[75] As in the Mao era, local zealous party leaders out to impress upper-level superiors went further. According to Chen Suping, a Communist Party member elected by the village committee to direct birth planning in Da Fo during 1996: "The Dongle county government declared there would be no births allowed for the whole year. People were not allowed to conceive their first baby then. It was the harshest year for birth planning."[76]

The cadres who enforced the policy were relentless. Chen describes her efforts to make village women comply: "When I was director of the Women's Federation in the village, I accomplished everything the upper government asked me to do. I visited every household to explain the birth planning policy and to persuade people to accept it. I took women to the hospital to have the metal ring [intrauterine device] inserted in the uterus and to undergo the operation to stop the pregnancy. Everybody had to do this. I would not allow for any exception. In the beginning, a few women refused, but I led the birth planning cadres to bombard them again and again. I would continue to visit them until they could no longer resist. I always convinced everybody to go in the end."[77]

As Chen's testimony suggests, the campaign of 1996 was run in accordance with the superautocratic style of the Great Leap–era Maoists, playing to popular fear of punishment and pressing villagers to conform to its institutionalized robotic simplicity.[78] During this period, the bimonthly pregnancy test was rigidly implemented. Pregnant women, including those with only one daughter, were ordered to undergo abortions. "In 1996, there were many forced abortions," says Qin Yanrong. "That year, the government decided to have a year of no new babies."[79] The household furniture of all couples who violated policy was trucked away. Noncomplying couples were threatened with the destruction of their homes, and the tough new slogan "If you refuse to have an abortion, your house will fall!" was put into practice in Da Fo.[80] Villagers were indignant about this style of implementation, which did great damage to state–society discourse on rural birth policy.

The no-child policy itself also angered villagers: it seemed to invalidate the raison d'etre of the post-Mao regime, which was predicated on a reformist transcript that would allow rural people to gather food through farm work and free market enterprise, all for the purpose of recovering a good, family-centered

---

[75] White has identified four stages of the implementation of the one-child policy and characterizes the third stage (1989–1995) as "the revival of campaign methods" and coercion and the fourth as one of a change to a more humane approach. White, "Policy Case Study," 305. In the Da Fo area, the third stage clearly spilled over into the fourth and violated basic female rights to reproduce.

[76] Chen Suping, interview.   [77] Ibid.

[78] Or what Barrington Moore, Jr., has called "standardized automatic conformity"; see Moore, *Political Power*, 52.

[79] Qin Yanrong, interview.   [80] *Gai zha bu zha, fan dao wu ta!* Ibid.

life. The central goal in villagers' quest for children was not child bearing per se but rather the satisfaction of material sufficiency. In denying material well-being to villagers, Maoist radicals had impeded the ability of farm people to marry and find a good life in family. Bao Yuqing refers to this denial when he recalls: "Very few people got married in the Great Leap Forward years. People were so hungry they could not concern themselves with getting married."[81] From the end of the Great Leap famine, the acquisition of goods went hand in hand with reclaiming the traditional prerogative of marriage, so that any party-state activity that posed even the slightest threat to the material requisites for marriage and its objective – childbearing to ensure the joy and rewards of family – was taken as a renewal of the despotic attack on the most treasured aspect of life.

And indeed, the declaration of the no-child policy in 1996 gave Liangmen township birth-planning activists reason, and leverage, to execute greater claims on the finances of farm couples by raising the going rate for both childbirth permits and marriage certificates, thereby making it harder for young people to afford to marry and begin families. A wave of "pretended elope-ments" followed in 1996 and 1997, by means of which couples evaded the rising permit fees.[82] Ruan Xiufang, an agent of birth planning, recalls: "Bao Junqiang and his girlfriend ran away and got married outside of Da Fo. They did not come back until they gave birth to their first baby. At the time, they told the villagers that the child belonged to their relatives. They later paid some money to the village to have the second child. But they did not pay for the wedding and birth permits." Similarly, "Tang Yongrui also ran away with his wife. They also came back to the village after giving birth to their first baby. They did not pay for the marriage permits or birth permits. The village leaders came to their house and asked them to pay for these permits. Without the consistent pressure, and support, of the Special Task Force, there was not much the village leaders could do if they refused to pay for these items."[83] Clearly, too, women fought to free their bodies from state intrusion. In Da Fo, there was massive resentment of the bimonthly pregnancy test. Chen Suping explains: "Most women did not like the idea of being tested to see if they were pregnant. The village leaders in charge of birth planning had to escort doctors to each woman's household to test the woman in her house."[84] Hiding in the home and refusing to come to village headquarters or the township hospital for the test was a way of expressing disdain for the invasion of the womb by party cadres such as Chen.

---

[81] Bao Yuqing, interview.
[82] Tyrene White has documented the development of a pattern of secret marriages occurring outside the official registration process of the Bureau of Civil Affairs. White, "Domination, Resistance, and Accommodation," 109.
[83] Ruan Xiufang, interview.   [84] Chen Suping, interview.

The mothers of Da Fo infants also resisted pressure to go back to work soon after giving birth, as mothers had been forced to do in the Great Leap. "They knew how to take good care of themselves," Ruan Xiufang says. "They wanted to take a good rest when they gave birth to a child. They would not do any work, and yet they would eat well and rest well. In the days of the collective, women would continue to work very hard after they gave birth to their babies, and they competed with other women to see who could work the hardest for the collective. Today we do not have the collective, and people are spoiled."[85] In little ways like this, women put greater distance between themselves and the politics that had once tethered mothers to collective fields shortly before and after birth, jeopardizing their health and that of their infants.

Implicit in the birth-quota propaganda of Beijing birth-planning cadres was the notion that having too many children posed a "problem" for farm couples. The center's propaganda warned that raising multiple children would be a monumental burden and played to fears that poor village couples might have to give up their offspring to relatives, child peddlers, or state adoption agencies. Da Fo's people did not accept this logic. It was an insult to their intelligence, for in local memory the major factor compelling farm couples to give up their children to outsiders since the birth of the PRC had been the radical encroachment of the central party-state on family-based entitlements, a process that ran amok in the Maoist famine of 1958–1961.

The history of the struggles mothers underwent to keep their young children during the throes of Mao's famine has yet to be written. In 1960, during the worst grain shortages of the Great Leap, some families had no choice but to give away their children to save them from starvation. There were at least six of these cases in Da Fo village.[86] One of them was that of Chen Suping's younger sister. She explains the circumstances: "In 1960, we faced a severe grain shortage in this area. There were families who had too many children and were afraid that they might not be able to provide their children with enough food to survive. Some of them were given away to people who did not have children and were sent to places where they had a better chance of survival. It was not an easy decision, and it was made mostly out of the parents' concern for the well-being of their children. My parents gave my younger sister away to a family in Jilu village, Hebei province. My younger sister was one year old. It was 1960." Chen's uncle also gave away two sons. "It was a very difficult time," she remarks.[87]

Occasionally, a family who had to give up a child in the throes of the Great Leap was able to use its material gains in the reform era to arrange a recovery. Ruan Xiufang, for example, helped her son return to Da Fo, building him a new house and sponsoring a community homecoming.[88] Sadly, however, many

---

[85] Ruan Xiufang, interview.   [86] Ibid.; Chen Suping, interview.   [87] Chen Suping, interview.
[88] Ruan Xiufang, interview.

parents who gave up their children to save them from the Leap famine were unable to recover them. And even in cases with a fairly happy ending, regrets and guilt over giving up children lingered on. Fifty-five-year-old Ruan Shunhe, for example, lost a fourteen-year-old sister to the Leap famine. In the hunger of 1960, when Ruan was six years old, Ruan's parents had given away his sister to a farm family in Hebei for fifty *jin* of corn on the assurance that the receiving family would take care of her; in the end, she married the son of the receiving family. Ruan says that he cried very hard when his parents were forced into this act. Forty years later, he continued to harbor guilt and regret over losing his sister, even though she had survived and found a good husband.[89] The struggle of Da Fo couples to keep their children in the 1990s reflected, in part, a desire to exorcise this traumatic past.

For similar reasons, Da Fo parents displayed steadfast loyalty to children born "out of plan." In many accounts of village China, the "throwaway" children are second and third daughters, and some Da Fo women did abort their second baby if it was female in order to try again for a son. But by the mid-1990s, most expectant mothers who underwent prenatal exams taking the form of ultrasound testing chose to keep the second female baby as well. Rarely did they give away second or third daughters, and even when they did, they went to great lengths to place them with nearby relatives from whom they could later retrieve them. Apparently, there was a great demand for these so-called *hei haidz,* or "black" (illegal) children. According to Ruan Xiufang, the mother of a son, who secured authorization to adopt a female baby, "It was very difficult to find anybody who would give up her baby daughter to others."[90] Partly because parents did not need to provide a dowry or build a house for daughters, young women became more valuable in the reform period, when the bride price for scarce marriageable Han females soared.[91] In Da Fo, the parents of sons frequently paid handsome prices for engagements to twelve- and thirteen-year-old daughters. This demand was fueled in part by the growth of globally connected cities full of prosperous bachelors: increasingly, many of Da Fo's daughters left to marry such men in Beijing, Tianjin, and Qingdao, crossing the rural-urban divide and accelerating the imbalance in male-to-female sex ratios back in the countryside. Da Fo's poor bachelors faced a dwindling pool of potential marriage partners, compelling some of them to purchase brides from young women sold into Da Fo from the poorest areas of rural Tibet.

The rising material value of daughters does not in and of itself explain the phenomenon of favoring female offspring, however. The determination of Da Fo villagers to keep second and third daughters also seems attributable to human impulses that were inseparable from popular memory of the Maoist disaster. Many of Da Fo's young mothers were the daughters of aged mothers

---

[89] Ruan Shunhe, interview.   [90] Ruan Xiufang, interview.   [91] Ao Jinfang, interview.

who had struggled to feed, protect, and keep them in the "throwaway years" of the Great Leap famine. These same daughters, in their thirties when the one-child campaign was cranked up in the 1990–1995 period, gratefully followed in the footsteps of their mothers, whose loyalty and sacrifices had taught them the value of keeping children – including daughters. It was not just motherhood that was being recovered. Many of the mothers who opted to keep their second and third daughters were seeking to recover their own childhoods, which had been cut short and severely diminished by the struggle to survive the poverty, disenfranchisement, and despair that had defined the long aftermath of Mao's great famine.

For mothers, keeping daughters involved taking charge of the most valuable resource of the household: children. And in Da Fo, this act was inseparable from natural instincts to incorporate children into a process of making do in everyday life. Seen in this context, it seems that holding on to extra daughters in particular was a way of rejecting birth planning as a tool of state power, of repudiating the kind of "programmed citizenship" that began in the simplified schemes of the Great Leap – day care centers, public dining halls, and work camps – and then reappeared in the authoritarian birth-engineering institutions of the post-Mao period.[92]

There was another hidden factor stoking popular anger over the 1996 no-child birth-planning campaign in Liangmen township. The campaign unfolded in a context that recalled the discriminatory birth order of the Great Leap famine, when local party leaders with connections to commune power begat children while making it impossible for ordinary villagers to procreate. Across the second decade of reform, including the year 1996, the Dongle county and Liangmen township leaders who imposed the center's harsh policy were able to get away with violating the one-child policy. According to Lin Zhiyan, the director of the Liangmen village Women's Federation, these officials "told the government their first child had died. But in reality, they hid their first child with their rural relatives. Then they had their second child. A few years later, they would tell the government they had adopted an orphan as their child. In fact, they were just adopting their hidden first child. The government officials turned a blind eye to this practice."[93] Yet these same officials opted to implement birth planning by force. To people in Da Fo and other border area villages, the unfairness of this violent 1996 campaign was in keeping with the biased politics that had inhibited child bearing in the Great Leap.

In the wake of the 1996 no-child campaign, Da Fo's farmers increasingly turned from deferential appeals to the use of contentious retaliation and threat against the village-level agents of Liangmen township government and its Special Task Force to win the freedom to procreate and hang on to their

[92] For the conceptual underpinnings, see Scott, *Seeing like a State*, 347–349.
[93] Lin Zhiyan, interview.

children regardless of whether they were borne within the state's plan. Their loosely constructed anti–birth-planning movement threw up a number of challenges to party-state efforts to effect strict compliance with the center's rigid birth regulations: physical resistance, public shaming, death threats, and arson punctuated the everyday operations of Da Fo Public Security, whose members were the eyes and ears of the township birth planners.

To begin with, Da Fo's farmers increasingly confronted the young toughs in the Special Task Force, initiating shoving matches, fistfights, and other physical altercations rather than simply fleeing persecution. After five years of sharp conflict and resistance, the Special Task Force rarely attempted to seize members of households with more than two sons, for these households joined together to challenge the seizures of kin with physical force.

Villagers also counterattacked the Da Fo party leaders who were connected with the Liangmen township Birth Planning Agency. The major target of this attack, which was anonymous and highly symbolic, was Bao Zhanghe, the head of Da Fo Public Security and the secret informant who ratted out pregnant couples and directed the Special Task Force to their homes. In the aftermath of the 1996 no-child campaign, Bao Zhanghe woke up one morning to find that someone had thrown a dead baby on top of his house. This highly public curse implicated Bao in the deaths of aborted fetuses, and it also symbolized an ominous fate for his children: the dead baby on Bao's housetop was a sign that his family line would be extinguished. At this point, Bao Zhanghe began to rethink his collaboration with the Liangmen township's birth-planning cadres. But it was too late. On another morning, Bao arose to find a paper funeral wreath placed on his courtyard door, which implied that his time on earth had expired and, further, that he was scheduled to experience a violent ending. Bao understood that indignant villagers saw him as a walking dead person. He was shocked by this shameful act. It drained him emotionally and put him in a state of acute anxiety.

These threats were followed by assaults on Bao Zhanghe's right to live in his native Da Fo village. Villagers set fire to Bao's house on three separate occasions. One of the arsons completely destroyed the gate to his front courtyard. Frightened, Bao fled Da Fo for long stretches of time, abandoning the village virtually completely for more than ten years following the third arson. Recalling this ordeal in late 2008, Bao lamented, "The arsons did great mental damage to me and my family. We lived in fear that serious enemies could set fire to my house any time they wanted. I could not live in Da Fo anymore. In some years, I did not even come back to celebrate the New Year. That is how hard life became for me."[94] Silent contention from below had expelled Bao Zhanghe from the village. With his exile, the Liangmen township

---

[94] Bao Zhanghe, interview.

birth-planning force lost its key local informant, giving couples more time and space to exercise their right to procreate.

Villagers' increasingly violent resistance to the center's one-child policy in 1996 and afterward could not have succeeded without the cooperation of village party leaders, who ultimately backed off rather than strictly enforce the policy. "We only asked people who were pregnant for the second or third time to undergo abortions," Chen Suping explains.[95] She resigned not long after the campaign subsided, expressing guilt and sadness over her stressful role as an enforcer. Chen and the other agents of birth planning were reluctant to actively embrace the strict and draconian enforcement of birth planning. They not only allowed villagers to carry on some of their secret forms of everyday resistance, such as flight, they also shunned certain forms of collaboration with the township birth-planning force. Da Fo's party secretary and his deputy were aware that the existential dilemma of tillers left them no choice but to produce one or more sons. They understood that in the eyes of farm people this dilemma had been created largely by continuing Central government discrimination against rural dwellers.

Pang Siyin, the Da Fo deputy party secretary in 1995, gives us a sense of the gap between the center and villagers:

The most difficult task facing village leaders today is the birth planning. Villagers have practical difficulties in their lives. Nowadays, we have the individual household farming. Each person is supposed to look after his own household. Those who do not have children or do not have sons in front of them face a big predicament now. Farmers do not enjoy pensions or medical care like the government employees. The one-child policy was created by the Central government and by people in the cities. They do not understand the difficulties of the farmers. They talk about the difficulties of the nation if population growth is not slowed. But are they willing to give up their retirement pensions and medical benefits to help the nation out? Why should they ask only the farmers to sacrifice for the interest of the nation? That is what made birth planning very difficult to implement. The Central government does not understand the villagers' practical problems and has not done anything to help villagers solve their practical problems. The government only wants to get money and grain from the villagers.[96]

Chinese villagers who participate in interviews sometimes omit the obvious; because everyone knows it, they see no reason to voice it. What Pang Siyin, whose father died while making steel in Lin county during the Great Leap Forward, omitted to say is that he and his Da Fo counterparts all know that the major worry in the lives of fellow villagers under individual household farming was about what might happen if there were another serious food shortage like the Great Leap famine. Bao Zhangchen put it this way: "We farmers have too many burdens on our shoulders. If there were a food shortage like the one in the 1960s, we think that we would suffer an even worse disaster."[97] The farmers of

---

[95] Chen Suping, interview.   [96] Pang Siyin, interview.   [97] Bao Zhangchen, interview.

Da Fo expect no help from the center if such a famine occurs. As Bao Dongwen says, "The government's decision to disband collective farming showed us that the government could not be trusted in the long run."[98] With the end of the collective, the old guarantees of the Maoist commons (which were minimal) disappeared, so that producing more children seemed to be the only way to guard against family misfortune in a future disaster.

Because the Da Fo party leaders were aware that many villagers saw the freedom to procreate as essential to sustaining household security in another famine, they could not fully embrace birth-planning efforts to curtail that freedom. Such a stance would have cast them as the agents of a potential recrudescence of the hunger and loss of the worst years of Communist Party rule. They feared that the revved-up birth-planning campaign of the early 1990s might direct protest against them, making them targets of resentment for years to come – or even popular retribution.[99] This local, largely unspoken knowledge of the past motivated Da Fo's party leaders to allow and even support the feigned compliance of villagers. Seared into the living memory of individuals and family, and shared by the community, such knowledge was powerful because it was based on a traumatic political experience that no one could forget and that could be mobilized against those who did not take its lesson to heart.

Bao Jinzhuang's testimony helps to make this unspoken understanding plain. Four years old when the Great Leap Forward began, he later became a key member of the Da Fo village committee, and between 1993 and 1995 he was in charge of birth planning. Says Bao:

I am forty-one years old now. There are six people in my family, including my wife and four children. Today, despite the government's one-child policy, people of my age all have at least three or four children, and some have five or six. After the land was divided to individual households to farm, nobody took the birth planning very seriously. The Da Fo leaders did not want to take it seriously either, because if they did the farmers would not obey them.

The village leaders did not want to make enemies among their neighbors. Once you make an enemy on a serious matter like birth planning, the hatred could carry over to the next generation. This has already been proven in the past. Look at the Da Fo leaders who made enemies in the past. They are still more or less isolated in the village today. So no village leader would dare to enforce government birth planning anymore. If they offended villagers for the sake of government policies, they would have to face retribution from villagers alone, and they would be left without government backup once they were no longer in a village leadership position. If the leader were no longer in office, he would have to bear the cost of such an attack himself.

Take Bao Zhilong, for example. Bao Zhilong's enemies were made when he was in office many years ago, in the late 1950s. But they came back to haunt him recently, and he got no compensation from the government. Given the precedent of Bao Zhilong

---

[98] Bao Dongwen, interview.   [99] Ruan Bingyong, interview.

and his generation of former village leaders, no village leader would push government policy as Bao's generation did.[100]

This fear of retribution was widespread among Da Fo's leaders. The former head of its Public Security unit explains how memory of the Great Leap's damage has operated in Da Fo over the long term to condition villagers' relationships with their leaders – and vice versa:

The village is laden with contradictions and conflicts. Some of the conflicts and hatreds date back to the Great Leap Forward and then later to the Cultural Revolution. In a village where people live in the same place for so many years, generation after generation, the hatred as well as the gratitude accumulates. If someone did something good for me, I will remember it and try to return the goodness in the future when I am able. On the other hand, if somebody did something bad to me, I will remember this too; and I will seek an opportunity to get even with him. If I cannot do it in my lifetime, my children will be told the story of my mistreatment, and someday my children will get even with these people. Once the seed of hatred is planted, it is very difficult to dig it up. This social fact has conditioned the behavior of our village leaders today. They dare not enforce the government policies by force, for once they are not in power, they would be especially vulnerable to the villagers' retaliation. That is why the Da Fo leaders do not do too much about birth planning."[101]

This fear for personal safety, in combination with the center's sporadic push to strictly enforce its policy, helps explain the two opposite modes of behavior on the part of Da Fo party leaders in the course of this campaign, and also the trajectory of policy enforcement/policy heedlessness in family planning. The campaign not only wore down some local party leaders, it also produced worries that strict enforcement would damage their standing in the village and, as after the Great Leap, make them targets of future retaliation – all of which argued for a retreat whenever villagers adamantly challenged enforcement.

In the end, Da Fo's villagers more or less compelled the Da Fo and Liangmen birth-planning activists to accommodate their defiance of the no-child policy with what the local party leaders called a "bottom line" local policy. Qin Yanrong, the female director of birth planning in Da Fo after the no-child policy fiasco of 1996, reflects on this local adaptation of state birth-control policy, finding its impetus in the great fear of child death: "If I do not take birth planning seriously, the upper government will not be happy with me. But if I push the birth planning too hard, the villagers will not be happy with me. I have to be reasonable with both the upper leaders and the villagers at the same time. I will be living in the village all of my life, and so will my family and my children. I want to make things as easy and smooth for my fellow villagers as I can." She explains the impossibility of changing villagers' minds about their need to have more than one child: "People want to be reasonable with me too. If you force them to have only one child, they will not understand. They believe

---

[100] Bao Jinzhuang, interview.   [101] Bao Peiji, interview.

that only one child is too few and that their child needs a companion. Farmers also want to have more than one child because they are afraid that the child might die later on. The bottom line is that every family needs at least two children, one of which has to be a boy. We all accept this bottom line, and we operate on this bottom line whenever possible. The bottom line is very important for the villagers and the village leaders. If we crossed the bottom line, it will be a big problem for the villagers and ourselves, and it will arouse public anger in the village."[102]

Around 2000, the Da Fo party leaders attempted to thwart flight by allowing prospective runaway couples to give birth to more children on a "stay and pay" basis, and from this point on couples resisted the one-child policy by paying fines to local village leaders. The fines often busted household budgets, but villagers strove to pay them nonetheless. The act of paying the fines guaranteed their infants would not be reported to the upper government, because, according to Yu Meijin of Liangmen village, "the village leaders kept the money for themselves, and when the upper-government leaders came to inspect birth planning [the village leaders] would ask those with more than one child to leave the village and hide with their relatives in other places for a few days."[103]

The system of hidden fines reduced fights with leaders in Da Fo and Liangmen, but it also dealt a blow to the center's birth-planning policy. Ironically, the 2006 Central government's elimination of the agricultural tax further undermined birth planning, for with the loss of tax revenue Liangmen township leaders suddenly were pressed to meet the government's annual revenue goals. From this point on, they came to the villages to encourage farmers to pay fines in exchange for a birth permit. In Da Fo, they clearly targeted households with two daughters and no sons. For example, Pang Yonggang originally had one daughter. Pang had paid a fine of 4,000 yuan in hopes of giving birth to a son, but the second child was a daughter. According to Pang Siyin, the father of Pang Yonggang, "They did not have any further interest in paying more fines, but the township government leaders came to them to ask them to have a third child and to pay a five-thousand-yuan fine. The township government leaders knew that I would like to have a grandson. And it was the end of the year, and the township government was looking for money to celebrate the New Year and to find ways to meet their annual quota. So I agreed. It turned out that my daughter-in-law's third child was a boy. We are very happy that we paid the fine."[104] Desperate for revenue, the leaders of nearby Shangcun township threw caution to the wind and began encouraging farmers in Wangguocun to produce another son even if they already had two sons.[105] Rescinding the agricultural tax, therefore, had an unintended consequence: it gave rise to a new bout of township government rent seeking in a different policy arena and to a collapse in local efforts to enforce limits on population growth. In speaking of this

---

[102] Qin Yanrong, interview.   [103] Yu Meijin, interview.   [104] Pang Siyin, interview.
[105] Yan Hailian, interview.

collapse, Qin Yanrong, the director of birth planning in Da Fo in the 1996–2011 period, laments: "The township government fines are supposed to stop people from having more children, not encourage them to produce more children. The birth planning work today has defeated the real intention of the central and provincial government policy."[106] Referring to the demographic consequences of the center's unwillingness to check this local state reliance on revenue collected from birth-planning fines, Yu Meijin of Liangmen village points out, "Nobody knows exactly how many people there are in our village now, and even the village leaders do not know."[107] Some villagers claimed the Henan government leaders actually knew about rural population growth, however. According to Zhao Junjie, a People's Liberation Army (PLA) veteran from Puyang county, the Henan population was one hundred million around 1990, and it grew by twenty million over the following two decades, but the provincial leaders told Beijing that it still was one hundred million because they feared higher-ups would punish them for failing to enforce birth planning. "This," according to Zhao, "was like the Great Leap Forward, when the Central government lost control of the lower level of government."[108]

– – –

Both the persistence of deeply ingrained patriarchal ideas about the importance of sons and the need for a larger family labor force to help with household farming once the collective collapsed influenced child-bearing decisions in Da Fo village. But Da Fo's farmers also needed more sons to protect them from the political jungle that evolved under Communist Party rule. The rise of the Liangmen township Special Task Force highlighted this need and also spurred villagers to fashion multiple weapons of resistance to the township officials charged with enforcing the center's birth-planning policy. This unfunded mandate not only fostered corruption among township and village collaborators, it also fanned violence against villagers. The center's sudden 1996 no-child policy campaign was a rerun of the impetuous, fundamentalist regimentations of the Mao era, reviving memories of when the Great Leap famine and the superautocratic work style of Maoist fanatics deprived ordinary villagers of the ability to procreate.

If Da Fo's farmers embraced corruption to produce more sons – and daughters – they nonetheless held Communist Party leaders responsible for taking advantage of them, and they spoke contemptuously of such leaders at both the top and the bottom of the party-state hierarchy. Ruan Xiaokang, one of Da Fo's farmers, said of officially tolerated disobedience to the birth-planning laws: "Actually, none of the villagers followed the government's birth planning laws. Birth planning was a complete failure in Da Fo village. The only tangible result

---

[106] Qin Yanrong, interview.   [107] Yu Meijin, interview.   [108] Zhao Junjie, interview.

here was that the Communist Party descended into complete moral bankruptcy. The Da Fo village leaders and Liangmen township leaders used birth planning as a means to get rich at our expense. This did not stop population growth at all. It only made the people hate the government and its officials more. The people who designed and implemented birth planning policies did not know anything about rural Chinese people; and that is why they failed."[109]

The statist demographic policy of Deng and his men reflected the legacy of the same political system that had planned the production of crops, steel, and other goods in the Great Leap, and was driven by a secretive autocratic politics in which rural people were again denied voice.[110] Though this ill-conceived policy was intended to help the CCP maintain stability and regain legitimacy, its coercive implementation traumatized countless women and their families, transporting them back to the Leap's assault on child bearing and motherhood. Clearly, the policy backfired, igniting resistance to its local agents. In the aftermath of the 1996 attempt to crush the efforts of farm couples to freely beget more children, the villagers of Da Fo made efforts to evict the village-level informants of the Liangmen township Special Task Force, fatally weakening the township's birth-planning offensive. Da Fo's farmers believed they had the right to make their own child-bearing decisions, and their resistance reflected this belief. Da Fo's married couples treasured the unique personal identities of their children, both sons and daughters, who in the Maoist past had been subjected to hunger, given up to famine, and, in many cases, deprived of the chance for an uplifting education.

[109] Ruan Xiaokang, interview.
[110] On this point, see Wang et al., "Population, Policy, and Politics," 118 and 126.

4

Rural Schools and the "Best Citizens of the State"

*The Struggle for Knowledge and Empowerment in
the Aftermath of the Great Leap*

Mao Zedong's Great Leap Forward was a threefold war on Chinese villagers: a war for their resources, their bodies, and their minds. To capture the minds of village people, the Communist Party attacked the values and personal identities of the rural schoolteachers who stood for pluralistic discourse and fought against the reach of the imperious central party-state.[1] In Da Fo, local party leaders loyal to Mao attacked the very people who, in the Republican period, had championed the efforts of villagers to stand up against Kuomintang state corruption and repression.[2]

THE IMPACT OF THE GREAT LEAP FORWARD ON DA FO'S TEACHERS

In the early 1950s, the Communist Party set out to improve rural education, and the county party leaders set up a Teacher's Training School in Dongle county. According to Zheng Bingzhang, a graduate who went on to teach in Zhaozhuang village, the school graduated only fifty teachers in the years 1951–1955, and most villages were without qualified teachers. The situation deteriorated after 1955, and the school system collapsed during the Great Leap Forward.[3] The Communist Party victory spelled trouble for Da Fo's vibrant system of schooling. The trouble actually began as early as 1951, before the so-called honeymoon phase of party rule, when the imposition of Mao's *tonggou tongxiao* (unified state purchase and sale of grain) policy on the Dongle county countryside had a devastating impact on rural education in general and on Da Fo's private school in particular. Prior to 1949, Da Fo village's school had been

---

[1] See Lewis, *Writing and Authority*, 109, 262–263, cited in Rosen, "State of Youth," 7.
[2] Cf. Thaxton, *Salt of the Earth*.   [3] Zheng Bingzhang, interview.

supported by voluntary private grain contributions from its big landowners, artisans, and small farmers – particularly from members of the dominant Bao lineage. Its teachers had a good track record of sending graduates on to Shangcun high school and the Kuomintang-managed postsecondary colleges, including the Daming Seventh Normal College – the regional college of first choice for young aspirants to teaching careers and official positions in the Nationalist government in the early 1930s. Teacher salaries, often paid in kind, were critical to sustaining the competitive position of Da Fo's school, and they constituted the largest part of the school's operating cost. The *tonggou tong-xiao* policy – a veiled form of procurement – placed unbearable pressure on this system. Once the policy was implemented in the Da Fo area, villagers had little, if any, grain left over to give to the village school or its teachers. From this point on, teachers were at risk, for pay and food were increasingly uncertain.[4]

At the inception of the People's Republic of China, less than 10 percent of the rural population in Dongle county was literate, and illiteracy rates among local party leaders in Liangmen township villages were very high. In Da Fo, 80 percent of the party leaders, including party secretary Bao Zhilong, were illiterate. In this situation, the Communist Party lacked the educated base needed to impose its collective fiscal model in the countryside, where family land holdings, cropping patterns, harvest yields, grain storage places, grain measurement standards, kinship alliances, and periodic market calendars varied from village to village, creating a bewildering obstacle to what James C. Scott calls "fiscal legibility."[5] Initially, illiterate township and village party leaders had little choice but to rely on the intelligence of literate schoolteachers and principals to help them realize Mao's goal of building state power in the countryside, so that teachers in Liangmen township, including those in Da Fo, were invited to lend their talents and energies to the task of improving rural public education at the grass-roots level. Although teachers and principals initially endorsed this goal, they were disappointed by their encounter with the mobilizational strategy of the Mao-led party-state.

There were two problems. First, as Glen Peterson has pointed out, Chinese villagers wanted their children to study with teachers who could meet expectations of cultural literacy, social mobility, and economic ascent, and Da Fo's farmers also had these expectations.[6] Yet teachers – now designated *gong ban* ("permanent," government-salaried employees) – were asked to abandon the goal of securing the future of individuals and families and, instead, in the words of Pang Lianggui, "to teach according to the government's will, and to think about the state's interest first."[7] In the period 1951–1955, Da Fo's teachers were preoccupied with attending county- and township-level meetings to study

---

[4] I am indebted to Glen Peterson for helping me work through this understudied development. Personal correspondence, October 3, 2010.
[5] Scott, *Seeing Like a State*, 35, 39.   [6] Peterson, "State Literacy Ideologies," 118.
[7] Pang Lianggui, interview.

Central government documents and socialist philosophy, the purpose of which was to train them to help the Maoist party-state convey norms and skills conducive to pinning farmers down in agriculture, boosting production for state benefit, and complying with the *tonggou tongxiao* policy.[8] Many of the teachers in Liangmen township were offended by this dumbed-down educational system, which they thought was designed to serve the production and regimentation goals of the party-state, and which they knew was transforming them into the local agents of an apartheid divide between rural and urban China. In Da Fo, the teachers were at the mercy of the illiterate party leaders, for they were chosen to teach only if the Peasant Association demonstrated they were "good people" (for the revolution); were paid only 18–29 yuan per month; and had little chance of moving up in their careers without strict adherence to the party line on education.

Hence there was a second problem. The teachers were skeptical of, and often uncomfortable with, the political work style of the leaders who pushed Mao's policies. As I have shown in *Catastrophe and Contention in Rural China*, teachers in the Liangmen–Da Fo area were accustomed to expressing dissent through written poems, scrolls, and doorway couplets reflective of the ancient wisdom of virtuous governance. The illiterate army of party stalwarts in this triprovincial border area were suspicious of written knowledge and, following Mao, placed great faith in the efficacy of simple speeches and songs, pictures and posters, and popular theater as a means of eliciting popular support for the collectivization of agriculture.[9] As collectivization deepened in the 1951–1955 period, party leaders used simplified oral discourse to cover up their grab of public goods. The schoolteachers saw through this corruption and were positioned to expose it, though they dared not do so.

The fear of speaking out was constant, but pride in the New China – in combination with the pressure from party superiors – prompted more than a few teachers to let their guard down. In the 1957 Hundred Flowers Campaign, for instance, the Dongle county party leaders, heeding the Mao-led center's instructions, called on teachers to demonstrate loyalty to the New China by raising criticisms of the Communist Party that would help its cadres improve their performance. At the time, the Liangmen party secretary held a meeting of all the teachers, during which he gave a "mobilizing speech" appealing to the teachers, as government functionaries, to criticize party policies. Teachers remember that speaking out was mandatory. Silence was taken as a form of

---

[8] See Peterson, "State Literacy Ideologies," 95, 98, 113–114, 117–119. Cf. Shue, who argues that the party's effort to capture agriculture in the first decade produced "encystment" and entrapped rural people in a cellular economic system more directly under the control of the party. Shue, *Reach of the State*, 132–133.

[9] Cf. Peterson, "State Literacy Ideologies," 99–101. Also see Kwong, who argues that Mao opted for mass campaigns instead of book learning to effect ideological education and elicit popular support. Kwong, *Chinese Education in Transition*, 76.

subversion, an inaction by people who wanted to see the party rot and fail. Consequently, there was an explosion of antiparty yammer and loathing.

Zheng Bingzhang, a Liangmenpo graduate of the Dongle county Teacher's Training School, reluctantly joined in the conversation. Assigned to Zhaozhuang village in Luyuan township, Zheng taught Chinese language, mathematics, and common sense – and common sense told him to keep his mouth shut about politics. Nonetheless, recalls Zheng, "In 1957 the party secretary came to talk to me many times, and I felt I had to say something in the end. Therefore, I said that farmers did not have enough to eat, and the party needed to give farmers more grain to eat so that they would have the energy to work in the fields. That was the only criticism I had to offer.... For that one criticism I was labeled a rightist. At the end of the campaign, they charged me with challenging the party's grain policy, and with standing on the side of farmers instead of the side of the party and the state."[10] Along with several hundred other schoolteachers, Zheng was condemned at a big meeting and then paraded around Dongle county in a tall paper hat with the characters "rightist" inscribed on it. Zheng Bingzhang was not beaten, but other teachers were, and Zheng remembers that the ones who beat them were chosen by the party leaders. Dismissed from his teaching position, Zheng joined scores of teachers who were sent back to their native villages to reform through manual labor. A similar fate awaited Bao Zhongxin in Da Fo, who scribbled a series of cartoons lambasting the food privileges of the corrupt Dongle county party secretary and who was ordered to clean Da Fo's streets without pay in consequence. He had to poach the crops of the collective to survive.[11]

The antirightist campaign that grew out of Mao's deceptive Hundred Flowers "opening" was the beginning of the end of the center's "noble experiment" with rural public education. Committed to the rapid industrialization of rural China and faced with the political cost of feeding "rightists," Mao and his allies in Beijing and Henan subsequently began the Great Leap Forward by cutting back spending on local public schools and literacy programs; in the end they favored urban schools and failed to improve rural education, thereby perpetuating inequality between rural and urban China.[12] The impact of the Great Leap on education in Liangmen township and Da Fo village was disastrous. It dismantled the institutional foundations of village schooling and brought chaos, pain, and loss to schoolteachers. With the commencement of the Great Leap, teachers who had ascended the ladder of educational success and won esteem for the teaching posts they had obtained beyond the confines of Da Fo were sent back to the village to work in the collective fields as serfs under illiterate Maoist party leaders. Such was the fate of Bao Zhongxin. A graduate of Liaocheng Teacher's Training School, Bao had risen to become

---

[10] Zheng Bingzhang, interview.
[11] Bao Zhongxin, interview; related in greater detail in Thaxton, *Catastrophe and Contention*, 144.
[12] Cf. Kwong, *Chinese Education in Transition*, 68–71, 82, 92, 98.

a middle-school teacher outside Da Fo before being returned to Da Fo's collective fields as a "peasant" in the Great Leap.[13]

With the revival of the antirightist campaign during the second year of the Great Leap, teachers in Dongle county were subjected to a pincer attack – a deliberate attack through political labeling and an indirect attack through hunger. Da Fo's teachers were not allowed to teach at all, and they were humiliated in everyday work life. Bao Zhongxin tells us his fate: "I was twenty-six years old when I was labeled a rightist in the Great Leap Forward. My father was labeled a rightist too. In 1958, I was still teaching, but I was ordered to participate in steel making in Lin county. After this I was labeled a rightist, and I was not allowed to teach anymore. I was sent back to the village. After I returned to Da Fo, my father and I had to sweep the streets as rightists. I did all of the sweeping because I did not want my father to do it. We did not have enough to eat at the time. I ate a lot of the green crops in the fields. In 1962, I began to teach again. In 1977, I received a notice from the government which said that I had not been a rightist since 1966, but no one informed me of this for eleven years. I was wrongly treated as a rightist for a long time after I had been cleared."[14] Although the Central government under Deng Xiaoping formally removed the "rightist" label from teachers in the early 1980s, many teachers suffered this stigma well into the reform period. Some Da Fo teachers were not cleared of "rightist histories" until they cleared themselves. This struggle to clear names and restore honorable reputations continually dredged up and kept alive the memory of the Maoist Leap and its offensive against reputation and subsistence.

In 1959–1960, Da Fo's teachers faced a severe food crisis. Most remember that they could not get enough to eat. Emaciated by hunger, Ruan Song pilfered a few ears of corn from the collective fields on one occasion, for which he was fired from his teaching job by Da Fo party boss Bao Zhilong and the party leaders. Facing starvation, Ruan Song migrated to Shanxi, where he survived the famine by working as a carpenter. When he returned to Da Fo to reclaim his teaching position toward the end of the famine, Bao Zhilong and the party leadership accused him of "illegal flight" and determined he had to come back to the village as a farmer.[15] Well into the third decade of post-Mao reform, such memories still overwhelmed the details of Maoist progress: "I do not remember the details of the Great Leap Forward," says Wei Dongmei. "My only memory is that I was hungry all of the time."[16] To cope with the raging hunger of 1960, teacher Wei Dongmei ate tree leaves, while her future colleagues scavenged the village for anything resembling food. To pursue scavenging, they had to quit teaching. Their students also quit school to search for food; the dropout rate skyrocketed as the economy went into a free fall. Apparently, even the more

---

[13] Bao Chengling, interview.   [14] Bao Zhongxin, interview.
[15] Ruan Shifan, interview; Bao Huajie, interview.   [16] Wei Dongmei, interview.

fortunate students felt the pinch of famine. One was Bao Dongwen, who was studying in Da Fo and had hopes for a bright future when the famine struck. "In 1960," testifies Bao, "I passed the exam for advanced primary school in Liangmen. However, I was able to attend for only a year. It was a very difficult time economically. We did not have enough food to eat. I felt hungry all the time. Many people stopped coming to school.... When you were hungry you did not think about studying. You thought about how to get food to eat."[17]

Indeed, Da Fo's teachers were frustrated because they could do little about the politics inhibiting the ascent of their students, which meant they could not create educated networks to challenge local power. Few of Da Fo's top middle-school graduates were able to attend Liangmen high school, in part because the Liangmen People's Commune party leaders determined who would go to high school. Zheng Shumin, who was five at the outset of the Leap, managed to get through middle school with flying colors. But when Zheng and the thirty-seven graduates took the high-school entrance exam, only seven were chosen, and Zheng was not one of them.

On the one hand, the commune leaders never published the results, leaving disappointed students without any basis for appeal. One the other, the leaders' decisions were colored by their own angry memories of Great Leap–era transgressions. Although they told Zheng Shumin that he was not chosen because he needed to stay in Da Fo to help his father with farming and to earn work points for his family, the decision was guided by a serious black mark on his political record: in 1960, during the desperation of the famine, Zheng Yunxiang, the father of Zheng Shumin, had led fifty-three hungry villagers in an armed raid on the sorghum crops of a nearby brigade, incurring the wrath of the commune leaders, including Da Fo party boss Bao Zhilong, who at the time was the vice-director of the commune. Although the elder Zheng had been punished, commune leaders had not forgotten or forgiven this transgression, and so Zheng Shumin was made to suffer for his father's political sin. Zheng spent the next twenty-five years of his life farming poor collective land in dreary solitude, bitter over this lost chance for a better life and a place in a network of enlightened and educated villagers.[18]

The Great Leap devastated both high-school and college education in Dongle county, making an ascent into a secure teaching position nearly impossible. Without the grain to feed students and teachers and with facilities in disarray, every college cut back its enrollment. In 1961–1962, for example, Dongle county had only one high school and 150 graduates, only three of whom were admitted to college. Bao Jingpu, who had wanted to become a teacher, recalls that many of those who did not get in had to return to the villages and farm, suffering "a big disappointment." A few became part-time

---

[17] Bao Dongwen, interview.
[18] Zheng Shumin, interview; also see Thaxton, *Catastrophe and Contention*, 178–179, and Cf. 240.

farmers and teachers. To recover food security, many teachers, including those in Da Fo, had to resign from teaching to till small parcels in the years after the famine.[19] Bao Tianhai, for example, had been teaching primary school in Sanlizhuang and later in Dingqiao village. In 1962, after he learned that Liu Shaoqi had approved private household plots, Bao had to give up his teaching post and return home to Da Fo. His children were too young to farm, and his teaching salary was too low to buy enough food for his family. "If I had not gone back home to farm the land," says Bao, "my family would have gone hungry."[20]

Speaking of the long-term impact on the school and its students, Bao Yingjie tells us that after the Great Leap Forward, some of the people who had left school to find more food returned to school, "but most did not."[21] In reality, there was a dire shortage of teachers, and the few prospective teachers lacked students to teach. This, too, made it difficult for teachers to recover their profession and its empowerment, which pleased Da Fo's Maoists, who did not want to see the development of a critical mass of educated young people capable of reasoning and arguing with them. In this and other ways, the imprint of Mao's Great Leap, especially its exaltation of an unscientific, cretinous approach to rural society and economy, inhibited the revival of rural education well into the Cultural Revolution and even the first decade of post-Mao reform.

In the decades following the Great Leap disaster, Da Fo's teachers were marginalized economically and suffered unbearable social insecurity, in part because they were fastened to socialist colonized agriculture. Those who had lost urban *hukou* (household registration) to being labeled "rightists" in the second year of the Great Leap were stuck with agricultural *hukou*, and this, according to Bao Sheping, "affected their livelihood greatly."[22] Worries over livelihood overrode the practical requirements of concentrating on school work and classroom teaching performance.

Although the Maoists proclaimed that village schoolteachers did not need to worry about farming their own land or making enough money to survive, Da Fo's teachers were so materially deprived that they had to engage in "gray zone" money-making activities to cover the costs of maintaining the village school. They helped run a village farm of three *mu*, raised a hundred goats per year, and produced and sold earth salt on the black market. "All teachers and students participated in these projects," recalls Bao Chengling, who taught in Da Fo's shabby post–Great Leap schoolhouse.[23] In the early years of reform, roughly from 1982 to 1985, teachers were given their share of land to farm, and they became preoccupied with cultivating crops on their small family parcels in order to maximize food production for household security. Because most teachers were paid as long as they showed up in the classroom (which did

[19] Bao Jingpu, interview.   [20] Bao Tianhai, interview.   [21] Bao Yingjie, interview.
[22] Bao Sheping, interview.   [23] Bao Chengling, interview.

not necessarily involve faithfully teaching their courses), teaching remained a largely secondary source of income.

By 1990, many Da Fo's teachers were working harder at farming than at teaching. In the early 1990s, just when farm households began sending their children to primary school, holding out hope they would someday attend middle school and high school and even go on to college, increasing pressure was put on Da Fo teachers to prepare students to do well on examinations. With obligations to cultivate their family parcels and to attend to animal husbandry enterprises like raising piglets, however, many teachers had little if any time for self-improvement. They found it difficult to deepen knowledge of their key subjects and even to prepare adequately for their daily teaching assignments. They were still struggling with the daily legacy of the damage the Great Leap had done to rural education.

GRIEVANCES UNDER REFORM

At the top of the list of all teacher grievances was the salary injustice they had suffered under the Maoists and Deng Xiaoping alike. In the Great Leap, Bao Zhilong and his party-based network of young know-nothings had simply told teachers that they were to eat the same amount of food as other villagers from the same communal pot. Withholding of pay became a weapon to punish teachers who were labeled rightists, regardless of their performance. Nor were Da Fo's teachers paid well in the aftermath of the Great Leap. Despite the teacher shortage in Liangmen township in the mid-1960s, the salaries of the teachers were extremely low, so that even today they complain about the egregious salary injustice of the Maoist past. Whereas *gong ban* teachers, officially speaking, made about 30 yuan per month and were entitled to retirement packages, in the Da Fo area local party leaders made teachers accept *minban* status as a precondition for employment, and this put their appointments under brigade-level illiterates. (Teachers who had agricultural *hukou* were called *minban* teachers; this distinction would later become important.) The *minban* teachers were paid 4 yuan per month, plus work points that fluctuated with annual harvest yields. Nearly all of the *minban* teachers aspired to become *gong ban* teachers in the years between the end of the Great Leap and the end of the Cultural Revolution, but the odds of this transition were slim. The only way for Da Fo's teachers to change their status from *minban* to *gong ban* was to succeed in the stiff competition for acceptance to a teacher's training school, of which there were only a few in the Hebei-Shandong-Henan border area. Although those who earned diplomas and achieved *gong ban* status felt good about being paid a monthly salary, even their salaries were not linked to classroom performance, and they had little motivation to perform well in the late Mao era or the early years of reform.

The situation worsened in the late 1990s. Beginning in late 1998, the teachers in Liangmen township were not paid their regular salaries on time.

By the summer of 2000, their regular salaries had not been issued for ten full months. The testimony of Pang Lianggui, a longtime, highly accomplished Da Fo math teacher, indicates that teacher indignation over the withholding of pay was inseparable from outrage over mistreatment by township government, which Da Fo's teachers associated with the remains of the commune-based tip of Maoist state aggrandizement. Here is Pang's recollection, offered in July 2000:

We have not been paid for more than ten months. During this summer, we teachers started to plan for a strike with teachers from other schools. We have been planning steadily for this strike. Because we have not been paid for the longest period compared with other townships, the Dongle county officials have used us as an example to hold out to the other townships. They told the teachers in the other townships, "Look, the teachers in Liangmen township were not paid for more than ten months, but they are not making any noises." I think it is very unfair for the leaders to use us this way. Liangmen township government should be criticized for not paying the teachers for a long time. We are angry not only because we were not paid, but also because we were treated very unfairly by the Liangmen commune government leaders. Before the wheat harvest this summer, the Liangmen commune leaders gave themselves and the people who worked for the commune government one *jin* of tea, ten *jin* of sugar, and five hundred yuan for the summer. We teachers are considered commune government employees, but we got nothing.

Of course, we must be careful about collapsing time, for not all of the teachers who complained about salaries in the 1990s were classified as rightists in the Great Leap, and some of the teachers were resentful about the betrayed promises of the communal era – not the specific injustices of the Great Leap episode. Perhaps this is why Pang Lianggui repeatedly used the term "commune" to refer to the township government, though this Maoist structure had not existed for many years.[24]

In the political thinking of Da Fo's teachers there was a causal relationship between the withholding of teachers' pay and the insatiable demands of township government officials. This relationship aroused indignation, as Pang made clear: "Teachers' salaries are in the budget of the state government, which is guaranteed. But the Liangmen township government went into debt, and so it embezzled the money earmarked for teachers' salaries. This is outrageous. In the past, this would have been a serious crime. But today it is common practice among township governments. The township government spent more and more money, and therefore its leaders need to extract more money from people. But they could not do this because most farmers were nearly broke. When the township leaders did not have money, they nonetheless wanted to drink and eat, and to ride in fancy automobiles. They do not know how to reduce their costs. I do not see how we can go on like this as a nation."[25]

---

[24] Pang Lianggui, interview.   [25] Ibid.

By the summer of 2000, many of Da Fo's teachers were angry with the government, but few were inclined to stand up for their rights. The memory of the fate of outspoken "rights-conscious" teachers in the Hundred Flowers, and again in the Great Leap, lingered on to inhibit collective action in the reform period.[26]

The issue of unpaid or irregularly paid pensions also became a sore point with Da Fo's retired teachers in the 1990s. Bao Jingsheng, the head of the village primary school for a stint in the late Mao period, had worked very hard to improve schooling in Da Fo. However, Bao was angry because his 400-yuan monthly pension had not been paid regularly between 1995 and 2001. During this period, Bao and several other retired teachers frequently organized themselves to protest against Liangmen township government for not paying their pensions regularly. With each protest act, they were able to get some of their retirement money restored, but the irregularity of payments resumed not long after a string of small victories.[27]

Withholding of back pay and pensions provided a moral basis for teacher discontent, but Da Fo's teachers were also offended by the official attempt to take more and more resources from their students – the children of their relatives, neighbors, and fellow farmers. At the outset of the reform period, there were no school fees. As getting rich became the mantra for personal achievement and national glory, however, Liangmen township education officials hankered to join the ranks of the nouveaux riches. School fees in Da Fo skyrocketed, while expenditures on the improvement of schooling fell precipitously. The attempt of Liangmen township leaders, in collaboration with the Dongle county education authorities, to turn rural schooling into a squeeze racket at the expense of both students and teachers compromised the integrity of Da Fo's teachers and threatened to damage their reputations in the eyes of students and their parents.[28]

In the years 1994 to 1996, when teacher pay was being withheld, the Dongle county Education Bureau officials and their agents in Liangmen township imposed a seemingly endless train of ad hoc fees on village schools and students.

[26] Of course, the memory of Maoist-era injustice was not the only factor structuring reluctance to join in protest against the Liangmen township authorities. There were other reasons, some more immediate and primary. Some Da Fo teachers, being part-time farmers, were aware that if they pushed Liangmen township leaders too hard to come up with back pay, the latter might well use this as a pretext to increase the grain tax that was due in July 2000. Some were nearing the end of their teaching careers, and so they also were fearful that involvement with a strike would give the township leaders an excuse to label them troublemakers and possibly dismiss them, thereby obliterating their claims to a pension and wrecking their hopes for retirement. Pang Lianggui, interview.

[27] Bao Xianpu, interview.

[28] Cf. Kipnis and Li, who report that funding for rural schools in Shandong still comes substantially from nontransparent miscellaneous fees charged to individual households by local officials. Kipnis and Li, "Is Chinese Education Underfunded?," 338–343.

In Da Fo, students were required to pay for test papers, homework notebooks, training manuals for test taking, and more. Most of these materials were produced by the Dongle County Education Bureau. Seeking money from students, its cadres trucked these materials en masse to each township education bureau, and the township leaders sent them on to village schools. When the materials reached Da Fo, the agents of the education bureau announced that students were required to purchase them. While the school put up the required sum, the task of actually collecting the money from students was assigned to the Da Fo teachers, who suffered the ire and complaints of students and parents.

This put teachers in an awkward position and often set parents against them. According to Pang Lianggui, parents didn't understand that teachers were "caught in between these two sides" and did not benefit personally from collecting the fees. "The Dongle county education officials are only after profits from their newfound printing businesses," he explained. "The quality of their products is very low, while the price is outrageously high. The number of tests we have here would surprise anyone. The Dongle County Education Bureau and Liangmen Township Education Bureau each has its own set of examinations, and each wants us to buy its materials for mid-term, end of term, quarter-term and monthly exams, for promotion exams, contest exams, and many others. Each of these exams costs students at least four yuan per exam. To administer these exams and ask students for the money is a dreaded task. Some parents cursed us for doing this."[29] When Hong Kong was returned to China in 1997, the Dongle County Bureau of Education officials asked the village schools to celebrate, whereupon they published some celebration guides and pressed the schools and students to bear the cost of acquiring this propaganda. Da Fo's teachers scoffed at these fees, and their resentment was compounded by the knowledge that the fees did not, by and large, go to education. According to Pang Lianggui, "More than two-thirds were spent on drinking and eating by the township and county education bureau officials," including former Da Fo party secretary Bao Zhilong and Bao Chengling, the Mao-era Da Fo school principal.[30]

By the mid-1990s, the Central government's unfunded policy mandate for a nine-year compulsory education program in rural China had produced high tuition fees at Da Fo's school. Rising tuition became a source of teacher and farmer discontent, for it proved to be a factor contributing to the high drop-out rate, which in turn exacerbated the crisis in youth education.[31] In 1998, some 98 percent of school-aged children were entering Da Fo primary school – a seemingly impressive figure. But approximately 25 percent of these children did not finish elementary school, and only 50 percent of those who did finish

---

[29] Pang Lianggui, interview.   [30] Ibid.
[31] On the problem of high tuition fees at all levels of the educational system, see Rosen, "State of Youth," 165–166.

actually qualified for middle school. Astonishingly, 70 percent of those who entered middle school dropped out. The major factor fostering the high dropout rate was soaring tuition.

The data from Da Fo on the actual burden of tuition as a percentage of household income are sketchy, so the extent to which tuition per se figured into the high dropout rate is unclear. Yet all Da Fo villagers, both haves and have-nots, complained that high tuition fees constituted a significant barrier to an education-powered escape from poverty. The Central government, though propagandizing its post-1978 commitment to improving rural education, did little to eliminate this barrier in the poor villages of Henan, Yunnan, Gansu, and other rural interior provinces until January 2007, when Beijing rulers declared they were going to abolish school tuition fees up through grade nine.[32] In Da Fo's case, the burden of tuition combined with the burden of state taxation, and other pressures, to compel many families to give up on schooling their children. With household income under pressure from grain-tax claims and with the price of grain dropping off, many farmers were pressed to a point where cutting expenditures on education became a seemingly rational choice for holding off debt and holding on to money to pay taxes, birth-planning fines, and medical bills. For the most part, Da Fo's teachers supported high tuition, because they reasoned that tuition increases meant higher salaries for themselves. Nevertheless, after 1995 they too grew angry over tuition raises, because some of their favorite students could not keep up with the hikes. Bao Huajie explained, "As a teacher, I am better off than most other villagers, but I cannot afford my own son's education. My second son graduated from middle school, but he could not afford to go to high school."[33] Many other Da Fo families were in a similar predicament.

When children did not finish primary school or dropped out of middle school, they were unable to compete in a money-based economy, and many of them thus were confined to back-breaking farm work. This fate occasionally stirred deep regrets in their parents. Da Fo's Pang Weiming, a farmer for nearly fifty years whose daughters dropped out in the Deng era, explains that he dropped out of middle school during the Great Leap Forward. As a middle-school student, he had held urban *hukou* status and been provided with a grain ration by the government, but he remembers being "hungry all the time," and feeling as if he was "starving to death." When he returned to Da Fo, he lost his urban *hukou* and regained rural *hukou*. Had he finished middle or high school, Pang explains, the government would have given him a job in an urban area, but in Da Fo he had to farm. "That was the first great mistake I made in my life," he says.[34] Farmers like Pang saw traces of their own traumatic past in the failure of their children to escape farm drudgery through educational success,

[32] Personal correspondence with Steven I. Levine, spring 2014, and see Hannum and Adams, "Beyond Cost: Rural Perspectives on Barriers to Education," 11–12.
[33] Bao Huajie, interview.   [34] Pang Weiming, interview.

and for this reason they expected more of Da Fo's schoolteachers and were embittered by the failure of the Deng-led center's system of rural schooling.

FORMS OF TEACHER RESISTANCE IN THE 1990S

Da Fo's teachers mounted everyday resistance to their mistreatment by village and township Communist Party leaders in the 1990s. This resistance, which was linked to the memory of the impact of the Maoist past on teaching as a means of survival and popular empowerment, took a variety of forms.

In the late 1980s, the issue of salary grievance surfaced in Da Fo. During the first decade of the Deng Xiaoping reforms, teachers had been told by Dongle county leaders that a raise was in the cards. It did not materialize. (Later, after the protests began, teachers learned that the Puyang government had actually given the Liangmen township leaders the money for a salary boost; they concluded that the township leaders had embezzled it.[35]) Angry about losing the promised raise, teachers took action. "The Liangmen township government did not give us the raise, so we organized to petition the prefectural government in Puyang," said Pang Lianggui, "and we demanded that the Puyang leaders tell the Liangmen township government leaders that they had to give us the raise."[36] In the end, this protest worked, and the raise was issued. Da Fo's teachers were relieved, but they were aware that without institutionalized legal rights, petitioning and demonstrations could not ensure fairness from township officials in the future.

A second aspect of salary-related protest involved an attempt to link pay to teaching performance or, to put it another way, to separate teaching from government-prescribed goals for labor production and propaganda work. For decades, Da Fo party boss Bao Zhilong and his clients had opposed teacher pressure for such a change, primarily because they had relied on politics, rather than competitive education, to keep cadre leadership positions within the circles of their poorly educated family networks.[37] In 1990, this situation began to improve with the ascent of Wen Xiuyin – a former *minban* teacher who had lost his younger brother to the food crisis of the Great Leap – to the position of acting chief of the Educational Commission of Liangmen Township Government. At Wen's urging, a plan was conceived to base teacher pay largely on performance. The plan struck a death blow to the Mao-era system in which teachers were rewarded largely on the basis of extra-classroom, politically correct networking.

The compensation mechanism, known as *gongzi huo yong* (flexible wages), had seven components or categories for pay, rewarding educational credentials, hours in the classroom spent teaching, seniority, and homeroom service. In

---

[35] Pang Lianggui, interview.   [36] Ibid.
[37] Cf. Ruf, *Cadres and Kin*, and Bossen, *Chinese Women*, 333–334.

addition, performance credits included bonuses for lesson planning, grading homework, and, most important, high student scores in township- and county-wide examinations. Teachers were awarded 45 yuan each month if their students came in first in the township-wide examination and 35 yuan for a second-place finish. If students performed below the average exam score, however, teachers had money deducted from their monthly paychecks. A final category recognized teacher research. Here, then, was a clean break from the "better Red than competent" politics of the Great Leap and Cultural Revolution.

Da Fo's teachers were elated by most of these changes, but their implementation was slow and ridden with conflict. Meanwhile, government withholding of back pay led to collective action in the summer of 2000, when teachers organized a one-day strike to recover eight months' back pay.[38] Led by Pang Xianrong, the teachers were able to draw in scores of their counterparts from other Liangmen township villages. When the township leaders got wind of the planned strike, they attempted to squelch it by threatening to round up the ringleaders, but Pang and his comrades stayed the course. The Dongle County Education Bureau removed the township education chief and began negotiations with the teachers, at which point the teachers, basking in their small victory, returned to their classrooms with their pay.[39]

The issue that came the closest to prompting teachers to invest in a contentious uprising against the Liangmen township government was the official suspension of pensions. As William Hurst and Kevin J. O'Brien have found, pensioner protests by and large occurred "in response to crises of subsistence" and were fueled by a sense that China's socialist state had betrayed its obligations to retirees.[40] As previously noted, in late 1994 the retired teachers in Da Fo and scores of teachers in Liangmen had not been paid their pensions. After a round of fruitless complaints to township leaders, the retired teachers joined together to elect representatives to visit with government leaders in Dongle town, Puyang city, and Zhengzhou, the provincial capital. In these meetings, the Liangmen teachers engaged in petitioning to express their grievances over the withholding of their pensions by township government leaders. Not long afterward, township leaders were ordered to pay the pensions. They came up with all but one month of the withheld pension payment.

Complaint via petition gained popularity after 2001, as Da Fo's teachers relied on it to press their claims for a "just pension." In a few cases, the retired teachers apparently used it to settle long-standing disputes over pension claims. Thus, after working with other retired teachers to win back his own pension in 1994–1995, Bao Huajie began pressing for his father's pension. "My father was a teacher, and he died in 1974," says Bao. "According to the government

---

[38] Bao Zhongxin, interview.   [39] Ibid.
[40] O'Brien and Hurst, "China's Contentious Pensioners," 360.

policy, my mother should have continued to receive his pension as financial compensation to the family of a retired teacher. However, from December 2000 to 2001, my mother did not get her monthly compensation."[41] Bao and his mother filed a complaint and petitioned for redress. The two of them were able to get the township government to pay back the withheld pension and to resume the regularly scheduled pension payments in early 2002.[42] Fearing that such petitionist claims could open a Pandora's box, Liangmen township officials moved to settle them discreetly.

Perhaps the most telling example of how the Great Leap legacy influenced petitioning involved a struggle against the longtime Da Fo principal, Bao Chengling, which exploded in 1996. Haughty and undemocratic, Bao never called a meeting, and he was known for his temper tantrums. As in the Great Leap period, Bao Chengling attempted to expel and exile teachers who spoke out against him. Bao Huajie, a teacher who became one of his targets, recalls, "I was the school's accountant. He took money from me, but he did not give me the receipts for his expenses." Angry, Bao Huajie quarreled with Bao Chengling, and Bao Chengling insisted that Bao Huajie go teach in Daweicun, a miserably poor, thief-infested village near Da Fo. "All of the teachers and village leaders opposed his decision," but the township government backed Bao Chengling. The teachers petitioned the township government, and Bao Huajie managed to keep his job "after a fierce struggle."[43]

The immediate trigger for the 1996 protest was Bao Chengling's withholding of teachers' salaries. In this period, the Liangmen township leaders often borrowed money from the teacher-salary pool and used it for their own purposes, including throwing banquets to which Bao Chengling was invited. Bao, the conduit for the Liangmen township salary pool, followed suit. The teachers protested to the Liangmen township government education bureau, and they sent a representative to the Dongle county government to express their grievances. Back in the village, they engaged in heated debates with Bao. At year's end, he was compelled to pay them and forced to apologize.[44]

What seemed like a momentary spat provided the impetus for a protracted movement to hold Bao Chengling responsible for the moral decline of educational leadership and for the perpetuation of autocratic and arbitrary decision making. It was a movement back toward popular Confucian concepts of school governance that had prevailed in the Republican era, when Da Fo's teachers had brought glory to the school and insisted on honor and integrity in leadership.[45] For the next two years, 1996–1998, the teachers mounted resistance to Bao Chengling, aiming to replace him with a teacher who revered education and would govern with a more democratic work style. They were led by Bao Sheping, a teacher (and local party member) with a reputation for generosity

---

[41] Bao Huajie, interview.   [42] Ibid.; Pang Mingfan, interview.   [43] Bao Huajie, interview.
[44] Ibid.   [45] Cf. Thaxton, *Catastrophe and Contention*, chapters 1 and 2.

and integrity. During the Cultural Revolution, Bao Sheping had been an outstanding student in the Da Fo middle school, recommended by his teachers for high-school placement. Party boss Bao Zhilong vetoed the recommendation, however, declaring that the younger Bao could not go to high school because he was the son of a rightist – Da Fo's courageous Great Leap–era dissident Bao Zhongxin. This decision set the stage for a long quarrel between Bao Sheping, on the one hand, and boss Bao Zhilong and the old-guard Maoists who took over village education, on the other.[46]

When Bao Sheping moved against the Mao-era principal in the reform era, a silent memory fueled this resistance, intensifying the emotions of its teacher activists and reminding them of the need for integrity in leadership, the loss of which was associated with a hardly bearable past loss. Tang Fuyan, who was seventy-nine years old in 2003, gave voice to this memory. Though Tang Fuyan never went to school, Tang's son graduated from middle school around 1958, after which he was sent to Lin county to make steel during the Great Leap Forward. Looking back on this most traumatic episode of the Maoist era, Tang Fuyan voiced a memory that all of Da Fo's teachers also held: "Bao Chengling became the village school principal after the Great Leap Forward. I think he was very corrupt when he was the head cook [in the public dining hall] during the Great Leap Forward. Even though he said that he was clean, and never took any money from the public, I believe he was more corrupt than any village leader at the time."[47] Mao's Great Leap had placed integrity and insatiable greed in sharp conflict, and in order to transition to a more open, democratic school system, Da Fo's teachers had to wage this battle to combat greed's corrupting influences in educational leadership circles. It was important to oust Bao Chengling, for he was one of the last remaining clients of Bao Zhilong, who had overseen the overthrow of integrity and allowed his cronies to set village education on a course of stagnation that continued to hinder the chance for genuine reform.

Shortly after Bao Sheping and his allies ousted Bao Chengling, several of Da Fo's teachers found themselves caught up in yet another struggle against institutionalized greed, this one occurring at the county level. The target was Huang Xiangjun, the director of the Dongle County Education Bureau. In 1998, the Central government issued an order to reform the rural schools by converting qualified rural schoolteachers into government-certified schoolteachers. In principle, this reform was designed to weed out bad teachers and was supposed to provide all teachers a chance to qualify for state certification. However, Huang Xiangjun manipulated this policy to line his own pockets. On the one hand, Huang set up a teacher retraining program and charged each teacher 10,000 yuan to participate, luring many to join it with the promise of government teacher status on finishing the course. He recruited approximately

---

[46] Bao Sheping, interview.   [47] Tang Fuyan, interview.

170 Dongle county teachers into this program (by corrupt means – a subject addressed in a later section of this chapter), thus pocketing more than a million yuan (US$125,000) after expenses. In the process, Director Huang allowed some of the least qualified, most corrupt of the Mao-era teachers to achieve certification simply by paying the 10,000 yuan retraining fee – Bao Chengling among them. Meanwhile, better-qualified, more industrious Da Fo teachers who could not afford to pay were left out in the cold.

To make matters worse, during his tenure Huang Xiangjun required village middle-school graduates to pay 10,000 yuan per year to attend the only high school in Dongle county. He also permitted the underqualified children of more than a few superrich families to gain admission by paying a higher tuition fee, the price of which Huang arbitrarily decided. This process triggered memories of the arbitrary selection of high-school and college-bound students by local party leaders during the Mao years. All through the late 1990s, rumors of Huang's corruption swirled throughout the towns and villages of Dongle county. Teachers in Da Fo village were furious with Huang, yet neither the Dongle county government nor Puyang municipal education bureau leaders took action to stop him. In the end, Huang Xiangjun got into trouble because of an anonymous letter-writing campaign by teachers in Da Fo and scores of other villages, all of whom accused him of wrongdoing and insisted on his removal from office. Some teachers sued Huang, and some even went to Beijing to report his corruption to the Central government. Beijing sent a team of investigators to Dongle county around 2000, but its leaders exonerated Huang. "He was exonerated not because he was not guilty, but because he had a very powerful network of protection," declares Bao Dongwen. "After he survived the investigation, he decided to resign from his office as the education chief. It was a very smart move. When he was in office, people could accuse him of corruption. Once he left office and he was no longer an official, people could not charge him with corruption."[48]

Clever Huang continued to wield enormous influence over education, and, like many local education officials in rural China, Huang fattened himself and his network from "reform." In 2007, the Central government started to prohibit rural public schools from charging students tuition and fees. Having lost this source of "rent," before leaving office Huang Xiangjun started to promote scores of private primary and middle schools in Dongle county. In this fuzzy transition from a public to a private school system, Huang made himself and some of his cronies the "secret shareholders" in the private schools. This maneuver put even more money in Huang's pocket. The private schools got a 300-yuan stipend per student, and Huang's people managed this stipend. The private schools also received a subsidy for providing students with meals and lodging, and Huang's people managed room and meal plans. The private

[48] Bao Dongwen, interview.

schools were allowed to charge students tuition, and Huang's people took care of this, too – tuition was 3,200 yuan per year and rising as of the summer of 2011. According to the local rumor mill, Huang was on his way to becoming the richest man in Dongle county.[49] Meanwhile, Huang Xiangjun had "retired" with a full government benefits package, and he was never required to make amends for imperiling the livelihood of Dongle county's deserving teachers, including Da Fo's Bao Sheping.

CASE STUDY: BAO SHEPING AND THE GREAT LEAP LINK TO TEACHERS' REFORM-ERA SUFFERING

In 2008, at the age of fifty, Bao Sheping was serving as the Da Fo primary school principal and working as a farmer in his native Da Fo. He struggled to get by, in part because his principal salary was only several hundred yuan per month. This paltry compensation was, according to Bao, the result of the reform-era Central government's failure to adequately compensate rural schoolteachers for the sacrifices they had made during the decades of Maoist rule.[50]

The existential dilemma of Bao Sheping was linked to the fate of his family in the Great Leap Forward – particularly to the Leap famine. Born in 1959, Bao was a descendant of a family of People's Liberation Army (PLA) veterans and esteemed schoolteachers. His father, Bao Zhongxin, fought with the PLA in the civil war before attending teacher training school in Shen county, Shandong province. After two years of teaching primary school there, he rose to become a vice-principal. But Bao Zhongxin left Shen county on a sour note, having been disciplined undeservingly for the indiscretions of the principal he worked under. Back in Da Fo, he became vice-deputy of the Dongle county Education Research Department. Teacher Bao was known for imparting Confucian ethics to his pupils. He was proud that he had succeeded in coaching many of his students to practice honesty in everyday relationships.[51] Bao also believed in virtuous governance. This, plus his embracing of honesty, got him into political trouble. During the Hundred Flowers Campaign in 1957, Bao joined forced with twenty-seven others to write big-character posters criticizing the Dongle county party magistrate and his deputy for giving themselves special food privileges. Bao also sketched a cartoon that portrayed the magistrate as a tiger who needed to be tamed. For this, he was labeled a rightist and subjected to public struggle and shaming. Bao was spared only because he found a protector in Bao Huibin, a powerful upper-level party member and veteran.

In 1959, during the Great Leap famine, Bao Zhongxin got in political hot water again. That year's antirightist movement was driven by Mao's call to seize all the grain that farmers were allegedly hiding from the state. Bao and

---

[49] Ibid. [50] Bao Sheping, interview. [51] Bao Zhongxin, interview.

other teachers openly supported Pan Fusheng, a moderate, high-ranking Communist Party leader who was attacked by Wu Zhipu, the Henan provincial party secretary who imposed Mao's Great Leap agenda on the villages.[52] In this period, some of the teachers who joined this opposition petitioned higher-ups to reverse the course of the Great Leap – but Mao did not heed their pleas. In the throes of this struggle, Bao Zhongxin assumed a pivotal role in Da Fo teachers' efforts to stop the Leap by writing a big-character poster that criticized party activists for violating the standards of the Communist Party. He acted out of anger and necessity: he was starving, and his grandfather had weakened and died as a result of Great Leap austerity. Bao was publicly criticized, labeled a rightist, suspended from his teaching post, and sent to perform slave labor on an irrigation project in Ji county. On returning to Da Fo in 1960, he had to work alongside farmers, surviving on unripened crops secretly nibbled in the collective fields. He was also required to repent by sweeping the streets and cleaning latrines.[53]

The rightist label stigmatized Bao and his family as a "bad element" household and tarnished their honor, both individual and professional. Growing up with the pain of his father's Great Leap fate, Bao Sheping committed himself to restoring his father's reputation and returning his family to respectability. He studied to become a teacher, making sure he did not get involved in politics. After completing a middle-school education, he was asked to serve in Da Fo's expanding school system in the late 1970s. He was hired as a *daike zhiqing*, or *daiqing* teacher, essentially an educated urban youth working in the countryside. Bao Sheping worked his way through high school and completed his college degree by correspondence in the first decade of reform, yet he could get work only as a poorly paid teacher, and even when he managed to secure the principalship in Da Fo in the late 1990s, his salary remained so low that he had to rely on farming to meet his household's consumption requirements.

In his quest for safety, Bao Sheping joined the Communist Party and followed government policies, keeping his independent thinking to himself. He lived by example, becoming one of the first to pay taxes, and he did not support tax evasion.[54] He earned the respect of his peers and was on good terms with most village and township leaders, seen by many as a small, benevolent sage. But Bao Sheping's appearance of success and fulfillment under Communist Party rule was deceiving. He did not have the money to purchase a new house, pay for his children's wedding expenses, or cover the costs of a decent funeral. More troubling, the Great Leap fate of his father had left him so marginalized economically that he lacked the money to address the central problem of his life: he was not yet a *gong ban* teacher, and he had failed to get his status changed in the 1980s and 1990s because he could not afford to do so. The concept of a *daiqing* teacher existed only in Dongle county, where

---

[52] Ibid.   [53] Ibid.; Bao Zhongxin, interview.   [54] Bao Sheping, interview.

minban were essentially farmers who also taught school and higher-status *daiqing* teachers with nonagricultural *hukou* were hired under the expectation that they would eventually find work in urban areas. After 1980, the collective was disbanded, and the Central government allowed *minban* teachers to acquire nonagricultural *hukou* and become state-employed teachers. The *daiqing* teachers fell through the cracks.

By the third decade of reform, there were some 220 teachers in Dongle county who were or who once had been *daiqing*. Fifty had become full-time government teachers, either through personal connections or by means of payments made to corrupt education officials. The remaining 170 were fired between 2001 and 2005 due to a sweeping Central government mandate to weed poorly trained teachers out of the rural schoolteachers – a sweep that affected a huge number of *minban* teachers deemed unqualified as well, abandoning them "without pensions, health care or dignity" after they had "given their best years to poorly paid teaching." Many of their jobs were given to officials' "kin and cronies, ignoring qualifications and seniority."[55] Bao Yanzhang, who had served as a *minban* teacher in Liangmen village, remembers that many rural teachers had their status converted to that of government teachers, and they gained high salaries, retirement packages, free medical care, and other benefits. But "those who were denied the opportunity were left with nothing."[56] In Da Fo, a number of teachers were disqualified from converting their status on the basis that they had violated the government's one-child policy. Like most other farmers, *minban* and *daiqing* teachers in Da Fo most often had more than one child.[57] Among the 170 dismissed teachers, only Bao Sheping and two others remained active in Dongle county educational circles; all had become school principals and were able to stay on in this new role – though at one-fifth the salary of ordinary schoolteachers.[58]

What Bao Sheping and his dismissed colleagues did not know was that a corrupt ruse had robbed them of the opportunity to regularize their status and secure their futures. In 1998, when the national Ministry of Education issued its new directive mandating that all qualified rural schoolteachers were obligated to become full-time government teachers *without exception*, the directive made it clear that *daiqing* teachers were to be treated the same as rural schoolteachers. But at the time, Huang Xiangjun was Dongle County Education Bureau chief, and he took advantage of vague loopholes in the directive to exclude the *daiqing* teachers from the reform – and then secretly withheld the quota for the 220 *daiqing* teachers and used it to line his own pockets. As we have seen, Huang set up a "training class" in Dongle county and invited all prospective candidates to take his class in order to become full-time, well-paid government teachers. He charged each participant 10,000 yuan. When Bao Sheping

---

[55] Cf. this section and its quotes with the thrust of Chris Buckley, "Chinese Teachers Oppose CCP."
[56] Bao Yanzhang, interview.   [57] Ibid.   [58] Bao Sheping, interview.

and his colleagues later investigated this matter, they learned that Huang Xiangjun had not received any new, additional quota from the upper-level government and did not have any quota to expend from his county position. Where, then, did the money come from to fund 220 training-class graduates as full-time government teachers? According to Bao Sheping, "The 220 quota Huang used was the quota that belonged to us."[59] Bao Sheping and other *daiqing* representatives also discovered that Chief Huang had manufactured the pretext on which they had been dismissed. "There was no such provision in the policy," Bao explains. "We should not have been dismissed for violating birth planning policy." Bao and his colleagues were the victims of corruption – and lying and deceit, the plague of the Great Leap episode, was back.[60]

Bao Sheping did not know this full story when he joined scores of other rural schoolteachers in Dongle county to petition the county and upper government – but he knew an injustice had been done. He and others from Da Fo joined at least 100,000 rural teachers who had been dismissed and who launched a national movement of petition appeals, protests, and demonstrations. In fact, when he was first approached by several dismissed teachers to discuss the matter in the summer of 2006, he refused to take on the leadership role they wanted him for. He feared dismissal from his position if the government discovered he was an organizer. But he did agree to serve as a liaison worker in the petition movement, contacting other Dongle county teachers to inquire whether they would participate. He found former *daiqing* teachers who had become farmers in Liangmen and poverty-stricken Daweicun. Most were desperately looking for work as substitute teachers in different villages. Bao persuaded six of them to contribute 50 yuan to the campaign.[61]

In 2008, Bao Sheping joined twenty other *daiqing* teachers to petition the Dongle county government, demanding justice. Unsatisfied with the empty promises of the county government head, they visited the municipal and provincial petitions offices. The officials told them they would discuss the case with their superiors, but that because it was Olympics Season and the Central government wanted to create a climate of harmony and peace, it was imperative the delegates go home and curb their appeal for the time being. Bao Sheping and the others decided to temporarily suspend the campaign. Meanwhile, they gathered information that revealed what Huang Xiangjun had done with the Central government funds intended for their promotion.[62] That fall, they decided to move forward with their petitions again – and to take them to Beijing if necessary. Township leaders put pressure on Bao Sheping to convince the others to give up the petitioning effort and encouraged him to reveal the names of the teachers' leaders. Bao told them nothing. But the environment for petitioning became increasingly repressive. One group of petitioners reached Beijing, only to be kidnapped and returned by Henan provincial government

---

[59] Ibid.   [60] Ibid.   [61] Ibid.   [62] Ibid.

officials. The Liangmen township representative in this group was sent to prison and had languished there for more than a year at the time of interview.[63] Liangmen government leaders bragged openly about this case and proclaimed that other petitioners would meet the same fate. Outraged, Bao responded: "The township leaders have openly violated our right to petition the government. They are government officials, but they do not observe the law themselves."[64] Shortly after this, Bao and his cohorts began mobilizing 170 of the *daiqing* teachers to converge on Dongle county town to demonstrate and petition. At this time, the government officials began mentioning them in official speeches that touted "the importance of unity, harmony, and security" and "stressed the importance of preventing the petition efforts of rural schoolteachers and *daiqings*."[65]

Rebuffed at every turn, Bao and his colleagues moved up to the provincial level, joining several thousand other rural schoolteachers and principals in late 2008 to petition in Zhengzhou, the provincial capital. At this point, the drive overlapped with a larger group of 100,000 dismissed schoolteachers who had been to Zhengzhou many times. These teachers, too, had been dismissed on the pretext that they had violated birth-planning policy. Some of them were from Liangmen township, including Huang Bingwen, a *minban* teacher dismissed in 1982. In that year, the Central government informed the Henan provincial government and the Dongle county government leaders that there would be no more hiring of *minban* teachers after November. The policy said nothing about dismissing those who already were *minban* teachers. Shortly thereafter, however, Huang Xiangjun and the Dongle county Bureau of Education leaders pressured the village school principals to require each *minban* teacher to write down on a sheet of paper how many children were in their families. Teacher Huang Bingwen recalls that he wrote down that he had two children, and then, a couple of days later, the principal in Liangmenpo, as well as his counterparts in scores of other villages, "announced that the government had decided to fire all of the teachers who had a second child since Deng had imposed the one-child policy."[66] According to Huang: "Everybody who faithfully reported their children was fired. Those who did not faithfully report their children survived. Only the honest people were punished by the policy."

For the next eighteen years Huang Bingwen had to work as a farmer, and so did most of the 200,000 *minban* teachers who were dismissed on the pretext of violating birth-planning policy. This dismissal, and the political deception surrounding it, pricked a memory of the dark Maoist past, when in the Hundred Flowers Campaign Mao and the Communist Party had pressured rural teachers in particular to faithfully report their thoughts and activities to the party-state and then used the guarded information to cashier those who honestly spoke out – a ploy that created a political climate in which corrupt

---

[63] Ibid.   [64] Ibid.   [65] Ibid.   [66] Huang Bingwen, interview.

local party leaders could push Mao's Great Leap Forward. Angered by the repeat of this kind of ruse, Huang Bingwen and the other dismissed teachers kept their powder dry for more than two decades, but in 2005 they began to organize to petition the Henan provincial government to revisit the 1982 dismissal. They discovered, as Bao Sheping did, that the Dongle county and Liangmen township education leaders had lied and distorted the policy, using birth planning as an excuse to fire them in order to replace them with their relatives and friends. They actually found, in one case, that a relative of one of the local party leaders had started taking the salary of the dismissed *minban* teachers at the age of five! This galvanized more and more ex-*minban* teachers to petition to be restated as *minban* teachers with full compensation. Dongle county officials pushed back hard, sending a ban to compel petitioners to return home and monitoring the activities of former *minban* teachers. "They tried very hard to prevent us from joining in petitions and demonstrations," Huang Bingwen remembers.[67] The local government leaders were fearful that the deception of 1982 – and all the benefits they had derived from it over two decades of reform – would be exposed to higher-ups.

Similarly, the Henan provincial party secretary – who would not have wanted to either reinstate or compensate the 100,000 teachers at his doorstep – refused to take them seriously. Incidents of official discouragement, repression, and Central government encouragement of "interceptors" infuriated Bao Sheping, and his unhappiness made him all the more determined to get justice. "The government leaders got very nervous," Bao Sheping explained. "They did not know how to handle our case. It was very hard for them to say we were dismissed wrongly. If they admitted this, then they would have had to compensate us financially, which would require a lot of money." Yet Bao knew the state *had* the money, and hence he and the others vowed to persist even in the face of political closure. "If we do not do anything about it, nothing will happen," Bao said. "And so I am willing to go all the way to the end." His small salary was, by this time, being paid out of Da Fo budget funds – well outside the official system – leaving him no way to retire. "I feel that we have been mistreated for all these years. We need to get justice from the system. The Chinese government is rotten. I do not know if its leaders will ever be able to redeem themselves. It will be hard to deal with such a corrupt government by routine methods."[68] But in the end, Bao had to give up petitioning for *daqing* teachers, because the Liangmen township government leaders threatened to dismiss him from his job. "I do not want to lose what I have," he explained, "for something that I might not be able to get in the future."[69]

Bao Sheping's loss of faith tells us a great deal about the legacy of the Great Leap among teachers in Da Fo village. The repression and disappointments his father experienced reverberated through Bao Sheping's life, shaping his

---

[67] Ibid.   [68] Bao Sheping, interview.   [69] Ibid.

opportunities and attitudes toward the wisdom of taking positions against the state. Yet cautious Bao Sheping had also absorbed his father's Confucian ethics, and when he applied such principles of honesty and justice to his own life, they led him into a struggle against the corrupted Communist Party educational system and against its leaders. In the end, his fate was similar to that of his father, whose Great Leap petitioning was also rejected and suppressed. The repression of the petitionist protest and demonstrations of Bao Sheping must have dredged up the memory of his father's fate – and yet these memories only made him more determined to continue. In the end, when he failed, the failure stripped any faith in the government that he had once possessed.

THE STRUGGLE FOR THE RETURN OF BENEVOLENT AND REASONED GOVERNANCE

As Taiwan-based political scientist Chih-Yu Shih has pointed out, the moral framework and the shared moral symbolism through which rural people learned about authority, responsibility, and virtuous conduct was thrown into crisis in the Maoist era. The decline of moral leadership in China actually was inherent in the Mao-led Communist movement, but, as Shih has argued, it accelerated on a vast scale in the Great Leap Forward (not the Cultural Revolution),[70] for it was in the Great Leap that the perversion, corruption, and violence that were part of the DNA of the Mao-led Chinese Communist Party (CCP) were unleashed in the countryside. The Confucian ideal that leaders should conduct themselves as good *en ren*, or benefactors, and should uphold, through everyday practice, codes of virtuous conduct was lost in the Great Leap and its famine. Da Fo's teachers welcomed the reformist agenda of Deng Xiaoping because they wanted to change this climate and restore the moral order that Bao Zhilong and his ignorant and immoral party clients had all but destroyed in the Great Leap and its turbulent aftermath.

In Da Fo, the moral pretense of the Maoists had nothing in common with the customary moral codes of conduct to which the Republican-era village elite had subscribed. From the end of the Great Leap, Da Fo's teachers had been waiting for a chance to separate from the institutionalized, dominant Communist Party vandalism and savagery that followed the Leap famine and its tragic spinoff – Mao's Great Proletarian Cultural Revolution. The Deng reform gave them the chance to openly initiate this separation and reverse the course of Maoist degeneration. From 1982 until 1995 and increasingly thereafter, small groups of Da Fo teachers began to step forth to challenge the conduct of village party leaders, and thus to present themselves as newly enlightened local elites who could offer an alternative to the incompetence and insensitivity of Bao Zhilong and the party leaders who had taken advantage of villagers in the past.

[70] See Shih, "Decline of a Moral Regime," 275.

They were aware this would not be an easy task. The conduct of Da Fo party leaders was habitual, embedded, and tethered to their performance in Mao's great disaster; it was not simply or merely the product of a "policy cycle."[71]

Seeking to reclaim the mantle of moral leadership through both education and example, Da Fo's teachers focused on raising popular consciousness of several precepts of virtuous rule, and they repeatedly informed Bao Zhilong and the Da Fo village party secretaries who followed in his steps they would hold them to such precepts. To begin with, they insisted that leaders should rule through benevolent moral conduct, just as the scholarship of distinguished China historian John King Fairbank would anticipate.[72] *Catastrophe and Contention in Rural China* demonstrated that Da Fo's pre-1949 educated and open-minded "first-pole" returning teachers who became Communist Party leaders had a history of benevolent conduct.[73] Many villagers saw them as patrons on whom they could depend in difficult times. In the mid-1990s, Da Fo's teachers were intent upon reviving this tradition. Many of them drew from their own salaries to assist villagers who were in need of help. Pang Lianggui and several other teachers gave money toward the cost of school tuition to children whose households were too poor to pay, for example. Bao Chenxia, another teacher, helped students acquire pens and notebooks.[74]

Above all, the teachers of Da Fo's school strove to be role models simply by working hard for their students. They took teaching seriously and were proud that their students ranked in the top 1–2 percent in the exams administered by the Liangmen Township and Dongle County Education Bureaus. Their teaching did not stop in the classroom, moreover. They encouraged students to be good people and to be kind to others. It seems that the memory of the past, when the Da Fo party leaders had abandoned humane conduct and embraced the savagery of the Maoist Leap, was a factor motivating this revival of compassion and charity. Pang Lianggui spoke of making up for the "lost years" by helping schoolchildren whose families could not spend as much time as needed with them, remembering with painful regret that he had been unable to care for his own son in the Great Leap because he had to spend almost all of his time working in the collective fields.[75] Da Fo's teachers frequently admonished party leaders for not caring enough about the village school and not doing enough to help students with the most pressing of needs, including schoolroom space and essential school facilities. (When I first visited this village in 1989, its schoolrooms were devoid of desks and chairs, and its roofs leaked rain onto students and teachers. This neglect began with the deterioration of the schoolhouse in the Great Leap and continued for nearly a decade after the commencement of reform.)

---

[71] On this point they would agree with ibid., 289–291.
[72] See Fairbank, *United States and China*, 59, and Shih, "Decline of a Moral Regime," 273.
[73] Thaxton, *Catastrophe and Contention*, chapters 1 and 2.   [74] Pang Lianggui, interview.
[75] Ibid.

After Bao Sheping replaced the old Maoist principal in 1998, the generosity of the teachers took on a collective dimension and was extended to other teachers in and beyond their own circle. When teacher Pang Chunhai broke his leg, all of the faculty helped pay his medical bills; they also sent money to a sick teacher in Beiba village. When disaster struck different parts of China, Da Fo's teachers thought of their countrymen: during the severe acute respiratory syndrome (SARS) crisis, every teacher contributed 20 yuan to help the government stem the epidemic.[76] Bao Sheping worked to secure money for upgrading the school from an outside educational foundation and from the Puyang city government, and Bao and his teachers helped rebuild derelict classrooms, plant trees, and pave village roads.

In addition to demonstrating generosity, Da Fo's teachers insisted on recovering the pluralist discourse that had been lost to the furious intolerance of Mao years. Most of them voiced strong preferences for the right to express divergent ideas. According to Bao Zhongxin, by the end of the Mao era, "Confucian ideas and ethics were no longer [all that] important in China. Actually, however, we still teach some Confucian ideas to our students, such as 'I can learn something from a group of three people.' This Confucian idea is right. Different people know different things, and we should be prepared to learn from anyone who knows something we do not. This is a reasonable attitude, and we want our students to adopt this kind of attitude."[77]

One particular memory of Mao-era intolerance fed this yearning for pluralist discourse. It concerned Bao Yingqing. A graduate of Dongle County Teacher's Training School in the late 1940s, Bao Yingqing had taken a teaching position in Xinglong, where he had become an outstanding teacher by the early 1950s. When Mao encouraged teachers to speak their minds in the Hundred Flowers Campaign of 1957, Bao made a remark in his classroom that "the United States had a longer system of railway track than China." On catching wind of this remark, the Mao-influenced principal, Bao Chengling, accused Bao of "admiring American imperialism," and during the abrupt change that ushered in the antirightist campaign of 1957–1958, Bao Yingqing was labeled a rightist. He suffered from this label all through the Great Leap.[78]

By 2001, the Confucian concept of honesty was being revived and emphasized in some of China's most prestigious universities, reflecting the determination of presidents, deans, and some faculty members to deal a serious blow to the habitual lying that had ruined state and society in the Maoist era. There is no evidence that this movement back toward honesty found its way down the educational hierarchy into Da Fo. But, by the same token, Da Fo's teachers struck up their own unofficial campaign to promote honesty as a primary virtue in leadership and governance. Of all the values that mobilized their passions, honesty seemed near the top of the list. One aspect of Great Leap–style

[76] Pang Yingfang, interview.   [77] Bao Zhongxin, interview.   [78] Ibid.

dishonesty reappeared in the process of educational reform: this was the official pressure to falsify records in order to exaggerate school development. This pressure recalled the *fukua feng*, or wind of exaggeration, that had been a major factor in turning the Great Leap into a disaster.[79]

In 1998, for instance, Henan provincial education leaders came to Liangmen township to push the Central government's nine-year compulsory education policy.[80] Subsequently, all schoolteachers in Da Fo village and other Liangmen township villages were asked to participate in falsifying records to demonstrate the township had achieved compulsory education. In Da Fo, as in other villages, a full semester was wasted on falsifying such records, as both Dongle county and Liangmen township leaders ordered village teachers to lie to Henan provincial government officials about dropout and graduation rates. Teachers also were pressed to say they were paid in a timely fashion each month, even though their paychecks were not showing up. Anyone who told the truth was fired and left to find a market for his labor outside the teaching profession, just as dissenting teachers who spoke the truth about inflated harvest yields, inadequate food provisions, and hungry absentee students in the Great Leap period had been penalized with dismissal and exiled to labor camps. Furthermore, these same township education officials attempted to turn the Henan provincial government compulsory education campaign into a cash cow, requiring each Da Fo student to pay 25 yuan for education equipment needed to meet its requirements. Da Fo's teachers saw the township party leaders as shameless degenerates, a judgment they and their predecessors had bestowed on the commune-level party leaders in the Great Leap Forward.

In the Great Leap, diligence and careful attention to detail had been overthrown for carelessly imagined large-scale projects and quick leaps into fast-paced production. Under the leadership of Bao Zhilong, the "bigger is better" ideology of the Maoists replaced the small arts of household agriculture with a careless frenzy to take over more land and produce more grain for the commune-based arm of the Maoist state, the folly of which culminated in the waste associated with "shooting up satellites" and the production of more poverty and suffering. As I documented in *Catastrophe and Contention in Rural China*, Da Fo's Maoists silenced village party leaders, teachers, and farmers who advised caution in deep plowing, well digging, and diverting skilled tillers to the work camps associated with the Great Leap campaign to industrialize the countryside. And throughout the Great Leap, party boss Bao Zhilong and his comrades were oblivious to the Confucian wisdom (and common sense) that

---

[79] For the seminal insight on this, see Bernstein, "Stalinism, Famine, and Chinese Peasants," and for confirmation, see Lu, "Weixing Shi Ruhe de Shang Tiande," and Yang, *Tombstone*. Also see Xu, "Erecting a Tombstone," 100.

[80] On official chicanery with the nine-year compulsory education policy, Cf. Rosen, "State of Youth," 166–167.

to take on more than can be managed is to invite carelessness, irresponsibility, and failure.[81]

In Da Fo, the durable memory of the social consequences of the careless "shooting up of satellites" coexisted with teachers' desire to the return to diligence and to strive for small, day-by-day classroom gains. Just why this was the case is not so hard to fathom, for to many teachers "spectacular Maoism" was synonymous with great suffering – and death. Bao Jingsheng underscored this point when he recalled:

Nobody in my family died during the Great Leap Forward. However, we did not have enough to eat, and yet we still had to work harder than normal. At the time the local leaders called on us to "launch satellites," which meant to achieve unusual accomplishments. They called on the teachers to participate in the steel making campaign. Those who had wheelbarrows were required to transport iron ore over bad mountain roads to Shire, in Lin county. We were there for four and a half months. We did not sleep much at night, and we did not get the wheat bread they promised us.[82]

The recovery of diligence was an important goal for Da Fo's teachers in the post-Mao era. They purposely reengaged village leaders and villagers in everyday conversations, both inside and outside the school, about the wisest approaches to crop development and management of their saline ecosystem. They emphasized that the rise of wheat and corn yields from late-collective-era highs of approximately 300–350 *jin* per *mu* to 600, 800, and then 1,000 *jin* per *mu* in the early 1990s was the result of recovering the arts of soil management (carefully applying time, labor, and enriched compost to familiar small plots of land) that had been neglected in the Great Leap era. Referring to the impetuous, careless well-digging scheme of Great Leap party boss Bao Zhilong, Bao Qiaoai, one of the village's most respected teachers, said, "The most crucial factor is that we have enough water and fertilizers. During the collective era, we dug shallow wells. However, when there was a drought and we needed to irrigate the fields, the wells ran dry. We did not possess the knowledge or the equipment to dig the wells deep then. But today we can dig the wells over one hundred meters deep, and there is always water in the well; and chemical fertilizers are widely available."[83] This teacher–villager discourse on the importance of diligence in crop land management became a counterpoint to reliance on Da Fo Communist Party leaders who, in the late 1990s as in the Great Leap era, were known to carelessly disseminate information about seed selection and chemical fertilizer via quick drive-by megaphone pronouncements.

---

[81] For this wisdom, see Ebrey, "On Farming," 188.   [82] Bao Jingsheng, interview.
[83] Bao Qiaoai, interview. As we learned in Chapter 1, chemical fertilizers were not widely available to ordinary farmers in the first years of reform, and the consequences of the failure of the state to make them available at the outset of the leap into capitalist-style market economy were destructive for many tillers.

Da Fo's teachers also were successful in behaving as diligent professionals for their students. Two changes made this possible. After 1990, teachers were no longer chosen by the village party leaders. Graduates of teacher training schools in China's northern interior, they were by and large free to teach students to think for themselves within the parameters of a depoliticized academic curriculum (which nonetheless excluded the history of the Leap famine), and some taught students not to blindly copy others. Increasingly, the monogenetic ideology of Maoist production achievements was discarded for the intellectual development of the individual student, with payoffs for productive teachers. In addition, teachers were charged with giving care to their own development, so that they could better serve their students. Still required to study government policies and documents, the purpose of this study changed in the Deng era. "We had to understand the government educational policies," said Bao Chenxia, a fifty-six-year-old graduate of Puyang Teacher's Training School, "and we had to do this to improve our teaching."[84] From 1990 on, teachers focused on the arts of diligent study, and innovative teaching methods gained momentum, the purpose of which, according to Bao, was to challenge students in the classroom and enable them to score in the top tier of Liangmen township examinations.

The post-Mao period also witnessed a revival of respect for open, fair-minded learning and for the wisdom of well-educated members of the village. Da Fo's teachers more and more frequently drew on their own understandings of Confucian norms to combat the Maoist practices that had undermined the shared quest for truth and the integrity of each individual: the public criticism session of the Great Leap Forward and the big-character poster of the Cultural Revolution. During the Great Leap, the public criticism session had more or less replaced the village schoolhouse (which party cadres had reconfigured for use as a public dining hall) as the arena in which formal learning took place. In the new Maoist "school arena," Da Fo's party leaders not only were intolerant of teachers who questioned the pitfalls of the collective, they also made false accusations against those who doubted their understanding of the virtues of Maoist doctrine. Bao Yingjie, who remembers that teachers had a hard time during the Great Leap because they did not have enough to eat and were subjected to indignities, like cleaning the dirt toilets, voiced support for Deng Xiaoping's move to discontinue the public whip of Maoist terror: "The leaders today are better than those during the Great Leap Forward. They do not debate people by public criticism, and they leave people alone most of the time."[85]

In the reform era, Da Fo's teachers rejected the politics that made it impossible for locally educated people to speak their own minds about center policy without becoming the targets of the defamations that poisoned Mao-era

---

[84] Bao Chenxia, interview.   [85] Bao Yingjie, interview.

relationships with power. To be sure, some teachers expressed ambivalence about the end of the Mao-led revolt of the masses, but they also understood the dangerous nuances of this revolt. Wei Dongmei dispelled the Maoist myth that the big-character poster had infused "democracy" into the Cultural Revolution and entailed a popular, risk-free process of discourse:

During the Great Leap Forward, there were people who were labeled rightists because they criticized the government leaders. They were labeled rightists because the Central government allowed them to be labeled. Today, they would not label us that way. It was a little bit different in the Cultural Revolution, when the government encouraged people to criticize their leaders. We could write big-character posters to anonymously criticize our leaders. But even that was not risk free. If you caused your leaders trouble, the leaders would deal with you one way or another.

I do not know how to judge Deng Xiaoping's decision to repeal the right to write big-character posters. When people had the right to write the posters, the officials could not abuse their power. But, at the same time, people could use the posters against people like me. Today, people no longer can use big-character posters, and I do not need to worry that my students would use it against me.[86]

Virtually all of Da Fo's teachers were hurt by local party leaders corrupted by the Communist Party's taste of absolute power in the Great Leap. They knew that the big-character poster of the Cultural Revolution was just another pretext for advancing the cause of Maoist fundamentalism against those who spoke for a variety of folk beliefs over the uniformity of Maoist propaganda and for the integrity of individuals over the Maoist abstraction of class enemies.[87] Many of Da Fo's teachers cheered the Deng Xiaoping attempt to stop the anti-Confucian, antihumanitarian Cultural Revolution practice of slandering those who were educated. Bao Huajie was voicing the bitter memory of the great majority when he said: "I think that it was a good thing that Deng Xiaoping abolished the big-character posters. The big-character posters could easily ruin someone's reputation. We do not need to worry about big-character posters today."[88]

Even the Da Fo teachers who did not actively endorse the struggle of the reformers against slanderous Maoism still preferred more free speech. Speaking of Deng's decision to remove the big-character posters, Bao Zhongxin declared, "It was wrong to stop people from airing their opinions. I am for people's right to use whatever forms they can invent to air their opinions against leaders. When America invaded Iraq, all other countries had demonstrations against the U.S. government, but the Chinese government did not allow its people to demonstrate."[89]

---

[86] Wei Dongmei, interview.

[87] On this point, I am indebted to Scott's lead in "Hegemony and the Peasantry," and to Thurston, *Enemies of the People*, 55–95.

[88] Bao Huajie, interview.   [89] Bao Zhongxin, interview.

THE QUALIFIED LOYALTY OF RELUCTANT REBELS

Some China scholars argue that the development of rural educational institutions during the late Mao era laid the foundations for the economic progress and social uplift of the early reform era, which Deng Xiaoping undercut by dismantling the collective foundations of rural education.[90] If we take a close look at the relationship between rural schooling and occupational success for the first generation of post–Great Leap famine school-age children in Da Fo – those who were approximately ten to thirteen years old in the 1972–1975 period – a somewhat different picture emerges. On the one hand, the post-Mao Central government neglect of Mao-era school arrangements did not always seriously affect the life chances of the children who had received a middle-school education. Many of Da Fo's middle-school graduates went on to find a future in the evolving political economy of reform at local, regional, and national levels. As of 2004, Bao Sheping, the son of Bao Zhongxin, was the Da Fo school principal. Bao Junli, the daughter of Bao Wenfang, had graduated from Sangqiu Teacher's College to become a teacher in Shangcunji middle school.[91] Middle-school graduate Bao Jinlin, the son of Bao Zhenmin, had found a job in the Songcun Credit Association, while his brother Bao Jingru had secured work in the Dongle County Police Department.[92] Bao Xianzhi, the son of Bao Mingxian, had become the vice-director of the Dongle County People's Hospital.[93] The list goes on. The interview data indicate that many of these reform-era "winners" were connected, even if only minimally, to evolving Communist Party networks of power[94] and had relied on historical ties to the party to weather the worst storms of Maoist rule. Most of these winners honored Da Fo's teachers and had a stake in educational reform.

On the other hand, the oral history interviews reveal a strong countertrend. Apparently, the neglect of rural education in the reform period compounded the desperate situation of many young villagers whose families had barely survived the Maoist disaster, and this neglect put them at odds with the post-Mao order. I met up with this countertrend in the summer of 1993, while traveling from Anyang City to Dongle county town. Around ten o'clock in the morning on August 26, 1993, the 1950 vintage Russian vehicle in which I was traveling was stopped by three young highway brigands who were posing as members of the traffic police. They demanded money in exchange for passage over the bridge linking Chu Wang town in Neihuang county with Dongle county and Da Fo village. Unfortunately, the young, spunky Chinese driver of my vehicle sprang out of his seat and challenged the highway brigands to a fistfight, bringing me face to face with my cowardice. I feared I had seen my last

[90] Han, *Unknown Cultural Revolution.*   [91] Bao Wenfang, interview.
[92] Bao Zhenmin, interview.   [93] Bao Sheping, interview.
[94] As Friedman, Pickowicz, and Selden found for Wu Gong. *Revolution, Resistance, and Reform,* 262.

day on earth. Fortunately, the confrontation was eventually defused with peace offerings of cigarettes. What happened after this mid-morning interruption of my usual Beijing–Da Fo travel routine was even more eye opening. On arriving at the Dongle county seat and joining the Communist Party–appointed county magistrate and his staff for a noontime banquet, I mentioned the youthful highway bandits to the magistrate. He quickly dismissed the incident as if it had been an exceptional bleep in a new world of ordered reform, declaring that he, in any event, had little power over the rise of highway brigandage – a phenomenon that agitated the teachers in Da Fo village – and he made no mention that for uneducated youth, crime was an optimal strategy of survival, as law enforcement was lax or could be bought off.

The three highway brigands were school dropouts. Their turn to rural crime was predictable, for they had no degree credentials, no skills, no competencies, and no station in life that would allow them to become productive villagers able to take care of themselves, enter into marriage, and settle down as farmers with commitment to family, village, and community. The rural schools of both the late Mao era and the early Deng era had failed these young outlaws. In Da Fo, as in scores of other villages in Dongle county, undereducated primary-school and middle-school dropouts followed a similar course, turning to a host of rural criminal activities in order to survive. In more than a few cases, they had entered into crime only in an effort to garner enough money to give themselves and their families a chance to live a normal life within the village.

By 2000, rural China's system of public village education had become the Achilles' heel of the post-Mao economic reform, further complicating the prospect for a democratic future. In Chapter 1, we saw that the first long, rising wave of youth crime was complex and that it crashed down on Da Fo and its sister villages in the first decade of reform, posing a threat to everyday safety and order for Da Fo's teachers, petty traders, and farmers. Da Fo's teachers were upset and alarmed because they knew that if the reform-era rural education system failed, then another wave of youth crime would follow. By 2000, another wave was indeed in the making, posing a challenge for both local society and the local police. This wave of everyday crime threatened Da Fo inhabitants' ability to protect their personal property and to receive relatives and friends from other villages. Forty-six-year-old Bao Huajie, a graduate of Dongle County Teacher's School, spoke of this latest wave when he complained: "We have had a lot of crime in the village. Many people have lost oxen, motor carts, and grain to thieves, and people feel insecure in the village. Three to four years ago, in 2000, people did not dare to walk on village streets. At that time, one of my relatives, a twenty-six-year-old woman, was coming back to Da Fo and she was robbed in the fields outside of our village."[95]

---

[95] Bao Huajie, interview.

Rural crime apparently made it difficult for the teachers to fulfill their professional mission, especially their goal of reversing the moral degeneration of the Maoist era. Wei Dongmei, a fifty-three-year-old female teacher in Da Fo, made this point: "We always teach our students to be honest, to not lie, and to assist those in need of help. We teach our students not to engage in any illegal or immoral activities. However, we are not always effective. We are only one force; and there are many other forces at work in educating students. Sometimes, the other forces can be more powerful than us."[96] Bao Jingsheng echoed this local knowledge when he said: "Teachers have attempted to teach students to be honest. But teachers' influence on students is very limited in today's world, and the students have many bad examples they can learn from society. The criminals and corrupt officials are educating students and the younger generation of villagers in their own way."[97]

Pang Jinshan was one of Da Fo's young criminal magnates. By 2001, Pang, who was notorious for kidnapping and selling women, had become a thorn in the side of the Dongle county police. The police feared Pang, in part because he had built a huge following among young people and in part Bao Yinbao, the alleged leader of a "black gang" (*hei bang*) in Dongle county, showed young people that it was possible to continuously engage in drinking, banqueting, and frequenting prostitutes in Dongle county town without having graduated from middle school, high school, or college and without doing any work.[98]

By 2000, a growing number of Da Fo's young criminals were on the most-wanted list of the local police. They were "targeted people" in the computer-based data files of the Ministry of Public Security *hukou* police, who attempted to tighten control over suspected criminals after the Tiananmen uprising.[99] Da Fo's teachers were uneasy with this process, because the police expected them, as government servants, to act as public security informants at the village level, where party-state monitoring was relatively weak. This official expectation implicated the teachers in the unpopular practice of controlling the movement of the poorest, least secure members of the village – a practice that had been responsible for restricting the mobility of disentitled and desperate villagers in the Great Leap and its aftermath. Da Fo's teachers did not want to be implicated in inhibiting the freedom of such targeted criminals, for the teachers understood that the fate of these young people was tied up with the failure of Communist Party leaders to provide them with an alternative to a life of hardship, uncertainty, and crime – that is, to provide them with an education. Nonetheless, the teachers had little choice in the matter, because any suggestion that they were not on the side of "stable order" – that somehow they might shield targeted elements by withholding

---

[96] Wei Dongmei, interview.   [97] Bao Jingsheng, interview.   [98] Bao Qingchao, interview.
[99] Cf. Wang, "Reformed Migration Control," 126–127.

information – would risk a police investigation and thus possibly jeopardize their most treasured gain under the post-Mao reform: the ability of their dependants to garner state-based employment and hence to be granted urban *hukou*, the permits that gave them a chance to find greater security and success in relatively prosperous cities.

By 2000, the children of many of Da Fo's teachers had graduated from middle schools, high schools, and professional schools to find state employment or government-connected jobs. They had become middle-school teachers, county government clerks, education-bureau staff, and public security officers in Dongle county town, Puyang city, and Anyang. Some had become construction company managers or construction workers in cities like Zhengzhou, Tianjin, and Beijing, a few having secured jobs in Chinese construction companies operating in Saudi Arabia, Africa, and Latin America (in some cases earning 100,000–150,000 yuan per year). One took a degree from the Henan Jiaozhou Mining School to start up a gemstone business in Zhengzhou, another from the Zhengzhou Railway Technology School to join the China Railway Tunnel Construction Company in Zhengzhou, another from the Henan Teacher's College to win a teaching position in the Henan College of Science and Engineering in Xinyang, another from the Changsha Central South Technology University to become Bureau Chief of Puyang City's New Hi-Tech District, another from the Henan Medical College in Kaifeng to become a physician in Kaifeng, and another from the Zhengzhou College of Technology to serve in the Dongle County Electricity Bureau. Others had experienced an even more extraordinary ascent: Da Fo's Pang Zhong, the son of Pang Zhangling, had graduated from Liangmen high school, taken a PhD in the PLA Commander's Training College (*zhihui xueyuan*) in Nanjing, and then risen to Commander of the PLA Division Headquarters of the Shenyang Military District.[100] Predictably, these young adults' Da Fo–based parents, who had sacrificed to enable their ascent and its promised advantages – better housing arrangements, marriage proposals, better health care, and the chance for their grandchildren to go to high school and even college – were not about to put it at risk by failing to cooperate with the public security probes of village criminals and fugitives.[101]

In this and other ways, Da Fo's teachers and some of their ascendant students were tethered to, and served, the reform era party-state. They constituted about 2 percent of Da Fo's inhabitants, but they were an important, seemingly obedient local subgroup. At least half of them were members of the Communist Party, and they facilitated its agenda by calling upon farmers to

[100] Pang Zhangling, interview.
[101] For a strong statement to this effect, see Bao Yutang, interview. For an account of just how much parents have sacrificed to help their children with this ascent and of the danger of having this educational-based ascent ruined by association with criminal youth, see Chen, *Colors of the Mountain*.

pay their grain taxes, writing slogans to promote birth planning, and pressing villagers to fill in the forms for compulsory education.[102] Materially speaking, life had improved for many of Da Fo's teachers in the post-Mao era. By 2000, most were far better off than their Great Leap–era counterparts – some of them earned fourteen times more income than teachers made in the Great Leap, at least seven times more income than the contemporary village party secretary, and a tad more than the official salary of the head of the Liangmen township government. Further, they were assigned to their positions and paid by the Dongle county government, and thus no longer vulnerable to dismissal on ideological grounds, as had been the case in the Great Leap and the late Mao era. Hence, as elucidated by Suzanne Ogden's insightful scholarship, Da Fo's teachers, like Chinese intellectuals in society at large, wanted to be included in the establishment because the party-state held and dispensed the funds they needed for survival.[103] Not everyone celebrated this inclusion, however. Along with their counterparts in Dingcun, some of Da Fo's farmers resented its teachers. They complained about government officials not doing anything to help ordinary villagers, and when teachers argued that Deng Xiaoping's methods were good, they argued back, declaring that Deng was good for them only because their salaries had been raised so high.[104]

In comparison with ordinary farmers, therefore, Da Fo's teachers apparently had not completely lost faith in the Communist Party, and they were more than willing to give the official agents of reform a chance. They did not always join angry farmers in their Orwellian rantings about the "pigs" in Liangmen township government. Many were on the same page with Pang Yingfang, a fifty-two-year-old graduate of Dongle Teacher's Training School, who said, "I do not agree that the township government leaders are like pigs. If that were true, then all people who did not work manually like farmers would be pigs. I still think that most township government leaders are good people, and their jobs are important and difficult."[105] Fearing the conception of the state as a piggish force might revive contentious memories rooted in the predatory Maoist past, Pang Yingfang spoke for the majority of teachers: "Teachers in our village are 'the best citizens of the state.' They work hard, and they obey laws. We talk about the importance of obeying the government in class and to individual students outside the classroom."[106]

If crime were to feed into banditry and rebellion, then the party-state that provided Da Fo's teachers with job security and impressive salaries could be seriously challenged, forcing them to choose between a corrupted and stalled reform – and the disorder it, in combination with the powerful heritage of the Maoist past – had spawned and the uncertainty of rebellion. For many, rebellion seemed an unacceptable choice. "We teachers are not rebels," says Wei

---

[102] Bao Huajie, interview.   [103] Ogden, *Inklings of Democracy*, 322.
[104] Zhang Junfa, interview.   [105] Pang Yingfang, interview.   [106] Ibid.

Dongmei. "We have benefited from the status quo. I do not like Revolution. Revolution will not do any good for China."[107]

Precisely because Da Fo's teachers wanted to preserve the gains of reform – precisely because they, as students of Communist Party history, knew that rural schoolteachers had been forced to make a choice between the Nationalist Party and the Communist Party in the pre-1949 period and that the choice, while beneficial in the short run, proved disastrous after the Mao-led revolution was in power – they almost always voiced support for the policies issued by the central party-state. Many publicly declared that a good citizen should go along with government policy, even when it is not necessarily right for his or her interest. "China is a big country. We cannot just obey the policies that are suitable for us," remarked Pang Yingfang. "We have to obey them all. Whatever the state wants us to do, we normally must do it."[108]

But why did Pang Yingfang insert the word "normally" in this homage to power? Pang knew, as all of Da Fo's teachers do, that within the village their privileged relationship to state power was compromised by a well-known abnormality: many of Da Fo's farmers had voiced support for a rebellion against Da Fo party leaders and their superiors in Liangmen township. Farmers no longer associated the lowest formal tier of the party-state with benevolent order. Instead, they equated it with predatory corruption and with the insecurity and crime that awaited so many of their underschooled and unfortunate children. To be sure, as late as 2005, the "best citizens of the state" professed loyalty to the Central government, and they endorsed the center's rhetorical support for village and township elections in the hope that Da Fo might achieve a democratic transition that would prevent crime from feeding into banditry and possibly becoming entwined with rebellion and insurgency. Nonetheless, teacher cynicism over crime, and the perception that corruption within the hierarchy of the central party-state had cued, and thus caused, corruption at the county, township, and village levels, weakened their trust in single-party rule. This, in combination with the teachers' valuing of critical thinking and pluralist discourse, neither of which China's authoritarian rulers appreciated, sharpened the contradiction at work in their identity as servants of the party-state within the village,[109] encouraging them to voice thoughts they otherwise might have kept to themselves. Thus, teacher Wei Dongmei was hedging her bets when she said, in reference to teacher support for state policy, "I believe that teachers should follow government policies even if the policies disagree with our interest."[110]

Actually, teachers did more than drag their feet. As the corrupted private takeover of rural public education continued, many principals of Liangmen township public schools came under pressure from teacher exodus to private

---

[107] Wei Dongmei, interview.   [108] Pang Yingfang, interview.
[109] I am indebted to Ogden for helping me better grasp this point. See *Inklings of Democracy*, 288.
[110] Wei Dongmei, interview.

schools, and hence from declining student enrollments, which in turn meant they lost government funding for their schools. In mid-2009, the principals struck back. When a private school from eastern Dongle county sent a car to the Liangmen township villages to advertise its school with loudspeakers, slogans, and banners, the principal of Liangmen village school, Deng Zhihu, gathered ten principals in the township to attack the vehicle. They tore away its banners and damaged the car badly. The police were called to investigate, and a Dingcun village shepherd who had witnessed the incident came forth to implicate the principal of Dingcun, whereupon Deng Zhihu advised all of the principals to flee. The Dongle county government was compelled to negotiate the sticky situation. The "best citizens of the state" were implicated in a serious crime, which actually was the product of anger over the corrupt ruse of Huang Xiangjun, the Dongle county Education Bureau chief, who was using privatization to fatten himself and his cronies. To hush up the incident, the Liangmen township government was ordered to cover the cost of the damages; the police persuaded the private school to drop charges against the principals; and the township leaders also paid for the expenses the principals had suffered while in hiding.[111] Following this incident, the conflict over Central government policy sharpened, and teachers grew ever more distrustful of greedy, deceitful local government leaders. Increasingly, they shared political sentiments that could not be found in public exchanges about the Communist Party's system of rule. Bao Jingsheng was expressing such when he echoed this hedged loyalty to the party-state: "Some people called the Liangmen township government leaders 'pigs.' The township leaders were supposed to make life better for farmers. But they did not do a good job. While it may be true that they behave like pigs, people should not say this publicly."[112]

There are many things Da Fo's teachers, and the parents of their prized students, were reluctant to express publicly, including their disdain for the idea that the one party-state is a political meritocracy run by leaders who share their dream for a better life.[113] Clearly, what was good for the upper-level party leaders was not good for teachers and their students, or so they intimated. They did not see Dongle county Education Bureau leaders, such as Huang Xiangjun, as qualified, competent, virtuous public servants, standing above corruption, fraud, and vice. Their repulsion and anger with these leaders extended upward, suggesting that popular support for the ideal of an authoritarian political meritocracy crashed against the actual practices of unaccountable big shots with ties to Beijing. In 2007, for example, the Chief of the national State Food and Drug Administration, Zheng Xiaoyu, was sentenced to death for issuing licenses for sale of fake medicines and defective medical equipment after receiving substantial bribes from the illegal manufacturers – an abuse of office that

---

[111] Tan Zedong, interview.   [112] Bao Jingsheng, interview.
[113] For this view, see Bell, "What America's Flawed Democracy Could Learn"; Compare with Minxin Pei, "The Myth of Chinese Meritocracy."

resulted in deaths of people not only in China but also in countries to which the faulty products were exported.[114] Da Fo's teachers, and the parents of rising students, applauded the sentence, for they understood that Zheng, who had risen through the ranks of the state-owned pharmaceutical companies, had been corrupted by the kleptocratic system that he had pledged to reform.[115] In this latter case, as with the case of Huang Xianjun, the avaricious official who turned the Dongle county Education Bureau into his own jackpot, villagers guardedly expressed contemptuous sentiments for the so-called public servants appointed by the CCP, and were unhappy that the center had not addressed the systemic corruption enveloping its reform.

– – –

The heritage of the Great Leap disaster left many teachers in the Da Fo area in deep poverty, and material recovery under the Mao-led party-state was a long ordeal, with little if any support from the government for teacher well-being or skill improvement. Post-Leap salaries were paltry, and they remained low and put teachers at risk in the early post-Mao decades. Though teachers were angry over government mistreatment, their memory of the Mao-era fate of "rightists" remained powerful, making them reluctant to stand up for their rights. Nonetheless, teachers increasingly turned to protest under reform, striking and petitioning for back pay and just pensions. Within the village, a day-by-day struggle to replace the old-guard Maoist principal unfolded – a struggle influenced by memory of the principal's misdeeds in the Great Leap. Da Fo's teachers wanted to restore Confucian moral order, and they preferred to practice generosity, tolerance for different viewpoints, kindness, and honesty in relations with villagers and higher-ups. Yet the latter was not an easy task under China's corrupt single-party system of rule.

The fate of Da Fo bears similarities to that of the pre-1910 Mexican village depicted in B. Traven's jungle novel, *Government*.[116] Ruled by baseborn, unethical, and conniving petty bureaucrats, the Mexican Indian villagers suffer under small-fry secretaries who abuse their students, falsify reports intended to facilitate the federal mandate of universal literacy, and turn the local school into a self-serving racket – practices familiar to villagers in Da Fo. There were differences, however. In the case of post-1978 Da Fo, many of the party leaders profiteering from such "governance" were the agents of a state-building process that had ruined the lives of teachers and students. The plight of Da Fo villagers in the reform era invited resistance because the politics of rural education reflected the antagonistic state–society relationship that formed in the Great Leap attack on knowledge, because the schools were still

---

[114] On this point, see "Former SFDA Chief Executed for Corruption" and, better yet, Black, "China Ex-Food and Drug Safety Chief Sentenced to Death."

[115] Bao Yutang, interview.   [116] Traven, *Government*.

influenced by party leaders implicated in the Leap disaster, and because the Deng-led center did not support parental desires to overcome the debilitating legacies of the great famine through improved access to rural schools. Also, unlike rural Mexico after 1910, when the triumphant Constitutionalists made rural schools "the arena for ... negotiations over power, culture, and knowledge" and empowered teachers to win villagers over to a regime-supportive national identity by enlisting them in efforts to promote academies, trade unions, and civic festivities,[117] Mao's Communist Revolution placed schools in the hands of corrupt fanatics, and the post-Mao reformers failed to transform rural schools in ways that persuaded a majority of villagers they could gain from party-guided development and regime continuity.

On the face of it, Da Fo's teachers were loyal to the Deng-led party-state, and many of them benefited from reform, which seems to have been integrating them into China's apartheid political economy, with its perks and privileges. Indeed, they paid homage to power, and they collaborated with public security. Yet they also had serious qualms about reform, especially the rising wave of rural crime and official corruption. They understood their fate was interwoven not only with the formal structure of increasingly hollow village and township Communist Party governance but also with the informal community networks of family, friends, and farmers with whom they interacted daily. Their great fear was that the rise of crime – which they attributed to center policy failures and high-state corruption, not just to the culture of local party leaders – would leave them no choice but to break with the central party-state and collaborate with popular stirrings against official corruption. In reality, Da Fo's teachers and farmers feared the problem of institutionalized corruption might lead rural China into another great disaster. It is to the problem of corruption that we now turn.

---

[117] See Vaughan, *Cultural Politics in Revolution*, chapter 1.

5

Official Corruption and Popular Contention in the Reform Era

At the turn of the twenty-first century, the central problem facing Da Fo villagers was political corruption. Hu Jintao, the chairman of the Chinese Communist Party (CCP), visited Xibaipo village in Hebei province in December 2002, where he gave a passionate speech about the critical urgency of fighting corruption in China. According to one report, Hu subsequently stated in a special emergency meeting of the Politburo: "It is not a few local governments, but most of the local governments; it is not a few officials, but most of the officials who are corrupt and suppressing people with state power. Are they not forcing the people to rise up to overthrow the Communist Party?"[1] In *Origins of the Chinese Revolution*, Lucien Bianco reminds us that corruption – not simply social misery and the destabilizing consequences of the Japanese invasion – proved fatal to the Nationalist government.[2]

Some Da Fo farmers, including those who had supported Mao's pre-1949 insurgency, said the fate of the corrupt Communist Party would be the same as that of the Kuomintang. Worried about this possibility, and using corruption as a pretext to put his own clients in key positions, in 2013 Xi Jinping kicked off his presidency with a vow to pull out all stops in fighting official corruption. The ensuing offensive, reminiscent of Mao-era anticorruption campaigns, was orchestrated to present the supreme leader of the Communist

---

[1] Sheng, Liu, and Xie, "Linshu 'cunguan' Tuiwu Junren da Liucheng."

[2] Bianco, *Origins of the Chinese Revolution*, 195. On this point, also see Wright, *Promise of the Revolution*, 6. Perhaps more than any other political scientist, Oxford University–based scholar Vivienne Shue understands the critical importance of official corruption in the exit of the Kuomintang and in the growth of popular discontent with CCP rule. See Shue, "Legitimacy Crisis in China?," 35–36.

Party as a man of the people and, according to Andrew Wedeman, to "build legitimacy."[3]

Building legitimacy through campaigns that did little to actually change the corrupt habits of Mao-era rule was difficult, however. Beijing's failure to institute such change is an important reason why the post-Mao period, including the reign of Deng Xiaoping, saw an explosion of popular resistance to corruption. In the Liangmen township–Da Fo village area, this resistance was charged by memories of Communist Party rule in Mao's great famine. It seems that there was nothing like the outbreak of Deng-era corruption, and resistance to it, at play locally in the initial phase of post-Stalinist USSR politics. Why the difference?[4] For one thing, Nikita Khrushchev apparently ran a very tight ship. His party – and the KGB – relied on internal administration to regulate official corruption. In contrast, Deng and his men failed to revive the CCP central disciplinary committee, whose authority to root out corruption had been seriously compromised by Mao's support of arbitrary and brutal local party networks in the Great Leap episode. Indeed, this key committee was defunct in Dongle county and in the Liangmen–Da Fo area during the first fifteen years of reform. For another thing, de-Stalinization in the USSR was not accompanied by the rapid, unfettered monetization of the politial economy, as occurred in the People's Republic of China (PRC), where the Deng-led center urged local officials to get rich, and then allowed them to generate wealth by virtually any means possible. For yet another thing, Khrushchev retained collective agriculture and the state farm system, which helped check official corruption, but Deng disbanded the collective and switched to quasi-private forms of rural collective enterprise that, in Da Fo and elsewhere, opened up new opportunities for cadre malfeasance and jobbery, thereby reviving popular memories of the small forms of corruption that had exacerbated scarcity in the Great Leap. Resistance to corruption in Deng-era China also was influenced by the memory of the role of top-level leadership in past suffering, for, as stated previously, Deng was directly implicated in Mao's Leap famine. In contrast, Khrushchev, although charged with sending cadres to the countryside to actualize collectivization, was not directly implicated in Stalin's 1932–1933 terror famine, and after 1944 he had worked to put subsistence grain consumption on par with grain extraction for state goals, thereby altering the utterly ruthless pattern of Stalinist plunder in the rural interior.[5] Finally, Da Fo's history helps us

---

[3] Andrew Wedeman, "Eight Questions: Andrew Wedeman, China's Corruption Paradox"; Branigan, "Xi Jinping Vows to Fight 'Tigers' and 'Flies' in Anti-corruption Drive"; and Oster, "President Xi's Anti-Corruption Campaign Biggest since Mao."

[4] I am indebted to Mark R. Beissinger, Thomas P. Bernstein, and Steven I. Levine for providing some of the clues that helped guide the development of this comparison. Personal correspondence, June 1–10, 2014.

[5] Here I have relied on Alexander Pantsov, personal correspondence, June 11, 2012; on comments by Nicholas Werth, who more or less agrees that Khrushchev was not directly responsible for the 1932–1933 Stalinist famine (Conference on "Communism and Hunger," Holodomor Research

understand why resistance to corruption welled up so quickly in reform-era China. Whereas Khrushchev attempted to make the police more professional and "more accountatable to the community,"[6] Deng did little to upgrade the inexperienced local police forces replacing Mao-era militias. Consequently, corruption rapidly infected local police systems, and because the police were on the take and not fully invested in protecting the corrupt local party leftovers of the Mao period, villagers could resist such leaders without automatically triggering all-out police repression.

A PATTERN OF CORRUPTION

The corruption enveloping Da Fo village and Liangmen township in the reform period had its roots in a pattern of political decay that began with Maoist revolutionary mobilization in the 1950s. This pattern persisted into the era of post-Mao reform, giving village and township power holders the opportunity to plunder without penalty.[7] Corruption was also the product of the habitual work style of the commune and brigade CCP leaders who pushed the Great Leap Forward, a style that had crystallized during the Great Leap famine, when Bao Zhilong and his party-based clients took as much food as they needed from the public dining-hall kitchens, solicited gifts from production team leaders in return for exempting them from public criticism, and issued favorable job assignments to friends, clients, and cronies. Corruption persisted in part because the national-level CCP failed to reform its system of governance.[8] The Communist Party was especially remiss in creating disciplinary mechanisms for controlling the political corruption of its subcounty agents in the countryside.[9] Instead, corruption was sustained and encouraged by patron-client ties within the party-managed state.

With the death of Mao and the withdrawal of the Deng-led center's support for the commune, moreover, many subcounty party leaders began to fear that the ship of state was on the verge of collapse. The fear of losing power in the transition to reform gave impetus to an insatiable, aggravated form of corruption that was utterly oblivious to any notion of right or wrong.[10] Having no confidence that the Central government would last, key local party leaders increasingly aimed to squeeze as much as they could get from their appointed

and Education Consortium, CIUS, University of Toronto, September 26, 2014); on Gibney, "Nikita Sergeyevich Khrushchev,"; and on Hornsby, *Protest, Reform, and Repression in the Soviet Union*, 157, 178, 187–188.

[6] See Shelley, *Policing Soviet Society*, 38–39.   [7] Lu, *Cadres and Corruption*, 27–28, 611–663.

[8] Cf. Gilley, *China's Democratic Future*, 45.

[9] Sun, *Corruption and Market*, 160–161, 169–171.

[10] I am indebted to Felice F. Gaer for this line of logic, which she presented in reference to corruption and human rights abuses at Brandeis University, February 28–March 2, 2002.

positions before the regime collapsed.[11] In the Da Fo–Liangmen township area, party leaders embraced predatory corruption.[12]

Thus, in Dongle county, a pattern of poorly regulated party-based corruption continued on into reform, mutating into what Minxin Pei has called "decentralized state predation."[13] If the demise of the people's commune and the redistribution of the collective means of production to farm households pointed to a weakening of central party-state power in the countryside, party leaders in Da Fo and Liangmen nonetheless relied on the power structures and political networks of the Maoist past to sidestep the administrative controls and subvert the ideological spirit of the Deng Xiaoping reform.[14] They took advantage of the climate of reform, scheming both to garner resources from the upper-level administrative hierarchy and to amass fortunes by plundering village-level communities.[15]

As we will see shortly, in the Da Fo area, this plunder invited acts of resistance, led by individuals and groups. Much of this resistance was rooted in popular Confucian norms that the Communist Party had suppressed in the Great Leap and that, in the case of Da Fo, were revived without official authorization. Whereas resistance-related claims seem to have tipped in the direction of a popular demand for the local party leaders to honor such norms, the actual resistance coming out of Da Fo was fairly minor in comparison to the scale of corruption itself – and, in any event, the corrupt acts of local party cadres made it all but impossible for the party to reclaim its legitimacy through economic performance or a functional Confucian reform within the party itself. In short, there was no transition to Confucian-cued governance, either democratic or dictatorial, and in consequence corruption remained a highly explosive issue with villagers.[16]

LEVELS OF CORRUPTION AFFECTING VILLAGE LIFE

Corruption involves the deviant use of public office for personal gain by, in this case, party-based politicians who willfully failed to uphold duties associated

[11] Gaer's logic and this point find support in the research of Han Dongping on the post-1978 political worldviews of rural Shandong officials. Han, *Unknown Cultural Revolution*, 180.

[12] See Bernstein, "Instability in Rural China," 106, for an intelligent statement on the center's role in this process.

[13] Pei, "Rotten from Within," 322.

[14] On this point, I am indebted to Auroe, "Towards a Chinese Sociology," 4–5.

[15] On the seizure of resources, see Thaxton, ISA Paper; Friedman, personal correspondence, 2004; Friedman and Selden, "War Communism," 3; and Friedman, "China Transformed," 6. On the phenomenon of leaders grabbing collective assets to which previously deprivatized villagers were entitled during decollectivization in Hungary, see Hann, "Idiocy of Decollectivization," 16, 20, 25.

[16] Cf. Holbig and Gilley, who seem to grasp that the CCP was unable to make such a transition. "Reclaiming Legitimacy," 410.

with their formally appointed positions.[17] In the reform period, corruption permeated virtually every level of Communist Party–structured power and rule; the chances of being imprisoned for it were exceedingly slim.[18] It affected the material well-being of individual farm households at every level of their interaction with government and cast a dark cloud over state legitimacy. In Da Fo, people spoke of corruption as a cancer.

Reform-Era Corruption at the Village Level

In Da Fo, Bao Zhilong and the old-guard Maoists seized on the hurriedly conceived and loosely supervised upper-level directives issued in the early transition to reform in order to pursue gains similar to those derived by means of corruption in the Mao period. Boss Bao and his cronies moved quickly to subvert three of the central goals of policy reform: (1) the division of the crop lands among individual farmers, (2) the provision of private housing spaces to families in need of them, and (3) the creation of township- and village-level enterprises designed to provide individual farmers with home-based work and village governments with much-needed revenue.[19] Hence, in Da Fo, the popular memory of reform was decidedly at odds with the official rendition of what supposedly unfolded in Chinese villages in the transition from collective to market, particularly in the key issue areas of land, housing, and enterprise.

In the chaos of the changeover to assigning individual parcels of land to individual farm households from 1982 through 1985, Bao Zhilong allowed village party leaders to take slightly more land than was given over to ordinary villagers. Worse, boss Bao retained 100 *mu* of prime crop land for the village. Actually, most of this land was rented out to people with special connections to Bao, people who in the rush of the land division had already grabbed a little more land than others. Unbeknownst to others, those who "rented" the 100 *mu* of prime croup land did not pay any rent. The grain yield on this land amounted to 80,000 *jin* annually. Boss Bao and his clients and cronies used this grain to serve the interests of their own network, breaking a host of formal rules. They did not pay taxes on the harvest; they used the proceeds from it to purchase farm implements and tractors for themselves; and they drew on the grain and the money from it to bribe the village accountant, Ruan Tianming, to overlook transfers of the rent money for informal political ends.

This corruption was discovered by villagers only after Bao Xuejing, a former People's Liberation Army (PLA) solider, returned to Da Fo to farm a share of land in the 1985–1990 period. In mid-1989, after the first arsons struck Great Leap–era boss Bao Zhilong and the old-guard Maoists, Bao Xuejing was elected village party secetary by Da Fo party members. He exposed the hidden

[17] Cf. Scott, *Comparative Political Corruption*, 4–5.
[18] Less than 3 percent, according to Pei, "Corruption Threatens."
[19] On this goal, see Oi, *Rural China Takes Off*, 20, 23–24.

100-*mu* plot and decided to alter this system of bogus redistribution. On learning of its existence, villagers were aghast. They supported Bao Xuejing, who proposed to take back the land and allocate it to individuals who would pay 150 *jin* in return for farming it. Although Bao Xuejing gave the old "renters" the right of first rental, all of them refused. Instead, they aligned with ex-party boss Bao Zhilong to overturn Bao Xuejing's decision. "After that," says Bao Xuejing, "I began to have trouble with some of the people in the village government."[20]

Ruan Tianming, the Da Fo accountant, refused to cooperate with Bao Xuejing. Acting on secret instructions from Bao Zhilong, Ruan wrote a letter to Cheng Weigao, the Henan provincial party secretary, listing "ten crimes" of the new party secretary, including sexual misconduct, illegal occupation of public building lots, and the theft of 10,000 yuan from the public till. The letter triggered a joint provincial and county government investigation of Bao Xuejing. Personal visits by Dongle county CCP secretary Jiang Zimin were followed by visits from the Dongle county police and audits from the county audit bureau. In the end, Bao Xuejing was cleared of all charges. Nonetheless, within a few years, Bao Xuejing had been dismissed from his post for refusing to carry out a complicated township-level scheme to redistribute 100 *mu* of village land to apple tree cultivation. Bao Shunhe, one of Bao Zhilong's clients, agreed to do it, and he replaced Bao Xuejing.

Just as Da Fo's farmers wanted to regain the freedom to farm their own land, they also longed to acquire building lots on which to construct homes for their offspring, an essential part of rebuilding close family ties and reestablishing the spaces in which family members could converse, care for one another, and celebrate life's precious moments. Such spaces had been invaded and altered, sometimes radically, in Mao's post-1949 confusion of governance with revolution. During the collective era, village party secretaries had held power over public lands reserved for allocation to individuals in need of home building lots. In Da Fo and countless other villages, the old-guard Maoists apportioned these lots in a discriminatory manner to create followerships and to control people who were not in their political favor, so that the practice of building lot allocation constituted a form of graft that farmers deeply resented.[21] Voicing such resentment over how Bao Zhilong had routinely practiced this form of corruption, Bao Jianzhuang recalls that he and his four brothers asked Bao Zhilong for building lots but were denied this right for years. Later, after his wedding, Bao Zhilong granted Bao Jianzhuang "a building lot with a huge sinkhole in it," which he worked three years to fill. Others who wanted building lots gave Bao Zhilong gifts, but Bao Jianzhuang refused. His refusal to give Bao Zhilong a gift explains, Bao Jianzhuang says, why he got "just about the worst

---

[20] Bao Xuejing, interview.
[21] For the conceptual basis, see Key, "Techniques of Political Graft," 40–41.

lot in the village." He concludes: "I think that many people in Da Fo hated Bao Zhilong for this kind of work style. If he had treated everybody the same way, I would not hold any grievance against him today."[22]

Such arbitrary graft continued into the early 1990s, mutating into naked money-based corruption. In the 1989–1992 period, when decollectivization accelerated, the Da Fo party leaders claimed village lands for building lots. Party secretary Bao Shunhe claimed that anyone could purchase a building lot for 300 yuan. In reality, he maintained the corrupt process of allocating building lots put in place by his patron, Bao Zhilong, transforming only its techniques. Whether or not a person really was in need of a building lot, he could not acquire one if he could not afford the gifts needed to get on the list of potential buyers. Further, Bao Shunhe actually sold the village building lots to buyers at different prices, so that his friends and favorites paid less than 100 yuan per lot, while others had to pay the full 300 yuan. Finally, some people were sold bigger pieces, whereas others got smaller pieces for the same price.[23] Villagers were unhappy, claiming there was no fair play in the process.[24] In the end, the behavior of Bao Shunhe triggered a frenzy of speculation in prime farm lands, as people with money and connections purchased bigger pieces and then subdivided them into small strips for resale. This "reform" of the building lot allocation process only reminded villagers that Da Fo's party leaders were determined to serve their favored clients first and had little, if any, sense of duty toward those who were marginal to their networks – as had been the case in the Great Leap.[25]

The early reform era renewed hope that local village leaders might embrace the experiment with a township- and village-level enterprise system, thereby stimulating new jobs and market prosperity. But, as Jean C. Oi has noted, few of China's rural people had the capital to start up rural enterprises of any scale.[26] They required loans, some of which were from government banks and arranged by county and township officials. Sensing Da Fo was a likely candidate for such a loan, village and township leaders saw a chance to gain funding for a model brick factory, noting that Da Fo had been host to such a unit under party boss Bao Zhilong in the late collective era.[27] But in leaping to embrace the enterprise system, the local party leaders leaders took Deng Xiaoping's command to get rich quickly literally and engaged in aggravated embezzlement. The loan for the new model enterprise system was regarded as a source of what Alan P. Liu calls "legitimate loot" for party cadres who were accustomed to

---

[22] Bao Jianzhuang, interview.   [23] Ruan Shifan, interview.   [24] Ibid.

[25] In constructing this argument, I have benefited from Heidenheimer, "Perspectives on the Perception of Corruption," 155–160.

[26] Oi, *Rural China Takes Off*, 67.

[27] On the practice of creating fraudulent models to mobilize resources for lower cadres in charge of such, see Liu, "Politics of Corruption," 492.

putting the gains of collective enterprise in their own poor, though privileged, pockets.[28]

To his credit, party boss Bao Zhilong had helped establish the "first" brick factory in Da Fo in 1973 – though actually the factory had a sporadic history dating back to the Republican era. For the next two decades, this factory produced the only industrial source of cash income for the village; output floundered in the late 1980s. In 1993, a CCP work team from the Dongle County Finance Bureau settled in Da Fo for five months. The deputy head of this team, Lin Yunding, got along well with villagers, whose hopes were raised by his suggestion that Da Fo rebuild its brick factory and enlarge its capacity to supply an expanding market. Bao Haifeng, the head of the village, helped spread word of Dongle County Finance Bureau's promise to support the enterprise with a start-up grant of 30,000 yuan. Villagers endorsed the plan. Assuming the grant was guaranteed, they began to dismantle the old factory while making plans to build the new one. However, after tearing down the old factory, villagers were told by Da Fo party leaders that Liangmen township leaders had embezzled the 30,000 yuan while it was en route to the village leadership. As of 1995, villagers were left without any factory. The old one was gone, but the new one could not be constructed without the promised grant.

Bao Haifeng tells us how villagers felt about the affair: "The villagers are angry with us now. They thought we were too soft and failed to fight with the township government for the money. You see, our Da Fo party secretary was a little bit too timid. He was afraid of losing his position. He did not dare challenge the commune leaders. As the head of the village, I could not do too much without his approval. If I had overreacted, the party secretary might have interpreted my good intentions in the wrong way."[29] Many villagers saw this complicity through the prism of the loss of the Great Leap past, when brigade party leaders all too readily embraced the false promises of commune developmental schemes that made for social ruin.[30] Understandably, this incident tainted the Communist Party as an unreliable ally in the quest to promote minimal prosperity, thus engendering another collapse of trust.

Many of the corrupt practices of reform-era governance in Da Fo were traceable to the degeneration of the Communist polity in the Mao years, especially the corruption that all but destroyed virtuous rule in the Great Leap Forward.[31] The corrupt practices in this pattern by and large were not the by-product of mutually beneficial two-way transactions between party leaders and village dwellers. They reflected a nontransaction type of corruption associated with the predatory controls over public resources that characterized the Mao era, when, as Yan Sun has put it, the name of the game was "power for

---

[28] Ibid., 500–501.   [29] Bao Haifeng, interview.   [30] Bao Mingpu, interview.
[31] Cf. Friedrich, "Corruption Concepts," 118, which reminds us that in the thinking of Machiavelli, Montesquieu, and Rousseau, corruption was a force that threatened to destroy virtuous political order.

money," not the money-for-power rules that came with economic liberalization and the increase of opportunities for corrupt exchanges between higher-ups and grass-roots hustlers under reform.[32] In other words, corruption in Da Fo was the product of top-down power relations, and it benefited mainly local crony networks such as that of party boss Bao Zhilong, leaving villagers to suffer its cost and further damaging the reputation of the Communist Party in their eyes.

Reform-Era Corruption at the Township and County Levels

Historically, the mandate to govern was to be won by ensuring that villagers' minimal subsistence requirements were met. Da Fo's farmers shared this moral preference, which charged leaders with placing the harvest claims of farm households before those of the state.[33] This charge required leaders to favor villager rights to a "moral share" of the grain harvest, a practice that was to be governed by honest conduct in addressing the issue of food scarcity. The Great Leap, which had tied mass political mobilization to party-driven falsifications of harvest surpluses, all but obliterated the obligation to practice this moral economy.[34] At the outset of reform, Da Fo's farmers still held bitter memories of losses stemming from the failure of Da Fo party boss Bao Zhilong and Liangmen commune leaders to speak truthfully about harvest output, to stand up against the rigid procurement claims of Wu Zhipu and the Henan Maoists, and to relieve the food crisis when the Leap famine hit home.

The memory of official separation from this basic principle in the 1958–1961 famine was revived again in 1992, when skyrocketing tax demands threatened the right of Da Fo's farmers to a fair share of the harvest, and it structured popular interpretation of a leadership quarrel over tax relief. In March 1992, temporary vice party secretary Bao Yibin was implored to look into the possibility of grain-tax relief. Bao submitted a written request for relief to the Liangmen township government. The request stated that Da Fo was due a tax-quota reduction because of its infertile saline land base and its flood-related crop losses in 1991 and 1992. The Dongle county government determined that township officials had overtaxed the village, and the Liangmen township government responded by authorizing a reduced tax quota for Da Fo village. The purpose of this reduction was to provide grain-tax relief to hard-pressed farmers. However, Da Fo's party leaders, themselves pressed to comply with the township grain-tax quota, feared that if they forthrightly informed villagers of the amount of the approved reduction, the villagers would prove even less willing to cooperate with tax collection, and the leaders consequently would be unable to secure their own salaries from the township. So they lied. They denied that the written appeal for tax relief had been approved. They even

---

[32] I am indebted to Yan Sun for helping me grasp this point. See *Corruption and Market*, 22–25.
[33] Cf. Scott, *Moral Economy*, 40, and Thaxton, *Catastrophe and Contention*.
[34] Cf. Lu, *Cadres and Corruption*, 93.

schemed to divide the amount that was to be reduced – or returned by way of a rebate of sorts – among themselves on collecting it. When Bao Yibin and other Da Fo party leaders openly quarreled over the issue of how they were going to divide the loot from this hushed-up tax rebate, the disagreement spilled into the public arena. Villagers sensed that Liangmen township leaders had taken too much, that Da Fo's party leaders were dividing the sum due struggling farmers among party-based friends and favorites. In the absence of open, honest communication about state claims on the harvest, people imagined the worst. They felt they were once again dealing with the same kind of state fabrication that had led to outlandish claims on the harvest and placed them in the grip of Mao's great famine.

In 1998, following the lead of other townships in Dongle county, the Liangmen township government concocted a scheme that would have required Da Fo's farmers to give up their freedom to independently decide which crops were to be planted – a throwback to the blind commandism of the Great Leap era. Seeing that Da Fo's farmers had planted sweet melons with good returns since 1995, the township officials pressured Da Fo party secretary Bao Shunhe to "encourage" all villagers to expand melon production. Township officials promised that growing more melons and shipping melons to Tianjin and other big cities of North China would earn villagers a lot of money. They hid the fact that they were going to impose an extra tax on this crop.[35] This tendency of township officials to blindly push for specialization in crops that would provide fast, superabundant returns and to simultaneously ignore the actual impact on the incomes of farmers was clearly a legacy of the Great Leap.[36]

Da Fo's farmers refused to heed the command to embrace this officially contrived melon-growing mania. As consumers, they preferred a more cautious, selective melon-production strategy. Although it was true that melons had done very well, allowing growers to earn up to 1,500 yuan per *mu* in the years 1995–1997, melon growing entailed risks to which township officials were oblivious. Such risks showed up in 1998, when competition from growers in Daming, many of whom sold their melons under the Da Fo sweet melon brand name, caused the market price to drop from 1 yuan to forty cents per *jin*; when rainy weather shrank the wheat harvest and diluted the sweetness of melons, reducing consumer demand to the further detriment of growers; and when an outburst of crop theft caused growers, who already were sleeping all night in the fields, to suffer losses to melon pilfering. Furthermore, the Liangmen township government had done nothing to improve the roads that would connect Da Fo's melon producers to regional city markets. Villagers informed the Da Fo party secretary and his superiors in Liangmen township that they would decide what and when to plant.

---

[35] Bao Shunhe, interview.   [36] Cf. Yang, *Calamity and Reform*, 32, 65, 112, 238.

The growth of Liangmen township government during the reform era also annoyed many villagers, whose perception of this process was informed by memories of the spurt in local state building and the proliferation of cadres in the years leading to the big commune government units of the Great Leap. "The government," according to Ruan Shifan, "has become bigger and bigger since Deng Xiaoping took power in 1978, and it has proven less and less effective in recent years." Comparing the present with the past, Ruan continued: "In 1978, Da Fo village had only six village leaders, and all of them had to work in the fields for a stint during the year. No one was a full-time village leader. Today, we have fourteen village leaders, and all of them receive a full-time salary. But they do not do anything for the village or villagers. They only work for the township government." The township, headquarters of the former commune, had suffered similar growth, from twelve officials in 1978 to more than 150, and whereas the former officials "rode bicycles to the villages and ... talked with villagers all through the year," today's officials were strangers. Dongle county also had suffered an expansion of officialdom. The Public Security Bureau had grown from twenty-eight people who "solved almost one hundred percent of all criminal cases in the county" to more than 300 who could "hardly solve any cases." The reason for the growth, Ruan Shifan concluded, was not need, but corruption: "Each township party secretary and township government head wants to give his family members, and his relatives, a government position, and this has increased the number of people in local government."[37]

In speaking of the growth of the township government, and specifically the taxes on the wheat harvest and the fines imposed in the name of birth planning, Da Fo's farmers cynically asked, "Where does the money go?"[38] In the summer of 1998, Da Fo party secretary Bao Shunhe gave a strikingly candid answer to this question. According to Bao, "When paying taxes, villagers pay a lump sum to the Liangmen township government grain station. In fact, the lump sum covers many different categories – the national state tax, the township government levy, the village government's portion to pay the salaries of village leaders, and the share needed to cover the operational costs of village and township government. However, we do not dare tell the villagers how much we collected for each category, because many villagers would be angry if they knew the township government took far more than the state tax. There are more than one hundred people working in the Liangmen township government today. The government also owns cars and jeeps. The township government leaders also eat and drink a lot. All of these costs have to be borne by tax grain taken from villagers."[39]

Da Fo's farmers were not opposed to the growth of township government per se. Rather, what made their blood boil were the banquets of Liangmen

[37] Ruan Shifan, interview.   [38] Ibid.   [39] Bao Shunhe, interview.

township leaders. In the course of securing compliance with reform-era policies that mandated tax payments, birth-planning fines, and high tuition charges, swarms of township-level cadres descended on Da Fo and ate villagers' food. The banquets brought up the painful memory of the Great Leap–era pig-outs of commune leaders who had consumed plenty of superior food while farmers suffered from runaway procurement and the depleted food supply of the public dining-hall system. Banqueting stood near the top of the list of the most intolerable acts of official corruption, or so proclaimed Bao Sheping, Da Fo's respected schoolmaster: "What we mean by corruption," says Bao, "is mostly eating a free banquet.... [This is why] we are not happy with government officials. They talk a lot but do not do much to help people. Yet they eat our food for free. Everybody hates this.... Most villagers say that the township government leaders are like pigs. They will leave here after they get fat."[40] Thanks to Frank Dikotter, we know that rural people used this same kind of language to complain against cadre feasting through Mao's great famine, when they dubbed party activists "pigsty cadres" after the character in the famous Ming dynasty novel *Journey to the West* who was half human, half pig, and, according to Dittoker, "legendary for his laziness, gluttony, and lust."[41]

The connection between Mao's "pigsty cadres" and the corrupt, grasping cadres of the reform era worked against the CCP attempt to reclaim legitimacy in Da Fo village and in much of the deep countryside, both in the Mao years and afterward. Let us clarify the connection, which has escaped scholars of present-day contention. In the aftermath of the Great Leap famine, farmers in Henan, Anhui, and Jiangsu complained that a new rich group of county- and commune-level cadres appeared in the countryside, in part because the cadres had gained from promoting a radical agricultural transformation – the Great Leap – that was in *their* interest rather than the interest of tillers. Representing the predatory expansion of the party-state into rural society, these cadres lived in comfortable county and township government houses, wore sporty Mao jackets and leather shoes, and ate high-quality wheat and rice during banquets that were convened on any pretext. They also celebrated the Spring Festival with liquor and foods that farmers could only dream of – fish, pork, duck, and premium beer and wine – a pattern that started in the secret kitchens of the Great Leap. Meanwhile, in this same period, farmers attempted to survive in shabby, decimated abodes, donned patched clothing and went barefoot, and got by on coarse gruel and sweet potatoes. Most could barely afford to celebrate the Spring Festival.[42]

Although some of the newly rich local party leaders were to be punished in the 1960–1961 Anti-Five Winds Campaign, most were reappointed after a

---

[40] Bao Sheping, interview.   [41] Dikotter, *Mao's Great Famine*, 194.
[42] Personal correspondence with Liu Woyu, University of Iowa, April 9, 2012, and Liu Woyu, "Prelude to the Cultural Revolution," manuscript in progress, April 9, 2012.

short period of "rehabilitation" in CCP-directed Learning Classes,[43] after which they resumed their corrupt behavior, which included embezzling village funds, using brigade and commune bricks and lumber to build new houses, traveling to cities for opera and other forms of entertainment, and hosting banquets for visiting "comrades."[44] In Da Fo, CCP bosses Bao Zhilong and Bao Yibin engaged in all of these activities, and ordinary farmers especially remember the banquets and drinking of party leaders in this period, including the bash thrown by secretary Bao for "friends" from Tibet. At the brigade level, and especially in Liangmen township and Dongle county, the pigouts continued, epitomizing the socioeconomic gap that had been created by powerful cadres in charge of the supercollective of the Great Leap. Farmers not only resented this gap, they also feared that the banquets surrounding each post-Leap campaign might presage another movement that cadres would use to plunder what little they had left after the Leap calamity.

The conventional wisdom is that Mao subsequently went after this corrupt new class in the Socialist Education Movement and in the campaigns of the Cultural Revolution, but this wisdom does not hold up against the oral history or the archival data. Although Mao Zedong did rail against corrupt cadres who were "taking the capitalist road," in the run up to the Cultural Revolution Mao refused to cashier the brigade, commune (township), and county party cadres who had unlawfully stripped farmers and the collective of grain and capital in the Great Leap, allowing the party secretaries who were positioned at critical nodes in the party-state hierarchy to stay in office and, in turn, scapegoat local party leaders.[45] Most of the big shots who had enriched themselves through building up the collective got off with minimal punishment, so that Mao actually saved this new rich class of upper cadres in rural China – a history by and large ignored by New Left PRC scholars.

Thus it is not surprising that the renewed outburst of banqueting among local party leaders angered and frightened villagers in Deng-era Da Fo. This form of corruption stirred memories of Mao-era plunder and loss, when county-, commune-, and, to a lesser extent, brigade-level party leaders relied on the political economy of the collective to embrace gluttony and bolster their material portfolios at the expense of tillers.[46] Worse, it underscored a systemic pattern of Communist Party rule that the intellectually fashioned Deng-versus-Mao contrasts of how rural China is ruled ignore: for the most part, the cadres

---

[43] Personal correspondence with Lu Huilin, Beijing University, April 9, 2012.

[44] The seminal work on village China by Chan, Madsen, and Unger helps us understand, through the political life of Qing Fa, the resiliency of the newly privileged cadre class in the postfamine period. *Chen Village*, 61–65.

[45] See ibid., 65. Friedman, Pickowicz, and Selden shed light on how this Maoist failure worked at the ground level. *Revolution, Resistance, and Reform*, 68–70. Liu Woyu's dissertation in progress offers a brilliant study of this Maoist retreat, "Prelude to the Cultural Revolution."

[46] On pigging out and overeating, see Chan, Madsen, and Unger, who show that Chen villagers resented the Mao-era cadre privilege of "eating big," that is, banqueting. *Chen Village*, 62.

who gained from corruption in the reform period *also* got off scot-free. Although expressing concern about corruption, Deng Xiaoping and the post-Deng Central Committee reformers, like Mao, failed to place any significant institutionalized democratic constraints on Communist Party corruption, thereby allowing the great leap into capitalism to widen the socioeconomic gap that was first created by state power during the Great Leap into socialism and death. Of course the difference was huge: few died from the corruption of the second leap – that is, the post-Mao reform. But, on the other hand, in both cases farmers felt betrayed, and in reform-era Da Fo, the CCP lost the chance to reclaim legitimacy based on a deep-reaching anticorruption performance.

When I first visited Dongle county in the mid-1980s, this socioeconomic gap was barely visible to me, because the county and township leaders did not seem to be affluent. The gap was there, however, and I was unknowingly introduced to it through county banquets sponsored to honor a foreign guest, some of which drew swarms of kin and cronies of the CCP power holders who received me. The relaxation of Central government controls on local county resources, the coming of globalization, and the attempt of the Liangmen township government to gouge villagers via taxes and fines widened it, giving further impetus to the formation of an official political class of nouveaux riches increasingly alienated from outlying villages, most of which had suffered disentitlement and deprivation in the Mao years.

Between 1993 and 1998, the Dongle county government leaders used tax revenue to modernize the living quarters of county government offices. The Liangmen township leaders followed suit. In these years, they moved into ostentatious two-story Western-style houses situated in the upscale section of Dongle county town, which as recently as 1985 had been home to earthen roads and wooden buildings dating back to the Ming dynasty. People in Da Fo took notice of this change. Local gossip targeted the Liangmen township leaders who arranged to be picked up from and delivered back to their homes in fancy vehicles, the cost of which was borne by villagers.[47] Pang Siyin, former deputy party secretary of Da Fo, commented on this change in the lifestyle of government leaders, which in the eyes of villagers led to a corrupt local polity of nouveaux riches: "The Liangmen township government leaders are all rich now. They have built very beautiful foreign-style houses for themselves. They did not derive a lot of money from their official salaries. So where did they get the money for such extravagent buildings? They eat, drink a lot, and do nothing. They have to be corrupt to live the lifestyle they live."[48]

Paralleling the widening material gap between the villagers and township rulers was a breach in normative understandings about the purpose of local subcounty government. When Liangmen township officials built extravagant government offices while neglecting to add village school classrooms and pay

---

[47] Bao Yibin, interview.   [48] Pang Siyin, interview.

village teachers, Da Fo's farmers had difficulty conceiving government as a resource for the poor or for mutual empowerment. They were reminded of the Maoist Leap, when cadres built palatial commune buildings and engaged in official business that excluded the poorly connected and the poor. When township leaders used taxes extracted from farmers to buy imported world-class sport utility vehicles to speed them away to sow wild oats in fancy hotels, disco bars, and brothels – rather than build macadamized roads and health clinics for people who otherwise had to negotiate rutty dirt trails on foot or by bicycle – villagers were inclined to see government as a "rat" or a "pest," which is why even under reform they still equated the Liangmen township government with "pestilence." They had also applied this term to commune governance during the Great Leap calamity.

Corruption extended to the county level, implicating the Central government. In 2001, Beijing started to pay attention to the so-called *sannong wenti* crisis, which focused on the slow growth of farm income and the widening gap between the rural poor and the urban rich. The essence of this "crisis" was political, for Beijing was worried that a decline in farmer income coupled with comprehensive structural change in the agricultural sector would widen the rural-urban gap, increase rural discontent, and foster political instabililty.[49] The Central government began to invest money in the poor interior provinces, making Dongle county and Liangmen township eligible to apply for development grant money. Their joint proposal to build wells aimed to improve irrigation in saline lands straddling the old course of the Yellow River. Over a million yuan poured into Liangmen township government.

There were two problems, however. First, the farmers in Liangcun, Dingcun, and Da Fo already had enough wells: they had dug them themselves over the first fifteen years of reform, a process officials in Beijing knew nothing about. Worse, the project was a ruse. Liangmen township officials threw a few "implementation dollars" at it, staged a helter-skelter bout of well digging, and then displayed indifference when the wells failed, recalling a frenzied, error-prone well-digging scheme that crashed in the crisis moments of the Great Leap Forward.[50] In addition, the township leaders favored some villages over others. According to the terms of the grant, the money was to cover all the costs of a project, especially for poor villages, but, according to Pang Yuefei (whose grandfather died in the Great Leap), the Liangmen township leaders charged farmers in out-of-favor, poor Da Fo 2,000 yuan per well for drilling wells they did not need while exempting politically favored, richer Weicaicun from any such fees.[51] Da Fo's farmers, aware of the center's gift to the county and township, assumed the township leaders had stolen most of the grant funds. They were angry with the township leaders, but they also were exasperated by

[49] Tian, "Agrarian Crisis," 47–51.   [50] Cf. Thaxton, *Catastrophe and Contention.*
[51] Pang Yuefei, interview.

Beijing's failure to forge new institutional mechanisms for distributing the money in a transparent, efficient, and fair manner.

By the second decade of reform, the vices of modernity had engulfed Dongle county and Liangmen township. By 1994–1995, township leaders were following the cue of Dongle county party secretary Zhen Fengshen, a well-known womanizer and patron of county restaurants employing young prostitutes, who set a bad example for township- and village-level cadres.[52] Da Fo's inhabitants found such behavior, which was underwritten by resources taken from poor farmers, both offensive and painful – they referred to Zhen as one of the county's "three pests." With the weakening of the party-state controls that had imprisoned people within the collective, a growing number of tales of official indecency circulated among mobile villagers. Many focused on the insatiable sexual desires of township and village party leaders. To more than a few Da Fo farmers, the root of such behavior lay in the base habits that formed in the Great Leap period, leaving China with a depraved polity. They said the township government leaders, like their commune predecessors, represented this depravedness. As Bao Xianpu put it, such behavior had "ruined the party leaders."[53]

The explosion of licentious behavior extended to Da Fo leaders in the roaring 1990s, disgusting conservative farmers. Rumors of the Da Fo party secretary's three extramarital affairs, all of which occurred during his tenure of office, swirled. It was said that secretary Bao Shunhe, after being caught in the act of copulation with one woman, had to pay 3,000 yuan to compensate the husband.[54] Equally dismaying, Bao Chengling, the corrupt Mao-era school principal whose tenure lasted into the mid-1990s, became a known gambler, a patron of restaurant prostitutes, and a pursuer of his neighbor's wife.[55] Many villagers concluded that Bao had tarnished the nobility of the teaching profession and set a harmful example for village youth. They suspected that his misconduct was underwritten by the kickbacks derived from helping the Liangmen township government leaders cover up their educational resource-skimming racket, which correlated with high student tuition and low teacher pay between 1988 and 1998.

Da Fo's farmers often cursed Liangmen township party leaders in private for the moral failure that accompanied the fleecing of the village. In speaking of the moral character of Zhao Shunchuan, the Liangmen township party secretary, and Yan Zedong, the head of the township government, Bao Timing, a leading Da Fo critic of party leaders, pointed to a deepening fault between villagers and the local state: "These two people," declared Bao, "are the most hated persons in the whole of Liangmen township." Bao continued: "They are greedy and corrupt. Under them, the township government has done hardly any good for

---

[52] Bao Yingjian, interview; Ruan Guobao, interview; Bao Guozheng, interview.
[53] Bao Xianpu, interview.   [54] Bao Wenfang, interview.   [55] Bao Timing, interview.

the people. These two leaders have extracted money from farmers, and they have used the money to purchase cars for their own use. Every day after work, they drive to Daming, or to some town, to entertain themselves in restaurants and dance bars where they sleep with prostitutes. We have been told that the Liangmen township leaders know how to economize. But they cannot provide their own food, and they eat at restaurants and attend banquets daily. They have abused their own wives by sleeping with mistresses or prostitutes. If the villagers of this township ever get the chance, they will slice these leaders to death."[56]

It is important to stress that this pattern of corruption was institutionally embedded and at work at the county level, because Dongle county leaders often turned a blind eye to what their clients in Liangmen township did with public funds. Farmers in Da Fo and surrounding villages saw the rot in the institutional design of the party-state, not just in the flaws or greed of a few individual officials – and they understood the police were implicated in the rot. Take the case of the nude dancing in the Cangji temple, for example. In 2005, a local historian persuaded the Dongle county government to invest in the rebuilding of the temple in nearby Weicaicun as an attempt to attract tourists. The project flopped, but within a year, Weicaicun party leaders had quietly secured the tacit approval of Liangmen township leaders to stage nude dancing under seven huge tents within the temple complex. The Weicaicun party leaders and the Liangmen township police worked together to sustain this lucrative undertaking, with police tipping off the dancers when upper-level government officials were coming to investigate.[57] A story that the police elicited sexual favors in exchange for protecting the managers of these young dancers was circulated by a Liangmenpo villager charged with driving the dancers from Shandong into Dongle county and Liangmen township. Those who heard this story said the driver told it to illustrate "the kind of police we have in China now."[58]

In Dongle county, Maoist rule imparted a legacy of violent factionalism at the township level. Many villagers traced the origins of factionalism within Liangmen township government to the repressive atmosphere of the Great Leap, when farmers who refused to give up their entitlements to family and food were publicly punished; brigade leaders who did not inflate harvest claims were beaten; and commune leaders who did not embrace the antihoarding campaign of Maoist Wu Zhipu were arrested and even driven to suicide. This violence was revived and expanded during the Cultural Revolution, when villagers took revenge on their Great Leap tormentors; Red Guard factions engaged in violent feuds; and the ultra-Maoist Red Artists and their commune-level allies tortured people they branded as "counterrevolutionaries." In the long aftermath of the Great Leap, villagers lived in constant fear of being

[56] Ibid.   [57] Zhou Jian, interview.   [58] Ibid.

affected by the warfare of higher-up party factions. Da Fo's inhabitants increasingly spoke out against the official infighting that made it difficult for them to go to Liangmen township leaders about the wrongdoings of village leaders, or of township leaders themselves. They insisted that Liangmen township leaders should resolve disputes among themselves, between themselves and villagers, and among villagers via a peaceful and consensual mode of rule.

Between 1993 and 1995, a poignant episode of violent factional rule ripped apart the Liangmen township government. In 1993, Wu Shunchang, the Communist Party chief of Liangmen township, swore brotherhood oaths with party secretaries in different villages. These secretaries protected each other and worked together in various shady dealings, a collaboration that worked against villagers' efforts to approach Liangmen township leaders with complaints and grievances against official corruption. In 1994, Yan Zedong, then the head of Liangmen township government, attended a banquet in Wanxiuzhuang village, where Lu Helin – one of Wu Shunchang's sworn brothers – was party secretary. During the banquet, Lu Helin became inebriated, and he stood up and bellowed out that the Liangmen township government owed him a transformer and that Wu Shunchang, the former Liangmen township party chief, supported his claim. This was a grievance over the spoils of reform: possession of an electrical transformer would have given Lu Helin a share of the money to be made from the electricity grid that was being installed in Dongle county. When Yan Zedong told Lu Helin that he should get the transformer from his patron Wu Shunchang, not from the township government, the newly appointed Liangmen township party secretary, Lu Wanxiao, stood up and yelled that whoever questioned Wu Shunchang's word was as good as fatherless – a bastard.

Soon, a shouting match between Lu Helin and his "brothers," on one side, and Yan Zedong, the head of Liangmen township government, on the other, degenerated into a profanity-laced argument and then a fistfight. Villagers looked on with disbelief as Yan Zedong was beaten by Lu Wanxiao and his sworn brother Lu Helin. Badly injured, Yan Zedong managed to return to Liangmen township government headquarters, whereupon he called on others to fight for him. The fight traveled to Wanxiuzhuang, then to Liangmenpo.

Fed up with this fraternal warfare, people from several villages in Liangmen township, joined by counterparts in Da Fo, filed a lawsuit against Lu Wanxiao and Lu Helin. They also lodged a complaint with the Dongle county government. The county officials merely ordered the two party leaders to reform and reflect on their behavior – a response that echoed the way in which such matters were managed in the Great Leap. They were not punished in any way for assaulting the head of the Liangmen township government. As a result, the esteem and authority of the Liangmen township party and government leaders was badly damaged. Villagers felt that there was no one to whom they could turn who would deal with disputes over corruption, either between them and officials or among officials themselves. As Ben Hillman's work illustrates, local state leaders frequently clashed over the spoils of reform, but the battle to build up patronage networks by capturing the tools of development did not, as Hillman claims, invariably promote stability at the local state level. In Liangmen township, it exposed the corruption and chaos surrounding reform, and it reminded villagers that the chaos within the domain of the party-state could hurt innocent bystanders.[59]

Corruption and the Liangmen Township Police

In the 1990s, everyday conversation in Da Fo increasingly focused on the relationship of Liangmen township leadership to the rise of crime. Villagers insisted that leaders should use power to inhibit official corruption and obey the laws themselves, so that they and their offspring would not be tempted to engage in crime and lawlessness. Yet according to villagers, the most corrupt political unit of Liangmen township was its police force. In the collective era, the formally constituted police apparatus of the local state was located within the Dongle county government, not the commune. With the deconstruction of the commune, a new police force emerged in Liangmen township during the first decade of reform. Recruited largely from local society, the members of this force were accountable only to the Liangmen township officials to whom they were connected by ties of kinship, patronage, and party. Their primary mission was to maximize revenue collection for people in their network. Da Fo's farmers saw this new police force as intrusive, parasitic, and incompetent. By the mid-1990s, villagers were using the metaphor of a "spreading cancer" to describe the corruption of the police.

Two aspects of police support for the unethical conduct of Da Fo party leaders upset villagers. First, the Liangmen township police were partisan in handling long-running disputes over property rights with village party leaders. Some of these disputes extended back to the Great Leap. During the Great Leap, Zheng Ziwen's family home had been dismantled while he was doing forced labor at a factory in Anyang. In the early 1980s, Zheng Ziwen moved to reclaim the wooden beams and belongings taken from his house, all in anticipation of reclaiming his family housing site. Party boss Bao Zhilong took this action as an affront to his authority, and he reported the incident to the Liangmen township police headquarters. Subsequently, the police came to Da Fo to arrest Zheng Ziwen. After serving a ten-day sentence, Zheng was arrested a second time by Dongle county police and sentenced to fifteen days in prison for seizure of "collective property." He also was fined 200 yuan. All of this transpired during a political moment that few missed: in this same period Bao Zhilong and the Da Fo party leaders were busy grabbing the property of the former collective for personal use, before that property was to be put up for sale

[59] Hillman, "Factions and Spoils," 1–8, 15–17.

to all comers in a public auction. Yet not one of these old-guard Maoists was arrested by the police. Villagers suspected the police were on the take.

The Liangmen township police also collaborated with Da Fo party leaders to deny farmers the right to freely articulate proposals for a more feasible and equitable land distribution process. In early 1990, a great debate unfolded in Da Fo over the best method of redividing the land. Bao Xuejing, the Da Fo party secretary mentored by Bao Zhilong, opposed the debate. But in a September 1992 meeting, Ruan Guobao, a member of the tenth production team, which had the most people and the least land in Da Fo, proposed that the land be reallocated on the basis of equal shares for everyone. He also suggested that the land be redivided in one or two blocks, as opposed to multiple tiny strips, so as to make cultivation more efficient, and that the money households paid to Da Fo party leaders to purchase land for new homes be placed in a transparent account for well improvement. This proposal was reported to the Liangmen township police by Bao Xuejing as an "act of opposition to land reform."[60] Party secretary Bao Xuejing told the township leaders that Ruan was mobilizing public opinion against further division, when in fact Ruan was only advancing the debate over the strategy of division. The Liangmen township police arrested Ruan Guobao and detained him for eight days, during which time they handcuffed him, tied him to a tree, and compelled him to apologize to everyone in Liangmen township through a loudspeaker. In the end, Ruan was let go with a 300 yuan fine. After Ruan sued the township government in Dongle county court, the government returned the 300 yuan. Nonetheless, the township party committee suspended Ruan's party membership pending a hearing of the Disciplinary Committee, which promised to rectify Ruan's case only if he would keep quiet – a promise it did not keep.[61]

In voicing complaints about how the deviant behavior of the police affected their well-being, Da Fo's famers mentioned four specific grievances, first among them the proliferation of police fines imposed on them for allegedly violating tax and birth-planning policies.[62] The Deng-era devolution of state power had been accompanied, for these farmers, by the rise of entrepreneurial brokers within the ranks of the police.[63] The police frequently used the money obtained from the fines to build expensive houses, purchase imported automobiles, build new roads for police use, and acquire modern surveillance and tracking equipment to squeeze villagers.[64] While traveling south of Da Fo, I once observed a police officer sporting a newly imported speed radar gun, pointing it at all moving traffic. Even slow-moving motorcyclists and tortoise-paced bicyclists became prey.

In the absence of a developed legal system, the Liangmen township police also engaged in the selling of detection, enforcement, and settlement services to

---

[60] Ruan Guobao, interview.   [61] Ibid.   [62] Pang Cunbin, interview.
[63] Cf. Duara, *Culture, Power, and the State*, 251.   [64] Ruan Guobao, interview.

villagers. On the one hand, the police nearly always demanded payments to cover the costs of gas, food, beverages, and other expenses in the course of investigating village-level complaints and conflicts. On the other hand, they were in the habit of accepting gifts in return for allowing villagers who were arrested or placed on police "most wanted" lists to escape the consequences of their allegedly uncivil behavior. Those who did not pay found it difficult to enlist the police to address their claims.

After the division of the land in the 1982–1985 period, scores of minor disputes over the use of irrigation facilities erupted in Da Fo. As in the Republican era, many farmers held three and four strips of land scattered across the territory of the village. Each time a family attempted to irrigate its land, its members had to carry their mechanical pumping equipment from one strip to another and queue up for a turn to use the wells for irrigating their fields. Many farmers had to stand in line for long hours to guard their equipment, and some chose to sleep in the fields through the cold of night, so critical was the timing of irrigation for wheat. Tensions over well use ran high. Quarrels over who was next in line were common. Some escalated into fistfights and knife fights, leaving grudges that fueled battles and wreaked havoc with intravillage harmony. In the spring of 1993, for example, members of Da Fo's eighth production team got into a brawl over the use of wells. That winter, the losers sabotaged eight wells, casting stones into the shafts and impairing the well-use rights of farmers in six other production teams.[65] Desperate to resolve these conflicts, some villagers called on the police to intervene. In a 1992 incident, the grandson of Bao Hexian broke into the home of Ruan Bingyong, slashing Ruan with a knife in a dispute over irrigation and well use. Ruan went to the Liangmen township police. The police, seeing little to be gained, refused to come to Da Fo to investigate the case. Bao Hexian verbally agreed to pay for the medical costs of treating Ruan's wounds but ultimately did not pay. Unable to afford a lawsuit, Ruan could not obtain justice.

Worse yet was the police habit of covertly requiring "dirty gifts" as a precondition for settling civil and criminal cases, particularly those in which there had been a clash with the police officers investigating the case. In Da Fo, villagers saw these gifts as a form of parasitic corruption that they had no choice but to accept. During the reform era, Bao Xuecheng and his younger brother, Bao Shuangcheng, destroyed the home of Bao Zhanghe, assaulted the police who came to arrest them, and then fled the village for several months. When the two fugitives returned, they told others they had made peace with the Liangmen township and Dongle county police by issuing gifts. Stories about the gifts flooded the local grapevine. One was that they had concealed a gift of 2,000 yuan to the county deputy police chief in the bottom of a chicken egg basket and that the deputy later was seen distributing the eggs to his dining-hall

---

[65] Pang Cunzheng, interview.

staff. Bao Xuecheng and Bao Shuancheng were taken off the police wanted list, and the police left them alone.[66]

The rising incidence of crime and theft in Da Fo presented the township police with opportunites to solicit bribes – a third popular complaint. Between 1988 and 1998, there were several dozen cases of theft per year. Farm implements, motor carts, household electric wires, irrigation pumps – all were fair game. By 1993, seven out of ten young males in Da Fo were armed with homemade pistols capable of killing people, and it was said that many of these youths had masterminded robberies in and around the village. The Liangmen township police repeatedly came to Da Fo to arrest scores of armed youths for robbery. Yet every young person arrested managed to get out of the township jail within a few days merely by paying a fine to the police, often as small as 50 yuan, but in some cases as much as 300 yuan.[67] Corruption structured police relations with these young petty criminals to the point that some of them came to believe they could get away with murder, buying their way out of any jail sentence.

Officially, the Liangmen township police proclaimed their support for the economic policy of the Central government, which encouraged free enterprise and market participation. But Da Fo's farmers experienced a different reality. On the one hand, they faced shakedowns when they attempted to establish business companies. The police conspired with the Liangmen Tax Bureau to demand an under-the-table payment of 500 yuan per quarter on factory start-ups, as happened to the Da Fo owner of a cement pillar factory in nearby Shangcunji, who was able to reduce the extortion fee to 200 yuan per quarter by inviting township officials and police officers to a lavish banquet. Speaking of this shakedown, Bao Xieji said, "This is what we call corruption." On the other hand, some farmers-turned-petty traders voiced anger over the Liangmen township police demand for protection money and the lack of a police shield for trade-related travel. The police collected fees to ensure the safety of market travel, and even then they often left villagers at risk in their travels to and from markets. Some Da Fo farmers who lifted their households from poverty via market-focused business enterprises during the first decade of reform had to discontinue their profitable ventures for lack of protection. In the early 1980s, for example, Bao Zhenghui made profits by riding a bicycle to a host of markets to purchase grain and peanuts, selling them back in Da Fo. But with the rise of highway robbery in the late 1980s and early 1990s, Bao grew fearful: "They stopped me and asked me for money," says Bao. "So I did not dare to continue to do that business anymore."[68] Ruan Fen was more explicit. After getting rich via trade in pigs to the north and west of Da Fo during the first decade of reform, Ruan also grew apprehensive: "I used to go to these dangerous places, but I dared not go there anymore, because I did not want to lose my life for sake

---

[66] Bao Zhigen, interview.   [67] Bao Peijian, interview.   [68] Bao Zhenghui, interview.

of money."[69] Villagers who made this choice invariably blamed the Liangmen township government and cursed Deng Xiaoping and his successors for not affording them the protection they needed to pursue off-farm income.

According to Yasheng Huang, an MIT-based expert on Chinese political economy, the fortunes of village-based small business folk who had done well in the 1980s fell off in the post-Deng years, in part because the center failed to provide private-sector loans in poor rural places.[70] This seems to have been the case for the Da Fo area, too. Here, the villagers who hit it rich in the post-Deng years were not small merchants with capital but rather a tiny handful of people who used their party and army ties in Shijiazhuang and Baoding to win out in the dirty and dangerous recycling business. Collecting discarded metal, plastics, and wood, and reselling through recycling centers, in a few cases they raked in 300,000 yuan per year (about US$50,000).[71] Lack of capital was an obstacle to market entry, therefore. Yet the center's failure to reform official corruption was equally important. The failure was reflected in cell-phone messages circulating among Da Fo area villagers who had "difficulty" in transitioning to the market. One read: "Sun Yatsen led the migrant workers, Mao Zedong led the poor peasants, Deng Xiaoping led the small peddlers, and Jiang Zemin led the corrupt officials."[72]

If, as Dali Yang has argued, Central government refomers made progress in constructing market-sustaining reforms in the second decade of reform, in the deep countryside this process was encumbered by entrenched political forces.[73] In the Da Fo area, the police arm of the dominant party-state failed to provide the elementary security that is essential for a functioning market economy. The popular retreat from the market was linked to this failure. Da Fo's farmers say there was no ground-level regulatory protection for rational, risk-taking petty trade. In reality, the local police forces practiced hidden forms of corruption that were antithetical to market development.

Despite the market reforms, the post-1978 Central government did not allow a completely free market system to develop in rural China, and this political factor worked against farmers producing for the market. There were two reasons for this government restraint – or interference with market progress – which occurred in a pronounced way in 1998, a year after Deng Xiaoping died. First, in 1998, the Central government leaders grew fearful of

---

[69] Ruan Fen, interview.

[70] Yasheng Huang argues that the fortunes of village-based small business folk who had done well in the 1980s fell off in the Jiang Zemin decade, in part because of the rise of urban-based state technocrats who curtailed state loans to the private sector in poor rural places such as Da Fo and in part because the Jiang-led CCP placed the leadership of rural financial reform in the hands of corrupt CCP-led local governments, whose officials turned the screws on people who were desperate for credit. Huang, *Capitalism with Chinese Characteristics*, 109–125, 151–157. Da Fo's reform-era history resonates with Huang's thesis.

[71] Bao Wenfang, interview; Ren Gaixiu, interview.   [72] Jiang Chuanxi, interview.

[73] Yang, *Remaking the Chinese Leviathan*, 2, 292–296.

dependency on food imports. They worried globalization would jeopardize food security. Therefore, they discouraged tillers from transitioning out of farming to off-farm enterprises by cutting back on privately driven grain price incentives and by forgoing subsidizes to farmers, both of which would have made it easier to exit full-time agricultural production. Second, around the same time, the Central government, as part of its plan to reform the state-owned factories, fired factory workers who were former tillers, sending them back to rural farms, where they were again bound to the land by the household registration system, or rural *hukou*. In other words, the party-state found it easier to prevent a spike in unemployment and discontent by deploying (and reemploying) people who worked in state enterprises back to the countryside, where they had little choice but to engage in farming to survive. In both of these ways, the state addressed its own anxiety over falling grain production by rewedding farmers to full-time farming, and of course this meant that they had less time and less capital for pursuing off-farm activities.[74] The Central government's signals that farmers should stay farmers allowed police to take advantage of people who wanted to risk escaping farm work by engaging the market. Thus, the center's push back to farming gave the police leeway both to refrain from protecting farmers who engaged in the market and to take advantage of them.

Despite the dangers of traveling to and from markets, many of Da Fo's small traders saw the risks of market entry as tolerable in comparison to the market closure their families had endured under the CCP-led Bureau of Industry and Commerce in the Great Leap Forward. Yet the implication of the police in the illegal predatory activity of *hei bang* (underworld gangs) in the post-Tiananmen period further infuriated them. Between 1990 and 2000, neighboring Wei county, in Hebei province, became a den of brigandage. As desperate young males turned to highway robbery, petty traders coming from Da Fo and its sister villages were victimized. In 1993, for example, Ruan Bingyong of Da Fo was passing through Tang village with his coal cart, and people came out onto the street to pull most of his coal off the cart with metal hooks, chasing Ruan for several li.[75] Although the police actually knew the names and whereabouts of the culprits, they did nothing to stop the rise of this form of robbery. Villagers suspected police collusion. They wondered why the same police managed to show up in force to impose birth-planning measures and fines on law-abiding folk. They worried that this lapse of law enforcement signaled village youth, including Da Fo's school dropouts, that crime paid.

---

[74] Oi, "Two Decades of Rural Reform," 622–623, and Lin, "Rural Reforms and Agricultural Growth," 35–40, esp. 38. I am indebted to Pamela Ban for her insightful summary of the Lin–Oi argument on this matter. Ban, "Chinese Economic Reform," 245–246.

[75] Ruan Bingyong, interview.

RESISTANCE TO POLICE CORRUPTION AND THE DISORDER
AND LAWLESSNESS OF REFORM

As reform-era corruption intensified, farmers, peddlers, and small merchants across the Hebei-Shandong-Henan border area began to challenge the behavior of the police. In Da Fo, people refused to cooperate when the Liangmen township police came to investigate alleged crimes, including theft of electricity poles, wires, and transformers, and, importantly, arsons targeting the households and standing crops of the village's old guard Maoist leaders. Increasingly, they called on Da Fo's martial artists, rather than the police, to settle disputes over property boundaries and land usage.

More and more, Da Fo's poor farmers took flight from police arrest rather than give into fines and bribery. By 2001, this strategy of resistance had produced a cast of twenty "missing fugitives" at any given time in the course of a year. The fugitives came back only to celebrate the Chinese New Year, incognito. Of course, for a few, corruption was a "weapon" for coping with this situation.[76] Among the farmers who could afford to do so, some just kept paying fines and providing gifts to the police. Still, the trend was toward flight, often reflecting the inability of hard-pressed households to meet the insatiable demands of the township police.

After 2001, Da Fo's farmers exercised a third strategy of resistance, stoked increasingly by their distrust and contempt for the police: they boycotted the recruitment drives of local public security forces. Seeing the police as a hopelessly self-serving instrument of corrupt Communist Party rulers, fathers increasingly warned their sons of the danger of working for local public security. They worried that police service would corrupt their male offspring, damage their family reputation, and expose their sons to popular ire.

Influenced by Qiu Xiaolong's *Death of a Red Heroine* (2000), a novel that details the commitment to crime stopping of a poet-turned-honorable-detective who had to work within the CCP-governed police state, I was skeptical that all policemen were content with keeping authoritarian order in the countryside. After all, police corruption was systemic, the product of superior-dictated low pay, and disrespect of the police often grew out of township- and county-level CCP officials sending the police to stifle protests against the misrule of these very officials.[77] In the 1985–1995 period, I discovered that some policemen lived among villagers and that each morning they had to pull their fatigued bodies out of bed, put on the same timeworn uniform, and travel on their own to thankless jobs. Hence I was equally skeptical that Da Fo's farmers all saw the police as egotistical, parasitic, and heartless; I questioned whether they would

---

[76] Cf. Scott, *Weapons of the Weak*. On corruption as a weapon of the weak in rural China, see Zhou, *How the Farmers Changed China*, 53–55, 140–141, 186–188, 222–223, 242–243.

[77] This skepticism resonates with a pioneering work on police discontent in urban China by Scoggins and O'Brien, "China's Unhappy Police," 5–18.

rule out the possibility that some members of the police would be willing to take a stand against bad government.

I decided to test my skepticism by asking villagers to do their own political analysis of the story of Tian Tejie, a member of the vice-squad of the Public Security Bureau in Wushan county, Sichuan province. On September 22, 1998, officer Tian murdered Cai Jun, the corrupt magistrate of Wushan county, a CCP leader who was bitterly resented by local people who had suffered under his tyranny. Cai Jun was discovered to have vacationed in the United States during the Wushan flood crisis of 1998, raked in 70 million yuan per year from taxpayers without returning a cent to the public, spent money designated for road development on luxury cars for himself and his network, and even started an ostrich farm for his own pleasure. Not surprisingly, therefore, people actually praised Tian for killing Cai Jun, petitioned the High Court of Chongqing to take mercy on Tian, and then, after Tian was executed for the killing, lined the streets of Wanzhou to pay silent tribute to their newfound hero, who, they said, had expressed their enmity toward corrupt officials.[78]

In discussing this incident, Da Fo's farmers refused to believe that Tian Tejie would have acted out of anything other than raw self-interest. They could not accept the concept of an honorable policeman, and they would not accept the argument that inspector Tian could have been driven by his conscience to kill a CCP county leader. Bao Guihang spoke for all of the Da Fo interviewees on this point, bringing us back to the dangerous political sentiments that stir beneath the surface of politics in rural China:

I do not think that you can find anybody in Chinese society who would tell you that the police are good people. Everybody knows that they are very corrupt. They are only interested in money. I do not know what to say about the case of the Wushan party secretary who was killed by the policeman. From what I know about China, I do not believe either of them to be good. The party secretary must have been corrupt. He must have gathered a lot of money through his position. People around here say that if you bring a machine gun to the Dongle county government and begin to shoot indiscriminately at everybody inside the county government building, you can rest assured that you will not have killed an innocent person. So I have no sympathy for the party secretary who was killed by the police officer.

At the same time, I do not think that the police officer killed the party secretary for any good reason. I think he was as bad as anyone else in the police force. I do not think there is anybody who is good in the police force. I think that officer Tian went to the party secretary's home to blackmail him for money. He knew, like everyone else, that the secretary had a huge amount of money. All the government officials have a huge amount of money, which they stole from the people. They did not earn the money through honest means. So why not blackmail the secretary to give him some money?

I do not think the police officer meant to kill the secretary. Rather, the secretary did not want to give up his money and got into a fight with the officer, and in the process the

[78] From Liu Bai, *The Wushan Governor's Murder*, 1–10.

officer's identity was revealed. At that point, the police officer had to kill the county party secretary to protect himself.

Was the execution of the police officer justified? Why should he have been pardoned for what he did? Killing a bad person out of evil intent does not turn the killer into a hero. He did not kill the party secretary out of any public spirit. He killed him to get money.

I have no sympathy for government officials, or for police officers. It was great that the police officer ... killed the party secretary. I do not think anybody felt a loss for his death. As for the police officer, I do not think we need to show any sympathy for people like him, either. He must have done a great deal of bad things in his life.[79]

This antipolice refrain – or rant – was manifest in the interviews of Pang Junshan, Bao Chaoxiang, and Zheng Huiqing.[80] To a man, each of these Da Fo farmers, all of whom were in their mid-fifties and had sharp minds, rejected the idea that Tian Tejie had good intentions, and each of them agreed with Pang Junshan when he said: "I never seek help from the police. I do not think they want to help you in the first place. If you ask for help, they would want money from you. I do not have any faith or trust in the police and government officials now."[81] But it was the commentary of Zheng Huiqing – a fifty-eight-year-old farmer who as a ten-year-old boy had survived the great famine in Da Fo by eating the green crops in the collective fields, and who was not a member of the party-state – that exploded the notion that the CCP-led police state had managed to reclaim legitimacy. After expressing contempt for both Cai Jun and Tian Tejie, Zheng had this to say: "I have not seen the police do anything good for anyone in my life. We can live without these police officers and we can live without the government officials. They live off the people without doing anything good for us. They both deserved to die."[82]

Farmers in the Da Fo area more and more engaged in direct challenges to the fist of township power. Increasingly toward the end of the second decade of reform, the township police were greeted by numerically superior popular forces when dispatched to defend the predation of village and township leaders. The corrupt Communist Party secretary of Luzhuang, for example, was beaten so severely by indignant villagers that he almost died. Dispatched to Luzhuang to arrest the assailants, the police quickly withdrew because too many villagers were implicated in the beating, and they united to shield those who were responsible. Summarizing the political significance of this incident, Da Fo's Bao Wenfang said: "In China, when too many people are involved in a crime, it is no longer a crime, and the law cannot punish the majority in this situation."[83] Of course, villagers still feared the police. But they had the power of numbers, and they increasingly used this power to check police support for systemic corruption.

---

[79] Bao Guihang, interview.

[80] Pang Junshan, interview; Bao Chaoxiang, interview; Zheng Huiqing, interview.

[81] Pang Junshan, interview.   [82] Zheng Huiqing, interview.   [83] Bao Wenfang, interview.

Indeed, the interviews on popular attitudes toward police reflected a total loss of trust in the government. As Zhou Jian, a formerly persecuted "rich peasant" from Liangmenpo, put it: "Today we cannot trust the government and the police anymore."[84] Some Da Fo area farmers, including Zhou, went further, voicing dangerous political thoughts. According to Zhou: "One PLA veteran in Liangmenpo said that he did not think there were any good officials in the government now. He declared that all they do is eat and drink at the people's expense. He wished that he could gather all of them together and machine-gun all of them to death, because he believed they deserved to die. I cannot tell you who said that, but I agree with his assessment. I am willing to back up what I am telling you with my own signature. I only wish that I would be able to go on the Internet to curse Hu Jintao and Wenjia Bao. I would tell them that their talk about a harmonious society is just nonsense."[85] Apparently, it was not just PLA veterans who felt this way; Zhou Jian himself said, "If someone gathered up all of the corrupt government officials, particularly those at the township bureau and deputy bureau chief level and above, and used a machine gun to shoot each one, none of the officials would be wronged."[86] That is, even a random shooting of higher officials would hit every mark, and no innocent would be killed, because no government officials were innocent of corruption.

LOCATING THE ROOT OF CORRUPTION AT THE TOP AND SEEING THROUGH THE CENTER'S ANTICORRUPTION FANFARE

If no government officials were innocent, then villagers apparently had an understanding of the politics engendering corruption that transcended local power. In *The China Survey of 2008*, two-thirds of respondents saw corruption as a "serious problem," but public opinion poll data indicate that people tend to express greater satisfaction with the Central government than with local government and pin blame for corruption more on local officials. As Robert Harmel and Yao-Yuan Yeh point out, the nature of authoritarian rule itself structures such judgments.[87] Although Central government politicians set the policy course, local party leaders implement policy, and rural dwellers who only hear of policies from above but see and feel the effects of implementation from close range naturally tend to blame local power for faulty performance. China's Central government rulers also have an advantage, for they can, and do, use their propaganda machinery, including state media, to bombard the populace with anticorruption hyperbole, thereby focusing blame for shorting of policy enforcement on local officials while obscuring the corrupt dealings of

---

[84] Zhou Jian, interview.   [85] Ibid.   [86] Zhou Jian, interview.
[87] Harmel and Yeh, "Corruption and Government Satisfaction in Authoritarian Regimes," 15–19.

their own descending vertical patronage networks.[88] Reflecting this center effort to disseminate the image of a divided state, many villagers in the Liangmen township–Da Fo village area pinned blame for corruption more on local officials than on higher-ups. But in this rural locality, popular anger over official corruption was dangerous precisely because some of these same villagers extended their critique of it to officials at the pinnacle of CCP power.

To villagers, corruption started with top-rank Communist party leaders who operated through networks within the organizational empire of the party-state. They had little faith, therefore, that President Xi Jinping, would, as Xi promised in 2013, actually root out corruption by rounding up all of the "big tigers" – high-ranking corrupt officials – because they reasoned that Xi would have to target himself and his own network in order to eliminate the cause of corruption. I was surprised that farmers in this relatively poor and distant border region were so aware of the national structural dynamics of corruption. They gained such knowledge in different ways, including rumors and word-of-mouth reports from their upwardly mobile urban-based children, some of whom had found their way into the secretive, innermost workings of the reform-era state. Zhou Zhian was privy to one such report, which implicated the top-level CCP leadership in translocal corruption and factional struggles for national supremacy. In the year before Xi Jinping succeeded Hu Jintao, Zhou had this to say:

Lai Changxing was a farmer in Fujian province. However, he was able to make a lot of money smuggling gasoline, cars, and other items from Hong Kong into China. According the Central government, his smuggling operation netted eighty billion yuan, and Lai Changxing was able to avoid taxes on this entire sum. Lai Changxing was protected by the police. His smuggling operation flourished when Jia Qinglin [the trusted lieutenant of Jiang Zemin] was party secretary of Fujian province. When Jia Qinglin was promoted to the standing committee of the Politburo, Xi Jinping, the current deputy president of the Chinese government, became the party secretary of Fujian.

Both Jia Qinglin and Xi Jinping protected Lai Changxing's smuggling business. Lai Changxing built a Red Mansion and hired some of the most beautiful women in China to work there as prostitutes. Lai Changxing then invited officials from the central and provincial governments to stay in his mansion on a regular basis. All of the officials who stayed there began to collaborate with Lai Changxing, and Lai Changxing provided the officials with money to bribe their superiors in order to get promotions. Li Jizhou, the police chief of Fujian province, was thus promoted to deputy prime minister of Public Security in Beijing.

When Lai Changxing's smuggling operation was exposed, Li Jizhou actually alerted Lai and helped arrange for him to flee to Canada. The Chinese government negotiated with the Canadian government to extradite Lai Changxing back to China. It took almost ten years to get him back. He was sentenced to life in prison. There were rumors that

---

[88] Ibid., 17. This finding resonates with the work of Li Lianjiang. Yet Li also finds that local people did not fully trust that the center would hold the feet of its cadre base to the fire of strict policy implementation. Li, "Political Trust in Rural China," 228.

both Xi Jinping and Jia Qinglin, two of the top nine Central government leaders, were involved in Lai Changxing's case, and tried hard to prevent Lai's extradition. This is why I do not place any hope in Xi Jinping or the Chinese government for that matter.[89]

Zhou's knowledge of the hidden vine of systemic power and corruption came from a trusted source. Zhou's talented descendant, Zhou Xiaoan, graduated with a B.A. degree from a Chinese university at the moment when the case of criminal mafia billionaire Lai Changxing broke out in Fujian province. At the time, the Central government could not use the local officials or police to investigate, partly because they were entwined with Lai's network. Beijing, therefore, set up a special training unit in Zhengzhou and recruited a bevy of college graduates to investigate the case. Zhou Xiaoan was one of the recruits. Zhou Xiaoan subsequently told Zhou Zhian about the case, and with this knowledge, recalls Zhou Zhian, "I began to understand Chinese politics more."[90] In predicting China's political future, Zhou Zhian takes issue with the notion that the center is above corruption or will be able to hold. "I do not think the government has a good prospect of surviving long," says Zhou. "So many people hate the government and government officials. I fear that once the government collapses, it will be very bloody. Those who have suffered at the hand of the officials or the police will seek revenge amid the chaos. A lot of officials will have to pay a high price for their past wrongdoings."[91]

Rural people saw through the fanfare of the center's anticorruption effort. The effort was, in their eyes, designed to keep the system of CCP rule in place, and rarely instituted meaningful change. As mentioned previously, the 2007 execution of Zheng Xiaoyu, the corrupt National Food and Drug Administration czar, was applauded by many of Da Fo's farmers, some of whom knew that families across China had suffered from fake drugs and faulty medical equipment. But these same farmers expressed great anger at the Hu Jintao center, saying Beijing did not go far enough. They wanted a crackdown on corruption that would go beyond singling out one specific leader and would clean up the systemic institutional dynamics of corruption.[92] In the absence of such, they grew cynical about the center's anticorruption strut, equating it with artful deception of genuine reform.[93]

They also saw the favoritism exercised behind the fanfare of "reform." Between 2007 and 2011, for example, Liu Yuan, the former Lieutenant General of the People's Armed Police and a PLA political commissar, began to present himself as an anticorruption fighter, quoting Mao on the importance of fostering a corruption-free CCP. But Da Fo's farmers knew better. They knew Liu Yuan – the son of Liu Shaoqi – as a princeling raised in Zhongnanhai and

---

[89] Zhou Zhian, interview.   [90] Ibid.   [91] Ibid.   [92] Bao Yutang, interview.
[93] Liang Jing has argued that the political reason for Hu Jintao's anticorruption orders was not to attack systemic corruption, but rather to revive a secretive dynastic police unit in order to shore up his own authority and preserve CCP rule. Liang, "From Ruling by Rhetoric to Ruling by Secret Police."

an official who secretly gave away state land to Hong Kong tycoons in order to become a shareholder in Yaxiya LTD, a monopolistic export-import company and supermarket complex; he was also known to be an obsessive womanizer during his tenure as deputy mayor of Zhengzhou. Rumors of Liu Yuan's corrupt rise circulated on village grapevines, informing all that the center's anticorruption operation excused higher-ups with political legacies and a place in the existing system.

Farmers in the Liangmen–Da Fo area also understood the explosive contradiction built into the center's anticorruption campaigns. Many agree with Minxin Pei, who has pointed out that the top leadership cannot preserve its system of rule by seriously fighting corruption because popular involvement in this fight might spiral out of control and destroy the Communist Party itself.[94] In commenting on the campaign of Chongqing party chief Bo Xilai, a member of the Politburo and Central Committee, against police corruption and police-mafia operations in the Chongqing area, Wang Guojing, a farmer in Liangmen village, confided: "I often laugh at the corrupt officials, because they have stolen so much money from the common people they will never be able to spend it all. Wen Qiang, the police chief of Chongqing City, was executed recently. Wen and his wife had hidden more than 20 million yuan in a pond, and he was a charged with protecting criminal gangs and raping a college student. When this Wen Qiang was executed, the people in Chongqing celebrated with firecrackers and banners. Actually, the people did not know much about Wen Qiang, and few bore a personal grudge against him. They were angry with the Communist Party and the government. On the surface they were celebrating what Bo Xilai was doing to a government official, but underneath they were celebrating the killing of Communist Party officials. Most Chinese government officials were like this Wen Qiang. They have stolen money from the government and the people, they live in the best houses, drive fancy cars, and eat at expensive banquets, and hence are the targets of popular hatred."[95] Allowing this hatred from below, tied up with memories of suffering from the hushed-up corruption of the Maoist past, to suffuse reform from the top was dangerous for the CCP.

Ironically, it was equally dangerous to forgo an effective war against corruption, for without a deep-seated reform the politics of corruption called up resentful memories of the harmful corruption of the Great Leap episode, including the delegitimating reign of party-structured gluttony. Indeed, no sooner did Xi Jinping call for top officials to curtail feasting in luxurious restaurants, in full view of popular media, than did party cadres across China shift their banquets underground into government canteens that rivaled five-star restaurants with private rooms and the best chefs,[96] thereby replicating in a more spectacular manner the pattern of lavish feasting within the secretive

[94] For Pei's view, see Schiavenza, "Why Xi Jinping's Anti-Corruption Campaign Is Hollow."
[95] Wang Guojing, interview.   [96] Zhai and Chan, "Officials Go Undergound."

eating quarters of the cadres responsible for the Great Leap and its hunger. Beijing's failure to prevent this shift, to take a different path of rule, is an important reason why farmers such as Zhou Zhian say they do not place any hope in Xi Jinping or the center.

To many local people, the top-down single-party system, however loosely structured, threatened to destroy order, hurling them back into the Great Leap era, when local party leaders violated any and all rules in order to develop the national state on which they depended. Da Fo's farmers, like their counterparts in surrounding villages (quoted in this chapter), believed that by turning a blind eye to corruption, Central government leaders and Liangmen township leaders fostered alienation and contempt for government rules. Ruan Shifan commented on why more and more people turned away from playing by any rules in the reform era: "The party leaders did not follow the rules themselves. They always have been quick to abuse the rules in order to benefit themselves. So why should the villagers abide by the rules?"[97] This logic resolated with popular Confucian precepts that called for rulers to abide by the customary rules.[98] The Maoists had jettisoned such precepts, and neither Deng nor his successors had restored them in township-level governance. This political situation, according to Bao Guoshan, had left the countryside without political order and created a world in which "everyone tried to do things his own way" and in which "farmers were becoming lawless people."[99] This slide into moral disorder stimulated and justified forms of contention against the corruption of township-level power holders and their accomplices within and beyond Da Fo.

CORRUPTION, MEMORY, AND CONTENTIOUS RESISTANCE

In Da Fo, the corrupt acts of reform-touting CCP power holders triggered resistance, generating more than a few episodes of "conscious hostility."[100] Most of this resistance fell short of rebellion against village, township, or Central government leaders. Increasingly, however, it was characterized by irreverent responses to the corrupt acts of the powerful, precisely because those acts touched the lives of farmers in a way that activated enduring memories of past party-state abuse and ruin.

In the second decade of reform, the Da Fo party leaders who had corrupted the land-division process became the targets of this contention, which took several forms. Boss Bao Zhilong, who had arbitrarily allocated prime crop lands to his network, was subjected to verbal insult and character assassination – the

---

[97] Ruan Shifan, interview.
[98] Cf. Fu, *Autocratic Tradition*. Villagers repeatedly expressed frustration with leaders breaking rules and laws, and implied this leadership behavior to be a major obstacle to democratic discourse and harmonious order – RT.
[99] Bao Guoshan, interview.
[100] This term is from Hilton, *Bond Men Made Free*, cited in Guha, *Elementary Aspects*, 21, 27.

weapons villagers had used in the 1960s to punish boss Bao for his Great Leap sins. Bao Haizhen, a production team leader who had taken more than his fair share of land in the division of 1982, had his wheat fields torched in 1993 and again in 1995, when he lost ten *mu* of his crop to arson.[101] According to Bao Wenfang, "Some villagers believed that Bao Haizhen had gotten more than his share of land. But this was only one reason why people torched his wheat crops." By 1995, Bao Haizhen had become a full party member, and he was known for his unilateral, arbitrary work style. Rumors swirled that Bao was going to become the Da Fo party secretary and that he would manage the village in the arbitrary manner of Bao Zhilong. In the absence of any democratic check on Bao Haizhen's ascent, villagers turned to the match to warn leaders of turning the clock back to Mao-era methods of rule.

In the Da Fo area, popular struggle with township officials focused on a number of corrupt invasions of family and village life, but the struggle to sustain trade within the space of the customary periodic village market was exceptionally contentious. As we have seen, the Liangmen township leaders approached market development in a manner not too dissimilar from that of the commune officials they superseded. With Deng Xiaoping proclaiming that to get rich was glorious, they sought to rope in and remake markets, hoping to fill their own pockets by manipulating commodity prices and licensing space to small traders. Hence, the mid-1990s witnessed another attempt to supplant Da Fo's old periodic market with a new market. By 1994, the Liangmen township leaders had made progress in setting up a new market in neighboring Liangmenpo, which operated on the same days as the Da Fo market. Disheartened villagers saw this progress as a step back toward the market closure of the Great Leap era.

When Da Fo's party leaders did little to effectively thwart the Liangmen township government's attempt to diminish and usurp Da Fo's market, a group of villagers took matters into their own hands. In late 1994, Tang Dafa and Ruan Yunchang, along with twenty other market brokers, evicted township level business tax collectors from Da Fo, and they subsequently barred the collectors from entering the village.[102] In the year to follow, these brokers were joined by fifteen Da Fo merchants who refused to pay any tax on income from their stores and stalls. From 1995 to 1998, Liangmen township got nothing from these proprietors. Still, the township government pressed for progress. In the summer of 1995, its officials incensed villagers by proclaiming that Da Fo's market "no longer existed."[103] Such boasting was premature. Liangmen township leaders then attempted to kill Da Fo's market once and for all by concocting a road-building project that would have bypassed Da Fo.[104] Shamelessly, these same Liangmen township leaders dispatched agents to Da Fo – and every village of the township – requiring each household to contribute 20 yuan per member to the

---

[101] Bao Shunhe, interview; Bao Wenfang, interview.   [102] Pang Siyin, interview.
[103] Bao Guanjun, interview.   [104] Pang Liangfeng, interview.

project. Da Fo's farmers boycotted the levy, chastized the Da Fo party leaders who did not join the boycott, and then enlisted their counterparts in other villages to sue the township government over it. Consequently, the plan was shelved.[105]

In late 1995, a delegation of villagers reminded Da Fo party secretary Bao Shunhe that the market had played a role in their escape from Mao's Great Leap war on their existence. Apparently, they struck a shared chord. According to secretary Bao, who had been only six years old at the time of the Leap famine, the delegation made him remember the famine – and the market: "I felt hungry all the time.... During the time of the worst food shortages, villagers were permitted to do whatever they wanted on the market. There were many businesses on the market. People sold bread, turnips, and sweet potatoes on the market in order to earn some money to make a living. The market certainly helped people in the past."[106] In short, Da Fo's party secretary understood that villagers could not afford to sit by and allow the reform-era township government to take away this life raft of the past.

In the 1998–2005 period, the popular struggle to prevent Liangmen township leaders from taking over markets in the name of development spread to other villages with kinship and market ties to Da Fo. One contentious episode in particular sent a chilling message to Liangmen township officials. Around 2001, farmers in neighboring Pingyuandi village, Guanjun township, Wei county, joined in a collective anticorruption action with their counterparts from surrounding villages. Their target was Guo Jiaoao, the head of Guanjun township government, who had plans to replace a local periodic market with a market of his own. In the Great Leap era, Guanjun's party leaders had wanted to impress their superiors with spectacular economic feats. According to Wu Anwen, a local village leader, this behavior reappeared among reform-era township leaders. Guo Jiaoao, recalled Wu, "wanted to show the upper government leaders that he did something special to develop the economy in Guanjun township. So Guo opened up some new market areas that conflicted with existing periodic markets. Many villagers were angry with him."[107] The heated arguments over Guo's attempt to minimize the old market system and rake in money from a new officially systemized market produced a standoff, and so, according to Wu Anwen, villagers moved on their own: "They organized and taught Guo Jiaoao a very big lesson. One day when Guo Jiaoao was taking a nap, they stole into the bedroom of his home, grabbed him by the legs and arms, and then carried him all the way to the market. There they lifted him up and heaved him high into the air in front of a huge crowd of market spectators. He was thrown high into the air many times, and he was totally

---

[105] In the end, only two villages, Weicaicun and Liangmenpo, signed on to it. Both were closely connected with Liangmen township leaders by ties of marriage and political geography, and both stood to benefit directly from the road-building plan of the township.

[106] Bao Shunhe, interview.   [107] Wu Anwen, interview.

powerless to stop this. The farmers did not beat him. They just threw him up into the air a dozen times, playing with him and humiliating him. Guo Jiaoao lost all face in public. When the story of this incident reached the Wei county government, the head of the township was transferred to a different place."[108]

This contentious action was neither authorized nor cued by official policy, yet it did not violate the law. The Guanjun township police could not do anything about this contention; Wei county leaders were careful not to intervene in ways that would have offended the challengers; and Beijing did not know or care about the popular seizure of a dispensable township leader. People in Da Fo took heart that acting on impulses to defend the market, as an arena of both popular trade and collective action, paid off.

This is not to say that popular contention was cued solely by politically induced material loss or, or for that matter, by supportive messages from sympathetic authorities. As the work of Jean-Louis Rocca would suggest, the corruption of local party leaders was also a profoundly moral problem, for the political legacy of the Great Leap calamity combined with the lumpy process of transition from commune to township rule to produce a bevy of officials inclined to serve only their own party-based networks and to trample the normative aspirations of rural dwellers.[109] Bruce Gilley has pointed out that contention in contemporary China often stems from the tension-ridden gap between corrupt party leaders and country dwellers, a gap due to debased leadership norms that work against consultation with the rural poor.[110] While I agree with Gilley, it is important to emphasize that the history of this gap did not start with reform.

As the work of Perry Link would suggest, rural China under reform still faced a core normative crisis – and Beijing was implicated in this crisis. Although Central government rulers propagated Confucian ideas of clean, good paternalistic governance,[111] they did little, if anything, to actually instill Confucian norms among the party-state's agents in the remote countryside. Judging from the oral history data on Da Fo and Liangmen township, the folk Confucian precepts for morally proper governance, which came under attack in the Maoist era, had not been internalized by the reform-era Communist party's subcounty political base.[112] If they chose to – and in Liangmen township they frequently did – local Communist Party leaders could ignore the anticorruption pronouncements of Hu Jintao, Xi Jinping, and other Central government leaders. In contrast, farmers in Da Fo and other Liangmen township villages retained preferences for many of the popular codes of official conduct that were violated by the Maoist fundamentalists in charge of the commune during the

---

[108] Ibid.
[109] Cf. Rocca, "Corruption and Its Shadow," 403, 411–416, and Gilley, *China's Democratic Future*, 43–59.
[110] Gilley, *China's Democratic Future*, 5–7.
[111] On this point, see Baum, "Obstacles to Political Reform," 5.
[112] Cf. Link, "China's Core Problem," 189–195.

Great Leap. When Da Fo and Liangmen township leaders violated these codes in the reform period, they raised memories of past misconduct, thereby exacerbating the CCP's legitimacy crisis. The Da Fo farmers who suffered these violations increasingly voiced a desire for righteous self-governance.

I focus below on four of the Confucian codes of conduct at the core of villagers' pro-Confucian thinking about politics and proper governance: Da Fo's farmers expected their leaders to practice *honesty, forthrightness, compassion,* and *good will* in their dealings with villagers. The contentious performances of villagers spoke to this expectation.

One example of villagers' perceptions of officials' disconnect with honesty comes from 1992, when Liangmen township tax demands threatened Da Fo farmers. Recall that in March 1992, villagers had implored temporary vice party secretary Bao Yibin to look into the possibility of grain-tax relief. The county granted the relief, and township leaders were ordered to reduce the tax burden and rebate a portion of the collected tax. But the Da Fo party leaders lied to keep villagers in the dark about the approved reduction, and then openly quarreled over how they were going to split the money that should have been returned to the villagers. Catching wind of this quarrel, Da Fo's farmers sensed an injustice. In the absence of honest, open discourse about tax claims, they imagined the worst. Gripped by fears of the same kind of state fabrication that had produced outlandish claims on the harvest and delivered them into hunger in Leap famine, they moved to challenge the lie enveloping the rebate appeal.

Bao Haifeng, at this point a member of the Da Fo Village Committee, called on villagers to make leaders act on the truth. Bao twice forced his way into vice party secretary Bao Yibin's home, each time verbally accosting him for conspiring to corrupt the grain-tax process. When Bao Yibin bolted his courtyard door, Bao Haifeng stood outside on the public street, cursing Bao Yibin and challenging him to come out and fight. In this struggle against party dishonesty, Bao Haifeng drew on villagers' memories of the poisonous reputation Bao Yibin had acquired by repeatedly lying about food availability during the Great Leap, and thus more effectively appealed to villagers to join him in throwing stones at the vice-secretary's house. Dismayed over this contentious outburst and his failure to win Village Committee support for land redivision, Bao Yibin resigned his position.[113]

---

[113] Ironically, it was party secretary Bao Xuejing – not Bao Yibin – who had blocked the county government–approved plan for a tax rebate. The rumor that the Da Fo party leaders *already* had divided up the amount to be rebated among themselves was also inaccurate. In the absence of honest, transparent politics, the persistent memory bias implanted by party-based corruption of the food allocation process in the Great Leap overwhelmed political thinking about the present, and popular imagination about reform-era corruption ran wild, stoking contention informed by a troubled past. On the purpose and power of memory bias, and on the persistence of memories designed to allow us to revisit the traumatic past to protect ourselves in the present, see Schacter, *Seven Sins of Memory,* 174–175, 191, 205–206.

Da Fo's farmers also expected village leaders to make themselves available for mutual discourse and *forthright* conversation. Historically, mutual discourse was intimately connected to the process whereby village leaders moved resources out of the village to town- and city-based authorities without producing disobedience and unrest.[114] The Maoist pressure on village party leaders to extract and deliver grain to the state had altered the process of engagement: in the Great Leap, boss Bao Zhilong and his allies procured and stored harvests for the state by force, abandoning forthright discourse with farmers over their view of this procurement. Even when villagers were facing starvation, they could not engage commune and brigade leaders in open, forthright conversation about using available locally stored grain to relive hunger. To raise this issue was to question the violent processes whereby the Maoist state had attempted to legitimate appropriation by altering or ignoring popular consciousness. People who did so were labeled "rightists" and were suppressed.

In the aftermath of the Great Leap famine, Da Fo's farmers attempted to reengage Bao Zhilong and party leaders in conversations focused on access to the tax grain placed in Da Fo's grain storehouse. Villagers wanted to make sure the grain was there so that they could fall back on it in case of a famine or some other disaster. In 1967, during the Cultural Revolution, villagers sought out Bao Zhilong and the party leaders to publicly debate the issue of who was to have a key to the public grain storehouse. Because Secretary Bao and his followers had secretly skimmed publicly stored grain for personal use during the famine, in the decade to follow, distrusting Da Fo farmers required Bao and the party leadership to make two keys to the grain storehouse lock, one of which was to be placed in the hands of a representative chosen by ten production team leaders in public meetings. Until the reform era began, this representative slept in the grain storehouse every night, so that party leaders could not gain entry without public conversation and popular agreement.

In theory, reform had removed the local Maoist leaders who closed off conversation and ruled through defensive references to party authority rather than mutual discourse and forthright interaction with villagers. In practice, however, Da Fo witnessed renewed two-way discourse only at the outset of reform. For a while, the home courtyard of the Da Fo party secretary became the locus for a stream of conversations with villagers with queries, needs, and demands, but this stream began to dry up in the late 1980s and early 1990s at around the same time that the popular oversight of grain appropriated by party leaders was discontinued.

In the years following the disbandment of the collective, Da Fo's denizens began to store grain in private households. The problem was that between 1985 and 1990, Da Fo party secretary Bao Zhilong followed suit, and he also

---

[114] In constructing this section, I have benefited from reading Sabean, *Power in the Blood*, 5, 22–25.

stored the collected tax grain in his home – as if it were his private property. Worse yet, Bao Zhilong stifled all inquiries about the amount of grain or its availability, and his successor, Bao Shunhe, refused to even discuss whether there was enough grain available to provide relief in an emergency – a practice that Liangmen township officials tolerated. When Da Fo's farmers showed up at the home of the party secretary, they were invariably told he was not at home. Villagers were incensed. Even Pang Siyin, the Da Fo deputy party secretary after 1988, said that it was wrong for Bao Zhilong and his successors to hold all of the grain in their homes. Pang critized the Liangmen township leaders for helping to dismantle village forums that had facilitated checks on leaders' skimming of grain in the postfamine period.

Da Fo's farmers concluded that party leaders had adopted new tactics to continue a long-standing pattern of corruption. The question was, how could they contest this latest failure of party leaders to practice forthright conversation about food security? The answer was obvious: if party leaders did not have houses, then they could not store the public tax grain in spaces to which only they had access. Arsons aimed at depriving Bao Zhilong and his men of their houses, therefore, were deployed to address the renewed illegitimate domination of the party-state. In *Catastrophe and Contention in Rural China*, I pointed out that the arsons of the reform period, including those targeting the home of Bao Zhilong, were acts of revenge against unapologetic perpetrators of the Great Leap's carnage. On further reflection, it also seems that the arsons were tactics of powerless villagers who were desperate to make reform-era party leaders conform to the legitimizing dynamics of a renewed discourse over food security. Those who abandoned this discouse paid a dear price – the house of Bao Zhilong, who sought to exercise power without discourse, was torched on three separate occasions between 1989 and 1993. (Although this might seem an odd strategy – burning the private spaces that housed the public grain jeopardized the grain – it also assured villagers that boss Bao and his cronies would not get the grain, either.)

Da Fo's farmers also repeatedly stressed that leaders should practice *compassion* in their relations with ordinary villagers. Liangmen township leaders frequently acted as if they were oblivious to this popular Confucian principle of virtuous governance well into the second decade of reform. Reform-era violations of this principle – and the persistence of unhappy memories of the Mao era – sometimes moved villagers who otherwise would have accepted the behavior of officials who delivered inequity and unfairness to embrace contention.

A month after the Spring Festival of 1998, popular resentment toward the privileged, corrupt order of Liangmen township government exploded. An Zhenlin, the new head of the Liangmen township government, was seized in a marketplace and humiliated before a teeming crowd. What triggered this contentious incident? In my travels in Dongle county, I frequently noticed that Henan villagers, like their counterparts in other poor interior provinces, lacked up-to-date ambulatory medical services. Most of them transported sick relatives to distant health clinics on crude wooden stretchers, in wheelbarrows, on bicycles, and even on their backs – an exhausting, snail-paced process that precluded timely treatment. Frequently, these makeshift arrangements were passed by the speeding, comfortable motor vehicles of the state – upscale jeeps and SUVs in which Liangmen township officials such as An Zhenlin traveled. In the reform era, people from Da Fo and surrounding villages sometimes solicited rides for their sick relatives from the drivers of such officials as the latter slowed down to navigate heavily trafficked market places. In March 1998, as An Zhenlin's personal jeep was passing through Wanxiuzhuang market, a few villagers hailed it and appealed to him to take a sick person to the hospital, located on the route to the township government. The leader not only refused, he also yelled that not just any lowly bumpkin could ride with someone of his high rank. Taking offense at An's disdainful, uncompassionate remark, farmers emerged from the market crowd to seize him. Several of them threatened to give him a beating him on the spot.

An Zhenlin managed to escape, but then he made a big mistake. On returning to his vehicle, An told his driver not to stop for any group of low-life farmers the next time he encountered a market crowd. Instead, he should just "run over the poor bastards" as, at most, An would have to pay them a few thousand yuan for compensation. The driver leaked the township leader's mean-spirited words, and the violent statement traveled fast on the local grapevine. Within a few days, when An's vehicle slowed down to weave its way through a teeming marketplace, he was seized and humiliated. This time, farmers made him crawl under the legs of various people in the market to avoid a severe beating while they shouted that he had lost his humanity. An became an object of popular disdain and ridicule in villages across Liangmen township. People in Da Fo learned about this incident from Bao Timing, a leader of Da Fo's growing tax-resistance movement.[115] They recalled their mistreatment by Great Leap party leaders who had denied them sick leave from the sites of forced labor and prohibited them from traveling to health clinics and hospitals usually reserved for high-ranking party cadres, and they concluded that An Zhenlin got what he deserved.

Da Fo's villagers also believed that leaders should be kindhearted and demonstrate *good will*, correspondingly upholding the golden rule of local political culture: *Leaders should not do any unnecessary harm.* If the logic of this preference had its roots in popular Confucian wisdom, the obsession with it stemmed in part from memories of its overthrow in the Great Leap era. The hope for a world without state harm was a major reason why Da Fo's villagers initially endorsed the Deng Xiaoping–led reform. Yet the Liangmen township leaders delivered a great deal of unnecessary harm to villagers in the reform era.

[115] Bao Timing, interview.

To be sure, by the early 1990s the oppressive Maoist climate had dissipated somewhat, and the Liangmen township leaders had less control over the economic lives of farmers. But Liangmen party leaders were not inclined to give up the habits of the Maoist past simply because reformers in Beijing had crafted new policies. When the township leaders could not persuade villagers to cooperate with their attempts to implement their versions of reform policy, they continued to resort to physical abuse, illegal detention, and public struggle as methods to enforce public compliance. In some cases, Liangmen township leaders reactivated these Maoist weapons to actualize corruption. Between 1990 and 2000, for example, the township leaders frequently charged villagers fees to "participate" in study sessions and public criticism sessions aimed at securing compliance with reform policies from taxation to birth control to tuition payments. Da Fo's farmers were frustrated by the harm delivered by this kind of reform-era extortion. I do not know if they mounted concerted resistance to it, but they were occasionally inspired by stories of how people in other villages and markets rose up to negate the delivery of harm through public criticism. Bao Shuangcheng descibed the formation of bottom-up contention against this corrupted mechanism of party-state domination in nearby Wanxiuzhuang, where villagers attacked the authority, status, and will of township officials who had used public criticism to hurt them. According to Bao, the people of Wanxiuzhuang were more courageous and more unified in their opposition to official corruption and abuse. Bao gives one example of their opposition to an official who had forced villagers to pay to participate in humiliating public criticism sessions: "When the Liangmen township leaders came to Wanxiuzhuang to enforce birth planning policies, they often took villagers to township government headquarters to attend public criticism sessions. They asked villagers to pay fifty yuan a day for attending these sessions. Sometimes they also beat up people, ordering them to crawl on the ground and bark like dogs. They did this to humiliate villagers. But people in Wanxiuzhuang later tricked the head of Liangmen township government. They invited him to a banquet in their village, but then they began to beat him. He had to hide under a bed and beg them for mercy. The villagers did not let him off easy, however. They made him crawl on the ground and imitate the barking of a dog also. Only then did they let him go. Later, the township government leaders, who had lost face, reported this matter to the Dongle county government, but the county leaders did nothing about it."[116]

The Deng-led condemnation of Mao-era mechanisms of public regimentation and repression did not automatically engender political change. Deep in the countryside, the habits of Mao-era party rule still persisted, and villagers saw those habits of CCP leaders as a continuation of the corrupt and coercive past. But villagers were determined to resist the will of party rulers and to stop them from practicing the kind of Mao-era politics that had delivered their

[116] Bao Shuangcheng, interview.

households into harm's way. In the Da Fo area, reform-era corruption was met with small counterpunches to the powerful. And just as Da Fo's farmers attended periodic markets and learned about incidents of resistance, empowering them and teaching them that collective action mattered, the seemingly isolated incidents of resistance to widespread, unending corruption that took place in Da Fo were repeated in scores of border area villages, and the news of them spread along the market, making them less than "isolated."

– – –

The post-Mao period, with its semi-reformed economy and its decentralized authoritarian thrust, gave rise to mutated forms of corruption.[117] Yet the origins of reform-era corruption in Da Fo lay not only in Beijing's plan to create a less despotic, more productive and efficient political economy but also in the embedded, corrupt, party work style that had crystallized in the Great Leap Forward and devastated villagers – a style that higher-ups in Beijing and Henan province failed to correct.[118] In Da Fo, the decision to restore party boss Bao Zhilong and his network to realize party-structured order toward the end of the Cultural Revolution, and the failure of the center to remove these village-level agents of corruption and catastrophe in the early 1980s, positioned them to grab the prizes of unregulated econonomic decollectivization locally and to build up new "official markets" at the expense of old popular village markets, all of which further undercut the Commmunist Party's ability to regain legitimacy.

Corruption in the first two decades of the Deng-led reform was systemic.[119] In places such as Da Fo village and Liangmen township, local party leaders appointed by higher-ups sought to bolster their gains at a cost to villagers. Distrustful of distant Central government politicians, they practiced a "grab what you can grab now" politics under the radar of reform. Such aggravated corruption stirred up popular memories of the traumatic losses of the Great Leap past and, in turn, ignited protest and contention against village and township party leaders whose brazen misdeeds raised popular fears of similar losses in the present.[120] In targeting such local party leaders, people in Da Fo understood they were taking on the microlevel agents of corrupt Beijing politicians who had designed reform as a tool of CCP power and monopoly and whose halfhearted efforts to constrain the corruption of its local political base only damaged its own authority.[121]

---

[117] Pei, "The Long March against Graft."   [118] Cf. Lu, *Cadres and Corruption.*

[119] Kwong, *Political Economy of Corruption.*

[120] For the conceptual underpinnings of this argument, see Kleinman, "How Bodies Remember," 703–723, and Jing, *Temple of Memories,* 67.

[121] For a counterview, see Landry, *Decentralized Authoritarianism,* 259–260, which argues that local party-state corruption has not seriously damaged the upper end of the CCP. Cf. Manion, *Corruption by Design.*

Contrary to conventional scholarly wisdom, which holds that Chinese villagers drew a clear distinction between Central government rulers and local party-state leaders, with the former having good intentions to deliver good policies,[122] Da Fo's farmers judged the Central government by the quality of local officials and party leaders appointed by the center and its spiraling hierarchy. Some understood that corruption extended up and down this hierarchy. They viewed the party-state as rotten from top to bottom, as a critically ill patient with layered secondary infections. While many farmers acknowledged the anticorruption sentiments of Hu Jintao, Xi Jinping, and other Central government leaders, they blamed higher-ups for lacking the integrity and will to discipline corrupt subprovincial and subcounty party leaders. Yan Chunjian points to this lack of integrity and will on the part of Beijing rulers when he says: "I do not know why more people do not blame the Central government for the official misconduct at the grassroots level. Should the Central government do something to control the official corruption? Of course. But most people do not have any way of knowing about the corrupt relationship between the Central government leaders and the local government. Of course it also seems that the Central government does not necessarily control local government officials very well."[123] While acknowledging that limited knowledge of the systemic nature of authoritarian state power makes villagers vulnerable to Beijing's efforts to encourage them to blame local officials for misrule, Yan Chunjian was explicating the link between the center and local government corruption.[124] Still other Da Fo farmers understood the politics behind this scapegoating, which Mao had used to shift blame for his Great Leap famine onto local party leaders, and which Communist rulers in Beijing subsequently borrowed to excuse the institutionally based corruption of the reform era. Of course, a few quotes can only begin to challenge the received academic wisdom that the center is far away and good, while the local party leaders are up close and bad, but the evidence from Da Fo urges us to look more systematically at the top-down nature of party-state corruption in order to grasp the deep legitimacy crisis in the countryside.

In Da Fo, the social costs of reform-era corruption paled in comparison to those of the Maoist past, particularly the party-centered corruption that exacerbated Great Leap era suffering and loss. Nonetheless, villagers saw the corrupt acts of reform-era cadres through the memory of forms of corruption and

---

[122] Li, "Political Trust in Rural China," 228–238, and O'Brien and Li, *Rightful Resistance*, 39, 45–46.

[123] Yan Chunjian, interview.

[124] Compare with Baum, "Obstacles to Reform," 8. In reviewing Chen Guide and Wu Chundao, *Will the Boat Sink the Water?*, Baum argues that the Central government plays on the anger of rural people against corrupt and capricious local rulers, and also on their ignorance of the wider structural dynamics of the political system, to contain local protest and contention. Baum's reading is somewhat consistent with O'Brien and Li, but their argument is more refined. Cf. O'Brien and Li, *Rightful Resistance*, 38-39, 20, 42–46, esp. 44.

coercion institutionalized by the Maoists, and their imaginations sometimes magnified the threat such acts posed to livelihood and security, activating an arsenal of weapons of resistance that had survived many decades of terror and tyranny.[125] The contentious performances of Da Fo area farmers, triggered by the corrupt acts of local party leaders, were not authorized by Central government leaders. Nor were they energized by a heartfelt belief in the supportive ethical rhetoric of Beijing power holders, designed to encourage the rural poor to concede that the center had the moral authority to govern even while its local party base relied on corruption to deprive them of full political rights. The performances were influenced, and significantly cued, by long-embedded habits of party-state rule that threatened to close off life chances, and they were informed by popular Confucian folk norms that were at odds such habits. In Da Fo, this contention had a dual purpose: to prevent local party networks from reconstructing another deadly form of dictatorship and to pursue a democratic alternative to a one-party state that, while open to globalization and to experimenting with "guided democracy," was determined to maintain its monopoly on power and on the political economy that bolstered that power.

---

[125] I am indebted to Steven I. Levine for helping me develop this point. Personal correspondence, January 31, 2003.

6

The Rise of the Electricity Tigers

Monopoly, Corruption, and Memory

In his 2002 warning on pandemic corruption, Chairman Hu Jintao focused mainly on local governments and local officials, as if only they, and not Central government politicians, were giving villagers cause to resist the party-state. The thrust of the Deng and post-Deng reform, however, was to restore CCP control at the central and local levels, and this entailed supporting local strongmen such as Da Fo party secretary Bao Zhilong. In this respect, reform actually involved a political restoration of party-centered power as opposed to the charismatic-based power of the Mao period, and Beijing relied on recycled Mao-era officials and local party leaders in hinterland villages where the legitimacy crisis stemming from the Great Leap's damage persisted. This process favored political hustlers who had been in leadership positions previously, and they often became the ground-level agents of Beijing politicians in charge of important sectors of the reform-era political economy.

Sure enough, Da Fo's farmers say that reform-era corruption was structured in part by big-name Chinese Communist Party (CCP) officials in charge of centralized state monopolies. They point out that the extension of state monopoly into the hands of party boss Bao Zhilong's local political network engendered a pattern of audacious rent-seeking at both the macro and micro levels, and their stories reveal that this pattern stoked memories of Great Leap–era domination and abuse.[1] Indeed, in some important ways, corruption in the village was a direct result of the monopoly power of the CCP.

---

[1] I am indebted to Yan Sun for helping me sift through the corruption literature to arrive at this point. See *Corruption and Market*, 8, 15–16. However, the narrative here does not fully support Yan Sun. It suggests that corruption stemming from the private capture of state assets and public services in China spawned forms of corruption that were as audacious and brazen as those in rural Russia under reform. Cf. Sun, *Corruption and Market*, 8. On the conception of bureaucratic

Popular experience with the Central government control of electricity stemmed all the way back to the 1950s when the Mao-led CCP – following Lenin, who took electricity as an icon of modernity – promised to provide rural China with electricity to promote development and alleviate poverty. While the Great Leap saw the construction of miniature hydroelectric power stations in parts of the rural interior, the center did not invest in these stations. The Maoist emphasis, instead, was on commune-supervised electricity-driven water conservancy projects and irrigation wells. The primary beneficiaries were official networks and a few farmers in communes and model villages such as Dingcun in Liangmen People's Commune. In the end, the Leap experiment with electricity was not designed to serve the needs of rural household consumers; only a few villages and households in Dongle county were heated or lighted at night or benefited from electric-powered shops, schools, and wells. By the time the Leap failed them, Da Fo's farmers understood that socialism plus electricity privileged a few party-connected people in localities with thick official representation and that they still lived in one of many pockets of poverty and darkness.[2]

In the first decade of the post-1978 reform, Central government officials sought to address this darkness, which reflected the fact that China was still a very backward country. The problem was how Deng's men went about it. Apparently, they restructured the delivery of public services and the distribution of public goods in ways that produced what Yan Sun has termed "joint monopoly."[3] Officials at the very center of the CCP-directed political system allowed local party cadres and their clients to seize economic power, so that in Dongle county, strategically positioned township and village party activists were free to reap profits and reconstitute the basis of their local power. Consideration of the experience of Da Fo with joint monopoly helps to reveal the links between macrolevel "reform" as dictated by the Central government and the government's microlevel agents in the deep countryside, as well as the fate of ordinary villagers who had to put up with these agents. In Dongle county, the everyday interaction of farmers with the local agents of the Central government Ministry of Electricity played a crucial role in shaping popular discourses about the reform-era state and its programs for promoting rural development.

Deng and other top CCP officials understood electrical power as central to economic development. During the first two decades of reform, China's economic growth was substantially dependent on the ability of CCP officials to manage the massive consumption of electricity in both city and countryside. By

---

capitalism and rent seeking, see Wedeman, "Looters, Rent-Scrappers, and Dividend-Collectors," 457–478. For support of the comparison with Russia, see Friedman, "China Transformed," 6.

[2] In constructing this section, I have benefited from several sources, not all of which are in agreement: Becker, *Hungry Ghosts*, 255; Chan, *Mao's Crusade*, 54; Lippit, "The Great Leap Forward Reconsidered," 92–113; and especially Pan, Peng, Li, et al., "Rural Electrification in China," 1–14; Cf. Brown, *City versus Countryside in Mao's China*, 103–104.

[3] Sun, *Corruption and Market*, 14.

the mid-1990s, the fear of serious power shortages associated with stampeding energy consumption of urban-based manufacturing and rural-based developmental enterprises gripped senior CCP politicians and economists in Beijing and Shanghai.[4] Understandably, Central government reformers focused on the delivery of this public utility to the agricultural interior, in part because they understood electrical power as key to rural economic development and in part because they equated the delivery of electricity with modernity and material improvement, a process that supposedly would prompt rural people to identify the Communist Party as *the* beacon of national progress. In the Da Fo area, as in countless interior communities, electricity was key to the efficient irrigation of farm lands and the improvement of harvest yields, to the lighting of homes and schools, and to the running of factories. Yet it was the agents of the National Electricity Company, a vertical state monopoly dominated by the network of CCP autocrat Li Peng (who also helped engineer the Tiananmen Square bloodbath of June 4, 1989), who became the major beneficiaries of Deng Xiaoping's effort to modernize the agricultural sector and industrialize the rural economy. In time, the role of these agents in delivering electricity came to remind Da Fo's farmers that the post-Mao center, like its predecessor, had failed to nurture and defend locally voiced standards of accountability, honesty, and fairness for petty officials, party secretaries, and their clients.

REFORM CAPTURED BY NONREFORMERS: THE LI PENG ELECTRICITY EMPIRE

The issue of electricity posed a special difficulty for Central government reformers and rural farm people. In the collective era, electricity was managed by the Ministry of Electricity and Irrigation. Headed by the Stalinist-trained electrical engineer Li Peng, in the aftermath of the Cultural Revolution the ministry was focused on both the construction and management of electricity. A decade after the dismantlement of the collectives, around 1989–1990, Li Peng, as China's Prime Minister, presided over the splitting of this ministry into two parts.[5] A powerful Beijing politician who by and large opposed economic reform, Li Peng, along with his family and their clients and cronies within the central party-state hierarchy, ran the newly formed Electricity Management Bureau (*Dianyebu*), which took the lead in managing the delivery of electricity to the countryside. Although the Electricity Management Bureau was formally separated from the old state ministry of electricity – and strictly speaking its subcounty agents worked for themselves rather than the collective – in reality this particular bureau remained an enterprise of Central government monopoly

---

[4] Cf. French, "China's Boom Brings Fear of an Electricity Breakdown." For a wonderfully insightful paper that lends powerful support for the interpretation I have given to this section, see Chen, "Taming the Electric Tiger," 2–3, 7, 10–15, 18–24, 31.

[5] Chen, "Taming the Electric Tiger," 19.

managed by the National Electricity Company, a reform-era vertical command structure with Li Peng at the top.

For the first two decades of reform, the national structure of the Ministry of Electricity was in the hands of Li Peng and linked to hard-liners in the security apparatus, which gave Li and his network an empire when it came to leveraging the energy-driven requirements of China's economic development. In the 1990s, the Ministry of Electricity was renamed the Zhongguo Guojia Dianli Gongsi (National Electricity Company). This company, still under the direction of Li Peng and his network, took complete responsibility for the supply of electricity to the prefectural level throughout China, leaving the governance of appointments, day-to-day supply operations, and pricing decisions in the hands of county- and township-level Communist Party officials and leaders who were, on the instructions of Li Peng himself, encouraged to build up their own small model electricity power plants. In this experiment, Li Peng continued to occupy the apex of a vertical state monopoly, but the structure of the monopoly allowed for extreme decentralization of central party-state energy operations in the towns and villages of the deep rural interior. Although Dongle county and Liangmen township government received some energy supply from the national electricity grid supervised by Li Peng's network, the local Commmunist Party leaders in charge of these units were instructed to be self-reliant, so that at the bottom of this public utility system the leaders responsible for creating electricity plants and acquiring and meeting energy demands were allowed to earn money for themselves by selling electricity.[6]

In effect, this Li Peng–orchestrated Central government monopoly, with tight controls at the top and loosely structured operations at the bottom, gave local party leaders the leeway to increase supply and, in turn, to enrich themselves by deciding the price of electricity without any popular oversight. This process encouraged an explosion of corruption within the CCP-ordered electricity bureaus at the lower county and subcounty rungs of Li Peng's far-flung electricity empire. In an important sense, therefore, this system replicated the impetuous political economy transformations of the Great Leap Forward, when the Mao-led center more or less granted autonomy to the people's commune without giving the local commune leaders the funds or wherewithal to promote development – a process that nudged cadres at the lower tip of the socialist state to garner money, capital, and property from villagers, and to do so without any political accountability. Thus, on the surface, the reform-era county and township electricity bureaus had autonomy and apparently used it to violate Central government attempts to make them comply with the "just" supply of this all-important public good. But in reality the center, with Li Peng at the helm, actually *granted* this autonomy and turned a blind eye when it came to how local Communist Party–appointed officials and agents implemented its developmental agenda.

---

[6] Li Peng D, Confidential Harvard University source.

Furthermore, during the first twenty years of reform, there were no laws governing this process, which gave rise in many parts of rural China to officially sanctioned local "electricity mafias" whose agents used their power to serve themselves through unregulated, often brazen forms of corruption that recalled the corruption of cadres in charge of the grain monopoly of Mao's Great Leap Forward. This process unfolded from the very outset of reform in Dongle county, Liangmen township, and Da Fo village.[7]

Between 1996 and 2002, the People's Republic of China (PRC) moved toward a nationwide grid system, incorporating the county and township electricity plans into a unified supply plan. In this period, the State Council replaced the old Ministry of Electricity with the State Power Corporation (SPC), which, in Xu Yi-chong's words, actually was "hived off of the older ministry"[8] and which remained dominated by Li Peng's core network. Though Li Peng's national monopoly was challenged by Zhu Rongji and later Wen Jiabao, Li successfully seized control of the most important of the new regional power companies in China – the Huabei Dianli Gongsi, or North China Electricity Power Company, which took charge of electric power in Beijing and all of Hebei, Shandong, and Henan, the region of China where most of the electricity plants that supplied the "teeth of industrial development" were located and where the density of reform-era heavy industrial development was the greatest. Higher-level party leaders, including Deng Xiaoping, deferred to Li's authority, expertise, and power in the energy domain, and so Li Peng was able to appoint his son, Li Xiaopeng, as the chief executive officer of the North China Electricity Power Company. Li Peng and his family became major stockholders in this key regional company and gained significant control of other energy sources, such as coal and thermal energy.[9]

Despite the movement away from the early reform-era model of decentralized electricity plant development toward five key regional companies tied to a national grid, two things remained unchanged. First, the Li Peng family empire by and large remained intact, and in some respects spread between 1995 and 2008. In this period, Li Peng used his clout to push through his pet Three Gorges Dam project, which left millions of "relocated" farm residents along the Yangtze River homeless, damaged the geological template, polluted the ecosystem of southeast Sichuan, and destroyed the cultural heritage of the Yangtze River Valley.[10] In the same period, Li Peng wielded his power to make his son Li Xiaopeng the chairman of Huaneng Power International Group, which was the regional power corporation responsible for electricity development and delivery in Hebei, Shandong, Henan, and metropolitan Beijing – and hence for all practical purposes blanketed most of the North China macro region,

[7] Ibid.   [8] Xu, "A Powerhouse Reform," 132–133.
[9] Li Peng D, 2010; personal correspondence with confidential Harvard University source and with Han Dongping, Warren Wilson College, December 17, 2010.
[10] Zeng, "Li Peng Ji Qi Fubai Jia."

including the border area in which Dongle county and Da Fo village are located. Listed at twenty-fourth on the *Fortune List of China's Top 100 Companies*, by 2009 the Huaneng Power Group had become the biggest electric power enterprise in all of Asia, assuming responsibility for electricity grid management and thermal power plant development from Beijing to Singapore – and delivering massive damage to river ecologies and river-dependent farmers throughout mainland Southeast Asia.

Li Peng also drew his daughter, Li Xiaolin, into the highly politicized world of energy development. In 2004 Li Xiaolin moved into the chairmanship of the China Power International Development Corporation, another one of the five regional power-grid companies designated by the State Council.[11] As the chief executive of this Hong Kong–based corporation, Li Xiaolin became the point person for managing the financial, logistic, and diplomatic dimensions of property acquisition and development, construction operations, and foreign trade endeavors of several of the five regional grid corporations. This Li Peng family–based network spearheaded the PRC's vault to energy superpower status in global energy supply, as its corporate leadership maneuvered to finance and construct coal power plants and hydroelectric dams in a sprawling empire from Southeast Asia to Africa. In project after project, the Li Peng energy power elite was involved directly or through subsidiaries in exporting the kind of developmental conquest that marked its energy operations in China, benefiting its own interest at the expense of rural people living under corrupted political systems.

In short, Li Peng's offspring became the dominant "princelings" (*taizidang*) of China's energy sector in the reform period, playing a critical role in controlling the lifeline of the national economy, in promoting China's global rise, and ultimately in stifling reform to conserve their monopoly of the electrical power sector. Although Li Peng and his network of clients paid homage to market reform, they actually used their dominant position within China's energy sector to hijack the promarket proposals of reform-minded rivals within the Central government in order to suppress market competition in this critical sector, thereby maintaining a monopoly that had its origins in the highly centralized planning system of the Maoist era.[12] Following Deng Xiaoping's 1992 Southern Tour, in which Deng called for a renewal of market competition, Li Peng mobilized his protégés, including Hao Yan, Zou Jihua, and Cai Songyue, to endorse Deng's logic, and they apparently seized leadership of the reform process.[13] "Yet," as Ling Chen has pointed out in her seminal *China Journal* article, "instead of focusing on introducing competition into generation and distribution, they diverted attention to maintaining the national integration of power transmission."[14]

---

[11] Peh, "Corruption: 'Princelings' Rule China's Corporate World."
[12] Chen, "Playing the Market Reform Card," 69–71, 73, 80–81.   [13] Ibid., 98.   [14] Ibid., 85.

There was a second continuity. The move toward a unified, more tightly integrated national monopoly with regional companies did not significantly alter the power structure of the CCP-controlled electricity monopoly at the local rural level, for there, most of the Communist Party officials and leaders who had become the semi-private owners of electricity plants, transformers, and stations in the early reform period stayed in power, and they and their networks of clients, while paying homage to structural reform, maintained a great deal of autonomy when it came to the local supply, delivery, and price of electricity. Thus, it is important to emphasize that the electricity bureaus within the Hebei-Shandong-Henan border area, including those in Dongle county and Liangmen township, continued to operate as semi-private monopolies even after they came under the influence of the Huaneng Power International Group headed by Li Xiaopeng. Farmers in villages such as Da Fo therefore had no choice but to purchase electricity from this noncompetitive system, which favored local party leaders who wanted to use the semi-privatization of the public utility system to serve their own monetary interests.

In this joint monopoly, those who controlled electricity at the local level had the tacit support of the Central government, for the Beijing-headquartered State Grid Corporation, which worked with the five key regional power companies, had to gain State Council approval for investment and construction of power plants in all regions. With this in mind, it is not surprising that the official, rapid post-2002 push for water-powered and coal-fired power plants and hydroelectric dam stations was accompanied by the forced takeover of prime town and village lands, the eviction of farmers from ancestral fields without monetary compensation sufficient to offset the resulting existential threat, the embezzlement of funds designated for relocation and resettlement of homeless villagers, and demands that soaring electricity bills be paid by farmers now dependent on regional cum local power grids for electricity supply.

Throughout rural China, this exploitative pattern of development was accentuated because many of the blueprints for power plants were implemented by county and township leaders who benefited from attendant land theft, which was central to the accumulation of local state wealth. The leaders facilitated the plants by undercompensating farmers for their land and then pocketing most of the money, a process they spurred by hiring thugs to drive farmers off of their lands and then calling in police forces to suppress those who protested this aggrandizement. As a result, there were belligerent confrontations between farmers and the local county and township agents of the power plants, and the incidence and scale of violence surrounding the face-offs increased after 2002. The collective uprisings in Qingfu, Da Shu, and Shunhe in Sichuan (2004), in Shengyou village in Hebei (2005), and in Dongzhou in Guandong (also 2005) all were reported as disputes with corrupt, land-grabbing local officials pure and simple, but actually each one had its origins in the frustrated attempts of farmers to prevent local party leaders charged with advancing the center's mission to develop water-powered and coal-fired electricity plants from usurping farm lands without adequate consultation and compensation. The case of Shengyou, where hundreds of hired thugs killed six village protesters, apparently grew out of the Huaneng Power International Group's decision to press ahead with development of the Dingzhou power plant. Li Xiaopeng's powerful North China regional network was rumored to have been responsible for suppressing this popular response to state-framed modernity.[15]

In 2006, mounting resistance to this pattern of brazen land theft prompted Beijing to verbally assert its right to regulate compensation for the local official acquisition of land, and in 2006–2007 Beijing and its Ministry of Land Resources sought greater control over land seizures for development.[16] In 2008, the Central government and some of its provincial arms passed laws to compensate farmers for the occupation of agricultural lands given over to electricity plants, power pylons, and electricity poles and wires, and it attempted to deepen reform by requiring punishment of illegal occupants. Yet the responsibility for enforcing such laws fell to the agents of the National Land Resource Bureaus within each local prefectural government, and these agents still had to deal with powerful, deceptive officials in the county and township electricity bureaus. Furthermore, Beijing's paper reforms did not spell out legal processes for personal litigation, so that individual farm households remained vulnerable to land seizures for power plant development. When the issue of energy development moved villages to defend their lands, Beijing's rulers chose to accommodate the powerful cartels within the state electricity sector whose patrons were, after all, significant players in China's economic rise.[17]

The great majority of rural dwellers in the Hebei-Shandong-Henan border area experienced Beijing's mandate for energy development through their daily encounters with the ground-level agents of this specific public utility sector *after* the plants were constructed and *after* their localities were tied to a particular regional electricity grid. At this point, rampant corruption enveloped the delivery of electricity services to the rural interior villages, increasing the risks to the livelihood of farmer-users in places such as Da Fo. As Akhil Gupta has shown for village India, it was precisely through conflict-ridden encounters with the corrupt practices of local public utility agents within this kind of joint monopoly that Da Fo's farmers, as consumers, formed their perception of the translocal reform-era CCP-led national state and voiced concerns about its harmful conduct.[18] These encounters, and the resistance they spawned, were seldom reported in even trustworthy sources on China, such as *South China Morning Post*, *Southern Weekend*, and *China Digital Times*. But by asking Da Fo's farmers how they experienced these encounters, we learn that their perception of the agents of state energy monopoly was conditioned by painful memories of

---

[15] "Li Peng's Son Implicated"; Divjak, "Another Angry Protest in China."
[16] Naughton, "Assertive Center," 1–10.   [17] Confidential Harvard University source.
[18] Gupta, "Blurred Boundaries," 83–84.

the past – a past that reached all the way back to the Great Leap Forward and raised fears of another round of harm at the hands of the bullies who delivered it.

THE RISE OF THE ELECTRICITY TIGERS IN DA FO VILLAGE

With the disintegration of the Liangmen People's Commune after 1978 and the renewed practice of household-based farming, popular demand for electricity boomed in Dongle county. The profession of electrician thus became an attractive occupation. The multilayered approval process, which involved licensing, regulation, and delivery of utility services to the villages, was governed by Communist Party officials in Beijing, Zhengzhou, Dongle county, and even Liangmen township itself.

Coming under the rule of this revised state-run public utility service, people in the deep countryside saw two important changes. First, there was a change in the trajectory of payment for the cost of electricity. In the collective period, the village, or brigade, paid for the cost of electricity to the Dongle County Electricity Bureau, and individual electricians could not make any money to speak of from the electricity bills of individual farm households. After the collective was disbanded, the Da Fo village party leaders contracted the transformers to individual electricians, and the electricians, who had to register with the county electricity bureau, were allowed to sell electricity to individual farm households. Essentially, the Dongle County Electricity Bureau sold electricity to the electricians in charge of transformers, and the electricians would set rates over and above the price for which they had purchased this right to resell electricity to villagers. Consequently, Da Fo's farmers were at the mercy of the individual electricians who owned the transformers. Whenever a farmer needed to irrigate his fields, he had to ask the electrician to come and help connect his pumps to the transformer, and the decision to come – or come on time – was solely that of the attending electrician, who rarely brooked contention over the charge for usage.[19]

It is important to emphasize that farmers in Da Fo saw the resulting price burden as the product of national politics. "The high price of electricity," says Bao Dongwen, "has been a national problem. Nobody wanted to pay the initial cost of electricity. But we only complained privately, and nobody took action to go to the county Electricity Bureau to fight this 'tiger'"[20] – a term that signified danger and possibly death to villagers. (Though not understanding the principle of electricity, villagers knew it could kill if mishandled, and so parents in the Liangmen–Da Fo area warned their children of the dangers of electricity, using the term "tiger" to scare them into not playing with it. This was the original reason why they used the nickname of "electricity tiger" to refer to the Bureau

---

[19] Bao Dongwen, interview.   [20] Ibid.

of Electricity and the electricians.)[21] We must be clear about why villagers were reluctant to fight this tiger: it operated in accordance with Robert Klitgaard's classic formula: monopoly + discretion – accountability = corruption,[22] and many of its local agents were party-approved hustlers who were not beholden to any democratic norms of responsibility. After 1998 or thereabouts, it became even more difficult to contest this monopoly, because for the most part the power of appointing electricians, which previously had been in the hands of Da Fo party leaders, was given over to Liangmen township government, so that the great majority of the electricians had a good relationship with the township government, whose leaders had an interest in supporting the electricians who were challenged from below. The commune had been disbanded, yet somehow power devolved back to the barely reformed township-level government, which, on the issue of how this joint monopoly worked locally, seemed to operate with the old dictatorial powers of the commune.

Second, the people who became township-level electricians by and large joined the ranks of a small group of rich people in rural China. Thus, although there was little change in who exercised power over the electricity monopoly, the local operatives of this monopoly used their positions and power to generate economic growth – and villagers saw them as the partisan agents of such growth. A Liangmenpo farmer explains that farmers near and far came to regard these agents of monopoly, who "made good money in the thirty years since reform," as "tigers" "because they have a monopoly over electricity, and everybody has to obey them."[23]

So why did people have to obey these tigers? In Chinese culture, the word "tiger" symbolized power, for the tiger, not the lion, was the king of the jungle, and the tiger could deliver deprivation as well as wealth. People in Da Fo also seized on this term experientially. They were inclined to obey the tiger out of fear – partly out of fear that a jolt of electricity could hurt their children who played around the transformers and wires, but partly out of another, historically conditioned fear: in the Great Leap, especially the anti-rightist campaign of late 1959, local party leaders were perceived as tigers on the prowl when they forced their way into homes to search for hidden grain, benefiting from the booty. No wonder that Da Fo's farmers both envied and feared the electricity tigers, who did not work under the hot sun, who were able to build some of the biggest homes in Dongle county, and who had the power to make or break the harvest fortunes of ordinary families.

These sentiments were felt in surrounding villages, as well. Lamenting that Deng Xiaoping had allowed "a few people to get rich at the expense of the majority of people," farmers in Liangmenpo included the electricity tigers among Deng's corrupt "friends" who were always "looking for money."[24]

---

[21] Tang Wuyi, interview.   [22] Klitgaard, *Controlling Corruption*, 75.
[23] Zhang Bingzhuang, interview.   [24] Zhang Heping, interview.

Bao Dongwen, a disgruntled Da Fo farmer, added a more explicitly political explanation for why these friends of Deng could look for money from this monopoly: "Electricity," says Bao, "has been a big issue in the village ever since the disbanding of the collective. It has not yet been resolved. People are angry with the price of electricity because the electricians, and the *officials* who were in charge of electricity, got rich at the expense of the people. I think that this is at the center of the major issues in China today. A small number of people take advantage of this public utility, and other public utilities, to get rich, and shift the cost onto the people."[25]

So who were the local people who took advantage of monopoly to get rich at the expense of tillers? Jonathan Unger has noted that many of the local Communist Party leaders who benefited from the deconstruction of the people's commune had held leadership positions under the Maost collective and that some became agents of corruption in the post-Mao period.[26] In the case of this particular sector of the economy, officials with close ties to the Deng-led center allowed local party leaders and their cronies to seize reform, and not only profit by such but also reconstitute the basis of their power. As Rasma Karklins has found for Eastern Europe, in Dongle county key agents in pre-reform-era Communist Party networks often joined with the state-appointed technocratic managers of electricity development to perpetuate their economic privileges and subvert the democratic input of villagers into the reform process, all in the name of serving the public good.[27]

As reform accelerated, people in Da Fo and Liangmen township jockeyed for official approval to become electricians, and some attempted to grab both the tools and the title.[28] By 1990, Da Fo village had six officially sanctioned electricians (or so it seemed). Several had jumped to the top of the small pile of the richest people in the village. Most of Da Fo's electricians were connected to the power network of the self-serving, corrupt, old-guard Maoists. Three of them were the sons of the most hated perpetrators of the Great Leap Forward's inhumanity: Bao Zhilong, the corrupt party boss of the Great Leap; Bao Yibin, the party secretary who had abused his own mother in the Leap; and Bao Zhigen, the pistol-toting rapist of the Leap era. Within a decade, these sons had established a monopoly over electricity distribution and delivery, taking full advantage of the Li Peng–influenced Central government failure to significantly reform the regulatory process of the Ministry of Electricity. As Ling Chen has pointed out, the electricity power bureaus were characterized by strong nepotistic politics, and the power sector was staffed by the relatives, friends, and

---

[25] Bao Dongwen, interview.

[26] Unger, *Transformation of Rural China*, 143; also see Gilley, *China's Democratic Future*, 257.

[27] Cf. Karklins, "Anti-Corruption Incentives," and Karklins, "Typology of Post-Communist Corruption," 22–32.

[28] Again, on the phenonemon of grabbing, see Friedman, "China Transformed," 6, and Pei, *China's Trapped Transition*.

cronies of corrupt power networks that managed it.[29] This was not reform at all, but rather a continuation of monopoly in the guise of reform.

By early 2000, virtually every farmer in Da Fo village had come to resent the social and political effects of this monopoly. They especially resented Bao Wenxing – the richest and the most powerful electrician in Da Fo and the son of the unprincipled Great Leap–era maniac Bao Zhigen, who had served boss Bao Zhilong by bullying and beating farmers whose collective work performances were displeasing. In the early phase of decollectivization, roughly 1978–1985, "rehabilitated" party boss Bao Zhilong still procured the village electrical transformers. With privatization, the transformers were purchased by individuals, and so in 1985 boss Bao Zhilong encouraged his client Bao Zhigen to borrow 2,000 yuan from his sister to buy a transformer for Da Fo village. This loan was matched with another 2,000 yuan loan from the village coffers. The two men thereupon bought the transformer "for the village" from the Liangmen township leaders, and in fact they were able to acquire it at half the market price. Shortly afterward, boss Bao Zhilong appointed Bao Zhigen's son – Bao Wenxing – to the position of Da Fo village electrician.[30]

The problem was that Bao Wenxing unilaterally decided how much he wanted to charge villagers for electricity. Bao dared to charge fees for his electricity delivery service higher than those of any of the other five Da Fo electricians.[31] After 1993, Bao Wenxing charged 1.4 yuan (or sixty cents) per kilowatt, compared with the fifty cents charged by the other electricians, and after 1997 Bao Wenxing's price jumped even higher in periods of peak use. If farmers argued with Bao Wenxing about the high price he charged, Bao would first shut off the electricity to their households while they were watching the television news. If they did not pay up, Bao would cut off their supply at critical moments in the planting, watering, and harvest cycle. Further, Bao Wenxing began to insist that every user had to pay before he could use the electricity. If a farmer said he would pay the next day, then Bao would reply, "Well, then you had better water your crop the next day."[32] Following this, Bao Wenxing enlisted local toughs to intimidate farmers to pay on time. During the collective period, young Bao Wenxing and several of his friends in the party's favor had studied martial arts under Ruan Tianbao, a celebrated martial arts teacher from Dongle county; later Bao Wenxing used these martial arts skills to bully villagers.[33]

By 1998, electricity had become so expensive that many Da Fo villagers had stopped using it to light their homes, switching back to the kerosene oil lamps that had been used in the mid-1930s, prior to the Japanese invasion.[34] One cannot help but wonder if this reversal reminded villagers of a similar, less distant disappointment. Some were old enough to remember that Dongle

---

[29] Chen, "Taming the Electric Tiger," 14–15.   [30] Bao Zhigen, interview.
[31] Bao Zhongxin, interview.   [32] Bao Hongwen, interview.   [33] Bao Wenfang, interview.
[34] Bao Dongwen, interview.

county had started its first electricity plant in 1958 and that for a while there were street lights and illuminated classrooms in a few state-favored places. Zhou Zhenmin, who was a nine-year-old schoolboy at the start of the Great Leap, recalls there was great excitement over this development.[35] But as the Great Leap created fiscal chaos, the government cut the funding for the plant. Suddenly the street lights were turned off, and students had to rely on kerosene lamps for nighttime classes because, remembers Tang Wuyi, "the lighting was too expensive."[36] Then, in a year or so, all of the lights went out and villagers were utterly preoccupied with survival. Recalling this dark period, Zhou Zhenmin says, "We did not have enough to eat. People began to collect tree leaves, and when they could not find leaves anymore, they began to eat tree bark."[37]

Bao Wenxing and several other Da Fo electricians also practiced favoritism. They allowed their friends and families to use the electricity first, making other farmers wait until they finished irrigating their scattered plots. Worse yet, they waived the fees for special customers, shifting the cost onto other villagers. "One year," revealed the Da Fo party secretary Bao Shunhe, the successor to party boss Bao Zhilong, "I was building a new house outside the village, and the electrician allowed me to use the electricity free at the time. Of course, in the end, he shifted the cost onto others."[38]

Bao Wenxing had grown so powerful and arrogant that he, like his father in the Great Leap, automatically bullied anyone who complained to or challenged him. Bao invented four ways of using his power to bully people. The first was to tell villagers that the supply of electricity was too low for the day, so that they could not use it to irrigate their fields. "By doing this," says Bao Hongwen, "he was sending a signal to the person that he was not happy with him, and that the person needed to plead with him and needed to give him some gift before he would be able to use electricity."[39] The second method was to challenge the person who wanted to use electricity. He would say, "Did you complain about the price of electricity? If you think the price is too high, why do you want to use it? You should not use it."[40] Bao often would make the complainants plead with him and kneel down before him in order to receive electricity. The third method was to falsely exaggerate the number of kilowatt hours a farmer actually used and then accuse the recipient of intentionally using a rigged meter to conceal actual use. False accusation had been one way local party leaders and their clients had dealt with "difficult" farmers in the Great Leap – and now it was back.

Finally, Bao Wenxing secretly hurt people who attempted to mobilize government to their side. One such incident provided Da Fo's farmers with material for sick comedy. Bao Zhenxian – its target – relayed it in disbelief. When Da Fo's electricians were wiring the village in the early reform period, Bao Wenxing

---

[35] Zhou Zhenmin, interview.   [36] Tang Wuyi, interview.   [37] Zhou Zhenmin, interview.
[38] Bao Shunhe, interview.   [39] Bao Hongwen, interview.   [40] Ibid.

ignored the plan's geographical details, stopping short of wiring certain houses. Bao Zhenxian was one of the farmers whose house was left out. Bao complained to the Liangmen township Bureau of Electricity officials, one of whom reprimanded Bao Wenxing for his negligence. This loss of face drew the ire of Bao Wenxing. According to Bao Zhenxian: "He tried to hurt me. Several years later, my mother had to pay over 200 yuan a month for her electricity bills. She was living by herself, and she could not figure out why the bill was so high. Eventually, a friend helped me figure this out. Bao Wenxing had intentionally connected my mother's meter with her neighbor's wire. There were eight people in my mother's neighbor's family house. My mother was paying for their electricity bill, while her neighbor was paying my mother's bill. When I found this out, I went to ask Bao Wenxing why he did this. He refused to admit it was his doing. He said that it was the fault of the township government. He was really disgusting."[41] This act stuck in the craw of Da Fo's farmers, for it recalled the politics of the Great Leap, when Bao Wenxing's father had retaliated against those who challenged his mean-spirited acts.

Many villagers dubbed Bao Wenxing the "electricity tiger," and others dubbed him the "electricity emperor," a reference to his predisposition for mastership, which, again, brought back the bad memory of his father's ruthless efforts to subjugate villagers in the Great Leap. One of his victims was Bao Chuanxi. According to Bao Hongwen, "If anyone complained about the high price of electricity, Bao Wenxing would bully him. Few dared complain. Bao Chuanxi, a farmer, complained on the back street about the high price in front of villagers. Bao Wenxing caught wind of the complaint. When Bao Chuanxi was about to irrigate his wheat fields, Bao Wenxing cut the electrical wires to the fields. An honest farmer, Bao Chuanxi did not want to provoke a fight. He pleaded with Bao Wenxing and offered to kneel down before him if he allowed him to use electricity to water the fields. But Bao Wenxing insisted he could not use the electricity. Bao Chuanxi had to ask many other people in the village to plead on his behalf. They told Bao Wenxing that Bao Chuanxi had a big family, and that if he did not allow him to use electricity to water his wheat fields, his family would starve, and that he should have pity on his family. In the end, he allowed Bao Chuanxi to apologize to him and use the electricity."[42] This incident raised anxiety. Bao's father had wielded absolute power over starving collective field workers in the Great Leap, and now four decades later his son had achieved a similar domination. Unhappily for Da Fo's farmers, the price of modernization during reform was submission.

Just about everyone in Da Fo was fearful of Bao Wenxing's violent temperament. He often stomped through the village proclaiming he was not afraid of dying, and on more than one occasion he showed up with a knife at the homes

---

[41] Bao Zhenxian, interview.   [42] Bao Hongwen, interview.

of individual farmers who had challenged him, threatening to kill them and their families. As of 2002, Bao Wenxing had not killed anyone, but Bao Hongwen confirmed that "everybody in the village believes that he will."[43] Bao Hongwen explained that Bao's behavior inspired comparisons to his father, who had frequently unleashed his temper on villagers during the Great Leap: "I am in the same kin group with Bao Wenxing. We are very close in blood. Therefore, many people in the village asked me to tell Bao Wenxing to stop bullying them, and to stop backing them into a corner. But I have not dared to talk with him about this yet. He is very bad-tempered, just like his father Bao Zhigen. He loses his temper very easily. He knows that I am close kin, but he will forget that if I make him angry."[44]

In *Catastrophe and Contention in Rural China*, I pointed out that although Bao Zhigen was a poor, violent rogue whom brigade and commune party leaders had feared, these same leaders frequently relied on Bao to do their dirty work in the Great Leap.[45] Bao Zhigen's behavior persisted into reform and seems to have been transmitted to Bao's son, a violent hustler turned powerful economic player in the subcounty electricity hierarchy. In Da Fo and many villages under Liangmen township, for example, Bao Wenxing trumped his father's unpopular track record. Whereas villagers had dared to beat up his father in the aftermath of the Great Leap famine, few dared take on Bao Wenxing, who was physically much bigger than his father and had some martial arts skills; villagers said he was "a good match for most people in Da Fo."[46]

It is important to emphasize that many Da Fo farmers hated Bao Wenxing in part because his bullying reminded them of their timidity in the face of the powerlessness engendered by Communist Party rule. Bao Zhenxian is pointing to this timidity when he says: "The people in the southwest part of the village all feared Bao Wenxing. He bullied everyone who used his electricity, but nobody dared to challenge him. If Bao Wenxing lived in the back part of the village he would have been killed long ago, because the people there are more daring, and they fight all the time. The people in the southwest care too much about face. Pang Deshi, a village teacher, looks smart and capable of taking care of himself. But he was beaten badly by Bao Wenxing, and he had to beg Bao to pardon him and allow him to use his electricity to irrigate the wheat. Pang Deshi is gutless. Bao Wenxing sees through people like him. That is why he beats them so badly." Speaking of how this continuity of Mao-era brutality was related to reform-era rule, Bao Zhenxian continued: "The Da Fo party secretary should have done something about it. But he did not do anything a secretary should have done. The police or the township government should have done something about it, but in fact nobody did anything."[47]

---

[43] Ibid. [44] Ibid. [45] Thaxton, *Catastrophe and Contention.*
[46] Bao Hongwen, interview. [47] Bao Zhenxian, interview.

Thus Da Fo's farmers were elated when, in May 2002, the Liangmen township leaders came to Da Fo to announce that they were going to attack the village bullies. The township leaders urged villagers to name the bullies in the village, and they left a box in which people could deposit the names of the worst bullies. They also said that villagers could talk to them or write them letters, on the promise of confidentiality. A few villagers took them up on this promise. But three months later Bao Wenxing was still stirring up mayhem, thus raising doubt about the ability of township leaders to afford protection. Said Bao Hongwen, "I do not know if anyone named Bao Wenxing as one of the bullies, or whether the Liangmen township leaders were on the side of the bullies. I feel that the township leaders, like the village leaders, would be afraid of somebody like Bao Wenxing. What if he threatened to kill *them* with a knife?"[48]

Why was Bao Wenxing a village electrician? Between 1990 and 2000, this question dominated village discourse about the rise of Da Fo's electricians. According to the Dongle County Electricity Bureau regulations, only certified electricians could serve as official village electricians. Each of the certified electricians was to receive a salary of 112 yuan per month, plus a bonus for every kilowatt of electricity used from transformers under his management. With this qualification in mind, beginning in the early 1990s a new list of five official Da Fo village electricians was drawn up. Those who were on it had the backing of the Da Fo Communist Party leaders. At the top of the list was the Da Fo vice party secretary; next came the head of the village; third was the son of the head of the village; and then came Bao Wenxing – increasingly known to all villagers as the "Electricity Tiger." In fact, however, Bao Wenxing was not certified.

In contrast, Bao Shuangcheng *was* certified, but his name was missing from the list. Bao Shuangcheng had served as an electrician for the village in both the late Mao and the early Deng eras, but he had been dismissed by the party-based network of electricians who began to manage the generation, transmission, and use of electricity under reform. During a brief stint as Da Fo party secretary in the early 1990s, his brother, Bao Xuecheng, had opposed and offended party boss Bao Zhilong and had quarreled with members of boss Bao's network. Afterward, Bao Xuecheng had been relieved of his position as party secretary and replaced by Bao Xuejing, a client of party boss Bao Zhilong. On failing to kick Bao Xuecheng out of the Da Fo party branch, the village party leaders transferred their anger to his brother, Bao Shuangcheng, and excluded him from the list of official electricians. They allowed Bao Wenxing, who was neither a party member nor a certified electrician, to stay on as a village electrician because Bao had ties to locally powerful CCP leaders.

From 1995 until 2002, Bao Wenxing concocted a host of schemes to fleece Da Fo's farmers. Beyond his price-gouging practices, about which Liangmen

---

[48] Bao Hongwen, interview.

township officials did nothing, Bao announced that he was going to construct a station to house and protect the transformers. He asked each Da Fo household to contribute money to the project. Villagers were appalled. One of them, Bao Mingchuan, sued Bao Wenxing in the Liangmen township court to stop the collection of money for the transformer station. The court decided the suit was justified, but it was too late, for Bao Wenxing already had collected the money, and he refused to return it. The station was never built. The township government did nothing to help villagers retrieve payment.[49]

In May 2002, under pressure from a deluge of complaints, the Liangmen township government leaders sent a team to investigate price gouging and extortion in Da Fo village. The investigators arrived with a tape recorder, and they took the testimony of villagers who were unhappy with Bao Wenxing. Within less than a month, however, these same Liangmen township investigators were playing the tapes secretly to Bao Wenxing himself. The electricity tiger had used his bonanza to bribe the township cadres in charge of the investigation with gifts of money and liquor. Bao Wenxing recorded the names of those villagers who had bad-mouthed him on the tape recorder, and rumors swirled about the fate of those who had spoken out. "He is going to cause these people a lot of trouble in the future," declared Bao Jingsheng.[50]

Nonetheless, complaints about the high cost of electricity persisted. In the summer of 2002, they leapfrogged Liangmen township government and reached the Dongle County Electricity Bureau, at which point the Dongle county authorities swung into action – or so it seemed. The Dongle County Electricity Bureau sent its own team of cadres to Da Fo to organize an election of village electricians. Bao Wenxing was not elected. Angered, Bao cursed in Da Fo's streets for several days. People shunned him. But Bao did not really need them. He used his connections in the Dongle county government and the Dongle County Electricity Bureau to overturn the result of the election. Within a few days, the county electricity bureau leaders put Bao Wenxing's name back on the authorized list of village electricians, and a county-level representative came to Da Fo to announce that Bao Wenxing was still one of the village electricians. "After all," reflects Bao Hongwen, "connections are more important than public opinion. I feel that there is no way we can fight bullies like Bao Wenxing."[51]

The everyday corruption of Da Fo's newly rich electricians alienated villagers, further tainting the reputation of the county and subcounty Communist Party leadership. In Da Fo, the cadres who benefited from this monopolistic variant of official corruption also were implicated in the deadly corruption of the Maoist disaster. Villagers took their monopoly control of electricity as evidence of the unfairness of Deng Xiaoping reform policy, which esteemed anyone who got rich by any means. Worse, they understood that Bao Wenxing,

---

[49] Bao Huajie, interview.   [50] Bao Jingsheng, interview.   [51] Bao Hongwen, interview.

the beneficiary of post-Mao crony capitalism, was able to use his newfound economic power to shield his father from suffering the consequences of the latter's Mao-era misdeeds and to dominate villagers in the same damaging manner as the Maoists. As a result, the center's attempt to restore its credibility locally by commanding the wonder of electrification sputtered, and villagers second-guessed the willingness of Beijing to reform its rural base and separate its modernity project from the unjust past.

Whereas some claim that the post-Mao Central government has regained legitimacy by delivering prosperity to the rural poor, Da Fo's dry-zone agriculturalists saw the reform-era center differently. The corruption of public energy supply not only sharpened the great divide between poor villagers and rich urbanites, it also created a two-tiered system of powerful haves versus powerless have-nots within Da Fo, weakening the ability of marginal tillers to produce the crops needed for family sustenance and permitting Bao Wenxing and the other prosperous electricians to live a lifestyle that set them apart from the farming poor. Da Fo's electricians were better able to take full advantage of public services such as transportation and medical care, and they were also able to use their material gains to engage in corrupt two-way transactions[52] that allowed them to circumvent the obligatory penalties of taxation, birth-planning regulations, and educational policies – penalties that most subsistence-level farmers were unable to avoid. Several of Da Fo's electricians, for instance, openly boasted of their ability to buy their way out of the birth-planning regulations, saying they could just come up with more cash to produce as many children as they wanted.

Da Fo's farmers resented this centrally designed corruption. Its local social consequences flew in the face of center's promise to close the gap between rural poor and urban rich. To villagers, Beijing had put its developmental program in the hands of party-connected wheeler-dealers who had a long history of abusing and cheating tillers – a move that did not engender trust in the center.[53]

The willingness of the Central government and its county-level units to tolerate the audacious corruption of Da Fo's electricity tigers undermined authority, tarnishing the reputation of the party-state from top to bottom and further damaging the legitimacy of the long arm of the central party-state.[54] Between 2001 and 2004, electrician Bao Wenxing not only cowed the Da Fo party leaders, he also got away with beating Liangmen township government leaders who came to control him. In the spring of 2003, for example, Bao Wenxing started a violent quarrel with the Liangmen township vice party secretary when the latter came to introduce the benefits of planting apple trees. Bao subsequently beat up the head of the Liangmen township Military Affairs Bureau over this same proposal. In the end, Li Mingde, the party secretary of

---

[52] Cf. Sun, *Corruption and Market*, 53–54.
[53] I am indebted to Jude Howell for helping me grasp this dynamic. See *Governance in China*, 239, n. 8.
[54] As Howell's work might predict. See *Governance in China*, 229.

Liangmen township, called in the police to arrest Bao and then came to Da Fo to announce that Bao Wenxing had again been dismissed as village electrician. Township secretary Li openly declared that he would resign if Bao were to continue as an electrician. But Bao Wenxing was later released without bail and was "rehabilitated" to the role of village electrician, and Liu did not resign.[55] Villagers cynically wondered: "Who really was in charge of government? Who actually had the authority to tame the roar of the Electricity Tiger and reform the politics that placed economic power in his hands?"

CORRUPTION AND THE ACTIVATION OF CONTENTIOUS MEMORIES

At the village level, popular anger with the utility monopoly designed by Central government power holders evolved its own forms of resistance and contention. Between 1995 and 2003, Da Fo's farmers waged everyday contention to resist the long arm of the electricity monopoly. They took aim at both its technical extension into their lives and its impact on their livelihood, and they challenged the brazen conduct of the Da Fo electricians appointed by boss Bao Zhilong and his cronies. Only rarely did they attack the electricians themselves. Rather, most attacks were against property. By 2001, the theft of electricity had become so common that nearly 70 percent of all electricity used by Da Fo's farmers in peak consumption time was stolen – a reaction to the failure of the Puyang city, Dongle county, and Liangmen township electricity bureaus to constrain the price gouging of electricians such as Bao Wenxing.[56] There was also an upswing in the sabotage of the transformers held by Bao Wenxing and the other thirty-plus electricians in Liangmen township, few of whom had a good relationship with farmers.

Though assaults on the electricity tigers were uncommon, there were occasionally direct physical challenges to Bao Wenxing and other local agents of the electricity monopoly. In some cases, the farmers who mounted the challenges stirred memories of the violent confrontations of the Mao years, especially the worst years of the Great Leap. In early 2000, for example, Bao Junling challenged electricity bully Bao Wenxing to a fight, threw him to the ground, and kicked him mercilessly in front of a huge crowd of villagers. This beating won Bao Junling great respect in Da Fo – he became a champion of the more timid farmers who hated Bao Wenxing.[57]

The importance of facing down bully Bao Wenxing cannot be overstated. Even in established democratic systems, bullying often scars victims for life, contributing to long-lasting feelings of disempowerment and self-disrespect.[58]

---

[55] Pang Siyin, interview; Bao Yingjie, interview.   [56] Ruan Zhanying, interview.
[57] Bao Hongwen, interview.
[58] Goldman, cited in Russell, "A World of Misery Left by Bullying."

The bullying tactics of Bao Wenxing were especially troubling for Da Fo's small farmers, because some had been bullied by his father in the Great Leap.[59] They still feared being targeted by this party-backed bully and hustler – a rational fear in an authoritarian political order whose local Communist Party leaders habitually relied on poor, macho rogues to bully farmers into submission. In the first decade of reform, a few of Da Fo's farmers saw in the collapse of commune mechanisms of domination an opportunity to stand up to Great Leap–era bully Bao Zhigen (Bao Wenxing's father). Many more timid counterparts were temporarily buoyed by the thought that their tormenter could no longer cow and insult them without penalty. For a while, they held their heads high in the presence of Bao. But with Bao Zhigen securing a niche in the electricity sector, and with his son gaining power over a utility instrument he could wield at his whim, the memory of the Great Leap resurfaced. Suddenly, reform portended a tortuous road back toward sheer powerlessness. No wonder that so many of Da Fo's villagers found hope for a more humane order in Bao Junling's beating of electricity tiger Bao Wenxing: it revived the prospect of getting beyond the disempowerment inflicted by the bullying of the past.[60]

Many of Da Fo's farmers remembered as well the Great Leap lesson of Tang Shu. Still living in 2004, Tang Shu offers a story that helps us grasp the continuing past in village China under authoritarian rule and understand the way in which popular knowledge of stories of past wrongs has influenced support for contention in the deep countryside. Tang Shu and many other Da Fo farmers hated party boss Bao Zhilong long before he played favorites in appointing electricity tigers such as Bao Wenxing, because boss Bao had relied on Bao Zhigen to impose the labor regimentation and hunger of the Great Leap. Forty years after the great famine, they still denounced Bao Zhigen as *touding shenchuang, jiaodi liudong, huaitola* (a person with a boil on his head and bad liquid dripping out of his feet, that is, with a totally infected and corrupted body). Bao Zhigen, according to Tang Shu, was "the biggest rascal in Da Fo":

He did not do any good his entire life. He was totally bad, and he is still bad today. During the Great Leap Forward I defied him all the time. He saw me as an enemy, like sand in his eyes. He sent me to work with Bao Peiyong in the fertilizer factory. This was a very filthy job. I had to collect all the night soil and manure from the village and turn them into fertilizer. Nonetheless, he said that I did not do a good job, and he threatened to cut off my food ration at the public dining hall.

I challenged him to give me one less bite to eat and see what I would do to him. He threatened to beat me, but I beat him first. He lost in front of everybody. But he did not want to admit defeat. He went back home and brought a butcher knife. He thought I would be scared of his knife. But I stood up in front of everybody in the village and pointed to my heart and told him to stab me in the right place. I said if he stabbed me in the wrong place, then he could not blame me for stabbing him back.

[59] Thaxton, *Catastrophe and Contention*.
[60] Cf. Fassin and Rechtman, *Empire of Trauma*, 161.

At the time, a big crowd was there watching us fight. His cousin Bao He told him to stop it. Bao He had served in the PLA. He saw the danger facing his cousin. He explained to Bao Zhigen: "Once you took up the knife, you gave the other person the right to defend himself by stabbing you, and you would die in vain because you were the first to threaten him." When Bao Zhigen heard this, he retreated to his house with the knife. That was exactly what I had in mind. If he had dared to stab me, I would have seized the knife and killed the rascal for the village. It was too bad I was not able to do that. Still, as a result of this confrontation, Bao Zhigen has always been frightened of me. Many villagers are afraid of him. But not me.[61]

In the heat of the struggles against electricity tiger Bao Wenxing, Tang Shu's story, buried in the unspoken community history of the Great Leap, resurfaced and found its way along the oral grapevine, reminding others that the Great Leap, for all its horrors, contained small but significant lessons of empowerment. Bao Junling's clash with Bao Wenxing drummed up the deep memory of Tang Shu's story about how everyday politics really worked under Mao. People remembered that courageous individuals could make a difference.

In the aftermath of Bao Junling's victory over Bao Wenxing, other Da Fo farmers stood up to Da Fo's electricity tiger, and they publicly denounced the way in which the center had spread its electricity monopoly in the countryside. Subsequently, Bao Wenxing paid secret late-night visits to the homes of those who followed Bao Junling's example, greeting them as "big brother," showering them with gifts, and imploring them to not make him lose face in public again. These popular acts of dissent and defiance were not sanctioned by sympathetic Central government reformers, and they certainly did not reflect the core values of higher-ups in the network of Li Peng's energy power empire. They drew collective support from the memory of a traumatic past in which regular people had demonstrated that survival had to come from the self-mustered courage to defy the uncurbed local minions of the high and mighty. Of course, defiant villagers were not able to overcome the corrupt and powerful system of CCP rule. They had to settle with small victories over the local agents of this system.

THE MYSTIQUE OF BENEVOLENT GOVERNANCE AND THE SHAM OF REFORM WITH RIGHTS

If, as Kevin J. O'Brien and Li Lianjiang argue, China's rural people see rulers in distant Beijing as benevolent and believe they can reach out to reform-minded allies in the Central government to exploit well-intentioned state policies and laws to resist injustice, then we should expect that Da Fo's farmers would have mobilized the official language and legal channels of protest to defend their rights to just and fair treatment by the agents of the electricity monopoly.[62]

---

[61] Tang Shu, interview.   [62] O'Brien and Li, *Rightful Resistance*, 2–4.

There is precious little evidence that they embraced officially sanctioned rights-based resistance, however. While doggedly pursuing various forms of everyday contention against the local face of Li Peng's far-flung electricity empire, they rarely engaged in protest aimed at bringing the central party-state into the bouts of anger directed against the village- and township-level agents of this monopoly. The intriguing question is *why* they did not root their resistance in some Central government policy–derived notion of reform with rights. There were, I believe, four reasons.

To begin with, Da Fo's farmers understood that the structure of the state electricity monopoly worked against their locating powerful allies within the Central government. They did not see Beijing leaders who had an interest in this monopoly as separate from provincial-, county-, and township-level leaders of the electricity bureaus. In popular thinking, all these leaders were part of the same corrupt *nomenklatura* of the central party-state, and they all stood to benefit from the official and technological power of the Li Peng family network. As patrimonial rulers, Li Peng and his cronies had extended the reach of their network into Dongle county by granting positions and privileges to followers who had a history of abusing party-based power. To little people without power, this empire was bent on conquest, and the delivery of electricity collapsed development with conquest. They saw local electricity tigers such as Bao Wenxing not as agents of a public good to which they had a just claim, but rather as cadres of a partisan conquest.

As in the Great Leap Forward, the center tacitly granted these local agents enough leeway to impose its developmental agenda, and neither its policies nor its legal edicts invited complaints from village- and town-dwelling simpletons who depended on this costly gift. How, in this situation, could Da Fo's farmers blame their woes on the local agents of monopoly pure and simple? In reality, not only did they see the CCP-led state as an aggregate, they also were able to unpack the state and grasp the triumphs of rival power networks within high policy circles.[63] To them, Li Peng was a powerful, cagey tiger within the gilded center, and Deng Xiaoping was ultimately to blame for allowing this tiger and his network to manipulate policy and monopolize the energy sector.

The evidence for villagers connecting local monopoly with central monopoly is not unequivocal. Some villagers – especially the electricians and their kin – were fearful of speaking openly about Li Peng. They asked not to be questioned about this powerful national CCP leader. Further, although just about every villager had heard the name Li Peng, and two-thirds of them knew Li had been the minister of electricity and premier, only a few expressed detailed knowledge of the connection between the local electricity bureau and the powerful CCP politicians at the top of the SPC, that is, the Li Peng network.

---

[63] Just as University of Chicago scholar Tsou Tang and his disciples have done. See Tsou, *Cultural Revolution and Post-Mao Reforms*, and esp. Fewsmith, *Elite Politics in Contemporary China*, 87–89.

Nonetheless, in reflecting on the corruption enveloping this system, Zhou Jian had this to say: "I have heard about Li Peng and Li Peng's family connection with electricity, and the generation and delivery of electricity to the country-side. Li Peng was the Minister of Electricity and Irrigation, and first got his reputation from this position. People in China knew Li Peng because of his special connection with Premier Zhou Enlai and his wife Deng Yingchao. He also was very closely connected with Deng Xiaoping. That was why he became Premier of China after the Tiananmen Square Incident. We villagers do not accuse Li Peng of being any more or less corrupt than Deng Xiaoping and his family."[64] Da Fo's Pang Liuxing continued this line of thinking: "I know," says Pang, "that Li Peng served as Minister of Electricity, and I also know he was well connected with Zhou Enlai and Deng Xiaoping. He was able to climb up to important positions not because he was capable but because of his close relationship with Zhou Enlai and Zhou's wife Deng Yingchao. He also was a close protégé of Deng Xiaoping. In 1989, Li stood with Deng and supported the suppression of the students in Tiananmen Square."[65] Tang Wuyi, who benefited from fifteen years of service in the Dongle County Electricity Bureau, doubted that Li Peng and his network could actually control the national electricity system, but then commented: "Li Peng may have many friends and family members working inside the national network of electricity. [After all,] the electrical utility system is still a state-owned monopoly, and it will continue to be a monopoly as long as the PRC still exists."[66] It seems, in the case of Da Fo, that many Da Fo farmers learned about the connection between national and local monopoly from their interactions with the village electricians themselves, including the complaints of the latter, who, along with some of the farmers, were unhappy that the capitalists, such as Li Peng and his network, were "connected with the state, like in Chiang Kai-shek's time, and hence used their power to dictate the price of electricity nationally and locally."[67] A few of Da Fo's farmers also under-stood the political intrigue surrounding the struggles for supremacy in this sector. After speaking of Li Peng's hold on this sector, Da Fo's Bao Wenfang said: "We did not hear much about Li Peng and his family for the last few years, but last year I heard on Central Television that Li Peng's son, Li Xiaopeng, was appointed deputy governor of Shanxi province. We wonder about the implication of this move. It could be the Central government's trick to get Li Xiaopeng out of his electricity industry, and to reduce Li Peng's family dominance in this sector. Or it might be a move by the Central government to promote his son to a more important position."[68]

Time and time again, Da Fo's farmers stressed that someone could become an electrician only if connected with the Communist Party, and this meant that

---

[64] Zhou Jian, interview.   [65] Pang Liuxing, interview.   [66] Tang Wuyi, interview.
[67] Bao Zhanghui, interview.   [68] Bao Wenfang, interview.

those who were successful were beholden to Deng, Li, and their political allies. Clearly, therefore, villagers understood that the odds against eliciting a benevolent response by appealing to higher-ups in the party-state hierarchy – tigers whose inherited grip on the state energy corporations gave them cause to stifle genuine reform – were substantial.[69] So much so that few of Da Fo's farmers were willing to take this leap of faith.

In Da Fo, a second factor seems to have inhibited the pursuit of contention in the name of the center: Da Fo's farmers did not know of any Central government laws to support their resistance against the agents of the Li Peng electricity empire. To the extent that it was even officially articulated, the law pertaining to the State Power Grid was more or less subordinated to the center's energy development policy, and so prior to 2005 Da Fo's farmers were not inclined to contemplate resistance based on legal regulations protective of their basic social rights – which of course included securing the electricity to irrigate their fields and grow their food crops. Apparently, the ambiguity built into the regulations pertaining to the energy sector allowed Communist Party officials at different levels enough maneuverability to sidestep popular attempts to hold them accountable to their own commitment to political stability at any cost. Understandably, therefore, villagers interpreted this ambiguity in a cautious manner: it gave them little confidence that higher-ups in Beijing stood ready to welcome a push against the electricity tigers in some imaginary public legal sphere.

Besides, there were rumors of the center feigning ignorance of grievances against the local agents of its power sector, of center-tolerated delays in processing deferential appeals, and of center denials of responsibility for what went on in conflicts over public utility operations at the local level. In Da Fo, this rumor-fed counternarrative undermined faith in the intrinsic goodwill of higher-ups and nudged farmers toward an inescapable conclusion: the self-serving interests of Li Peng and his patrimonial electricity network were very difficult to distinguish from the national economic interest, and because Li Peng's policy-centered network could do just about anything it chose in order to thwart challenges to the smooth functioning of its monopoly, the scope for legal action designed to exploit the gap between center policy and local practice was extremely small, if it existed at all. In this context, Da Fo's frustrated farmers understood that appealing even small grievances to the next plane of government could get them into big trouble, for such appeals would only bring them closer to a center whose key energy policy–making network operated without any significant legal constraint.

Whether a favorable view of the center – and the agents of its public utility sector – was fostered by policy-articulated reforms is not fully clear, but local knowledge suggests that official declarations of change alone did not convince Da Fo's farmers that Beijing was on their side. After 2005, for example, the

---

[69] Just as Kong Bo has argued, "Institutional Insecurity."

Central government attempted to more carefully manage electricity in the countryside. The price of electricity henceforth had to be within a range set by the Central government, the Henan provincial government, and the Dongle county government, and a price-monitoring agency was established within the county electricity bureau to make certain the price range was not exceeded locally. Use of electricity in the fields was to be managed differently: the electricity bureau was to bill only the electricians in charge of transformers, and the latter were to pay the electricity bureau on the twenty-seventh of each month – a system designed to deter electricians from overbilling individual farmers. To inhibit electricians from adding on charges to household electricity bills, the Dongle county and Liangmen township electricity bureaus had to provide Da Fo's farmers with a telephone number for reporting illegal activities on the part of electricians. Finally, the electricians were prohibited from charging farmers for the costs of burned-out transformers or new equipment.[70]

In Da Fo, six years after these policy adjustments, Bao Wenxing was still increasing the price of electricity without official permission. He was not alone. According to Bao Zhanghui, other electricians were adding on to the price, which the Dongle County Electricity Bureau had increased by five cents to sixty-five cents per kilowatt in 2010. "On top of that," testifies Bao, "the Da Fo electricians also added on to the price. My electricity came from the transformer managed by Pang Guolin. One of our electricians, he also is the village deputy party secretary. He managed three transformers in Da Fo. One supplies electricity for household use, and two supply it for irrigation. Pang Guolin is considered one of the best electricians in the village. Whenever he increases the price of electricity, he would tell us why. Last time, he asked me if I would object to him charging me seventy cents per kilowatt because he needed the money to buy equipment. What could I say? I did not want to make him angry. I wanted to irrigate my land without arguing with anyone."[71] Actually, Bao Zhanghui knew the unspoken reason for the price increase. According to Bao, Pang Guolin had a "very bad habit." He gambled a lot, and he frequently lost a lot of money. The price increase went to feeding this bad habit, and so those who suffered the increase were doubly unhappy with it. Bao Shepeng, who in 2011 still farmed his own strip of land on the side to survive as the Da Fo principal, reveals that this price gouging was not limited to Bao Wenxing or Pang Guolin. Said Bao, "I have a very low salary as principal. Farming provides some supplemental income for me. Because I farm I have to deal with the village electricians. I use the electricity from Zheng Xitang. Zheng is considered one of the better electricians in Da Fo. The worst is Bao Wenxing, but I do not use his electricity. But even Zheng Xitang always added on more money to his electricity. He added five cents to each kilowatt once, and in 2011 he added ten cents.

---

[70] Bao Shepeng, interview; Bao Shuangcheng, interview; Bao Chuanxi, interview.
[71] Bao Zhanghui, interview.

He said that he needed more money to buy equipment, like meters and other things. He asked us first. But who could tell him not to do it? It was not worth fighting with him. Our easygoing attitude has fed the appetite of the electricians' greed."[72]

Not one Da Fo interviewee reported using the telephone number to report electrician wrongdoing, in the face of either price manipulation or surcharges for equipment. And in the end, Da Fo's electricity tigers still managed to shift the cost of transformer damage to farmers. In 2010, for example, Bao Wenxing burned up his transformer by overloading its electric motors, then asked farmers to bear the cost of a new 7,000-yuan transformer. "Farmers are angry with him now," says Bao Shuangcheng, "but for some reason the Bureau of Electricity allowed Bao Wenxing to gather the money from villagers when his transformer was damaged."[73] The disciplinary innovations of the center did little to alter the influence of embedded, thuggish forces on the ground or to give farmers the political tools to effectively challenge such forces. Consequently, some of Da Fo's tillers were unhappy with the Central government leaders and mocked them with satirical commentary. Wondering why the leaders allowed subordinates in the utility sector to set prices at their whim, for example, Bao Zhanghui had this to say about Premier Wen Jiabao: "People in Da Fo say that Wen Jiabao's words do not amount to much. His words are like *leisheng da, yudian xiao* (like hearing loud thunder, but not seeing much rain). Some stupid people in the village do not understand this and think that Wen Jiabao is a good Premier. They did not know that his words have little impact on what really happens. He said the price of electricity would be unified nationwide. However, he has not been able to make this happen even though he is the premier of the nation."[74]

There was a third, even more fundamental reason for a lack of faith in Central government responsiveness. By 2008, political discourse among Da Fo's farmers centered on social suffering under state monopoly – not in some vague belief in the center. If anything, villagers were concerned with the "bad institutional faith" of Beijing politicians who spoke of virtuous governance while victimizing small people with big monopoly.[75] While preferring a beneficent center and higher-ups supportive of resistance to state monopoly, most Da Fo farmers experienced the electricity monopoly as an institution that put controls on their daily lives and, in some instances, put their lives in danger.

If Beijing leaders were so committed to conferring the benefits of this wonderful invention of modernity, then why did they allow local party leaders and their clients to implement joint monopoly in ways that enriched only them and that, in some cases, jeopardized the livelihood of even competent farmers? The electricity-powered irrigation of crop lands promised a future of freedom from

---

[72] Bao Shepeng, interview.   [73] Bao Shuancheng, interview.   [74] Bao Zhangui, interview.
[75] On institutional bad faith, see Bourdieu, Accardo, and Ferguson, *Weight of the World*, 205.

hunger, but what good did it do if the price of this gift from Franklin, Volta, Faraday, and Edison edged a farm household ever closer to the margin of hunger when nature was menacing, as was the case in the severe drought of summer of 2011? In this period, Zhou Jian, who tilled four *mu* in his native Liangmenpo and who was supposed to receive a government subsidy for low-income farmers but was ignored by local party leaders who gave the money to "people who were close to them," had to irrigate his wheat crop six times rather than the usual two times, and thus had to purchase three times the usual amount of electricity per *mu* at the same unadjusted, monopoly-dictated price just to break even. Zhou was lucky. According to him, "Eighty percent of the wheat crop died in the northern part of the village, and farmers there did not even get back the money they spent on irrigation, but the government would not do anything to help them."[76] Electricity – this scientifically derived source of modernity – was supposed to free tillers from the drudgery of working the bad earth, but what good was it if the party-supported bullies who delivered it beat villagers to a point where their bodies were broken, increasing the physical cost of working the land? These questions, generated from daily encounters with haughty electricity tigers such as Bao Wenxing, preoccupied Da Fo's farmers and their counterparts in nearby villages.

The equation of widely detested electricity tiger Bao Wenxing with a badly infected body echoed a popular vision of the brazenly corrupt and lawless manner in which this piece of the central party-state oozed and implanted its policy. Living under such a corrupt one-party state, whose leadership believed first and foremost in perpetuating its own power, Da Fo's farmers spoke of the center as "good" only out of a need to protect themselves against higher-ups who consciously violated the officially espoused mystique of benevolent governance – with its promise of a better life under reform – and they relied on this voice to disguise their great distrust of aggressive and arbitrary rulers in the center's energy council.[77]

And was this not the voice of a haunting past? Writing on the "bad faith" tillers felt for the Mao-era state during the collectivization of the 1950s, Allen Liu informs us that after a decade of change, facing the hurricane of the Maoist Leap, "they gave up . . . hope, saw their relationship with the state as zero-sum, and mobilized themselves to resist the state in whatever ways were at their disposal."[78] The spate of electricity thefts, the damaging of government power stations and transformers, and the rise of antiparty graffiti on the utility poles of

[76] Zhou Jian, interview.

[77] Cf. O'Brien and Li, whose model of rightful resistance is predicated on popular understandings of the center as "good" and "benevolent" and on an analysis of an undifferentiated center, that is, a center without key policy-contending factions and groups and a village world whose protest actors cannot identify different factions and groups in the central party-state. *Rightful Resistance*, 4–5.

[78] Liu, *Mass Politics in the People's Republic*, 36–37.

the electricity bureau in Dongle county and other counties of the border area portended a similar noninstitutionalized path of small acts of resistance. This resistance – and the indignation driving it – was promoted by the politics of a failed democratic republic that, as in the Great Leap Forward, included the rights of rural people in its quest for irreversible modernity only as an afterthought and that, in any event, was inclined to solve the problems of little people in terms that served its own presence. It reflected profound alienation from this state, which in the reform period mobilized the police to defend its monopoly powers.[79] Da Fo's Bao Shuangcheng is referring to the zero-sum politics surrounding the electricity monopoly when he recalls, "The poor farmers from Wei county were known for stealing the electricity transformers and the wires around Shangcunji. They could sell a transformer as a whole unit or break it up and sell the copper inside. In the end, the Dongle county police caught five of these thieves and executed them. Since the executions fewer people have dared to steal the transformers and wires."[80]

Thus towering over any of the above-mentioned reasons for villagers' reluctance to advance their struggles with the electricity tigers through center-approved modes of participation was a fourth explicitly political factor: the fear of state retaliation in the form of lethal repression. The electricity monopoly gave Li Peng's patrimonial network control over a critical sphere of the central party-state, and the family-managed regional grid corporations exercised virtual sovereignty over the rural populations subjected to their "infrastructural power."[81] The local CCP-appointed electricity bureau officials and agents in charge of the field operations of these corporations were eager to share in the enrichment generated by this sovereignty, and they were granted broad discretionary powers in using force to benefit from this domination.[82] With no institutionalized central party-state protections for protestors, Da Fo's farmers feared that a direct challenge could trigger a crackdown and that the center most likely would not take up their case. They knew that the Communist Party ruled primarily through force, not through fortifying the rights of ordinary people – and to Da Fo's electricians, as well as its farmers, Li Peng embodied this modality of rule. As prime minister, Li had responded to popular deferential protest in the capital with state force; as patriarch of the public electricity sector, he and his followers greeted local popular opposition to their corrupt monopoly with hired thugs and police force. As rumors of thugs and police putting down farmer protests over power plants in Sichuan and elsewhere found their way to Da Fo, its farmers worried about inviting a violent response from higher-ups, thereby jeopardizing the small gains won in the long post–Great Leap Forward struggles to thwart state extraction of village resources and clip the wings of village party leaders and their minions. Rather than

---

[79] I am indebted to Reid for inspiring this analysis. "Towards a Social History of Suffering," 350.
[80] Bao Shuangcheng, interview.   [81] Cf. Mann, *Rise of Classes and Nation-States*, 59–61.
[82] This section owes a great debt to Adams, *Familial State*, 16–17.

implore the center for help, Da Fo's farmers placed their bets on themselves and went on fighting the electricity tigers on home ground, in contested spaces free from upper-level power.

– – –

The first decade of the twenty-first century saw the publication of two important studies of Chinese politics, each of which addressed the issue of the tension stemming from the corrupt rule of the one-party state. According to Dali Yang, Central government leaders were making great strides toward creating a state supportive of a market economy, and were undertaking reforms that "helped enhance the efficiency, transparency, and fairness of the administrative state."[83] The post-Mao reform had created a powerful regulatory state whose technocratic leadership was committed to cracking down on corruption, forging a less arbitrary, more service-oriented bureaucracy, and providing some limited space in which marginalized nonstate actors such as Da Fo's struggling farmers could voice their demands for just treatment.[84] Yang makes a plausible case that central party-state reforms, often bearing the stamp of the State Council, were moving rural China away from the aggressive, self-serving corruption and gouge of Mao-era rulers and creating rational administrative capacities to combat local predatory forces[85] – a process that was important to gaining popular support, defusing social unrest, and setting rural China on a course of greater political stability.[86]

By way of contrast, Minxin Pei portrayed Beijing leaders as being more interested in preserving their own autocratic power than in pursuing genuine reform. To Pei, the Deng-led reformers shortened the reach of the lawless Maoist center but embraced short-term economic growth without undertaking the reforms needed to significantly promote competent, open, and just governance. The administrative tinkering of reform fostered an "illiberal adaptation" that actually strengthened the hand of Communist Party–based networks of cadres and cronies, encouraging decentralized forms of predatory corruption and, worse, ignoring the need to institutionalize measures of accountability for local party leaders. Instead of promoting a full-blown free-market economy, the Deng-led reform was "a mixing of command and control with embryonic market forces."[87] This flawed reform process more or less permitted Communist Party–appointed officials at each descending level of administration to collect rents from monopolistic controls over key sectors of the barely changed Mao-era command economy (banking, rail and air transportation, telecommunications, real estate, and energy power generation) through bribery and extortion.[88]

---

[83] Yang, *Remaking the Chinese Leviathan*, 290–291.   [84] Ibid., 291, 306, 312–314.
[85] Ibid., 220–223. Here, Yang gains support from Sun, *Corruption and Market*.
[86] Yang, *Remaking the Chinese Leviathan*, chapter 7.
[87] Pei, *China's Trapped Transition*, 206; Baum, "Limits of Authoritarian Resilience," 10.
[88] Pei, *China's Trapped Transition*, chapter 3, esp. 124–125, 145–147, 150.

The center's reliance on the same "local strongmen" to preserve its monopoly on power and to collect rents in these economic sectors created a dangerous contradiction: because these powerful local accomplices by and large operated as "independent monopolists," their predatory acts sapped the rent-based resources of the state, thereby weakening the center's capacity to manage its political base and legitimate its reform in the deep countryside.[89] Thus, in Pei's rendition, the Deng-era center's shrewd but nearsighted reform process moved China away from the Maoist past but stranded both rulers and ruled between that past and a yet-to-be-realized competitive market economy that included administrative oversight and popular checks on corruption, thereby fostering discontent and conflict and weakening the capacity of the center to govern.[90]

Both Yang and Pei capture a piece of the truth about how rural China has been ruled under reform. If, as Yang claims, the center seemed to be moving toward a market economy, in the vital policy area of public energy supply, a key central-level politician who played a pivotal role in forging the command economy of the Mao era maneuvered to shape the post-Mao reform process. In reality Li Peng's patrimonial network supported the concept of greater market competition only insofar as it served its own monopolistic interest. This network failed to institute effective procedures for controlling the predatory corruption of local, party-appointed state utility agents – the electricians who delivered this public good to Da Fo's farmers. As Ling Chen has shown, the capture of reform policy discourse and reform policy making permitted the left-wing conservatives in the central party-state – with Li Peng being one of their champions – to stifle the growth of a competitive domestic electricity market, a development that allowed the subofficials in charge of energy to collect rents from their monopolistic controls, just as Pei's work argues. However, the local strongmen who imposed these rents on villagers did not, as Pei's model assumes, act as "independent monopolists" pure and simple. Of course they committed wayward acts. But they were connected with patrons in the township and county electricity bureaus and relied on the supremacy of one-party rule to keep their positions and privileges, ultimately to compel farmers to submit to their charges.

Although reform is frequently represented as having moved rural China away from the terror and trauma of the Maoist past, this micro slide of reform in a key state-dominated sector of the economy reveals an otherwise hidden continuity with the combative, thug-based rule of the Mao era. As the case of Da Fo illustrates, the so-called reform of the public utility sector actually strengthened the hand of local strongmen who had been the most venal accomplices of Mao's leap into famine and who seized on reform to amplify "decentralized predation."[91] The revival of their intimidating methods of domination in turn revived popular memories of the disempowerment that went hand in

---

[89] Ibid., 12–13, 31–33.   [90] Ibid., 6–7, 13–14.   [91] The term is from ibid., 163.

hand with hunger and loss in the Great Leap Forward. In this situation, a fear of the return of the Maoist past gripped Da Fo's farmers; and it fed resistance.

With no Central government to actively support their desire to escape the tentacles of the state electricity monopoly, Da Fo's farmers grounded their resistance in low-profile challenges to party-backed bullies and chose to rely on their own devices. They did not implore the center to aid their struggle, and for good reason: their struggle challenged the "taking hand" of the state,[92] which in this case was connected to a crucial, technologically sophisticated network of stakeholders at the helm of what, according to Edward A. Cunningham, was "arguably the most politically critical sector of the economy."[93] How were ordinary people to escape the aggrandizement of this center-approved, growth-generating cartel and its corrupt, unaccountable local agents?[94] The risks of openly challenging the core mission of the state energy monopoly, of rising up to remove the local party leaders who delivered its corruption, as well as the multiple forms of corruption documented in the previous chapter, were too great. The economic grievances of villagers could easily be misconstrued as a direct challenge to the most important sector of the developing national political economy. In this situation, a set of local challenges seemed a safer way of checking the worst aspects of the administrative despotism of the center and the local toughs who aided its conquest of village China.

---

[92] Ibid., 34.   [93] Cunningham, "Energy Governance," 254.

[94] According to Naughton, the State Power Grid and its big companies made up the sector of the PRC economy that was the "least transparent." "Claiming Profit for the State," 4.

7

The Defeat of the Democratic Experiment and Its Consequences

Facing a continuing legitimacy crisis in the deep countryside, on November 24, 1987, the Deng Xiaoping–led Central government passed the provisional Organic Law on Village Committees, which mandated the formation of new bodies of local government through democratic procedures in China's 900,000-plus villages. Subsequently, the Ministry of Civil Affairs (MCA) set out to promote the democratic elections of Village Committees, the purpose of which was to liberate villagers from the coercive rule of Mao-era vigilantism and, according to Kevin J. O'Brien and Lianjiang Li, to "rejuvenate village leadership by cleaning out incompetent, corrupt, and high-handed cadres, all for the purpose of consolidating the current regime."[1]

Working with local government leaders and assisted by both the Carter Center and the Ford Foundation, the MCA attempted to promote several rounds of free and fair village elections in rural China. Between 1988 and 1998, its cadres sought to protect the young experiment in electoral democracy by providing secret voting facilities and legal oversight over violations of electoral procedures.[2] Their hopes buoyed by Beijing's professed support for Village Committees, Western observers concluded that China's rural people had become weighty actors in the local electoral process, benefiting from a reform that was making village leaders more responsive to a popular electorate.[3]

---

[1] O'Brien and Li, "Accommodating 'Democracy,'" 489. Also see White, "Village Elections," 264, and Gannett, "Village-by-Village Democracy," 3–4.
[2] Gannett, "Village-by-Village Democracy," 4–6.
[3] White, "Reforming the Countryside," 276–277; White, "Village Elections," 263–267; and Manion, "Electoral Connection," 737, 745.

Some even claimed the Chinese Communist Party (CCP) had planted the institutional seeds of local freedom.[4]

The problem with this view was that it was a view from above. It was not rooted in an understanding of how local Communist Party leaders shaped the democratic experiment as it unfolded day by day, election by election on the ground. It presumed that popular support for elections was nurtured primarily by reformers in Beijing and that local party branch leaders were capable of supporting the fundamental principles and procedures underlying electoral democracy. Neither of these assumptions turned out to be true in Da Fo village. Because Da Fo experimented with electoral democracy between 1988 and 1998, we can draw on its history to generate a worm's-eye view of why elections mattered to villagers, of how contentious the electoral process was, and of the very limited extent to which local party leaders were inclined to endorse core democratic ideas and procedures.

ORIGINS OF THE POPULAR DESIRE FOR DEMOCRACY

Historians of the origins of Mao's agrarian-based revolution argued that local elections in the World War II anti-Japanese base areas were orchestrated by the Communist Party and did not empower rural dwellers.[5] Similarly, political scientists who studied change in the post-Mao countryside argued that the experiment with electoral democracy reflected political alarm among both liberal and conservative Communist Party leadership circles in Beijing – that is, that it was not the product of popular demand.[6] Perhaps, as Wang Zhengyao, the key MCA official in charge of managing reform-era rural elections, claimed, rural people were not capable of imagining a democratic polity.[7]

Yet Da Fo's farmers had not forgotten their village's 1938 democratic election and its positive results. This election had replaced corrupt pro-Kuomintang village rulers and swept educated Communist Party leaders touting democracy into political office, suspending the claims of predatory tax agents and supporting a long-running struggle to remove the police arm of the national Kuomintang state from home, village, and marketplace. Rather than praising post-Mao policy reform for improving living standards, Da Fo's farmers gave the credit to their own protracted struggles for better treatment from the state – struggles that began in the late 1950s and were undertaken in response to the Communist Party's betrayal of the democratic promise of that wartime election.

---

[4] White, "Reforming the Countryside" and "Village Elections"; Gannett, "Village-by-Village Democracy," 9–10.
[5] A good review of this literature is in O'Brien and Li, "Accommodating 'Democracy,'" 467–469.
[6] Cf. Thurston, *Muddling towards Democracy*, x, and Manion, "Electoral Connection," 745.
[7] Cf. Thurston, *Muddling towards Democracy*, x.

Villagers who were sixty or older still remembered the antirightist campaign of 1957, in which Da Fo's Communist Party bosses used undemocratic methods to cashier anyone who spoke out against the Maoist drive toward deprivation and disentitlement. They remembered the Great Leap Forward as a campaign that brooked no tolerance for people who spoke out against food shortages and forced labor. They remembered the dismissed, banished, and starved teachers who spoke against Maoist-imposed hunger in the second antirightist campaign of 1959 as the leaders of a second, thwarted "democratic wave" within the village. They remembered the factional wars and violent polarizations of the Cultural Revolution, with its democratic moment giving way to the war communism and terror of 1970.[8] And they remembered the party-driven perversion of the reform process, when a handful of Da Fo's old-guard Maoist leaders collaborated with higher-level Liangmen township cadres to magnify a familiar pattern of corruption, often resulting in villagers' confrontations with township officials and the police arm of the state.

By the late 1980s, Central government leaders and village dwellers alike understood that such confrontations were spiraling out of control, giving rise to a wave of contentious political opposition. As we have seen, in Da Fo this contention took the form of militant tax payment refusals, backstage character assassination of party secretary Bao Zhilong and people in his network, and covert acts of arson targeting key old-guard Maoists. Da Fo's party leaders worried that the long memory of party-imposed terror and famine, unintentionally pricked by the reform process, was surfacing to complicate their hold on power. By 1990–1991, they were frequently convening closed party meetings to pass on Beijing's warning that local leaders had to guard against chaos and collapse. The November 1989 fall of socialist regimes in Eastern Europe particularly alarmed Bao Zhilong and his clients.

Beijing power holders used the term "chaos" to define the efforts of rural people to extend their post–Great Leap famine struggles to recover basic social entitlements and to experiment with small, autonomous forms of self-governance in the wake of decollectivization in the early 1980s. As Liu Yawei, the associate director of the China Village Election Project at the Carter Center for Democracy, pointed out, villagers' "creative initiatives" were "seized by the Central government in order to maintain social stability and raise revenue."[9] That is, China's post-Mao Central government reformers cautiously endorsed the electoral democratic experiment out of a faith that a party-framed, party-guided electoral process would make it possible for them to recover a mandate to govern and avoid overthrow from below.[10] Rural people in villages such as Da Fo did not share this faith, however.

---

[8] See Friedman, Pickowicz, and Selden, *Revolution, Resistance, and Reform*, and Thaxton, *Catastrophe and Contention*.

[9] Liu, "Statement in Roundtable," 1.

[10] Cf. Gilley's take on this in *China's Democratic Future*, 119.

Nor did they agree completely with Western scholars who attributed democratic inklings to global linkages. The latter saw rural people benefiting from a divided but internationally enlightened Communist Party leadership that had to seize on elections as an alternative to being ruined by rural-based revolt. They reasoned that villagers reaped advantages as Beijing reacted to new pressures to adapt to transnational financial institutions and global democratic norms. Disparate village dwellers, they argued, were exposed to global communication technologies that enabled them to learn about and act on shared grievances in a democratic fashion and to well-traveled individuals who spread information about the significance of democracy for human dignity and whose global reporting more or less raised the cost of regime abuse.[11] I do not doubt that such influences enhanced the prospects for democratic order in village China. But in remote Da Fo, the desire for democracy found its origins mainly in troublesome individual and family encounters with the politics of Mao's war on peasant life, which reached its zenith in the Great Leap Forward.

Actually, it was the bitter memory of Mao's terror famine that made the democratic ideal so appealing to many of Da Fo's farmers. They saw two encouraging consequences of electoral democracy, each rooted in the memory of the Maoist disaster. To begin with, elections were seen as a means of speaking out against powerful local and national Communist Party leaders who had suppressed local voices in the pseudodemocratic mass participatory campaigns of the radical past, including the Great Leap Forward. Da Fo's farmers targeted one powerful nationally prominent Communist leader in particular: Deng Xiaoping. They anticipated that the achievement of universal suffrage and individual voting would allow them to admonish him for his role in the Maoist state's tyrannical past. On my first day in Da Fo village, Zheng Tianbao, assuming that I somehow was a sanctioned agent of the Deng-led center, implored me to inform Deng Xiaoping himself that Zheng was ready to die for the right to voice his vote against Deng and his local party followers, who in Da Fo were understood to be minimally reformed Maoists. Local people were closely attuned to the opening of the post-Mao political system and to the possibility of gaining voice through voting. Zheng Tianbao and his disgruntled fellow villagers were anticipating that national and local party leaders would need to compete for their allegiances in the wake of the passing of the 1987 electoral law of the National People's Congress.

Bao Zhongxin, who had been labeled an intransigent rightist and beaten by the followers of Henan Maoist Wu Zhipu in the heat of the Great Leap Forward, was one of these democratic aspirants. Claiming he held no grudge against Chairman Mao, Bao said: "It was not his fault. It was Deng Xiaoping

---

[11] The clearest statement of such a process is in Markoff, *Waves of Democracy*, xv, 35, 130–139. For a powerful and convincing argument for the importance of international linkage in the formation of protodemocratic forces in authoritarian regimes, see Levitsky and Way, *Competitive Authoritarianism*.

who was in charge of the Central Party Committee that labeled so many people as rightists. Even though Deng rehabilitated us later, there was no reason for us to show gratitude toward the person who was responsible for us being labeled rightists in the first place. Those who expressed gratitude to him for their rehabilitation were being stupid and speaking without a clear mind. In fact, after Deng suppressed the students in Tiananmen, we all hated him. History will not treat him nicely."[12] Bao continued with his judgment of China's great reformer, *Time* magazine's one-time "Man of the Year":

Deng Xiaoping was the worst manipulator in Chinese history. He lied to Chairman Mao that he would never change his verdict on the Cultural Revolution. Everybody was aware of his promise. But he broke it after Mao died. This is unethical in Chinese politics. I do not know how he had the guts to do what he did and then face people across China. He spread so many malicious rumors against Chairman Mao. He said that Mao did not value intellectuals. However, it was Mao who invited Li Siguang, Qian Xuesen, and many others back from overseas. These intellectuals were able to live and work very comfortably in China under Chairman Mao's leadership. They made a great contribution to China's development. The Chinese rockets, nuclear bombs, and satellites were all built by these intellectuals and scientists. In contrast, despite Deng's apparent policy of favoring more educated people with material benefits, more educated Chinese people are leaving China – indeed more than at any other time in Chinese history. Is this not ironic?[13]

Bao Zhongxin's bitterness was personal. As a result of his being labeled a rightist, his children had suffered. In the Great Leap, they all had to settle in Da Fo under agricultural *hukou*, and thus they were denied the opportunities of city-based educations. During the Great Leap famine, their mother could not take care of them by herself. Bao Zhongxin coped with his children's misfortune by singing while chained to the collective fields. He was all but powerless to help them pass over the food crisis of 1960.

For Bao and many other Da Fo survivors of the Leap famine, electoral competition not only promised to punish those responsible for Maoist disappointments, it also offered an opportunity to elect leaders who would provide a warning system against future disasters. Needless to say, the people of this remote Chinese village had no inkling of Amartya Sen's work *Development as Freedom*, which argues that famine has never occurred in a nation with a working democracy.[14] Nonetheless, in the reform era Da Fo's farmers reasoned that elections would enable them to install leaders who would warn of impending famine or be thrown out of office. The logic of this preference for democratically structured discourse, guided by the memory of empty stomachs and starving offspring in the Great Leap disaster, conditioned the political psychology of Da Fo's farmers in the early reform period. Thus, most Da Fo

---

[12] Bao Zhongxin, interview. [13] Ibid.

[14] Sen, *Development as Freedom*. For an interesting, supportive critique of Sen, which concludes that his argument is by and large valid, see Banik, "Democracy, Drought, and Starvation."

villagers welcomed the democratic experiment because it offered an exit from an embedded single-party dictatorship whose leaders had a track record of insensitivity, injustice, and incompetence in times of crisis.

THE CORRUPTION OF THE VOTE: POPULAR PREFERENCES, PARTY PRACTICES

By 1989–1990, most people in Da Fo had come to perceive electoral democracy as a mechanism for combating political corruption, achieving community self-governance, and preventing a future, sudden disaster. Interviewees in Da Fo believed that rural citizens should have the right to freely elect and replace leaders who placed the goals of the party-state before the interests of local denizens. In spite of the challenges facing their community – poverty, illiteracy, and the lack of many basic modern conveniences – most of the inhabitants of Da Fo village envisioned a future democracy in their possession.

High-ranking party leaders saw indigenous village democracy that resonated with the urges of aspiring rural denizens as a threat to party dominance and rule, however. The 1987 Organic Law they crafted was, according to two of the most astute scholars of village elections in China, "maddeningly vague" when it came to the manner in which elections were to be conducted.[15] With this law, dominant local party networks were able to usurp the process of choosing Village Committee leaders. From the outset, Beijing more or less allowed entrenched Dongle county and Liangmen township cadres to preempt the process of replacing village leaders through elections.

To be sure, the Village Committee elections were held regularly in Da Fo, but the village party secretary more or less decided who the candidates for the Village Committee were, and Bao Haifeng, the head of the Village Committee, was a puppet of secretary Bao Zhilong and his successors. As a result, many Da Fo farmers saw the Village Committee as toothless. Some said that they did not pay any attention to it.[16] Many farmers knew that the internal party-controlled process of electing the village party secretary trumped the new parallel system of Village Committee elections, and they understood they were excluded from the former – a reality that continued to erode trust in village party leaders ten years after the Organic Law had passed.[17]

Between 1988 and 1998, people in Da Fo participated in several elections. However, over the span of five years, roughly 1993–1998, the glaring flaws of the electoral process under Communist Party rule shook popular confidence in the possibility that democracy – as they learned about it through local experience – could guarantee freedom, order, and security. To be sure, support for the principle that elections should provide a choice of more than just a single candidate was widespread among villagers. "For an election to be effective, the

---

[15] O'Brien and Li, "Accommodating Democracy," 487.   [16] Bao Shuqin, interview.   [17] Ibid.

people should be allowed to choose their own candidates," declared Bao Wenfang.[18] But between 1988 and 1993, the candidate for the Da Fo village party secretary position invariably was nominated by the Liangmen township party leaders, who then orchestrated the election of the one and only nominee.

In the first election of the early 1990s, only the fifty-six Communist Party members in Da Fo – 2 percent of the village's population – were permitted to vote for the candidate, a clear violation of the one-person-one-vote rule. The majority of villagers were disenfranchised, a process that was directed by the Liangmen township government, whose leaders sent party cadres to Da Fo to "help" village party members elect the upper-level party nominee. In the 1993 election of the Da Fo party secretary, for example, the township government nominated Bao Shunhe, then sent its own unit cadres to Da Fo to arrange his election, in which forty-three of fifty-six village party members participated. Thirty-nine voted Bao Shunhe into office – or so it was reported.[19] Few villagers saw the nominee as legitimate. Some said that a minimal step toward democracy could have been taken by allowing the Da Fo party members to nominate the village party secretary first.[20]

Yet most villagers wanted to liberate the entire nomination process from the field of *guanxi*, or connections, controlled by the party-state. Zheng Yunxiang underscored why villagers distrusted the "guided nomination" process run by the Communist Party: "The state should allow the people to nominate their own leaders. The leaders appointed for us in the last few years have not been good. The Liangmen township government leaders only appointed those who had connections with them, and the Da Fo party leaders who were appointed by the township government did not care what the villagers thought about them. They only cared if they could get a good deal out of the situation. Otherwise, they did hardly anything for Da Fo. If we could elect our own village leaders, we would elect those we trust, not those who have connections with the upper government."[21]

Other aspects of the democratic process disappointed villagers, as well. Da Fo's farmers understood campaigning to be an essential aspect of democratic politics. To their dismay, this aspect was absent in the elections of 1993 and 1996. Because the Da Fo Communist Party secretary was nominated by the Liangmen township party branch and was under no pressure to carry on a political conversation with villagers, the electoral campaign of 1995–1996 amounted to little more than Bao Shunhe, the party secretary, shouting from a loudspeaker that villagers were neither allowed to speak critically of leaders nor permitted to discuss any political issue with insiders or outsiders. Fearful of popular criticism, Secretary Bao and his subordinates discouraged the asking of questions. The unwillingness of the one and only nominee to allow voters to

---

[18] Bao Wenfang, interview.   [19] Bao Shunhe, interview.   [20] Bao Wenfang, interview.
[21] Zheng Yunxiang, interview.

evaluate his character and competence was taken as further proof that the party secretary was neither a good leader nor someone who put villagers before the state (or himself). The autocratic work style that had crystallized in the Great Leap years remained operative.

The absence of campaigning reflected an irony of post-Mao politics: there seemed to be more freedom, but people were not free to find out which particular leaders would be responsible to the community. Ruan Shifan represented the silent majority when he said: "To choose township or national leaders through elections sounds good, but it is not possible. We ordinary villagers do not know anyone up there. We do not know which leaders are good or bad. How can we distinguish the good ones from the bad ones? Elections will work only if they do it the American way and let each candidate tell the people what his policies are. After that we would know whom to choose."[22]

The notion of a secret ballot and a public vote count, supported by villagers, was also violated. The Liangmen township officials made little effort to ensure the secrecy of the ballot in Da Fo's three elections. The adapted technique of voting was a kind of "roving ballot box," and it undercut privacy. In the 1996 election of both the Da Fo village chief and the Village Committee, for example, the Liangmen township Communist Party leaders came to Da Fo to administer the process. Operating according to township instructions, Da Fo party leaders gave each adult villager a ballot, after which they carried a ballot box to each household and told residents to choose a candidate.[23] Bao Xuejun, a forty-one-year-old farmer and sojourning bread seller, described what happened: "Some villagers did not know how to read, and others had no interest in the elections, and they asked the village leaders to fill in their ballots for them. In the end, therefore, we had no way of knowing who filled in the ballots. It was a mess. But Da Fo was not alone. It was about the same in other places."[24] Bao Dongwen adds: "Before the election they already had selected the candidates for us to choose. Even if we did not choose the one they had selected, in the end they would just say that the one they had selected was elected by majority vote. Therefore, the election was useless."[25]

Many of Da Fo's farmers concurred. They said they did not participate in the 1996 election because the CCP had preempted the nomination process and used a ballot system that required villagers to choose only from the party's stable of candidates.[26] This system engendered fear among would-be voters and discouraged voting for actual preferences, because the Da Fo party leaders were offended if farmers did not select the names on the roving ballot.

[22] Ruan Shifan, interview.   [23] Pang Siyin, interview; Bao Dongwen, interview.

[24] Bao Xuejun, interview. This sentiment was voiced by many farmers, including Bao Dongwen, interview, and Bao Shuqin, interview.

[25] Bao Dongwen, interview.   [26] Bao Xuejun, interview.

As Bao Dongwen hints, the vote-counting process in Da Fo was also seriously flawed. In 1993, when Bao Shunhe, the client of old-guard Maoist Bao Zhilong, was elected as Da Fo party secretary, the Liangmen township leaders took away all of the ballots without even telling village party members the election results. The vote tally was never publicized, prompting ordinary villagers to point out that they did not know whether the party secretary in fact had been elected or appointed by the township government. Many villagers suspected the latter, and they said the village's democratically elected candidate was prevented from taking up the post of party secretary by the Liangmen township leaders.

In this 1993 electoral season, the same Liangmen township government leaders who came to Da Fo to preselect their own candidate for village party secretary confused the issue by casually telling ordinary villagers that they could vote for whomever they trusted. Then, after counting the ballots behind closed doors at the Liangmen township government offices, the secretary of the township CCP committee paid an unexpected, low-profile visit to Da Fo to ask Bao Timing, one of the maverick leaders of the underground movement against unfair taxes and rash state birth-control measures, if he would serve as the village party secretary. Bao Timing had apparently won as a write-in candidate. "I was told," recalls Bao Wenfang, "that Bao Timing got more votes than most of the other party members in the village."[27] This was the sort of outcome that both Da Fo village and Liangmen township leaders had feared – and for good reason. Surprised by this little rebellion within their rigged electoral system, Liangmen township leaders and those at higher levels blocked Bao Timing from assuming the position. The antidemocratic forces were able to hang their hat on a salient issue: Bao Timing, they argued, was disqualified because he had violated the state birth-planning policy. At the time, Bao had six children, while Central government policy allowed no more than two children. Consequently, according to the village grapevine, Bao Shunhe, the favorite candidate of township power holders, was installed as Da Fo party secretary even though he had fewer votes than Bao Timing.[28]

Thus, as of 1998, there was no institutionalized democracy in Da Fo. Open democratic elections were subverted by official power and the Da Fo party secretary installed through manipulation of the system. The corruption of the electoral process and the imposition of Bao Shunhe as Da Fo party secretary through noncompetitive elections deepened widespread distrust of Communist Party–guided democracy. Despite the fact that Bao Shunhe belatedly offered villagers some relief from the claims of township government, allowing some tax evasion and occasionally permitting avoidance of birth quotas, the electoral process reinforced popular suspicion that the secretary would, in situations where push came to shove, sacrifice the interest of villagers to the interest of

---

[27] Bao Wenfang, interview.   [28] Ibid.

the party-state. Bao Shunhe himself confirmed this suspicion: "I believe," he declared after his 1996 electoral victory, "that as village party secretary I have to implement the party's policy in the village, and that is why I was chosen to be the party secretary. We are working for the Communist Party first and for the villagers second."[29] The "democracy" of China's single-party dictatorship – not the pluralist urges of villagers – had triumphed.

Popular faith in elections slipped. In Da Fo, the majority of farmers questioned whether elections could produce accountable leaders. Some of them, like thirty-eight-year-old Bao Junwei, a hard-pressed tiller and migrant laborer, gave up on party-guided democracy and said that only "real democracy" mattered. As Bao's testimony illustrates, he was able to connect the dots linking authoritarian party-based leadership to ineptitude, corruption, and the failure of the economic promise of reform, and his thinking about electoral democracy was in part a product of his ability to interact with peers and learn about politics beyond the confines of the village:

In our village, most villagers do not like the leaders, because they are incompetent and useless. The village leaders were supposed to lead us to prosperity, which has been the slogan of the rural reform. But they did not do what they were supposed to do. They only thought about themselves. They wanted to make money so that they could bribe the upper-government leaders to protect their positions. They want to be leaders, but they did not do what leaders should do to lead. I do not read newspapers or books. But I talk with people when I work outside the village, and when other people talk about politics I join them if I am in a good mood. Nowadays, all of the officials in China are corrupt. You would not necessarily know this if you stayed in the village all of the time. But once you are outside the village, and you hear people talk about it, you know just how corrupt our country is. Everybody wants money, and they find all kinds of reasons to get it. If you know somebody, you will be able to get things done. But you have to give the person who helps you a lot of money. We all hate this system. But we have to play within it. When everybody operates through bribery, the whole society becomes corrupt.[30]

Bao continued, deriding the CCP-guided democracy that sustained this system:

I do not believe in democracy. It is a mere formality. There has not been an open election in our village. The government has appointed a few people as candidates, and then put them on the ballot. On election day, village leaders would go to each household and tell people to vote on the candidates. Da Fo village does not have a public place where the elections can take place. Moreover, we have no regular procedures for the elections. In the end, we do not even know how many people have voted. So after the elections were held, the so-called election representatives would announce that the candidates had been elected. The elections were akin to child's play. If this is democracy, then it will not work.

I think that the current village leaders do not want real democracy. If there were real democracy, then they would not be able to get elected. In a real democracy, it is possible for really competent people to get elected. I think that the reason Da Fo is doing so

---

[29] Bao Shunhe, interview.   [30] Bao Junwei, interview.

poorly now is because we do not have competent leaders. Da Fo is a huge place with a lot of people, and there are competent people here. If these competent people were village leaders, then Da Fo might become a good village again.[31]

Precisely because the Da Fo elections of 1993 and 1996 did not produce competent or accountable winners, villagers were reluctant to comply with the policy commands of local party leaders. Their sense of disempowerment brought up the memory of the undemocratic politics that gave rise to the famine of the Great Leap Forward. At the center of this memory was the Communist Party suppression of any effort to hold a popular referendum on the incumbent brigade leaders who were unprepared to admit the errors that had turned collectivization into deadly folly. Bao Wanxuan recalls: "During the Great Leap Forward, village leaders mostly were appointed by the village party secretary. There were no elections. People who were the leaders were not necessarily more capable people. They were people who were willing to please the upper leaders and obey orders, and," laments Bao, "most people dared not challenge the leaders."[32]

In commenting on the attempt of the MCA to promote local self-governance via village elections since the late 1980s, several political scientists have pointed out that where elections were effectively orchestrated, the party-state was able to align with farmers to foster democratic village governance and protect villagers against the predatory designs of township rulers.[33] Xu Wang, a Princeton-trained political scientist, has summed up the premise of this school of thought: "The state and the peasants havebeen mutually empowered," he said, for the elections *supposedly* made the party leaders more responsive to village demands and simultaneously strengthened the capability of the central party-state to work with independent, village-based civil associations in carrying out policy locally.[34]

At first, Da Fo's farmers also saw democracy as a pathway to mutual empowerment of society and the state. They had embraced elections as a mechanism not only for constraining the despotic reach of corrupt township rulers but also for bringing forth alternative leaders who would responsibly help the village secure a measure of self-governance, in which policy implementation would be based on institutionalized mutual consultation. However, in manipulating the electoral process to preserve the autonomy of single-party command, the Liangmen township leaders debased this mutuality.[35]

As Robert Pastor's work would anticipate,[36] Da Fo's flawed elections actually inhibited stable leadership and incited powerless villagers to find alternative

---

[31] Ibid.   [32] Bao Wanxuan, interview.
[33] Cf. White, "Reforming the Countryside," 273–277; O'Brien, "Implementing Political Reform," 33–59; O'Brien and Li, "Campaign Nostalgia," 177–178; and Pei, "Creeping Democratization," 65–79.
[34] Xu, *Mutual Empowerment*, 236, 244.   [35] Compare with Ibid., 231–246.
[36] Pastor, "Centrality of Elections," 5.

ways to get the attention of unaccountable party leaders. Maintaining stable party rule and building consensual order without democracy proved difficult for Da Fo's appointed party secretaries. In the absence of a government-sanctioned process in which villagers could elect leaders who would represent the interests of the village majority, a brutish factionalism arose in the 1990s. "The factional infighting in Da Fo is very tough today," related Tang Shu. "No matter which group is leading the village, the other groups in the village try to discredit it and try to make trouble for the leadership faction. Villagers do not try to contribute to the success of the village leaders. Instead, they gloat over the failure of the village leaders, so they can take their place."[37] Indeed, between 1968 and 1993, there were nine changes of party secretary in Da Fo, most coming in the 1989–1993 period. Each change was linked to the factional intrigues of people who were out to remove CCP bosses who had – or had not – collaborated with the schemes of Liangmen township rulers.

Villagers by and large remained alienated from the party-state–framed process of selecting village leaders. Without enforceable democratic elections, without the power of the ballot, villagers devised their own political weapons to fire unwanted party leaders. As we have seen, they resorted to arson to make office holding by appointed and privileged Communist Party secretaries a hazardous undertaking. When I conducted research in Da Fo in 1993, I saw forty charred red brick houses. The targeted houses were invariably those of Bao Zhilong and other old-guard party leaders or those with close ties to them.[38] According to Pang Siyin – the appointed deputy party secretary of Da Fo between 1988 and 1996, a widely traveled soldier, and one of the more open-minded village party leaders – the arsons were the product of the misrule of Da Fo party leaders:

In 1993, when the village witnessed forty-three arsons in a very short period, I was the deputy party secretary. At the same time, I was the head of the arbitration committee and the security chief in the village. Within about one month before the Spring Festival, at least forty-three arsons took place consecutively, one after another. The first arson started right in the middle of my courtyard. Somebody set fire to my big pile of firewood around eleven o'clock at night. After the fire at my place, twenty other fires were set in the village. Secretary Bao Zhilong's house was torched. That was the biggest fire of all. Along with his coffin, one wing of Bao Zhilong's house was completely destroyed. After Bao Zhilong's fire, there were as many as twenty-five more house fires. At this point, we realized there might be some people in the village who were discontented with the village party leadership. They wanted to use these fires to disturb the peace of the village and damage the image of the village leaders.[39]

In the reform era, arson increasingly became the weapon villagers used to let Da Fo party rulers know that they had not forgotten the perpetrators of the

---

[37] Tang Shu, interview.   [38] Cf. Thaxton, *Catastrophe and Contention*, 312–314.
[39] Pang Siyin, interview.

Great Leap's inhumanities. Thus the arsons of 1993, 1994, and 1995 were to show Liangmen township officials that actions could be taken to drive unaccountable village party secretaries from office. This silent contention from below, unmentioned in *People's Daily* and unreported by global news services such as CNN, did not go unnoticed in county seats, provincial capitals, or Beijing. Even China's high-ranking Communist Party leaders well understood that they were not immune to brushfires in the deep countryside.

THE SURGE OF MAO FEVER

As the prospect of a genuine democratic opening receded in Da Fo village, a flood of pro-Mao sentiments was sweeping the rural Chinese interior. Cao Jinqing, author of *China along the Yellow River*, discovered that some Henan villagers praised the Mao years as a way of underscoring their dissatisfaction and disgust with the income disparities, corruption, and political disorder of the reform era.[40]

During the 1995–2005 decade, roughly one in four of Da Fo's adult residents was in the grip of this Mao fever. Many of these villagers seemed oblivious to the mind-boggling legacy of Maoist political injustice. They were attracted by stories detailing the return of Mao worship in the Kaifeng area, some of which were passed on by Ru Xiangtian, the police chief of Dongle county. One story held that an image of Mao had appeared on the wall of a household, drawing local people, retired soldiers, and local officials to visit the "soul of Mao." Some of the visitors were said to have scrawled slogans on the walls of the house. "We Hope Chairman Mao Will Return." "Chairman Mao, We Working People Need You." "Those Who Wish to Rebel, I Am Your Guide – By Mao Zedong." "Long Live Chairman Mao!"[41] Many Da Fo inhabitants said they would have been better off if they had followed Chairman Mao's developmental track. They referred to the accomplishments of Nanjie village, a model factory town governed by party leaders who exuded nostalgia for Maoist collectivization.[42] Many proclaimed that a restoration of Maoist rule was the only way to save Da Fo and China from the chaos and uncertainty of reform-era politics.

By 2001, frustration over corruption, economic inequities, factionalism, and the defeat of electoral democracy had unleashed a surge of Mao fever in Da Fo. To many villagers, including even some of those who had suffered under Mao, Bao Zhilong and the strong-armed party leaders of the Maoist era now

[40] Cf. Cao, *Huanghe Biande Zhongguo*, 69–71, and on Mao nostalgia also see Chen, "New Perspectives on the Study of Chinese Culture and Society," Internet source.

[41] This episode of Mao worship in Kaifeng is also reported in Cao, *Huanghe Biande Zhongguo*, 168, 598.

[42] Cf. Ni, "Mao's Utopia Made Real," and Feng and Su, "The Making of a Maoist Model," 45–46, 48, 50.

symbolized a time when there was unity, stability, and a polity whose purpose was to serve the people. Even Tang Shu, who was burdened with bitterness over all that he lost in Mao's Great Leap Forward, including the chance to marry, declared: "Despite Bao Zhilong's personal shortcomings, Bao has been the best village leader so far. Nobody else was nearly as good as Bao Zhilong. Da Fo is a big village with many different small factions. It is very difficult to manage. Only Bao Zhilong was able to lead the village."[43]

That Bao Zhilong – the unredeemable Maoist who led Da Fo to disaster in the Great Leap, the target of popular indignation in the Cultural Revolution, and a key agent of aggravated corruption in the early Deng era – could be seen as offering a solution to the political disorder prevalent in the post-Deng reform period said a lot about the Communist Party's legitimacy crisis. The divisive, greed-stricken local party leaders of the reform era made the bad eggs of the Great Leap seem a better bet. This failure of popular memory played into the hands of protofascist power holders who sought to defeat positive democratic impulses and slow the pace of rural change.[44]

Given that Da Fo village was hurt by the Great Leap famine, how can we make sense of this nostalgia for Mao? In Da Fo, the people who said they were "sincerely missing Mao" had several things in common. Their fathers and older brothers had joined the CCP by 1945–1947, so that they by and large were entrenched in the party-dominant network by the start of the Great Leap Forward. For the most part, they had been able to rely on party connections to pass through Mao's famine without a traumatic family loss. Also, many of the nostalgists were twelve to fifteen years of age in the Great Leap. Although they, too, experienced hardship in the Great Leap years, they were not displaced to work sites where brutal conditions prevailed, and they managed to avoid the worst effects of hunger by eating the green crops standing in the fields. As the offspring of Da Fo party leaders, they identified with their minor Great Leap–era assignments in advancing Mao's agenda to make China a modern, powerful country, and hence their highly politicized adolescence provided what Fred Davis has argued to be "the prototypical frame for nostalgia for the remainder of life."[45] At the age of forty-five to fifty-five in the 1990s, a few were retired People's Liberation Army (PLA) soldiers who had helped end the chaos and paralysis of Da Fo's warring factionalism in the Cultural Revolution but who subsequently failed in their efforts to rein in and regulate party corruption and greed in the post-Mao reform. Their nostalgia for Mao was associated with collective order and security. They seemed ready to embrace

---

[43] Tang Shu, interview.
[44] Cf. Friedman, who calls this profascist phenomenon "chauvinist Leninism." *National Identity and Democratic Prospects*, 256.
[45] See Davis, *Yearning for Yesterday*, 57–59, quoted in Yang, "China's Zhiqing Generation," 6.

destructive violence to rectify the chaos and crime of the reform period.[46] Their insecurity over post-Mao economic reform was in part attributable to the fact that they had found job security in the Liangmen People's Commune factories between 1975 and 1984, and thus had eschewed farm life after their demobilization from the PLA. Their status fell when they were forced back into farming after the land was divided to the household in 1982–1985. They were also frightened by the prospect of runaway taxation, corruption, and the rising costs of farm inputs.

Fifty-six-year-old Bao Xuejing was one of the villagers "sincerely longing for Mao." His father, Bao Chengyi, joined the Communist resistance in the 1940s, and all of his father's brothers worked for the party-state. One, Bao Chenmei, was the founder of the Da Fo CCP; another, Bao Chengcai, became the deputy chief of the Anyang Grain Bureau; yet another, Bao Chengqi, became the deputy chairman of the Guangxi Provincial CCP Disciplinary Committee. Bao and his brothers had survived the Great Leap famine without great suffering. They remember Mao as a god whose army helped save them from the Henan Famine of 1942 and who, after coming to power, rescued poor farmers from disaster, as when the 1956 Wei River flood swept through Da Fo.[47]

Bao Xuejing had returned to Da Fo and worked with party boss Bao Zhilong in the late Mao years. But in the 1985–1990 period, he repeatedly spoke against corruption within village and township government. By 1995, Bao Xuejing was deeply troubled about the future of the CCP, but like other Maoists, he had not abandoned all hope. Influenced by political news flowing from the party-state, Bao concluded: "I think the Communist Party will collapse the same way the Russian Communist Party collapsed if we continue like this. However, this year the government told us there was a very good model party member whose name was Ren Changxia. Ren was the police chief of Dengfeng county, south of Zhengzhou. She did good things for the people. When she died the ordinary people mourned her death. She has been on the television for a long time since her death. It seemed to me there were still a few good party members. Maybe there still is hope for the party."[48] The hope could not be realized quickly enough for Bao, who, after a twenty-year stint as a worker in the commune paper factory, lost this status and had to take up farming, giving up the security of a state job for the uncertainty of harvest yields. Bao also was challenged by soaring taxes and the skyrocketing cost of chemical fertilizers. A return to Mao would be quite an improvement, he believed.

The nostalgia for Mao also seems to have been rooted in an unarticulated fear of loss. Many of the nostalgists were caught in a paradox. Although they had more food and better housing in the post-1978 period, they fondly recalled

---

[46] My thinking here has been influenced by Zhao and Bell, "Destroying the Remembered."
[47] Bao Xuejing, interview.   [48] Ibid.

the Mao era as a time when life was simpler, less stressful, and more secure. Perhaps this is true, for in that era they had benefited from positions within a privileged party-structured network. In the early reform years, some were able to use their Mao-era connections to find jobs, build houses, and secure property. But they were not prepared to generate wealth on their own.[49] Drawn to the privileged dependency of the past, and lacking self-confidence and initiative necessary to compete in the turbulence of a market-focused reform, many of them longed for a Maoist communality that had delivered security to those with ties to the political economy of commune and brigade and had enabled them to imagine they were superior to individuals who questioned their instructions on how to build a dynamic nation and live a good life. To some of the nostalgists, therefore, the outbreak of antiparty arson was a sign of oncoming anarchy. A return to strong-armed governance, they felt, would be better than no rule at all.

This pining for the restoration of a 1950s Maoist-style mobilizational polity, with its campaigns to ensure official accountability and correct official misconduct, was somewhat misleading, however.[50] The logic of Da Fo's nostalgists was based on a selective, incomplete, and jaded memory of the Maoist past – the product of the Communist Party's failure to discipline its subcounty agents.[51] Nostalgists claimed that the authoritarian political climate of Maoist rule made for anticorruption efficiency. Yet the structure of Maoist power in Da Fo engendered a specific kind of corruption – one that had benefited those who later became nostalgists. On the one hand, the inefficiency of the Maoist-style anticorruption mobilizations conditioned CCP secretary Bao Zhilong and his clients to expect that they would be restored to office in spite of campaign setbacks, thereby encouraging them to seek personal gain in between campaigns that would pay off enough to offset losses incurred in the next round. On the other hand, the Maoist campaigns drove party cadres to accentuate corrupt performances.[52] Campaigns were invariably followed by reevaluations and rehabilitations of corrupt village-level party leaders. In Da Fo, these same corrupt party operatives came to expect that they could either work around the campaigns or go along with the campaigns until they ended, at which point they would rebound.[53] In short, the "nostalgia" responses in this village, where the majority of farmers remembered the suffering of the

[49] Cf. Liu, *In One's Own Shadow*, 162.

[50] Cf. O'Brien and Li ("Campaign Nostalgia," 375–387), to whom I am greatly indebted, but whose arguments do not fully capture the essence of the puzzle of nostalgia for Mao, at least in Da Fo.

[51] See Barme, *Shades of Mao*, 39, and O'Brien and Li, "Campaign Nostalgia," 384, for the starting points to my argument here. On the overall pattern, see Chan, Madsen, and Unger, *Chen Village*, 28, 35, 177, 278–285, and Lu, *Cadres and Corruption*, 13.

[52] Lu, *Cadres and Corruption*, 114–115.

[53] I am drawing on Ngan, "Crystallization of Cadres' Working Style," for this line of analysis. Unpublished paper, Brandeis University, Fall 2004.

Maoist Leap, were not just the product of incomplete memory. They reflected a keen understanding of how the old-guard Maoists had ruined the majority of their fellow villagers and advantaged themselves and their families, and of Mao-era anticorruption campaigns, which functioned like a "closed loop" that was not subject to checks by villagers outside the circle of those within the loop.[54]

Under reform, nostalgic party leaders were threatened by the prospect of ordinary villagers using elections, laws, and more transgressive forms of contention to escape boss Bao Zilong's long-dominant network. Reform-era party leaders feared they would not be able to rely on rebound strategies mastered in the Mao era. The emotional investment of CCP leaders with ties to the local Mao-era dictatorship also contributed to Mao fever. It was not just that such people were favored in the quest to obtain adequate food relief, housing, education, and medical care in the Maoist years, or that they sometimes were able to connect their family-based economies to towns and cities. Da Fo's nostalgists still believed in Mao. They had a huge emotional stake in sustaining the idea that the Maoist developmental strategy, including that of the Great Leap, was the best way to construct a strong Chinese state. Their nostalgia for Mao was based on a past that differed from the memory of those who had suffered the most from Mao's socialist leaps and yet somehow managed to survive.

In Da Fo, nostalgia was linked to the desire of a small group of Bao-lineage party members to reestablish the supremacy of the CCP by silencing those who were inclined to express, if not act on, memories of the Great Leap disaster. This group sought to prevent any discussion of the famine – the most glaring and negative example of willful management of state violence against poor farm people for party goals. The Mao nostalgia not only reflected a desire to deny voice to those who were victimized by the Great Leap but also contributed to the reproduction of CCP hegemony by party-connected elements who conveniently held no memories of the Leap as a devastating famine.[55] For such people, the Great Leap was, at worst, a troubled experiment in an otherwise commendable developmental strategy.

In some quarters of Da Fo, by contrast, an incipient moral discourse ran counter to this spin. Fostered by resistance from below and decollectivization from above, this discourse called for the elimination of state violence against poor farm people. It sought to legitimate renewed bottom-up resistance to the violent state management of tax, birth control, and educational policy.[56]

---

[54] Thanks to Steven I. Levine for helping me sharpen this point. Personal correspondence, March 2014.

[55] See Weigelin-Schwiedrzik, "Trauma and Memory," 7. This is my extension of her logic.

[56] Here, I am indebted to Liu, *In One's Own Shadow*, 148–150; to Harrell and Lipman, *Violence in China*; and to Perry, "Rural Violence in Socialist China," 428–440, and "Rural Collective Violence," 175–192.

The reform era had given rise to resisters of various stripes, some of whom carried the memory of the Great Leap famine in their hearts. These resisters took their political cues from a popular cultural tradition that Da Fo's Maoists had attempted to suppress, and the nostalgists feared the reemergence of this tradition, which, as documented in Chapter 10, summoned rural people to defend themselves against abusive state power.

POLICE REPRESSION AND THE FATE OF CIVIL SOCIETY

Denied the ability to vote democratically for their preferred leaders, Da Fo villagers might have been expected to turn to civil protest, had it not been for the repressive influence of the police state. Ian Johnson's *Wild Grass* portrayed post-Mao China as a place where rural people were forging a civil society independent of the party-state, waging small-scale oppositionist struggles focused on the realization of legal rights, and creating the framework of rural self-governance.[57] For more than a few of Da Fo's farmers, the creation of public space free of the everyday pathological interventions of party-based rule promised a path away from the misrule of the Maoist past. But in Da Fo, police repression suffocated this civil society before it could fully be born.

By the mid-1990s, Da Fo was no longer a place where the Communist Party leaders could effectively repress every conflict that arose. Farmers challenged the reform wave of burdensome taxes. Women engaged in opposition to birth planning. Teachers challenged the usurpation of pay and pensions. For many people in Da Fo, this third path of civilian-based legal oppositionist resistance promised a form of governance that political scientists Jennifer Gandhi and James Vreeland call "institutionalized anocracy," that is, a hybrid form of single-party dictatorship in which the state would address and sometimes accommodate their demands without resorting to force and driving the opposition to outright rebellion.[58]

Between 1989 and 2004, small enclaves of enlightened Central government officials and scholars, including those connected with the State Council and the MCA, focused their efforts on promoting state policies that could facilitate such an accommodation and thus allow the party-state to better coopt rural civil society, lessening the chances that popular contention would evolve into rebellion from below. Post-Mao China's high-ranking, reform-minded officials attempted to steer the party-state and rural people along this path, all the while trumpeting harmonious political intentions and the start of a new age of pluralistic discourse and order. But the opposition forming in the sinews of Da Fo's emergent civil society was hard pressed to achieve its goal of altering the arbitrary and abusive style of CCP rule.

[57] Johnson, *Wild Grass*. For an insightful review, see Wasserstrom, "Reading China"; also see Sheridan, "Review of *Wild Grass*."
[58] Gandhi and Vreeland, "Political Institutions and Civil War: Unpacking Anocracy."

Despite the spate of small protest victories, documented in the early chapters, the subcounty agents of the party-state by and large relied on habitual methods of deceit and violence to deal with challenges to their authority – including force.[59] Though rural China seemed far better off in the reform era, in Da Fo villagers still lived under one-party rule, and township leaders still called on police powers to fend off, divide, and make opposition disappear, all while trampling on basic legal rights and repressing the quest for village self-governance.

Much of the field research on rural China has occurred in micro-level settings relatively free of police controls in the periods of investigation, and so the researchers who have provided commentary on the nature of the post-Mao polity have had little to say about the presence of the police in the lives of villagers. Yet the police have attempted to warn villagers against talking about the crises of rural governance. In the spring of 1998, prior to a summer research trip, the police came to Da Fo village on two separate occasions to caution villagers about speaking freely to me. They interrogated several farmers, insisting they provide information about my research agenda. Cautious villagers claimed they did not know anything. As in the Mao period, rulers sought to preserve state power by stifling storytelling that was not part of official memory, and villagers kept political emotions to themselves.

On arresting villagers, the Liangmen township police illegally detained suspects, denied them due process, applied torture to extract confessions, and imposed a spate of illegal fines as a precondition for release from jail[60] – all flagrant violations of the judicial review process to which rural people were entitled under the constitution of the People's Republic of China.[61] The police also occasionally destroyed evidence of their legal misconduct and threatened retaliation against people who sought to reveal it, including those who had opposed heavy taxes, birth-planning campaigns, high tuition, and the distortion of democratic elections. Some police cover-ups reportedly involved higher-level supervisory units, often after discussion with leaders of local CCP committees.[62]

Some of the Da Fo victims of police retaliation recorded the details of their ordeals with an eye toward suing both the Liangmen township government and its police. They wanted to use the law to fight against the illegal activities of township rulers.[63] Actually, however, they seldom went to court. After 2001, the police began arresting villagers who threatened to bring lawsuits against

---

[59] On this point, see Philip P. Pan, "A Trip through China's Twilight Zone" and "Chinese Peasants Attacked in Land Dispute."

[60] Bao Wenfang, interview.   [61] See Amnesty International Report, 51–52.   [62] Ibid., 51–54.

[63] On this trend, see Yu Jianrong, *Dangdai Zhongguo Nongmin de Yifa Kangzheng*. In reading this source, I have also relied on Li and Ou Bowen [O'Brien], "Dangdai Zhongguo Nongmin de Yifa Kangzheng," and personal communication with Kevin J. O'Brien; also see Yu, "Conflict in the Countryside," 148–153.

Liangmen township government officials, including the police,[64] and this pattern developed across Dongle county and in other parts of the Hebei-Shandong-Henan border area. One reason farmers found it useless to seek legal protection was that the salaries of court judges were paid through the collection of taxes by the Liangmen township and Dongle county leaders who were the targets of lawsuits. Deciding for plaintiffs against township and county rulers was not in the interest of the court.[65]

By early 2004, popular revulsion toward the police was widespread in Da Fo, in Dongle county, and in much of the northern Henan countryside, primarily because of violent police interventions in the attempts of villagers to replace discredited socialist dictatorship with community self-governance. Da Fo's inhabitants and their counterparts in surrounding villages and counties had a history of organizing collective opposition to oust bad rulers. In early 1998, news spread of police action to suppress this kind of opposition. According to Bao Wenfang, "In Neihuang county, people in Yixian village organized to overthrow the Communist Party secretary and the Village Committee. They set up a government themselves. However, the upper government officials later came to the village and told the villagers that their seizure of power was illegal. Subsequently, armed police entered the village on trucks to arrest eighteen of the rebel leaders. Nobody knows what happened to these leaders in the end – they disappeared. Neihuang County Television broadcast the incident for more than one week. The government has attempted to use this incident to scare people away from taking matters into their own hands."[66]

The police unit responsible for the roundup was the People's Armed Police. The principal instrument of central party-state repression in contemporary China, this force did not have legitimacy in the deep countryside. People in Da Fo saw its actions against villagers who engineered oppositionist struggles for self-governance as unrighteous. Having followed this incident in Neihuang via the local grapevine as well as on television, Bao Timing, Bao Wenfang, and their kindred spirits in Da Fo expressed sympathy for the arrested protest leaders, who were said to have been doing a good deed. They also scoffed at government media attempts to discredit the opposition, which they understood as an effort to frighten prodemocratic people like themselves away from doing the same thing.[67]

Such police repression flew in the face of popular democratic aspirations.[68] Da Fo villagers possessed greater political knowledge than they had at the start of the reform period. They drew strength and mutual protection from their collective actions and thus were more inclined to openly confront local party leaders who ignored or twisted state policy.[69] Yet many Da Fo farmers also were cognizant that those who dared to oppose state policy would be at

---

[64] Bao Shuangcheng, interview.   [65] Yu, "Liyi Quanwei He Zhixu."
[66] Bao Wenfang, interview.   [67] Ibid.   [68] Nathan, *Chinese Democracy*, chapter 6.
[69] O'Brien and Li, "Politics of Lodging Complaints," 773.

the mercy of high state power holders, and hence they would not automatically receive protection from political reprisal.[70] Villagers understood that when they, or their counterparts, acted on impulses to evict local party leaders and re-create forms of self-governance independent of party controls, such acts could trigger police repression. They worried that Central government rulers would not be capable of shielding them – or, for that matter, willing to shield them – from local police violence.

This political atmosphere enormously complicated the efforts of more liberal Beijing leaders and their allies in distant poor villages, townships, and counties to coopt popular opposition by peaceful methods.[71] The police used torture not only to extract confessions, but also as a form of extrajudicial punishment. Apparently, many police officers in Dongle county did not believe that torture was wrong. They saw it as a necessary and appropriate means of law enforcement.[72] The persistence of police interventions, therefore, made it difficult for members of Da Fo's emergent "civil society" to overcome everyday conditions of inequity and insecurity by engaging the overburdened operatives of reform – lawyers willing to bring corrupt officials to justice or journalists willing to report the truth about the usurpation of "real democracy." Such people existed, but few were to be found in Liangmen township, and most feared the police.

Seen from the vantage point of Da Fo's farmers, what Bruce Gilley has called the post-Mao movement from "political tumult to an ad hoc peace"[73] was really a weak Central government effort to address a pattern of direct police-state violence without correcting the political institutions that produced such violence in the first place. People in Da Fo understood this reality. They understood they were not operating in a postviolent socialist polity. They understood that below the high-sounding commitments of Beijing leaders to democratic and legal reforms, there persisted a legacy of sharp conflict between the police and country dwellers, which in the vicinity of Da Fo often occurred within a culture of party-state vendettas, denunciation of opponents, and destructive violence. The persistence of this culture continually compromised the path of democratic, legal, peaceful opposition, engendering a renewal of discourse on rebellion among villagers.

VILLAGERS' VIEWS ON REBELLION

Few of Da Fo's farmers wanted the guided democracy of the Communist Party, nor did they wish for the restoration of Maoist rule. What they wanted was to

---

[70] Cf. O'Brien and Li, "Villagers and Popular Resistance," 53–54, and Tsou, *Cultural Revolution*, xxiv, cited in O'Brien and Li, "Villagers and Popular Resistance," 54.
[71] The problem of police violence and torture is so rampant that Professor Cui Min of China's National Police College proclaimed that "torture and other illegal means . . . remains, as before, a principal basis for proving [legal] cases." Quoted in Tanner, "Torture in China."
[72] Ibid.   [73] Gilley, *China's Democratic Future*, 23.

engineer the removal of local party leaders who had violated the laws and trampled on democratic elections, ignoring voices for genuine political reform. In Da Fo, the success of the Communist Party's underhanded electoral tactics alienated villagers from elections and damaged the democratic prospect. Bao Zhanpo, who appreciated the freedom local farmers had gained under the Deng Xiaoping reformers, had grown cynical about elections. "I do not like the democratic elections," said Bao. "The elections were only a formality. All the leaders want is to line their pockets. They do not think about the village as a whole. It does not matter who gets elected or how they get elected. The leaders are no good. I do not care about elections at all."[74] This popular cynicism fanned villagers' deep-seated predisposition to oust party leaders through contention and compelled a few to risk punishment by talking about rebellion. Unlike in the Mao era, when local party leaders could use the mechanism of public criticism to humiliate and silence dissenters, Da Fo under reform proved to be a more openly contentious place.[75]

The Maoists had failed to eliminate ageless cultural understandings of justifiable resistance to authority. Da Fo's wisest farmers knew Mao's Cultural Revolution protestation that "to rebel is justified" was a mendacious replacement of the historical Mencian-Confucian narrative of a just rebellion.[76] To be sure, Mao's narrative of just rebellion confused many rural people, for they were being asked to give up the old narrative that equated rebellion with the right to defined one's livelihood and dignity, which the Maoists had attacked. In Da Fo, this confusion had to compete with memories of past suffering. The survivors of Mao's famine were driven by an indelible "emotional memory"[77] to cope with their traumatic past through contention rooted in the older, culturally based notion of a just rebellion. This memory was a political asset. People held on to it to prevent the postfamine state from fooling them again. It provided a compass for resisting rulers whose acts slit open barely healed wounds and portended a new round of injury, humiliation, and loss. It also guided them back to what they had learned from placing too much faith in the party-state's promise of a revolution that would restore benevolent governance.

The pre-1949 Communist-led revolution in Da Fo had shared two basic premises of the Mencian-Confucian idea of a just rebellion. The errant actions of China's rulers – Chiang Kai-shek and his key policy advisors – had produced

---

[74] Bao Zhanpo, interview.

[75] Cf. Friedman, Pickowicz, and Selden, *Revolution, Resistance, and Reform*, 63, and Thaxton, *Catastrophe and Contention*, chapters 5 and 6.

[76] For a study of how Maoist Cultural Revolution heritages shaped post-Mao protest and rebellion, see Perry, "To Rebel Is Justified," esp. 266. The issue of whether villagers subscribe to the the Mencian-Confucian idea of a just rebellion versus the Maoist idea of such, or a blend of the two, remains to be carefully researched by China scholars, and such research will be convincing only if it starts with an understanding of how the Mencian-Confucian paradigm differed from that of the Maoists and their brand of vigilante mobilization and violent justice.

[77] Cf. LeDoux, "Emotion, Memory, and the Brain."

a vast array of enemies in rural society, thus permitting the Mao-led CCP to unite many people from different walks of life against a tiny, self-isolating Kuomintang oligarchy. Even so-called landlords, minor gentry, and lower government officials had joined in the united front against the Nationalist government,[78] though of course their participation rested in part on the CCP's false promise of a so-called New Democracy. Moreover, the unrestrained, indiscriminate use of force by autonomous and inept Kuomintang national power holders had undermined the respect for human dignity and due process customarily accorded rural villagers.[79] All of these conditions enabled Mao and his party – after a brief, nearly fatal attraction to violent terror against affluent landholders and local elites – to win by deploying violence mainly against the most incorrigible Kuomintang militarists and their die-hard allies. It was the memory of this "just rebellion" of the pre-1949 Republican period that continued to frame much of the contentious political discourse among Da Fo villagers after Mao's death, not Mao's Cultural Revolution declaration that "to rebel was justified."

Mao, villagers knew, had omitted the fact that rural people invariably joined in rebellions only when time-honored deferential modes of peaceful dissent and protest had failed. Because Maoist rulers did not succeed in replacing the memory of this pre-Communist tradition of protest and rebellion in Da Fo, the possibility of a Mencian-Confucian–cued rebellion against the remains of China's failed socialist dictatorship was still alive. Many villagers expressed a belief that China's post-Mao rulers were taking them down with a sinking ship of state. Whereas some talked about rebellion, most saw it as a last resort. They were still holding on to faint hope for a democratic miracle.

Deng's reform was pregnant with paradoxes. While it failed to deliver the democratic institutions that could have alleviated popular anger, it also failed to preempt the moral basis for rebellion locally. Beginning with the second decade of reform and increasing as the CCP took over local democratic elections, therefore, Da Fo witnessed several waves of contentious disobedience. One, occurring at the village level, took on a life of its own in the early 1990s. Another in the late 1990s targeted the Liangmen township leadership. The third, more guarded expression of contention was aimed at the center, which increasingly became the focus of popular thinking about how to eliminate political injustice.

At the village level, popular determination to hold party leaders accountable for their wrongdoings produced a silent rebellion against CCP rule itself. In Da Fo, this rebellion took the form of character assassination and arson. In the wake of electoral closure, disgruntled villagers smeared human excrement on the doors of several party leaders and their clients. While in Da Fo, I noticed

---

[78] Van Slyke, *Enemies and Friends*, and Thaxton, *Salt of the Earth*.
[79] See Thaxton, *Salt of the Earth*, chapter 9.

that former party boss Bao Zhilong, one of the targets, had nailed a dead vampire bat on the wall of his inner courtyard, believing this would protect his household against the "evil" of this post-Mao "chaos." A spate of arsons, breaking out between 1989 and 1993, charred the homes of Bao and other key party leaders. The arsons warned of a far more dangerous fate, which had been visited on party secretaries in other places. The CCP secretary in Wangguo village, Shangcun township, made so many enemies that someone abducted his only son, who was never returned. The secretary was overwhelmed by anger, and he died of a heart attack. Afterward, his wife remarried. "His family was completely destroyed," recalled Bao Guanjun.[80]

By 1995, popular knowledge of violence against party secretaries in surrounding villages and townships had strengthened the resolve of Da Fo's residents to rebel against their secretary if he continued to blindly impose upper-government policy. According to Bao Guanjun, "Village leaders are unlike state leaders. They cannot run away. If they do anything bad, then villagers will retaliate. If villagers cannot retaliate today, then they will wait. The party leaders know there will come a day when villagers will be able to get even with them."[81] By the summer of 1998, the possibility of being relieved from his position or personally ruined by contentious acts from below had motivated Da Fo party secretary Bao Shunhe to pay more attention to village social forces and to balance the claims of Liangmen township power holders with the moral interests of villagers. Bao Shunhe put the matter this way: "I must accomplish as much as I can for the township government. If the township government leaders were behind me, then it would be easier for me to do the job for the government. On the other hand, I also have to balance the township government's demands with the villagers' interests. I cannot afford to ignore the demands of the villagers. I live in this village, and I cannot move away. I will not be village party secretary all of my life. After serving two terms as village party secretary, I will be like everybody else. Therefore, I must think about my own future. Also, if villagers become angry with village leaders they can retaliate against village leaders any time. They can do many things to hurt village leaders when they are no longer leaders. I cannot afford to make myself and my family vulnerable to the anger of villagers."[82]

By the turn of the twenty-first century, farmers in Da Fo were fed up with Liangmen township government. More than a few looked forward to the day when their struggles for just treatment might eliminate township rule. Ruan Shifan summed up the feelings of many villagers: "I think our country is finished. It is on its way to destruction. The most sacred government laws and regulations are violated by township officials. I [would] support a rebellion against the township government. The Liangmen township officials are the lowest officials in China. Yet they somehow live in two-story, foreign-style

---

[80] Bao Guanjun, interview.　　[81] Ibid.　　[82] Bao Shunhe, interview.

houses, and they ride in imported cars and jeeps. When farmers need their help and seek them out in the township government, they cannot find them there. If the villagers should rebel, they will kill all of these corrupt officials."[83]

To be sure, some contentious protest in Da Fo was still carried out in accordance with the publicized rules of the Central government. Villagers protested unauthorized tax extractions, scoffed at birth-planning fines imposed by Liangmen township leaders, and complained about high tuition, all the while blaming local party leaders for distorting the intent of center policy. Some of Da Fo's farmers placed faith in Beijing's promise to serve their interests and said local party leadership was the problem. Yet such faith often was voiced cynically: "No matter how stupid the Central government leaders might be," proclaimed Bao Shuqin, "they are concerned about the people. But it is not the same with local leaders. They worry more about personal gains."[84]

The inclination to blame local government leaders rather than superiors in the upper reaches of state power was rooted in a selective memory of the politics engendering the Great Leap–era mess. After each failed campaign, including the Great Leap, Beijing had cultivated this tendency by professing the benevolent intent of its policies and scapegoating its rural party base. The post-Mao center more or less continued this practice. Da Fo's farmers understood the politics underlying it: to implicate the center in the harmful acts of its local partisan base was dangerous. For many, therefore, selective memory resonated with political safety. Indeed, many fantasized that the center genuinely represented their cause, or at least represented them better than local party leaders, and so they said that a rebellion against the center would be in opposition to majority interest. However, a few did express varying degrees of support for a rebellion against the Central government.

At first, the experiment with village elections had raised hope that Beijing would become a benefactor of the rural poor. But in Da Fo the defeat of the democratic experiment dashed this hope. An alienated minority grew cynical about the so-called benevolent center. When Da Fo's farmers used the center's propaganda to challenge village and township leaders who twisted state policy, they were cognizant that those same leaders were the appointed agents of Beijing's system of one-party rule. As Hok Bun Ku has pointed out, China's farmers had to embrace the myth of a benevolent center standing apart from its decayed rural political base "not only to validate their resistance but also to play it safe."[85] For the most part, Da Fo's farmers cautiously kept their real feelings about center power to themselves. Nonetheless, by 1998 a growing number (but no more than 20 percent) were inclined to verbalize support for a rebellion against Beijing, whose officials, they said, had sown the seeds of their own destruction. Zheng Yunxiang, who had been cashiered for embracing an armed raid on another brigade's collective fields during the Great Leap hunger,

[83] Ruan Shifan, interview.   [84] Bao Shuqin, interview.   [85] Ku, *Moral Politics*, 168.

declared: "I have a lot of complaints against the Central government. Our country is in serious trouble. Nowadays many workers are out of work. Many farmers are not happy with the government. If there is a rebellion against the Central government, I will support it. The Central government has not done much for rural people. I think the leaders do not really care what is going on in the rural areas. In the past twenty years, we have gotten nothing from the government. Farmers like us are not troublemakers. Generally speaking, as long as we have enough to eat, we will not rebel. The Central government leaders know this. But if we farmers are outraged by something, we will rebel, and the leaders ought to know that we will not rebel without a purpose."[86]

But why this animosity toward the center? Many Da Fo villagers worried that the Central government, despite its opening to the world and despite its reformist domestic economic policies, had not remade its national institutional apparatus in ways that might relieve the psychic damage of the Maoist past or prevent its subnational operatives from imposing new traumas. In a world where aloof local party leaders with a Mao-era lineage were preoccupied with serving their own interests and pleasing superiors, villagers feared another cycle of party misrule, suffering, and justice-seeking revenge that only democratic elections could end. Most of them understood that only the top-level party leaders could authorize the institutional reform that would break China out of this cycle.

In the course of field work in Da Fo, I encountered Great Leap famine survivors who had difficulty in verbalizing pent-up frustrations over CCP misrule. Occasionally, unable to articulate their true feelings, they would just leave the household courtyard in which I was conducting interviews. More frequently, they would find a simple metaphor from nature to express long-imprisoned feelings. They often likened their relationship with Central government rulers as that of fire to water: the two could not mix. One would tend to destroy the other. By 1998, top CCP leaders also feared that a single spark in the rural interior might ignite a prairie fire capable of spreading all the way to the national capital. While on tour in Shenzhen, Qiao Shi, the former chief of China's national internal police, warned Central government leaders that state oppression was driving China's farmers to rebel and sweep away the government.[87] Nearly half of Da Fo's farmers agreed with his prediction. Ruan Shifan, who was among them, put it this way: "I think Qiao Shi is right. Farmers could rebel at any moment. There is some similarity with the conditions that led to peasant rebellion under past dynasties. The corruption is widespread, and villagers do not have any way to express their anger with government officials. We are like a pile of dry wood, which just needs only the touch of a match to start a big fire."[88]

---

[86] Zheng Yunxiang, interview.
[87] See *Cheng Ming*, and Liu, "Qiao Shi Jinggao Zhonggongguo Guanbiminfan."
[88] Ruan Shifan, interview.

While paying homage to the center as a parental benefactor, some rural people contemplated rebellion against power holders in faraway Beijing. Still, most Da Fo farmers were reluctant about embracing an open challenge to Beijing's authority. They would be drawn to rebellion only if they found no other way of averting the continuing abuse of one-party rule. Da Fo's Bao Guanjun was one of them. Seventeen years old when the Great Leap Forward began in Da Fo, Bao Guanjun became a production team accountant. He was able to survive the famine of socialist rule only because he secretly peddled grain purchased in Shandong. Liangmen People's Commune leaders caught him and confiscated his grain, which he retrieved with the help of friends. Aware that those who did not have such friends often did not survive the Maoist disaster, Bao remained haunted by memories of fellow villagers dying from starvation in 1960. Yet Bao's key memory centered on his conflict with Da Fo party boss Bao Zhilong. In the throes of the famine, in the spring of 1961, Bao Zhilong pressured Bao Guanjun to help him personally acquire more food. Bao Guanjun refused. The next year, boss Bao arbitrarily removed Bao Guanjun from his production team position, throwing him back into the ranks of farmers and leaving him to eke out an existence by working a tiny, infertile parcel and pilfering cabbages and sweet potatoes at night. By 1998, the painful memory of this terrible past, in combination with the persistence of the arbitrary, brutal, and corrupt work style of boss Bao Zhilong's reform-era successors, had driven Bao Guanjun to see China's single-party system as illegitimate. "This world," declared Bao, "is not fair to farmers. If the current situation continues, the farmers will rebel in the near future. If there is a rebellion, Da Fo's farmers will join it, and I will support it. We are extremely angry about what is happening in our country. It will take drastic measures to change the Central government. In 1989, when the students rebelled in Beijing, the government used tanks to kill them. It was very brutal. I think in order to change the government, the people will have to take the same measures."[89]

But villagers greatly feared such measures. Support for rebellion against the center surfaced mainly in a renewal of subaltern folk revelations. The first involved a resurgence in the popularity of Guangong, the War God whom Da Fo's farmers traditionally mobilized to mount a symbolic counteroffensive against the unwarranted acts of unrighteous imperial rulers.[90] Associated with opposition to state injustice well into the Republican period, this War God cult had been suppressed in Mao's Great Leap. In the early phase of reform, it made a comeback in Da Fo, as well as in many other Dongle county villages. By the late 1980s, Guangong could be found in the household shrines of most Da Fo farmers, and by 1995 farmers were looking to Guangong precepts to challenge the wrongdoings of local party leaders and the failure of Central government policy.

---

[89] Bao Guanjun, interview.
[90] Cf. Lewis, "Memory, Opportunity, and Strategy," and Thaxton, *Salt of the Earth.*

There was also a revival of legends of past rebels, including the epic tale *Shuihuzhuan*, celebrating the outlaws and rebels who had challenged the Song dynasty. Beijing attempted unsuccessfully to appropriate such legends. According to Ruan Shifan, "Recently, the television has been showing *Shuihuzhuan* (The Water Margin). It is about a peasant rebellion. The peasant outlaws in the story opposed the corrupt officials but not the emperors. This informed us that we had the right to rebel if the officials were corrupt, as long as we did not oppose the emperors [in Beijing]."[91] Through manipulation of the cinematic representation of *Shuihuzhuan*, Beijing attempted to divert popular anger against the system of state power sustained by corrupt higher-level officials, but Da Fo's farmers said the center could not alter their interpretation of *Shuihuzhuan* as a guide to the logical systemic target of a "just rebellion" – the center.

Geomancy pamphlets predicting the ruination of the Central government flourished. In the Da Fo area, people paid close attention to such portents, which were entwined with the misconduct of government higher-ups.[92] In early 2004, Bao Peijian showed up in Da Fo with a little underground press book titled *Qimen Dun*.[93] This book, which contained secret information about state misconduct, was disseminated widely in the Dongle countryside. Purchasers such as Bao often became self-appointed storytellers, conveying its central message. According to Bao, it would be impossible for the Central government to govern if all farmers were to read the book, because *Qimen Dun* revealed too much about government misrule. The pamphlet predicted an upheaval against the center to begin in the Year of the Chicken (2005) or the Year of the Dog (2006). It would usher in a sixty-year reign of apocalypse and rebellion, through which abused rural people would reclaim the Mandate of Heaven. Da Fo's farmers understood why *Qimen Dun* was banned by Dongle County Public Security.

Worse yet from the standpoint of the Central government, the decade following the defeat of the democratic experiment witnessed the spread of so-called counterrevolutionary slogans portending an end to Communist Party rule. Many of these slogans appeared in Da Fo village and across Dongle county – some on electrical poles, often the targets of an everlasting paint that had been applied through molding. According to Bao Zhanghui, a well-traveled sixty-three-year-old Da Fo farmer and chicken droppings merchant, one read "*Tianmei zhonggong, tuidang baoming!*" (Heaven is wiping out the CCP, and every party member should resign from the party to save his own neck!).[94] Yet another said that a savior had been born to show farmers and migrant workers a way out of Hell. Rumor had it that the first was the work of Falun Gong followers, whose secretive ranks included even alienated

[91] Ruan Shifan, interview.
[92] Cf. Gilley, who is superb on this point. *China's Democratic Future*, 103.
[93] Bao Guozheng, interview.   [94] Bao Zhanghui, interview.

local party members. The second slogan was not the work of Maoist nostalgists, for the savior was not Mao.[95] No one knew who put up the slogans. But, Bao Zhanghui concluded, "It had to be a lot of people, because the slogans were everywhere."[96] When the slogans appeared on the poles and walls of Da Fo, party secretary Bao Shunhe attempted to eliminate their message by painting a layer of black ink over each one. But the rains washed away the ink, and the original slogans came out again. The Central government, according to Bao Zhanghui, was losing control of rural China.[97]

– – –

Da Fo's farmers had learned over time that they could not be safe from the violent interventions of greed-driven rulers unless they replaced those rulers. Short of replacement, villagers harbored fears of a quick slip back toward the hunger of the Maoist past, delivered by embedded habits of draconian party rule. Of course, Da Fo's farmers had never heard of Amartya Sen or India's democratically structured famine safeguards, but their logic resonated with his wisdom: they saw elections – the mechanism for replacing abusive, unaccountable leaders – as the best hope for avoiding future economic setback and the kind of social ruin visited on them in the Great Leap famine.

In Da Fo, reform-era Communist Party village and township power holders dashed this hope by underhanded methods. Through manipulating the process of competitive nomination and balloting, they preempted the efforts of villagers to free themselves from autocratic and arbitrary rule. We can only hope that Xu Wang is correct in arguing that local "political reform has achieved significant progress in past years" – enabling villagers to evict worthless village party leaders, to establish village associations supportive of free speech and free assembly, and to make leaders more accountable and less abusive.[98] But because Li Lianjiang found that nearly five-sixths of the preliminary candidates in approximately sixty village electoral "contests" were nominated by either the CCP branch or the party-controlled township government,[99] perhaps Da Fo's electoral odyssey was not an oddity. Bao Yuwen spoke for virtually all of Da Fo's farmers when he said: "We did not have village elections here. The so-called democratic elections were arranged by the township government. Our votes were not important. The village leaders were appointed by the upper government."[100] As Li's work suggests, this democracy from above engendered distrust in the party-state.[101]

---

[95] Wu Anwen, interview.   [96] Bao Zhanghui, interview.   [97] Ibid.

[98] Xu, *Mutual Empowerment*, 14.   [99] Li, "Elections and Popular Resistance," 9–10.

[100] Bao Yuwen, interview.

[101] Li, "Elections and Popular Resistance," 11. Support for Li's analysis can be found in Bernstein, "Village Democracy and Its Limits," 29, 31–33, 36, 41. Manion suggests that elections fostering greater contestation and greater voter input also foster greater trust in leaders. Her

The efficacious democratic selection of local village leaders could have opened up a path toward greater popular satisfaction, and thus supplied a source of legitimacy for the CCP's discredited political system. But the party missed this opportunity.[102] Instead, Da Fo's election experience seems to support John James Kennedy's hypothesis that elections structured by a top-down, closed township nomination process offered Chinese villagers the certainty of a manipulated outcome, and thus produced dissatisfaction and discord.[103] All of this begs a crucial question: To what extent did the failure of effective democratic elections foster a kind of path dependency, complicating future reform and moving otherwise powerless rural players to take more political risks in defending their households against party-state rule? The oral testimonies suggest that the exclusion of villagers from free and fair elections produced frustration and alienation, drawing them into a political vortex that invited less deferential, more portentous forms of contention. This contention took the form of arson against the homes and property of village party leaders, outspoken challenges to township leaders, and symbolic declarations of the end of the CCP's organizational dynasty. Ground-level reform seemed a sham. Rural people felt betrayed. Many were gripped by fear of a recurring traumatic past, when the Maoist assault on democratic discourse engendered disaster. The testy and more tempestuous forms of contention documented in this chapter reflected this fear.

This last point should not be pushed too hard, because we need more verbal evidence that actually links the trauma of the Great Leap famine to present-day contentious attitudes toward local party leaders. To better grasp this link, let us return to the wisdom of Sen, who reminds us that famine poses a serious political dilemma for the state precisely because its effects move ordinary people to vociferously complain about "uncaring government" and even strike out against it.[104] With this in mind, we can see the link between the trauma of the past and the popular frustration stemming from the party's failure to deliver free elections and free discourse in the present in the testimony of Zheng Yunxiang, a Da Fo production team leader who was cashiered for secretly adding grain from the collective granary to the rapidly dwindling public dining-hall grain ration in 1959. When the Da Fo party brass discovered this secret, they reported it to the Liangcun People's Commune leaders, who conducted a witch hunt for the

---

intelligent work uses corruption as a proxy variable for popular perceptions of the unscrupulous acts of local party leaders, finding that 51 percent of respondents voiced broader trust in leaders over the period 1990–1996. In other words, competitive elections mattered. Manion, "Democracy, Community, Trust," 301–302, 307–308, 311. Nonetheless, Manion's conception of the context of elections is social, not political, and this social conception does not factor in attitudes toward local party leadership networks implicated in the venality and harm of the Mao era – in particular the great famine.

[102] I am indebted to Christianne Hardy-Wohlforth for helping me bring greater conceptual clarity to this conclusion. Personal correspondence, May 22, 2009.

[103] Kennedy, "Face of 'Grassroots Democracy,'" 457–459, 461, 478–479, 481–482.

[104] Sen, *The Idea of Justice*, 243.

villagers who had told Zheng Yunxiang and other production team leaders they were hungry. Zheng and two other team leaders were accused of stealing grain, forced to admit their error in public, and then compelled to carry a huge bag of grain on their backs from early morning until early afternoon – a humiliating and wrenching ordeal. Reflecting back on this episode, Zheng Yunxiang linked the Great Leap disaster to the inability of the villagers to replace leaders through free speech and free elections and to the legitimacy crisis of an undemocratic, uncaring CCP-led government in the reform period:

We think the state should allow the people to elect their own leaders. The leaders appointed for us by the township government in the last few years were not good. The township government leaders only appointed those who had connections with them. These leaders do not care what villagers think about them. They only care if they can gain something for themselves. If we could elect our own leaders, we would elect those in whom we trust, not those with connections to the upper government. During the Great Leap Forward we could not openly criticize the village leaders. Of course we can criticize them openly now, but this is of little use. Right now, we are in a mess because the appointed leaders do not abide by the law themselves. When they do not abide by the law people have no respect for them, and do not want to listen to them. We Chinese believe that when the government leaders do not do the right thing, they do not have the right to rule at all.[105]

Zheng Yunxiang said the village, township, and other government leaders feared rebellion (especially another Cultural Revolution) because angry villages would show no mercy. Of course, such talk is cheap. But in the end, the defeat of the democratic alternative, along with the continued plague of corruption, seemed to legitimate rebellion against the CCP-controlled government. It also seems to have poisoned the soil in which local democracy could grow, making it difficult for some villagers to escape the labyrinth of political emotions associated with memories of Mao-era excesses.[106]

Although rebellion was tempting, the majority of Da Fo's farmers were reluctant to endorse – let alone embrace – it. They understood that rebellion did not promise a more secure, better life. To rural people, a just rebellion could originate only in folk Confucian norms that gave rulers many chances to right their wrongs, and such norms were supportive of peaceful modes of conflict resolution. In Da Fo, therefore, villagers sought to redress the wrongs of rulers through historically legitimate forms of deferential protest, presenting higher-ups with an opportunity to renew the arts of responsive, virtuous governance.

---

[105] Zhang Yunxiang, interview.

[106] As John Markoff points out in reference to *Democracy in America*, Tocqueville had argued that the transition to democracy was comparatively easier in America than in his native France, in part because the memory of the cataclysmic violence and terror was still alive in France and therefore acted as a constraint against a peaceful democratic experiment inclusive of basic civil rights. Markoff, *Waves of Democracy*, xiv. Da Fo's history seems to reflect this wisdom, a point to be taken up in the Conclusion.

FIGURE 1. Dai Ruifu (the author) before the "people's heaven" – the earth's harvest – circa 1989

FIGURE 2. The entrance to Da Fo village, Dongle county, Henan province

FIGURE 3. The rhythm of rural life: a farmer on the way to market, during first decade of reform. The Mao-led Communist Party banned such market travel in the Great Leap Forward

FIGURE 4. The author, Dai Ruifu, with an aged survivor of the catastrophic past. Puyang county, Henan province, first decade of reform

FIGURE 5. Cutting the June wheat harvest

FIGURE 6. A family bringing in the harvest. Families were deprived of their claim on the harvest during the Great Leap Forward; husbands and wives often were separated for long periods, with men working in far-flung labor camps and women left to bring in the harvest for the collective

FIGURE 7. A village threshing and milling ground

FIGURE 8. A wagon driver and August corn, Da Fo village, 1990

FIGURE 9. A farmer on the move with his companion

FIGURE 10. A small, early-morning market, Da Fo village, 1990

FIGURE II. Selling peppers and garlic in a village lane

FIGURE 12. Chilling out on a hot summer day. Read the text, and then decide just who is chilling out

FIGURE 13. A small temple, rebuilt by villagers themselves in the aftermath of the Maoist assault on religion and culture. Hebei-Shandong-Henan border area, first decade of post-Mao era

FIGURE 14. A rural villager and Dai Ruifu (the author), Hebei-Shandong-Henan border area, first decade of post-Mao era

8

Contentious Petitioners and the Revival of Mao-Era Repression

With democratic elections scuttled, villagers had to find ways to make higher-ups aware of their grievances. In the mid-1990s, Da Fo's people joined a growing chorus of protesters who engaged in petitioning county, provincial, and national ruling groups to voice their claims. In time, petitioning evolved into a protest movement that occupied center stage in the contentious resistance of rural people. In rural Henan province and Da Fo village, people from all walks of life turned to this form of protest, an important subset of them consisting of survivors of the Great Leap famine.

The petitioning system in China had deep historical and cultural roots. Partly through struggle and partly though dynastic practice, rural people had established their right to petition the powerful. Confucian writings portrayed the common people imploring the emperor for redress of grievances by submitting petitions, sometimes hovering outside the imperial palace with their letters and memorials. As one reform-era Chinese lawyer who had experience in helping petitioners put it, the common people did not always have a sophisticated understanding of the law, but they knew they could petition, and they subscribed to the Confucian notion that appealing to higher-ups in a deferential manner would result in fair treatment.[1]

In the Hebei-Shandong-Henan border area, this ageless petitioning system lasted into the Republican period. Between 1931 and 1935, for example, minor gentry, small landholders, schoolteachers, and semi-peasant salt makers in scores of villages successfully petitioned the Dongle county magistrate over the illegal, violent intrusions of the Central government's salt-tax police into the household-centered economy of earth-salt producers. Da Fo's semi-farmers made an important contribution to thwarting the expansion of Kuomintang

---

[1] Davis et al., "We Could Disappear at Any Time," 1, 3.

Central government fiscal controls.[2] Apparently, the petitioning system, in combination with popular collective action from below, worked rather well into the middle years of the Republic of China, when the Japanese invasion destabilized the Nationalist government and introduced the savagery and chaos that gave the Mao-led Communist Party its chance to seize power through agrarian-based insurgency.[3]

The petition system was revived in the reform era. Supposedly, the Chinese Communist Party (CCP) leaders in Beijing wanted to use it to provide rural people with the institutional means to remonstrate against the wrongdoings of local government officials and, simultaneously, to generate accurate, ground-level information about popular grievances in the countryside. This form of limited, vertically structured participation was designed to promote two-way trust between the center and country dwellers, to foster political stability, and to ensure the survival of single-party rule. Scores of rural people in Dongle county embraced petitioning. Some of them lived in Da Fo. Yet their petitions were aimed at a specific failure of the Central government itself – not at the failure of local government leaders to abide by center policy guidelines. Moreover, high-level CCP leaders in Beijing not only took this particular group of petitioners as a potential threat, they also brought pressure on local government leaders to comply with orders to thwart petitioning without addressing core demands. Thus, as the voices of Da Fo's petitioners reveal, the center itself weakened what Hiroki Takeuchi has termed "the institutionalization of remonstrative political participation"[4] and made it all but impossible for rural people to realize their claims through this seemingly approved official channel of politics. Ironically, the center's failure to support a functional system of remonstration alienated a key subgroup of petitioners who were far better equipped than ordinary farmers to drum up the instability feared by leaders in Zhongnanhai.

PETITIONING IN THE MAO AND REFORM ERAS

The rise of the petition movement in the post-1978 reform era must be understood against the backdrop of the transformation of the petitioning system in the first two decades of Maoist rule.[5] In June 1951, the Communist Party–directed Council of Government Administration, which subsequently became the State Council, started "formalizing the already common practice of

---

[2] Thaxton, *Salt of the Earth*, 73, 80, 130–131, 253–255.

[3] On this point, see Johnson, *Peasant Nationalist and Communist Power*, 1–2, and Thaxton, *Salt of the Earth*.

[4] Takeuchi, *Tax Reform in Rural China*, chapter 4.

[5] For two excellent articles on this backdrop, see Minzner, "Xinfang," and Qin, "Bridge under Water."

approaching party officials with complaints."[6] This was the inception of Communist Party efforts to monitor dissent in the countryside and exploit the petitioning system to serve the party's own brand of revolutionary justice. To be sure, rural people engaged in petitioning in the early 1950s, but in the context of the emergency national security measures put in place by the Communist Party in the aftermath of the civil war and the Korean War, petitioning was increasingly subordinated to political campaigns designed to promote national security and the collective political economy on which Maoist state power rested.

There were, it seems, two political obstacles to petitioning. First, the early Communist Party directives for handling petitions were penned in a way that made party disciplinary committees and public security offices the final arbiters of petitioner complaints and claims.[7] This raised the stakes of petitioning for villagers who had grievances against the wrongdoings of local party leaders. In Da Fo and much of Dongle county, party leaders had intimate connections with public security personnel,[8] a conflict of interest that did not bode well for petitioners. Furthermore, Mao Zedong, with his faith in Communist Party-led mass line politics, did not fully appreciate the dynastic process whereby rural people registered dissent through petitioning. In the early 1950s, as Mao increasingly relied on provincial- and county-level party cadres to pass up popular complaints about state policies, he and the Central Committee were instructing those very same cadres to pressure villagers to embrace collective agriculture – a radical change that tillers opposed. Thus, it is not surprising that subnational Communist Party cadres who dealt with petitions on the ground in rural provinces and counties far removed from Beijing were not inclined to dignify and address complaints expressed via petitioning.[9] In 1955–1957, when villagers rose up to protest the household dispossession engendered by their encounter with Mao's socialist agenda, the number of petitioners who jumped over local government complaint offices and took their petitions for justice to higher-ups, including those in Beijing, rose substantially.[10]

Between late 1957 and late 1959, Mao Zedong set the tone for the suppression of petitions stimulated by his march toward agricultural collectivization. In the spring of 1957, Mao unfurled the Hundred Flowers Campaign, which called for non–party members to express their criticism of cadre misrule, including the abuse of farmers in the course of appropriating their harvests for the collective. In this period, the number of complaints and petitions in Dongle county increased.[11] In late 1957, however, Mao reversed this campaign, with predictable consequences in the countryside. In Dongle county, local party leaders subjected those who had admonished them to stinging public criticism, declaring them "rightists." The Maoist center, with general party

---

[6] Luehrmann, "Officials Face the Masses," 32.   [7] Cf. Ibid., 33.
[8] Thaxton, *Catastrophe and Contention.*   [9] Luehrmann, "Officials Face the Masses," 37–39.
[10] Ibid., 41.   [11] Ibid.

secretary Deng Xiaoping leading the charge, turned a blind eye toward this process, which had a chilling effect on petitioning.

Further damage was done to the petitioning system in the Great Leap Forward, resulting in widespread suffering. Between mid-August and late October 1958, Mao and key Central Committee members received written petitions from rural farmers in Henan province. Some of the petitions, written by members of the Communist Youth League, pleaded with central party leaders to correct problems created by party cadres in charge of the Great Leap locally. One, addressed to Tan Zhenlin,[12] on whom Mao closely relied to push his Leap policies, complained that cadres were falsely overreporting the harvest output so they could justify appropriating more of the harvest for the party-state and thereby ingratiate themselves with superiors.[13] Yet another, sent directly to Mao on October 20, 1958, documented cadre abuse of farmers who did not want to enter the people's communes and beatings of those who insisted on accurately reporting harvest output. For the first time, this second petition revealed the severity of the consumption problem engendered by the transfer of the means of production to commune-level party leadership and by the crackdown on petty trade conducted without official permission.

Operating on the premise that petitions reflected the complaints of a rural minority – and failing to locate the causes of the unfolding calamity in his own policies and the corrupt work style of his party base – Mao Zedong ignored the requests of petitioning tillers and teachers for an independent Central government investigation and directed his followers in the Communist Party provincial party committees, including the Henan Party Committee, to look into the complaints. This act placed the decisions on petitions in the hands of the same subnational party hierarchy whose conduct had spurred them, and these leaders frequently invoked party-contrived public criticism to silence the petitioners.[14] As a result, the ageless practice of addressing the misrule of the powerful through deferential petitions was surrendered to the offensive of Maoist-style war communism.[15]

Whereas many of the offices that were to receive petitioners and their complaints were shut down during the Cultural Revolution, the late Mao–early Deng transition witnessed a revival of petitioning in Dongle county. The first three years of the post-1978 reform saw the party-state reinstituting complaint offices and training cadres to handle petitions, most of which focused on injustices suffered during the Cultural Revolution.[16] Some of the petitions

---

[12] My data on this are weak but resonate with the scholarship of Meisner, *Mao's China and After*, chapter 4, and with Luehrmann, "Officials Face the Masses," 41; also personal correspondence with Dongping Han, August 22, 2011.

[13] Yu, *Dayuejin Kurizi Shangshuji*, 41–43, 61–64.

[14] Cf. Thaxton, *Catastrophe and Contention*, 1–3.

[15] Yang, *Calamity and Reform*, 1, and Thaxton, *Catastrophe and Contention*.

[16] Luehrmann, "Officials Face the Masses," 45–49, and Luehrmann, "Facing Citizen Complaints," 855.

coming out of villages in the vicinity of Da Fo apparently fell into this category –
or so it would seem from officials in charge of Letters and Visits, Communist
Party–screened journal articles, and reports made by Chinese academic investigators. To be sure, much of this official information was accurate and provided
new insights into center efforts to reinstitute the petitioning system after 1978.
It was based, however, on two highly dubious assumptions. The first was that
the petitioning of the post-Mao years, and especially the petitions addressing
Cultural Revolution grievances, was unrelated to social suffering in the Great
Leap Forward. The second was that the revival of the state-controlled Letters
and Visits system, with its multilevel complaint bureaus, *in and of itself* inspired
rural people to contentious action and permitted them to "bargain" for justice
with officials, a process that supposedly proved efficacious for villagers and, in
the end, demonstrated that it was more effective in engendering reform than
more direct challenges to single-party rule.[17]

For the most part, these assumptions were derived from studying petitioning
through official sources, not from in-depth investigations of the life experiences
of petitioners. By exploring the encounters of individual petitioners with state
power, we can more fully appreciate the emotional and psychological factors
motivating relatively powerless individuals to seek justice through petitioning.

A PETITIONER'S LIFE

In theory, the petitioning system was to provide a transmission belt between
rural people with grievances against local party leaders and higher-ups in the
reform-era regime, so that the CCP could achieve legitimation in the aftermath
of the Mao-era clampdown on petitioning. But did it actually function this
way? To address this question, let us take up the case of Bao Zhifa, a People's
Liberation Army (PLA) veteran. We want to know if Bao's case was in any way
linked to an individual experience with the Great Leap famine and whether his
memory of this episode of suffering and loss conditioned his petitioning; we will
then try to understand what his case indicates about the petitioning process in
post-Mao China.

In 2008, at the age of fifty-eight, Bao Zhifa was working as an unskilled
manual laborer on a construction project in Jinxi, Shanxi province. Living in
shabby mobile shelters and eating poor food, Bao led a hard life. He undertook
construction work during sojourns from Da Fo, leaving in the spring after
feeding and weeding the wheat crop, in the summer after bringing in the wheat
harvest, and again in the fall after gathering the Indian corn. Bao Zhifa worried
about his future. He was getting older. Age and work were taking their toll on a
body that already had suffered the privations of the Great Leap famine and a
decade of demanding military service. Yet Bao also held out hope for a better

---

[17] Cf. Xi, "Collective Petitioning," 62–63, and Tarrow, "New Contentious Politics." To some
    extent, Luehrmann shares this premise, but her careful, splendid scholarship is far more cautious
    on this point. Cf. Luehrmann, "Officials Face the Masses," 83–86, 110–112.

life: "Most people my age would not work outside of the village anymore. If they did go out to work, they would not do hard work. I do not think that I will be able to work for many more years. My hope is that I will not need to work more than two more years. I just need to pay a little bit more to qualify for a military pension at the age of sixty. I would be able to receive about 700 yuan a month when I reach the age of sixty. With that money, I would not need to work outside of the village anymore."[18] But four years later, in the summer of 2011, Bao Zhifa was still chasing temporary jobs in the construction sector, this time in Shandong province.

Bao was no stranger to struggle. Mao's Great Leap had driven his father, a former smallholder, into deep poverty, and it had ripped Bao's family apart. With no ties to the party-state, his father was unable to hold the family together in the Leap famine. At the height of the famine, when Bao Zhifa was ten, his mother had to save his emaciated second sister by giving her up to a farmer in Liuzhuang, Hebei province. That same year, in order to improve her own chances of survival, his mother left Bao's father to marry someone else in Sijiakou village, Qinji township, Wei county. "My mother left without my father's knowledge," recalled Bao. "My father was away working in Hebi city at the time. He was transporting various items with a wheelbarrow. After my mother settled down in Sijiakou, she came back to Da Fo to divorce my father. Her excuse was that she could not live harmoniously with my father."[19] But behind the excuse was the great famine, which had created intrafamily discord over how to cope with the fate of the children.

In 1967, at nineteen, Bao Zhifa joined the PLA. He was chosen from among a hundred or more young people in Da Fo who wanted to join up; the army would take no more than four recruits from each village. According to Bao, the army was very popular in China then because it offered an escape from the lingering hunger of the Great Leap famine and "provided young people an opportunity to see the outside world." In Bao's case, army service was also a key to coping with the social ramifications of losing a parent. "I was allowed to join the army," recalled Bao, "because my mother left my father and me. I did not have a mother in Da Fo at the time. This made life very difficult for me. When other young people returned home each day, their mothers had prepared lunch or dinner for them. I did not have that. At the age of nineteen, other people's mothers would start looking for a wife for their sons. I did not have a mother to do that for me. If I had stayed in the village, I most likely would not have been able to get married in the end. I think this was one of the main reasons why the village leaders sent me, instead of someone else, to the PLA."[20]

Speaking of the trauma of 1960, Bao recalls: "When I was ten years old, during the Great Leap Forward, my mother left my father with my two younger sisters. My first sister was only eleven years old, and my second sister was only

[18] Bao Zhifa, interview.   [19] Ibid.   [20] Ibid.

one year old. I have been angry with my mother all of my life. She left me when I was barely ten, turning me into an orphan."[21] Bao recalls that being an orphan in the village was "hard" – so hard that he never got over it and was still defined by this politically delivered social trauma in the summer of 2007, when he despondently revealed that he had attempted to get beyond it on many occasions by undertaking efforts to reunite with his mother. When Bao was nineteen, his mother's second husband was killed in an accident while digging an irrigation well for the collective. "At that time," reveals Bao, "I was hoping that my mother would come back to my father again. But I was not able to make that happen."[22] Bao did not give up, however. After joining the PLA, he asked his commanders for help in bringing his mother back to Da Fo. A small PLA reconciliation team found the matter to be very complicated, especially since Bao and his mother had residence permits in different provinces. After sending out a letter and then making an inquiry in Sijiakou village, the team leaders gave up. Bao did not. After returning home from army service, he tried for a third time to convince his mother to reconcile and return to Da Fo. Hardened by her grief over the failure of her husband to keep the family together during the famine, she would not budge, and so Bao returned to Da Fo without her. When interviewed in the summer of 2007, Bao Zhifa still longed to reunite with his mother, who by this point was seventy-nine years old and threatening to outlive her dejected son.

Though it was small consolation, Bao Zhifa recalled that at least he had been able to rely on army service to escape the dead-end bondage to Da Fo's saline collective lands in the Mao years. The PLA took him out of the village and set him on a path that led to Pakistan.

The Pakistan National Defense Highway

In 1963, at the height of the Cold War, Pakistani Prime Minister Bhutto and People's Republic of China (PRC) Premier Zhou Enlai signed a contract for China to build a highway for Pakistan. This highway was of strategic importance to both nations. Pakistan was one of the few countries through which China could gain access to international diplomatic channels and to the global economy, so Beijing agreed to pay all of the costs of the highway project. Nearly five hundred kilometers long, it had to be built in challenging high-altitude terrain.

The project gained momentum in 1967–1968, when China's relationship with India and the Soviet Union grew tense and rumors of an anticipated surprise Soviet attack on China in the Xinjiang area were rife. When the border

---

[21] Ibid. According to Kay Ann Johnson, the term "orphan" was commonly used by villagers to describe the kind of one-parent abandonment experienced by Bao Zhifa. Personal correspondence, March 29, 2009.

[22] Bao Zhifa, interview.

war between India and Pakistan broke out in 1971, China withdrew its PLA construction workers, and the highway work was temporarily halted. It picked up again in 1974, when Premier Zhou Enlai, worried that India and the Soviet Union might attack China on two fronts, agreed to accelerate the Pakistan highway project on the condition that China be allowed to use the highway and to ship supplies to Pakistan. Using "retired" PLA soldiers to carry out large-scale construction projects in China and abroad was a common Central government practice.[23] By early March 1974, therefore, scores of retired PLA soldiers who were scheduled to return home after the end of their normal required tour of duty were sent off to build the highway in Pakistan's mountains. At this time, Bao Zhifa and his counterparts in a PLA construction division volunteered to go to Pakistan to work on the highway, a mission that lasted until September 1976 and resulted in the completion of the Karakoram Highway, sometimes called the Ninth Wonder of the World.

Bao Zhifa was one of 10,000 PLA veterans sent to Pakistan as "civilian workers" in the early 1970s. Eight hundred of these workers were from Puyang, two hundred from Qingfeng, and another two hundred from Dongle county, all in Henan province.[24] Like many impoverished and desperate young PLA recruits, Bao Zhifa "volunteered" for the Pakistan national defense highway project largely because the work offered food security – a precious ticket out of the dearth that continued to stalk village China in the post–Great Leap decade. The pay for Bao and his fellow volunteers was 45 yuan per month, enough money to purchase twice the food available per person per day back in Da Fo village. Also, at the time, the Central government had ordered thirteen provinces to provide food for the operations in Pakistan, and workers' rations included protein-rich grain, meat, and vegetables.[25] Bao Zhifa recalled, "That was the best food I ever had in my life."[26]

This comment should not be taken lightly. Other ex-PLA "civilians" who served in Pakistan and later joined in petitioning had a similar story. Referring to the food crisis of his household in the immediate post-Leap period, Pang Siyin had this to say: "Not many people in China ate well at that time. Young people wanted to join the army because the army provided better food and other opportunities for rural people. Most urban people spent only 7 yuan a month on food. The government spent 15 yuan per month on our food. When we went to Pakistan, the food was even better. There were several dishes for each meal, and plenty of canned beef, pork, and fish. Before we went to Pakistan we had never eaten that well."[27] Zhang Jieming of nearby Shangcunji village has a similar story. In December 1970, Zhang, who remembers eating tree bark and collecting wild vegetables to cope with hunger after his school's public dining hall collapsed in the Great Leap, joined Construction Unit 544 to

---

[23] See Diamant, *Embattled Glory*, 64–65.   [24] Pang Siyin, interview.
[25] Bao Zhifa, interview.   [26] Ibid.; confirmed by Yan Hailian, interview.
[27] Pang Siyin, interview.

build barracks for the PLA in Xinjiang, and thereafter went to Pakistan. He recalls: "Many people wanted to join the army at the time because the army ate better than we did at home. Before we joined the army, we mostly ate porridge. But once we joined the army we were able to eat as much bread as we liked, and there was plenty of rice also. We were happy with the food in the army."[28] Lest we think that young villagers joined in defense of Mao's imaginary nation, let us listen to Bao Hongwen, who lost his father to the Great Leap famine. Bao joined the PLA in 1970, nearly ten years after the Leap famine ended. At the time, he still lived on a damaging mono diet of sweet potatoes and was so poor that he and his wife could not afford even one piece of wooden household furniture. "I did not join the army for any high idea," says Bao. "I joined because I was told that the army provided better food. The food in the army was one hundred times better than the food we had in Da Fo village."[29]

For this subset of Great Leap–era survivors, the CCP apparently regained a measure of legitimacy in the opening months of the Pakistan highway campaign. This legitimacy was based on providing soldiers with a fair share of food in exchange for helping Beijing build goodwill with a troubled, strategic state, and it produced high army morale before ground-level troubles in Pakistan engendered more trauma.[30]

The Pakistan highway project was carried out in an unfriendly local environment, and it required great sacrifice. For one thing, neither the regimental commanders nor the rank-and-file soldiers such as Bao Zhifa were recognized as people with needs and rights. Because they were actually serving in the army longer than the law of the PRC required, the Central government took secretive measures to deny that the project and its personnel existed. During the three-year stint of 1974–1976, no commander or soldier was able to visit his family, and no member of Bao Zhifa's construction unit was allowed to get married. At one point, Bao's regimental commander appealed to Chen Muhua, a Politbur-eau member, to relax this rule, but he was told that revolutionary soldiers should never ask for special consideration. "That was the culture of our army and our nation at the time," recalls one of Bao Zhifa's comrades.[31] In 1976, a massive earthquake devastated Tangshan. The top five commanders of Bao's regiment all lost all of their family members – and yet due to the secrecy of the Pakistan mission, not one of them was allowed to return home to bury their dead kin.[32] Bao and his highway worker peers hold bitter memories of the inhumanity of this culture of sacrifice for Maoist state goals, and they all understood the political origins of this inhumane denial: at the height of the Great Leap famine, the institutionalized practice had been that villagers who had joined Mao's industrial army on far-flung reservoir- and road-building

---

[28] Zhang Jieming, interview.   [29] Bao Hongwen, interview.
[30] I have benefited here from Gilley, *China's Democratic Future*, 5.   [31] Yan Hailian, interview.
[32] Ibid.

work sites were not allowed to return home, even if their parents died, without permission from party leaders.[33]

The promise of food security also turned out to be a problem. Working at extremely high altitudes, the young soldiers were unable to eat fresh vegetables, and, more important, the bread and rice could not be fully cooked because the water reached a boiling point only at 70°C (158°F). So while some of the soldiers say that they ate well, still others frame their days in Pakistan through a memory of intestinal diseases related to "too much uncooked bread and water."[34] Though food supply from China to the workers was prompt most of the year, collapsing mountain slides and melting snow occasionally blocked and washed out roads for four to six weeks, requiring both commanders and ordinary soldiers to improvise for survival. This was difficult, in part because the local people were hostile to the volunteers and the project. Tang Yintang recalls: "During one month when we did not have any food supply from China, we had to buy flower, vegetables, and meat from the local merchants. But the Pakistani merchants were very bad. They supplied us with flour with mildew in it. Most of us were poisoned by the bad flour. Many people vomited. In the beginning, we did not know why we were sick. Only after a month or so did we discover our sickness and vomiting was due to the moldy flour."[35]

Indeed, the local people themselves posed a formidable problem for this secret PLA mission. They caused trouble by stealing equipment (gloves, hammers, and shovels), by threatening to sue PLA soldiers if they took the tree branches and twigs from forests to start camp fires, and by adding water to the gasoline the PLA bought locally. This latter act shut down the petro-powered stone drilling operations for days and weeks. Thus, Pang Siyin was understating the problem when he recalled, "They never cooperated with us."[36]

But the greatest challenge was terrain. Building the Pakistan national defense highway required PLA construction workers to risk life and limb working in dangerously jagged and vaulted mountain terrain. The day-to-day work was backbreaking, and the physical aches and pains that resulted from it stayed with Bao Zhifa and his army comrades for decades after their arduous tour of duty. Bao Zhifa blamed his poor health and chronic joint pain on his tour in Pakistan.[37] But he was fortunate compared with those who did not survive: "More than a hundred of our comrades [188 in reality – RT] died there. Some were killed by the explosives used to blast the mountains. Others were killed by mudslides. Still others by traffic accidents." Bao retains graphic memories of gruesome traffic accident scenes – of trucks falling into deep river gorges, of truck driver's bodies broken into small bits, of nurses going down into the river gorges to retrieve body parts and sew them back together, and of tearful burials in forlorn, makeshift cemeteries.[38]

---

[33] For this information I am indebted to Bao Jingshen, interview.   [34] Zhang Jieming, interview.
[35] Tang Yintang, interview.   [36] Pang Siyin, interview.   [37] Bao Zhifa, interview.   [38] Ibid.

Jeremy Brown has shown that top party leaders came to fear potentially damaging popular reactions to accidents in the reform period and that this fear is rooted in the Mao era, when accidents that affected countless families were kept secret by party leaders.[39] The post-Mao center's attempt to cover up, and keep out of public knowledge, the abhorrent PLA accidents of the post-Leap famine period was shaped by a deeply embedded modality of rule, one that extended back to the Great Leap itself, when party leaders regimented rural dwellers in military-style units to complete large-scale construction projects (roads, mountain passages, dams, iron refineries) at breakneck speed and failed to report accidents stemming from pressure on underlings to meet deadlines and goals. Moreover, it appears that the reform-era pattern of top-level power holders sacrificing powerless young people for their own gain[40] has an echo in the fate of the former Pakistan highway accident victims, the great majority of whom were vulnerable and impressionable young people.

Pang Siyin, a member of an engineering brigade sent to Pakistan, holds a memory of one such trauma, witnessed by all of his comrades: "We simply blasted a highway through the middle of the mountains. We would dig a big hole into the mountain, and then fill the hole with tons of TNT. We used trucks to carry the TNT into the mountain. One blast, and half the mountain would be blown away. Normally, we would wait twenty-four hours after a blast before we entered the site to clear away the debris. But one platoon leader wanted to hurry the project. He ordered about forty soldiers to come right away to work with the debris. However, the aftershock of the blast continued after the soldiers entered the work site. They were engulfed by the collapsing mountains. All of our men tried desperately to rescue the soldiers, but we were able to rescue only two of them. They had been shielded by a big slab of stone. All the rest were crushed by the stones. In the end, we were not even able to recover their bodies."[41] Such accidents were the product of the lingering Maoist work style of rash advance that infused the campaign of the Great Leap Forward, engendering its disaster. The habit of impetuosity – of blindly hurrying the daunting task of altering natural landscapes at the risk of seriously harming the rural people who volunteered to construct the roads, dams, and mines demanded by Mao's developmental transcript – persisted.

Da Fo's Tang Yintang was fourteen years old when Mao's rushed collectivization ruined village China. Hungry all the time in the Great Leap years, Tang remembers: "I always collected grass seeds on the way home from school. My mother would grind the seeds to make a flour for bread. I also remember that we ate cotton seeds that were very hard to digest. And like many other people, I ate raw squash in the fields."[42] Tang's father died after the famine subsided, and Tang did not want to stay in Da Fo. He joined the army and ended up in

[39] Brown, "When Things Go Wrong," 11–12.   [40] On this point, Cf. ibid., 15–22.
[41] Pang Siyin, interview.   [42] Tang Yintang, interview.

Pakistan. The occasion when forty soldiers died in the mountain blast described earlier by Pang Siyin is vividly etched in Tang's memory: "One time, one of these intended TNT charges did not blast as planned. According to the code of conduct, we should have waited for another full day before going back to work at this site. But the commander was in a hurry to finish the project. He ordered his men to enter the site to start working there only thirty minutes after the planned TNT blast was to occur. Not long after the soldiers entered, the explosion occurred, and all of the soldiers were buried on the site. It was the biggest accident of the entire Pakistan highway project. It was a very sad event."[43]

The Party-State Betrayal and the Emergence of Petitioning

Normally, PLA construction workers involved in high-risk international highway and railway projects, such as those in Pakistan, Tanzania, or Zambia, were treated as national heroes, and the Central government took care of them after their return to the PRC, either by compensating them handsomely or by finding them jobs in state-owned enterprises. But Bao Zhifa and his comrades returned to China from Pakistan in the middle of what he termed "an untimely mess." While en route by train from Pakistan to the PRC in early September 1976, Bao and his fellow soldiers learned that Mao Zedong had died. They worried about the future of the Central government – and about their own fate.

"Just as we had suspected," recalled Bao, "there was something happening in the Central government. There was serious infighting among the top leaders. Hua Guofeng arrested Chairman Mao's wife and other top leaders, and he proved to be a conspirator from the start."[44] Because the Central government leaders were involved in factional struggles in this period, no one in the state paid attention to the returned Pakistan highway workers. Most were sent back to their native villages, and no special arrangements were made for them. Jobless, most were left to scratch out a living in villages where farmers had yet to recover from the devastation of the Great Leap famine. "We were very upset with the government for neglecting us from the beginning of our demobilization," said Bao.[45] Feeling betrayed and facing a bleak future, Bao Zhifa and his comrades in several different provinces started to demand that Central government leaders explain why they had been neglected rather than rewarded for their sacrifices in Pakistan. Seeking compensation for their national service and their economic losses, in the second decade of the post-Mao reform, Bao Zhifa and scores of ex-PLA Pakistan highway construction workers began to petition the state.

Like his counterparts, Bao Zhifa had not been adequately compensated for his service in Pakistan. In 1997–1998, therefore, he joined with other

[43] Ibid.　　[44] Bao Zhifa, interview.　　[45] Ibid.

Henan-based PLA veterans of China's secret Pakistan highway project in a province-wide petitioning movement designed to advance claims for compensation from the state. By 2001, this petitioning initiative had become a national movement, as PLA veterans from Jiangsu and Henan – the provinces from which most of the veterans hailed – were joined by thousands of their counterparts from Gansu, Sichuan, Shanxi, and Hubei provinces. There were nine hundred of these petitioners from Henan province, and more than three hundred of them hailed from the villages of Dongle county and nearby Puyang. At least twenty were from Shangcunji, four from Liangmen township, and three from Da Fo village. In petitioning the state, Bao Zhifa and these veterans were not suing any individuals or government officials, nor were they expressing any grievances against any local government or its leaders. Instead, Bao Zhifa explained, "What we have been trying to do is to find out what was the Central government policy toward people like us. What standard has the government set for treating workers who had performed services for the state but have not been adequately compensated in the past? We have not been asking for special treatment in any way. We just want fair compensation within the legal boundaries of the Chinese work law."[46]

According to Bao, the Chinese legal codes regarding work compensation had specific stipulations for different types of working conditions. When they worked in Pakistan in the 1970s, he and his fellow soldiers were at an altitude of 4,700–5,300 meters above sea level. "Under Chinese law," Bao explains, "one year of working at such a high altitude was equal to three years of service credit. We worked there for three years, so we earned nine years of work credits." Though they had had the status of civilian workers, the families of the soldiers and officers had received military subsidy pay.[47] "During the 1970s," Bao continued, "the state did not have any law that allowed the government to dismiss workers. Once a worker was hired, he would enjoy lifelong employment. Therefore, we should have been government employees once we were hired." Instead, they had been returned to their villages and ignored.[48]

During his Pakistan tour of duty, Bao Zhifa had learned how to drive a truck, a skill in high demand in the PRC in the late Mao years. In early 1978, he was hired by the Liangmen People's Commune Truck Team Unit, but as a storekeeper, not a driver, because he was not able to convert his army driver's license (acquired through a tour of service the state did not openly acknowledge) into a civilian permit. When the collective disbanded in 1982, the minor commune employees all had to return to Da Fo to farm their share of land, and Bao Zhifa was no exception. Shortly thereafter, however, Bao managed to convert his army license into a civilian permit, and he started driving for a private entrepreneur in the slow months of the agricultural cycle, transporting

[46] Ibid.　　[47] Ibid.　　[48] Ibid.

coal from Shanxi to Shandong and fruit from Guangdong to Henan. The private trucking operation did not meet official standards, so the drivers had to work mostly at night to avoid police inspection. On each long-distance hauling trip, Bao and two other drivers were crowded into a small front cab whose bouncing inflamed the chronic aches and pains he had acquired in Pakistan. In this period, Bao Zhifa was paid 100 yuan per trip, while the private truck owner got rich.

Bao recalled this experience in categories that did not resonate with Deng-era tributes to market glory: "When I learned how to drive in the army, I thought I would drive for the state or the government. But the state did not want to use me, and it did not give me a job. At the time, drivers were scarce in China. People who returned from the army with a driver's license all got a good job. I and my comrades, however, happened to be caught in the Central government's internal struggle, so we were denied the opportunity to work for the government. For the government jobs, workers only needed to work an eight-hour day, and there were many other benefits like paid medical leave, paid holidays, paid medical insurance for families, as well as retirement benefits. The private entrepreneurs did not give any of these benefits. I worked for them for nearly twenty years, until 2000. Eventually, my eyes turned bad, and I could not see clearly. I was too worried about having an accident to continue. In all of this time, I did not receive any government subsidy, and the state did not give veterans like us any formal help."[49]

Embittered by this betrayal, Bao Zhifa explains why he and his fellow veterans were petitioning the government: "Because of this mistake on the part of the state [in not providing government jobs], we suffered and our families and our children all suffered negative consequences. If we had been awarded with jobs after we returned from Pakistan, our living conditions would have been different and our families would have been facing very different circumstances. Now, however, we are older. We do not seek to force the government to give us jobs. But we are demanding that the government compensate us for our losses over the past thirty years in accordance with the law."[50]

According to the PLA veterans of the Pakistan highway campaign, the legal codes pertaining to government work and compensation in the 1970s stipulated that a worker's monthly salary could not be less than 60 yuan. Even if they had been paid the minimum wage in the intervening decades, Bao and his counterparts had calculated that each one of them deserved a total compensation of 300,000 yuan in missed salary over the thirty-year period. If the state could not compensate that much, they argued, it should have cared enough about them to come up with some kind of substantial compensation package. Most of the veterans, such as Bao Zhifa, were getting older and facing a future in which they would not be able to work any longer. Bao Zhifa spoke for

49 Ibid. 50 Ibid.

the majority when he said, "The state has to provide support for our livelihood. We will not stop petitioning the government until they do something for us."[51]

Through a ten-year petitioning experience involving multiple exchanges with ex-PLA survivors of the Pakistan national defense highway project, the leaders of the petitioning effort came up with four goals, each reflecting a demand for just compensation for their sacrifice in the post–Great Leap years. Guo Xingyun, an army veteran from Wangguo village in Shangcun township, Dongle county, and one of the petition writers, sums up the four core demands of the petitioners:

We demand that the Central government treat us as retired workers, and that we receive the standard retirement package of the government, which would be 2,000 yuan.

The Central government should compensate us for all medical problems stemming from working in the high-altitude and hazardous terrain of Pakistan, including lung disease, high blood pressure, and chronic arthritis. Many of us have lost the ability to work because of these diseases. We need government relief.

The returned soldiers involved in building the highways in Tanzania and Zambia were assigned to work for state-owned enterprises even though they were abroad for only two years. We worked in Pakistan for four to six years, so we should be compensated like the returned soldiers from Tanzania and Zambia.

Because we are older, we should be compensated now. We do not want to be treated like the veterans of the Korean War, who were kept waiting so long that most of them had died by the time the government recognized their sacrifice.[52]

In all of the petitions, the veterans of the Pakistan strategic highway campaign made reference to a Central government promise that, in their eyes, justified their core goals, especially the goal documented by Neil J. Diamant: a state-backed, post-service social ascent.[53] Guo Xingyun explains:

Another important point we made in the materials we submitted is that in September 1976, Wu Guixian led a Central government delegation to visit us in Pakistan. Wu said that our work in Pakistan made an important contribution to the friendship between Pakistan and China, and that we had added glory to Chairman Mao and our great motherland. Wu said the state would in turn take care of our families. Wu then promised: "When you return home upon completing your mission, the state and the government will make a good arrangement for you." Wu Guixian's speech buoyed our hopes and lifted our spirits. She made the speech on behalf of Chairman Mao and the Central Military Committee. But twenty-nine years after her speech we still are waiting for the government to carry out her promise.[54]

(Wu Guixian was the head of the Factory Workers Revolutionary Committee in the Cultural Revolution, and later a deputy premier of the State Council.[55])

---

[51] Ibid.   [52] Guo Xingyun, interview.   [53] Diamant, *Embattled Glory*, 363.
[54] Guo Xingyun, interview.   [55] See *Gongyi China: Persons of Modern Times*, April 26, 2005.

WHY DID PETITIONING EXPLODE IN THE SECOND DECADE OF REFORM?

The belief that the Central government owed veterans for their sacrifices is underscored by Neil J. Diamant, whose *Embattled Glory* shows that, to a limited extent, PLA veterans had mobilized to make the state deliver even during the Mao era.[56] So why did this particular version of contention explode in the second decade of reform, from roughly 1995 to 2005, rather than in the late Mao–early Deng transition? Kevin J. O'Brien, Lianjiang Li, and Mingxing Liu have given us part of the answer. In the early years of reform, around 1982, the Central government began to recognize petitioners as good citizens in pursuit of virtuous governance. This constitutionally sanctioned change, however ambiguous in language, rippled along the grapevine in city and countryside, gaining traction among people who had ties to the party-state but who felt they were victims of administrative injustice. By the late 1990s, the returned Pakistan soldiers were calling themselves "citizens" and reading this change to justify their petitions to Beijing.[57] In addition, the national leadership change from Jiang Zemin to Hu Jintao, who wanted to gain popular support and defuse rising discontent in the interior, mattered greatly. With Hu and Wen Jiabao reaching out through Communist Party–controlled media to those who had been marginalized under reform, more and more rural people took up petitioning in the expectation that Beijing would assist them in resolving disputes and grievances. The returned Pakistan soldiers joined in this "high tide," which peaked in the years 2003–2005. But in mid-2005, the Hu-led center started to rely on police force, public security offices, and local county officials to suppress petitioning.[58]

Local knowledge suggests that the differential impact of the Deng-led economic transformation and rising discontent over the corruption swamping reform produced a convergence of interest among the Pakistan-returned soldiers, who saw the challenge of petitioning from different angles. We can divide this subset of petitioners themselves into two crude groups: winners and losers. By the late 1980s, the first group of returned Pakistan soldiers included a few people who were doing well under reform and who now had the time and the money to invest in the petitioning effort. The veterans from Jiangsu, and to a lesser extent from Henan, were included in this group. The monetary gains they made from engaging the market were used to purchase the time to organize petitioning, and so they slowly but surely contacted scores of returned veterans

---

[56] Diamant, *Embattled Glory*, 153–159, 363, 375–377, 386–387.

[57] As O'Brien, Li, and Liu make clear, the Central government advanced this notion of "legitimate petitioners" in order to help them "monitor local authorities as well as prevent and clean up forms of misconduct that damage regime legitimacy." O'Brien, Li, and Liu, "Petitioning Beijing," 6. So the center did not fully anticipate legal petitioners using its rule changes to fight against its own center-based injustices.

[58] O'Brien, Li, and Liu, "Petitioning Beijing," 11–12, 20–22.

across different provinces. The interview data make it clear that these people were not mainly petitioning in reaction to reform-era deprivation. Instead, as the testimony of Guo Xingyun, a native of Wangguocun, indicates, they engaged petitioning to maintain their integrity, to make higher-ups acknowledge – and even demonstrate gratitude for – their sacrifices for the nation over a lifetime.

In the late 1980s and early 1990s, Guo Xingyun was able to earn a great deal of money by purchasing corn from farmers and selling it to pharmaceutical companies. He explains the mindset behind his petitioning activity: "My life is improving each year. I embraced petitioning not because I need financial help from the state. The reason is that my comrades and I made great contributions to our nation. If we can get some money from the government as a kind of recognition for our sacrifice in the past, it would be a good thing for us."[59] Guo was unhappy with the Central government, partly because he saw too many corrupt officials. However, he had sacrificed so much for the state, and he was not yet ready to give up on the center.

Many of the Pakistan-returned soldiers who had lost out in reform did not share Guo's optimism, however. They were petitioning for material gain, and they saw a government-sponsored retirement package as a life raft designed to help them survive the unfair steamroller of reform, which had benefited corrupt Communist Party officials, not ordinary people such as themselves.[60] I was surprised to learn that some of the veterans of the Pakistan highway adventure blamed their inability to secure a job with the government on high-level corruption, thereby linking their fate to the root of the CCP legitimacy crisis. Tang Yintang was one of them. According to Tang: "The government should have reserved the positions for us, but it did not. Instead, it allowed the different government officers and officials to recruit their own relatives and friends."[61] Fed up with corruption and favoritism, and finding it difficult to keep their households above water, Pakistan-returned soldiers such as Bao Zhifa primarily sought compensation from sheer necessity. Unlike many of their well-to-do counterparts, they had soured on the Communist Party–led political system. Petitioning was a way of delivering trouble to the officials who had delivered so much trouble to their lives.

A Pattern of Systemic Political Repression

Over several decades of reform, roughly 1985–2011, the PLA veterans of the Pakistan national defense highway project took their petitions to four different levels of government. Although they responded to the "high tide" and accelerated petitions to the center in the early Hu Jintao era, they actually made an

[59] Guo Xingyun, interview. [60] Yang Hailian, interview. [61] Tang Yintang, interview.

appeal to Central government leaders as early as 1985–1986, and only after this was thwarted did they start to petition the subnational leadership.

In 1985–1986, Puyang's Zhao Junjie, who was in touch with Jiangsu-based returned Pakistan soldiers, came to Dongle county to mobilize veteran support to petition Beijing. At this point, a delegation of the soldiers went to talk with Chen Muhua. An alternative member of the Politburo in the Cultural Revolution, Chen Muhua had worked in the Ministry of Foreign Economic Relations and visited with the PLA "volunteers" when they departed for and returned from Pakistan.[62] Acknowledging their sacrifice, Chen Muhua subsequently wrote a letter to Chen Junsheng, the general secretary of the State Council in the 1985–1988 period, requesting that the Central government help the veterans resolve their problems. Chen Muhua's star was on the wane by this point, however, and Chen Junsheng, who was on his way up to the Central Committee, scuttled her request, instructing his subordinates to "not open one more window for this kind of thing."[63]

Only after this rejection did the veterans of the Pakistan highway-building ordeal begin to petition the authorities in Dongle county, Puyang City, and Henan province. Bao Zhifa and the PLA veterans visited the Dongle county Office of Petitions and Grievances many times between 1988 and 2005. The county government finally responded in 2006 by arranging to make a 50-yuan-per-month grant to each of the petitioners. This paltry sum – the same amount the government offered people living below the poverty line – offended the veterans. They were also upset to learn that the money came from the county, not the Central government. Bao Zhifa declared: "What we did while in the army had nothing to do with the local government. We did work for the Central government. Therefore, it is the Central government's responsibility to take care of us, and to do something to recognize our contribution to the state."[64] Indeed, the subsidy was issued by Henan and Dongle officials who wanted to "comfort" the complainants so they would not petition Beijing. It had nothing to do with genuine concern for the injustice that lay behind the petition of grievances.[65] The calculation behind this approach became more apparent when the Dongle county Petitions Office followed up on the first subsidy payment by informing the veterans they should refrain from any further petitioning – the 50 yuan was, officials said, a lot of money for *little people like the veterans*.

When Bao Zhifa and the other petitioners protested, the Petitions Office officials refused their entreaties and mobilized to prohibit the veterans from advancing their petition up the next rung of the Henan provincial government hierarchy. According to Bao, the Dongle county Petitions Office agents watched them constantly and intercepted them when they attempted to petition the

---

[62] On Chen Muhua, see Lee and Stefanowska, *Biographical Dictionary*, 69–72.
[63] Yan Hailian, interview.   [64] Bao Zhifa, interview.   [65] Ibid.

upper government offices.[66] Pang Siyin, a veteran of the Pakistan highway-building project, confirms this was the case, and he adds that Liangmen township leaders collaborated in this county-ordered suppression: "The township government assigned specific people to watch us all the time. Each village has a township government official assigned to it. That official is responsible for making sure that none of us is involved in petitioning. Some people refer to this as the black list of the township government."[67]

In the meantime, Zhao Junjie urged his comrades to join with their counterparts in Puyang to petition the Puyang City government. Zhao was able to organize thirty people, mostly from Shangcunji in Dongle, to petition the Communist Party's Bureau of Labor Affairs. At first the bureau leaders agreed to pay the petitioners 500 yuan per man per month. But in time the Puyang Communist Party leaders suspended this payment, issuing the promised 500 yuan only to those from Puyang proper, where there was a critical mass of organized veterans. The veterans from Da Fo, Shangcunji, and other villages in Dongle county were unhappy with this arbitrary process, which they repeatedly challenged. Although the Puyang leaders promised to review the decision, they simultaneously asked Dongle officials to take the veterans back to Dongle and to prevent them from engaging in more petitioning.[68]

Thrown back into Dongle county, Bao Zhifa and returned veterans were assured by county leaders that the 500 yuan monthly stipend would be paid to compensate them. In time, however, they discovered that the Dongle county officials were funding the monthly stipend by illegally shifting money from other sources: half of the 500 yuan came from money earmarked for low-income paupers,[69] and the other half was taken out of a fund designated for injured and disabled veterans.[70] Knowing they were getting the money illegally, the returned Pakistan veterans all shared Pang Siyin's worry that "these benefits could be taken away any time."[71]

This worry drove a contingent of the Dongle county veterans to continue petitioning. In 2007 they came up with a plan to skip over the Puyang City government, which had administrative power over Dongle county, by sending a small delegation to visit their old PLA regiment commander in Tangshan. They asked him to help them present their petition materials to upper-level government leaders. In time, the leaders of the army unit were asked to help pass the petition material upward to Henan provincial and Central government offices, but this unit had been transformed into a police force, and its leaders betrayed the petitioners by passing the materials to the Puyang City government.[72] Once again, the Puyang leaders called on Dongle county party leaders to return the

---

[66] Ibid.   [67] Pang Siyin.
[68] Tang Yintang, interview; Guo Xingyun, interview; Pang Siyin, interview.
[69] Pang Siyin, interview.   [70] Bao Zhifa, interview.   [71] Pang Siyin, interview.
[72] Guo Xingyun, interview.

petitioners back to their home village and to keep them from entering Puyang City to petition.

On taking their grievance to Zhengzhou, the capital of Henan province, the petitioners ran up against the intransigence of provincial officials. "If someone petitioned the provincial government against the city or county government," said Bao Zhifa, "the *xinfang* [Letters and Visits] office would receive you and then call your county government to come and take you back home."[73] Bao and the veterans learned that the Dongle county government received a negative performance report from Henan province for each petition delegation that came to the capital. Under threat of penalty for too many negative reports, the Dongle county Office of Letters and Petitions stepped up efforts to dissuade the veterans from petitioning, after which Bao and his colleagues became apprehensive about approaching the authorities in Zhengzhou.

A year or so later, when Bao Zhifa and provincial representatives of the Pakistan highway builders first contacted Central government officials about their claims, they discovered that the Communist Party Secretary of Henan province had withheld information about their case from Beijing by issuing an order regarding their petition: he had placed a prohibition on communication about their work in Pakistan because, he said, it was a "national secret." The secretary then had attempted to buy the silence of the returned highway workers by approving payment of a subsidy of 50 yuan per month to each of the veterans. The payment did not immediately reach Bao and his comrades, however.[74]

When the payment did show up, Bao and his fellow veterans used it to pay for writing the petition materials and delivering more petitions to Zhengzhou – and to Beijing.[75] "We all believed it would work in the end," declared Bao. "The injustice that befell us will be corrected, and we will not give up until the problem is solved. There are so many of us involved, I do not think the Central government can ignore us continually. The Central government now has money, and it has not always spent it on the right thing. So why should we keep quiet about our contribution to the state any longer?"[76] Indeed, they did not keep quiet. From 1992 to 2004, Bao Zhifa and the veterans of the Pakistan highway campaign made twelve trips to Beijing to report their grievances to the Central government. They made little progress in this period, and the Central government began to suppress petitioning after 2005.

Under pressure from Bejing and Zhengzhou, in mid-2008 the petitioning system more or less collapsed in Henan province.[77] With the Olympics on the horizon, Xu Guangzhun, the Henan Communist Party secretary, sought to

---

[73] Bao Zhifa, interview.　[74] Ibid.　[75] Ibid.　[76] Ibid.

[77] Conflicts between CCP leaders and returned veterans had a long history, but in this case we can see how the center's pressure exacerbated, and even caused, such conflict. Cf. Thaxton, *Catastrophe and Contention*, 82, 177, 253–267, 310, and Diamant, *Embattled Glory*, 66–69, 175–176, 320, 328–329, 361–362, 366.

curry favor by promising there would be no petitioning of Beijing in 2008. Xu subsequently ordered all Henan provincial, city, and county officials to make sure that no petitions were forwarded to the Central government Office of Letters and Visits.[78] In subsequent months, the Dongle county government intercepted the soldier-petitioners who were departing for Beijing, and Bao Zhifa and his comrades were thrown into uncertainty. "We did not know what would be the best way to proceed," said Bao.[79] The movements of Bao and his fellow PLA veterans were closely monitored by public security. The antipathy of the Central government toward what essentially was a supralocal form of deferential protest recalled the exclusion of the Great Leap, when the Communist Party suppressed petitioning in order to push ahead with a corrupted, repressive model of national progress.

The ex-PLA Pakistan national defense highways returnees ramped up their petitioning in the post-Olympics years, traveling to Beijing in the second half of 2009 to present a petition to the Central Military Commission (CMC) of the Central government. Given the difficulty of skirting the thugs assigned to restrain petitioners from appealing to the center, of combing through the maze of bureaucracy to file a petition with the correct office, and of finding even one important sympathetic official, it may seem surprising that Bao Zhifa and this group of rural Henan petitioners managed to gain access to the power center of the CCP in the first place. They did so by putting a connection to good use. Zhao Junjie, the Puyang-based organizer of the petitioning veterans, had been the bodyguard of a key PLA regiment commander, and Zhao had befriended the commander's son, Song Feng, who later worked for the CMC.[80] When veterans in Puyang county began organizing to seek their retirement benefit, they chose Zhao as their representative. The Jiangsu veterans, having been put off for two years by the Central government, sought Zhao's help, and he agreed to take the case to Beijing. Even so, access in and of itself did not necessarily equal victory. After futile appeals to the CMC, Zhao Junjie won an audience with his former commander, Wang Xiyang. Wang agreed to help, but his appeals to the CMC fell on deaf ears. Afterward, around 2005–2006, the Henan provincial government and Puyang city government discouraged peaceful petitioning of any kind and told Zhao they could not come up with the money to help the veterans' cause. Later, through a tie to a friend who had risen to become a PRC ambassador, Zhao connected with Xinhua News Agency reporters who wrote reports on the sacrifices of the Pakistan highway volunteers, thereby bringing pressure on the party-state to help Zhao's comrades. Even so, from 2008 on, the Puyang city government leaders put Zhao under house arrest, cutting him off from the outside world for several years. They allowed him to resume his representation of the petitioners only when,

[78] Personal correspondence, confidential source, March 17, 2009.   [79] Bao Zhifa, interviews.
[80] Zhang Jieming, interview; Zhao Junjie, interview.

following his containment, scores of his Pakistan-era comrades began taking matters into their own hands, petitioning high officials in Beijing and Zhengzhou.[81] As for the Da Fo–based petitioners, the CMC spokesman told them his committee had reported their issue to the State Council, but Pang Siyin, and other veterans, believed this was a lie, as the necessary paper trail was missing[82] – and, in any event, the CMC never got back to them with an acceptable solution.

Bao Zhifa, Pang Siyin, and the other petitioners did learn two political lessons from their petitioning effort. The first was eye opening – and disheartening. Late in the petitioning drive, the veterans discovered in one of the documents issued by the National Bureau of Petitions and Letters that they had not exactly been lied to: their case had reached the State Council, and Hu Jintao, the General Secretary of the Communist Party, had seen and studied one of their petitions. Hu had personally scribbled a question to his subordinates on the petition of 2003: "Why," Hu wrote, "can we not solve the problems of these people? Their problems do not appear to be against government policy. Are the officials in charge of this case doing their job properly? Should we not seriously do some kind of analysis of their problems? We keep talking about taking care of people's problems, but if we do not do any real work to solve their problems, then what is the point of talking about taking care of the problems?" While impressed by Hu's note, the veterans were depressed by the result. As Guo Xingyun, a key petition activist, put it in 2005: "Hu Jintao is the highest leader of our party and our country. Despite his written comments on our petition materials, our problems have not been solved yet. Our problem is too big for any individual to effectively solve it, including General Party Secretary Hu Jintao."[83]

The second lesson was even more alienating. Upset with the petitioning and wary of the PLA petitioners, the CMC leaders plotted to demobilize them. Pang Siyin explains: "They ordered the Henan provincial officials to take us back to Henan and solve the problem locally. The provincial government could not solve our problem, however. Our problem is not a provincial-level problem. It is a national problem, because it involves people from several provinces. We are becoming more and more frustrated with the Central government's inaction. If they do not want us to petition then they should solve the problem nationally."[84] The former deputy party secretary of Da Fo village, Pang Siyin, was as frustrated as Bao Zhifa, for he had given sixteen years of his life to the Communist Party and had only a 40-yuan pension to show for his service and sacrifice. The Dongle county and Liangmen township leaders constantly warned Pang against petitioning, and in the end he concluded that petitioning in and of itself would not work. "I knew it was useless to petition the local government," says Pang. "The

---

[81] Zhao Junjie, interview.   [82] Pang Siyin, interview.   [83] Guo Xingyun, interview.
[84] Pang Siyin, interview.

government would not change just because a few people were petitioning. I knew this from working inside the government."[85]

Indeed, Bao Zhifa and his fellow petitioners were even more dismayed when they discovered that the center's suppression was entwined with party-based corruption. "When someone petitioned the Central government against the provincial government decision, the *xinfang* office in the Central government would record some of the negative points for the provincial government," says Bao. "I was told that if there were more than ten petitions from one province, the head of the highest court in that province had to go to Beijing to explain why there had been so many petitions from his province." This put pressure on provincial and local government officials to allow fewer petitions, which fostered a system of bribery in which lower officials paid upper-level petition office officials to omit the visits of petitioners from official records. The petitioners would be sent home, their complaints unregistered.[86]

Historian Qin Shao has pointed out that widespread institutional corruption more or less turned the petition system into a trap for petitioners prior to 2004–2005.[87] Yan Hailian, of Yuanchao village, tells us how Beijing used subnational Communist Party operatives to stifle petitioning in this period: "On one occasion, our comrades chose a delegation of four people to petition in Beijing. We decided that we would go to Beijing separately to avoid discovery by the Puyang and Dongle county governments. Therefore, we decided to leave Puyang for Beijing at midnight. However, right before the bus was to depart, four people boarded the bus [that I planned to take to Beijing]. They told me that I could not go." These individuals turned out to be employees of the Puyang government. When Yan Hailian told them he could go to Beijing any time he wished, the head of the Puyang Bureau of Petitions and Correspondence got on the bus. He and the other officials insisted that Yan "come down to talk with them more about our demands," and in the end he was persuaded to leave the bus and talk with them. "They sent me back to my home village in a car," he says. "The three other delegates were intercepted by other officials as well."[88]

On their next attempt, sixteen ex-PLA petitioners from Dongle and Puyang escaped the local government and made it to the Bureau of Petitions and Correspondence in Beijing, but Dongle county officials tracked and intercepted them. After buying the Dongle petitioners "a good meal," they purchased train tickets and escorted them home. The Puyang petition leaders were similarly intercepted by officials from the Puyang Bureau of Petitions and Correspondence. They were taken to a restaurant as well, but they were not returned to Puyang right away. Instead, they were taken to a hotel in Beijing, and then given a week-long sightseeing tour of Beijing, all expenses paid. Back in

---

[85] Ibid.   [86] Bao Zhifa, interview.   [87] Qin, "Bridge under Water."
[88] Yan Hailian, interview.

Puyang, they were given 200 yuan each. "They used these methods to soften our resolve," Yan Hailian says.[89]

Increasingly frustrated with the closure of the official channels of petitioning, in early March 2010 Qiu Heqing and Gao Yimin of Shenglian township, Dongle county, went to Beijing to explore a legal solution to the veterans' grievances. They arrived on March 5, when the People's Congress was in session, and stayed for three days, all the while attempting to persuade delegates to include their demands in a bill and thus reward their sacrifice in Pakistan through a new law. But they were not allowed to approach the delegates attending the Congress. In the end, they mailed their petition materials to Premier Wen Jiabao, addressing their letter to "Brother Wen Jiabao."[90]

There was no response. The petitioning veterans understood that Beijing's leaders were worried more about maintaining "social stability" than about acting on their appeals and that the center's spending priority was for internal security.[91] National power failed them.

Before moving on, let us sum up the case to this point. The case of petitioner Bao Zhifa suggests that traumatic family experiences in the Great Leap episode, in combination with individual sacrifices for the party-state in the postfamine decades, drove petitioners to take matters into their own hands. That is, they were not merely reacting to post-Mao reform policies that offered them the opportunity to advance new claims.[92] The case also suggests that reform-era officials at key rungs in the hierarchy of state power responded to claims for "compensatory justice" with hollow, useless sympathy. Bao Zhifa's case begins to demonstrate that growing party-state repression of petitioners in the Hu Jintao era originated at the very pinnacle of China's authoritarian political system. In a manner somewhat reminiscent of the way Mao handled petitioners in the Great Leap crisis, the post-2005 center dealt with the upswell of petitioning by deporting petitioners from Beijing, leaving them to face local officials who had a stake in making them suspend contention. In the end, this suppression took over the process whereby the reform-era Central government was to address the claims of rural people through nonelectoral channels and compelled some of the most loyal servants of the party-state to question the integrity of the center.

Regime Intransigence and the Suppression of Petitioning by the Central Government

Why was the CCP-led Central government unwilling to honor the claims of this subset of rural petitioners? Given the leadership's obsession with "stability," and given the role of ex-soldiers in upending different regimes during the

---

[89] Ibid.   [90] Guo Xingyun, interview.   [91] Zhao Junjie, interview.
[92] For this view, see O'Brien, "Rightful Resistance," 42.

twentieth century, the party's failure to deliver on its promise of a pension and security is hard to understand. After all, in Russia, where the tsarist autocracy's limited pensions had long been a thorn in the side of veterans, used-up army soldiers switched sides and paved the way for the October 1917 Bolshevik Revolution.[93] In Germany, where the Weimar Republic betrayed the promise of pensions for those who had sacrificed in the Great War, hastily discharged army veterans joined paramilitary groups supportive of the fascist seizure of power.[94] And in Republican China, the Mao-led CCP rose to power on the wings of carelessly dismissed warlord soldiers and Kuomintang Army conscripts and officers.[95]

So, again, why on earth did the post-Mao Central government flirt with the risk of alienating this subset of soldier-petitioners? There are at least two plausible explanations. The first involves regime fear of the past. To begin with, the cases of Bao Zhifa and the Pakistan-returned "volunteers" threatened to open up a long-tabooed subject: the link between suffering in the Great Leap famine and the sacrifice rural people had to make to survive Maoist rule after the famine. Perhaps higher-ups thought that denying the pension claims of the veterans of the Pakistan highway project was a way of containing a memory-fed critique of the socialist state. Letting this history out of the closet was dangerous, for it would have revealed a socially harmful pattern of single-party rule. Also, the fact that rural people still held the PLA in greater esteem than the party and that army veterans had suffered far more than party leaders in the Great Leap famine meant that people in the countryside would be far more interested in, and sympathetic toward, the plight and actions of the restless veterans.

The preceding explanation is not totally convincing, however. If the CCP-led center wanted to contain memories and to keep ordinary folks from connecting the dots, then all it would have had to do was to quietly buy off this limited subset of PLA petitioners – a feasible expenditure for a regime with a full coffer and a means to shut them up once and for all. The CCP could have presented this as a special case, playing on public respect for veterans and their need for pensions, and then touted its reputation for paternalistic governance. So a second explanation seems plausible. Lumping Bao Zhifa and his fellow veterans together with other petitioners was an act of regime stupidity, of needless fear and worry that addressing the claims of this subset of petitioners would open the floodgates for all others seeking redress from the Central government.[96]

[93] See Wirtschafter, "Social Misfits," 215–235, and Wade, *Russian Revolution*, 127–128, 137.

[94] See and compare Du Quenoy and McCartney, "Alienation of Soldiers," 1–9, esp. 2–5; also see Hudson, "The Poppy vs. the Pension," 27–32.

[95] See Bianco, *Origins of the Chinese Revolution*, 180–185; Cf. Fan, *China's Homeless Generation*, 71–72.

[96] I am indebted to both Michael Szonyi and Steven I. Levine for making me think harder about this matter. Personal correspondence, August 12 and September 28, 2013, respectively.

Whatever the answer, judging from Yongshun Cai's study, *Collective Resistance in China*, the result of the petitioning of the Pakistan-returned soldiers seems to have replicated that of other petitioners, including teachers and migrant workers: endless waiting for some meaningful official response, useless Central government reaction, and then Beijing and Henan provincial government repression.[97] Failure to settle the claims of the PLA veterans hurt the party's legitimation project in Da Fo and in scores of other villages and towns where the veterans of the Pakistan highway campaign lived.

The PLA veterans' case also posed a serious challenge to a ruse foisted on China's rural people by Central government leaders from Mao Zedong to Deng Xiaoping to Hu Jintao: the scapegoating of local party leaders, who allegedly screw up Beijing-designed policies that reflect the center's benevolent intentions. This process of shifting the responsibility for bad central policies onto the party's local cadre base was perfected by Mao himself in the aftermath of the Great Leap disaster, which Beijing politicians pinned on small-fry party leaders. Ever since, the ruse has remained robust: when central policies rouse popular ire, the center claims that the wayward acts of local party leaders have undermined its virtuous intentions.

Yet the petitions of the returned PLA Pakistan highway builders all but made it impossible for Beijing to convincingly blame local officials, for the petitioners' beef was not with local officials. Rather, they were calling on the Central government itself to repay sacrifices for which the center was responsible. In an important sense, they were attempting to break an unwritten Central government rule of silence about past *national* state injustice. The case of the PLA soldiers who had volunteered to serve in Pakistan illuminated an inconvenient political truth: whereas the Central government touted petitioning as means for ordinary rural people to remonstrate for Beijing's intervention against the wrongdoings of local officials, the returned soldiers were pleading for the center to address its own malfeasance. Beijing could not politically afford to let these people win, because their petitioning gave credence to the idea that the key to just governance was a more responsive center, not merely the correction of local cadre behavior.

Thus, acknowledging the claims of the returned Pakistan soldiers would have admitted a pattern of institutional-based injustice at odds with what Vivienne Shue has termed the center's effort to cultivate a "mystique of benevolent governance."[98] Throughout most of Chinese history, cultivating this image was a two-way process: high officials had to create trust among rural dwellers, demonstrating through practice that if the latter gave up something of value, the officials would, in turn, address popular claims for fair treatment. This reciprocal process helped create the basis for the center's identity as a *fumu*

---

[97] Cf. Cai, *Collective Resistance*, 66–67, 192–193, 196–197.
[98] Shue, "Legitimacy Crisis in China?," 35, 36–39.

zhengfu, that is, a government that acted as a reliable parent-modeled patron in its relationship with rural people. The notion of Beijing as a caretaker of rural subjects was at the core of the discourse whereby rulers historically effected hegemony and legitimation. As we have seen, post-Mao Central government leaders needed to revive this image of the Communist Party, for the Maoist Leap had damaged it – and in some rural places ruined it.

Yet the claims of veterans such as Bao Zhifa and other Pakistan national defense highway workers cast doubt on the Central government's commitment to reclaiming this authenticating identity. After all, if the center had failed to take care of army veterans who had given their all to its cause, why would villagers without army-centered profiles in sacrifice imagine that the Communist Party leaders in Zhongnanhai would take care of them? The center had promised reward and a better life in return for the sacrifices of this subset of veterans. The veterans had delivered; the center had not. Surely, Beijing did not want its rural subjects to gain knowledge of this default, which did not jibe with the party-state image of a stable paternalistic order. Indeed, although Da Fo villagers said they hated mainly local party leaders, some also confessed that because the Central government no longer cared about people who had sacrificed to build the socialist state, they were no longer confident that its leaders could be trusted to serve their interests. Some of these skeptics were farmers, teachers, and veterans. All held Bao Zhifa and the other returned Pakistan soldiers in high esteem. All understood that Beijing leaders tolerated petitioning mainly to defuse and deflect challenges to their power, and all more or less concurred that pressing higher-ups to create a genuinely benevolent political system was dangerous, because if push came to shove, the higher-ups in the Communist Party would chose power over benevolence.

Economic and Emotional Roots of the Quest for Compensatory Justice

If Bao Zhifa and his comrades were disappointed with Mao-era betrayal, they were also motivated by the impact of the state's fiscal organization on their life chances. The needs of the reform-era state were at odds with those of their households, and the decisions of party-state politicians were exhausting their ability to reconcile the benefits of support for state policy with the costs of family security.

Many of the petitioning veterans, such as Bao himself, were minor party members who more or less eschewed self-advancement and went along with "politically correct" policies in order to satisfy the government to which they were connected. Bao Zhifa had been one of the very first Da Fo villagers to pay the grain tax in the first decade of reform, when so many of his Da Fo counterparts refused. In the late 1980s, when Da Fo party leaders came under pressure from higher-ups to promote birth planning in the village, Bao Zhifa asked his wife to undergo an operation to prevent future pregnancies. Consequently, the couple had only one son and one daughter in a village where four children was the household norm.[99] Bao had worked outside the village to earn money to pay high school tuition for his son and daughter, but neither finished middle school. Bao kept his mouth shut about the shoddy performance of the public school system, even though it had failed his children. With this track record, good soldier Bao Zhifa did not seem a likely candidate for joining what had the potential of becoming a highly contentious petitioning movement. But he did, in part because he resented being short-changed by a state that was growing in wealth and grandeur – a state for which he had sacrificed before and after Deng's rise and China's opening to the world.

After all, when Bao Zhifa retired from military service, he still had to work to survive. Because the Central government had reintroduced household-based agriculture, he had to take up farming. For two decades, roughly 1982–2005, Bao Zhifa worked the tiny plot of bad earth allocated to his household, harvesting 700–800 *jin* of wheat per *mu* annually. Apparently, he had little room for error. "My wheat did not do well compared with others," he said. "I would have to sell most of the crop in the end, and so we did not eat so well."[100] As of 2005, Bao was barely able to break even as a farmer, and he occasionally fell into debt.

I was surprised to learn that Bao Zhifa lived so close to the margin, for a wheat yield of 800 *jin* per *mu* was more than a sixfold increase over the crop yield on this same tiny strip of land in the Republican era.[101] Moreover, Bao Zhifa managed to produce another 9,000 *jin* of corn per year, selling it at a profit of 4,000 yuan. Why, therefore, was Bao finding it difficult to break even in farming? He described the situation: "When we have a good harvest, and the price of grain is good, we will be able to make a few thousand yuan from the fall crop. If the weather is not good, and the price of grain is not good, we do not make any profit at all. We farmers always are the ones who end up losing. The state has been very smart. Its leaders said they exempted farmers from all taxes, and they also gave farmers a subsidy for working the land. However, the government did not lose any money. The officials got it all back through setting the price of the production materials that farmers must purchase." Bao Zhifa went on to explain that the state set the price of chemical fertilizer, diesel fuel, and pesticides, all of which were frequently hiked; additional costs were associated with breaking up corn stock in the fields, plowing under the land following a harvest, buying and planting seeds, harvesting and transporting corn. "In fact," Bao said, "all the money I made while working outside of the village was spent on farming. I brought back all of the money I made from working for subcontractors in Shanxi. By the time I was getting ready to go back to work outside of Da Fo, all of the money had been spent. I had to take 500 yuan from my savings to pay for the costs of going out to work for the subcontractors

---

[99] Bao Zhifa, interview.   [100] Ibid.   [101] Cf. Thaxton, *Salt of the Earth*.

[who paid only half of transportation expenses]. If I could not go out to work and make some money, I do not know how I would survive in the village."[102]

In the first two decades of reform, Bao Zhifa relied on off-farm income to offset the cost of cultivating his fields, and he so he wore several hats: he was a farmer, a truck driver, and a migrant laborer. As we have seen, Bao could not earn a living wage by driving for private entrepreneurs.[103] After giving up on driving, Bao Zhifa built houses and high-rise apartments in Beijing for 17 yuan per day for three years, but he gave this work up too, for he was too old to endure the demands of the long days. In 2006, Bao found work in Tianjin loading trucks, but this too was short lived, in part because Bao injured his shoulder, in part because his aging body was not up to the demands of the labor. "I am too old to work like that now," he said. "Nowadays, all of the work out there is like that."[104]

It is in this political and economic context that we must understand the petition struggle of Bao Zhifa and the Pakistan national defense highway PLA volunteers. Many, but not all, of the petitioners were driven by an existential dilemma and by resentment of the Central government, whose leaders had ignored rural poverty as well as the sacrifices of the returned highway workers, suppressing their petitions for just treatment while sitting on top of US$2 trillion in foreign reserves, much of which was lent to wealthy nations. This, along with the corruption of Communist Party leaders, was what Bao Zhifa alluded to when he said that the Central government leaders had not always invested state wealth in the right ways.[105]

In short, a sense of betrayal, combined with the urgency of finding a way to live a decent and dignified life in his graying years, put Bao Zhifa in the ranks of the Pakistan highway petitioners, both in Da Fo and in Henan province. Yet the question remains: Why did Bao, after joining with other petitioners, become an earnest petition activist only in 2007–2008? After all, the petition movement had been in motion for many years. One particular encounter with post-Mao Communist Party power holders stands out as having been influential. This incident occurred in 2007, when Bao Zhifa's mother died. It unfolded in a way that rocketed him back to all of the unforgotten suffering associated with his mother's departure from Da Fo at the height of the Great Leap famine and her subsequent permanent abandonment of young Bao.

During the New Year celebration of 2007, Bao Zhifa's mother fell and broke her hips and legs. Subsequently, Bao suffered a dual insult. First, the Communist Party authorities in Guanjun township, Hebei province, did not tell Bao right away that his mother had fallen. By the time he learned of the accident, she was already dying, and she passed away right after Bao and his wife and son arrived in Sijiakou village. After her death, Bao Zhifa and his mother's Sijiakou family

---

[102] Bao Zhifa, interview.   [103] Ibid.   [104] Ibid.
[105] Liang, "2009 'Chuanzhang' Hu Jintao de Zhongguo Dalu."

decided to bury his mother secretly in the ground, for Bao Zhifa himself did not want his mother cremated, as Central government policy mandated. They met with a second insult, however. Seven months later, a small team of Guanjun township funeral reform activists discovered the illegal burial and ordered Bao and his sister to dig up the mother's body and pay to cremate it. They complied in order to avoid a fine of 4,000 yuan, which neither Bao Zhifa nor his sister could afford.

Frustrated that he could not put his mother to a peaceful rest and put the Great Leap past behind him, Bao grew angry over state funeral policy. For one thing, he was compelled to leave his mother's ashes in the Guanjun township cremation factory, whose officials charged him a fee of 30 yuan per month for storage. Bao said, "We should not have left her ashes there. My mother had daughters. If they did not want to take care of her ashes, then I would take her ashes back to bury her in my own land in Da Fo."[106] But this required official state paperwork, and Bao waited for official permission that never came.

After his mother's death and the difficulties with her burial that followed, Bao Zhifa became even more determined to seek justice through petitioning. Apparently, he wanted to settle scores with the higher-ups as well as make them compensate him for his sacrifices in the line of duty in distant Pakistan.

Choosing to Defy the State

We now turn to an intriguing question: Why did Bao Zhifa and his fellow veterans press ahead with petitioning even in the face of Central government repression? To be sure, Bao and his comrades did not set out to defy the state. In petitioning, they were pursuing their quest for compensatory justice within culturally conditioned channels. After all, the reform-era center had encouraged people to air grievances through these channels. Perhaps the veterans were also influenced by the change in the political culture of the state, for in the past the state had appealed to its own functionaries to make personal sacrifices for the good of the nation. When Communist Party officials shared hardship with the rural people, which they in fact did in Dongle county during some of the Mao-era campaigns, this kind of appeal had traction with many Da Fo farmers – especially demobilized veterans. But with corrupt reform-era officials grabbing an ever greater share of national wealth, and with the socioeconomic gap between officials and villagers widening year by year, Bao Zhifa and his comrades wanted to be compensated for their past sacrifices from the burgeoning treasury of Beijing power holders.

Moreover, there were deeper psychological forces underlying their protest. It seems that the challenges of army life – especially the everyday brushes with death blasting tunnels through the dangerous mountains of Pakistan – taught

---

[106] Bao Zhifa, interview.

Bao Zhifa and his comrades to persevere in the face of impossible odds. Apparently, Bao and other petitioners drew on this lesson of deep survival under seemingly impossible conditions to sustain their petition drive in the face of state pressure to give it up. Laurence Gonzales sums up the life lesson of this subgroup of petitioners in *Deep Survival* when he writes: "Survivors always turn a bad situation into an advantage or at least an opportunity.... They plan for and have an earnest hope that they will manage. But they do not care overly much that they might not. They accept that to succumb is always a possibility and is ultimately their fate. They know that safety is an illusion and being obsessed with safety is a sickness. They have a frank relationship with risk, which is the essence of life. They don't need others to take care of them. They are used to caring for themselves and facing the inherent hazards of life. So when something big happens, when they are in deep trouble, it is just more of the same, and they proceed in more or less the same way: they endure."[107] In other words, for the returned Pakistan soldiers, petitioning was synonymous with survival, with making do under the continuing political extremity of Communist Party rule.

As a PLA veteran, Bao had a strong community group behind him. In line with the wisdom of Robert E. Lane,[108] we might expect that Bao's determination to seek justice through petitioning was also anchored in his associational solidarity with other PLA soldiers who had served in Pakistan. Many of them, along with Bao, had been neglected by post-Mao reformers – they were treated as trash left over from an antiimperialist country that no longer existed. Bao and his comrades were proud of their sacrifices, however, and felt they were entitled to compensation for their service in Pakistan. Apparently, they saw themselves as part of a collective battering ram that could knock down the doors of a secretive, unsupportive single-party system whose higher officials would be reluctant to turn army veterans – people who knew how to use weapons and wage war – into contentious rebels. Of course this political thinking was not readily apparent in their approach to the powerful, but it infused their petitioning with an explosive potentiality, and they seemed to sense they could make the most of it.

Bao and this particular subgroup of petitioners also held a wild card they could use to enhance their petitioning. They had come to understand how the government maneuvered to exploit rural dwellers in the process of manufacturing "social stability" – a code word for keeping autocratic party leaders in power. Recognizing that the state was not a paternalistic political partner, they saw through its worn-out promise that the next round of party-orchestrated change would point rural people toward an ordered, secure, and happy life. This accumulated, evolving knowledge of the reform-era state as an exploiter was empowering, for Bao and his fellow veteran petitioners understood they

---

[107] Gonzales, *Deep Survival*, 239–240.   [108] Lane, *Political Thinking*, 274.

could use it to maneuver against Beijing leaders. In reality, the unwillingness of Central government politicians to seriously address the claims of the returned Pakistan soldiers backfired. The official pretext of maintaining "social stability" by suppressing the petitions not only offended the soldiers' sense of justice, it also fueled the determination to stand up to those in power.[109]

Of course it might seem that the center's repression did not backfire, because the state never really acknowledged the petitioners or paid the restitution they deserved and, in any event, was able to do so without triggering any explosion against its unhelpful policies. This interpretation is flawed, however. Between 2004 and 2007, there was an explosion of petition-related protest by retired PLA soldiers in various provinces. Some of these petition movements took the form of marches, sit-ins, and riots, and some snaked their way up to Beijing, where veterans clashed with police agents in front of the PLA's General Political Department and, in some cases, were beaten by agents of the Central Military Commission.[110] According to Wu Baozhang, a former Xinhua News Agency correspondent, some of the veterans openly questioned "the absolute power of the CCP," thereby creating bad publicity for the party-controlled political system.[111] In the Da Fo area, petitioners got wind of this bad publicity and hence began to understand that they shared many of the same grievances as their demobilized comrades who had served in the Korean War and the Vietnam War. As more and more veterans came together through petitioning efforts, they began to learn that the Central government had broken its promise to take care of them *as a group* and that joining in collective resistance paid off.[112]

The oral testimony of Bao Lintang, one of Da Fo's retired soldiers, makes this point. Bao served in a PLA artillery unit in the last year of the 1979 Vietnam War, which Bao says was an unjust war, designed to "bully the Vietnamese people" in order to give certain PLA army commanders a chance to promote their careers.[113] But Bao was even more peeved by the false promise of the CCP leaders who praised the war. According to Bao, Henan provincial governor Cheng Weigao had promised the retired Vietnam soldiers jobs in the state enterprise system, but, Bao recalls, "Nothing happened. No one assigned a job to us." Consequently, Bao Lintang and five hundred veterans started petitioning Dongle county party leaders, Zhengzhou officials, and the Central

---

[109] Cf. ibid. for some of the conceptual starting points here. This is Diamant's logic, too: *Embattled Glory*, 134–136, 141.

[110] "Up to 2,000 Retired Soldiers Protest in Central Beijing"; Lim, "2,000 Retired Servicemen Stage Protests in Beijing"; and Lim, "China Veterans Stage 2,000-Strong Protest." Cf. Diamant, who says the police moved in and relied on coercion to ship the veterans "back to wherever they came from." *Embattled Glory*, 392–393.

[111] Qu, "New Army Regulations," 19.

[112] Cf. Anthony Kuhn, "Beijing Wary of Rising Tide of Veterans' Discontent," 2, and Chan, "Abandoned by Motherland They Served," 2, 1–3.

[113] Bao Lintang, interview.

Military Committee offices in Beijing, only to discover that there was no unified government policy on the same issue that had riled the veterans of the Pakistan highway project. There was a silver lining in the cloud of their disappointment, however. "The good thing for us," recalls Bao, "is that we eventually hooked up with other retired soldiers who were involved in the Korean War, those who supported the Vietnamese Resistance War against the United States in the 1960s, those went to Pakistan to build the national defense highway, those who were involved in the fight with the Soviet Union [over] the Zhenbao Islands, and also those who were involved in testing nuclear bombs and rockets."[114] In the course of waging petition struggles, these veterans formed close bonds and drew on organizational strategies and the disciplinary habits they had learned in the PLA, all of which led top CCP leaders in Beijing to worry that the veterans would link up and engage in a unified rebellion.[115]

Fearing "chaos," in August–September 2005 the Hu-led Central government initiated a crackdown on the petitioning veterans, using police force to break up their demonstrations and sit-ins and sending tens of thousands back to home towns and villages on buses and trains – a panic-borne action that did little to dissuade the ex-soldiers.[116] Pang Siyin, the reform-era Da Fo deputy party secretary who, at age nine, suffered hunger in the Great Leap, then joined the PLA for survival, and later helped build the Pakistan national defense highway, underscored this point when he said: "The Central Military Committee was very upset with our petitioning, but there was nothing they could do about people like us."[117]

With the key disciplinary instruments of Mao–era CCP control – the militia patrols and the public criticism sessions – disbanded locally, Da Fo's returned PLA veterans had less fear every year of engaging in open conversations with their peers inside and outside of Da Fo and Dongle county, and engaging in petitioning enabled them to accelerate the evolving process of learning about the state itself as a source of injustice. In this context, Bao Zhifa and his counterparts in Da Fo were more inclined to aggressively pursue their deferential quest for compensatory justice, and this approach sometimes produced results, even if they were small victories. In mid-2008, for example, Bao Zhifa and the returned Pakistan soldiers discovered that although Dongle county had allocated funds to each township for veterans of the Pakistan highway campaign, the veterans in other townships had been paid twice the amount as those in Liangmen township. Subsequently, Bao and other veterans went to Cui

---

[114] Ibid.
[115] *Economist*, "China: Beware of Demob"; on the reportage on this danger by the Hong Kong press, see Diamant, *Embattled Glory*, 361, 381.
[116] Cf. Lim, "2,000 Retired Service Men Stage Protests," 1; Chan, "Abandoned by Motherland They Served," 2.
[117] Pang Siyin, interview.

Baogang, the CCP secretary of Liangmen township government, and aggressively appealed for equal treatment and received it – a minor triumph that encouraged them to continue their struggle.[118]

Finally, for veteran army petitioners such as Bao, men in the autumn of their lives, age seemed to be an important factor in their finding the courage to press on with petitioning in the face of state repression. A host of disappointing interactions with local Communist Party leaders over a long span of life had taught Bao Zhifa and his comrades that resignation in the face of party authority seldom paid off. With age came an understanding that acceptance of state logic would not get them out of the situation in which they were stranded, and in this wisdom the returned Pakistan soldiers found the courage to stand up for their own notion of what was fair and just. Of course, Bao Zhifa and his comrades wanted to make the most of their last years on earth, and many said they feared getting sick in old age. But, on the other hand, they apparently no longer feared the threat of death that lurked in the background of state efforts to discipline and contain their contention. The desire to reclaim individual dignity negated this fear. Bao and his comrades needed to let the state know that they existed and had to be dealt with, individually and collectively.

My sense is that Bao Zhifa and many of his fellow veterans were no longer afraid of standing up for justice because they had already come to terms with a question that surviving decades of dehumanizing treatment under the Communist Party had planted in their consciousness, namely, "What else can the party and its police agents do to hurt us that they have not already done?"[119] They had already endured the denial of food during the Great Leap, of communication with kin while on tour in Pakistan, of work opportunities on returning from Pakistan, of the freedom to produce the number of children they needed for the family workforce, of any basic legal protection against the exploitation they endured as migrant laborers, and of dignifying funeral practices. They must have concluded there was little the state had left to deny them (though of course the state could have imprisoned them on charges of disturbing public order).

To Bao and his hardened comrades, therefore, a setback in petitioning to right past wrongs was just that – a temporary reversal best dealt with by a guffaw about official abuse and a return to the drawing board of revved-up defiance. Life under the party-state had taught them to question its modality of rule, and their petitioning was intricately entwined with making a transition from being victims of this state to becoming survivors in their own right. Continuing with petitioning in this respect was hardly experienced as "contentious bargaining" within the institutional web of the Communist

---

[118] Bao Zhifa, interview. [119] Neil J. Diamant, personal correspondence, March 24, 2009.

Party–controlled petitioning system.[120] It was, instead, mainly about firming up the inner will to survive, about facing down Communist Party dictatorship even if it meant extermination, for that was the only way the returned veterans of the Pakistan front could face death with dignity.[121] To be sure, the Da Fo–area veterans did not take up violent forms of resistance involving direct challenges to state authority described in other chapters of this book, but they actually were playing for keeps, and given the dynamic of the past even this form of protest could jump onto an insolent, militant track if the state were to mishandle it.

PETITIONING AND POPULAR THINKING ABOUT STATE POWER

Recently, Beijing officials in the State Petitions Office admitted that 80 percent of the petitions submitted to the State Petitions Office were based on legitimate claims,[122] and even the Petitions Handling Office of the Ministry of Public Security confirmed that the cases of most petitioners seemed reasonable.[123] Yet Yu Jianrong, an astute scholar of the petitioning system, found that less than 1 percent of the cases were ever resolved and that the system was incapable of enabling petitioners to realize their claims.[124] Bao Zhifa and the returned Pakistan soldiers, in other words, suffered the same fate as most petitioners.

Da Fo's inhabitants, and especially its farmers, drew two lessons from the fate of the Pakistan-returned veterans, each of which shaped how they saw higher-ups in Beijing. First, they increasingly asked themselves: If local party members such as Bao Zhifa could not win the support of the Central government through deferential petitioning, then what chance did ordinary nonparty villagers without a record of serving the government have in appealing to the center for justice? The answer given by the great majority of Da Fo interviewees was "none." This explains why so many Da Fo villagers saw petitioning as useless – a phenomenon that originally baffled me, for it was clear that scores of villagers had reason to press claims by petitioning. Put another way, most of the petitioning in Da Fo originated with claimants who still had some hope for justice, and who at one point were small-fry functionaries in the socialist state. The majority of Da Fo's farmers did not share this history or this hope.

Second, most Da Fo villagers concluded that the reform-era petitioning system had become a tool for maintaining the apartheid system constructed during the period of Maoist rule. Rural people in Da Fo and elsewhere had

---

[120] For scholarship that takes this imaginary political process model for real, see Xi, "Collective Petitioning," 61–70. The term "contentious bargaining," which implies a process of mutual accommodation between those with and without power, is from Xi, *Social Protest and Contentious Authoritarianism in China*, 189–194, 204–207, esp. 204; also see Tarrow, "New Contentious Politics," 7–10.

[121] Here too, I have benefited and borrowed from Gonzales, *Deep Survival*, 213.

[122] Yu, *Xinfang Zhidu Diaocha Ji Gaige Silu*.   [123] "Call to Scrap 'Zero Petitions' Target."

[124] Yu, "Xinfang Zhidu Pipan"; Yu, *Xinfang Zhidu Diaocha Ji Gaige Silu*; Yu and Pei, "Seeking Justice," 1; and Yu, "Social Conflict," 7–10.

good reason to fear the Hu Jintao–led center's quest for "zero petitions," for this quest not only encouraged subordinates to suppress petitioners, it also stirred memories of state abandonment in the Great Leap famine, when Mao and his fervent cadre base had closed ranks to feed themselves first, to wall off rural people from state food supply, and to repress a petitioning process that could have bridged the provisioning gap between poor rural dwellers and comparatively well-off urbanites with party-bestowed privileges.

To argue that recent Communist Party efforts to quell petitioning have reminded rural people of an embedded apartheid and the hunger it engendered in the Great Leap may seem far-fetched. Perhaps it is. When farmers in Da Fo were asked if they thought China could have another great famine, 70 percent of them of them said they felt this was unlikely. However, when they were asked if the state would help them in the event of another great famine, a significant majority agreed with Bao Dongwen, who declared: "If only a small part of the country were to suffer a flood or drought, the state might help a little, but if there is a large-scale famine, I do not see how the state will help. The state has become more ruthless today. We farmers are the ones who will suffer in the end."[125] By suppressing the right of the Pakistan-returned veterans to petition, the center pricked memories of Great Leap–era repression and called forth deeply ingrained fears of having no legitimate means of effective remonstrance in the face of another great subsistence crisis in the countryside.

– – –

To sum up, the center under Hu Jintao handled the petitions of veterans in roughly the same way that Mao had handled the pleas of desperate Great Leap–era petitioners: he and other Central government politicians sent them back down the party hierarchy, blindly trusting that local party leaders would somehow restrain and resolve the restive popular urges that produced them. Yet the center's attempt to fend off the petitioning of the PLA veterans who had sacrificed themselves on the Pakistan highway project proved counterproductive. Suppressing the petitioning of this subset of contentious rural people damaged the reputation of the Central government leaders as benevolent allies and created a dangerous rift in relations with otherwise loyal foot soldiers of the state. For petitioners like good soldier Bao Zhifa, Beijing's intolerance for petitioning raised the stakes of pursuing justice through deferential channels. In the beginning, the soldier-petitioners were neither disrupting the functions of government nor looking to challenge the system of Communist Party rule, but in suppressing their right to make claims on the debt owed them by the center for their sacrifice in Pakistan, Beijing politicians schooled the veterans in the Janus-faced culture and corrupt inner workings of China's authoritarian state.

---

[125] Bao Dongwen, interview.

In reality, the decision to suppress petitioning, including that of the veterans of the Pakistan national defense highway project, was taken in 2005, when Hu Jintao and the top CCP leaders in Zhongnanhai assigned public security forces to play a central role in supervising the petition system.[126] From this point on, growing knowledge of the center's hand in the ensuing repression seems to have lessened the faith that Bao Zhifa and his colleagues originally had in the leaders at the top of the political system: it told them that the Central government, not local government leadership, was their problem. Thus it undercut, in a rather dazzling manner, the center's effort to shift blame for the maladies of reform from its "good" policies to the distortion of such by unsupportive cadres. To a man, the petitioning soldiers knew that Beijing had pressed provincial, county, and township leaders to suppress petitioning, turning those leaders into its hunting dogs whose promotions under the Cadre Responsibility System depended on strict compliance with Beijing's orders.[127] In the end, therefore, Da Fo's solider-petitioners came to understand that the petitioning system was rotten from top to bottom.[128] Even General Party Secretary Hu Jintao could not make it work. In practice, his regime proved unable and unwilling to convert the petitioning system into an instrument of popular empowerment and an effective alternative to the rule of law.[129]

Without this conversion, the suppression of this traditional form of protest was risky, for it invited rural people to challenge the mandate of the center through riot and rebellion. The outbreak of rebellion in historic China, and in much of the agrarian world, was often the result of the state repression of a train of routine deferential protests, giving the powerful ample warning of large-scale upheavals against their failure to regain high moral ground though virtuous governance. By resorting to suppression and ignoring this potential metamorphosis, the Hu Jintao center undercut the efficacy of what Ho-fung Hung has termed "state-engaging protest,"[130] leaving the ex-PLA veterans of the Pakistan highway campaign to rely on their own devices in challenging the state's failure to care for is subjects. In the end, therefore, the center's handling of this tool of governance served to promote the instability its leaders wanted to avoid.[131]

---

[126] O'Brien, Li, and Liu, "Petitioning Beijing," 1–2, 20–22; also see Minzner, "Xinfang," 178.

[127] On the Cadre Responsibility System, see Edin, "State Capacity," 35–36, 38–39, 42–45, 50–52, and Whiting, "Cadre Evaluation System."

[128] For the same understanding, see the work of folklorist Sara Meg Davis, "A System Rotting from the Ground Up."

[129] For the case for a Communist Party–engineered institutional conversion, see Xi, "Collective Petitioning," 55, 70. The theoretical underpinnings of this argument are in Thelen, "How Institutions Evolve." A summary of these underpinnings can be found in Pierson, *Politics in Time*, 137–138. For the notion that the *xinfang* system has provided an alternative to the rule of law, see Minzner, "Xinfang," 115–117, 103, 155.

[130] Cf. Hung, *Protest with Chinese Characteristics*, 148, 151, 166, 192, 200.

[131] This conclusion resonates with Minzner, "Xinfang," 178–179.

Indeed, suppression backfired in two ways. First, it strengthened the resolve of the petitioners, whose ranks, as we witnessed, were filled with survivors who did not fear the risks of petitioning.[132] Their brushes with death in Pakistan had prepared them to meet the setbacks of life with focus and resolve.[133] Suppression also reminded veterans like Bao Zhifa that they would be on their own in a crisis – in this case, that the state would leave them to die a miserable death, alone in old age. To survive the Great Leap famine as ten-, eleven-, and twelve-year-old children, they had been forced to rely on themselves. As we have seen, Mao's leap into famine had turned Bao Zhifa and some of his desperate peers into orphans, and Bao saw the world through the unhappy long-term memory of this devastating experience. When the state under Hu Jintao invoked the model of repression followed by Mao in the Great Leap, it unwittingly charged this memory, informing Bao and the other returned Pakistan soldiers that politics had not changed all that much and telling them they had to rely on primordial instincts to survive. Without this memory, their situation would have seemed hopeless.

So what did this memory teach? That strength and survival were enhanced with numbers, and that people who fought battles alone often were lonely victims. This is why Bao Zhifa continued to try to reunite with his mother, why he joined the PLA and went to Pakistan, and why he decided to work with fellow petitioners. The center's suppression therefore made petitioning ever more attractive for Bao Zhifa and his counterparts. As Tang Yintang, one of Bao's fellow soldier-petitioners, pointed out: "Individual petitioning is useless. There are too many individuals petitioning the government. It is beyond the government's capacity to deal with all of the injustices in such a complex system of governance. In order for petitioning to work, there has to be a critical mass of people involved."[134] In the summer of 2011, a rumor spread among the veterans of the Pakistan highway project that the petitioning would continue in the face of repression, and, further, that the government might accept all of their core demands in the end. The rumor had little to do with faith in the center. Rather, it struck a chord with faith that individuals could better survive and succeed together.

---

[132] On the regime's long-standing fear of veteran-driven contention, see Diamant, *Embattled Glory*, 361.

[133] Cf. Gonzales, *Deep Survival*, 175, 180. For the literature that presupposes that the state handling of petitioning, through restraints and repressive techniques, somehow has strengthened the center's legitimacy, see Luehrmann, "Facing Citizen Complaints," 865, and Cai, "Local Governments," 41; Cf. O'Brien, *Popular Protest*, 17–23. Although O'Brien says that the faith of protestors and petitioners in the center sometimes produces desired results, he also shows that repression can backfire and erode faith in the center.

[134] Tang Yintang, interview.

9

Migration and Contention in the Construction Sector

The second decade of the Deng-led reform brought up bittersweet memories of the Great Leap Forward, when Da Fo's famers were promised that the change-over to the commune would deliver a better life, only to be flattened by a dwindling food ration and exhaustion from overwork in the collective fields. The disbanding of the collective was more than welcomed by villagers, many of whom equated reform with permission to rescue themselves from the restrictive and demeaning labor regime of the Mao era. With reform, Da Fo's farmers were quicker to rise for work each morning, more eager to engage tilling and petty trade, and more hopeful that each day's increment of labor would distance them from the damage of the past.

This hope was still alive in the mid-1990s. But, as we have seen, fifteen years of reform had resulted in a renewed tax burden, another radical assault on procreation, and a rise in tuition payments – all piled onto, and entwined with, the fines, bribes, and extortions of Liangmen township leaders and public security forces. By 1995, Da Fo's farmers were working longer and harder to feed the rent collectors of the reform-era political system, and daily survival was again encumbered by a single-party state whose agents were undermining democratic institutional experiments and closing down avenues of supposedly legitimate remonstration. Fortunately, the existential dilemma of Da Fo's farmers was not as dire as in the Great Leap, for they now had the option of exit: they could flee with minimal penalty. Flight, therefore, became the order of the day. Increasingly, as the second decade of reform wore on, Da Fo's hard-pressed farmers joined in the greatest internal migration in human history, supposedly stimulated by the pull of reform policy.

PUSH FACTORS

By the early twenty-first century, approximately 120–130 million rural migrants had left the countryside to find work in emerging towns and cities benefiting from

China's economic boom.[1] Of the forty million migrants laboring in the construction industry, nearly 70 percent were of rural origin.[2] Few of them held the residential permits required to stay in the cities without police harassment.[3] These illicit rural migrants built the airports, train station platforms, superhighways, five-star hotels, department stores, high-rise apartments, and power plants that would make for eye-popping development in Beijing, Tianjin, Qingdao, Shanghai, and many of China's metropolitan zones. By 2001, seven in ten of Da Fo's farmers had joined this rural-to-urban migration. The majority of them sought work in the construction industry.

Few of Da Fo's migrant farmers had finished primary school, and some had never been to school, which made them less educated than the average migrant worker. Nationally, 71 percent of the migrant construction workers were between the ages of 15 and 29.[4] Only half of Da Fo's migrant labor force was in this age group; the other half was between age 30 and 63. Of the 33 migrant workers interviewed for this chapter, the average age was 47, which increased to 50 when the two youngest (17 and 21 years old) migrants were taken out of the sample. In fact, many of the migrant farmers in this older group were aged 55–57, and they had worked in construction for 20–25 years.

Many of Da Fo's migrant workers were unskilled, and most had to work under unscrupulous labor contractors without a written labor contract. Their "opportunity" to pursue off-farm income in richer, coastal provinces was seen as liberating by the propagandists behind *People's Daily* and was hailed as a progressive, humane solution to the problem of rural surplus labor by Western economists. Farmers in Da Fo – the victims of Mao's commune-era lockdown – welcomed the freedom to escape the stifling, institutionally imposed "serfdom" and dearth of the brigades.[5] Yet their memory of the process whereby they took up migration does not exactly resonate with the official narrative, which omits the process whereby the center literally left impoverished villagers no choice but to become the reserve labor force for its development plan. In actuality, the center's reform discriminated against poor tillers and criminalized their attempts to wring a living from the land. Under Deng, the state turned farmers into floaters and more or less compelled them to become members of a "disposable labor force."[6] Many of Da Fo's floaters had little choice but to accept insecure jobs and paltry wages in urban-based industries that were only

---

[1] The figures vary considerably. See Xiang, "Migration and Health," and Cai, Du, and Changbao, "Regional Labor Market Integration"; for the outer limit, which is 150 million, see Lary, *Chinese Migrations*, 155.

[2] Human Rights Watch, *One Year of My Blood*, 2:1, and Guang, "Guerrilla Workfare," 482, 497.

[3] See Guang, "Guerrilla Workfare," 486; Cf. Wang, "Renovating the Great Flood Gate," 362–363.

[4] Human Rights Watch, *One Year of My Blood*, 2:2.

[5] On the demeaning and impoverishing effects of this serfdom, see Thaxton, *Catastrophe and Contention*, and on the resulting system of rural-urban inequality, see Whyte, *One Country, Two Societies*, 1–12, esp. 1, 7, 9, 11.

[6] Solinger, *Contesting Citizenship*, 45.

superficially advantageous. The path of migrant work led many into an ordeal that in some ways mirrored the state-orchestrated insecurity of Mao's Great Leap Forward.

During the first decade of reform, many Henan farmers preferred to stay in their home villages and recover the family-based entitlements they had lost to Maoist collectivization in the early 1950s. They had hopes of becoming competent, mobile farmers, able to produce food for family consumption and to garner off-farm to reinvest in agriculture. Indeed, even if the farmers had wanted to leave, they would not have been able to spare the time. After the land was divided up in Da Fo in 1982, its farmers had little time or energy to work outside Da Fo after working in the fields.[7] According to Bao Liming, "In the early days of reform, when the land was first divided, we had to do all the work in the fields by hand."[8] In the mid-1980s, I witnessed farmers themselves pulling heavy ploughs – in place of oxen and other beasts of burden – a pattern that did not significantly fade in Da Fo until ten years later.

This handicap on working the land was linked to politics. As we have seen, when the Da Fo Communist party leaders disbanded the collective, they did not distribute its public assets to farmers, but rather took tractors and farm tools for themselves. By the late 1980s, population had nearly doubled compared with the late 1950s, and few of Da Fo's farmers had enough land to farm. Worse yet, they had little capital to invest in the land they did receive through reform, so that they were short when it came to purchasing seeds, tools, pesticides, and above all chemical fertilizers, which the government began to import into Dongle county from Japan and Europe between 1983 and 1985. Although grain yields improved gradually over those of the Mao era and procurement prices improved somewhat, yields were still low, and the price of grain was unpredictable – and often low – in part because the state was buying grain abroad instead of purchasing it from Chinese farmers.

Virtually every interviewee recalls that in this situation, farming did not pay – and that this situation was the product of the center's policy of neglecting and discriminating against the agricultural sector. With reform, most of Da Fo's tillers became better able to provide their families with enough to eat. Nevertheless, many say they were short when it came to buying clothes, paying medical bills, and taking care of school tuition. Only a few could sell enough surplus grain to cover all of the costs of farming.

As a result, Da Fo's farmers had little choice but to leave the land and seek off-farm employment, either locally – where those with connections to local party cadres were favored[9] – or in far-flung cities. Ruan Liqin, a thirty-seven-year-old Da Fo migrant worker at the time of the interview, offers his take on the politics that drove villagers to join the exodus to urban construction

---

[7] Bao Liming, interview.   [8] Ibid.
[9] On this process and its complexity, see Guang, "Guerrilla Workfare," 23–25, and Zhao, "Rural-Urban Labor Migration," 7.

sites: "The government," says Ruan, "has not invested much in the countryside in the reform period. . . . The government did not do anything for farmers. We could not make any money from farming. Therefore, we have to support agriculture by working in the urban areas."[10] Many other farmers who floated from village to city, and then from city to city, looking for construction work also said that they had no choice but to leave Da Fo to make the money to purchase the necessities of life and sustain the farm activities on which they depended for food.[11]

There was a second "push factor" at work. This was the failure of the Liangmen Township and Village Enterprise (TVE) system, which Central government leaders touted as a key to reforming the rural economy. Bao Xiaojian explains: "There is no township enterprise here in Shangcun, and this is the reason people have to go out to work in the urban areas. It would be much better and much easier if they had something to do here locally."[12] In the first decade of reform, there was a state-owned wine factory in Dongle county. By the mid-1980s, some of Da Fo's young farmers had found jobs in this enterprise, which dated back to the Mao era. The winery workers enjoyed permanent job security, free medical care, and a pension package that guaranteed 70 percent of regular pay. In the first reform decade, however, the state replaced this system with one that permitted the managers to assume de facto ownership of the winery and gave them the right to dismiss workers at will. The new Communist Party–appointed manager fired most of the workers and then defaulted on a promise to continue the medical insurance and retirement benefits of the dismissed workers, who responded by organizing a collective-action lawsuit against the new management. The handful of new factory leaders plundered the winery. They stopped producing any wine and sold tons upon tons of stored wine, which allowed them to live in luxury by marketing the leftover "public assets" of the previous regime. In speaking of this injustice, Da Fo's Bao Zhanpo, one of the dismissed wine factory workers, explains how this plunder drove him to seek work in faraway urban areas: "Since I lost my job in the winery," says Bao, "I had to come back to Da Fo to farm the land and to work outside the village on construction to make ends meet."[13]

In combination with the center's failure to provide skills training for poor young farmers, the shortfall of farm income and the plunder of township enterprise gave rise to a wave of petty theft in the Chinese countryside during the years 1980–1985. As we have seen, rural farmers began pilfering the one item they most desperately needed to make their worn-out lands serve the consumption requirements of their households: chemical fertilizer (see Chapter 1). Recall that the center responded to this rise in rural crime with repression, which culminated in the Strike Hard crackdown on Da Fo's petty

---

[10] Ruan Liqin, interview.   [11] Zhang Wenjie, interview.   [12] Bao Xiaojian, interview.

[13] Bao Zhanpo, interview. On the laid-off (*xiagang*) state workers under post-1978 capitalism, see Solinger, "New Crowd of the Dispossessed," 50–54, 59–62.

thieves between 1983 and 1987. Many of Da Fo's younger farmers were arrested and imprisoned for pilfering state-monopolized commodities. This state criminalization of desperate popular efforts to increase agricultural output for basic food security angered and frightened Da Fo's farmers. To avoid the fate of their imprisoned counterparts, scores of Da Fo farmers began to search for construction work in unfamiliar cities like Beijing, Tianjin, Qingdao, and Taiyuan. Working in the cities was better than languishing away in a prison for four, five, or ten years of one's life. Thus, the authoritarian response to efforts to cope with the transition away from collective agriculture to household-based farming became yet another hidden political factor pushing Da Fo's farmers to join the floating army of migrant workers.

THE LIMITS OF LABOR MOBILITY

The reform era reinstated labor mobility and renewed the hope of Republican-era freedom – an era when rural people had been able to exercise the right to seek food security beyond the boundaries of home villages and nearby market towns.[14] Strictly speaking, Da Fo's farmers were free to move out of the village in search of food security after 1978, and they initially welcomed the opportunity to escape poverty, corruption, and a dead-end future under village party leaders. By the mid-1980s, many Da Fo farmers had settled into a routine of leaving Da Fo to work in distant venues much of the year, then coming home in early February to celebrate the Chinese New Year, in late May to help bring in the wheat harvest, and again in the late October–early November planting season.

In pursing this path, they encountered terms of work life that replicated some of the worst features of labor injustice in the collective era – particularly the episode of the Great Leap Forward. Labor mobility brought Da Fo's farmers into contact with party-connected agents who took state-ordered reform as an opportunity to exploit migrant construction workers for their own ends, often imposing some of the same debilitating and humiliating terms of work that had defined life under corrupt and callous brigade and commune leaders at the height of the Mao-era apartheid.

Bad Wages, Bad Food

In the Mao era, Da Fo farmers who were drawn into the Liangmen People's Commune's extravillage industrial work projects by the promise of higher wages and food security met with great disappointment. At the height of the Great Leap Forward, the Communist Party leaders in charge of these sites frequently broke this promise and defaulted on payment of a "living wage."[15] The problem of nonpayment of wages to migrant laborers surfaced again in the

[14] See Solinger, *Contesting Citizenship*, 31.   [15] Thaxton, *Catastrophe and Contention*.

reform period, when party-connected subcontractors frequently defaulted on wages owed for completed projects. Forty-nine-year-old Bao Jiansheng began migrating for work in 1988. He worked in Tianjin, Beijing, Xingtai, Shijiazhuang, Handan, and Dongle county. Bao says: "Twice I was not able to get any salary after I did the work for the subcontractor. One time the subcontractor did not pay me after I did the work for him. This was in the Xingtai steel works. The other time was in Shijiazhuang. Each time, the amount was one season's salary – about 500 yuan. It was a lot of money at the time. I do not think that I will ever get the money back. I cannot find these subcontractors anywhere. Their homes in the countryside were deserted. Their neighbors said they had moved to the cities, and they did not know where. Many of these subcontractors made money by exploiting farmers like us either by not paying us properly or by running away with our salaries. This kind of practice was very common in the 1990s and in the early 2000s."[16]

Some of Da Fo's migrant workers attribute this pattern of development to the wolfish nature of Communist Party–guided reform. Bao Zhanghe is one of them. Born in 1948, Bao was orphaned at age ten, when his mother died in the first hunger wave of the Great Leap. Ten years later, in 1968, Bao turned to migrant work in order to escape the poverty of farm life in Da Fo, working in Anyang, Beijing, Tianjin, Shanxi, and Shenyang for forty years of his adult life. In the summer of 2007, Bao had just returned to Da Fo from Tianjin, where he had been cheated out of 8,000 yuan in wages by a subcontractor. According to Bao, "[The subcontractor] used to be a farmer himself. But now he has a lot of money. He has a driver, who drives a Mercedes-Benz for him. He has a big house in Tianjin, and he has a big house in Xinhua village. His money all came from exploiting the workers. He did not pay his workers."[17]

A seasoned veteran of migrant construction work, Bao Zhanghe links the politics behind this practice to the Central government's turning a blind eye to ties between the subcontractors, thugs, and the police: "Many of these subcontractors are people in charge of criminal gangs. In Tianjin, I saw a subcontractor known as Dongbeihu (the Tiger from the Northeast). He hired all kinds of migrants who were looking for work. Once the workers came under his sway, they would lose the freedom to leave. He had many thugs in his service. The workers could only work – they were not allowed to talk to one another or to anyone outside of the construction site. At night, their doors were locked, and no one was allowed to get close to their living quarters. After a few months, they would beat the workers so badly that the workers would decide to run away to save themselves. In this way, he did not need to pay the workers.

---

[16] Bao Jiansheng, interview.
[17] Bao Zhanghe, interview. The Great Leap famine, and the long dearth to follow, apparently left some villagers so desperate that they accepted the dirty work of the state to survive. Note that this Bao Zhanghe is the same individual who secretly reported pregnant couples to reform-era township birth-planning officials, as documented in Chapter 3.

The subcontractors like this Dongbeihu had connections with the police. Therefore, they had a free hand to do bad things."[18]

In organizing the construction industry, the Central government separated management companies from labor companies, allowing the latter to operate free from government oversight.[19] In this situation, the contractors and sub-contractors were able to shift the risks of their dealings onto migrant workers, covering food and/or housing in exchange for worker agreement to defer wages until the end of the contract. In a sense, therefore, Da Fo's migrant workers, much like their counterparts from countless Chinese villages, "consumed their earnings" in meals supplied by labor contractors.[20] Surely in some cases the food provided by the contractors was of better quality than that of the Great Leap era, and of course the public dining-hall system was, technically speaking, a thing of the past. But was the past really the past? Fifty-seven-year-old (in 2009) Bao Chaoxiang, who worked on the construction of the Beijing International Airport after planting his fields with winter wheat in late 2008, explains how the labor contractors organized the allocation of food on the template of the supposedly defunct Mao-era system and turned it to their advantage: "I went there with nine other people from Da Fo," says Bao. "They provided us with lodging, but they did not provide us with food. They gave us a plastic credit card with money on it. With this card, we could get food from the public dining hall there. We could eat what was available there, and they would deduct the money from our pay. It cost us about 400 yuan per month. That was a lot of money."[21] Though they were paid, the migrant workers expended much or even most of their earnings on food costs dictated by their labor bosses – who were Communist Party appointees.

The subcontractors who did supply food often provided the cheapest food possible. Some of it was barely edible and comparable to what farmers had fed their pigs.[22] More than a few of Da Fo's migrant workers paid to purchase additional, more palatable food on the market outside the construction site. But they could not purchase additional food if their wages were not paid. The withholding of wages thus left them without disposable cash and put their immediate day-to-day health at risk, compelling them to work with undernourished and fatigued bodies.[23] The food problem – documented by a 2008 *Human Rights Watch Report* – was serious.

Overwork and Exhaustion

Many of Da Fo's migrant construction workers fell victim to the overwork and physical exhaustion that epitomized work life in the Great Leap era. For Da Fo

---

[18] Bao Zhanghe, interview.
[19] Personal correspondence with Sarah Swider, December 31, 2008.   [20] Ibid.
[21] Bao Chaoxiang, interview.   [22] Cf. Human Rights Watch, *One Year of My Blood*, 2:13.
[23] Cf. ibid., 3:8.

migrant workers, one important thread linking the past to the present involved the schedule of work.[24] In both the Mao and post-Mao periods, the agents of Communist Party–guided industrial development required displaced farmers to work continuously, without any rest breaks whatsoever – often denying them any opportunity for deep sleep or sick leave. In the colonized space of Liangmen People's Commune, Da Fo's farmers worked for fifteen to twenty hours per day, for seven to ten days running.[25] More than four decades later, this same practice persisted for Da Fo's discontented migrant workers.

Let us listen to Ruan Jingwei, a thirty-six-year-old migrant worker whose twenty years under hard-driving subcontractors jeopardized his health and jolted his faith in the will of reform-era rulers to create a humane path of economic reform. After graduating from Shangcun middle school in 1988, Ruan started working on construction sites in Shanxi. He was only sixteen years old. He recalls:

We worked there for a full year. The work was unbelievably hard and exhausting. We got up before dawn, and we worked until it was too dark to continue. We worked at least thirteen hours a day.

The food was not good at all. In the morning, it was porridge and pickled vegetables with bread. For lunch, we had water and bread, with one poor vegetable dish. We were told that we would be paid three yuan per day at the time. However, at the end of the year we each got only 500 yuan. The subcontractor had a very dark heart. He was greedy. He found many ways to take money out of our pay. He wanted us to work continuously. If one of us did not work as hard as he thought we should, he would deduct our pay. Moreover, when it rained and we could not work, he wanted us to pay for our own food.

We had no weekend off, and we had no days to rest except when it rained or snowed and the severe weather conditions would not allow us to work. The subcontractor did not care about the safety and health of the workers. He was only interested in making more money. Many workers were injured and had some health problems as a result of long hours of continuous work.

The time between our two meals was also too long. I suffer from chronic stomach pain, and I have a stomach ache constantly. I have back problems too. I suffer from back pain almost every day, and sometimes I cannot stand up straight because of the pain.

One day we were laying the foundations for a tall building in Shanxi. We started working [again] right after lunch. By 4 PM we were so tired and hungry. But the subcontractor refused to allow us to take any rest break or to eat anything. He patrolled the work site, all the while yelling and cursing us in order to make us work harder and faster. He did not beat anybody that day, but he never stopped yelling and cursing. He called us all kinds of names, repeatedly insisting that we finish laying the foundation that day. Otherwise, he yelled, we would mess up his schedule, and we would be responsible for his loss and we would not be paid in the end if he lost money. We worked that day until twelve midnight, when dinner was served and we were permitted to stop working. I felt as though I was

---

[24] For this concept of "quantum entanglement," see Stott, *Ghostwalk*, 194–195.
[25] Thaxton, *Catastrophe and Contention*.

dying. I was so exhausted I did not eat anything, and I fell asleep with my clothes on right there at the work site.[26]

To get a better feel for why this practice stoked nearly as much indignation as nonpayment of wages, we need to listen to another of Ruan Jingwei's experiences with subcontractors – this one with Bao Chenzhong, from Ruan's native Da Fo:

In 2003, we were working in Crouching Tiger Park (Wohushan) in Taiyuan city. Bao Chenzhong was the subcontractor for that job. He hired forty people from Da Fo to do the project for him. Bao Chenzhong got the project in Taiyuan, and then his wife quickly rented a bus to take us there from Da Fo. We left after dawn, and were on the bus for more than ten hours. When we got here it was four o'clock in the afternoon. As soon as we got off the bus with our luggage, Bao Chenzhong asked us to start working right away. We did not have the time to unpack our stuff. We worked there until four the next morning before we were allowed to stop. We were so tired that first day, we did not eat, did not even unpack our belongings. Instead, we just fell asleep on the ground. At eight o'clock the same morning, after less than four hours of sleep, Bao Chenzhong and his wife woke us up to start working again. His food was very bad too. We worked like this without any distinction of day or night for seven days. We were completely exhausted. Some people fell asleep standing up, while working with their shovels.

By this point, I had worked under this Bao Chenzhong for sixteen years. In these years, I saw his heart become darker and darker. Over the years, his greed grew to the point where he was willing to kill people to get money. How could he turn his fellow villagers into slaves like that? How could he do that to people from the same village as him? I finally woke up to reality. I refused to work for him anymore after that. He is so inhuman, nobody from Da Fo wants to work for him anymore. Even his nephew refused to work for him. His heart is too dark. Everybody in Da Fo knows this. His car, his money – all were paid for with our sweat and blood. I will not forget this fact.[27]

The disallowance of work breaks, the denial of sleep, and the shouting a of profanities at workers in order to goad them into greater sacrifices to build infrastructure for state-guided development recalls the tempo and tone of Chinese Communist Party (CCP) cadre abuse of Da Fo farmers who were conscripted to work for the collective during the Great Leap, when farmers lost faith in socialism. Whether the replication of this abusive pattern in the reform era produced swells of alienation across the villages of the border area remains to be established. But Da Fo migrants such as Ruan Jingwei have an interesting political take on the issue. In reflecting on his experience, Ruan says: "When I was growing up, I saw many Communist Party propaganda films about how landlords oppressed the poor farmers, and how the capitalists and landlords forced workers to do more work in order to squeeze more money out of them. Now it has been my turn to experience capitalists and landlords in real life. I think that the subcontractors I have worked under are far worse than the

---

[26] Ruan Jingwei, interview.   [27] Ibid.

capitalists and landlords described in the Communist films. These are very bad people. They do not have a human heart at all. They do not care if we live or die. They just want their money, and they only want more money. They already have money, but they want more, still more."[28]

Ruan Jingwei's statement implies that the incentive for cruelty under state capitalism was different from that under socialism, with the dark side of fidelity to Mao-era ideology giving way to the dark pursuit of money in the Deng era. This may be true, but it is important to keep in mind that under one-party rule both incentives unleashed a desire to dominate and fleece country dwellers and that rural people who needed to move to survive were hurt in both systems.

Renewed Confinement

The assumption that the growth of the market and the boom in Chinese business has resulted in greater labor mobility than was the case in the Mao era permeates virtually all scholarship on rural China, and indeed, this assumption finds impressive support in some of the interviews with Da Fo's migrant workers. There is no question that most farmers have been able to leave the village for the cities. Da Fo's migrant workers also claim, however, that some of the city-based labor contractors placed severe restrictions on their right to freely leave the workplaces to which they have migrated. They say the subcontractors in particular violated their right to abandon construction work that proved unbearably exploitative. This renewed confinement seems to have replicated some of the most draconian features of the political controls on poor, desperate farmers who had no choice but to "volunteer" to work on the construction projects of the commune in the Great Leap period.[29]

Two aspects of this phenomenon jump out of the interview data. One involves the attempt of migrant workers to flee unbearably heavy work assignments. In the reform period, many of the construction sites were characterized by heavy workloads, and the migrant workers often fled the work sites, leaving the contractors to search for replacement workers. In this respect, there was unrestrained labor mobility at a number of the sites at which Da Fo's farmers worked. Bao Guoshan informs us, for example, that this pattern more or less characterized the Tiananzhuang brick factory site, a few dozen li from Yuema city. Yet many Da Fo migrant workers found that exiting this work site was not so easy. The work load was so heavy, and the pay was so uncertain, that the half-dozen Da Fo migrant workers who went to this site – after scores of migrants from other villages had fled it – eventually could not tolerate the work. When the Da Fo workers prepared to flee the site, brick factory manager Xu Dacheng confiscated their cooking pots and pans so they would think twice about fleeing.[30] After Bao and the other migrants returned to Tiananzhuang,

[28] Ibid.   [29] Thaxton, *Catastrophe and Contention*.   [30] Bao Guoshan, interview.

Xu Dacheng refused to pay them their promised salaries. In three months of confinement at this site, Bao and his colleagues spent 100 yuan each on essentials, and then they had to purchase train tickets for the trip back to Da Fo, so that by the time they arrived back home each migrant worker had only 100 yuan left.[31]

In the Great Leap, the CCP leaders in charge of the commune work camps had also frequently attempted to restrict the mobility of camp "volunteers," invoking pay cuts, confiscating cooking utensils, and hunting down workers who attempted to leave the camps – and all the while turning the commune work sites into a penal colony that was, in many respects, a makeshift prison. Many Da Fo migrant workers testify that this pattern of regimentation and rule reappeared under reform.

One place where this happened was in Jindong county, where Da Fo's Zhou Chunxue began work in 1982 at the age of thirty-one. One of Da Fo's poorest farmers and an orphan of the Great Leap's carnage, Zhou went to build an apartment complex to house the Public Security staff of Jindong. During his first season working for the contractor, in 1982, he was shorted on his wages. He returned to work for the same contractor after the spring festival, in part because he still intended to get the back pay he was owed. Again, he was cheated on his wages. The contractor told him he had no money to pay, because the Public Security Bureau leaders would not pay him. Zhou recalled:

I had no way of knowing whether what he told me was true or false. There was no way I could find it out. There was no place for me to go to get justice. I did not have a contract with him. It was an oral agreement between him and me. There was no evidence of how much I had worked for him or of his promise to pay me for extra work. In China at that time, you took somebody's word as being as serious as a written contract. I did not even know where I could go to complain about this matter. The only option to me, it seemed, was to quit working for him. Therefore I declared I was leaving.

However, he wanted me to continue working for him, and he would not let me leave. I ran away, but he chased me with a knife. I was running toward the train station, and he caught me and grabbed me. I was scared. He accused me of leaving the work site without finishing my job. People surrounding us watched him abuse me and did not come to my aid. He grabbed me and dragged me back to the construction site, and then he forced me to continue to work for him. I was not paid for the work I had done for him, and, moreover, now I had lost my freedom to leave. There was no place for me to get help. I never thought that something like this could happen to me in my own country.

In the end, one of my fellow Da Fo villagers implored him to let me go, and he allowed me to leave. However, he did not pay me for any of the work I had done. He owed me 3,100 yuan. That was a lot of money for a farmer like me. Afterwards, I went to ask him for the money many times, but he refused to pay me. Each time he said that I was a bad worker and should not be paid. Each time, I was treated like a beggar, and I had to plead with him for mercy. I felt angry. I worked for him like a slave, and I was not paid.[32]

[31] Ibid.   [32] Zhou Chunxue, interview.

Zhou Chunxue's ordeal begs the question: have rural migrants actually enjoyed unrestricted labor mobility under reform? For the most part, Da Fo's migrant workers were able to exit the village, but many were tethered to new urban work spaces. They were subjected to a form of internal colonization that reproduced the same kind of "bonded labor" regime that Anita Chan has discovered in the work factories of Guangdong, including the military-like regimentation of labor that infused CCP–worker relations under the commune.[33]

The Dangers of the Work Site

The market liberalization of the post-Mao era was accompanied by a state default in policy regulations governing treatment of the floating workforce entering the construction industry. Although Dorothy J. Solinger has shown that an official People's Republic of China (PRC) construction body attempted to rank-order and register the migrants who sought work in the towns and cities, her meticulous scholarship also demonstrates that many powerful labor bosses used informal networks to recruit migrant workers into the construction industry[34] and that the quantity and quality of state regulations under which the migrants labored declined in "a descending hierarchy of subcontracting."[35] It seems that Da Fo's migrant workers were near the bottom of this hierarchy. With the Central government turning a blind eye toward the contractors, the latter frequently took advantage of the farm-based migrant workers, throwing safety measures to the wind and compelling the migrants to work under conditions that posed a serious threat to their physical well-being.

We know from the history of Da Fo and Liangmen People's Commune (and from data on many other interior rural Chinese localities) that during the Great Leap Forward, local party whips in charge of the Liangmen commune labor force drove farmers to perform exceedingly dangerous work assignments on extravillage construction sites.[36] The logic of Great Leap schemes to introduce modernization by frantic measures that shifted the risks of construction and development to the rural poor seems to have become the basis for the core operational codes of the reform-era construction industry, wherein contractors and subcontractors fashioned ad hoc and arbitrary work rules and used their power to overthrow practical technical knowledge, all the while pressing migrant workers to perform within a highly simplified labor framework.

The testimony of Da Fo's Ruan Qiuyong underscores this point. The migrant workers' discriminatory power, however elementary, was the only thing ensuring their physical safety at the work sites, where militant labor bosses threatened them. Ruan highlights one of his ordeals with his boss in Taiyuan,

---

[33] Cf. Anita Chan, "Regimented Workers," 12–16.   [34] Solinger, *Contesting Citizenship*, 211.
[35] Ibid., 212.   [36] Thaxton, *Catastrophe and Contention*.

the capital of Shanxi province: "The contractors forced us to do dangerous jobs. We all worked in the open. One time it was raining very hard, but the contractor would not allow us to stop, and he insisted that we continue to work. The steel lift got wet. We knew that the brake did not work when it was wet. I knew it was very dangerous to operate the machinery under these conditions. Nonetheless, the contractor still insisted that I operate the machinery. I refused. He then threatened to cut my pay and to apply other penalties. However, I knew my life was more important than money."[37]

As Lei Guang has pointed out, when migrant workers fell victim to life-threatening accidents, the investigating authorities seldom did anything to help the workers secure compensation from employers, and they made no effort to enlist the efforts of the district or city government to address the shoddy safety regulations at construction sites.[38] Hence, migrant workers such as Ruan Qiuyong had no choice but to flee dangerous work spaces like this one and return to their native Da Fo, where many of them attempted to eke out an existence by tilling the land. Recalling his return to Da Fo around 2004, Ruan says: "My life did not improve at all. My family and I were barely able to get by."[39]

A World without Doctors

The early reform-era Central government decision to gear its public health-care plan to serve city dwellers with the privilege of urban *hukou*, or household registration permits, left rural-to-urban migrant workers without basic health care. The migrant workers in the construction industry were especially vulnerable when it came to injury or illness. They not only were excluded from formal medical care services, they could not count on government to enforce the laws and regulations that obligated employers to arrange medical treatment for work-related health problems.[40] Not surprisingly, therefore, Da Fo's migrant workers say they had to fend for themselves and pay for all medical services, which they rarely could do, because they were frequently cheated out of their earned wages by the contractors.

Da Fo's migrant workers faced two "everyday health problems." One centered on the poor food regime of the workplace. Most of the workers had to eat the cheapest food available – usually noodles in water – and only rarely were they able to obtain vitamin-rich vegetables. This deprivation weakened

---

[37] Ruan Qiuyong, interview.   [38] Guang, "Guerrilla Workfare," 493–494.
[39] Ruan Qiuyong, interview.
[40] On the failure of the government to create institutional arrangements to cover migrant workers and to enforce its own protective laws and regulations, see Xiang, "Migration and Health," 1–17, 21–22, 29, esp. 21. On the prohibitive cost of competent medical care, see Yip, "Disparities in Health Care," 154–157; also see Solinger, who was one of the first to document this policy gap and failure and its negative consequences for the well-being of migrant workers in *Contesting Citizenship*, 265–266.

their immune systems and increased their chances of succumbing to all kinds of unanticipated illnesses. It also increased their vulnerability to the severe air pollution, to the viral flus sweeping their damp and chilly workplaces, and to the mosquito-borne diseases they encountered at the work sites.

There were other problems, including a lack of emergency medical facilities. Even when an injured migrant worker was transported to a hospital by fellow workers, the victim was often received by a half-hearted nursing staff and a physician ill-equipped to handle traumatic injury. Pang Zhongmin explains how the tragedies of the work site created a climate of fear of catastrophic injury among many of the migrant workers, including Pang himself: "I had to leave Tianjin after two months there. One of the workers died on the construction site. He was assigned to work on the roof of the house. He took a pail of cement and climbed on top of the roof. The roof was composed of a very thin layer of fiberglass, and he stepped on it and fell through it. The house was not very high, but he fell off head first. When he hit the ground, he was able to stand up again, but then he fell down immediately. I was right there at the time. We carried him to the hospital on a cart, but he died there. The doctor was not able to do much for him. Watching him die like that, I was so greatly shocked that I could not work anymore. The image of him dying was in my mind all of the time, and we all knew it could happen to any one of us. He was single, and he did not have a family. But I had a family to look after, and I could not risk my life like that. The incident affected my view of life a great deal."[41]

Traumatized migrant workers had no means of finding psychiatric assistance in the aftermath of such horrific experiences on construction jobs. In the course of chasing jobs in construction from 1981 until 1992, Pang Zhongmin, who was in his thirties at the time, worked extremely hard in brick making, and on two occasions he fainted while working in this industrial sector, each time falling into a deep ditch filled with filthy, polluted water and nearly dying. His parents implored him to discontinue the work. But Pang Zhongmin was from a poor farm household that had barely survived the dearth of the Great Leap and had yet to recover from Mao's great famine, and Pang's role in counterattacks on Great Leap–era party boss Bao Zhilong in the late 1960s had left him without any allies in the Da Fo village power establishment. Working outside Da Fo under subcontractors was the only way he could survive – and so he continued to work in the brick-making industry, for a while.

Still, Pang's two brushes with death, plus the constant loud, grating noise of the brick-grinding machine he operated daily, finally got to him. Pang says he developed a psychological reaction to the brick construction site. As soon as he heard the grinding machine, he would develop a splitting headache, and his fear of falling again would overtake him. In the end, he was forced to give up his job at the brick factory, mainly because he had no one to turn to for mental health

---

[41] Pang Zhongmin, interview.

care – that is, no one to provide the therapeutic remedy to his anxiety-stimulated panic attacks over working in the factory.[42] As Nancy Chen has pointed out,[43] many Chinese have experienced mental breakdowns engendered by the cruel pressures of reform-era development. Da Fo's migrant workers were no exception. In fact, some of them seem to have lived on the edge of madness.

When pushed over the brink, they were left to fend for themselves, in part because the state-directed post-Mao capitalist psychiatric hospitals did not keep pace with the wave of mental health problems in the construction industry, but mainly because the post-Mao authorities did not recognize the suffering of construction workers such as Pang Zhongmin as a product of the industrial storm of state-filtered global capitalism.[44] Much like their counterparts who went mad in the frenzied rush of Great Leap industrialization, most rural-based migrant workers had to rely on family and especially on friendship networks to provide relief from their breakdowns. But there was a difference – and it is important to keep this difference in mind, for only by doing so can we fully appreciate the local challenge to Communist Party rule to be documented in the next chapter: Da Fo's migrant workers had escaped the tight draconian political controls associated with the commune-dictated labor assignments of the collective era, and, moreover, they quickly moved to create small groups of friends who would help one another cope with and survive the demands of labor bosses.

The Great Fear: Accidental Deaths and the Connection with the Great Leap Past

The great fear among Da Fo's migrant workers was meeting death on a distant, unknown worksite without the knowledge of family. Because the construction companies could be seriously penalized if there were two or more recorded deaths, unrecorded work-related accidents were not uncommon, and rumors of the disappearance of dead workers' bodies traveled the sites.[45] Accidental death in the unsecure, coercive industrial work sites had been a curse in the Great Leap, when, according to Tiejun Cheng and Mark Selden, the rush to speed up industrial development prompted the state to accelerate labor recruitment; this, in combination with the development of rural famine, produced a flood of desperate migrants in search of any kind of work in the cities.[46] The Great Leap and the emergency produced by its famine gave Public Security cause to suspend the *hukou*, or household registration system, under which the police

---

[42] Ibid.   [43] Chen, *Breathing Spaces*, 108–109.

[44] On both of these points, I have benefited from ibid., 108–109, 122, 135–137, 154.

[45] I am indebted to Sarah Swider for helping me construct this section. Personal correspondence, April 16, 2012.

[46] Cheng and Selden, "China's Hukou System," 664.

had the power to grant the internal passport, which permitted the rural poor to pursue rural-to-urban migration – and meet with accidental deaths that were just waiting to happen under this poorly regulated system of rushed development.[47]

Some of Da Fo's migrant workers who went to do construction work in the Beijing area recall a similar phenomenon in the post-Mao period. For example, while digging the foundation for the new Public Security Bureau building in Shunyi county, just outside Beijing, Zheng Huiqing witnessed several deaths. When the sandy ground around the Shunyi construction site caved in, three migrant workers were buried alive, after which the boss instructed the subcontractor and the workers to run away. This first encounter, says Zheng, "was a very scary experience for me, so I did not go out to work again until 1998." In 1998, Zheng began work in Beijing on a seventeen-story building called Jinyu Dasha. Toward the end of the first month, Zheng Huiqing witnessed two workers fall to their deaths.[48] In both of these cases, the employer–contractor was obligated to get the rural migrant workers temporary resident cards. However, according to Zheng Huiqing, the police and the government allowed the subcontractors to lure the migrant workers to Beijing without documentation, and the government failed to enforce its own rules. The Da Fo migrant workers, and many of the workers who died in the accidents, were never given temporary resident cards (temporary *hukou*).[49] In this situation, the contractors stood a much greater chance of avoiding responsibility for employee deaths when the government officials arrived to investigate an accident. In the case of the two workers who fell to their deaths on the Jinyu Dasha project, the boss of the work site panicked and ordered everyone, including the subcontractor and all of the migrant workers, to flee the site. He got off scot free, while the two migrant workers lost their lives and their identities. In fact, they were treated as if they had not existed. With no one to claim their bodies, they became missing persons whose families could not provide them with proper burial.[50] Traumatized by witnessing such job-site deaths, Zheng Huiqing said that he was gripped by anxiety while doing construction work.[51]

[47] Chan and Li, "Hukou System," 218–820, and Dikotter, *Mao's Great Famine*, 234–235, 269–273.

[48] Zheng Huiqing, interview.

[49] According to Mallee, nearly two-thirds of the migrant workers were issued such cards, or permits, in the 1990s. But Mallee also notes that the system of reform-era regulations opened the door to corruption and that the fundamentals of the *hukou* system were unchanged. Mallee, "Migration, Hukou and Resistance," 96, 99.

[50] According to Sarah Swider, the relatives and friends who worked on job sites brought pressure on contractors to negotiate settlements with the families of accident victims, but clearly this was not always the case. This also partly explains why Da Fo's migrant workers preferred to work for local subcontractors and with peer groups from the Da Fo area. Sarah Swider, personal correspondence, April 16, 2012.

[51] Zheng Huiqing, interview.

I do not know if Da Fo's migrant workers experienced such trauma in the cities during the late 1950s, but villagers still wonder what happened to those who never returned to Da Fo after taking off for urban construction work in the Great Leap period. In any event, the pattern of abuse, trauma, and reported deaths of unknown workers sent to the rural construction sites in this border region and outside it during the Great Leap resonates with the pattern documented for the reform era. In short, the reform-era CCP-led political system structured a labor regime based on Great Leap–style regimentation, with its agents and networks getting the lion's share of the benefits and the migrant workers getting the short end of the stick. Whether we are dealing with a true "continuity" from the Great Leap, and hence path-dependent causality, rather than a correlation that stems from just standard exploitative practices, is of course an important question. But there are more than a few threads of the specificity of the Great Leap legacy, suggesting that the roots of the ruthless labor system in which Da Fo's migrant workers struggled to survive lay in the dark Maoist past.

STRATEGIES OF CONTENTION, TOOLS OF RESISTANCE

In response to unbridled subcontractor exploitation and to the lack of state protection of basic rights, Da Fo's migrant workers forged a number of tools to resist employer-contrived injustice in the first two decades of reform. Unrepresented and battered, they often took matters into their own hands and acted individually – and increasingly collectively – to assert their claims to be paid a living wage and to be treated fairly in their relations with the contractors and subcontractors who harnessed their labor power.

In the process of defending their rights, Da Fo's migrant workers came up with various strategies of contention, all of which involved local interaction with the power holders in the construction industry and many of which increasingly were played out in regional and national urban arenas. Four of these strategies are present in the interviews of the cast of characters making up Da Fo's floating population. Not surprisingly, the main stream of contention more or less centered on the polarized conflict over payment of wages, and this issue often was entangled with resistance on many other fronts.

The danger of engaging in strikes at the construction work sites, which could trigger beatings by subcontractors or reprisals by the police or thugs, compelled many of the Da Fo migrant workers to find a less direct way of engineering work stoppages. Some found a way to carry out a stoppage without formally declaring one, by, for example, secretly stealing machine tools that were critical to the continuous functioning of construction. Those who remained on the work site often seized on the theft and the missing tools to express their grievances, hinting in the course of heated conversations with frustrated subcontractors that the tools might be "discovered" on the site if only the subcontractors could find their wages. The workers from Da Fo also saw the stolen tools as collateral to be held against promised wages: if the wages were not paid, then they would at least have the tools to sell, and they would be able to use the money as a means of recovering part of their wages – which, after all, they reasoned had been stolen by the subcontractors. Da Fo's migrant workers and the subcontractors all understood the dynamics of this more or less silent, low-profile tit-for-tat game. During the Great Leap, villagers under Liangmen People's Commune had similarly stolen brigade construction tools and materials to cope with nonpayment of wages, and so, on this aspect of not being paid, too, an earlier, parallel history returned in reform.[52]

To counteract subcontractors' tendency to disappear with the funds they received from superiors, Da Fo's migrant workers also initiated their own system of monitoring the subcontractors, essentially stalking them to ensure that wages were issued promptly after the subcontractors received their money from upper management. This strategy often involved heated verbal confrontation. Pang Zhongmin made sure that he listened to what the subcontractor wanted from him, and he always worked hard and long, demonstrating he was doing his best. But Pang also was gripped by worry over not being paid, and so during his construction work he pursued a strategy of total engagement with the subcontractors. Pang tells how he used this strategy of contention, and why he choose to embrace it:

As soon as I saw the subcontractor get the money to pay workers from his sources, I would follow him to his office or home. I would tell him that I wanted to be paid my salary right away and in full, right there. Usually, the subcontractor would refuse to pay me there. But I would tell him that if he did not pay me there immediately then I would yell and tell everybody to come and get his money. If the other construction workers heard me yelling, they would all come and demand payment from him, and he would not be able to get away with his plan to run away with everybody's salary. In most cases, the subcontractor was compelled to pay me. As soon as I got my salary paid in full, I would quit that construction job, and then come back later, or find a job in another place. If one were careful and observed what was going on, one would be able to protect one's interests. Therefore, I always got my salary while working outside of Da Fo during my travels as a migrant worker.[53]

In *The Contentious French*, Charles Tilly notes that a major characteristic of popular contention in pre-1850 France involved convergence on the residences of those who had wronged the poor.[54] This strategy of resistance was at the core of migrant worker contention during the reform period. Da Fo's poor, mobile semi-farmers pursued it individually and in groups. Seldom noted by global scholars or reported in the Chinese press, this strategy of garnering wages was honed in remote villages and towns with barely visible threads to

---

[52] I am indebted to Dorothy J. Solinger for inspiring me to think harder about this issue. Personal correspondence, June 14, 2009.
[53] Pang Zhongmin, interview.   [54] Tilly, *The Contentious French*, 392.

metropolitan construction sites, and it was increasingly taken up by Da Fo's migrant workers in the 1990s. Bao Ruimin, who had been a victim of the Strike Hard Campaign and who later had to employ this strategy in order to cope with being cheated out of his wages after working in Tianjin, recalls the circumstances that drove him to adapt it, as well as how he pursued it with others in Yueguang, Daming county, Hebei province:

We were trying to get our salary back from this [subcontractor] Deng Zhenxu at the time. We went to his home village. The first time we went there was right after we finished planting the wheat in the fall. Ruan Hongqiao, Ruan Zhanfang, Ruan Zhangzhen, and I went there together from Da Fo. Deng Zhenxu was not there. Only his wife and children were home. We had to return empty handed.

On December 20 we went to Yueguang again. Again, however, Deng Zhenxu was not at home.

The third time we went was on Chinese New Year's eve. Four of us from Da Fo joined with two other migrant workers from Pingyuandi. We had worked with these two migrant workers on the construction project in Tianjin. They had decided to go to Yueguang on that day, and they stopped by Da Fo to ask Ruan Hongqiao if he would go with them. We all decided to come along. We also made a decision that the six of us would stay there as long as it took to get our money back. Otherwise we would celebrate the Chinese New Year in Deng Zhenxu's home.

The six of us rode our bicycles to Daming, and we arrived at his village around 11 o'clock in the morning. He was not home. There were a dozen other migrant workers in the village waiting to get their money back from him.

The six of us entered his house and then settled down. We did not eat lunch. His wife cooked some food for her two children and herself. We watched them eat while we waited. Deng Zhenxu came home around six o'clock in the evening. He assumed everyone would have left by then. He was a little surprised when he saw us there. He asked his wife to cook some food for us to eat. We told him we would celebrate the Chinese New Year with him there in his own home if we were not paid that day. We said we would eat their dumplings that night. We would not eat all of the dumplings, but we were prepared to eat half of their dumplings and leave the other half for them. This was something no Chinese would want to have happen to him. One cannot allow anyone else to eat New Year dumplings in their home. It was not a Chinese custom for that to happen.

Still, Deng Zhenxu insisted that he did not have the money to pay us. Consequently, we just sat there quietly. By nine o'clock that evening, I told the five others to bring our bicycles into the house and to get ready to spend the night. At that point, Deng Zhenxu realized that we were determined to celebrate the Chinese New Year in his house. He got up, and he told us that he would go to his friends to borrow money to pay us. He went out for a while, and he came back with three hundred yuan. He gave each of us 50 yuan and promised that he would pay us back the next year. We felt that he did not have the money to pay us there. We understood that it was not easy to borrow money from others that late on the Chinese New Year. He still owed me three hundred yuan, and I and the others did not get our money back from him until New Year's Eve of the following year.[55]

---

[55] Bao Ruimin, interview.

Thinking about this resistance more systematically, it is important to emphasize that most of the Da Fo migrant worker confrontations with subcontractors, construction company managers, and the authorities were peaceful, and intentionally so. The interviews make it clear that the workers rarely used profanities and nearly always demonstrated respect and paid homage to their employers. The pipe dream of just about every interviewee was to find a kind, fair subcontractor – a good, dependable patron.

Thus, even when disputing arbitrary, stubborn refusals to pay them overdue wages, most of the migrant workers from Da Fo village attempted to fight for their rights by a strategy of nonviolent, deferential, lawful engagement. After all, Da Fo's migrant workers, like those from countless other interior Chinese villages, were aware of the power of subcontractors, contractors, and their hired goons – not to mention the police – and they invariably sought to avoid the kinds of contentious acts that invited beatings, imprisonment, or sudden banishment and return to the countryside.

But what they sought did not matter. Increasingly, in the late 1980s and early 1990s, their attempt to avoid, or rein in, the arbitrary and brutal treatment of contractors and subcontractors proved futile. The story of Da Fo's Zhou Chunxue illustrates the kind of setbacks they encountered in a world where the state placed few, if any, constraints on subcontractor greed and savagery, and it helps us grasp the process whereby the subcontractors/contractors and the courts battered many of the migrant workers, turning them into radicalized proletarians without any basic human – not to mention civil – rights.

At age fifty-four in 2006, Zhou Chunxue was one of Da Fo's poorest farmers. Zhou's household had been reduced to near ruin in the Great Leap, and his family had yet to fully recover from the impact of the famine. Zhou never went to school. He never gained literacy. He never obtained a skill. He never got married.[56] And he could not find local off-farm work that would enable him to survive and help support his aging father.

When the collective disbanded and the land was divided in the early 1980s, Zhou Chunxue began to seek work outside Da Fo. He wandered to Anyang and to other secondary North China cities in search of work on construction sites. For the first three years, he befriended a decent subcontractor and did well. In 1986, however, an Anyang-based subcontractor arbitrarily shortchanged Zhou on his promised salary. After Zhou expressed his dismay, the subcontractor promised to pay Zhou back by the end of the year. But he broke his promise. "So," says Zhou, "in the end, I left him."[57]

After a series of run-ins with other unscrupulous subcontractors in his native Henan in 1987, Zhou Chunxue begged his way to Yongji City, Shanxi province:

When I reached Yongji, a person asked me why I did not work to make money to buy food. He said that I was young, and I should work, not beg. He also asked if I was willing

[56] Zhou Chunxue, interview. [57] Ibid.

to work for food. Of course I wanted to work, and in fact I was looking for work at the time. But I did not know how to find work. He took me to a brick factory to make bricks. My job was to ship the bricks to the drying places. I never worked that hard in my life. We worked extremely hard every day. It was the most strenuous work I had ever experienced. We sweated a great deal, and we had to drink a lot of boiled water. One day it was my turn to go with another worker to fetch the boiled water. The boiled water pail turned over, spilling the scalding water onto my leg. My leg was seriously burned. The subcontractor did not want to pay for the medical expenses. He actually cursed me for being careless.

The owner of the brick factory intervened and gave me 15 yuan. He said I could leave and go take care of my problem.

I went to the hospital to seek the treatment. But without a deposit the hospital refused to treat my burn wound. The doctors and the nurses ignored me. Therefore, I went to the Yongji township government to complain about my treatment. But the township government leaders said they had nothing to do with this matter. The subcontractor, they said, was not under their jurisdiction. Even if he were a local person, they explained they were not a court, and they could not address disputes of this kind. At this point, the township government said that I could go back to the hospital and get some shots. I was in severe pain, and I went to the hospital again. After giving me a painkiller injection, the nurses said I should leave the premises.

In the meantime, I was told that there was no way I could win if I were to sue the subcontractor. It would be hard for me to win the case single-handedly in a place far away from home. But I did not believe that. I sued the owner and the subcontractor in the county court for their failure to treat my injury. The brick factory owner and the subcontractor were called into court to face my complaint. They lied. They said that I was a bad, lazy worker, and also a troublemaker. The court said it would investigate the matter and dismissed us. I did not trust that they would investigate the matter. Even if they did, I was not convinced they would find out the truth of what transpired in the brick factory. I felt they would not give me justice.

Worse, once I stepped outside of the county court, the owner and the subcontractor threatened me. They said that if I did not leave Yongji as soon as possible, they would break my leg or neck. They said they meant it. They said that they could do it in a way that nobody would know what had happened to me, and that I would disappear from this world without a trace. I knew that these people could do this to me, or that they could hire some thugs to do something to me, and my family in Da Fo would not know what happened to me.

Nevertheless, I decided to fight them in the Yongji city court, which was higher than the county court. I was angry, and I was hungry, but I wanted to fight for justice. I went to the court and waited my turn in line to tell the judge about my suffering and the injustice I had endured. But before I was able to speak in court, I blacked out completely. The court officers took me to the hospital, and I was given a shot. I regained my energy. But the court officers really did not care about my health or hunger. They just wanted to get rid of me so that I would not further burden them. They asked me where I came from, and I told them. They said they would arrange to send me back to Da Fo. But they only took me as far as Handan, which was still a few hundred li from my home. I walked and begged my way back home. I was completely disappointed by the legal system. I was not able to get justice there.[58]

---

[58] Zhou Chunxue, interview.

Zhou Chunxue confided that he probably would have killed the Yongji brick factory owner and the subcontractor if he had not been escorted back to Handan by the court officers. By this point, Zhou had become so frustrated by his bad experience at the hands of urban-based subcontractors that he expressed blind hatred for the people of the cities, and he fantasized violent revenge on them, taking a page from a Henan newspaper article as his model for future justice: "There was a story in the newspaper about a migrant worker from Henan," says Zhou. "He worked in Beijing for a while, but he was not paid. He was frustrated and angered by his mistreatment, but he did not have the money to return home. In the end, he stole an automobile. He steered it to the Wangfujing commercial area of Beijing and drove it through a crowd. He killed three persons, and he injured many others. In court, he said that he had found that nine of ten urban people had a 'black heart,' and that they abused rural people. He hated the rich urban people. Since Wangfujing was where the rich people went, he decided to kill as many as he could. I agree with his action. We Henan farmers are not bad people, but we cannot take all of the abuse without fighting back. It is true that many Henan villagers have become criminals. They steal, rob, and kill urban people. However, we cannot blame Henan people alone for this. The city-based subcontractors abused us first, and they turned us into criminals. They are only harvesting what they have sown."[59]

The pattern of subcontractor deceit, trickery, and abuse also created alienation and cynicism toward government, which posed a problem for the center. On giving up on the courts, Zhou Chunxue had this to say about the lack of official support for migrant claims against subcontractors in 2006:

There were many stories in China about rural migrant workers who worked for long periods for a subcontractor, but whom, in the end, the subcontractor refused to pay. This has become a national problem. Two years ago, in 2003–2004, Wen Jiabao, the premier of the Chinese government, pleaded on state television on behalf of the workers to be paid. At time, I began to wonder – What kind of a premier is this?! Could he not do something more powerful than that? Why should he plead with these illegal subcontractors? Could he not order the police to arrest all of these illegal subcontractors? Isn't the government supposed to protect migrant workers like me who are powerless and helpless in dealing with these rascals?

There were other stories that some rural migrant workers snapped when they were not paid, and in the end stabbed to death every member of the subcontractor's family. In this kind of case, the government executed the unpaid workers as quickly as possible. But this same government never helped us migrant workers when we needed help in dealing with these rascals.[60]

Such anger does not seem to be the result of increasing rural-urban inequality or of urbanites getting richer than rural farm people pure and simple.[61] According to Martin King Whyte, much of the resentment that has driven

---

[59] Ibid.   [60] Ibid.   [61] Whyte, "Views of Chinese Citizens."

protest in post-Mao China has its root in procedural injustice rather than experiences with socioeconomic inequality and the injustice of poverty per se.[62] This finding rings true for the Da Fo migrant workers who have gained some ground under reform. It seems that cruel and humiliating mistreatment by the ground-level cadres of the reform-era construction industry, when coupled with official procedural injustice – specifically the complicity and/or failure of the courts – contributed to Zhou Chunxue's dangerous political mind-set. And this mind-set led him to a conclusion that poses a problem for political stability. On speaking of such mistreatment, Zhou provides a solution that has implications Beijing's rulers surely do not want to hear: "What can I do to deal with a person like that? I came to understand why other workers killed their subcontractors, and I understand now why the heroes in the *Shuihuzhuan* (The Water Margin) killed the bad people and people in China still called them heroes."[63]

Whereas physical altercations taking the form of shoving matches, fist fights, and melees also shaped contention over wage injustice, the migrant workers from Da Fo did not intentionally engage in these actions to seriously injure or kill the subcontractors who had cheated them. They did, however, rely on physical tools of resistance, specifically on a traditional form of combat, to secure promised wages – a theme to be taken up in the next chapter. Their clashes with subcontractors by and large occurred in villages and towns far away from the construction sites in Beijing, Tianjin, and other urban spaces, often pitting local clients of the contractors against Da Fo migrant workers, who entered the home villages and towns of the subcontractors as outside complainants – as was the case in Xingtai, where several of Da Fo's workers were injured, and in Wei county, where, after heated arguments with the subcontractor, some of the Da Fo workers were threatened with bodily harm if they ever returned.[64]

One surprising aspect of these migrant worker challenges is their long-term nature. They not infrequently involved a migrant worker seeking out a subcontractor to demand back pay ten, eleven, and twelve times over a decade or more. Apparently, the Da Fo migrants who led this protracted struggle for wage justice learned two important lessons. The first was to travel to the subcontractors' home villages and towns in groups of five, six, ten, and twenty. It was not safe to go out alone, and it was even less safe to fight alone. They also learned to not fight over small grievances. Better to save their bodies for the battle over the most egregious mistreatment – invariably, nonpayment of salary.

The struggle to secure a living wage also took the form of flight. Bao Yuwen, a poor Da Fo farmer who did not get paid by his boss, says, "I have good skills,

---

[62] Ibid., 33–34.   [63] Zhou Chunxue, interview.
[64] Ruan Faxiang, interview; Zhou Chunxue, interview.

and the contractors and subcontractors normally have to treat me well. If they do not treat me well, I would look for a job elsewhere."[65] Some of Da Fo's migrants felt that flight was the only way they could survive. Fifty-eight-year-old Bao Wenpu tells us, "I worked in Tianjin once. The subcontractors were from the Baoding area. They were worse than the Japanese. They forced people to work for fourteen hours a day without any rest breaks. They cursed the workers all the time, urging them to work harder and harder. The food they provided was bad. I could not stand it, and so after one month I ran away."[66]

For most of Da Fo's migrant workers, flight from the workplace was not the norm, however. Why? The answer is complex, though grounded in the simple existential dilemma of the workers. To begin with, the rate and massive volume of rural-to-urban migration worked against construction workers who made the quick decision to move to other job sites. This was especially true for those without skills, which was the case for most of Da Fo's wondering semi-farmers. Finding another job in an overcrowded industry was exceedingly difficult. Many of Da Fo's migrant laborers were therefore reluctant to "jump ship." I was astonished to discover that nearly half of Da Fo's migrant workers not only stayed with subcontractors who failed to pay them for months on end but also returned to work for the same subcontractors after taking a temporary six- or nine-month "leave" spurred by disgust over unpaid wages. Many went back to labor bosses they knew on the slight hope they might be able to retrieve overdue wages.

One might surmise that the authoritarian structure of the workplace itself also worked against flight, and indeed this was the case. Many work sites were patrolled by guards hired by the construction companies. After 2004, some of the subcontractors and their armed retainers confiscated workers' state-issued identity cards in exchange for making temporary residence arrangements for the Da Fo workers, making it more difficult for workers to walk away from the job site.[67] But it seems that a more important second factor mitigated against flight: the fear of stepping back out into the world of pickpockets, robbers, and con artists who were ready to prey on the migrant workers.

Bao Xiaojian, a twenty-one-year-old migrant worker, says that his brother did not like working in Beijing construction because the urban people looked down on construction workers and saw them as inhuman. But that was not the real problem. Referring to the years 1998–2001, Bao says, "My brother was cheated when he answered an advertisement which said migrant workers would be paid 1,300 yuan per month after signing up for a training program. When he went there the people said he had to put down a 600-yuan deposit. For the first few weeks of training, there was no pay. After several weeks, my brother realized that fewer and fewer of the applicant workers were showing up at the

---

[65] Bao Yuwen, interview.   [66] Bao Wenpu, interview.
[67] Chan found this kind of restraint much earlier. See Chan, "Boot Camp at the Shoe Factory."

job site. He was not sure what was going on. He left and lost 600 yuan."[68] In this same period, Bao Xiaojian himself suffered the fate of many other naive and good-hearted migrant workers when he became the victim of street-level con artists. "A couple asked me for help," recalls Bao. "They said they had lost their son, and they needed money to purchase train tickets to look for him. I gave them ten yuan. But I later realized that I had been cheated by them. There are many people doing this kind of thing in the cities. It was their profession."[69]

A fourth factor inhibiting flight was the fear of being swept up in police dragnets. If the migrant workers could not quickly land a new job on leaving a previous one, they could find themselves wandering for days and weeks across city landscapes. This state of drift made them vulnerable to police round-ups of migrant workers, for many of them, like their counterparts from across China, lacked residence permits.[70] In the first half of 2000, Beijing police rounded up 180,000 migrants and locked them up in preparation for deportation back to the countryside, a practice that continued in the post-2000 period despite the fact that the State Council had abolished the law that authorized the repatriation of internal migrants back to their home counties and villages.[71]

Da Fo's migrant workers lived in fear of deportation. For most of them, a forced return to rural farming was out of the question: they depended on income earned in the construction sector to sustain the economy of the household farm itself. By 2000, the great majority of Da Fo's mobile farmers counted on income from construction to cover 60 percent of their basic household budgetary needs, up 10 percent from 1990. Those who were paid relied on this income to purchase seeds, chemical fertilizers, insecticides, and tools for cultivating their family fields. And city-based construction work served another purpose: nearly half of the migrant workers had to earn money in construction work to pay for the medical prescriptions, treatments, and hospital visits of aged parents, wives, and children back in Da Fo – and, if possible, to cover their own health crises. Seen in this context, an empty-handed return to the village was not only a blow to the male migrant workers' efforts to put food on the table and steer clear of health-cost–related debt but also a blow to their pride and self-esteem. The work in the city was hard, yet even with its injustices and injuries, it allowed Da Fo's farmers to hold out some hope for a better life. To return empty-handed to the village was to return to a poor, fragile existence.

SUBCONTRACTORS, CRONY CAPITALISM, AND THE INHERITED PAST

Many accounts of migrant construction work in the reform era underscore the differences from the Great Leap past – including the workers' newfound

---

[68] Bao Xiaojian, interview.   [69] Ibid.   [70] Cf. Guang, "Guerrilla Workfare," 495.
[71] Van Luyn, *City of Floating Peasants*, 89.

mobility and the opportunities they acquired to obtain off-farm income. To be sure, there was a break with the past, but it was not a clean separation. As we have seen, urban construction work was in some ways just as restrictive for Da Fo's migrant farmers as the collective era had been for them and for their parents. The patterns of collective-era exploitation continued to play themselves out in worker treatment. This should come as no surprise, considering that many of the subcontractors who supervised workers had themselves been schooled in the work habits of CCP cadres and that regulations governing work were not earnestly enforced by officials.

At the outset of reform, many contractors were CCP officials who used their political power and leverage to form construction companies, which in turn allowed them to establish monopolies over the construction business in urban-cum-regional core market networks extending out to the rural county and subcounty level. The subcontractors usually were clients of these powerful actors. Bao Zhanghui, whose education was delayed because of the Great Leap famine, had to plow the land, pull donkey carts piled with black-market grain, collect chicken droppings to sell as fertilizer for melons, and steal grain from the collective fields to survive the post-Great Leap decade. Sixty-three years old when interviewed in the winter of 2008, Bao Zhanghui has deep knowledge of how the rural political economy has evolved in the Henan countryside under reform, and so his take on the construction business in neighboring Wei county, where many of Da Fo's migrant workers had hooked up with subcontractors, is worth noting: "Bo Deli, the party secretary of Dalu village, in Shiruan township, Wei county, was known as a very powerful person in that area. He had three construction companies himself. He had connections with the police and with criminal gangs in Wei county. He had a monopoly over the construction business. In the last couple of decades, when a new county party secretary came to work in Wei county, he and his officials had to visit Bo Deli first in order to get off to a good start in governing the county."[72]

The excessive greed of the subcontractors – and of their politically connected patrons – was not a product of reform pure and simple, but rather the result of a CCP work style that stretched back over time to the crisis of the state-owned construction companies in the immediate aftermath of the Maoist disaster, when the Great Leap famine had strained state finances to the breaking point, leaving many companies without capital and thereby encouraging their managers to engage in various scams. The most common scam was to publicize unfunded projects, offering contracts that were in reality not backed by collateral. As a result, the subcontractors often were underpaid by CCP-based managers, and they frequently passed their losses down to other subcontractors and to poor migrant workers at the bottom rung of the hierarchy. Apparently, the Communist Party never forged any mechanisms for reversing this practice,

---

[72] Bao Zhanghui, interview.

which by the reform period had become self-reinforcing. Under reform, the older "political market" for free labor exploded, with contractors and subcontractors taking as much profit as they could and refusing to share the returns fairly with migrant workers.

The nonpayment of wages in the reform period was, in short, path dependent, the product of a political complexity that had its roots back in the failure of Mao-era state building and industrialization.[73] In reality, the corrupt, fiscally strapped Mao-era state was implicated in the nonpayment of wages to the rural migrant workers who left the villages to work in Beijing, Tianjin, and other North China cities.[74] We cannot grasp the reform-era dilemma of Da Fo's migrant workers without reference to this temporal dimension of politics, for their plight was partly the product of a hard to detect "long-term causal chain" (to borrow Paul Pierson's concept)[75] extending back to the Mao period.

Ruan Shaoqing, who was ten years old when the Great Leap propelled rural China into famine, helps us grasp this chain. After the famine, Ruan's family barely had enough to eat, in part because production team grain was insufficient, and so Ruan was one of the first to leave Da Fo to search for work in the urban areas. In 1969, at the age of nineteen, Ruan began temporary work under a subcontractor in a Tianjin construction company. "The subcontractor was Zhang Bohai, from Zhangbeicun," remembers Ruan, "and I went with him to Tianjin in February. I decided to ask for my pay in July of that year. The job was yet to be finished, and the company changed the management leadership at that time. The company leaders said that they did not know anything about the previous agreement and refused to pay me for the work I had done for the other leaders. In the end, I was shortchanged, and I lost six months of salary. I asked for the money several times, but I was not able to get it from the new leaders. I did not know what had happened. At the time, I was dealing with subcontractors. Later, I also was cheated a couple of times by them. The subcontractors short changed me, and I lost several months' salary. That was very common. Sometimes the subcontractors did not get paid from the company they worked for. The big company could declare bankruptcy, and the boss would run away with the money. So we cannot always blame the subcontractor."[76] Indeed, this is one of the reasons Da Fo's cheated migrant workers often were reluctant to sue the subcontractor in court – they would have to pay the cost of the suit, and besides, the subcontractor might have been swindled himself.

The 2008 *Human Rights Watch Report* on Beijing's failure to rectify the problems created by the state-ensnared construction industry located this

---

[73] Interviews with Ruan Liqin and Ruan Shaoqing; personal conversation with Sarah Swider, September 9, 2008; Pierson, *Politics in Time*, 1–4, 38–34; and North, *Institutions, Institutional Change, and Economic Performance*, and "Transaction Cost Theory of Politics," esp. 362.

[74] I am indebted to Sarah Swider for this insight. Personal conversation, September 9, 2008.

[75] Pierson, *Politics in Time*, 3.   [76] Ruan Shaoqing, interview.

failure in an embedded pattern of state capitalism. Maurice Meisner has argued that this pattern is best understood as "the creation and functioning of a capitalist market [that] is closely entwined with the political power of the Chinese Communist Party."[77] Whereas Meisner's conception holds that the post-1978 global capitalist order more or less "overwhelmed" the socialist ends of the Deng-led reform, Da Fo's migrant workers saw the process differently. They trace reform-era crony capitalism to the entrenched party-state control of the construction market, linking the magnified suffering of migrant workers in the post-1978 period to the less visible suffering of workers under pre-1978 socialist rule, when temporary workers of rural origin were organized by local, rural-based subcontractors with a vague relationship to general contractors obligated to state-owned enterprises.[78] To them, Beijing's rulers created a long-range pattern of abuse. The first significant labor law was passed only in 1995,[79] after which the CCP paid attention mainly to the laws pertaining to the state-owned enterprises and government offices. Referring to the dilemma migrant workers, Da Fo's Ruan Jingwei recalls, "The Central government [still] allowed the private enterprises to abuse the law without doing anything about it."[80]

Although many of the Da Fo migrant workers recognized CCP entanglement with this crony capitalism, they were fearful of challenging it, because they knew this would put them at risk. It was not a matter of expressing a right backed up by law. Even if they had the right, they feared the consequence of exercising it.[81] Actually, some of the migrant workers simply were unprepared to grasp what was being done to them, let alone grasp whether they had a right to do anything about it. Speaking of the migrant workers he had met in the course of his construction work, Bao Chunlin put it this way: "In many cases, the rural migrant workers did not know what was going on when the subcontractors did not pay them, or made life miserable for them. The worker would blame himself for having bad luck. In fact, these bad subcontractors were connected with the police, and the police would protect them even if the migrant workers went to the police to complain; and in most cases, the workers did not know how to complain before the police."[82] No doubt crony capitalism was, as Meisner has argued, part of the problem. But the essence of the problem was that the Communist Party–based "capitalists" who dominated the construction market were too ready to use force – of both formal police units and

[77] Meisner, *Mao's China and After*, 8–10.
[78] Sarah Swider, personal correspondence, July 30, 2014. According to Kang Chao, these temporary, vulnerable construction workers constituted 44 percent of the construction industry work force in the 1960s; see Chao, *The Construction Industry in Communist China*.
[79] I am indebted to Mary Elizabeth Gallagher for this point, and for nudging me to think harder about how the coming of law worked, or did not work, for Da Fo's migrant workers. Personal correspondence, July 28, 2015.
[80] Ruan Jingwei, interview.
[81] On the concept of government-bestowed rights to resist, see O'Brien and Li, *Rightful Resistance*.
[82] Bao Chunlin, interview.

informal thug groups – to impose their parasitic demands on migrant workers. And this is precisely what Mao's cadres had done to exploit the conscripted farmers they mobilized to work on the construction projects of the people's commune.

Which brings us to an intriguing finding. As we learned in the previous chapter, whereas the Central government passed regulations providing more protection for the rights of petitioners,[83] and whereas petitions to the State Office of Letters and Visits in Beijing proliferated between 1995 and 2005, Da Fo's migrant workers by and large eschewed this form of deferential protest – for two reasons.

First, they say that many of the petitioners were people who still held out hope that the Central government would enforce the laws acknowledging their right to a living wage. They, on the other hand, had given up hope, preferring to pursue their struggle for wage justice through low-profile forms of resistance that did not directly engage official channels of redress and possibly also invite police tracking and repression. The reason so many of them pursued their bosses at home was that they agreed with fifty-eight-year-old Bao Yuwen, a carpenter who worked on many construction sites over the years of reform and was cheated out of his wages on more than one occasion. Bao explains: "No government office would help me with this kind of problem. I did nothing else but work fourteen hours a day, but in the end I was not paid. The subcontractors ran away with the money, and got rich in the process. Many other people had a similar experience. This happened because the government did not do enough to protect the workers. It is a big problem in China. I am very angered by this problem."[84]

Second, the migrant workers from Da Fo did not, in any event, trust that the Offices of Letters and Petitions would process their claims swiftly, fairly, or efficiently. They looked upon the CCP officials in charge of these offices with suspicion. To them, the officials were more concerned with controlling petitioners than with helping them, and they knew that the officials had enlisted thugs to silence those who petitioned and had collaborated with local "retrievers" to send the petitioners back the countryside. Petitioning was, to them, too risky.[85]

Although a few of the Da Fo migrant interviewees spoke of suing the subcontractors, the vast majority did not have the time or money for such an undertaking. Furthermore, few trusted that the courts would be able to enforce their legal claims against the subcontractors.[86] Instead, in the mid-1990s they

[83] Davis, "A System Rotting from the Ground Up."   [84] Bao Yuwen, interview.
[85] On this point, also see the careful and grounded interviews of petitioners by Davis, "A System Rotting from the Ground Up." Her documentation of the violent ways in which the post-1978 reform state dealt with migrant petitioners in Beijing resonates with the voiced fears of Da Fo's migrant workers. Cf. Davis et al., "We Could Disappear at Any Time," 1:4.
[86] Ruan Shaoqing, interview.

began to put their trust in a hidden, culturally rooted means of contention for dealing with officially tolerated injustice – a means we will learn about in the chapter to come.

– – –

To sum up, the post-1978 reform offered a way for Da Fo's farmers to escape the serfdom and poverty of the Mao-era collective. The switch to a state-dictated version of household-based farming left many of Da Fo's capital-short, land-short tillers with little choice but to search for work in an urban construction industry designed to serve the party-state's goal of industrial growth and national grandeur. The great majority of the Da Fo–area migrant workers pursued this strategy of survival. They found a rather false liberation from the Maoist past, however. Though better off than their counterparts who had suffered in bondage to Mao-era collective fields, many of Da Fo's migrant workers fell victim to a reform-era version of bonded labor and had to survive in segregated urban work spaces patrolled by subcontractors whose treatment recalled the work style of Communist Party cadres in the Great Leap: lying and betrayal, verbal insults, and physical abuse of the people who were sacrificing to realize what Dorothy Solinger calls the regime's "passion to industrialize ruthlessly."[87]

The Central government leaders fed this passion by fostering an urban labor market that discriminated against migrant workers. On the one hand, they organized the construction industry in a manner that put the party-connected contractors, subcontractors, and migrants into an informal, unprotected market. On the other, they "reformed" the *hukou* system in a way that made for an "unregulated mobility" and transformed the migrant workers into transient outsiders.[88] This "reform" put Da Fo's floaters at the mercy of predatory contractors. Under it, they were hard pressed to independently find employment, and the employers – and the developers they served – were entwined with the party-state. The same ruthless modality of rule that drove Da Fo's workforce over the brink in the socialist Leap of the late 1950s, therefore, resurfaced in the reform era, this time evolving into a greedy, mean version of capitalist development – a development that more often than not left migrant workers, who had few institutionally guaranteed rights, with empty pockets. Trapped in this venal system, Da Fo's migrant workers could have turned to urban crime, but few did. As in the Great Leap, the Central

---

[87] Solinger, *Contesting Citizenship*, 37.
[88] Cf. Wang, "Renovating the Great Flood Gate," 360–363; Brown has shown that this pattern of the CCP treating migrant workers as "illegal immigrants in their own country" has a lineage back to Mao-era discriminatory mechanisms of *hukou* and grain rationing, both of which were implicated in the Great Leap disaster. Cf. Brown, *City versus Countryside in Mao's China*, 1, 5, 10–12, 20–38, 41–42, 51, 69.

government argued that the local party leaders – or in this case, the subcontractors – were venal, while its own intentions were good. Yet in reality the reform-era construction industry was configured by the center's policy, and so Beijing was implicated in the false promise of wages.[89]

Whereas previous scholarship has focused on the rising inequalities between poor, interior-based farmers and rich, coastal-based urbanites,[90] Da Fo's migrant workers do not fit neatly into either category. For decades, they lived a back-and-forth existence between their farms and urban construction sites. Hence, they had to maneuver for their livelihood within the least secure tier of what Martin King Whyte has termed a "three-caste system"[91] – an apartheid system that was far worse than apartheid in Afrikaner-ruled South Africa, where black migrant workers benefited from powerful trade unions, space for street-level discourse and concerted resistance (including spontaneous work stoppages), and apparently, in some cases, the freedom to pick up and return to their homelands with saved wages.[92] As bonded laborers with few of these assets, Da Fo's migrant workers shared a great fear of becoming displaced persons.[93] For many, the experience in the construction industry sector only intensified this fear.[94] Subjected to theft of wages by contractors and subcontractors who frequently were connected with the Communist party-state, the migrants grew angry not only over rank inequality but also over the revival of exploitative labor practices that had originally crystallized in the episode of the Great Leap – practices that compounded the difficulty of finding adequate security and minimal dignity under reform.

The Ministry of Labor officials appointed in the Deng era failed to dismantle forms of labor management that were embedded in earlier Mao-era socialist dishonesty, trickery, and chaos, and this failure fostered great worker distrust in the national state.[95] This systematic process ultimately left some of Da Fo's

---

[89] From Sarah Swider, personal correspondence, December 31, 2008.

[90] On the complexity and nuances of this gap, see Sicular et al., "Rural-Urban Income Gap," 102–103; Davis and Wang Feng, *Creating Wealth and Poverty*; and Wang, *Boundaries and Categories*.

[91] Whyte, *One Country, Two Societies*, 15. On the persistence of the state-originated *hukou* system that helps perpetuate this caste system, see Mallee, "Migration, Hukou and Resistance," 99–100; Zhao, "Rural Urban Migration in China," 6–9, 16–17; and Chan and Buckingham, "Is China Abolishing the Hukou System?," 582–583, 587–588.

[92] Denise Walsh, personal correspondence, February 4, 2009, and September 12, 2011. Cf. Worden, *Making of Modern South Africa*, 134, 140, 143; Clark and Worger, *South Africa*, 71–73, 91, 99; Thompson, *History of South Africa*, 208–209, 224–225; and Bozzoli, *Theaters of Struggle*, 88–89, 96–97, 190–192.

[93] As He Qinglian's work on China's "peasant problem" would suggest. "Relationship between Chinese Peasants' Right to Subsistence."

[94] Ibid., 77–79, 81.

[95] As Pu Ngai and Lu Huilin have pointed out, the dismantlement and corruption of the labor subcontracting system began in 1958 at the outset of the Great Leap Forward. Pu and Lu, "Culture of Violence," 146–147.

migrant workers to rely on a cultural weapon of self-defense that local Communist Party leaders and their high-positioned allies in Beijing had good reason to fear. If, as Pu Ngai and Liu Huilin have shown,[96] some construction industry migrant workers resorted to self-destructive actions such as suicide to protest the broken promises of contractors and their thugs, Da Fo's migrant workers took another path, mobilizing a physical form of self-protection that had been around for millennia to secure their wages. The violent imposition of the Great Leap and its debilitating hunger more or less precluded engagement with this form, but in the twenty years after the Leap famine, and continuing well into the first decade of reform, rural people in Da Fo and scores of surrounding villages started to resurrect it to combat the aggressive habits of unreformed power.

---

[96] Ibid., 154–157.

The Rise of the Martial Artists and the Two Faces of Mafia

Notwithstanding the Chinese Communist Party (CCP) subversion of the electoral process, the repression of petitioners, and the exploitation of migrant workers, reform-era Da Fo underwent a subtle but profound change in its politics. The Central government wanted to restore the party's hold on local society, but in the Da Fo area the overall balance of power shifted in favor of a seemingly new social force. The shift, however, was orchestrated by the bearers of an age-old rural culture, and they were influenced, and to some extent driven, by memories of Great Leap–era harm. Operating on an alternative social compact and within a new state–market political economy, the leaders of this counterforce occasionally challenged Da Fo's party leaders for control of village politics. In time, their transvillage networks also penetrated the local police forces ensuring CCP control of the countryside, and so there was cooperation as well as conflict with official power.

In the Great Leap Forward, the Maoists had banned martial arts training in Dongle county and its villages. Furthermore, most of the farmers who knew martial arts and taught it to villagers were so emaciated and fatigued that they had no time to practice this activity, let alone to teach it to younger villagers. As a result, few of Da Fo's young villagers learned the arts of self-defense. Its families were more and more at the mercy of village Communist Party bullies who relied on brutal methods to rule. In the two decades following the Great Leap, most Da Fo farmers and their teenage sons were still caught up in a low-grade famine and had to live with long-term poverty and physical diminishment. Under the collective, they received 100 *jin* of grain per capita less than they needed to meet the minimum annual requirement for grain consumption. Most of them lived on sweet potatoes and other inferior tubers to survive. The teenage children who helped them with planting and harvesting were often very thin and weak, and thus unable to fully engage in family agricultural tasks. Once Da Fo party boss Bao Zhilong regained power in the last years of the

Cultural Revolution, moreover, farmers' fears of having to deal with commando Bao and his brutish clients and cronies were renewed.

In this political situation, many farmers and their children felt humiliated. To build up their bodies, they entered into secret pacts with some of the older martial arts teachers in Da Fo and scores of border area villages. Du Yufeng, who was fifty-three years old when interviewed in the summer of 2008, gives us a hint of how this process unfolded in Pingyuandi village: "I was working with Zhang Kaifa in the collective fields during the Cultural Revolution years. At the time, I was fourteen years old. I was very thin and weak. Zhang Kaifa suggested that I should study martial arts to get myself stronger. He said he would be willing to teach me. This Zhang Kaifa liked to tell us stories about his youth during the breaks in the fields. He said his teacher was a great martial arts master. He claimed that he had become very powerful, and he said that one time he had been able to get away from forty people who had wanted to beat him up. I thought that was an amazing feat. Therefore, I started to learn martial arts from him. He would teach me during the breaks while working in the fields. At night, I would go to his house after dinner. The two of us would talk about martial arts skills in his courtyard. He demonstrated to me how to stand and how to strengthen my legs and arms."[1]

More than a few of the young men who turned to martial arts masters did so mainly for health reasons. They were not looking to become athletic boxers pure and simple. Instead, they were stepping back into traditions of martial arts training that had been passed on by their fathers and uncles, who told them, as Bao Xianyong recalls, "that martial arts were an important way to maintain good health"[2] Nonetheless, some of the teenagers who had survived the Great Leap and its famine also took up martial arts to defend their families against institutionalized brutality. When Du Yufeng was five years old, his father pilfered crops from the collective wheat fields in order to avert starvation. He was caught by party leaders and dragged to the public criticism grounds. During this ordeal, Du Yufeng heard people making jokes about his father and was overcome with shame – shame that was reinforced when the police repeatedly showed up to take Du's father in for questioning in subsequent years. Pingyuandi's teenagers would mimic the honk of the police car to young Du each time they encountered him. When Du Yufeng began to study martial arts, he did so because he "wanted to fight [his tormentors] to stop the teasing and shaming." Becoming a fighter brought him the respect he craved, and afterward few dared to taunt Du.[3]

A similar pattern unfolded in Da Fo village, where young survivors of the great famine took up martial arts to defend their families against toughs connected with party boss Bao Zhilong and his clients in the reform period. Under the leadership of skilled martial artist Bao Yinbao, a network of sworn

---

[1] Du Yufeng, interview.   [2] Bao Xianyong, interview.   [3] Du Yufeng, interview.

"brothers" took shape and began to fight back against the local Communist Party power holders. Bao Yinbao became a patron, and many villagers were only too happy to become his clients in exchange for the martial artists' assistance in reclaiming their ancient entitlements, from the right to build houses on their own land to the ability to travel, market their goods, and form networks of mutual support. By the late reform period, this patron–client network had matured into a rural mafia that mobilized violence for its own ends – a mafia torn between its loyalty to fulfilling the needs of local tillers and the demands of its involvement with government via corrupt ties to the police state.

HOW MARTIAL ARTISTS SUPPLANTED COMMUNIST LEADERSHIP IN DA FO

To grasp this temporal process, let us listen to Bao Yinbao, who became the leader of the martial artists in Da Fo and scores of surrounding villages in this remote triprovincial border area in the 1990s. Bao Yinbao left school in 1979 at fifteen, the same year his family began fighting with another Da Fo family. "My family had few people," he remembers, "and we could not defend ourselves." While only his father, sister, and elder brother could fight – Bao Yinbao himself was "too young to be of much help" – "the other family had more people, and beat us very badly." The village had no police presence at the time, and as for the party leaders, "there was nothing they could do."

The family that beat up Bao Yinbao's family was that of Bao Haifeng, who subsequently had been chosen Da Fo village chief by party secretary Bao Shunhe, the client of Great Leap boss Bao Zhilong. Bao Haifeng, had a big family and several brothers behind him, and he beat many Da Fo families into submission in the last years of Maoist rule. However, not every one of them gave up. Some decided to settle the score in a way that led them to self-defense training beyond Da Fo. Bao Yinbao explains, "I decided to leave home to study martial arts in order to someday avenge my family." He left home to attend a martial arts school in Yuncheng, Shandong province – the hometown of Song Dynasty rebel Song Jiang. There, Bao Yinbao learned of the *Shuihuzhuan*, a novel that tells the story of Song Jiang and his 108 brothers. Bao received strenuous training at the school, whose teachers imposed strict discipline backed by beatings. He became one of the school's first three hundred graduates. "Today," he says, "Yuncheng Martial Arts School is the best in China." After four years, he left to study in western Shandong with Dai Weijian as one of a group of student recruits who showed great potential. Bao spent another four years studying with Dai Weijian.[4]

---

[4] Bao Yinbao, interview.

According to Bao Fengyi, the mother of Bao Yinbao, young Bao was humiliated by the beating delivered by party-connected bullies, especially because his brother and sister had suffered serious injuries. Bao's anger over the beating drove him to earn money by mending old shoes and repairing umbrellas by day on the streets of Heze, in western Shandong, to pay for study with a martial arts teacher in the evenings.[5] The nighttime training became an obsession, and he embraced each session with great concentration. By the time Bao departed Heze, he had found a survival tool he could rely on to defend his family and meet the challenge of local bullies without fear.

Having transformed his body into a "weapon of the weak,"[6] Bao Yinbao returned to Da Fo village in 1986. He quickly challenged all of the alleged martial arts experts in the Da Fo area, as well as in Liangmen township, Dongle county, Wei county, and the greater Puyang area. Few dared to fight Bao, but those who did learned their lesson. Bao quickly earned a reputation by defeating Ruan Qingyuan, the son of powerful martial arts teacher Ruan Tianbao. He was later ambushed by Ruan Qingyuan and forty of his students, but he escaped. "In the first few years, when I came back to Da Fo from Shandong, I beat so many martial artists in this area," Bao Yinbao remembers. "Looking back, today, I should not have done that. Once I earned the reputation of being number one, I should have fought less. I was too proud at the time, and I wanted to beat anyone who claimed they were good in martial arts."[7]

As Bao Yinbao's reputation spread to surrounding villages and counties, people from near and far came to the Da Fo area to befriend him, because, Bao says, "Once they were my friends, they felt I would be willing to fight on their behalf." Bao made many friends and became "sworn brothers" with a number of people, following the practice "passed down from the olden times" and modeled on both the *Shuihuzhuan* and the *Sangguo Yanyi* (The Romance of Three Kingdoms), in which three men swear an oath "that if one of them died, the other two would risk death to avenge him."[8] By the end of the first decade of the reform era, farmers, small business folk, and even real estate developers were seeking Bao Yinbao's friendship. Many of these suitors wanted Bao to serve as their bodyguard and retainer. With the breakup of the collective and its common lands, fights over property rights, petty theft (which had been rampant after the great famine), and robbery of people who had to travel to dispersed fields and markets became common, partly because neither the local party-state nor the Central government organized effective protection for the rural people in this remote border area.

Who were these young martial artists who flocked to Bao Yinbao's side? Most were young men of a social background similar to his own. The Great Leap had decimated many of Da Fo's families, leaving a large number of

---

[5] Bao Fengyi, interview.   [6] Scott, *Weapons of the Weak*.   [7] Bao Yinbao, interview.
[8] Ibid.

households with only one male child or with one or two thin, weak, sickly offspring. This put these small families at the mercy of the callous Communist Party leaders who enlisted local militia bullies to maintain their hold on power. In the postfamine decades, Da Fo farmers pined to produce as many sons as possible. By the time the 1978 reform commenced, some households had three and four sons. They by and large could stand up for the family against Da Fo party leaders, who no longer had an organized, ruthless militia to do their bidding. The party leaders, therefore, attempted to coopt strong-armed, multiple-son households, leaving smaller, weaker families to fend for themselves in skirmishes with leaders over tax, birth planning, and tuition grievances and in feuds with some of the larger, stronger families. The weaker households with only one son, or with two weak sons, were extremely vulnerable. From 1978 to 1985, when there were only a few police in the Da Fo–Liangmen area, Bao Zhilong and the other Da Fo party leaders stepped back and allowed the larger, stronger families to beat the weaker ones. The Liangmen township government did little to protect or compensate the weaker, shredded families.

Violence had different victims in the reform era. Smaller families whose fathers or sons were injured badly had to suspend work in the fields for long periods. Moreover, this phenomenon occurred simultaneously with the Deng Xiaoping–orchestrated *yanda* campaign that reframed the desperate efforts of these undercapitalized, undermanned farm households to resurrect family-based agriculture as "criminal,"[9] thereby pushing poor farmers off of the land into the cities. Many of the younger males (usually aged fifteen to twenty-two) from these marginalized, battered families set out to acquire martial arts skills that would enable them to defend their families against further violence, taking refuge in martial arts orders that provided a bond of friendship and hence a surrogate version of protective family life. As we have seen, Bao Yinbao himself came from such a small, weakened family. Du Yufeng reports of Pingyuandi village: "Most people who were eager to learn martial arts in our village were people who did not have any brothers. They felt that they needed to learn martial arts to make up for their disadvantage vis-à-vis other villagers, which came from being the only son of their households."[10]

Bao Yinbao and his network of martial arts friends stepped into the evolving political vacuum to assist people who felt vulnerable. Within a decade, they had established themselves as the willing patrons and protectors of both poor farmers and well-to-do folks who were benefiting from economic reform, in both Da Fo village and beyond. These strong young men became – perhaps not always in a premeditated manner – contestants for local power in two other ways, as well, challenging the abilities and the attempts of Da Fo's old-guard Maoists to impose their designs on villagers. In each instance, they moved to

---

[9] Of course, throwing fertilizer from government trucks was "criminal," but the *yanda* public security forces ignored the severity of the crime, not to mention the political pressure driving it.

[10] Du Yufeng, interview.

correct an injustice that had been in place since the Great Leap, and which Deng Xiaoping and his high-level officials had not fully corrected in the remote countryside.

First, Bao Yinbao and the martial artists supported and in a sense symbolized the efforts of poor farmers to regain direct mastery over their land, especially to work and utilize their farm lands without party interventions that had characterized the Great Leap era – and this included the right to build houses on farmlands allocated to them in the 1982–1985 land reform. Bao and most of the people making up his band of brothers were impoverished small tillers themselves, people who, at an early point in the reform process, wanted to develop private household lands, undertake side occupations, and pursue the market in order to benefit their own households. In reality, they were fighting for their right to liberate the family farm as a productive unit from the Da Fo party leaders who had managed land for the commune.[11] They used their martial arts skills to finish the post-1978 land-reform process, carrying out, in the words of one scholar, "a de facto privatization of Chinese farming."[12] Far from being an agent of the concentration of state power, in these early years the Bao Yinbao brotherhood helped to break up the collective and weaken the ability of village- and township-level Communist Party leaders to call on the police powers of county, provincial, and national authorities to automatically enforce regimentation and appropriation locally.

As we saw in Chapter 2, in the mid-1980s, Bao and some of his sworn brothers also stepped into a long-running struggle against socialist state extraction. This struggle – initially led by returned People's Liberation Army (PLA) veteran Bao Timing – intensified in the early 1980s and exploded in 1986–1987, soon after Bao Yinbao returned home. That year, his antitax activity established him as a key leader of antistate appropriation in Da Fo and encouraged other farmers to follow his lead. It also made him de facto leader of an emergent parallel system of informal power in the village – a system that village-level Communist Party leaders could not effectively counter.

Bao explains that he "refused to pay any taxes" when village chief Bao Haifeng, came to collect soon after Bao Yinbao's return from Shandong. Recall that it was Bao Haifeng, whose family had fought with Bao Yinbao's and driven him to study martial arts in the first place. On Bao Haifeng's insistence that the taxes be paid, Bao Yinbao "beat him up very badly." The village leader returned with several members of village government to fight Bao Yinbao, and he threatened them with a knife. Bao Yinbao remembers, "One of my friends and I each had a knife in our hands, and we declared that if they dared to fight with us, we were ready to kill them and kill the entire family of each one of them. I made this threat, and I meant it." Bao Haifeng called in the police

---

[11] On the preference for individualistic and independent household farming, see Nee, "Peasant Household Individualism," 172, and Netting, *Smallholders, Householders*, 250–252.
[12] Smil, "China's Food," 118.

from Liangmenpo, but they knew of Bao Yinbao's reputation and dared not act against him. "It was a fight between the villagers," he says. The police chief advised Bao Haifeng to find a peaceful resolution to the dispute. After a few days, "Bao Haifeng sent one of the elders in his lineage to talk with me. He said that Bao Haifeng and his family did not want to continue the feud and wanted peace. I told him that he could tell Bao Haifeng that I wanted peace, too. But I said that if he caused me any trouble, my friends and I would wipe him and his whole family out completely. After that, we did not fight with one another. But I did not pay any grain tax either."[13]

In the Great Leap and for many years to follow, young farmers such as Bao Yinbao had been powerless to defend themselves against the verbal and physical abuse used to enforce the grain appropriation schemes of Da Fo's Maoists. Now the political psychology that had helped sustain this system had changed. Courageous, entrepreneurial individuals were no longer afraid of encounters with powerful Communist Party leaders who had previously used brutish methods to seize grain needed for family subsistence. Bao Yinbao had challenged this system. Scores of his Da Fo counterparts welcomed this challenge. They understood Bao had been successful by fighting fire with fire, not by consulting some tax adjustment edict of the Central government. More of them wanted Bao's powers.

While Bao Yinbao became the leader of this shift, he was by no means the first Da Fo villager to be successful. The martial arts renaissance in reform-era Da Fo has clear roots in the Great Leap and the efforts of powerless teenagers to advance the material interests of their families in an imperfect Hobbesian world. Ruan Gaiwang, who had survived by joining with other Da Fo children to eat the standing green crops of the collective during the Leap famine, testified in his sixtieth year: "I studied martial arts when I was a teenager, right after the Great Leap Forward. Many of us studied for reasons of self-defense. There were a lot of fights in Da Fo during the collective era. People quarreled with one another over work points, and over the distribution of grain and produce. However, if you knew martial arts, others would only yell at you and not beat you. They were less likely to attack you. After the collective disbanded, there was even more fighting in the village. Villagers stood up for family justice more and more often. In the early years [of reform] the fights were over grain taxes, and sometimes over birth planning issues."[14]

After 1978, Da Fo's old-guard Maoists began to pull back from using brute force to squeeze taxes out of farmers in possession of boxing skills, in part because they did not possess those skills themselves and in part because they no longer could enlist the militia or the police to enforce party-orchestrated public struggles against those who stood up to them. By the 1990–1995 period, the successful tax resistance of a few martial artists had spread. Ordinary farmers

[13] Bao Yinbao, interview.   [14] Ruan Gaiwang, interview.

who were kin and friends began to call on Bao Yinbao and his network of martial artists to act on their behalf. This resource gave many of Da Fo's formerly defenseless farmers the capacity to threaten collective action when confronted by the Communist Party's village- and township-level tax agents.

THE FORMATION OF A PATRON–CLIENT NETWORK OF MARTIAL ARTISTS

We need to know when and how the Bao Yinbao brotherhood morphed into a mafia, so let us begin with an understanding of what this mafia was. As we have seen, Bao's brotherhood had its roots in the concept of a physically empowered individual, capable of fending for himself and his family against arbitrary state force – a concept that had been overthrown by the Communist Party and its violent political base in the Great Leap. Bao Yinbao and his friends started out as a loose confederation of martial artists intending to once again put this concept into practice. The power vacuum stemming from the collapse of the collective magnetized other villagers to their cause. During the era of conflict over grain taxes, birth-planning, and government-monopolized agricultural imports described by Ruan Gaiwang, "people fought with their bare hands."[15] This gave the upper hand to the martial artists, in part because the reform-era township police force was relatively new, weak, and somewhat intimidated. The quick transition to a market economy overseen by a party-state that had destroyed the arts of administrative governance, and whose agents by and large were oblivious to the rule of law, was also a crucial factor in the mafia path of the Bao Yinbao brotherhood, for this brotherhood was only providing the protection its members, and many other rural people, were seeking to survive market entry in a system where the party-state still held more than a few monopolistic advantages and was quick to impose rents on new businesses.

Still, what explains the development of a secretive relationship with local power, particularly the police, that will be documented in the pages to come? There are, I believe, two answers to this question, one of which can be found only in the oral history testimonies of Bao Yinbao's sworn brothers. According to Ruan Xiaokang, a close friend and former student of Bao Yinbao, "Most of our sworn brothers in the government felt insecure about their positions, and that was why they wanted to make sworn brothers with us."[16] In other words, in the early, uncertain years of reform, the fear of political collapse and social disorder drove the police to align with Bao. Then, toward the end of the 1990s, after the Deng-led reformers had established police order locally through the *yanda* campaign, the police were in a position to provide capital to Bao Yinbao and to afford his network advantages over competitors. This more or less sealed the tension-ridden alliance with local power – an alliance in which Bao Yinbao

---

[15] Ibid.   [16] Ruan Xiaokang, interview.

and his friends occasionally intensified the powers of a local police force with which they were reluctant to deal in the first place but from which they gained hidden support for illegal business operations benefiting their own network.[17]

This does not mean that the primary focus of Bao's politics was on his relationship with formal local power nor that his network formed a political economy that served only its own interest, excluding villagers from its gains and benefits at every turn. Carl Lande, Eric R. Wolf, and James C. Scott have shown that politics in agrarian societies often works through informal groups held together by a host of instrumental relationships, which social scientists term "patron–client relations."[18] The rise of Bao Yinbao reflected this kind of instrumental relationship. Scott's description of patron–client relations more or less captures the pattern of Bao's relationship with the hundred-plus people who studied under him in the reform period. Bao was "a powerful figure . . . who delivered security and benefits to his followers."[19] They in turn demonstrated fidelity and supported Bao and his goals.

Over time, Bao and members of his core martial arts network gained access to training spaces in Da Fo village. They were able to establish a strong cluster of primary and secondary subclients within the village and eventually within many of the surrounding villages – Pengdi, Pingyuandi, and Yuezhuang in the Hebei-Shandong-Henan border area. Operating on the basis of instrumental friendships established with scores of Da Fo farmers in the 1980s, Bao Yinbao was able to provide or help villagers gain scarce material goods and much-needed services that had been lost or severely depleted in the Leap famine and the two decades of dearth that followed it.[20] Yan Chunjian, a forty-one-year-old poor farmer in Yuezhuang and member of Bao Yinbao's network, explained in 2008: "Our goal is to expand this network. Our daily economic activities are centered around this network. We spend a great deal of energy and money and we make great sacrifices for this network, and we get substantial rewards from this network."[21]

At the village level, Bao Yinbao's ascendancy seems to have fueled a "rights movement," helping villagers realize they were no longer at the mercy of previously dominant local party leaders, who had ruled Da Fo with impunity, ignoring social norms of compassion and justice. Bao and his lieutenants became experienced at putting an end to the disorder and mistreatment of farmers by party secretary Bao Shunhe and his mentor, the previously dominant party boss, Bao Zhilong. As the work of Eric Schickler would suggest, the

---

[17] In constructing this section, I have benefited from Chubb, *Mafia and Politics*, 6–12, and Gambetta, *Sicilian Mafia*, 184.

[18] Lande, *Leaders, Factions, and Parties*; Wolf, "Kinship, Friendship, and Patron-Client Relations"; and Scott, *Comparative Political Corruption*.

[19] Cf. Scott, *Comparative Political Corruption*, 92.

[20] On the importance of patrons delivering services to their clients, see ibid., 92–94.

[21] Yan Chunjian, interview.

rise of Bao Yinbao created another layer of power within the institution of reform-era local government, especially at the county level.[22] The presence of this parallel network blurred the dividing line between official and counter-official forces, making it more difficult for the agents of the distant Central government to implement their agenda at the county and subcounty level. The people who had been marginalized and mistreated in the Great Leap had insinuated their way into the lower tier of the reconfigured political order. They had their own ideas of what was best for their village counterparts when it came to political change.[23] They were not just responding to the policy-driven economic dynamics of reform or to the policy-crafted institutional adjustments evolving at various levels of the Communist Party–controlled system; they were emerging as an intermediate network of entrepreneurs who thought of serving the ends of their own brotherhood first. Consequently, they sometimes stood for but other times stood against the interests of the local farming populace. Their network of toughs took on a mafia-like quality.

The efforts of Bao Yinbao and his network involved the recovery of family-controlled farming activities and family-centered off-farm jobs, the provision of basic forms of protection and security, the repair of damaged and frayed social relief arrangements, the restoration of socially acceptable conflict management and dispute resolution practices, the setting up of industrial enterprises with connections to the market economy, and, in some cases, the encouragement and support of members who attempted to start up small business ventures incurring political risk. By 2000, Bao and his clients had also gained a measure of control over the transportation system and the communications network linking Da Fo and surrounding villages to the developing provincial infrastructure of reform – and ultimately to the national economy centered on megacities, including Beijing, Tianjin, and Qingdao. Finally, and significantly, Bao Yinbao and his friends were able to gain favor with Communist Party–appointed police operatives in scores of border area counties. This hidden alliance gave them access to official political resources and capital and enabled them to call on agents of the local police to support their efforts to stake out economic terrain and, in the process, empower themselves and their followers.

Basic Subsistence Services, Everyday Livelihood

The lack of clear legal protections for rural property owners under reform engendered popular distrust of the state and its commitment to keep its local agents from interfering with family-held lands, personal property, and land-use practices. The Bao Yinbao–led martial artists and the mafia that formed around their activities restored this trust in several ways. First, the network played an

---

[22] Schickler, *Disjointed Pluralism.*
[23] In developing this argument, I have drawn on Pierson, *Politics in Time,* 137–140; Schickler, *Disjointed Pluralism*; and Thelen, "How Institutions Evolve."

important role in the efforts of farmers to build family houses on family lands. This became a highly contentious issue in Da Fo, Pingyuandi, and Yuezhuang villages, where the martial artists were based. In the Mao era, the commune government did not allow farmers to build houses on their lands. Villagers were to live collectively, and private homes were destroyed, their materials used by the collective. With decollectivization, tillers regained the right to work on household plots, but the land remained state owned and managed, and villagers did not enjoy the right to use the land as they saw fit. Even in the early 1990s, it remained an ordeal for farmers to obtain permission from local party leaders to build private homes on their land. After 1995, the Liangmen township government gave in to great pressure to allow construction of houses on land previously cultivated. Township officials approved applications for building lots in return for under-the-table fees. Most farmers in the vicinity of Da Fo had no choice but to surrender to this system of bribery. But the members of Bao Yinbao's network, with good friends in the township government and the police bureau, avoided these fees, thus regaining their land-use rights without penalty.[24]

The Bao Yinbao–led martial artists also provided jobs for insecure farmers. After returning to Da Fo, Bao Yinbao became an itinerant martial arts teacher, providing lessons to border-area youth in return for small fees, gifts, and meals. A few of his friends followed suit. Several did well after opening martial training academies. Sun Deshi, one of his sworn brothers, started an academy in Anyang. Enrolling two thousand students, Sun accumulated more than 30 million yuan in assets.[25] In the reform period, Bao Yinbao started a number of businesses, including a coal mine in Jiakou county, Shanxi province. Bao hired Da Fo's Ruan Xiaokang as a the mine's manager, and the two men hired another twenty farmers to open up this coal mine. An illegal criminal undertaking of sorts, it used Sichuan migrant workers to do the dangerous work of bringing up the coal. Like so many small-scale mines, this one had atrocious working conditions and bad accident rates, so that its managers were reproducing the exploitation that poor farmers suffered at the hands of the party-state.[26]

A few of Bao Yinbao's martial artist clients also were able to piggyback on Bao's entrepreneurial successes, saving enough money and acquiring enough knowledge about how to negotiate the treacherous political terrain between township government leaders and local farmers in faraway places to start up their own business operations. Bao Xianyong, whose uncle had been Da Fo's oldest martial arts master in the pre-1949 period, went to work in urban construction around 1980, but he found job security only after he became connected with Bao Yinbao and his friends in the early 1990s. "As Bao

---

[24] Yan Chunjian, interview.   [25] Bao Yinbao, interview.
[26] Ruan Xiaokang, interview. I am indebted to Steven I. Levine for helping me develop this point. Personal correspondence, September 28, 2013.

Yinbao's friend," says Bao Xianyong, "I worked with him on his coal mine to make money. Then I was able to start my own iron-ore mine in Shanxi with his help and connections."[27]

The failure of the township and village enterprise system in the Dongle–Wei county area nudged many Da Fo farmers into black-market activities bound up with theft, requiring protection from members of the Bao Yinbao–led mafia and their friends in the uniformed local police. Yan Chunjian, of Yuezhuang, got to know Bao Yinbao through his martial arts training in the 1982–1985 period of land division, after which Yan took up farming. Barely able to produce enough grain for household consumption and looking to avoid work in Tianjin construction, Yan Chunjian first sought off-farm income by raising pigs. That did not work out. Yan then joined with his uncle to start up a new business in dog meat in the Da Fo–Yuezhuang area. This business found a regional, national, and international market. By 1995 Yan and his uncle were buying dogs from people in this interior border region, processing them, and then selling the meat to Korea as well as cities in Northeast China. When they killed off most of the dog population in the border area, they started to steal dogs from the Tianjin region, and so they ran into trouble with the Tianjin police for operating an illegal enterprise. But Yan's martial artist friends in the local police force tipped Yan off, enabling him to flee with his uncle. Yan explained that being on the police's "wanted" list circumscribed his freedom somewhat, but he could travel within Wei county, where he had "many friends." These friends "spent a lot of money on [his] behalf, bribing police officers with meals and paying their travel expenses."[28]

Yan Chunjian was able to remain in business not just because the Deng Xiaoping–led reformers had relaxed limitations on market activities or because the rural economy was in private hands, but because Bao Yinbao and his men had succeeded in planting "private networks" within public coercive structures. Distant, urban-based police units could no longer automatically compel local forces to do their bidding, as had been the case in the Mao era. In the Great Leap, outside security forces had worked hand in hand with Mao-loyal militia, and police forces could subject black marketeers to savage public criticism and distant labor camp sentences. Now, however, the local Dongle county police stood to benefit from protecting tough, local entrepreneurs who less feared national power. Those in Bao Yinbao's mafia not only were able to secure protection from their well-positioned friends, they also could make outsiders pay for meddling in market space.[29]

---

[27] Bao Xianyong, interview. [28] Yan Chunjian, interview.

[29] E. J. Hobsbawm reminds us that *mafioso* leaders such as Bao Yinbao have appeared and thrived in such space. In developing this point, I have benefited from Hobsbawm, *Primitive Rebels*, 30–51; Gambetta, *Origins of Mafias*, 2, and "Mafia," 128; and Shvarts, "Rational Mafia," 69–71.

Protection and Security

The Da Fo–based martial arts teachers and their students in other villages offered protection to villagers faced with daily threats from both arrogant local Communist Party leaders and the savagery of the labor market. This protective shield appealed to farmers who had long been abused by local party leaders and to those who now faced uncertainty and danger in migrant work. Between 1985 and 2000, the Da Fo area was swept up in a martial arts craze. With subsistence and strength regained in the first reform decade, and with money saved from handiwork and petty trade, young farmers increasingly took up training under Bao Yinbao and other master teachers. Again Da Fo village and Dongle county became the site of *gongfu* contests. Between 1985 and 1990, scores of families sent their sons to train under Bao Yinbao. They made it difficult for boss Bao Zhilong to rule by brute force. They frequently challenged Bao Zhilong and his clients, occasionally threatening to beat their sons if they attempted to complicate efforts to regain household security.[30]

Their involvement with the Dongle county police, where their alternative network of sworn brothers was nested, gave them the power to counter the efforts of Da Fo party leaders to keep them subservient. In response to a 1989–1993 wave of antiparty arson within Da Fo, the police invariably arrived far too late to find any suspects. They were not inclined to faithfully investigate and frequently allowed their "friends" to get off with a token fine. In the village, the martial artists' use of violence to achieve their version of reform and their "submerged power" were generally understood to be acceptable when compared with the arbitrary, wicked violence imposed by Bao Zhilong and his network.[31]

The most pressing need of many of Bao Yinbao's clients was to secure wages earned in the construction industry. Some of the farmers who learned martial arts used this skill to stop subcontractors from cheating them out of promised salaries and to protect themselves from the wolfish order of the Communist Party's version of statist economic development. After dropping out of middle school, Bao Jianjun, a student of Bao Yinbao, worked in urban construction, suffering under the harsh labor regime documented in the previous chapter. Yet Bao was able to successfully deal with the threat of salary nonpayment by taking action to defend his claim. As Bao remembers it, "I nearly always got paid my salary. ... One had to be smart while working outside of the village. There were a lot of bad people out there who were prepared to take advantage of you if you gave them the slightest opportunity. Of course, in my case, I would beat the hell out of the people who wanted to cheat me, and so the subcontractors had to think twice if they did not want to pay me any salary."[32]

---

[30] Cf. Thaxton, *Catastrophe and Contention*, 215–216.
[31] The term "submerged power" is from Fentress, *Rebels and Mafiosi*, 155.
[32] Bao Jianjun, interview.

Many Da Fo farmers sent their sons to study martial arts for this very reason – to give them the necessary skills to endure the hardships and injuries they encountered on construction job sites. Their neighbors followed suit. Farmers in Yuezhuang village paid for their sons' martial arts training in the Tian Shi Martial Arts School in Anyang to defend themselves in their encounters with powerful construction industry tigers beyond the village.[33] Ruan Xiaokang, who studied martial arts with Bao Yinbao in Da Fo and then ventured out to work in construction, became "stronger and quicker" through his training. When he was attacked at a construction site in Shanxi, he fended off five assailants before his friends came to the rescue. "Without martial arts training," he says, "I would have been killed that day."[34] When migrant workers from Da Fo were cheated out of their wages, they could summon their sworn brothers from Da Fo itself and from other nearby villages and townships to confront the subcontractors who stole their labor power, ripping away their sense of self-worth. Mobilizing small groups from their martial arts networks, therefore, became important in the violent struggle to survive in "harmonious China."

Crisis Social Relief

The dearth of the Great Leap, along with the starvation-related deaths of household members and the shredding of families, left many farmers with no one to depend on for a loan to get through hard times. Few friends or neighbors had the strength or the means to help them provide their kin with funeral rites and burial services. Bao Yinbao's friends began to address this issue, and they were seen by fellow villagers as making up for the sins of a state that had stripped farm families of the ability to engage in various forms of joint family self-help and friendship-based caring that had been at the center of Han village civilization. Accordingly, Bao Jianqiao, who recalls he was weak and in poor health "all of the time" in the last years of Maoist rule, learned martial arts to build up his body at the behest of his father. In the process, Bao found friends in martial arts circles, in both Da Fo and the wider border region.[35] These friends, he explains, "will always lend us money if they have it, and they will not ask us to pay the money back before we have it." Access to such generosity is no small matter in a rural area where bank loans to farmers are unheard of.

Bao's jubilation over finding "brothers" among his fellow martial artists was conditioned substantially by his belief that "One simply needs friends to do many things in the countryside. A person without friends in the village will find life very difficult. Quite apart from playing and drinking, one just needs friends to help with life." To Bao, this friendship-based assistance included help with building a house, preparing for the marriage of a child, and, more than

---

[33] Yan Chunjian, interview.   [34] Ruan Xiaokang, interview.   [35] Bao Jianqiao, interview.

anything else, making funeral arrangements for loved ones. In the Great Leap, people like Bao could not call on friends to spread the word that a grandparent, parent, spouse, or child had died, to dress the body of a dead relative, or to put a deceased family member in a coffin and carry the dead person to a burial spot. The Maoist state undermined these practices. Families began to solicit the help of Bao Yinbao and his friends and followers in recovering ancestral burial grounds and reinventing precollective mourning rituals and customary funerary passages of close kin into a tranquil celestial kingdom. (I will return to this subject later in the chapter.)

Conflict Management and Dispute Resolution

In an insightful essay, Judith Chubb points out that highly personalistic mafia networks flourish in environments characterized by the disintegration of customary political arrangements and the penetration of market networks in an age not yet dominated by a modern national state, that is, not regulated by the rule of law. Mafia gained respect and legitimacy with local people as they began to "seek ways to regulate the intense war of all against all, which would otherwise tear the society apart and threaten its own position."[36] This search led mafia into conflict management and dispute mediation where the central state was mistrusted and incapable of coping with complex social and political conflict.[37] The Da Fo–based "mafia" that centered around Bao Yinbao dealt with these services in the reform period, mediating and resolving conflicts even at a transcounty level.

By 1992, Bao Yinbao and his band of martial artists had gained respect and esteem throughout the village. They had begun to supplant the CCP leaders previously charged with mediating and resolving disputes. When property rights and land-boundary disputes between villagers arose, Bao and his followers stepped in to settle them.[38] People outside Da Fo sought them out to mediate disputes too, especially the ones that threatened to tear society apart. Speaking of the post-Deng period of reform, in the summer of 2008 Bao Yinbao declared: "I have a big reputation as a martial arts master, and villagers also respect me. When there was a fight in Da Fo village, they often came to me to settle their disputes. When I came out to help them settle their disputes, they usually listened to me. This has been very common. Even people from other places came to me for help when they were in disputes with others. A few days ago, two parties got into a fight on Highway 6 in Daming county. One of the parties was from Henan province, and the other was from Hebei. The Hebei party got reinforcements from the Handan area, and the Henan party got reinforcements from the Puyang area. The fight appeared to be very menacing and they did not

---

[36] Chubb, *Mafia and Politics*, 6, 11.   [37] Ibid., 11–12.

[38] See Thaxton, *Catastrophe and Contention*, 316.

know how to end the conflict. In the end, they came to me. Because I knew both parties, I was able to settle the dispute for them. I reasoned with them and convinced the side who was at fault to give the other party some money for a banquet. They agreed, and the dispute was resolved."[39]

Influence over Rural Transport and Communication Networks

In southern Italy, the mafia brotherhoods formed not out of pathological criminal designs but rather in response to the popular need for protection of commercial pathways in a rocky transitional period.[40] The Sicilian mafia became an independent supplier of protection and services in a region where the state could not be trusted. The mafia used the power of its network to generate profits from overseeing the flow of market-bound commodities.[41] The Da Fo–based mafia functioned in a similar manner. With the disbanding of the collective and the failure of the Central government to lawfully regulate regional and provincial transportation and communication, Bao Yinbao's network was able to operate in the interstices of state power and modify transportation fees to local petty traders, allowing them to circumvent the claims of the greedy party-driven state on goods in transit. Bao Yinbao himself provides an example of this practice: "A few years ago, in 2005, the government built a new bridge in Shangcun with a bank loan. In order to pay back the loan, the government set up a checkpoint at the bridge to collect money from cars and trucks. For a truck the fee was 60 yuan. However, I started to work that highway at night. I charged the truck drivers only 50 yuan, and I would get them through the checkpoints. The drivers wanted my service because they could save 10 yuan. The people who were working the checkpoints knew my reputation, and they wanted to become my friends. So they allowed me to pass through the checkpoint without paying the fees, and then I would collect the 50 yuan from each driver. When I was not busy with anything else, and when I needed money, I would do this on the highway, and I could make a few hundred yuan each night."[42]

Whereas this might be taken as extortion pure and simple, Bao's network was providing a popular, lower-cost alternative to the squeeze of the local party-state, whose police agents charged transportation tolls on the public. The police members of Bao Yinbao's "soft mafia" also helped farmers whose motor carts were confiscated for not being properly licensed to retrieve their carts with minimal fines and to use cell phone technology to alert Bao and his brotherhood to the whereabouts of traffic police with modern radar guns.

---

[39] Bao Yinbao, interview.
[40] Gambetta, *Origins of Mafias* and *Sicilian Mafia*; see the review of Gambetta in Shvarts, "Rational Mafia," 76–77. On the mafia as a violent business enterprise engaged in territorial expansion, also see Lupo, *History of the Mafia*.
[41] Shvarts, "Rational Mafia," 77–78.   [42] Bao Yinbao, interview.

Many of the brotherhood members were on police wanted lists. Moving incognito from village to village, Bao's men used a secret internal cell phone number system to avoid arrest when they traveled on the main county highways.

This was not violent mafia collusion with officials pure and simple. It was a parallel system that was in competition with the local party-state and its police machinery. One of Bao Yinbao's friends elaborates how this system benefited its members: "Bao Yinbao," says Bao Xianyong, "takes the trucks to pass through the checkpoints at Shangcun bridge. This is easy money for him. Because I am his friend, I was able to drink with the people who worked at the checkpoint too, and in the end I also was able to become friends with these people. So I also take trucks through the checkpoints now and then, particularly on the nights when Bao Yinbao was away. I made quite a bit of money doing this. Of course I have to take the people who man the checkpoints to eat and drink a lot, and in this way we share the benefits together. This is how Chinese society operates today."[43]

Nonetheless, Bao Yinbao did in fact collude with officials, and this collusion proved crucial for business in the transport sector. In 2008, during his prison stay (more on this later), Bao was able to start up a bus company with lines running from Shangcun township to Shijiazhuang and Tianjin. Bao paid 670,000 yuan for a fifty-seat bus, and while Bao himself put in 100,000 yuan, he tells us that "two of my police friends put up 500,000 yuan, and another put up the rest of the capital."[44] The company had the earmarks of mafia, or so Bao revealed at the time of its launch: "As soon as my buses start running," he declared, "nobody will be allowed to run the same bus line anymore. I do not need to beat anybody. I just need to tell the other bus company owners that I have chosen this line, and they will have no choice but to give up and find other routes. Yesterday, I went to Qingfeng county to tell my friends to make sure that when my bus arrives the passengers will be channeled onto my bus first. This is how I will do business."[45] Bao Yinbao's dominance over the key bus transport routes was secured through hidden connections with public force. "According to the government's code of conduct," says Bao, "the government officials are not allowed to run private businesses, but many of my police friends are still doing it. They cannot publicize it. The deputy police chief of Dongle county is my sworn brother, and the two officers who are buying the bus line with me are the heads of Dongle county public security force and the chief of the Shangcun township police. When these police friends of mine travel to Shijiazhuang, they call me to see if my friends can make arrangements for them, and I usually can find some of my friends to provide a banquet for them."[46] In short, with the threat of public force on his side, Bao did not need

---

[43] Bao Xianyong, interview.   [44] Bao Yinbao, interview.   [45] Ibid.   [46] Ibid.

to beat anybody, for local people knew which buses were secure and which ones were subject to "visits" from Bao's friends.

THE RISE OF VIOLENT ENTREPRENEURS

Da Fo farmers saw Bao Yinbao's help networks as a superior alternative to the physical abuse and material deprivation they had known under Mao-led socialism. Bao and his men gained respect and honor by upholding the moral economy claims of villagers.[47] But the members of the rural mafia network also got involved with the actual economic lives of villagers, helping them to navigate the cutthroat economy of the reform era even as they launched enterprises of their own.[48] And in these endeavors, they used violence to ensure their success. Many of these "violent peasant entrepreneurs" became powerful brokers negotiating the tricky juncture between neglected and distressed agrarian resource landscapes, on the one hand, and the capital-starved provincial-, county-, and township-level officials charged with promoting development on the other – and using force as a tool of these negotiations.

When Bao Yinbao started a small illegal coal mine in Shanxi province, in 2001, he did not have to rely on force to make it possible. He had connections. Because the Central government did not want to issue licenses for coal mine adventures to individuals – and because starting an enterprise in a province other than his own was against the law – Bao Yinbao went through "friends" in the township, county, and provincial governments. He spent 40 percent of his profit on bribes to officials, including the center's inspectors. (Success made it difficult to escape Beijing's radar.) "I had a sworn brother in the provincial supreme court," says Bao, "and he wrote a letter and made a few telephone calls for me to the county government. With his letter and phone calls, I did not have any problem from the county government. The county leaders contacted the township government leaders for me." Apparently, the demand for coal was high, due in part to the multiplication of poorly regulated, carbon-dioxide–spewing coal-fired power plants serving the energy demands of city dwellers. Between 2007 and 2008, the price of coal went from 170 yuan per ton to 800 yuan per ton. In this period, Bao's profits skyrocketed.

Bao Yinbao operated this illegal Shanxi coal mine, employing desperate Sichuan migrant workers without the formal approval of the Central government, with the assistance of local state leaders, who informed him and his clients ahead of time about central and provincial inspections so they could seal the openings of these unsafe, unregulated mines to conceal them from the

---

[47] On the fight for moral economy, see Scott, *Moral Economy*, and Scott, "Moral Economy as an Argument."

[48] This same path was taken by the mafia in postwar Sicily. See Blok, *Mafia of a Sicilian Village*, 7–8.

inspectors. When the inspectors left, Bao quickly started up operations again.[49] "Many county and township government leaders wanted to use me to make money," Bao Yinbao explains. "When I started a business in my name, the capital was mostly from the heads of county government and township governments. They all held shares in my businesses. When I made a profit, I had to share it with them. Nowadays, all the government leaders want to make money, and they are involved in all kinds of business activities secretly and sometimes illegally. The Central government has issued orders forbidding government officials and offices from running business operations. However, many of them still do secretly."[50]

Bao Yinbao and his highly skilled clients also occasionally served the interests of powerful real estate developers, so that they became the retainers of rising local wealth in the border area, which sometimes made for conflict with poor farmers. A Wei county real estate tycoon, Qi Bantian, hired Bao and his friends to kick people out of their homes and throw them off of their lands: "Qi Bantian needed somebody who had good martial arts skills. He heard about my reputation and came to ask me to work for him as his bodyguard. He put me and my friends up in the best hotel in Wei county, and he covered rooms, meals, and drinks. I helped Qi Bantian make a great deal of money in a few years, because I could do things other people could not do."[51] Bao Yinbao paid friends in his network handsomely for their assistance with the evictions, and he was able to collect 40,000 yuan in return for his services. He used this money to open up a restaurant and a liquor store in Puyang, where he had "friends" who allowed him to use buildings free of charge and who arranged for him to avoid taxes on these operations.

Doing business offered a way out of Mao-era poverty. After all, in the Republican era, Da Fo's people had depended on private trade and small business for survival.[52] But the reform-era Da Fo entrepreneurs did not benefit from a legal framework capable of providing orderly and civil market competition. As Minxin Pei has pointed out, the assumption that once market-geared dealings replaced the state-planned economy "everything would be smooth sailing" proved false.[53] The creative urges of small businesspeople ran up against political constraints. In the villages and towns of the Hebei-Shandong-Henan border region, the competition to start, sustain, and grow small business operations was razor-sharp, and new entrants were vulnerable to various attacks. In this situation, businesspeople attempted to secure the services

[49] Bao Yinbao, interview.   [50] Ibid.   [51] Ibid.
[52] On this point, Cf. Parris, "Rise of Private Business Interests," 262–264; on the importance of petty trade for the economic security of small farmers, see Huang, *Peasant Economy*, and Thaxton, *Salt of the Earth*; and on Da Fo, see Thaxton, *Catastrophe and Contention*, chapters 1 and 2.
[53] Pei, *China's Trapped Transition*, 29.

of the Da Fo–connected martial artists. Some embraced violence as a means of dealing with competitors.

To illustrate, let us consider Du Yufeng of Pingyuandi village in Hebei province. A martial artist who began to develop a substantial following among young people in surrounding villages in the transition from Mao to Deng, Du reports that he, too, was a fierce fighter who "was willing to fight for my friends." According to Du, his reputation rose after 1978, and he was recruited by businesspeople looking to secure a dominant market position in the amoral postreform world where, he says, "people were only looking after themselves," because "the collective security and the collective mindset formed during the collective era disappeared very quickly." In this competitive atmosphere, Du Yufeng formed a small private militia, and Du and his followers were hired by some businessmen to beat up their competitors in order to drive them out of business and by others to back them up in retaliatory actions. "I would go with my friends with knives to tell the competitor that he could not conduct business there anymore," he remembers. "I said that if he continued to operate there, he would be cut by my knife-carrying friends." Though he was "mostly bluffing," the threats were effective – and lucrative. "I made a lot of money doing this for people." Young people who needed employment came to live with Du Yufeng. "When I worked the streets," he remembers, "they would follow me everywhere," and "I could easily gather a couple of hundred people to fight." By 2008, Du Yufeng had a three-story fortress and a retinue of a dozen people living with him and drawing a daily pocket-money allowance, as well as a full-time chef to keep them well fed. "They are not obligated to do anything in particular," he says, "but when I need them they must fight for me." He surrounded his house with a moat and purchased a big, fierce Tibetan Mastiff for 200,000 yuan (US$30,000), which he treasured for protection, and in which he took great pride. The dog, according to Du, "is like a Lion. He can kill a person very easily. Yet he is extremely loyal to his owner. No one dares to beat him, including my wife and followers. Only I can play with him or beat him." Du also owned several upscale automobiles, including an imported Land Rover. The license plate on his Land Rover read 00004, which, he says, "is a number usually reserved for the county government leaders, but when my driver is driving me around the police will not stop me, because they are aware of my government connections." "I know many government leaders, including police leaders," he says. "They are my friends. When I need help, I can get them to help me. When they need help, my friends and I will help them." [54]

This mafia side of rural China's market expansion, structured by the violent interventions of martial artist leaders such as Du Yufeng, is by and large invisible to outsiders. Visitors inquiring how Du acquired his wealth would be taken to Du Yufeng's Tea Shop in the town, which sells attractively

---

[54] Du Yufeng, interview.

packaged green tea. Du might even praise the Deng-led reform for making it possible for him to find a niche in the green tea market. This scripted "green tea story" is how Du Yufeng started off the interview, but only a careful reading of the tea leaves reveals how he actually obtained his house, his big car, or his ferocious Tibetan friend. The shadow business of mafia was not a topic easily broached with outsiders.

THE BROTHERHOOD BECOMES A MAFIA

In *China's Trapped Transition*, Minxin Pei has linked the rise of a "decentralized predatory state" to the loss of faith in Mao-era ideology among CCP cadres and to the collapse of Central government arrangements for monitoring and regulating the agents of the party-state locally.[55] This pattern of rule has, according to Pei, fostered the growth of local mafia states in which criminal elements have secretly forged alliances with corrupt subnational officials, thus making the CCP-led local government the captive of dark, violent, social forces.[56] Pei, as well as Yu Jianrong, has provided ample documentation for this pattern. Yet his analysis also reveals that some of the local mafia kingdoms were not in the hands of base elements pure and simple. Rather, they were shaped by rural people who at first had attempted to eschew criminal activity.[57] This latter insight is helpful in understanding the political and social origins of Bao Yinbao's martial arts network and the pivotal political role it assumed in local, regional, and possibly national politics. The so-called soft mafia of Bao Yinbao had its origins in the family angers, political chaos, and social vulnerabilities prevalent in the aftermath of the Great Leap disaster, followed by the demise of the collective.

The Iron Bond of Friendship

Martial arts training offered young fighters an honorable identity that the Maoists had equated with disobedience and disloyalty – the identity that Erik H. Erikson found is often connected with the youthful "craving for locomotion."[58] According to Erikson, "It is clear that societies offer any number of ritual combinations of ideological perspective and vigorous movement (dance, sports, parades, demonstrations, riots) to harness youth in the service of their historical aims, and that where societies fail to do so these patterns will seek their own combinations."[59] In the collective era, and especially the Great Leap and the Cultural Revolution, the Maoists had attempted to harness youthful bodies to campaigns designed to serve the fantasia of war communism. The chance for youth to participate in empowering physical activity was lost to the

[55] Pei, *China's Trapped Transition*, 156–166.   [56] Ibid., 160.   [57] Ibid., 161.
[58] Erikson, *Identity, Youth, and Crisis*, 243.   [59] Ibid., 243–244.

exhaustion of work in the collective fields and to the frenzy of public criticism sessions and party-orchestrated parades targeting "class enemies." This state-orchestrated process was aimed at creating a political identity that superseded family- and friendship-based identities, and at making it difficult for young villagers to resist the outbursts of party-state violence against their families.

The revival of martial arts training not only required Bao Yinbao and his peers to submit to challenging techniques of defending the body against attacks by party-recruited bullies, it also required fidelity to those who took up this art, teaching them that they were no longer alone and encouraging them to remake themselves through new friendships.[60] Apparently this lesson stuck, for long after achieving fame and fortune, Bao Yinbao still believed that his greatest fortune was friendship. In June 2008, Bao declared: "I am very keen on friendship. I help my friends when they need help from me, and I am willing to do anything for my friends. Friends are my life. Many people compared me to Song Jiang, the rebel leader in the Song dynasty who was from Yuncheng, Shandong. I like Song Jiang's style of treating friends well, and making a great number of friends everywhere."[61]

Wu Anwen, a farmer turned martial artist in Pingyuandi village, explained why *yiwu huiyou*, or making friends through martial arts, became so important in the early phase of reform: "Those who did not have any brothers, or had only a few brothers, in the countryside were often the targets of bullies. Those who took up martial arts could fight several people, and, at the same time, they could make many friends. If you can accomplish things with the help of your friends, other people would think you are resourceful, and they would not bully you. They would respect you." Wu says of himself and the other "brothers" in the branch of Bao Yinbao's network that he belongs to: "Anyone who is accepted into a branch has to be accepted by everyone in the entire network. We treat each other like real brothers. Actually, these people are more important to me than my real brother. We take an oath to join the group, like in the olden days. We pledge to defend each other like blood brothers. We will live together and die together. Because I have this kind of connection with seven people outside of Pingyuandi village, nobody will dare to bully me."[62]

In speaking of the importance of friendship, many of Bao Yinbao's martial arts clients equated friends with a "stairway to heaven": "When you have many friends, you can stand on earth and reach heaven," they said. Still others said that friends were like wind and like rain, so that people in Bao Yinbao's network could manufacture wind and rain, and thus depend on the force of friendship to produce returns for all to share.[63] And one of them confided that as long as they cultivated their friendships and maintained their connections

---

[60] I have benefited from Erikson here. Ibid., 245–246.   [61] Bao Yinbao, interview.
[62] Wu Anwen, interview.   [63] Yan Chunjian, interview.

with their friends inside the Liangmen township and Dongle county governments, they could get away with just about anything short of murder.[64]

The Code of Honor and Violence

Anton Blok has argued that *mafioso* in Sicily thrived in a subculture of violence and that mafia leaders gained respect in part because they were predisposed to use physical violence without conscience.[65] This logic does not describe the norms of the mafia-style patron–client newtork of Bao Yinbao, for Bao and his key followers placed great emphasis on the importance of using their physical skills only as a last resort in disputes and conflicts with adversaries, and on showing mercy to opponents who had given in to the threat, or limited application, of martial arts force. To be sure, Bao Yinbao and his tight circle of friends gained authority by mastering the arts of physical force. Yet Bao initially secured his reputation as a man of honor by upholding a strict code of conduct that was taught by Da Fo's older martial arts masters and that Bao, in his interaction with martial arts teachers in the Yuncheng Martial Arts School, had taken to heart. This code, which the martial arts teachers required their students to honor as a precondition for training them, obligated Bao Yinbao and his friends to heed two commandments: "Do no unnecessary harm with your martial arts skills – especially do not use your physical skills to bully others" and "Do all you can do to avoid fighting with others, and use the threat of physical force to settle disputes peacefully."[66]

The Da Fo martial artists who were most respected by villagers and by their peers were those with the best skills who were also best able to exercise restraint in using force. Bao Xianlong said: "My elder brother, Bao Xianli, was a much better student than I am, and he is less aggressive than I am. He does not fight with people. He is highly respected in the village. In the countryside, people respect those who have martial arts skills. But they respect you more if you do not fight with other people."[67] In contrast, Bao Xianlong himself had lost the respect of many villagers because he, unlike his brother, was in the habit of picking fights with too many people. Many of the martial artists interviewed said that they had entered into compacts with their teachers obligating them to refrain from doing any harm or from menacing others. Apparently, this pledge was reinforced by their teachers, who refused to get involved in any fights provoked by their students and by their families, who supported their training.[68] Bao Jianqiao explains: "My father encouraged me to study martial

---

[64] Ruan Xiaokang, interview.   [65] Blok, *Mafia of a Sicilian Village*, 211.

[66] Interviews with Bao Yinbao, Yan Chunjian, and Wu Anwen. The logic is in line with those who have stressed that the virtue and honor of *mafioso* leaders were derived from the careful, timely threat of physical violence rather than the application of "actual physical violence all the time." See esp. Hess, *Mafia and Mafiosi*, 62.

[67] Bao Xianyong, interview.   [68] Du Yufeng, interview.

arts, but at the same time he constantly reminded me that I should not fight with anybody. Otherwise, I would earn the reputation as a troublemaker."[69]

Sparing adversaries who have submitted in order to minimize the risk of future acts of revenge was a lesson Bao Yinbao learned in his martial arts training. Most of the time, Bao was able to gain popularity and expand his network of devoted followers by putting this lesson into practice, even in the course of highly emotional confrontations. He tells of one adversary who, on being defeated, knelt in front of Bao and begged for his miserable, doggish life to be spared. Bao Yinbao told his friends to open the gate and release the man. "He had already submitted to us without fighting," he explains. "So why should we have needed to beat him up?" Bao Yinbao summarizes the anecdote with the statement: "I want to practice wisdom. I do not want to make any enemies unnecessarily. I want to turn enemies into friends – friends who will help me succeed in what I want to accomplish in life."[70]

Villagers saw such merciful behavior of Bao Yinbao and his cadres through a contrasting memory of the Great Leap past, when Da Fo's party leaders beat and brutalized those who kneeled down in the public criticism sessions. They remembered that party zealots had taken this submission as a sign of weakness – as inviting more thrashings to "raise the morale" of the timid farmers the cadres held in contempt. The local Maoist state had allowed its village-level activists to physically abuse farmers to a point where they severely injured them, thereby damaging their ability to perform fieldwork and carry on assignments crucial to securing food, so that the arbitrary beatings of the past were, in the eyes of some villagers, equated with a dangerous state threat to the "moral economy" of the household.[71] Bao Yinbao and his fellow martial artists were aware of how previously powerless villagers saw the brutal local enforcement agents of Maoist policies. Their parents and grandparents had been the objects of such beatings. Understanding the damage that could be done to their good names by mean-spirited treatment of those who submitted to the demonstration of their magical skills, Bao and his men treated young villagers who thought they could defeat them with mercy. This practice protected them from character assassination and enabled them to present themselves as people who would not jeopardize the livelihood of other tillers – at least in the Da Fo area.

In the Mediterranean world, the word "mafia," which in popular usage meant a "fraternity of respected characters," gradually was interpreted by northern Italian jurists and journalists in the service of the national state to become synonymous only with the threat to public order posed by violent criminal elements.[72] As Pei has demonstrated, this language of the high modern state is precisely the language that has been used by the People's Republic of China (PRC) Ministry of Public Security to describe the "scourge" of mafia

---

[69] Bao Jianqiao, interview.   [70] Bao Yinbao, interview.
[71] On moral economy, see Scott, *Moral Economy*.   [72] Hess, *Mafia and Mafiosi*, 2.

bastions in reform-era China, and Yu Jianrong's writings on mafia also resonate with this depiction.[73] But this is not how villagers saw the use of martial arts skills by Bao Yinbao and his band of brothers. They weighed the *restrained* use of physical force by Bao's martial arts cadres against the *wanton* use of force against their families and fellow villagers in the CCP-orchestrated public criticism sessions that defined normal "discourse" in the Maoist Leap as well as against the beatings delivered to them and many of their kin by the party's birth-planning agents in the post-Mao period. The "scourge" of this self-defense force acquired some legitimacy with poor villagers, who saw Bao's martial arts network as providing an honorable solution to the lack of protection from unaccountable, abusive local party leaders who stood to benefit from the center's brutish path to modernity.[74]

Popular Contention and Collective Action

Social science work on agrarian-based mafia seldom mentions "mafia" support for popular contention against local state injustice. The chiefs of mafia networks are instead depicted as aligned with local official power against ordinary villagers and, simplistically, invariably pitted against the rural poor. Yet the struggle of the Bao Yinbao–led martial artists to open up market space previously captured by the commune – and to freely engage in interactions with villagers in periodic rural markets – posed a threat to the ability of local party leaders to exercise power and control over rural subjects, occasionally putting the martial artists in conflict with officials in charge of Liangmen township and Dongle county government and, for that matter, with many other local governments in the triprovincial border area.

Historically, the market provided an important source of community in rural China.[75] With the reform-era revival of periodic market trade, Bao Yinbao and his entrepreneurial friends made frequent appearances in the markets of Da Fo, Shangcunji, and Liangmenpo after 1978. They rubbed shoulders with famers coming from surrounding villages, listening to marketgoers articulate grievances against village leaders and township officials, and, in some cases, witnessing or even joining in impromptu concerted actions against township-level political authorities. This frequenting of local periodic markets, sometimes as small business entrepreneurs, put Bao Yinbao and his network in touch with popular challenges to township government officials. When they returned to their dispersed home villages, they frequently told family, friends, and followers

---

[73] See Pei, *China's Trapped Transition*, 160–161; and compare with Yu, "Hei'e Shili shi Ruhe Qinru Nongcun Jiecheng Zhengquande."

[74] On the unresolved crisis of modernity, see Qin, "China's Economic Miracle." On the Communist Party itself as the source of disempowerment and suffering in village China, see Friedman, "Persistent Invisibility of Rural Suffering."

[75] Skinner, "Marketing and Social Structure in Rural China" and "Chinese Peasants and the Closed Community."

about these challenges – and thus rural people quickly got wind of what happened in the marketplace from these martial artists on the go.

They also tacitly supported popular contention in the marketplace. The martial artists were familiar with the marketplaces in which contention occurred, and they were on friendly terms with many of the farmers who took over these spaces during the key incidents of contention – marches, demonstrations, boisterous debates, shoving matches, and public seizures of township officials. As far as I can determine, they by and large did not intervene on behalf of the local state to repress popular challenges to its domination of market space. In effect, they silently abetted market-connected farmers who refused to accept the domination of township and county rulers. We have seen one example of the sort of contention martial artists supported – the 1998 incident when farmers pulled the Liangmen township government head from his Jeep in the Wanxiuzhuang marketplace and punished him for his callous, arrogant refusal to help a person in need of medical attention by giving him a choice: he could receive a severe beating from local people skilled in using the force of their fists (the martial artists) or he could crawl through a gauntlet of "lowly bumpkins" in the marketplace on his hands and knees. Choosing the latter, the government official lost face, becoming an object of popular disdain and ridicule. Farmers in Da Fo learned about this incident from some of the martial artists who had witnessed it and whose fists had been used to back up the threat against the official. (See Chapter 5 for a fuller description of the Wanxiuzhuang marketplace incident.)

In the contentious moments of reform, rural people came together to teach humility to haughty, party-based officials whose inherited modality of rule blinded them to the shared rights movement forming around the market community. The Da Fo martial artists were not heavily invested in this community struggle, but as friends – and in some cases teachers – of many of the farmers who challenged the Liangmen township officials who attempted to usurp or obliterate Da Fo's market or who treated farmers' problems with utter contempt, the martial artists were positioned to protect the villagers who confronted township-level power holders. The martial artists, with their connections to county-level police, constituted an alternative source of power that Da Fo's farmers could use to protect themselves if necessary – and everyone knew that if township officials attempted to repress market conflicts, the martial artists might be called on to mediate. Dongle county party leaders often chose instead to defuse such contentious episodes by arranging for township leaders to be transferred to other posts.

HOW MARTIAL ARTISTS SEE THE STATE

How did the Da Fo martial artists, some of whom had close ties to tillers, see the post-Mao state? And how did their actions affect the previously dominant position of the CCP and, in turn, the legitimacy of the party-led state? These are important questions, for historically in rural China the involvement of martial artists – people who specialized in the delivery of physical violence – was intimately connected with contentious politics, and imperial ruling groups sought to regulate the weaponry of skilled fighters to preserve their own dominance. Indeed, Peter Lorge has argued that the progressive sophistication of martial arts–based tactics, weapons, knowledge of fighting, and mental toughness was associated with the overthrow of the ruling imperial center from the Zhou dynasty and the Warring States period.[76]

To Bao Yinbao and members of his network, the party's leaders represented the pathetic agents of bad, useless authority, embodying a standard of moral behavior well beneath that of Bao's sworn brotherhood. Bao Xianyong, whose grandfather was a famous martial arts master in the Hebei-Shandong-Henan border area in the Republican period, summed up the critique: "Within the village, nobody pays much attention to the village leaders anymore. Bao Shunhe, the Da Fo party secretary, knows that he is not respected by villagers. So he is quiet, and he keeps a low profile in the village. He seldom tries to help people with their problems. He is very different from the old village leaders, who, in the years after Liberation, wanted to build up the village and make it a better place. Bao Shunhe no longer has that desire, and he does not have the ability to even conceive of how to create a better future. In reality, therefore, Da Fo does not even have any leadership at all. Everybody looks after themselves, and many people have tried to become friends with Bao Yinbao because he has many connections outside of the village, and he is more able to deliver assistance to villagers than the village leaders. That is why Bao Yinbao is popular with villagers."[77]

By the end of the third decade of reform, the Da Fo Communist Party stood in stark contrast to the influence of the community of martial artists. The latter was a natural home-grown force, the former an in-house appendage of outside power. The latter operated through a patronage network anchored in bonds of friendship, the former through a patronage system based on state-dictated obligations subject to bribery, manipulation, and the betrayal of friendship. The brotherhood mustered physical force to ensure the capacity of farmers to associate with people of their choosing. The party used force to deter villagers from associating with one another. The martial artists were involved in trade networks that opened up opportunities for some villagers to earn a living, while the village party leaders did little, if anything, to enable farmers to escape poverty. Whereas the martial artists provided villagers with a way of defending their interests against the predatory designs of Da Fo party leaders within the village, the latter still looked to fatten themselves through ties to township leaders and often colluded with this level of state power – the level of the Mao-era commune and its calamity.[78]

---

[76] Lorge, *Chinese Martial Arts*.   [77] Bao Xianyong, interview.
[78] In constructing this section, I have benefited from Hall, "Patron-Client Relations," 511–551, and Pitt-Rivers, *People of the Sierra*, 33, 138–139, 200–201.

The CCP's village leadership had lost its authority. The neo-Leninist nature of the local polity had been replaced by a multipolar system of more spontaneous political competition involving the village school principal and teachers, the returned PLA veterans, and the martial artists and their network as well as the local party leaders. The Da Fo village party leadership was unable to meet all of the challenges of these groups, whose members held powerful memories of the cost of submission to party rule in the Great Leap era. In this situation, local party leaders became utterly dependent on upper-level state force to ensure their survival and power – and this dependence set the stage for contentious struggle with the next level of state power.[79] The Da Fo–based martial artists perceived the Liangmen township government as a predatory, commune-era relic. Many of the martial artists, much like most of Da Fo's farmers, said they would never find peace or achieve prosperity as long as the township government persisted in robbing villagers of their resources and directing its police agents to injure those who disobeyed its directives. The legitimacy of local party rule had all but vanished at this level.

The coercive handling of birth planning in particular had done irreparable harm to the Communist Party's reputation. As we have seen, after the collective disbanded, there was a lot of fighting locally over Liangmen township government grain taxes, birth planning, and education surcharges. Ruan Gaiwang recalls that "people fought with their bare hands," which gave the upper hand to the martial artists for the first two decades of reform, in part because the reform-era police force was still relatively new and weak.[80] Beginning with the third decade of reform, the Central government attempted to improve its relationship with farmers by eliminating grain taxes and tuition charges. Villagers welcomed these policy changes, but the changes left the township leaders with fewer ways of squeezing revenue from the villages. According to Wu Anwen, of Pingyuandi in Guanjun township, "The local township government could no longer get money from farmers by adding on to the state taxes," but "the greed of the local government was still there." Thus, "When they could no longer get money the old way, they found many new ways to get money from the rural people."[81]

One way involved using the police to generate revenue. Once the township government beefed up its police force, it began to arrest more and more people who were involved in fighting – either in civil feuds that had nothing to do with the police or in fights over police enforcement of a host of township government regulations, including those pertaining to licensed highway travel and legalized procreation. This made it more costly for the martial artists to deliver their stock in trade. As Ruan Gaiwang put it, many of his brothers found that it cost a lot of money to get out of trouble with the police. Although many in Bao

---

[79] Cf. Dickson, "Dilemmas of Party Adaptation," 153–154. [80] Ruan Gaiwang, interview.
[81] Wu Anwen, interview.

Yinbao's brotherhood were undaunted, some found that they "could not afford to fight anymore."[82] Bao Xianyong spoke for these disgruntled brothers when he said, "The police just want to make money from the people. It seems that people are happy with the outcome of this process . . . but actually we hate the police for treating us like this. When the time is right, the people will fight back against the police." Bao made clear that he and his brothers would be leading this fight.[83]

Around 2005, the Liangmen township police – and police throughout the Hebei-Shandong-Henan border area – began to enforce a new way of getting money from birth planning, stoking greater popular hatred for party-dictated procreation regulations. In this period, the Guanjun township government repeatedly sent a twenty-man birth-planning enforcement team to arrest villagers who had more than one child. They took these people in to make the farmers' families pay for their release. The township enforcement team, which was ultimately backed by the township police, had the authority to seize whomever it pleased. The arrested parties – male and female, young and old – were thrown into a mass detention room. In some cases, the young sisters or elderly grandmothers of accused birth planning violators were seized and placed in the makeshift detention center, as well. "The reasoning behind this," says Wu Anwen, the ringleader of the Pingyuandi martial artists, "was that if you did not pay the fine, they would continue to seize your kin, and they would make life miserable for you and for your family." "Of course," exclaims Wu, "they also beat people once they were in their custody, and this illegal and brutal method worked for them. They usually would get the money very quickly from farmers who wanted to free their own people from this horrendous situation." In the eyes of Wu Anwen and most of his fellow martial artists, this practice "completely ruined the government's legitimacy in the countryside."[84]

In June 2005, the claims of the Liangmen township leaders escalated, and so did popular contempt for this level of CCP rule. In response to growing resistance to the enforcement teams, the township government disbanded the teams and imposed a quota on the villages to collect money based on birth-planning policy. In 2005, they asked each village party sectary to hand in 15,000 yuan. In 2006 the quota went up to 20,000 yuan, in 2007 to 25,000 yuan, and in 2008 to 28,000 yuan. "They told us," says Wu Anwen, the village chief as well as the martial artists' chief in Pingyuandi, "they did not care where we got the money from, and they sometimes wanted it in a hurry. They said if we could not get the money in time, then we could not continue to serve as village chiefs and party secretaries. For instance, this year, 2008, they wanted us to get the money in three days. But there was no way that we could get the money to them on time. Therefore, I had to pay them out of my own pocket first, and if I did not

[82] Ruan Gaiwang, interview.   [83] Bao Xianyong, interview.   [84] Wu Anwen, interview.

have it, I would have to borrow it from my friends and then try to collect it from farmers to pay back my friends. It is ridiculous, but this is how it works."[85] Actually, it did not always work this way. Wu Anwen was a sworn brother of Bao Yinbao and martial artists in several other border area villages. Some of Wu Anwen's sworn brothers had a reputation for fighting over family-planning issues in the previous two decades. Wu and his friends threatened to activate this reputation if the township leaders pressed on with their claims.

Double Identity of the Martial Artists

The Bao Yinbao–led martial artists held competing views of the Dongle county government. On the one hand, they had developed a host of collaborative relationships with leaders in this layer of state power. They saw their nested position within the county police force in particular as helping them preserve some measure of independence from the CCP-controlled national state, as well as enhancing their ability to benefit from supplying protection to key players in the market sector.[86] On the other hand, the submerged relationship with county-level power sometimes put Bao Yinbao and his sworn brothers in the uncertain, tension-ridden middle of conflicts with higher levels and farmers who stood to lose, materially and spiritually. There was local state pressure to breach the bonds of friendship with farmers, to serve the money-grabbing schemes of the powerful, and this elicited contempt for county leaders.

This double identity of the martial artists – the oath to honor friends in life and death versus the obligation to perform as public servants – was strained in 2006–2007. In February 2006, Beijing unveiled a plan to create a "New Socialist Countryside," the centerpiece of which was to close the gap between rich urbanites and the rural poor. The plan focused on rescinding agricultural taxes, making education affordable, and providing minimal health care. But it also called for new land-management practices to improve agricultural productivity, including the consolidation and preservation of farm lands, said to be a key to achieve spatial economies of scale in villages like Da Fo, where there were scattered strips of farm land. To save farmland, the center called for a ban on underground burial in the countryside. In the view of secular officials in Beijing, family graves were waste of farmland, so the prejudice of state policy was that farmers should be required to cremate their dead relatives, preserving more land for production – and state-framed development.

County-level compliance across the Hebei-Shandong-Henan border region varied considerably. Some leaders, such as those in nearby Qingfeng, ignored the state internment reform–particularly the push for cremation–and turned a blind eye towards the old burial practices, earning them praise from local

---

[85] Ibid.

[86] In developing this point, I have followed Gambetta's analysis of mafia. *Sicilian Mafia*, 253–254.

farmers. But in Dongle county and in neighboring Wei county, the county governments pushed this new agenda, leaving its implementation to township-level officials. In Liangmen township and in Shangcun township, Dongle county, the enforcement team was composed of unemployed young people who, according to Yan Hailian, "were connected with the township government leaders, and, in some cases, were the sons of the village party secretaries."[87] Farmers, including those with ties to Bao Yinbao's network, were incensed by their actions, which included digging up graves and violently disposing of dead bodies.

In Da Fo, and many other border area villages, death rituals, including funerals and burials, were designed to facilitate the passage through *yinjian*—the world after death.[88] The burial of the dead in the earth was of vital import-ance, because the ground was seen as a safe, peaceful space from which the soul of the deceased would begin its journey through this shadowy underworld, a potentially perilous adventure through a demonic universe dominated by imperial judges, spies, police, and guard dogs. Sending the soul on this journey required each family to present material offerings to these dark underworld cosmological figures. In Da Fo, and scores of its sister villages, the custom was for a surviving family member to place a fried cake or steamed bun in the hand of the deceased relative to appease the vicious barking guard dog Tiangou, one of many demonic spirits of the netherworld. If villagers could not make such offerings to these demonic forces, then the soul of the dead relative would not be able to effectively pass through this dark spiritual world to rebirth and eternal peace. The ghost of the deceased would drift about in this dark goblin region, inviting misfortune into the lives of living family members.[89]

Needless to say, Central government policy to prohibit burial, coupled with the forced cremation of the corpse, threatened this death ritual. The size of the fine for in-ground burials spelled bankruptcy for some households. The destruc-tion of the corpse through cremation, dismemberment, or both also proved traumatic. It made it impossible for villagers to prepare the body of the corpse for its passage to heaven, leaving the soul to wander through a demonic spiritual cosmos. This funeral reform process was all the more hated in Da Fo because its farmers had just begun to recover their ability to carry out the old burial customs, putting the memory of wandering famine ghosts from the Mao era behind them.

Elizabeth J. Perry has pointed out that as mechanisms of policy implementa-tion, the Communist Party's reform-era campaigns had resonances with the Maoist campaigns of the Great Leap but were managed in a more pragmatic,

---

[87] Yan Hailian, interview.
[88] I am indebted to Robert P. Weller for helping me grasp the concept of *yinjian*, and for helping me sharpen this section. Personal Correspondence, August 6, 2015.
[89] Thaxton, *Catastrophe and Contention*, 304–306.

less forceful manner.[90] Yet Perry acknowledges that the campaign for a New
Socialist Countryside was at times implemented "with callous disregard for the
desires of local inhabitants."[91] Indeed. To villagers, the campaign to clear the
ancestral grave lands seemed path dependent. It was highly impractical, and
the misconduct of the young ruffians who imposed it rivaled Great Leap–era
levels of sacrilege. In fact, the CCP attack on burial customs stoked memories of
what happened to dead bodies in Mao's Leap famine, when party leaders
shocked villagers by minimizing funerals and jettisoning old burial practices,
going so far as to destroy ancestral grave sites and dig up the dead in order to
expand the land available for agricultural production.[92] As in the Great Leap,
this reform-era assault on the corpses of kin was experienced as profane – as an
irreverent assault on a sacred Confucian-Taoist ritual, for in Confucianism
local community leaders were to practice respect and filial piety toward *all*
village subjects,[93] and this practice was to extend to expression of grief and
sorrow toward the dead.[94] In Taoism, which coexisted with this popular
Confucian precept of filial piety, funeral rites on behalf of ancestors were
critical to taking care of the soul, both in the here and now and in the afterlife,
and to ensuring its passage through a celestial bureaucracy guarding the entry
to Heaven and eternal harmony.[95] Digging up dead bodies and then torching
them in public made it impossible to exercise these rites.

   Within a few months after the burial policy began to be enforced in the Da
Fo area, Bao Yinbao and his friends were trying to persuade township government officials to build a memorial hall in each village with government money
so that farmers could store the ashes of their dead inside. They argued this
would make it easier to persuade farmers to accept the funeral reform policy.
The Dongle county government leaders and their counterparts in Wei county
refused to go along with this proposal. This unfunded funeral reform policy
subsequently became an instrument of official squeeze.

   The squeeze produced a bonanza for Liangmen township officials. The fine
for noncompliance with the cremation policy was usually about 3,000 yuan,
but officials often reduced it to 2,000. Liangmenpo's Zhou Jian recalls there
were sixty deaths in his village during the four years of strict enforcement. The
total amount of fines collected in this period was approximately 120,000 yuan,
so if we multiply this by twenty villages, the number of villages within Liangmen township, we get a figure of 2,400,000 yuan, which comes to well over US
$350,000. Most of this sum went directly into the pocket of Wang Jintang, the
deputy head of Liangmen township government and the official in charge of
enforcing the cremation policy. Wang was in charge of the group of young
thugs who enforced the policy. He allowed them to dig the buried corpses out

[90] Perry, "From Mass Campaigns," 30–31, 44–45, 50.   [91] Ibid., 41.
[92] Wang, "ABCs of Communization," 160–161.   [93] Bellah, "Father and Son," 103.
[94] See Confucius and Legge, *Sacred Books of China*, 466–488.
[95] Hardy, "Afterlife and Salvation."

of the deep earth, pour gasoline on them, and set them on fire – a fate visited on Ren Binghai, Ren Xuemin, Liu Lianzhang, Dong Huichun, and many other deceased villagers in Liangmenpo. Wang and his men were so greedy, so insensitive, that in at least two cases they actually came to the homes of sick villagers who were not dead yet to ask for a 3,000-yuan fine, as if the living patients had been secretly buried by their families. According to Zhou Jian, "many villagers were infuriated by this kind of outrageous behavior by the township government."[96]

As anger and resistance welled up in the villages, Bao Yinbao and his friends had to choose sides. The martial artists tell us that the Dongle county and Wei county government leaders were especially innovative in generating revenue from this funeral reform mandate of the center. To enforce compliance, they allowed the township governments to form Burial Law Enforcement Squads to descend on the villages. In many villages, farmers attempted to circumvent the policy by digging unusually deep holes in the land and skipping the construction of above-ground grave mounds in order to camouflage the burial of their family members. The Burial Law Enforcement Squads, working through party-based village informants, invaded the villages with long rods to test where the coffins were buried, dug them out, and set them on fire. In Pingyuandi village, a base of martial artist power, indignation reached a high pitch. Farmers fought daytime battles with the enforcement squads, prompting the latter to perform their profane missions under cover of darkness to avoid clashes with incensed villagers. Arrested farmers were fined 6,000 yuan (about US$750) and had to produce yet another fine to effect their release from jail. In some instances, the Burial Law Enforcement Squads pushed their luck. Sensing the importance farmers placed on being in possession of the whole body of deceased kin, some of the squad leaders started cutting off the limbs of the burned corpses. Farmers had to pay money to buy back the arm or leg of a loved one from these body snatchers.[97] The Pingyuandi martial artists entered this fray on the side of the farmers, using their contacts in the Wei county police force to tip off the timing of the Enforcement Squad coffin searches and occasionally fighting side by side with the farmers who took on these state-backed thugs. This action does not, of course, fit with the usual stereotypes of mafia, who are portrayed as the goons of the local state pure and simple.

The martial artists in the Liangmen township–Shangcun township area of Dongle county also sided with indignant farmers. In Yuanchao, farmers took matters into their own hands. Here, they dug up the roads leading to the cremation factory, so that the official trucks could not carry the dead bodies of their relatives to the factory and township leaders could no longer collect rents on this "service." Worse, from the standpoint of the CCP leaders in charge managing of this "enterprise," hundreds of farmers around Yuanchao

[96] Zhou Jian, interview.   [97] Wu Anwen, interview.

joined in an attack on the crematory factory itself, dismantling its big chimney, without which it could no longer function. "This action," according to Da Fo's Bao Yutang, "was the main reason why the cremations were suspended."[98] And threat of future collective action by local people who knew how to fight was an important reason why the township leaders did not attempt to restore the factory to working condition.

The Righteous Path of Contention and the Tragedy of Bao Yinbao and His Brotherhood

Mediating between villagers and officials in such conflicts, Bao Yinbao and his men worried that trouble with the reform-era center eventually would compel them to take up militant disobedience, following the path of Song Jiang and his band of outlaws. Although referring to the present, Bao Yinbao reasons with logic shaped by dynastic political time when he declares, "Many people have compared me to Song Jiang, the rebel leader in the Song dynasty." He laments, "But it is too bad that I am living in a time like this. If I were born during a time of war, I would be a big general, and I would be leading a hundred thousand warriors to fight our enemies."[99] Members of Bao Yinbao's martial arts network saw the CCP-led state as the enemy of poor rural people who were subjected to corruption that ran against the humanistic tradition (*rendao zhuyi*) of rural-based martial arts culture – a culture that celebrated principles of righteous brotherhood and physical self-defense against oppressors.[100] They subscribed to a transcript that challenged the center's right to rule.[101] Hence, they were predisposed to follow a leader such as Song Jiang, who had challenged dynastic power. Of course, few of the martial artists would openly declare their desire to realize this transcript. But some of Bao Yinbao's followers said that Bao could become a Song Jiang, or a Mao Zedong, if only he were not facing an authoritarian state with a powerful national army.[102]

Despite the voiced admiration for Mao Zedong, Bao Yinbao and his men were more attracted to another model of political order: the protofascist order fashioned by Yang Faxian, the Chinese leader of an 80,000-man ultrarepressive Japanese Puppet Army that held sway in the Hebei-Shandong-Henan border area during World War II. Headquartered in Da Fo between 1939 and 1945, this force evidently had its origins in a martial arts association based in Da Fo village. Old-timers recall that its members had studied martial arts under Bao Lan, a farmer who was "a very righteous person." A poor, uneducated youth of nearby Shangcunji, Yang Faxian had followed suit, taking up this exercise to defend himself and his family against Wei county bandits who stole crops and

[98] Bao Yutang, interview.   [99] Bao Yinbao, interview.
[100] Cf. Morris, *Marrow of the Nation*, 193–194, 196, 211–212.
[101] On hidden transcripts, see Scott, *Domination and the Arts of Resistance*.
[102] Wu Anwen, interview.

valuables in Da Fo and other villages. Under Yang's leadership, the martial artists gathered to recite an oath to invite Guangong (the War God) into their bodies, and they pledged they would "conduct martial exercises together, fight together, and enjoy prosperity together."[103] This historical paradigm, with its promised relief from suffering, held great attraction for Bao Yinbao and his men. By the mid-1930s, Yang Faxian was recruiting orphans, small-time criminals, and ex-Kuomintang soldiers with martial arts skills into his army. According to Bao Zhenmin, "Yang Faxian knew martial arts and was highly respected by the people of this border area."[104] Yang was popular before the Japanese arrived because, according to Bao Jingru, "Yang was very much like the Communists. He forced rich people to give him money, and he used the money to help the poor."[105] "He was trying to help the poor people," says Bao Zhenmin, "and he even set up middle schools which attracted students from rich families in this area."[106] In short, though Yang Faxian was a collaborator, his system was not based on a small number of misfits and dissenters.[107] It had broad appeal. In fact, the majority of people in Da Fo, and in hundreds of border area villages, held allegiances to Yang Faxian, whose regime, while subjecting Han opponents to abuse, promised greater security and fairness under indirect Japanese rule.

But Yang Faxian was brutal as well as benevolent. Staunchly anti-Communist, Yang Faxian not only buried alive seven members of Da Fo's underground CCP, his loyal fighters also foiled a Communist-engineered wartime plot to defeat them. In April 1941, the 773rd regiment of the 129th Division of the CCP-led Eighth Route Army sent 300 soldiers to pretend they were defecting to Yang's Japanese puppet force, so they could destroy his army from inside. One of the 300, Liu Zhishu, betrayed the plan. On discovering the ruse, Yang and his men shot all 300 soldiers. Afterward, Yang unleashed a reign of terror against Communist Party members in Da Fo, Weicaicun, Yuezhuang, and other villages. Subsequently, many people accepted the sovereignty of Yang Faxian, who became the head of Shangcun district in Dongle county and had the authority to "kill anyone he did not like."[108] To Bao Yinbao and many local farmers, Yang Faxian was on his way to becoming a Song Jiang under the umbrella of the Japanese occupation. But Yang made one fatal calculation: he listened to his advisor, Zhao Jinjing, who thought that the Communist Party would not be able to defeat the Japanese Imperial Army, and Yang decided to side with the Japanese.[109] Bao Yinbao did not want to replicate this mistake, for he understood that the reform-era CCP had superior

---

[103] Bao Zhenmin, interview.   [104] Ibid.   [105] Bao Jingru, interview.
[106] Bao Zhenmin, interview.
[107] In other words, Jean-Paul Sartre's conception, which takes collaboration as the product of a small minority of misfits, would not apply to this case. See Treat, whose reading of Sartre is astute. "Choosing to Collaborate," 83–84.
[108] Bao Zhenmin, interview.   [109] Bao Jingru, interview.

force and, in the words of Everett Zhang, would use its "power of death" to crush any challenge to its rule.[110]

Bao and his friends said they preferred to live by the moral code of their sworn brotherhood, and they equated this code with righteous conduct in the face of oppression. For this reason, they expressed great frustration, and even self-hatred, at their inability to conform to a code of righteous, nonaggressive behavior that could reduce conflicts with others and earn them self-esteem and honor. Bao's men said they were trapped in a hedonistic, violent political system. They expressed hatred for this system because survival within it has required them to violate the advice of their fathers. Speaking with regret, Bao Yinbao recalled his own father's advice to pursue a path of righteousness: "I learned a great deal from my father. He did not want me to do bad things in society. He warned me again and again. But I did not listen to him."[111] This is a common refrain among the martial artists. Wu Anwen, the chief of Pingyuandi village, said: "When the upper government leaders come to the village, I must eat and drink with them. I do everything with them – I have a public bath with them, go sleep with prostitutes with them, gamble with them, and sing songs with them to make them happy. I used to be a very righteous person. However, if you want to keep your righteous principles in today's world, you have to die from anger. That is how our society is today. The righteous cannot survive. One of my clan elders served as village chief before me. He died from anger, because he could not tolerate the lies and deception of the government."[112]

In failing to follow the righteous path, Bao Yinbao and his friends – increasingly despised for drinking and hiring prostitutes – felt they had undermined their ability to inspire others to moral action. They held the Central government responsible for this predicament. In spite of their self-hatred – and perhaps because they felt a need to right their own wrongful complicity with the center's system – they wanted to remove the political structure that compromised their ability to live out the codes of their fathers and their martial arts teachers. The need to feel moral also found expression in the desire of Bao and his men to speak truth to state power and to work closely with villagers to promote righteous governance. Those interviewed for this volume seemed angry that the Communist Party had steered reform in a direction that had forced them into a life of crime and dangerous collaboration with its local base. They felt Beijing had fashioned a political economy that left them with little choice but to collaborate locally with some of its appointed cronies – a collaboration that drove them into the mafia.

By 2008, Bao Yinbao and his followers were confronted with Song Jiang's dilemma. They lived in a corrupt, lawless system where, they said, "one could not find even one clean official,"[113] where "tough guys could get away with

---

[110] Zhang, "The Truth about the Death Toll of the Great Leap Famine in Sichuan," in Zhang, Kleinman, and Tu, *Governance of Life*, 72.
[111] Bao Yinbao, interview.   [112] Wu Anwen, interview.   [113] Bao Jiangjun, interview.

crimes,"[114] and where they could count on the police to help them in a time of trouble only if they paid them off.[115] But, by the same token, they were committed to fighting for those in their network, even if fighting got them into serious trouble with the police and landed them in prison. This was their greatest fear – the loss of physical movement, the source of their power. Caught in an emotional tug-of-war over their dual identities, Bao and his men expressed a desire to change the world through righteous struggle. This desire was summed up by Wu Anwen, one of Bao Yinbao's sworn brothers: "Bao Yinbao is a very capable person. If not for the suppression of the Communist government he would be a person like Song Jiang. Yet the Communist Party is too powerful for him to challenge. The Central government has a very powerful army, and Bao Yinbao cannot openly challenge the government. If there were a foreign invasion, he definitely would organize an army to fight the foreigners, and during the war he would use righteous slogans to organize his own army. He would use his own money to support his troops, and help the poor people and move from bandit to hero."[116]

While Central government force precluded an opportunity to mobilize against Beijing, we should not discredit the possibility of this hidden desire playing itself out locally, slowly expressing itself in violence against the next ascending level of the police system of party rule.[117] The Da Fo martial artists perceived the Liangmen township government as a predatory relic of the commune era. Many of them, like most of Da Fo's farmers, said they would never find peace or achieve enduring prosperity as long as the police agents of this level of power injured those who disobeyed upper-level directives and used birth planning and burial policy to extract money from villagers. Of course, given their secret connections with police insiders, Bao Yinbao and his sworn brothers were better able to cope with this system. But they, too, were occasionally arrested by the police, and many of them were fed up with paying off the police to get out of trouble.[118] Thus, Bao Xianyong spoke for his sworn brothers when he said, "The police just want to make money from the people. It might seem that people are happy with the outcome of this process, but actually we hate the police for treating us like this. When the time is right, the people will fight back against the police."[119] The time was not right, however.

INTO THE BLACK HOLE OF CHINA'S AUTHORITARIAN POLITICAL SYSTEM

By the spring of 2008, Bao Yinbao and several of his sworn brothers had become the objects of Henan police dragnets. They were living the life of

---

[114] Yan Chunjian, interview.   [115] Ibid.   [116] Wu Anwen, interview.
[117] In constructing this section, I have benefited from Scott, *Domination and the Arts of Resistance*, and Tilly and Tarrow, *Contentious Politics*, 89–93, 188–190.
[118] Ruan Gaiwang, interview.   [119] Bao Xianyong, interview.

outlaws, safe only within the confines of Hebei-Shandong-Henan border area villages where their network was entrenched. But in May, the machinery of China's multitiered police state caught up with Bao. He was arrested in Da Fo village after involvement in a fight that had occurred back in 2005. One person died and a dozen were badly injured. Bao apparently did not harm the person who was killed. Nevertheless, the victim's family claimed Bao was responsible, and the family had a relative in Henan provincial police headquarters, so that Bao was put on a police wanted list. For nearly three years, Bao's friends in the Dongle county police force provided him with immunity, protecting him by cell-phone warnings of police raids. But his luck ran out. Under mounting pressure from the Henan police, a county police squad arrested Bao when his cell phone was dead.[120] Shortly thereafter, Bao Yinbao was sentenced to three years in what he dubbed "the black hole" of official corruption – the Chinese prison system in which many of Da Fo's poor farmers, caught up in the dragnet of the *yanda* campaigns, had ended up.[121]

Yet Bao Yinbao was able to escape the fate of most farmers. In July 2011, after getting out of prison, Bao explained: "I did not suffer much in prison, mostly because I was well connected with police officers, and because my friends constantly sent money to me while I was in prison. Normally, prisoners had to suffer a great deal. Therefore, in order to have good meals in prison, one had to have a lot of money to buy food, and he had to make sure that the prison officials would be able to make some money."[122] Through friends who were police officers, Bao Yinbao was able to eat well, feasting on fried dough, turtle soup, and wine daily. His friends occasionally took Bao out of confinement to eat dinner, and he was able to enjoy a banquet once a week. One of Bao's sworn brothers, the deputy police chief of Dongle county, even celebrated special holidays with Bao outside prison, taking him to a fine restaurant on the Moon Festival. In fact, reports Bao, "the prison warden allowed me to take meals with him when I paid 400 yuan into the dining budget." And Bao could treat himself to a snack outside prison, because the warden allowed him to run errands and purchase various supplies.[123] By contrast, the imprisoned farmers did not have much to eat because the prison authorities took money out of the tight food budget and because the money that prisoners paid for food was pocketed by prison guards who did not tell their superiors.

Bao was also favored over other inmates when it came to communication with the outside. Fearing prisoners would secure information about their cases, the Dongle county police generally prohibited telephone calls to the outside. But in their desire to raise money, the police allowed prisoners to pay 500 yuan for minute-long calls. Bao Yinbao, however, was able to use the prison telephone any time, and he did not have to pay. "I was able to do this," recalls Bao,

[120] Bao Jinghe, interview; Bao Shuhe, interview.   [121] Bao Yinbao, interview.   [122] Ibid.
[123] Ibid.

"mainly because I had a sworn brother in county police headquarters, and he put in some good words for me with the prison warden."[124]

Bao was also able to use his network to avoid the most devastating aspect of prison life: prison farm labor. According to Bao, "All prisoners, once sentenced to a fixed term, will be shipped to different farms and factories to go through reform by physical labor. However, because I had connections with police officers, they told me I did not have to leave the county prison to go any-where."[125] In reality, Bao served time in a special "detention center" within the Dongle county prison, which was only for people waiting for trial, because his police friends allowed him to stay there.[126]

Yet what mattered most to Bao Yinbao was getting out of prison. Bao's case was serious, warranting three to seven years in prison, with a possible death sentence for murder. Bao and his friends used their influence, money, and power to change his sentence. Bao explains: "From the first day I was arrested, I started a very complicated operation to get out of prison as soon as possible. I gave money to the Dongle county police team that arrested me so that they would put favorable words in their report about my case." In fact, Bao had been arrested in his Da Fo home, but by paying off the police he was able to persuade them to change his "arrest" to a case of "voluntary surrender," which provided the judge an important ground for light sentencing. According to Bao, "I also gave money to the officials in charge of my case in the county prosecu-tor's office, and in the court house, and so the Dongle county court decided to give me five years' probation."[127] But the tide quickly changed. Upset by this light sentence, the victim's family sued the Dongle county police in Puyang city court. Bao and his men had enemies in Puyang, including its police force. Not wanting to lose the upper hand to Bao's friends in Dongle, they pushed for a heavy sentence. Subsequently, Bao's friends had to spend over 100,000 yuan to move the case back to Dongle county, where the judge, fearing he would lose his position if he upheld the probation verdict, changed the decision to three years with the possibility of release after two.[128]

In spite of this favorable treatment, Bao Yinbao was distressed by his prison experience. Bao's imprudence had put great pressure on his sworn brothers inside the local police force. They were honor-bound to protect Bao, but he had gone too far. Because his was a murder case, and because many of his friends had secured positions inside the police force prior to his arrest, they could do only so much in helping Bao without exposing themselves and threatening the autonomy of the Dongle county government.[129] Bao's prison activity also tarnished his image with poor farmers. The prison warden had implicated Bao in a form of extortion, pressing him to inform new prisoners they could talk with anyone outside for 500 yuan and then, if the prisoner put the money

---

[124] Ibid.   [125] Ibid.   [126] Ibid.   [127] Ibid.   [128] Ibid.
[129] Confidential interview, Shanghai.

into an account, urging Bao to find other ways to squeeze the unassuming family.[130] When Bao left captivity, therefore, he had to rebuild his reputation with local people, a task that was difficult.

Bao Hongwen, a poor Da Fo farmer who was on speaking terms with Bao Yinbao, actually disliked Bao and feared the latter's connections to power holders in Beijing. His story of how these connections formed in the reform period is revealing:

I know that Bao Yinbao is very well connected with criminal gangs. Bao Yinbao has a sworn brother who is the chief of a criminal gang in Beijing, and this chief has a brother who is a high ranking officer in the Beijing Military Command. With this officer's help, the chief was able to get many construction contracts in the Beijing area. He became the head of criminal gangs seeking his protection, and he often refused to pay his workers. Some of the Da Fo area people worked for him, and he did not pay them. So a few years ago they conspired to kidnap him. They brought him back to this border area. They were going to teach him a lesson by cutting off one of his limbs. But Bao Yinbao got wind of this kidnapping, and he seized on it to help himself by convincing the kidnappers to let the chief go without harming him. Because of this, the chief became a sworn brother of Bao Yinbao.[131]

Indeed, the chief stood by Bao Yinbao, greasing the institutional machinery of the prison system for his sworn brother. As soon as this Beijing mafia chief heard that Bao had been arrested in May 2008, he came to Dongle county and gave Bao 20,000 yuan, and he also paid off the prison warden to take good care of Bao. Speaking of this criminal network, with upward threads to state power in Beijing, Bao Hongwen fumed: "I do not like people like Bao Yinbao. As far as I am concerned, these people stand for some of the worst social injustices in China today."[132]

Politics in rural, seemingly remote Da Fo was connected with politics in urban China – and with national power. And yet politics here, in the deep countryside, was fraught with complexities and contradictions and with regime-damaging judgments of systemic power, even by those who benefited from this system. Indeed, Bao Yinbao's prison experience made him even more contemptuous of the "black hole" of systemic political corruption, intensifying his desire to escape this hole through rebellion. When Bao Yinbao departed prison, he had a contentious exchange with the warden, signifying that his attempt to survive the extremity of this system had not blinded him to its injustice: "When I left prison," says Bao, "the warden asked me if I had any reflections on my time in captivity. I said I had learned a great deal. I told him the police force itself was a black hole, but the detention center was the darkest place of all. I said, 'Unlike the police officers, who were in charge of important government functions and had ways of extracting money from society, you are

---

[130] Bao Yinbao, interview.   [131] Bao Hongwen, interview.   [132] Ibid.

left with only one way of extracting money – from prisoners. You steal money that is designated to purchase their food. Your people are unbelievable.'"[133]

Reflecting further, Bao Yinbao proclaimed official corruption in China to be an intractable problem. He had seen that poor farmers were confused and intimidated by the prison system, that they did not know how to use the legal system to escape it, and that the little money they could scrape up to help them survive the insatiable demands of its guardians ended up in a black hole that did not help them in any meaningful way.[134] The officials, Bao concluded, could not live without corruption designed to extract as much money as possible from powerless rural people. Bao Yinbao was alienated from this system – a system from which he and his men often prospered. Most interestingly, Bao defended the actions of his brotherhood, claiming that by colluding with local CCP-appointed officials despite their corruption, decadence, and violence, he and his men were helping the Central government leaders commit suicide – that is, they were contributing to the creation of a society and state in which total darkness prevails, and thereby making rulers so blind they could not see they were breeding the conditions for anarchy and a collision with dehumanized rural people. Of course this excuse was not convincing, especially for victimized farmers; actually, Bao's men understood they were not powerful enough to overthrow the center, and they knew they were implicated in its ability to persist in the short term. While they indicated they might turn against it and its black hole if massive state ineptitude, in combination with unrestrained state plunder and a supportive commitment from below, were to become the order of the day, their actions spoke louder than their words.

Aware of all this, Bao went on to say that China is going through a fundamental transformation that is pulling farmers outside their customary social networks, exposing them to a wolfish order centered on violence and money making, and he concluded with an insightful analysis of how state power works in China: "When I was young, I had a dozen people who were doing the fighting and killing with me. We traveled with a hundred others, and we were able to overwhelm other groups because we had greater force. The dozen loyal fighters were the core of my group. They were willing to follow me because I enabled them to profit from our activities. That is how it works. In a way, the government is the same. The higher the government organization, the darker it is."[135]

In the summer of 2008, this dark side of governance crashed down on Da Fo, on Dongle county, and on Henan province, angering Bao Yinbao and his sworn brothers, most of whom were against the Central government's engagement with U.S.-led globalization. They saw the center appeasing America's neoliberal order, and they were especially peeved by Beijing's all-out effort to achieve Olympic glory and engage in what they called the "nonsense of a one

---

[133] Bao Yinbao, interview.   [134] Ibid.   [135] Ibid.

world dream."[136] They were especially upset by the center's crackdown on pollution emissions in order to promote a clean environment in Beijing for Olympic visitors, for this crackdown pricked a bad memory from the Great Leap era, when the material structures of everyday life were destroyed by the sudden delivery of hyperidiotic policies linked to the command economy of the Mao-led center. Along with farmers in Da Fo, Liangmen, Liangmenpo, and other villages, they were infuriated with the CCP secretary of Henan province, who seized on the crackdown to promote his own career. He promised the Central government that Henan would contribute to improving air quality in Beijing by blowing up all of the brick factories in the province, after which he sent in vigilante squads to destroy these self-supporting private factories without compensating villagers – a move that forced poor rural Henanese to scavenge in nearby Hebei for bricks for home repair and construction.[137] Bao and his brothers had relatives who lost their livelihood to this ruthless opportunism, which also took its toll on their own local business enterprises. To them, the dark shadow of the Maoist past had rolled back over the countryside. The reformist center seemed ready to sacrifice anyone, any part of the other "unknown China" in which Bao and his sworn brothers had grown up and in which they and their families had to find a way to survive, all in order to preserve its own power and promote its own version of growth and grandeur – and this was precisely the same kind of politics that had delivered the disaster of the Great Leap Forward.[138]

– – –

In the reform era, the Da Fo–area martial artists played a role in the unfolding struggle against Communist Party authority in the village, constructing the body itself as a form of political counteragency.[139] The origins of this struggle stretched back to the Great Leap era, when disempowered farmers were unable to develop martial skills to defend themselves against the violence of party leaders and their network of thugs.[140] The Da Fo martial artists sought to rectify Mao-era domination by practicing their politics, as Bryan S. Turner would argue, "through their bodies."[141] To be sure, Bao Yinbao and his network practiced violence. They were, in a sense, practicing Machiavelli's "economy of violence," that is, their political behavior reflected the judicious application of force uninhibited by pride, malice, or personal revenge and was designed to curtail the despotism of the CCP – and to avert indiscriminate

[136] Bao Jianqian, interview.   [137] Zhou Qiutian, interview; Ruan Xiaokang, interview.
[138] Cf. Friedman, Pickowicz, and Selden, *Chinese Village, Socialist State*, and Dikotter, *Mao's Great Famine*, 133–136, 153.
[139] The concept is from Peterson, *Contemporary Political Protest*, 69.
[140] See ibid., 99, and Scott, *Domination and the Arts of Resistance*, for the logic here.
[141] Turner, *Body and Society*, 230.

escalation at a later point.[142] Hence they relied on martial arts and the norms passed on to them by its master teachers to settle scores with local party leaders who had brutalized their families in the Maoist Leap and after. In doing so, they managed to break the CCP's "monopoly on force" at the grassroots level.[143]

These martial artists' political beliefs were consistent with, and perhaps drawn from, the *Shuihuzhuan*, a cultural narrative that celebrated the notion of a "just rebellion" of the rural poor against state tyranny. Their mafia affinities notwithstanding, Bao Yinbao's brotherhood was formed on the basis of friendship bonds designed to offer mutual support against the aggrandizement of the powerful, and its members shared the same kind of collective rebel identity to be found in the *Shuihuzhuan*.

The martial artists derived their legitimacy substantially from supplementing kin ties weakened by the Great Leap's savagery and by the post-Leap decades of hunger and misrule with iron bonds of friendship. Though connected to county-level power, Bao Yinbao's brotherhood created a community-based alternative to centralized dictatorial policies that played into the hands of unaccountable local party leaders. Based in a transvillage self-defense network, the brotherhood held great appeal for vulnerable villagers who saw the CCP as an exclusive organization of violent ruffians.[144] By way of contrast, villagers initially understood that Bao and his friends were honor-bound to do everything in their power to resolve disputes peacefully, to lower the risk of conflict, and to include ordinary folk in their system of protection and patronage.[145] Bao's Da Fo–based martial artists also played a role in helping rural people reclaim the market as a transvillage space for contentious action, a territory wherein people from different villages could challenge the domineering and demeaning work style of CCP leaders.[146] Their support bolstered the confidence of the farmers who took charge of these explosive moral events and made the police think twice about using violence to suppress challenges to arrogant local officials.

Nevertheless, the fierce authoritarian political system in which Bao Yinbao and his brotherhood had to survive drew some of them into the hidden money-grabbing schemes of local power, and this process corrupted them and even required them to hurt farmers in far-flung villages. But what other choice did they have? The Communist Party failure to carry out a fundamental rural political reform and create a political economy in which the rural poor could relieve their suffering left people such as Bao Yinbao and his friends with a set of cruel choices. They could attempt to endure the back-breaking toil of farm

---

[142] For this reading of Machiavelli, see Wolin, *Politics and Vision*, 221–223.
[143] I am indebted to Peter Lorge for this phrase and for helping me grasp this important point. Lorge, *Chinese Martial Arts*, 237.
[144] Thaxton, *Catastrophe and Contention*.
[145] See Peterson, *Contemporary Political Protest*, 29–30.
[146] For this line of analysis, see ibid., 11–12.

life, striving to break even when faced with soaring costs of agricultural inputs and low, government-dictated grain prices. They could turn to petty theft of essential commodities monopolized by the party-state (seeds and chemical fertilizer) and risk the ordeal of imprisonment and torture. Or they could turn to migrant work, toiling as bonded laborers in an alien, unfriendly construction industry dominated by cutthroat contractors who were out to make as much money as possible, regardless of the consequences for workers. As Qin Hui has suggested, this cruel set of choices reflected the continuing crisis of late Qing governance – that is, the failure of post-Mao reformers bent on achieving a quick, ruthless modernity to end CCP privileges through empowerment of the rural poor.[147] Life in the brotherhood provided an alternative to the insecurity and suffering incurred from any one of these choices. Precisely because the CCP maintained this system, therefore, Bao Yinbao and his men had little choice but either to operate in the interstices of official power networks or to collude with party-based politicians located at crucial nodes in these networks.

In pursing this latter path of action, Bao and his men were conflicted. They found themselves committing thuggish acts against farmers and small business folk, thereby violating the martial honor codes to which they subscribed. They became, tragically, part of the violent system of Communist Party power, which in the case at hand extended all the way upward to Beijing and which, at bottom, perpetuated the suffering of ordinary farmers. Yet if Bao and his men were filling the power vacuum created by a profoundly flawed reform, they were only doing this to survive – though of course in doing the bidding of money-grabbing party leaders they also enriched themselves. As survivors of Mao-era suffering, they understood that the system was not designed to serve the rural poor, that it exposed innocent country people to the possibility of more pain, more suffering[148] – and Bao Yinbao himself saw this pain when the system landed him in its black hole. Bao and his friends hated this system, and the brotherhood they formed maintained a belief in the values that inspired Song Jiang. Given the complex political history of change and contention in Da Fo and the surrounding countryside, one cannot help but wonder what the future holds for the Communist Party and the rural areas it claims to have regained the right to rule but has yet to demonstrate it can govern.

---

[147] See Qin, "China's Economic Miracle."

[148] On this system, and its relationship to the continuing late Qing crisis in rural China in the post-2005 Hu Jintao era, see Friedman, "Persistent Invisibility of Rural Suffering," 2, 20–22.

Conclusion

Big Questions and Small Answers from Da Fo

A FISSURED LEGITIMACY

The story of Da Fo village, and its sister villages in this interior North China border area, sheds light on an important paradox of contemporary Chinese politics: the Communist Party–led Central government apparently has overall legitimacy nationally and yet hidden fissures in its legitimacy in the deep countryside. The case of Da Fo introduces us to political contention within one of these fissures. It tells us that we cannot grasp the genesis, or essence, of authoritarian China's unresolved legitimacy crisis without carefully studying the way in which memories of Chinese Communist Party (CCP)-inflicted suffering in the Mao era persist in the lives of rural people, providing the psychological and emotional bullet points that inform and direct defiance, resistance, and contention.

Many Da Fo survivors of the Great Leap–era famine remember it as the most traumatic episode of one-party dictatorship, retaining smoldering resentments of its horror. Reform-era Central government policies, and their local implementation, delivered new injustices, stoking fears of a repeat of past loss. Da Fo's inhabitants drew on memories of regime misconduct in the Mao period to protect themselves from the renewal of party-structured aggrandizement and lawlessness in the present. These memories of the traumatic past constitute what James C. Scott calls "weapons of the weak," and villagers relied on these weapons to bolster their quest for survival in the present.[1] Da Fo's history calls us to reflect on how this process factors into a type of grassroots contention that is suppressed but not fully controlled by the Central government, nor by its political base in the villages, towns, and markets of the

---

[1] Scott, *Weapons of the Weak*.

unknown interior – many of which were decimated, if not devastated, in the Leap famine and shortchanged by the post-Mao center.

THE FALSE PEACE OF REFORM AND THE ROLE OF EPISODIC MEMORY IN RESISTANCE

Bringing in the missing variable of episodic memory and studying the case of Da Fo, we can begin to grasp how memory of the Great Leap and its famine influenced resistance in the post-Mao period. The Deng Xiaoping–conceived reform sailed Da Fo's villagers into the headwinds of the Great Leap past, raising villagers' fears of once again being caught in a rapidly evolving political storm in which the sky would collapse and the land and life itself would be turned upside down. The fears fed into resistance, ongoing or otherwise.

The post-Mao reform fell far short of its goal of delivering an appealing peace to all villagers. To be sure, many welcomed reform as an end to the murderous politics of the Mao era, but in the Da Fo area the Deng-led Central government instituted its version of political order by imposing a reign of police violence targeting poor farmers who could not afford to pay the rents demanded by state monopoly. The so-called reform was, in one sense, a violent metamorphosis concealed within a party-state battle to restore the Communist Party's weakened hold on a restless, famine-ravaged countryside, and the Deng-led Strike Hard Campaign was carried out in a way that ultimately hindered the development of inclusive pluralistic discourse and the rule of law. The reform-era Central government crackdown on rural crime, resulting in part from the rush of center policy itself, actually followed Mao-era templates of campaign politics and piled a new trauma onto existing Mao-era traumas, sometimes reviving memories of the dehumanization of the Great Leap and its violent simplification of rural life.

The memory of life-threatening procurement in the Great Leap Forward influenced tax resistance in post-Mao Da Fo. While Da Fo's farmers, experts in agricultural efficiency,[2] welcomed the changeover to household-based farming, they soon rejected the heavy burden of local party tax assessments, coupled with the obligation to first pay grain due to the state at its own dictated price. Unable to keep what was rightfully their share of the harvest, they had no choice but to resist the Deng-era tax system in whatever ways they could devise. Surely they appreciated Beijing's 2006 agricultural reform policy, which abolished the tax on the harvest, but they saw this center policy as a belated concession made out of Beijing's fear of revolt from below rather than a voluntary act of beneficence.

The one-child policy, imposed on a rural society where the production of children was taken up to overcome the great famine's destruction of customary

---

[2] See Netting, *Smallholders, Householders*.

social insurance arrangements, stoked memories of the Maoist assault on motherhood and family well-being and continuity in the Great Leap episode. This impetuous, brutal policy hurled Da Fo's young would-be mothers back to the traumatic years their parents had endured in the great starvation of the Great Leap, when they lacked the time, nourishment, and energy to produce children as they saw fit. Moreover, the one-child policy did so in an utterly visceral and dehumanizing manner. Angry and resentful villagers mobilized to resist the local party leaders, special forces, and thugs imposing this policy, which often went hand in hand with rent-collection schemes that lined the pockets of local power. The one-child policy, from which local party leaders – as in the Great Leap period – often exempted themselves and their families, completely ruined the credibility of policy as a tool of Central government legitimation and intensified the hatred villagers felt for local party leaders who conspired with higher-ups to deny them the right to strengthen household labor forces and produce sons who would protect them against party-backed bullies.

Da Fo did not experience an impressive advancement in basic rural education during the first decade of Maoist rule. The historic entitlement of education and enlightenment was taken away by uneducated, ignorant Mao-era local party leaders, and the rural education system collapsed under the pressure of the Great Leap famine. In Da Fo, a reform-era struggle welled up to replace the principal of the local school, a corrupt old-guard Maoist. This struggle was rooted in grievances stemming back to the Great Leap, for the principal's stewardship reminded villagers of the link between corrupt autocratic rule and the hunger and loss that came with the Leap famine. This protracted struggle gained momentum under reform, when CCP-appointed educational administrators again marginalized teachers and pressed them to accept corruption, all the while threatening them if they did not comply with practices that worked against both their material interest and the development of a transparent and efficient system of education designed to serve their students – the same pattern of politics that had ruined Da Fo's teachers, students, and farmers in the Great Leap and its famine.

If, as Andrew Wedeman has argued, the Communist Party thus far has been able to keep regime-ending corruption at bay,[3] the predatory corruption in remote, poor, reform-era Da Fo proved destructive, undermining economic development and deepening a legitimacy crisis that villagers associate with the worst days of Maoist rule.[4] Its aggravated forms stirred memories of party-state greed in the Great Leap, igniting protest against village and township party leaders whose greed and banqueting stoked villagers' fears of reexperiencing the kind of suffering and sacrifice they had endured under corrupt,

---

[3] Wedeman, *Double Paradox*.

[4] Wedeman makes clear that the "economically destructive corruption" in poor, underdeveloped China resembles the corruption that cripples the rural poor in underdeveloped countries. Ibid., 5.

two-faced local party leaders in the Leap famine. The everyday challenges to the callous behavior of these corrupt CCP leaders reflected popular indignation over the renewed violation of the popular Confucian ethical codes of conduct that had been overthrown by Mao's local accomplices in the Great Leap. Da Fo's history also underscores the influence of Mao-era politics on popular judgments of the reform-era police force. Locally, the Deng-era police, like the militias of the Mao era, were held in contempt. They failed to fairly mediate property disputes extending back to the Great Leap episode and to protect market-bound villagers against known thievery, and they turned routine police work into money-making schemes.

This study demonstrates that the same local CCP leaders who benefited from the inequities and injustices of the Great Leap took charge of the state delivery of electricity services in the reform period, repositioning themselves to get rich at the expense of farmers. The voices of Da Fo villagers who were exposed to the autocratic, vertical extension of a key reform-era "public" monopoly suggest that the political economy of state monopoly, and the official corruption enveloping this monopoly, unfolded locally in ways that revived memories of the violent rule experienced by villagers in the Great Leap. The CCP's artificial reform of the electricity monopoly fueled everyday contention, pitting villagers against its ground-level agents, whose family reputations for venality extended back to the Great Leap and its overthrow of centuries-old local traditions of leniency and kindness.

The notion that the post-Mao/post-Deng leadership has learned from past mistakes, promoting harmony and stability by accommodating individuals and groups previously excluded and ignored, seems dubious. In Da Fo, some of the unenlightened performances of the Maoist past seeped into the reform period, impeding the introduction of democratic forms of participation. Da Fo's people welcomed electoral democracy in part because they remembered that local party leaders, appointed by higher-ups, had abandoned consultation and imposed Mao's will in the Great Leap, a process that dragged their families and friends into famine. Wanting democracy to prevent leaders from taking them down the road to another great disaster, villagers understood the CCP suppression of free and fair elections as an act that only made it more difficult for the party to restore its legitimacy and manage dissent.

Petitioning, too, was entwined with an incessant yearning to escape the social nightmare of the Great Leap and influenced by a protracted struggle for compensation for personal sacrifices for the party-state and its national security goals – sacrifices that were undertaken to deal with the food scarcity that persisted in the aftermath of the great famine. Yet, as with democratic elections, the struggle for inclusion was thwarted by higher-ups, including the leaders in powerful CCP-controlled military hierarchies and those in Zhongnanhai. By suppressing petitioning, the Central government not only alienated some of its most loyal supporters, it also elicited memories of Mao-era neglect and betrayal, for Mao and his cadres had suppressed petitioners who called attention to the hunger induced by the Great Leap. In short, in Da Fo the failure of what Jean-Pierre Cabestan has called "enlightened plutocratic authoritarianism"[5] or what Steve Tsang has termed "consultative Leninism"[6] kept alive the memory of the Great Leap as institutional closure, and more or less escalated the struggle to escape the claws of CCP dictatorship.

The testimonies of Da Fo's migrant workers reflect the challenge of surviving under a state-orchestrated system of apartheid. Deng and post-Deng rulers perpetuated this discriminatory system, which Qin Hui and other China scholars have described as a strict, regime-designed, rural-urban divide.[7] Situated at the bottom of a three-tiered apartheid system,[8] some of Da Fo's migrant workers hailed from households ruined by the Great Leap and its famine. Most of them found it difficult to sustain life in urban construction settings without official work permits. In this respect, their fate mirrored that of Great Leap–era counterparts, who fled the radical scarcity of the brigade in 1958–1959, when nearly ten million desperate migrants poured into cities only to discover how very hard it was to secure food without government approval to work in an urban area.[9] Clearly, Da Fo's mobile semi-farmers faced a regime whose agents used the *hukou* system to threaten repatriation to the countryside and thereby secure compliance with insufferable terms of work life, which, in many ways, resembled those of the militaristic labor regime of the commune.

Thus Da Fo's migrant workers provided dirt-cheap, if not free, labor for modern urban development projects run by contractors and subcontractors frequently connected with the party-state. They were left to their own devices to avoid the pitfalls of working in this capricious, seemingly lawless system. Thanks to Mary Elizabeth Gallagher, we know that the post-Mao period saw the transfer of some migrant worker disputes, and the process of resolving them, to institutional channels deemed legal by the party-state.[10] In contrast, Da Fo's migrant workers often bypassed the channels of the poorly regulated labor system of the Central government, resolving many disputes without formal institutional support – and with cunning and the threat of force.

The life stories of Da Fo's martial artists – termed the local "mafia" – are another aspect of life in the village that compels us to acknowledge the importance of memory of the Great Leap famine in the contention of rural people. These young men, many of them survivors of famine-damaged households, embraced martial arts to survive the disorder and tumult of the transition from Mao to Deng; they activated this weapon to protect their small, weakened

---

[5] Cabestan, "Is China Moving Towards Enlightened Plutocratic Authoritarianism?"

[6] Tsang, "Consultative Leninism."   [7] See Qin, "Nongmin Liudong."

[8] See Whyte, *One Country, Two Societies*, 1–12, 15, and Mallee, "Migration, Hukou and Resistance in Reform China."

[9] Cf. Li Ruojian, "Dayuejin yu Kunnan Shiqi de Liudong Renkou."

[10] Gallagher, *Contagious Capitalism*, 113–121, 132.

families against local party leaders who in the Great Leap and its aftermath had forced villagers into submission. Whereas Yu Jianrong has represented the mafia as a dark social force pure and simple,[11] Da Fo's history shows that the leaders of its martial arts confederacy were only taking advantage of the authority deficit created by the CCP's impressive record of misrule to create an alternative, parallel system of force and governance. To be sure, the leaders of this martial brotherhood occasionally hurt farmers, and they were aligned with the local police. Their understanding of politics in CCP-ruled China, however, was conditioned by a deeply felt affinity with the kind of rebellious challenges that historically surfaced in the moments of dynastic misrule. The leaders not only encouraged resistance to the taxation of tillers and the fleecing of migrant workers; they also voiced great anger over the party-state attack on ancestor worship, and more specifically over the party's disrespect for the culture of the physical body, because – in accordance with the logic of Bryan S. Turner – they counted on their bodies to defend themselves and their friends against the aggression of CCP rule.[12] Experiencing themselves as "rebels in waiting," the martial artists stood ready to challenge the very regime with which they were aligned in the event that the balance of power and force were to turn dramatically against Beijing.

THE CONTENTIOUS NEAR-FUTURE

The nature and pattern of resistance in reform-era Da Fo suggests that people in rural places damaged by the Great Leap disaster will continue to engage contention, for several reasons. Each, I submit, is linked to an insufficiently reformed modality of Communist Party rule, and each therefore is likely to produce conflict between the powerful and the powerless in the near future.

The work of Hiroki Takeuchi, which differentiates poor, agricultural, and nonindustrialized villages from wealthy industrialized villages, offers a clue to the first reason.[13] Located in the highly saline, poor soil interior, Da Fo village had to compete with richly endowed and industrialized periurban villages. Beijing's developmental strategy favored the latter while disinvesting in the former, continuing a pattern of state discrimination against poor northern hinterland localities documented by Kenneth Pomeranz,[14] dating from the late Qing and early Republican eras, reinforced by the Great Leap, and lingering on into reform. Da Fo's farmers had a long history of distrusting a political system that had repeatedly betrayed them, and the post-Mao reformers did little to change the politics making for this discriminatory rural-urban divide.

---

[11] Yu, "Hei'e Shili shi Ruhe Qinru Nongcun Jiecheng Zhengquande?"
[12] Turner, *Body and Society.*   [13] Takeuchi, *Tax Reform in Rural China.*
[14] Pomeranz, *Making of a Hinterland.*

In the Da Fo area, the post-Mao Central government leaders left the reigns of subprovincial local governance in the hands of an ignorant, bellicose political base whose wolfish habits of rule crystallized in the peak moments of the state-making campaign of the Great Leap Forward, unleashing a radical attack on the customary entitlements of the farm household and delivering villagers into deadly famine.[15] In Da Fo, this work style remains more or less unreformed, so that villagers who have been burned by it in the past most likely will be inclined to challenge the local party leaders who rely on it to deliver "reform."

Deciphering this political work style is essential if we are to grasp the ABCs of the Communist Party's modality of domination and rule. As Da Fo's history reveals, at its core are six deeply entrenched habits, each of which can all too easily evoke villagers' memories of mistreatment in the catastrophic past and, in the right situation, inflame defiance and resistance.

The first of these habits is autocratic, arbitrary, often lawless rule, a Great Leap–era practice hindering the revival of Confucian-inspired receptivity and even-handedness.[16] Apparently, CCP leaders at different levels interpret, bend, and sometimes just ignore the laws of the People's Republic of China (PRC) as they please to protect their privileges and preserve the party system of domination. This habit generated popular anger and opposition in reform-era Da Fo, and there is little reason to assume it will not continue to provoke resistance in the future.

The second habit is aggression and reliance on various forms of force to suppress opposition. Many of these forms originated in the Great Leap's unbridled savagery. In helping enforce the Deng-led center's Strike Hard Campaign and birth-planning scheme, Da Fo village and Liangmen township party leaders still engaged these forms when they could get away with it, reminding villagers that the Communist Party continues to recruit and rely on local party leaders who demonstrate a willingness to carry out policy by force, and that the repression of the present is descended from the crackdowns and cruelty of the past. This habit of rule by force most likely will continue to invite counter-force from below, especially in villages such as Da Fo where the state has thwarted democracy and development.

The third is corruption. This case study reveals that corruption is the product of uncontested one-party domination, party-state economic monopoly without popular democratic oversight, and feeble legal constraint. It also teaches us that corruption has a root in the run-up to the Great Leap, when local party leaders developed a strong sense of entitlement to the rewards of office and proved

---

[15] Thaxton, *Catastrophe and Contention.*

[16] On the role of this arbitrary work style in forming the current public security-run "garrison state," see Sullivan's important article, "The Chinese Communist Party and the Beijing Massacre," in Goodman and Segal, eds., *China in the Nineties*, 90–92, 100. On Confucian receptivity and openness, see Wong, *China Transformed*; Wong, "Taxing Transformations."

indifferent to the complaints of the victims of their greed.[17] In the Da Fo area, the reform-era revival of the institutionally based greed prevalent in the Great Leap famine stoked anger and resistance, and unchecked, brazen corruption motivated villagers to stand up to haughty Communist party leaders at the village, township, and county levels. This study suggests that as long as CCP leaders enjoy immunity from prosecution and punishment for the corruption hindering survival pursuits in poor rural villages such as Da Fo, the drumbeat of contention will continue, and possibly grow louder.

The fourth dimension of this habitual Communist Party work style is falsification and outright lying about performance. Institutionalized distortion, pervasive at the national and local levels, is seemingly inseparable from the political crisis of the Great Leap past. In 2013, for example, the Xi Jinping-led Central government initiated a campaign to refute the occurrence of a massive famine in the countryside during the Great Leap period. The intellectual clients of Xi's princeling order produced scientifically unsound journal articles to disprove the famine's death toll, and then falsely accused researchers who had used rigorous demographic methods to determine the number of starvation-related deaths of engaging in statistical lies and spreading ludicrous rumors,[18] all in an effort to put the disruptive memory of the great famine back into a regime-treasured Mao-era snuff bottle. This sophistry is an important tool of authoritarian security and stability. After all, as Amartya Sen's argument about the free press, elections, and famines reminds us, a regime can get away with imposing massive starvation as long as it does not manufacture a newsworthy famine.[19] Censoring press coverage and thwarting the electoral dismissal of its local accomplices, the Mao-led CCP was by and large able to accomplish this goal in the Great Leap and after, thereby avoiding significant political consequence for its famine crime; and post-Mao political leaders, and their intellectual minions, have sought to maintain this immunity. Their efforts to refute, and contain, the growing scholarly evidence that the CCP developed its political order in part by generating a massive famine must be placed in this context. In the end, they fear the unpredictable consequences of open discourse over a

---

[17] On the alienating and anger-producing consequences of "an entrenched sense of entitlement," see James, *Assholes*, 4–5. On the historical context of this sense of entitlement, see Friedman and Selden, "War Communism," 27. See also Thaxton, *Catastrophe and Contention*, 87–88. Melanie Manion has shown, statistically, that for all practical purposes most CCP leaders still enjoy virtual immunity from prosecution and punishment for their corrupt dealings. Manion, "Issues in Corruption," 5–7, 9–11, 14–15, 21.

[18] See Mao, "Lessons from China's Great Famine"; and especially the splendid essay by Anthony Garnaut, "The Mass Line on a Massive Famine," 1–10.

[19] See Sen, *Development as Freedom*, 4, 15, 150, 153, 160–168, 178–185, 188. I am indebted to James C. Scott for calling this point to my attention, and for making me think harder about how Sen's work relates to this case study. Personal Correspondence, September 6–7, 2015; I also am thankful for Steven I. Levine's input on this matter. Personal Correspondence, September 19, 2015.

persistent legitimacy crisis that, as this study shows, often influences grassroots struggles in parts of the deep countryside.

As Lester Thurow has pointed out, the phenomenon of falsifying information is embedded in China's single-party system, under which Beijing holds to the fire the feet of any provincial or county official who fails to report robust GDP-calibrated growth in his domain, which in turn blinds higher-ups to what is actually going on in rural places like Da Fo.[20] Consistent with Thurow's point, Da Fo's farmers tell us that this work style invites popular antiregime invective not only because of the social damage it delivers in the present but also because they still associate lying with suffering in the Great Leap, when the institutionalized exaggeration of harvest returns fanned excessive procurement and delivered their family members into famine and ruin.[21] According to Da Fo's farmers, in the summer of 2012 the grain harvest in the Da Fo–Shangcunji area was not good, but the local party leaders reported that farmers enjoyed an unprecedented bumper harvest, all in an effort to please superiors, offering proof that the work style of the radical past is still operative. Fearing a return of this past, and the systemic force behind it, villagers most likely will fight or take flight, and Da Fo's history indicates that either course of action can intensify conflict with power.

A fifth component of the CCP's work style is evasion of responsibility, the correlate of which has been the shifting of blame for errors onto lower-level functionaries or onto opponents. The CCP's failure to admit and address its own errors was a major factor cascading the Great Leap's folly and inducing the precipitous descent into hellish famine. The tendency to scapegoat overzealous grass-roots cadres and adversarial "rich peasants" took on an institutional life of its own after the Maoist calamity – not unlike the Stalinist response to the murderous famines of 1932–1933 in the Ukraine and Kazakhstan, both of which were the direct product of policy made in Moscow.[22] An important reason why Da Fo's farmers gave up on and then resisted post-Mao/post-Deng village and township party leaders was that they simply could not get them to listen to their grievances or to take responsibility for government error – the stencil of undependable rule in the Great Leap episode still influences how village China is ruled.

Finally, the expendability of any individual or group who might openly challenge the right of CCP leaders to exercise any of the earlier habits of rule

---

[20] Thurow, "The Emergence of China and the Global Economy," 2004. For a shrewd essay on how the Great Leap Forward-influenced GDP craze has produced a rapid, mindless housing construction economy and, consequently, a serious housing bubble in the PRC, see Evans, "The End of China's Economic Miracle."

[21] On the exaggerated output of harvest and its devastating human consequences, see Bernstein, "Stalinism, Famine, and Chinese Peasants."

[22] On the Ukraine case, see Dolot, *Execution by Hunger*, and Perloff, "Holodomor." On the Kazakhstan case, see Pianciola, "Kazakhstan and the Geography of the Soviet Famine."

must be emphasized. As the testimony of Bao Yinbao, the leader of Da Fo's martial artist network, reminds us, the CCP has a deep hole into which it can "disappear" people who challenge the rules of the party-defined political game, and the predisposition to do so echoes the Great Leap Forward, when the disappearance of expendable dissidents was common practice in the antirightist campaigns introducing and enabling the Great Leap and engendering its famine.[23]

Because the post-Mao Central government leadership has not methodically altered the habitual work style of its rural political base, and because villagers know that they might be seriously harmed if they do not stand up to the local carriers of this work style – the price of passivity in the Great Leap Forward – popular contention most likely will grow. As this case study demonstrates, some of the rural people who opted for contention have drawn on memories of painful encounters with past injustice to muster ever bolder forms of resistance to the networks making up the party's rural base. In the Da Fo area, this resistance, when met with repression, apparently raised the stakes of political conflict and increased the chances for attacks on power: government offices came under siege; officials suffered verbal ridicule, kidnapping, and physical harm; and local police forces were greeted with profanities, rocks, and pitchforks. Knowing what happened to the meek in the Great Leap and in the Cultural Revolution, rural people will be less and less inclined to allow themselves to be treated as sheep under the reign of a wolfish, degenerate local party base. [24]

For the most part, the CCP leadership in village China is not, and never has been, a genuinely esteemed elite. Instead, as the case of Da Fo illustrates, the local party leaders who took charge of the post-1949 village political economy were uneducated, crude fringe elements. They were not equipped to improve the quality of life for villagers. In spite of the dismantling of the Mao-era commune, the reform-era Beijing leaders apparently did not learn this lesson well. Guided by self-serving greed and the quest for promotion within the authoritarian single-party system, Da Fo's old-guard Maoists were allowed to stay in power, insinuating their old habits into reform-era political processes, organizing force to enrich their local networks, and collaborating with township and county leaders to practice rent extraction and maintain economic monopoly, all of this in order to generate a surplus for higher-ups and to limit challenges to the established system of domination and exploitation. Regardless of its reform-era Confucian rhetoric, in the Da Fo area Beijing and its Henan provincial clients actually relied on rough-hewn hustlers who, in the great leap into state socialism and then, twenty-five years later, in the great leap into state capitalism, secured gains through hidden party-state connections, not

---

[23] On this predisposition and the CCP's use of "disappearance" as a threat, see Teng, "A Hole to Bury You In."

[24] Just as the scholarship of Edward Friedman would suggest; see "Raising Sheep on Wolf Milk."

through open independent business ventures and/or professional merit. In this situation, accepting reform was easily experienced as being tantamount to accepting the continuity of an underhanded, stingy politics that, when played out locally, usually left villagers out in the cold. Da Fo villagers refused to accept this kind of politics, and they and their counterparts most likely will continue to do so.

This experienced political exclusion is why so many of Da Fo's inhabitants still fear they might encounter another serious crisis of subsistence under CCP rule.[25] According to Cormac Ó Gráda, for many decades after the Great Irish Famine of 1845–1848 survivors held dreadful memories of this horrible event, passing them on to their descendants and feeding resentments, emotional discourses, and conflicts over the role of Westminster policy makers in engendering this massive subsistence crisis.[26] The political turbulence of Ireland's postfamine century reflected a deep-seated need to keep alive the memory of the great famine as an event of unequal suffering and unjust death.[27] If even in democratic Ireland rural people were fearful of accepting that the national state was capable of liberating them from the terrible past, and of giving up a famine narrative through which they (or those who claimed to speak for them) could mobilize resistance to power and its version of progress, then imagine how much more potent such a fear is in Da Fo, in an antidemocratic PRC whose rulers have strived to erase the memory of a similar past.

As we have seen, this fear drove resistance against CCP-structured taxation, fueled mobilization for a democratic alternative to one-party rule, and gave impetus to migration to the city world. Such resistance was essential to survival, for the disaster of the Great Leap taught Da Fo's farmers that the right to live had to be won, and sustained, through struggle at the margins of a CCP-led "civilization-state" that Martin Jacques argues operates on the basis of "duties shown by cadres towards the people they represent"[28] but that actually has operated on the precivilization principle of "survival of the fittest" and treated rural people as fodder for state developmental goals. People in Da Fo, and their counterparts in many border-area villages, understand the danger inherent in CCP-directed civilization. They have drawn on a host of cultural weapons to resist its practices, which fly in the face of treasured Confucian codes of humane conduct, and this book's findings indicate they most likely will continue to do so.

This study of Da Fo also shows that the CCP-led Central government organizes force to maintain the exclusive prerogative of its officials to extract rents

---

[25] On the importance of subsistence first principles for tillers, see Scott, *Moral Economy*, and Diamond, *World until Yesterday*.

[26] Ó Gráda, *Black '47 and Beyond*, 212, 232.

[27] In constructing this section, I have benefited from Ó Gráda, "Famine, Trauma and Memory," 142; McLean, *Event and Its Terrors*, 151–163, 6–18; and Morash, "Making Memories," 49–53.

[28] Jacques, *When China Rules the World*, 274.

from rural people.[29] In China's authoritarian political system, upper party leaders, the chiefs in charge of rent collection in specific economic sectors, allocate a portion of the money generated from rents as patronage to party-based clients positioned at descending levels of their networks. Apparently, this is one reason why the CCP-dominated system has generated popular anger. Not only were Da Fo's farmers by and large excluded from the vertically tiered system of patronage; the reform-era center also did not afford them institutional arrangements for advancing a claim on the pool of government-collected rents, continuing a pattern of marginalization that has roots in the Mao era.

Relying on this top-down exclusionary system of patronage, the post-Mao center was challenged to bind rural people to its purpose, and so practicing legitimation in the wake of the Great Leap disaster proved difficult. Worse, as Da Fo's response to the CCP administration of the electricity monopoly attests, this system put villagers in a situation where they were more or less compelled to fight against the long, coercive arm of the party's rent collection empire. Without self-government, without an independent legal system, the fight was unfair and risky. But it is a fight in progress, and the fight most likely will continue, for many villagers have no other choice.

Da Fo's history teaches us that the law governing the right to resist the disquieting effects of state rent collection has been subject to interpretation by public security forces. In this political situation, resistance has proven danger-ous, because at the outset of reform Deng Xiaoping himself – the paramount leader of the CCP – allowed internal security to play the key role in resolving popular struggles against the rent-collection agencies of the party-state. Moreover, Deng gave in to the demand of these specialists in violence for a larger share of the gains and privileges from rent – a political development that is nowhere to be found in rosy academic portrayals of the Deng-led transform-ation of China.[30] Over time, therefore, public security became a racket, with its members gaining more and more from the CCP-led authoritarian system they served, and the justification for this increase became dangerously entwined with its role in preventing and/or suppressing the rise of mass protest over rent collection. Thus in 2010, for the first time, Central government leaders increased the budget of public security to a sum surpassing the national defense budget.[31] The decision to implement this increase was framed as if contention had originated in society rather than in the design of the CCP, which, as Daron Acemoglu and James A. Robinson point out, is first and foremost a powerful "extractive political institution," whose security affili-ates, one might add, secure the order that is necessary for state-driven growth.[32]

[29] On state force and rent, see North, Wallis, and Weingast, *Violence and Social Orders.*
[30] For a notable example, see Vogel, *Deng Xiaoping and the Transformation of China.*
[31] See Henochowicz, "Machine Guns"; also see Buckley, "China's Internal Security Spending."
[32] Acemoglu and Robinson, *Why Nations Fail*, 439.

Thus people in Da Fo and its sister villages faced a daunting political dilemma: if they challenged the center's rent collection work and, by extension, its vertical hierarchy of power, they risked drawing public security into the fray, a dangerous step because public security itself had become a key player in state-organized money grabbing. With villagers better able to ramp up their social defenses and with local party leaders becoming audacious rent collectors, sometimes backed by public security forces, clashes between villagers and local power were bound to increase. This in part explains why Tsinghua University sociologist Sun Liping, an expert on the persistent influence of the party-led state on daily life in rural China, discovered that the PRC saw 180,000 mass protests in 2010,[33] and it explains why Da Fo villagers held the police in contempt and said they would be better off without them. In the near future, therefore, we should be prepared for confrontations between protestors and police that rip through the official representation of reform as a CCP-engineered liberation from the disharmonious past, of a state no longer turning inward on rural people – as happened in late Qing, in the Republican period, and again in the Great Leap Forward.

THE STABILITY AND DURABILITY OF THE AUTHORITARIAN POLITICAL SYSTEM

The interesting question is whether the stability and durability of the Central government itself could be jeopardized by the microbursts of resistance occurring in villages and market towns of this distant North China border area. Or is contention mainly a local affair, with villagers holding local party leaders and local officials responsible for misrule while excusing distant, good-intentioned Central government leaders?

For many years, political scientists and economists have been telling us that CCP-led Central government stability and durability rests substantially on economic performance. As I pointed out in the Introduction, rural people, including those in Da Fo, are better off materially today than they were in the Mao era. Nevertheless, the persistence of the Central government is first and foremost dependent on guns and steel. In the PRC, political power grows out of the barrel of a gun, and the CCP has long had the guns. The CCP used its Mao and post-Mao campaigns to continually disarm village people, so that it is nearly impossible for any individual to secure a firearm of any sort. This ultimately is why people in Da Fo have been powerless to effectively stop the lawlessness that has infused the Strike Hard and birth-planning campaigns, and why Da Fo's Bao Jingjian said, "Without weapons in their hands farmers could not do much to overthrow the CCP."[34]

---

[33] See Orlik, "Unrest Grows as Economy Booms."   [34] Bao Jingjian, interview.

The most earth-shaking change in Chinese politics in the past century has been the forging of a national combat-ready state army, the People's Liberation Army (PLA), which Beijing's leaders most likely can rely on to put down any rebellion. Rural people, including those in the Da Fo area, understand this great CCP achievement. Hence they will be inclined to think twice about openly challenging the party with armed struggle. Furthermore, the Communist Party has constructed a vast, multitiered system of internal security, including an informal plainclothes police unit, a beefed-up Public Security Force, and the million-man People's Armed Police. This latter, mobile strike force, and local police and auxiliary thug forces in rural towns, can be called in to help suppress local insurgents if and when the main army should falter. These armed, guardian forces give the regime great resiliency.

But it is not just that CCP still wields superior force. An important change seems to have occurred in the reform era, particularly since the Tiananmen Square events of June 4, 1989. In contrast to the Mao-orchestrated collective era, when CCP leaders often responded to just about any challenge to the chaos manufactured by policy with kneejerk violence, post-Deng rulers in particular have practiced a more selective version of repression. As Minxin Pei has pointed out, the regime is learning how to repress with brains and fingers as well as thumbs.[35]

We saw this politics at work in the response to contention in Dongle county's Da Fo village and in Neihuang county's Yixian village. Here the center authorized the use of the People's Armed Police only when local people directly challenged the one-child policy or when farmers attempted to overthrow the party's system of corrupt power. By way of comparison, neither the center, nor the provincial, nor the county-level police forces were mobilized to suppress contention against haughty local government leaders in the instances where popular Confucian norms were at play and, importantly, did not pose a direct threat to high state policy or power. Higher-ups more or less turned a blind eye to these local, small acts of resistance to official wrongdoing. If this kind of popular resistance had reared its head in the Great Leap, its leaders would have been seized by militia, subjected to party-framed struggle sessions, and sent to labor camps or prisons – or worse.

The CCP also has pursued a strategy of preemptive protest, more or less seizing protest leaders before they can appeal to, and possibly organize, a mass base of support. Da Fo's history shows this strategy has involved abducting prominent regional and national protest leaders, spiriting them off to undisclosed spaces of detention, and keeping them under house arrest and cut off from their followers and the public. This strategy, energized in part by CCP fears of an Arab Spring, probably will stump the efforts of local protest leaders to organize and direct an insurgency against the center. The resiliency of the

[35] Pei, talk at Dartmouth College, 2008.

regime is dependent on this clever form of lawlessness, the art of which was botched in the Great Leap Forward, when rural people who swam against the Maoist tide were left to die while in illegal detention.

Yet another strategy of repression has complicated the ability of would-be rebels to mount a serious challenge to Beijing. In the reform period, a few mini-rebellions sprang up in the province where Da Fo is located. In response, CCP-led Public Security Forces imprisoned the leaders indefinitely and refrained from the spectacular trials and punishments that would have given rebel leaders name recognition with the public. Thus only a few farmers in Da Fo, or in other interior villages, were able to learn about the agendas and goals of rebel leaders who might have shared their sense of injustice. Not turning proto-rebels into high-profile martyrs gives the regime staying power, or so it would seem.

Political psychology also would seem to work against a rebellion from below. This factor is inextricably bound up with the painful, enduring memories of Mao-era suffering and loss, especially the Great Leap and its carnage but also the killings of stigmatized party-state enemies in the Cultural Revolution.[36] Many of the interviewees in Da Fo and the surrounding villages said that if the political lid constraining the angry memories of the inhumane treatment of the dark past were to come off, it would be a political disaster for everyone, both for them and for the CCP, because the explosion of contention would likely produce hateful, sweeping violence. Some intimated that if there were another Cultural Revolution (which Da Fo's farmers appropriated to settle scores with the party-based perpetrators of the Great Leap famine[37]), they would kill every last CCP official. Surely, whether one is a small-fry party leader in the Da Fo area or a party big shot in Zhongnanhai, this kind of talk offers a frightening counterpoint to the stability maintenance discourse of institutional power. Few villagers looked forward to an all-out war with the regime, however. Few, if any, saw the face of the regime as a silhouette with an inner promise of support from security personnel who might, as David Shambaugh has suggested, express "human empathy" for the opponents of the party, and thus help facilitate deliverance to a brighter future.[38] They understand that if the lid comes off, the pathological, brutal work style that the Communist Party perfected in the Maoist Leap, and then relied on to deal with the post-Mao crises of state command, will summon itself, making the massacre of June 4, 1989, look like a relatively benign affair.

Judging from the testimonies of Da Fo's Great Leap survivors, rural people most likely will be inclined to fight harder to hang on to the small material gains they have secured through everyday struggles since the end of the great famine, and will be reluctant to risk such gains by throwing in with oppositionist forces

[36] See Su, *Collective Killings in Rural China*, 257–260.
[37] Thaxton, *Catastrophe and Contention*, chapter 6.
[38] Shambaugh, "The Coming Chinese Crackup."

calling for a new political system offering greater liberty, greater participation, and greater wealth – Mao, after all, wore out such a promise in the Great Leap. In this situation, local people more than likely will opt to initially engage in cautious, deferential protest, thereby giving CCP leaders the chance to defuse conflict by prudently addressing the claims of the powerless.

Surely Beijing's current leaders do not want to turn back the clock to the Mao era, thereby jeopardizing the advancement villagers have made in the long aftermath of the great famine. They know the CCP cannot afford to flirt with rural-oriented policies that might seriously split its leadership ranks or create shared anger across wide swaths of the countryside, fostering the conditions under which rural people from different walks of life might unite against their system of rule. This is why, in the reform era, the Deng and post-Deng leadership invited greater popular input into the politics shaping the implementation of reform, though, as the case of Da Fo illustrates, this input often was conditioned by the locally based leaders of the party-state.

Perhaps the introduction of formal democratic mechanisms in an authoritarian political system can, in some cases, foster regime-supporting identities and defuse the ire that drives extrainstitutional challenges to established power.[39] The Deng-led CCP center apparently intended to create manageable channels for claims making, to provide local people with checks on unaccountable local power, and to inhibit the kind of unregulated contention that would spell trouble for Beijing.[40] In fact, people in Da Fo welcomed elections, for they feared that greed-driven local party leaders would transmute reform into another cataclysmic famine. They also welcomed petitions, for the most part following the center's rules of engagement, and they hoped that the creation of the Cadre Responsibility System would enable them to effectively plead with local party leaders to respond to reasonable demands,[41] thereby avoiding the disempowerment that came with the loss of petitioning rights in the Great Leap episode.

Perhaps Beijing's rulers had little choice but to experiment with political inclusion. At the village level, popular disillusionment with the CCP was deep, for, as the stories of Da Fo's survivors indicate, villagers still lived under a regime rooted in the Communist Revolution, which culminated in the Great Leap Forward, an experience so monstrous that its survivors could too easily connect the smallest wrongdoing of local party leaders in the post-Mao period with the crimes Mao's local accomplices committed in the course of imposing

---

[39] See Levitsky and Way, "Rise of Competitive Authoritarianism," 52–53. Cf. Geddes, "Why Parties and Elections in Authoritarian Regimes?," 5–6, and Brownlee, *Authoritarianism in an Age of Democratization.*

[40] Cf. Takeuchi, *Tax Reform in Rural China.*

[41] Cf. Xi, "Collective Petitioning and Institutional Conversion," 54–71; Dimitrov, "The Resilient Authoritarians," 26–27; and Dimitrov, "Popular Accountability and Autocratic Resilience," 40–50.

the great famine. The leaders of the post-Mao center had to find some way to persuade local people of their good intentions and trustworthiness. To their credit, the Deng-inspired reform-era leadership, including the Hu Jintao–Wen Jiabao team, attempted to do just that, apparently winning some popular support and trust in the short term.

The political economy of the reform-era merit-oriented educational system might further inhibit unified, rural-based resistance and rebellion. Da Fo, and most of its sister villages, have been stratified internally by a renewed merit-based occupational mobility. If sustained, this development will likely impede any kind of insurgent solidarity, even if there were a crisis of Central government command extending into the countryside. Whereas this study finds that rural education surely has not been a complete success story, a significant minority – at least 2 percent – of Da Fo's residents took advantage of the reform-era educational system to give their children a far better life than was possible in the Great Leap era and afterward.

Many of these children are now adults who have secured a niche in the rising middle class, some in cities within the Hebei-Shandong-Henan border area and others across China – and the globe. Da Fo's high school graduates have opened businesses, found jobs worldwide, and assumed various leadership positions in China. Likewise, its college and technical school graduates have engineered an impressive ascent. In some cases, Da Fo's graduates have even soared to command an important presence in the PLA.

Bao Yutang, a parent of several of these upwardly mobile graduates, is speaking for the group of Da Fo parents who have made sacrifices for such ascent when he declares: "My financial situation has been quite bad for the past few years because I have had to support my three children to finish their education. Now that I have fulfilled my duty as a parent, my children will live better than my generation. They have gotten out of the countryside, and no longer need to struggle in the village. Their children will be better educated and have better lives."[42]

People such as Bao Yutang seem reluctant to endorse the cause of village discontents whose children, as we have seen, have dropped out of school, ended up in prison, or lived the lives of mafia outlaws. We might expect these conservative villagers to support a right-wing CCP-led center in return for Beijing's retreat from direct interventions in their daily lives and its occasionally flamboyant "reforms" of official corruption and state monopoly. Such proregime sentiments have also been encouraged by CCP propaganda, which argues that utilitarian policy making has given rural people the chance to reclaim the mastery of material life and that the party is working to end the disorder of the past. As Jonathan Unger has reasoned, people in the thrall of this propaganda might stand with the center in a showdown with a rebel movement.[43]

---

[42] Bao Yutang, interview.   [43] Unger, "China's Conservative Middle Class," 43.

The variables of time, population movement, and state policy maneuvering also would seem to work against the memory of the Great Leap's anguish powering a rural-based rebellion arising against the Central government. Apparently, the older generation has, in some cases, transferred the memory of this state-inflicted disaster to its older children, but this transference apparently has not significantly affected the under-thirty-five generation, that is, the young people who were born during the post-1978 reform era. Even on hearing parents tell of Great Leap–era suffering, few of Da Fo's younger villagers took the stories to heart. In some cases, they either refused to believe the stories or chided their parents for allowing local party leaders to inflict the Leap's damage. In this respect, the shadow of Mao's Leap famine seems to be receding, making it more difficult for survivors haunted by memories of this institutionally induced calamity to use the past to mobilize youth against the regime. As more and more of the great famine's survivors die, this shadow will retreat even more, thereby decreasing the danger of youth joining a rebellion influenced by the catastrophe of Maoist rule, or so it would seem. Time, and politics in the time of reform, seem to be on the side of the regime.

Reform-era population mobility also seems to have worked against the formation of antistate contention based on the shared Great Leap memories of a critical mass of villagers. As more and more young people have moved out of Da Fo and nearby villages into towns and cities, the phenomenon of the "dying village," which characterizes many other parts of China's rural interior, has progressed to the point of weakening the potential for any dissident group to forge a united front against the regime based on Great Leap–era indignation and shared, combustible memories. In short, this finding too offers hope for regime continuity.

One school of thought, advanced by Barrington Moore, Jr., argues that imperial China was characterized by a highly exploitative system of power, with the Emperor being "a super landlord who collected grain from his subjects."[44] Whatever the accuracy of this assessment, Mao Zedong gained just such a reputation with many rural dwellers who managed to survive the great famine engendered by his party's terror and plunder. Indeed, some of Da Fo's farmers, including Bao Zhongxin, blamed Mao as well as his overzealous Henan provincial clients for the Great Leap's destruction, and thus for ruining the CCP's chance to gain legitimacy through virtuous governance.[45]

The important question, therefore, is whether the post-Mao CCP leadership has been able to restore the image of the Central government as an institution of good will. On the face of it, Da Fo's history suggests that Beijing has made some progress on this front. Whereas the majority of Da Fo area farmers attributed reform-era betterment to their day-to-day sacrifices, rather than help from the center or its appointed local party leaders, at least 40 percent

[44] Moore, *Social Origins of Dictatorship and Democracy*, 168.   [45] Bao Zhongxin, interview.

proclaimed Hu Jintao to be "the best Emperor in Chinese history." To be sure, they knew the Central government was still squeezing them. Nevertheless, the "tolerable squeeze" of reform seems to have made it more difficult for rural dissidents operating on memories of the Great Leap's intolerable plunder to draw people from differently endowed, differently fated villages into a rebellion against the center.

Thus, although this book demonstrates that memories of the terrible Maoist past still inform popular contention in the deep countryside, the post-1978 Central government apparently has begun to pass on a "mystique of benevolent governance"[46] to more than a few Da Fo area villagers. This mystique, with its prognosis of a future with humane treatment from imperial power, would seem to compete daily at the ground level with the memories rural people hold of the Maoist Leap as a war without mercy, giving both rulers and ruled the time that is needed to move out of the dark past.

This, of course, is the hope and ruse of higher-ups in Beijing, and the mantra of academic-based social scientists who, eschewing the study of politics from below, ignoring how memory of past suffering informs quotidian resistance in the present, and assuming that tomorrow will be the same as today, see the regime as resilient.[47]

BEYOND THE SMOKE AND MIRRORS OF REFORM AND THE ARGUMENT FOR REGIME RESILIENCY

Whether hope and ruse can actually carry China's authoritarian rulers safely through the next serious political crisis involving popular contention remains to be seen, however. There is no warranty ensuring the long-term workability of the above strategy of state-managed contention and stability. This book's data on ground-level contention in Da Fo village argue that the political situation in this rural locality is far more fluid and volatile than an analysis focusing on top-level institutionalized authoritarian power and policy making would suggest. If we listen carefully to the voices of individual villagers who still live in memories of Mao-era political suffering, we can detect a more complex representation of resistance as a continuing effort to end the institutionalized irrationalities of CCP rule. The question, therefore, is this: Is it possible that the microbursts of resistance in the Da Fo area, influenced by memories of Mao-era suffering and resentment, might jump out of the local fire pit in which they by and large are confined, and spiral out of control to threaten power holders in Beijing in a crisis moment of state command?

---

[46] This term is from Shue's brilliant essay, "Legitimacy Crisis in China?," 36.
[47] On authoritarian resiliency, see Nathan, "Authoritarian Resilience," 6–17, and Perry, "The Illiberal Challenge of Authoritarian China," 3–15, and "Cultural Governance in Contemporary China," 1–5, 29.

As mentioned earlier, Da Fo area villagers are keenly aware that power in the PRC grows out of the barrel of a gun and that the resiliency of the Central government is mainly dependent on its ability to keep modern weaponry out of the hands of ordinary people. In recent years, however, Public Security leaders have indicated that China is no longer completely sealed off from the international arms market and that every caution must be taken to prevent foreign arms, and underground homemade arms, from finding their way into the hands of rural people – recall that many of Da Fo's youngsters carried handcrafted pistols. The CCP has reason to fear such a development, for the desire of Da Fo area farmers to combat institutionalized corruption and privilege with machine guns and firing squads apparently is not unique.[48] And after all, the right to bear arms was a customary right that rural people exercised in late Qing and early Republican times, and villagers in Da Fo, and elsewhere, remember that this right was surrendered to the CCP-led antirightist campaigns of the Great Leap, making it more or less impossible for them to counter the force behind socialist expropriation with force.[49]

Of course rural people fear the possibility of regime counterviolence if the political lid were to come off. Nevertheless, few of the Da Fo survivors of the Great Leap's ruin were utterly dispirited and immobilized by this fear. Many were inclined to push the envelope of contention more than the paradigm of "authoritarian resiliency" would suggest. They tell us that living with the CCP, and surviving its error and oppression across many decades, wore away some of their fears of party rule. Many of these survivors of CCP rule were proven to be tough, resilient people. Having survived the extreme danger of the Great Leap as well as the Cultural Revolution, they took the post-Mao reform as a chance to show local party leaders they could not be broken, to find ways to recover family securities previously surrendered to the fear of party-state mechanisms of repression.

Apparently, therefore, the Da Fo area villagers whose interviews are recorded in this book were not incapacitated by the traumatic, disordered past. Instead, they seem to have found ways to carry on with their lives, and one such way was to take up resistance.[50] While this resistance was informed by the fear of a recurrence of Mao-era suffering, it also was the product of a resiliency developed through surviving the pathologies of Mao and post-Mao politics. Most important, its practitioners seem to have taken resistance as training to overcome the fear of standing up to party rule. Some of them experienced resistance as empowerment, so that resistance itself helped relieve fears of taking on the regime. To more than a few villagers, therefore, resistance promised a

---

[48] In October 2012, Louisa Lim, a University of Leeds–educated China specialist known for her astute news reports on the PRC, found travelers expressing a similar desire in Yan'an, the cradle of the Communist Revolution. Lim, "China's New Leaders Inherit Country at Crossroads."

[49] Cf. Thaxton, *Catastrophe and Contention*.

[50] This reading resonates with Southwick and Charney, *Resilience*, 1, 5–6, 53–55.

different political future, for it was seen as leading CCP-ruled China toward the fate of 1989 East Germany where, according to Jeffrey Kopstein, everyday contention managed to "wear down a despotic state over four decades and thus make its overthrow an appealing strategy in the first place."[51]

This study shows that villagers preferred deferential, nonantagonistic methods of choosing leaders and remonstrating with higher-ups. In the Da Fo area, Beijing failed to develop grass-roots institutional channels to accommodate this preference. The Deng Xiaoping center allowed its political base to hijack the village electoral process and refused to allow villagers to elect leaders "the American way," and the Hu Jintao center instructed this same party base to greet petitioning with repression.

In Da Fo, this Central government unwillingness to develop a functional conduit for rural people to have a political voice seems to have backfired, thereby weakening support for the regime. On the one hand, the defeat of the democratic prospect made villagers cynical of party-guided democracy. It also made them aware that if democratic impulses were to actually oust party-controlled village governments, the CCP would mobilize force to crush popular opposition and decisively end the so-called democratic experiment. On the other hand, the stonewalling and suppression of petitioning taught villagers that the CCP was not on their side, and thus weakened trust in national-level party leaders. As petitioners worked their way up the state hierarchy, they learned to deconstruct the bureaucracy under Beijing, just as Li Lianjiang has found in his work on petitioners.[52] Each step they took in dealing with the party-state hierarchy taught them that CCP politicians at its top – not the local government agents labeled by higher-ups as difficult to govern – called the shots.

In many agrarian societies, village dwellers have turned to resistance and rebellion only when their deferential appeals have been defined as subversive by rulers unwilling to make even minimal concessions. Witness Syria. The outbreak of the 2011 civil war originated in the refusal of Bashar al-Assad's regime, constructed around crony capitalists and brutal security forces, to heed farmers' deferential appeals for government help in the face of crop failures brought on by the regime's abandonment of subsidies for small farmers and its allocation of shriveling water resources to capitalist agrobusinesses as well

---

[51] Kopstein, "Chipping Away at the State," 393. Anyone who is familiar with defiance of police orders, fights with baton-wielding police forces, and fire bombings of special police tanks sent to quell protests and riots in China's rural towns understands how resistance in Da Fo resonates with the rise of contention in the countryside today. Cf. Lu and Ngai, "Unfinished Proletarianization," and Lu Huilin, lecture with film.

[52] See, especially, Li, "The Magnitude and Resilience of Trust in the Center," 3–36, and "Political Trust and Petitioning in the Chinese Countryside," 222. Cf. Li, "Political Trust in Rural China," 231–233.

as by devastating regional drought.[53] Could authoritarian China encounter a similar fate? Facing the rapid depletion of groundwater reserves on the arid north China plain, a phenomenon accentuated by the reform-era diversion of mountain-fed river runoff to urban water supply and by the insatiable water needs of hundreds of coal-fired electricity plants, some of Da Fo's farmers worried that drought, in combination with the party-state abandonment of tillers dependent on water-intensive double-cropping, might portend a comparable predicament and make them turn against the regime.[54]

If the lesson of the remonstrations of Da Fo's returned PLA veterans offers any clue to the future, the post-Deng national CCP leadership policy of exclusion might bring more and more protestors to realize that the principal problem is in Zhongnanhai, not merely, or simply, in the center's inability to overcome local government obstacles to policy implementation. The CCP-led center's strategy of scapegoating local party leaders for harm delivered to villagers – a strategy that was honed in the immediate aftermath of the Great Leap when Mao and his provincial clients shifted responsibility for the famine onto subordinates – is an open secret in Da Fo, whose farmers said the party should "change its work style, and not blame the problems of today on some other day or some other people."[55] I do not know how widespread knowledge of this regime-maintenance trickery is in the deep countryside, but its spread surely will attenuate the ability of Beijing leaders to wall off outrage over present-day injustice from memories of past suffering.[56]

In the meantime, as Carl Minzner has shown, the Central government's chosen top-down tool of rule, the Cadre Responsibility System, continues to create pressure on local party leaders to meet its goals, or give the appearance of doing so, if they are to survive and advance in the shark-infested, sycophantic CCP-run system of power.[57] This system often gives rise to local cadre abuse of the legal proclamations of the center itself and creates incentives for cadre abuse of rural people, compelling the latter to survive through contention. According to Minzner, many such protest leaders have learned the arts of political organization from serving in the armed forces[58] and, implicitly, bring these to bear in

---

[53] See Hinnebusch, "Syria," 95–99, 103; Edelen, "Resource Mismanagement, Climate and Conflict in Syria"; "Syria's Civil War Has Environmental Origins"; and, especially, Friedman's interviews of drought-devastated Syrian farmers who say they turned to resistance and insurgency only after the Assad regime turned its back on them. *Years of Living Dangerously*.

[54] Bao Xuejun, interview. Their worries are confirmed in "Water: All Dried Up"; in Qiu, "China Faces Up to Groundwater Crisis"; and in Foster, Garduno, Evans, et al., "Quaternary Aquifer of the North China Plain," 81–88.

[55] Bao Jingjian, interview.

[56] I am indebted to Felix Wemheuer's insightful article for helping me grasp this point. "Dealing with Responsibility for the Great Leap Famine," 184, 186, 188, 193–194.

[57] Minzner, "Riots and Cover Ups: Counterproductive Control of Local Agents in China," 57–61, esp. 58; see also Minzner, "Social Instability in China," 58–72.

[58] Minzner, "Social Instability in China," 70–71.

ramping up contention. Whether they would support a rebellion is partly dependent on CCP effectiveness in preventing PLA leadership corruption from alienating rank-and-file soldiers and veterans. According to James Mulvenon, the CCP leadership has not fully institutionalized anticorruption norms within the army.[59] Some Da Fo area veterans were angered by army corruption. A few were convinced that if there were a rebellion, "the soldiers will side with the farmers,"[60] as opposed to fighting for corrupt PLA officers.[61]

The "right wing populism" thesis makes good sense. But just because some rural people have found a niche in China's post-1978 urban political economy does not mean they are incapable of choosing to go along with a rebellion, were one to develop in the countryside. This book's findings on the center's tax, birth-planning, and education policies, and especially on the political economy of corruption, suggest that people from both rich and poor stations see CCP-led government as hopelessly corrupt and predatory and that in some cases this judgment extends to the center.

Thus it should not surprise us that President Xi Jinping's new 2013 antigraft campaign, in which he vowed to attack "tigers" at the top of the political system as well as small-time corrupt local party leaders, was taken as more of the "same old, some old" center's flawed policy behavior.[62] People in Da Fo and nearby villages complained that the post-Mao center has focused anticorruption work mainly on local party leaders rather than on princelings with ties to Beijing or on super-rich, super-influential higher-ups, most of whom are relatively immune from serious investigation of official wrongdoing,[63] thereby perpetuating the Great Leap–era practice of blaming lower-order subordinates to cover up center responsibility for corruption. As more and more rural people adopt the view that petty corruption of local party leaders and the grand corruption of the center go hand in hand, questions about the origins of systemic corruption will grow, giving villagers more reason to give up on Beijing and contest the prevalence of corruption at the top.

Of course it is possible, as Noah Feldman has argued, that the CCP will rise to meet the challenge of systemic corruption.[64] The comments of villagers warn against such optimism, however. Their view concurs with that of Roderick MacFarquhar, who has cautioned that General Party Secretary Xi Jinping represents a political system so corrupt that any serious effort at reforming it would threaten the regime itself.[65] To Da Fo villagers, MacFarquhar's wisdom resonates with the Chinese proverb *shang liang bu zheng xia liang wai* (If the

[59] Mulvenon, "So Crooked They Have to Screw Their Pants On," 1–8.
[60] Zheng Yunxiang, interview; Ruan Shifan, interview.
[61] Gan, "Retired Generals Point to 'Horrible' Graft in PLA."
[62] See Chen, "President Xi," and Greene, "Can Xi Jinping Really Fight Corruption?"
[63] For an excellent article on this, see Baaru, "Xi Jinping's Anti-Corruption Drive."
[64] See Subrahmanyan, "Feldman Examines Corruption and Political Legitimacy in China."
[65] See Yu, "Reform Unlikely Says China Expert."

upper beams are not straight, the lower beams will go aslant – If the leaders set a bad example, their subordinates will follow). This is why, notwithstanding the progress of reform, so many of the Da Fo area farmers said they were *still* searching for a Bao Qingtian, the legendary Song dynasty leader who waged an uncompromising war against crooked officials.

Although the right-wing populism narrative should not be dismissed outright, the memory of Great Leap–era corruption persists, and is sometimes inflamed by reform-era corruption, fueling a sense that the CCP is finished. Many Da Fo villagers saw the CCP-led center trapped in the system of corruption it created over many decades, and they said that blowback from this system might yet prove to be an insurmountable problem for Beijing; this is why they predicted that the fate of the CCP is that of the Kuomintang. Of course, these astute villagers might not embrace a rebellion against the regime – but they might not oppose those who start one, either.

Such a rebellion would be especially alarming to Beijing, for it would signal another Tiananmen, which after all was substantially caused by official corruption.[66] And Da Fo's history suggests it most likely would draw discontented teachers, migrant workers, and retired soldiers into its ranks, none of whom were in, or near, Beijing en masse to support the protest movement of 1989. Surely their involvement in such a challenge would add an element to the equation of mass contention that was missing in the spring of 1989. The post–Great Leap struggle to find justice has prepared Da Fo's teachers to play the role of the transvillage, transregional coordinators of an insurrection against regime corruption. Da Fo's migrant workers can quickly locate some of Beijing's high officials and officially connected nouveau riche networks, for they built the buildings in which the latter reside and work. The petitioning campaign of Da Fo's army veterans has taught them how to find the Public Security Offices and the Central Military Affairs Commission in Beijing. A few of its retired PLA veterans, who joined the army to survive the post–Great Leap dearth, served as bodyguards for key PLA generals and CCP leaders in Zhongnanhai, so they have knowledge of the compounds of the high and mighty.[67] They also know how to use AK-47s, know the whereabouts and workings of army munitions plants in North China, and know how to make it difficult for Beijing leaders to defend themselves by deploying army units from Baoding and other key North China garrisons. In short, all of these angry, mobile village people could, if the conditions were right, take part in bringing down the very system they helped build.

But why would they decide to fight? It is important to bear in mind that people from places like Da Fo cannot heal past traumas through involvement with mental health workers, truth commissions, trials of perpetrators, the arrests of higher-ups, forensic studies of the deaths of innocents, artistic

---

[66] Cf. Miles, *Legacy of Tiananmen*, esp. chapter 5.   [67] Bao Yutai, interview.

personal counternarratives, films such as Hu Jie's *Spark*, or eye-opening books –
Yang Jisheng's *Tombstone*, a documentary of the Great Leap Forward Famine
by a former New China News Agency reporter, is banned from publication in
the PRC.[68] Worse, when Great Leap–era survivors in Henan province have
erected food memorials and stelae to commemorate the lives of famine victims,
they have been scolded by cadres and paid "visits" by Public Security forces.[69]
Given the blockage of such choices, villagers most likely have stored memories
of past trauma in the gut.

One cannot help but wonder whether Beijing's leaders fear the example of
Ukraine, where President Viktor Yanukovich lost the struggle to assimilate
individual memories of the Stalinist-inflicted 1932–1933 Holodomor famine
into a hegemonic *supramemoria* of a "general tragedy" of the Ukrainian people
to democratic forces capable of narrating their own ethnic political history.[70]
My guess is they do not. Rather than open up discourse on the Great Leap
famine, Beijing's leaders most likely will attempt to move ahead with authoritarian rule by building a case that the famine was a national pan-Han tragedy
that everyone, including those within the party, wants to forget. This might
work. Yet Da Fo's history shows that individual encounters with the CCP-
dictated hierarchy of suffering in the great famine live on in memory. Thus
Oksana Zabuzhko's claim that the corrupt Ukrainian state (prior to the
2014 Revolution of Dignity) had a direct lineage to the Holodomor "when
the most ruthless prospered"[71] seems to resonate with what Da Fo's farmers tell
us about the political system of the PRC, where the party whose agents suffered
least, and often gained the most, in the great famine still holds power and rules
in ways that invite antagonistic resistance cum rebellion. It does not seem that
such a development is imminent; perhaps it is highly unlikely. But, looking at
contention in Da Fo, we can see that ascending small acts of protest are pushing
out from the magma within the vents of the Great Leap's destructive heritage.
To focus mainly on words and policies coming out of Beijing misses subsurface
pressures for genuine reform that are rooted in this particular authoritarian
system's catastrophic past.

Rebellions in rural societies by and large do not start overnight. They often
grow out of low-profile, restrained acts of resistance to a train of regime threats
to daily routines of livelihood. Reform-era China is no exception. An example,
right out of my field work, is worth consideration, for it reminds us how
different the world looks from the vantage point of rural people who might,
from the perspective of Beijing, or outsiders, be labeled "disorderly." In June
1987 I was doing interview work in Shadizhuang, Neihuang county, with Peter
J. Seybolt, a Harvard-educated China historian. To reach this remote place

---

[68] Cf. Yang, *Tombstone*.   [69] See "Nanfang Renwu Zhoukan."
[70] On the Ukraine case, see Motyl, "Deleting the Holodomor."
[71] See Baziuk, "Behind Ukraine's Protest." In developing this point, I also have prospered from
personal correspondence with Marta Baziuk, February 24, 2015.

required travel on dirt and sand roads. On June 1, as I was en route to the village, a small delegation of farmers suddenly emerged to plead with the Chinese driver of our Japanese minivan to stay off the road's edge, which state-owned buses and army trucks had trespassed, damaging the abutting peanut fields. Rather than respectfully heed this request, the driver, a CCP appointee, talked down to the farmers, giving them the impression he would follow his own rules of the road. I soon paid for his arrogance. Later in the day, after a sudden torrential rainstorm drove us from the village, our van returned to the section of the road where the farmers had implored the driver to spare the peanut crops. The road was not there, however. In its place was an eight-by-eight-foot hole, deep enough to wreck the minivan. Forty yards away, at the top of a hill, stood about twenty rain-soaked farmers, old and young. Wielding shovels, spades, and pitchforks, they stared at us with a silent warning: do not tread on our livelihood, do not test us. I had to join with the driver, and the minivan occupants, to fill the hole with hand shovels during a fierce rain and lightning storm.

These small acts of resistance, undertaken to maintain some measure of autonomy within the landscape of an intrusive authoritarian modernism, are an important part of the dynamic ebb and flow of low-profile contention in rural China. If an incipient rebel movement were to form in the deep interior, and if rural people join it, then some of these acts surely will find their way into it, and the aged villagers who personally remember the Great Leap disaster just might help it along.[72] Verbal firefights with village party leaders will be combined with kidnappings – already a trend in Da Fo and the border area. Township and county police forces will be met with the threat of counterforce by villagers capable of turning their bodies into missiles – clearly a progression in the works. Roads will be torn up and/or booby-trapped, and county, provincial, and national security forces will be slowed down, if not ambushed – already a dangerous undercurrent. Whether Beijing can stay ahead of such a protoinsurgency is an open question. I doubt that such a scenario will even develop, let alone begin to achieve the level of serious threat. But if it does, Beijing's local political base most likely will see an uptick in resistance, the arts of which have been developed by villagers who have survived many party-state campaigns, including that of the Great Leap, and who, if Da Fo's history is relevant, have concluded that Heaven will be on their side in wiping out the CCP.

Finally, whether the "mystique of benevolence" manufactured by reform-era Central government propaganda machinery can actually help Beijing's rulers survive a rebellion is uncertain. Reading the evidence from Da Fo, and other border area villages, suggests there are two problems with assuming the center

---

[72] I find it interesting, and relevant, that the woman who is pictured as a protest leader on the front cover of Xi Chen's *Social Protest and Contentious Authoritarianism in China* appears to be at least seventy-five years old.

will be able to hold on to power. They go to the heart of this book's argument that rural-cum-urban China is a highly contentious place and that the political stability manufactured by the CCP is, as Susan Shirk has argued, fragile.[73]

For one thing, the national-level CCP leadership ultimately rules much of rural China through the use of an informal thug base, which the party-state still relies on to contain and suppress popular contention in the crisis moments of rent collection and command. The hustlers and hooligans who make up this base have a long track record of trampling on the dignity of rural people who want little more than to be treated fairly, thereby inciting them to resistance, which the CCP frames as "disturbance and disorder" and then responds to with repression – a pattern of rule that hardly resonates with virtuous-cum-sturdy governance.

For another thing, we know from several protest incidents of the past decade that individuals who chose to stand up to police and thugs have galvanized the support of massive crowds. Thus far, the Central government has more or less contained such incidents. Nevertheless, as Wang Feng and Yang Su have pointed out, in the PRC "the measures of protest management are experimental and ad hoc, subject to the whims of the current 'emperor,' and void of a constitutional foundation or institutional guarantees."[74] In amplifying this point, even some of the Da Fo farmers who praised Hu Jintao pointed out that the "mystique of benevolence" is based on mere words and that Beijing's leaders have ruled in accordance with a restrictive systemic reality. According to Bao Xuejun, "Hu Jintao was like the emperors of the past – he was blind. He was unable to grasp what is going on in the countryside, because everywhere he went the lower officials already had made arrangements for him to see what they wanted him to see. In fact, Hu Jintao was not as smart as the emperors of the ancient past, for they disguised themselves and went to see what was actually happening in local society without letting the local officials know."[75]

Apparently, villagers saw Hu's successor in a similar light. Looking at the present through their past, it is easy to understand why they might conclude that Xi Jinping's campaign to foster a Mao-like personality cult and to embrace Mao as a caring, incorruptible, truth-seeking leader will likely make it more difficult for those at the top to grasp the danger in promoting submissiveness within the state as well as within society. Celebrating Mao could backfire,[76] especially in the parts of rural China where many villagers who were hurt in the great famine recall that Mao oppressed all who opposed him and created a political atmosphere that motivated *him and his followers*

---

[73] Shirk, *China – Fragile Superpower.*

[74] Wang and Su, "How Resilient China's Regime Is and Why"; see also Su and He, "Street as Courtroom."

[75] Bao Xuejun, interview.

[76] Compare with Brady's wisdom, "Xi Jinping's Challenge," March 25, 2015: Here I also am drawing on the wisdom of Bailey, *Kingdom of Individuals*, 9.

to present favorable pictures of development, when in reality there was decay and deprivation.[77] Da Fo's history hints that some local party leaders as well as many villagers fear re-victimization, and that Central government rulers who want followers to tell them what they want to hear, and who willfully ignore the faults of their political system, will only refresh the memory of past suffering and invite resistance. In short, while reform-era Beijing leaders have made progress in policing mass protest, it remains to be seen if they have fully escaped the trap of intolerance, misinformation, and "willful blindness" that facilitated the Great Leap disaster,[78] and that has proven fatal to more than one repressive authoritarian regime.

UNKNOWN CHINA, TOCQUEVILLE, AND THE UNCERTAIN FUTURE

To get back to the theme of this book, whether popular memory of Mao's Great Leap into folly and famine might actually influence the course of a transregional rebellion against the Central government is of course unknown. If the story of ground-level contention in Da Fo raises the specter of regime instability, we must heed the wisdom of Martin King Whyte and not leap to the conclusion that rural China is a social volcano pure and simple[79] or that a rebellion in this one region might spread and easily pick up support from discontented famine survivors in other regions.

Reflecting back, it seems that Da Fo village, located in a remote, grain-deficit border area with primitive transport links to interior regional cities, did not suffer nearly as much from the Great Leap famine as villages in regions with fertile grain lands and modern transport links to major urban areas. As Anthony Garnaut has demonstrated, the Mao-led CCP met its procurement goals by targeting rural communities in these latter regions, so that the intensity of the famine in some of them was greater;[80] indeed, the death rate in these some of these regions doubled, tripled, and quadrupled that of Da Fo, which lost only 6.8 percent of its population to the Leap and its famine.[81] We simply do not know if memories of the Great Leap episode still complicate party-state legitimacy and significantly influence day-to-day contention in the villages of these other severely damaged regions. We cannot, therefore, use the particular findings of this microlevel study of Da Fo to make reliable predictions about

---

[77] For the scholarship that resonates with their memory, see Becker, *Hungry Ghosts*, 83; Yang Jisheng, *Tombstone*, 104; and Dikotter, *Mao's Great Famine*, 89.

[78] See Dikotter, *Mao's Great Famine*, 84–85; and Bernstein, "Mao Zedong and the Famine of 1959–60," 424, 429–430, 432–433, 440–441, and 445.

[79] Whyte, *Myth of the Social Volcano*.

[80] Cf. Garnaut, who has helped me with this point. "The Geography of the Great Leap Famine," 323–327, 338–341.

[81] Thaxton, *Catastrophe and Contention*.

how the Great Leap episode, with its still understudied dimensions of space, time, and memory, might facilitate or hinder transregional-cum-national challenges to CCP rule, that is, the political stability of "China."

Nevertheless, if we place the findings on Da Fo in the context of the wisdom of Alexis de Tocqueville, it seems that two of the critical determinants of political instability and upheaval are present in this part of rural China, and hypothetically in some other unstudied parts of the countryside, and that the PRC's future will be affected by the way its national leadership addresses each of them.

The first, according to Tocqueville, is a closed political system under the leadership of autonomous corrupt aristocrats who live only for administrative privilege while feigning commitment to public service.[82] The phenomenon of ruling mainly for office-based privilege reflects the politics engendering the Great Leap disaster, and it resonates with the habits of power in reform era Da Fo – habits that have only fostered opposition to the Communist Party's version of order and justice and that point toward a future marked by greater conflict.

The second is the failure of the self-proclaimed forces of Liberation to accommodate the persistent memories of violence and terror unleashed by the Revolution they brought to power.[83] Tocqueville has taught us that this failure poisoned civil discourse and compromised the post-1789 democratic experiment in his native France.[84] Keeping this in mind, the story of Da Fo suggests that the CCP's failure to face up to the truth about the Great Leap Forward, to help the survivors of this catastrophe recover from its emotional and physical damage, has kept alive powerful memories of past individual and community suffering in the Mao era. These memories of "power without integrity," in combination with official practices that bring out the worst in all parties involved in contention, will only hinder the trust building that is essential for rural people to pay respect to the Communist Party's authority, increasing mistrust, contempt, and conflict, as has been the case with Da Fo.

One way out of this dual institutional dilemma would be for the CCP leadership to favor popular Confucian precepts supportive of pluralist discourse, tolerance, and dissent, so that rural people might begin to experience their engagement with party leaders in terms of a win-win proposition, slowly but surely giving up distrust of power – and the desire to avenge the past.

---

[82] See Richter, "Tocqueville's Contributions to the Theory of Revolution," 75–107. For the empirical support for this point, see Shih, Adolph, and Liu, "Getting Ahead in the Communist Party," 179–183. This seminal article demonstrates that the CCP relied on the Cadre Responsibility System to promote state fiscal growth and stability and that the CCP's leadership system itself did not actually promote economic growth. The latter came from the move toward household farming, labor mobility, and the opening to foreign direct investment, and in any event key CCP factions at the top of the centralized political system, apparently including "princeling" leadership factions, raked in the lion's share of goods from "reform."

[83] See Markoff, *Waves of Democracy*, xiv.   [84] Ibid.

Precisely because such precepts are, as Francis Fukuyama has pointed out,[85] compatible with liberal democracy, the CCP is unlikely to take this path. Thus grass-roots struggles to reclaim the basic rights for which Da Fo's inhabitants have been fighting probably will continue and, in some cases, gain force from obstinate memories of the painful lessons of Mao-era rule.

Of course, these two conditions alone are insufficient to trigger a massive transregional rebellion, let alone sustain a successful insurgency, against the Central government. But, as Bruce Gilley has argued, if a rebellion were to occur, some of China's rural people might see in it a chance to rectify a great historical injustice that still haunts the construction of a national political community founded on respect for individual human dignity and democratic empowerment.[86]

---

[85] Fukuyama, "Confucianism and Democracy," 20–33.
[86] Gilley, *China's Democratic Future*, 221.

Bibliography

Chinese Sources

Cao, Jinqing. *Huanghe Biande Zhongguo* (China Along the Yellow River). Shanghai: Wenyi Chubanshe, 2000/2003.

Cao, Shuji. *Dajihuang: 1959–1961 Nian de Zhongguo Renkou* (The Great Famine: China's Population during 1959–1961). Hong Kong: Shidai Guoji Chuban Youxian Gongsi (Times International Press), 2005.

Chen, Dabin. *Ji E Yinfa de Biange* (Reforms Originating from Hunger). Beijing: Zhonggong Dangshi Chubanshe (Central Chinese Communist Party History Press), 1998.

Chen, Tingwei. "1960 Nian Zhongnanhai Neide Yici Jiuzai Yingji Huiyi: San Nian Kunnan Shiqi 'Dai Shipin Yundong' Chutaiji" (The 1960 Disaster Emergency Meeting in Zhongnanhai: The Record of the "Substitute Food Movement" in the Three Difficult Years). *Wenshi Cankao* (Historical Reference Materials), No. 14, July 2010.

Chen, Yiyuan. *Jianguo Chuqi Nongcun Jiceng Zhengquan Jianshe Yanjiu: 1949–1957, Yi Hunan Sheng Liling xian Wei Ge'an* (A Study of Rural Grass-roots Administration: 1949–1957 [Li Ling county, Hunan]). Shanghai Shehui Kexue Chubanshe (The Academy of Shanghai Social Sciences Press), 2006.

Cheng Ming (Cheng Ming Monthly). Hong Kong, June 1, 1998.

Da Jihuang Dangan (The Great Leap Famine Archive). *Xin Guancha* (New Observations), 2000. www.xgcbbsindex.com/wh/famine//.

"Dianli Gongyebu Wenjian Guanyu Zhizhi Nongcun Yongdian Luan Shoufei de Tongzhi" (The Official Document on the Regulation of Illegal Utility Fees Published by the State Ministry of Industry and Electricity). *Nongcun Diangong* (Rural Electrician), Vol. 1, 1994.

Ding, Shu, and Yangyi Song. *Dayuejin–Dajihuang: Lishi he Bijiao Shiye Xiade Shishi He Sibian* (Great Leap Forward, Great Leap Famine: The Truth and Analysis in Historical and Comparative Perspective). Hong Kong: Tianyuan Shuwu Chubanshe (Greenfield Bookstore), 2009.

Fan, Ziying. "Guanyu Dajihuang Yanjiuzhong de Jige Wenti" (Several Commentaries on Research into the Great Famine). *Jingjixue (jikan) China Economic Quarterly*, Vol. 9, No. 3, April, 2010.

Fan, Ziying, Lingjie Meng, and Hui Shi. "Weihe 1959–1961 Nian da Jihuang Zhongjie Yu 1962 Nian?" (Why Did the Chinese Famine of 1959–1961 End in 1962?). *Jingjixue (jikan) China Economic Quarterly*, Vol. 8, No. 1, 2008.

Feng, Zhi, and Li Longjiang. "Dangqian Nongcun 'Cunguan' Fubai Wenti yu Duice" (The Current Problems and Coping Strategies Surrounding the Corruption of Local Cadres). *Lianzheng Wenhua Yanjiu* (Honest Culture Research), Vol. 2, 2012.

Fu, Lili. "Qianyi Nongcun Xuanju Zhong de Jiazu Liyi Jituan Xingwei" (A Study on the Behavior of Family Interest Groups in Rural Elections). *Xue Lilun* (Learning Theory), Vol. 10, 2009.

"Gansu Shengwei Jiancha Jiejue Tongwei Deng Sange Ciao de Naoliang Wenti" (The Communist Party Committee of Gansu Province Examination and Solution to the Conflict [Grain Riots] over Food Problems in Tongwei County and Two Other Counties). *Xinhuashe Neibu Cankao* (New China News Agency, Internal Reference Materials), March 5, 1960.

Gao, Hongbin. "Zhongguo Shenpan Weiyuanwei Zhidu Gaixing Hechu" (Reforming the Chinese Judicial System). *Falu Shiyong Yuekan* (Journal of Applied Law), No. 3, 2006.

Gao, Hua. *Zai Lishi de Fengling Dakou* (At the Fengling Ferry of History). Hong Kong: Shidai Guoji Chuban Youxian Gongsi (Times International Publisher), 2006.

Gao, Wangling. *Renmin Gongshe Shiqi Zhongguo Nongmin "Fanxingwei" Diaocha* (An Investigation of the Counteractive Behavior of Chinese Farmers during the Era of the People's Commune). Beijing: Zhonggong Dangshi Chubanshe (Chinese Communist Party History Press), 2006.

"Guanyu Jianguo Yilian Dang de Ruogan Lishi Wenti de Jueyi" (Resolution on Some Questions Concerning the History of the Party Since the Establishment of the People's Republic of China). *Renmin Ribao* (People's Daily), July 1, 1981.

Jia, Yanmin. "Dayejin Shiqi Henan Dajihuang de Balu Guocheng" (On the Exposure of the Great Famine in Henan in the Great Leap Forward). *Jiangsu Daxue Xuebao (Shehui Kexue Ban)* (Journal of Jiangsu University) (Social Science Edition), Vol. 13, No. 3, May 2012.

Li, Jun. *Congzhong Congkai: 1983 Nian "Yanda" de Beilun* (As Severe and Fast as Possible: The Paradox of the 1983 "Strike Hard" Campaign). *Nanfang Dushibao* (Southern Metropolis Daily), No. 6, November 7, 2008.

"1983 'Yanda' de Beliun" (A Paradox of the 1983 Strike Hard Campaign), *Nanfang Dushibao* (Southern Metropolis Daily), November 3, 2008.

Li, Lianjiang, and Ou Bowen (Kevin J. O'Brien). "Dangdai Zhongguo Nongmin de Yifa Kangzheng" (Villagers' Rightful Resistance in Contemporary China). In *Jiuqi Xiaoying* (The 1997 Effect), ed. Wu Guogang. Hong Kong: Taipingyang Yanjiusuo (The Pacific Research Institute), 1997.

Li, Qinggang. "Jin Jinan Dayuejin Kan Jiu Ruogan Wenti Zongshu" (Several Articles about the Great Leap Forward). *Dangdai Zhongguo Yanjiu* (Modern China Studies), Vol. 17, No. 1, January 2010.

Li, Ruojian. "Dayuejin Shiqi Jiceng Ganbu Xingwei Fenxi" (An Analysis of Grass-Roots Cadre Behavior in the Great Leap Forward). *Xianggang Shehui Kexue Xuebao* (Journal of Hong Kong Social Sciences), Winter, 1998.

"'Dayuejin' yu Kunnan Shiqi de Liudong Renkou" (The Floating Population in the Great Leap Forward). *Zhongguo Renkou Kexue* (Chinese Demography), No. 4, 2000.

"Dayuejin yu Kunnan Shiqi de Shehui Dongdang yu Kongzhi" (Social Turbulence and Social Control during the Great Leap Forward and the Period of Difficulty). *Ershiyi Shijie Pinglun* (Hong Kong: The Magazine of the 21st Century), Issue 62, No. 4, 2002.

"Zhibiao Guanli de Shibai 'Dayuejin' yu Kunan Shiqi de Guanyuan Zaojia Xingwei" (The Failure of Index Management [Targeting]: An Analysis of Systematic Fraud by Officials in the "Great Leap Forward" Movement and the Period of the Great Famine). *Kaifang Shidai* (Open Times), No. 3, March 2009.

Li, Zhiguo. "Dajihuang Niandai de Touqiang Xingwei" (The Activity of Theft and Robbery in the Great Leap Famine). Beijing: Yanhuang Chunqiu (Annals of the Yellow Emperor) No. 7, July 2009.

"Li Peng Jiazu Zhangkong Zhongguo Jingji Mingmai" (The Li Peng Family Control of the Economic Lifeline of the Chinese Economy), http://news.creaders.net/china/newsViewer.

Liang, Jing. "Cong Konghua Zhiguo Dao 'Dongchang' Zhiguo" (From Rule by Rhetoric to Rule by Secret Police). *Xinshiji*, January 26, 2010.

"2009 'Chuanzhang' Hu Jintao de Zhongguo Dalu" (2009: The Path of China under Chief Hu Jintao). *Nanfang Zhoumou* (Southern Weekly), March 19, 2000. Trans. David Kelly.

Liang, Zhiyuan. *Dayuejin Zhong Boxian Ganbu Zuofeng Wenti Jishu* (The Issue of Cadres' Work Style in Bo County during the Great Leap Forward). Beijing: *Yanhuang Chunqiu* (Annals of the Yellow Emperor), No. 10, October, 2009.

Ling, Zhijun. *Lishi bu Zai Paihuai, Renmin Gongshe zai Zhongguode Xingqi he Shibai* (History Is No Longer without Direction: The Rise and Fall of the People's Commune in China). Beijing: Renmin Chubanshe (The People's Press), 1997.

Liu, Fuzhi. "Yanda Jiu Shi Zhuanzheng – Ji Deng Xiaoping Tongzhi Dui Yanda De Zhuan Lue Jueci" (Yanda as a Form of People's Democratic Dictatorship – A Record of Deng Xiaoping's Strategic Policy of the Strike Hard Campaign). *Zhongguo Jianchabao* (China Procuratorial Daily), January 13, 1992.

Liu, Kunyuan. "Qiaoshi Jinggao Zhonggongguo Guanbiminfan" (Qiao Shi Warns People's Republic of China that Oppressive Government Is Driving People to Rebellion). *Zhonghua Pingshu* (China Comments), Issue 22, June 2008.

Liu, Yuan. "Dayuejin Yundong yu Zhongguo 1958–1961 Nian Jihuang-Jiquanti Zhi Zai de Guojia Jiti yu Nongmin" (The Great Leap Forward and the Chinese Famine of 1958–1961: State, Collective, and Peasants in the Centralized System). *Jingjixue (jikan) China Economic Quarterly* (Beijing University Press), Vol. 9, No. 3, April 2010.

Lu, Huiln. "Weixing Shi Ruhe de Shang Tiande, Xiangcun Jiceng Ganbu yu Dayuejin" (How Were the Satellites Launched? The Grass-Roots Cadres and the Great Leap Forward). *Nongcun Yanjiu* (Rural Studies) (in French) (2007). Originally an unpublished paper. Beijing University Sociology Department, 2005.

Lu, Xueyi. "Nongmin Zhenku, Nongmin Zhen Qiong" (The Farmers Live a Bitter Life, the Farmers Are Really Poor). *Dushu* (Readings), January 2001. U.S. Embassy-China.org.

Ma, Qianli. "Qunfang Budan, Daodi Nage 'huanjie' Chule Wenti? – Dui Liuxian Nongcun Laobing Quanfang Shijian de Huigu yu Sikao" (What Resulted in the Constant Mass-Petitioning? – A Review and Reflection on the Mass-Petition Incident of Veterans in Li County [Hunan]). *Zhongguo Xiangcun Jianshe* (China's Rural Village Reconstruction), Vol. 4, 2009.

Min, Shan, and Zhou Hongbo. "Lun 'Yanda' Zhong de Ruogan Wenti" (On Several Problems in the Strike Hard Campaign). *Fazhi yu Shehui Fazhan* (Law and Social Development), May 2002.

"Nanfang Renwu Zhoukan: 1959–1961 Niande Dajihuang Jiyi" (Memories and Recollections of the Great Famine of 1959 to 1961). *Southern People's Weekly*, No. 16, May 21, 2012.

"1983 Nian 'Yanda': Feichang Shiqi de Feichang Shoudan" (The Strike Hard Campaign in 1983: The Special Method in the Special Time). *Wenshi Cankao* (Historical Reference), Vol. 20, 2010.

Qin, Hui. *Gongze Zhimi – Nongye Jitihua de Zairenshi* (The Secret of the Commune – Reconsidering Agricultural Collectivization). *Ershiyi Shiji* (The Twenty-First Century). Xianggang Zhongwen Daxue Chubanshe (The Chinese University of Hong Kong Press), August 1998.

   Nongmin Liudong: Liangxing Xunhuan yu Xunhua (Peasant Migration: A Virtual Circle and Vicious Cycle). *90 Niandai de Nongcun yu Nongmin Wenji* (A Collection on Countryside and Farmers in the 1990s). Xianggang Zhongwen Daxue Chubanshe (The Chinese University of Hong Kong Press), 1998.

   Renmin Gongshe yu Chuantong Gongtongti (People's Commune and Traditional Community). Hong Kong: Zhongguo Shuping (China Book Review), No. 13, 1998.

Ren, Baoyu. "Caizheng Xiaxiang: Nongcun Jicheng Zhengfu Caizheng Hefaxing Wenti Yanjiu" (Finance in the Rural Areas: A Study of the Fiscal Legitimacy Problem of Rural Local Governments). *Huazhong Shifan Daxue* (Central China Normal University), 2007.

Shan, Hongxing. "You Nongcun Jihua Shengyu Weifa Xingzheng Yinqi de Sikao" (Reflections Upon the Illegal Administrative Activities of the Birth Planning Campaigns in Rural China). *Shehui Kexuejia* (Social Scientist), June 2007, supplement.

Sheng, Jianwei, Liu Guihe, and Xie Xiaolai. "Linshu 'cunguan' Tuiwu Junren da Liucheng – Shandong Sheng Linshi Xian Xuanba Tuiwu Junren Chongshi Nongcun Jiceng Zuzhi Diaocha" (Sixty Percent of the Elected Cadres in Linshu County Were Veterans – A Study of the Policy of Promoting Veterans into Local Party Cadre Positions in Linshu County, Shandong). NS, ND. *Shijie Ribao* (World Journal), December 31, 2002.

Song, Eva. *Xunzhao Dajihuang Xingcunzhe* (Looking for the Survivors of the Great Famine). New York: Mirror Books, 2013.

Sun, Zhiqiang. "Nongcun Cunweihui Xuanju Zhong de Wenti Qianxi" (A Study of the Problems of Rural Election Fraud). *Dazhong Shangwu* (Public Commerce), Vol. 8, 2009.

Tang, Zhaoyun. "San Nian Kunnan Shi Qi Nongcun Jihuang yu Nongcun Renkou de Guanxi" (Rural Famine and Rural Population in the Three Years of Hardship). *Jiangsu Daxuebao (Shehui Kexue Ban)* (Journal of Jiangsu University) (Social Science Edition), Vol. 12, No. 3, May 20, 2010.

Wang, Lihong, Yuzhan Liu, and Xiumin Zeng, "*Qianxi 'Dayuejin' Shiqi Lingdao Zhe de Shehui Xinli*" (Elementary Research on the Social Psychology of Leaders in the

Great Leap Forward Period). Jinan: *Shidai Wenxue (xia ban yue)* (Times Literature, second half of the month), No. 6, June, 2008.

Wang, Mingliang. *Xianshi Jichu Yu Lixing Sibian: Ping Yanda Xingzhi Zhengce* (The Foundation of Reality and Rational Thinking: Comments on the Criminal Policies of Strike Hard). *Xingshifa Pinglun* (Criminal Law Review). Beijing: Zhongguo Zhengfa Daxue Chubanshe (China University of Political Science and Law Press), 2005.

Wei, Xiangyu. "Wo Guo Nongcun Jiceng Fubai de Chengyin ji Yingdui Silu Tanxi" (A Study of the Causes, and of the Strategies of Coping with Corruption in Rural Chinese Government). *Fazhi yu Shehui* (Law and Society), Vol. 10, 2009.

Xia, Yong, ed. *Zhouxiang Quanli de Shidai* (The Era of Rights). Beijing: Zhongguo Zhengfa Chubanshe (China University of Political Science and Law Press), 1995.

"Xiaochu Nongcun Shehui Yige Bu Gongzheng Yinsu – Shekeyuan Yanjiuyuan Dang Guoyinig Tan Feichu Nongyeshui" (Eliminating an Unequal Element of Rural Chinese Society – The Opinions of CCAS Researcher Dang Guoyin on the Abolition of the Agricultural Tax). *Xin Jingbao* (The Beijing News), 2006.

Xiao, Jiansheng. *Zhongguo Wenming* (Reflections on Chinese Civilization). Hong Kong: Xinshiji Chubanshe (New Century Press), September 25, 2009.

Xu, Shan. "Zhongguo Shifan He 30 Nian" (The Anti-Criminal Campaign Style over Thirty Years). *Liaowang Dongfang Zhoukan* (Oriental Outlook), September 3, 2009.

Xu, Shan, and Ge Jiangtao. "Congqing Da Hejin Jin Xingshi" (Chongqing's Engagement in the Battle against Organized Crime). *Liaowang Dongfang Zhoukan* (Oriental Outlook), September 3, 2009.

Xu, Shan, and Yu Zhang. "Fanhei Fengbao Zai Shengji" (The Anti-Criminal Storm Upgrade). *Laowang Dongfang Zhoukan* (Oriental Outlook), September 3, 2009.

Yan, Lebin. "Guizhoude Dajihuang Niandai" (The Years of the Great Famine in Guizhou Province). *Yanhuang Chunqiu* (Annals of the Yellow Emperor), No. 5, May 2012.

Yang, Jisheng. "Dalao Dajihuang Jiyi" (In Search of the Memory of the Great Famine). *Nanfang Renwu Zhoukan* (Southern People's Weekly), No. 15, 2012.

Mubei: Zhongguo Liushi Niandai Dajihuang Jishi (Tombstone: A Record of the Great Famine in China in the 1960s). Hong Kong: Cosmos, 2008.

Yang, Kuisong. "Mao Zedong Shi Zenyang Faxian Dajihuangde?" (How Did Mao Zedong Find Out about the Great Famine?). *Caijing* (Caijing Magazine), No. 15, June 2012.

Ying, Bichang. "Xin Nongcun Shiye Xia Nongmin Xiwu de Renzhi yu Xingwei Yanjiu" (A Study of Peasants' Perceptions and Actions of Martial Arts from the Perspective of New Rural China). *Wuhan Tiyu Xueyuan* (Wuhan Institute of Physical Education), 2008.

Ying, Xing. "Shenti yu Xiangcun Richang Shenghuo Zhong de Quanli Yunzuo–Dui Zhongguo Jitihua Shiqi Yige Cunzhuang Ruogan Anli de Guocheng Fenxi" (Body and Power in Everyday Rural Life: A Process-Oriented Analysis of Several Cases in One Village during China's Collectivization Period) in *Zhongguo Xiangcun Yanjiu* (Studies on Rural China), ed. Philip Huang. Beijing: *Shangwu Yinshu Guan* (The Commercial Press), No. 2, 2003.

You, Wei, and Xie Ximei. "Yanda Zhengce You Fanzui De Xingshi Kongzhi" (The Yanda Policy and the Control of Criminal Cases). *Xingfa Pinglun* (Criminal Law Review). Beijing: Zhongguo Zhengfa Daxue Chubanshe (China University of Political Science and Law Press), 2005.

Yu, Jianrong. *Dangdai Zhongguo Nongmin de Yifa Kangzheng* (Peasant Lawful Resistance in Contemporary China) Changsha: Wenshi Bolan (Horizons of Culture and History), No. 12, 2008. (Originally read as ND, 1–8.)

"Dangqian Zhongguo Neng Bimian Shehui Dadongdang Ma – 2009 Nian 2 Yue 9 Ri zai Riben Zaodaotian Daxue de Yanjiang" (Can Contemporary China Avoid Social Upheaval? – A Speech at Waseda University in Japan, February 9, 2009).

"Hei'e Shili shi Ruhe Qinru Nongcun Jiecheng Zhengquande? – Dui Hunan 40ge 'Shikongcun' de Diaocha" (How Did the Dark Forces Invade the Basic Power Structure in the Rural Areas? – An Investigation of Unrest in 40 Hunan Villages). In *Lilun Cancao* (Theoretical References), No. 4, Zhonggong Fujianshengwei Dangxiao (CCP Fujian Provincial committee party school) Fuzhou, 2009.

Kang Zhengxing Zhengzhi: Zhongguo Zhengzhi Shehuixue Jiben Wenti (Confrontational Politics: The Essential Problem of Chinese Sociology). *Renmin Chubanshe* (People's Publishing House), 2010.

"Liyi Quanwei He Zhixu: Dui Cunmin Jili Duikang Jiceng Dangzheng Shijian de Fenxi" (Interest, Authority, and Order – An Analysis of Villagers' Collective Confrontations with Local Party and Administrative Units). *Zhongguo Nongcun Guancha* (Rural China Survey), Vol. 4, 2000.

"Xiangcun Zizhi: Huangquan, Zuquan he Shenquan de Lianjie" (Rural Self-Government: The Combination of Imperial Power, Clan Power, and Gentry Power). Yu Jianron's blog, http:///blog.legaldaily.com.en/blog/html/08/2443308-4022.html, November 2009.

Xinfang Zhidu Diaocha Ji Gaige Silu (A Survey of the Administrative Petitioning System and Thoughts on the Road of Reform). Beijing: Shehui Xingshi Fenxi Yu Ce-2005 (Analysis and Forecast of China's Social Development), 2005.

Xinfang Zhidu Pipan (A Critique of the Petition System). Speech at Beijing University, December 2, 2004. On Line (December 5, 2004), at www.yannan.cn/data/detail .php?id=4842; and in *Zhongguo Gaige* (China's Reform), No. 2, 2005.

Yu, Xiguang. "Dajihuang Zhongde Yinjing Canan" (The Tragedy of Yingjing County during the Great Leap Famine). *Jianghuai Wenshi* (Jianghuai Cultural History), No. 2, March 2013.

Dayuejin Kurizi Shangshuji (A Collection of Petitions Made during the Hard Times of the Great Leap Forward). Hong Kong: Shidai Chaoliu Chubanshe (The Tide of the Times Press), 2006.

Zeng, Jieming. "Li Peng Ji Qi Fubai Jia Zu De Qianjing He Chulu" (The Future of Li Peng and His Corrupt Family). Trans. TQ. Published in Taiwan, March 2008. www.secretchina.com/news/08/04/02/238816.html.

Zhao, Zongli. "Dajihuang Niandai Pohai Shangfang Zhe Shiliao" (Historical Materials on Persecuted Petitioners in the Great Leap Famine). *Yanhuang Chunqiu* (Annals of the Yellow Emperor), No. 7, July 2010.

Zhou, Changjun. "Boyi Chengben Yu Zhidu Anpai" (Negotiation, Cost, and Design of Institutions: An Institutional Economic Analysis of Strike Hard). *Xingshifa Pinglun* (China Criminal Law Review). Beijing: Zhongguo Zhengfa Daxue Chubanshe (China University of Political Science and Law Press), 2005 (also 2003).

Zhu, Liyi. "Nongwang Gaizao: Fubai Youliang de Lun Xiantu" (The Reform of the Electricity Grid Structure: The Phantom of Corruption). *Guancha yu Sikao* (Observation and Contemplation), Vol. 1, 2005.

English Sources

Acemoglu, Daron, and James A. Robinson. *Why Nations Fail: The Origins of Power, Prosperity, and Poverty.* New York: Crown, 2012.

Adams, Julia. *The Familial State: Ruling Families and Merchant Capitalism in Early Modern Europe.* Ithaca, NY: Cornell University Press, 2005.

Aizenman, N. C. "New High in U.S. Prison Numbers," *The Washington Post*, February 28, 2008.

Alexander, Jeffrey C. "Toward a Theory of Cultural Trauma." In *Cultural Trauma and Collective Identity*, ed. Jeffrey Everman et al. Berkeley: University of California Press, 2004.

Amnesty International Report. AL Index ASA 2001. *Amnesty International.* February 17, 2001: 51–52.

Auroe, Merle. "Towards a Chinese Sociology for Communist Civilization." *China Perspectives*, No. 52, March–April 2004.

Baaru, Sanjaya. "Xi Jinping's Anti-Corruption Drive – Rounding Up the Usual Suspects." *China Business Hand*, January 3, 2013 (online).

Babbie, Earl. *Practice of Social Research.* Belmont, CA: Wadsworth, 1979.

Bailey, F.G. *The Kingdom of Individuals.* Ithaca, NY: Cornell University Press, 1993.
  "The Peasant View of the Bad Life." In *Peasant Societies*, ed. Teodore Shanin, Baltimore, MD: Penguin, 1973.

Ban, Pamela. "Chinese Economic Reform." *Concord Review*, No. 1, June, 2011.

Banik, Dan. "Democracy, Drought and Starvation in India: Testing Sen in Theory and Practice." PhD Thesis, Department of Political Science, University of Oslo, 2002.

Banister, Judith. *China's Changing Population.* Stanford, CA: Stanford University Press, 1987.

Barme, Geremine. *Shades of Mao.* Armonk, NY: M.E. Sharpe, 1996.

Baum, Richard. "The Limits of Authoritarian Resilience." *CERI*, January 17, 2007. www.ceri-sciences-po.org.
  "Richard Baum on Obstacles to Political Reform in China." http://fivebooks.com/interviews/richard-baum, October 21, 2010.

Baziuk, Marta. "Behind Ukraine's Protest Are Memories of Moscow's Famine." *The Globe and Mail*, December 11, 2013.

Becker, Jasper. *Hungry Ghosts: Mao's Secret Famine.* New York: Free Press, 1996.

Bell, Daniel A. "What America's Flawed Democracy Could Learn from China's One-Party Rule." *The Christian Science Monitor* (Global Viewpoint), July 24, 2012.

Bellah, R.N. "Father and Son in Christianity and Confucianism." *Psychoanalytic Review*, Vol. 52, No. 2, 1965.

Bernhardt, Katherine. *Rents, Taxes, and Peasant Resistance: The Lower Yangzi Region, 1840–1950.* Stanford, CA: Stanford University Press, 1992.

Bernstein, Thomas P. "Farmer Discontent and Regime Responses." In *The Paradox of Post-Mao Reforms*, ed. Merle Goldman and Roderick MacFarquhar. Cambridge, MA: Harvard University Press, 1999.
  "Instability in Rural China." In *Is China Unstable?*, ed. David Shambaugh. New York: M.E. Sharpe, 2000.
  "Mao Zedong and the Famine of 1959–1960: A Study of Willfulness." *China Quarterly*, Vol. 186, June 2006.

"Stalinism, Famine, and Chinese Peasants: Grain Procurements during the Great Leap Forward." *Theory and Society*, Vol. 13, 1984.

"Unrest in Rural China: A 2003 Assessment." Center for the Study of Democracy, University of California-Irvine. April 13, 2004.

"Village Democracy and Its Limits." *ASIEN*, April 2006.

Bernstein, Thomas P., and Lu Xiaobo. *Taxation without Representation*. New York: Cambridge University Press, 2003.

Bianco, Lucien. *Origins of the Chinese Revolution, 1915–1949*. Trans. Muriel Bell. Stanford, CA: Stanford University Press, 1971.

Peasants without the Party: Grass-roots Movements in Twentieth-Century China. Armonk, NY: M.E. Sharpe, 2001.

"Tax Protest as the Foremost Expression of Peasant Resistance: China, 1900–1949." Paper presented at the annual meeting of the Association of Asian Studies, April 5, 2002.

Black, Lindsay. "China Ex-Food and Drug Safety Chief Sentenced to Death." *Reuters*, May 29, 2007.

Blok, Anton. *The Mafia of a Sicilian Village, 1860–1960: A Study of Violent Peasant Entrepreneurs*. New York: Harper Torchbooks, 1974.

Bly, Robert. *Iron Man: A Book about Men*. New York: Vintage, 1990.

The Sibling Society. Reading, MA: Addison-Wesley, 1996.

Bo, Kong. "Institutional Insecurity: The Key to Energy Security." *China Security*, Summer 2006.

Bossen, Laurel. *Chinese Women and Rural Development: Sixty Years of Change in Lu Village, Yunnan*. Lanham, MD: Rowan and Littlefield, 2000.

Bourdieu, Pierre, Alain Accardo, and Priscilla Parkhurst Ferguson. *The Weight of the World: Social Suffering in Contemporary Society*. Stanford, CA: Stanford University Press, 1999.

Bozzoli, Belinda. *Theaters of Struggle and the End of Apartheid*. Athens: Ohio University Press, 2004.

Brady, Anne-Marie. "Xi Jinping's Challenge Is to Be Strong Enough to Loosen Control." *Financial Times*, March 25, 2015.

Branigan, Tania. "Xi Jinping Vows to Fight 'Tigers' and 'Flies' in Anti-corruption Drive." The Guardian.com, January 22, 2013.

Braudel, Fernand. *Civilization and Capitalism, 15th–18th Century*, vol. 1: *The Structures of Everyday Life*. Trans. Sian Reynolds. New York: Harper and Row, 1985.

On History. Chicago, IL: University of Chicago Press, 1982.

The Structures of Everyday Life: The Limits of the Possible, vol. 1: *Civilization and Capitalism, Fifteenth–Eighteenth Century*. Trans. Sian Reynolds. New York: Harper and Row, 1981.

Brown, Jeremy. *City versus Countryside in Mao's China*. New York: Cambridge University Press, 2012.

"When Things Go Wrong: Accidents and the Legacy of the Mao Era in Today's China." In *Restless China*, ed. Perry Link, Richard Madsen, and Paul G. Pickowicz. Lanham, MD: Rowan and Littlefield, 2013.

Brown, Kerry. "Chongqing and Bo Xilai: How China Works." *Open Democracy*, August 6, 2012.

Open Democracy. 2012. Online. www.opendemocracy.net.author/kerry-brown

Brownlee, Jason. *Authoritarianism in an Age of Democratization*. New York: Cambridge University Press, 2007.

Brownwell, Susan. *Training the Body for China: Sports in the Moral Order of the People's Republic*. Chicago, IL: University of Chicago Press, 1995.

Buckley, Chris. "China's Internal Security Spending Jumps Past Army Budget." *Reuters*, March 5, 2011 ca.reuters.com; and *Chinh's News*, March 5, 2011.

"Chinese Teachers Oppose CCP." Topix China (posted in China Forum), February 6, 2009.

Bulag, Uradyn E. "Can the Subalterns Not Speak? On the Regime of Oral History in Socialist China." *Inner Asia* (Special Issue on Oral History), Vol. 12, No. 1, 2010.

Cabestan, Jean-Pierre. "Is China Moving Towards Enlightened but Plutocratic Authoritarianism?" *China Perspectives*, Vol. 55, 2004.

Cai, Fang, Yang Du, and Zhao Changbao, "Regional Labor Market Integration since China's WTO Entry: Evidence from Household Level Data." In *China: Linking Markets for Growth*, ed. Ross Garnaut and Ligang Song. Canberra: Australian National University Press, 2007.

Cai, Yongshun. *Collective Resistance in China: Why Popular Protests Succeed or Fail*. Stanford, CA: Stanford University Press, 2010.

"Local Governments and the Suppression of Popular Resistance in China." *China Quarterly*, Vol. 193, March 2008.

Chan, Alfred L. *Mao's Crusade: Politics and Policy Implementation in China's Great Leap Forward*. Oxford: Oxford University Press, 2001.

Chan, Anita. "Boot Camp at the Shoe Factory: Regimented Workers in China's Free Labor Market." *The Washington Post*, November 3, 1996.

"Regimented Workers in China's Free Labor Market: Military Discipline in One of Dongguan's Shoe Factories." *China Perspectives*, Vol. 9, January–February, 1997.

Chan, Anita, Richard Madsen, and Jonathan Unger. *Chen Village*. Berkeley: University of California Press, 1992 (and 2009).

Chan, John. "Beijing Abolishes Centuries-Old Agricultural Tax." World Socialist Web Site (wsw.org), January 17, 2006.

Chan, Kam Wing, and Li Zhang. "The Hukou System and Rural-Urban Migration in China: Processes and Changes." *China Quarterly*, No. 160, 1999.

Chan, Kam Wing, and Will Buckingham. "Is China Abolishing the Hukou System?" *China Quarterly*, No. 195, 2008.

Chan, Minnie. "Abandoned by the Motherland They Served: Families Struggle to Look after PLA Veterans as Rich China Turns Its Back on Military." *South China Morning Post*, March 22, 2010.

Chang, Jung. *Wild Swans: Three Daughters of China*. New York: Simon and Schuster, 1991.

Chao, Kang. *The Construction Industry in Communist China*. Chicago, IL: Aldine Publishing, 1968.

Chen, Da. *Colors of the Mountain*. New York: Anchor, 1999.

Chen, Ling. "Playing the Market Reform Card: The Changing Patterns of Political Struggle in China's Electric Power Sector." *The China Journal*, No. 64, July, 2010.

"Taming the Electric Tiger: The Paradoxical Role of the Chinese State in the Power Sector." Unpublished draft, Department of Political Science, Johns Hopkins University, 2007.

Chen, Nancy N. *Breathing Spaces: Qigong, Psychiatry, and Healing in China.* New York: Columbia University Press, 2003.

Chen, Pi-Chao. "Birth Control Methods and Organization in China." In *China's One-Child Family Policy*, ed. Elizabeth Croll, Delia Davin, and Penny Kane. Basingstoke, UK: Macmillan, 1985.

Chen, Yixin. "The People's Dictatorship against the People: The Criminal Charges during the Great Leap Forward." Paper presented at the annual meeting of the Association for Asian Studies, Chicago, March 26–29, 2009.

Chen Yung-fa. "New Perspectives on the Study of Chinese Culture and Society." Internet source.

Chen, Zhi, ed. "President Xi: Anti-Corruption Efforts Need to Draw on Heritage." *Xinhuanet*, April 20, 2013.

Cheng, Tiejun, and Mark Selden. "The Origins and Consequences of China's Hukou System." *China Quarterly*, No. 139, 1994.

Chin, Ko-lin, and Roy Godson. "China: Beware of Demob: A Reserve Army of Unemployed ex-Servicemen Worries China's Leaders." November 8, 2007. *Economist.com*

"China: Eight Guangdong Public Security Officers on Trial." *Asia/Legal Daily*, January 18, 2013.

"Organized Crime and the Political-Criminal Nexus in China." *Trends in Organized Crime*, Vol. 9, No. 3, Spring 2006.

Christie, Daniel, J., Richard V. Wagner, and Deborah Dunann Winter, eds. *Peace, Conflict and Violence: Peace Psychology for the 21st Century.* Englewood Cliffs, NJ: Prentice Hall, 2011.

Chubb, Judith. *The Mafia and Politics.* Ithaca, NY: Cornell Studies in International Affairs, 1989.

Clark, Nancy L., and William H. Worger. *South Africa: The Rise and Fall of Apartheid.* Harlow, UK: Pearson Education, 2004.

Coale, Ansley J. Concerns Rise over China's Mental Health Problem. Hong Kong: Radio Free Asia, October 12, 2004.

Rapid Population Change in China, 1952–1982. Washington, DC: National Research Council, 1984.

Confucius, and J. Legge, trans. *The Sacred Books of China: The Texts of Confucianism.* Delhi: Motilal Banarsidass, 1966.

Cunningham, Edward A. "Energy Governance: Fueling the Miracle." In *China Today, China Tomorrow: Domestic Politics, Economy, and Society*, ed. Joseph Fewsmith. Lanham, MD: Rowman and Littlefield, 2010.

Damousi, Joy. "Marriage Wars: Memories of Marriage to Australian Returned Servicemen, 1945–1965." Paper presented at the Frontiers of Memory conference, Institute of Education, London, September 19, 1999.

Davin, Delia. "The Single-Child Family Policy in the Countryside." In *China's One-Child Family Policy*, ed. Elisabeth Croll, Delia Davin, and Penny Kane. Basingstoke, UK: Macmillan, 1985.

Davis, Deborah S., and Wang Feng, eds. *Creating Wealth and Poverty in Post-Socialist China.* Stanford, CA: Stanford University Press, 2008.

Davis, Fred. *Yearning for Yesterday: A Sociological Analysis of Nostalgia.* New York: Free Press, 1979.

Davis, Sara Meg. "A System Rotting from the Ground Up." *Asian Wall Street Journal,* February 20, 2006.

Davis, Sara, Christine C. Goettig, and Mike Goettig, "'We Could Disappear at Any Time': Retaliation and Abuses against Chinese Petitioners." *Human Rights Watch,* Vol. 17, No. 11, New York, 2005.

De Bary, William T., and Weiming Tu, eds. *Confucianism and Human Rights.* New York: Columbia University Press, 1998.

De Certeau, Michel. *The Practice of Everyday Life.* Berkeley: University of California Press, 1984; chapter 3, "Making Do."

Deng, Yanhua, and Kevin J. O'Brien. "Relational Repression in China: Using Social Ties to Demobilize Protestors." *China Quarterly,* Vol. 215, September 2013.

Diamant, Neil J. *Embattled Glory: Veterans, Military Families, and the Politics of Patriotism in China, 1949–2007.* Lanham, MD: Rowan and Littlefield, 2009.

"Hollow Glory: The Administration and Conceptualization of Justice for PRC Veterans, 1949–1969." Paper presented at the annual meeting of the Association for Asian Studies, New York, March 27–30, 2003.

"Talking about the Revolution: The Draft Constitutional Discussion of 1954 and Its Implications for Historical Research." University of Pittsburgh Center for International Studies, Asia over Lunch Lecture, January 30, 2014.

Diamond, Jared. *The World until Yesterday: What Can We Learn from Traditional Societies?* New York: Viking, 2012.

Dickson, Bruce J. "Dilemmas of Party Adaptation: The CCP's Strategies of Survival." In *State and Society in Twenty-First Century China: Crisis, Contention, and Legitimation,* ed. Peter Hays Gries and Stanley Rosen. New York: RoutledgeCurzon, 2004.

Dikotter, Frank. *Mao's Great Famine: The History of China's Most Devastating Catastrophe, 1958–62.* London: Bloomsbury, 2010.

"Penology and Reformation in Modern China." In *Crime, Punishment, and Policing in China,* ed. Borge Bakken. Lanham, MD: Rowman and Littlefield, 2005.

Dimitrov, Martin. "Popular Accountability and Autocratic Resilience: Evidence from the Single-Party Communist Regimes in Eastern Europe and China." Unpublished paper, Dartmouth College, April 2009. Online. government.arts.cornell./edu...dimitrov-popular-acc

"The Resilient Authoritarians." *Current History,* January 2008.

Dittmer, Lowell. "China's Global Rise." *America's Quarterly,* Winter 2012.

Divjak, Carol. "Another Angry Protest in China." World Socialist Web Site (wsws.org), July 15, 2015.

Dolot, Miron. *Execution by Hunger: The Hidden Holocaust.* New York: Norton, 1987.

Dower, John W. *War Without Mercy: Race and Power in the Pacific War.* New York: Pantheon, 1986.

Du Quenoy, Paul, and H.B. McCartney. "Alienation of Soldiers: Did Soldiers Who Had Fought at the Front Feel Permanently Alienated from Civilian Culture?" In *History in Dispute,* vol. 8: *World War I,* ed. Dennis Showalter. Detroit, MI: St. James Press, 2002.

Duara, Pransejit. *Culture, Power, and the State: Rural North China, 1900–1942.* Stanford, CA: Stanford University Press, 1988.

Dutton, Michael, and Xu Zhangrun. "A Question of Difference: The Theory and Practice of the Chinese Prison." In *Crime, Punishment, and Policing in China*, ed. Borge Bakken. Lanham, MD: Rowan and Littlefield, 2005.

Ebrey, Patricia Buckley. "Confucian Teachings." In *Chinese Civilization: A Sourcebook*, 2nd rev. ed. Trans. Mark Coyle and Patricia Ebrey. New York: The Free Press, 1993.

Ebrey, Patricia, ed. *Chinese Civilization: A Sourcebook*, 2nd ed. New York: The Free Press, 1993.

Edelen, Kate. "Resource Mismanagement, Climate and Conflict in Syria." *Friends Committee on National Legislation*, January–February 2014. Online. fcnl.org/resources/.../...

Edelman, Murray. *Public Policy and Political Violence*. University of Wisconsin Institute for Research on Poverty Discussion Paper. Madison, 1968.

Edin, Maria. "State Capacity and Local Agent Control in China: CCP Cadre Management from a Township Perspective." *China Quarterly*, Vol. 173, 2003.

Engel, Susan. *Context Is Everything: The Nature of Memory*. New York: W.H. Freeman, 1999.

Erikson, Eric H. *Identity, Youth, and Crisis*. New York: W.W. Norton, 1968.

Evans, Bob. "The End of China's Economic Miracle." *The Wall Street Journal*, November 21, 2014.

Faber, Sebastian. "The Price of Peace: Historical Memory in Post-Franco Spain – A Review Article." Hispanic Institute, Columbia University, 2005.

Fairbank, John King. *The United States and China*. Cambridge, MA: Harvard University Press, 1983.

Fan, Joshua. *China's Homeless Generation: Voices from the Veterans of the Chinese Civil War, 1940s–1990s*. New York: Routledge, 2011.

Fang, Lizhi. "The Real Deng." *New York Review of Books*, November 10, 2011.

Fassin, Didier, and Richard Rechtman. *The Empire of Trauma: An Inquiry into Victimhood*. Princeton, NJ: Princeton University Press, 2009.

Feldman, Allen. "Punition, Retaliation and the Shifting Crises of Social Memory and Legitimacy in Northern Ireland." Paper presented at the Harry Frank Guggenheim Foundation Workshop on Revenge, Madrid, Spain, December 15–17, 1995.

Feng, Shizheng, and Yang Su. "The Making of a Maoist Model in Post-Mao China: The Myth of Nanjie Village." *Communist and Post-Communist Studies*, Vol. 46, 2013.

Feng, Xiaogang (with Zhengyun Liu). *Back to 1942*. China Lion Entertainment, 2012.

Fentress, James. *Rebels and Mafiosi: Death in a Sicilian Landscape*. Ithaca, NY: Cornell University Press, 2000.

Feuchtwang, Stephen. "Reinscriptions: Commemoration and the Transmission of Histories and Memories Under Modern States in Asia and Europe." Working paper, 2000.

Fewsmith, Joseph. *Elite Politics in Contemporary China*. New York: M.E. Sharpe, 2001.

Foer, Joshua. *Moonwalking with Einstein: The Art and Science of Remembering Everything*. New York: Penguin Books, 2011.

Fong, Mei. "China's Quiet Two-Child Experiment," *The Wall Street Journal*, November 13, 2015.

"Former SFDA Chief Executed for Corruption." *China Daily*, July 10, 2007.

Foster, Stephen, Hector Garduno, Richard Evans, Doug Olson, Yuan Tian, Weizhen Zhang, and Zaisheng Han. "Quaternary Aquifer of the North China Plain – Assessing and Achieving Groundwater Resource Sustainability." *Hydrogeology Journal*, Vol. 12, No. 1, 2004.

French, Howard W. "China's Boom Brings Fears of an Electricity Shutdown," *The New York Times*, July 5, 2004.

Friedman, Edward. "China Transformed." *University of Wisconsin Political Science Newsletter*, Fall 2004.

"Deng versus the Peasantry: Recollectivization in the Countryside. *Problems of Communism*, Vol. 39, No. 5, 1990.

"Maoism and the Liberation of the Poor." *World Politics*, Vol. 39, 1987.

National Identity and Democratic Prospects in Socialist China. Armonk, NY: M.E. Sharpe, 1995.

"The Persistent Invisibility of Rural Suffering in China." *Indian Journal of Asian Affairs*, December 2009.

"Post-Deng China's Right-Wing Populist Authoritarian Foreign Policy." In *China Review*, ed. Lau Chung-ming and Tianfa Shen. Hong Kong: China University Press, 2000, 1–26.

"Raising Sheep on Wolf Milk: The Politics and Dangers of Misremembering the Past in China." In *Totalitarian Movements and Political Religions*, June–September 2008.

"Why the Ruling Party in China Won't Lose." In *Political Transitions in Dominant Party Systems: Learning to Lose*, ed. Edward Friedman and Joseph Wong. New York: Routledge, 2008.

Friedman, Edward, and Mark Selden. "War Communism." Yale University Program in Agrarian Studies Colloquium Paper, October 23, 2004.

Friedman, Edward, Paul G. Pickowicz, and Mark Selden. *Chinese Village, Socialist State*. New Haven: Yale University Press, 1991.

Revolution, Resistance, and Reform in Village China. New Haven, CT: Yale University Press, 2005.

Friedman, Thomas L. *Years of Living Dangerously*. Showtime, April 2014.

Friedrich, Carl J. "Corruption Concepts in Historical Perspective." In *Political Corruption: A Handbook*, ed. Arnold J. Hedenheimer, Michael Johnston, and Victor T. Levine. New Brunswick: Transaction, 1990.

Froissart, Chloe. "Book review." (Kevin J. O'Brien and Li Lianjiang, *Rightful Resistance in Rural China*), *China Perspectives*, Vol. 4, 2007. http://chinaperspectives.revues.org/2723.

Fu, Zhengyuan. *Autocratic Tradition and Chinese Politics*. New York: Cambridge University Press, 1993.

Fukuyama, Francis. "Confucianism and Democracy." *Journal of Democracy*, Vol. 6, No. 2, April 1995.

Gallagher, Mary Elizabeth. *Contagious Capitalism: Globalization and the Politics of Labor in China*. Princeton, NJ: Princeton University Press, 2005.

Gambetta, D. "Mafia: The Price of Distrust." In *Trust: Making and Breaking Cooperative Relationships*, ed. D. Gambetta. New York: Basil Blackwell, 1988.

The Origins of Mafias. (Mimeo)Cambridge: Cambridge University Press, 1991.

The Sicilian Mafia: The Business of Protection. Cambridge, MA: Harvard University Press, 1993.

Gan, Nectar. "Retired Generals Point to 'Horrible' Graft in PLA." *South China Morning Post*, July 20, 2015.

Gandhi, Jennifer, and James Vreeland. "Political Institutions and Civil Wars: Unpacking Anocracy." Unpublished paper, August 30, 2004.

Gannett, Robert T. Jr. "Village-by-Village Democracy in China: What Seeds for Freedom?" Commissioned by the American Enterprise Institute, Tocqueville on China Project, April 2009.

Garnaut, Anthony. "The Geography of the Great Leap Famine." *Modern China: An International Quarterly*, Vol. 40, No. 3, 2014.

"The Mass Line on a Massive Famine." *The China Story*, Australian Center on China and the World, Posted, October 8, 2014.

Geeds, Barbara. "Why Parties and Elections in Authoritarian Regimes?" Manuscript, Department of Political Science, UCLA, 2006. Online. Revised version of APSA paper, Washington, D.C., 2005.

Gibney, Frank B. "Nikita Sergeyevich Khrushchev." Encyclopaedia Britannica, online, December 27, 2015.

Gilley, Bruce. *China's Democratic Future: How It Will Happen and Where It Will Lead.* New York: Columbia University Press, 2004.

The Right to Rule: How States Win and Lose Legitimacy. New York: Columbia University Press, 2009.

Goldman, Merle. *From Comrade to Citizen: The Struggle for Political Rights in China.* Cambridge, MA: Harvard University Press, 2007.

Gongyi China: Persons of Modern Times. April 26, 2005.

Gonzales, Laurence. *Deep Survival: Who Lives, Who Dies, and Why.* New York: W.W. Norton, 2003.

Gooch, Elizabeth. "Estimating the Long Term Impact of the Great Famine (1959–1961) on Modern China." Unpublished paper, February 11, 2014.

Goodspeed, Peter. "'Fewer Children – Fewer Burdens': Severe Birth-Control Measures Aim to Curb Demands of Swelling Population." *Toronto Star*, January 11, 1991.

Goodwin, Jeff, James M. Jasper, and Francesca Polletta. "The Return of the Repressed: The Fall and Rise of Emotions in Social Movement Theory." *Mobilization: An International Journal*, Vol. 5, No. 1, 2000.

Greene, Scott. "Can Xi Jinping Really Fight Corruption?" *China Digital Times*, April 4, 2013.

Greenhalgh, Susan. "Controlling Birth and Bodies in Village China." *American Ethnologist*, Vol. 21, No. 1, 1994.

"The Evolution of the One-Child Policy in Shanxi." *China Quarterly*, Vol. 122, 1990.

"Governing Chinese Life: From Sovereignty to Biopolitical Governance." In *Governance of Life in Chinese Moral Experience*, ed. Zhang, Kleinman, and Tu. New York: Routledge, 2011.

Just One Child: Science and Policy in Deng's China. Berkeley: University of California Press, 2008.

Greenhalgh, Susan, and Edwin A. Winckler. *Governing China's Population: From Leninist to Neoliberal Biopolitics.* Stanford, CA: Stanford University Press, 2005.

Greenhalgh, Susan, Zhu Chushu, and Li Nan. "Restraining Population Gorwth in Three Chinese Villages, 1988–93." *Population and Development Review*, Vol. 20, No. 2, 1994.

Gries, Peter Hays, and Stanley Rosen, eds. *State and Society in 21st-Century China: Crisis, Contention, and Legitimation*. New York: RoutledgeCurzon, 2004.

Guang, Lei. "Guerrilla Workfare: Migrant Renovators, State Power, and Informal Work in Urban China." *Politics and Society*, Vol. 33, No. 3, September 2005.

Guha, Ranajit. *Elementary Aspects of Peasant Insurgency in Colonial India*. Durham, NC: Duke University Press, 1999.

Guldin, Gregroy Eliyu, ed. *Farewell to Peasant China: Rural Urbanization and Social Change in the Late Twentieth Century*. New York: M.E. Sharpe, 1997.

Guo, Baogang. "Political Legitimacy and China's Transition." *Journal of Chinese Political Science*, Vol. 18, Nos. 1 and 2, Fall 2003.

Guo, Xiezhi. *China's Security State: Philosophy, Evolution, and Politics*. New York: Cambridge University Press, 2012.

Gupta, Akhil. "Blurred Boundaries: The Discourse of Corruption, the Culture of Politics, and the Imagined State." *American Ethonologist*, Vol. 22, No. 2, 1995.

Hall, Anthony. "Patron-Client Relations: Concepts and Terms." In *Friends, Followers, and Factions*, ed. Steffen W. Schmidt et al. Berkeley: University of California Press, 1977.

Hamber, Brandon, and Richard Wilson. "Symbolic Closure through Memory, Reparation and Revenge in Post-Conflict Societies." *Journal of Human Rights*, Vol. 1, No. 1, March 2002.

Han, Dongping. *The Unknown Cultural Revolution: Educational Reforms and Their Impact on China's Rural Development*. New York: Garland, 2001.

Hann, Christopher. "The Idiocy of Decollectivization." Yale University Agrarian Studies Program Colloquium Paper, 2011–2012.

Hannum, Emily C., and Jennifer Adams. "Beyond Cost: Rural Perspectives on Barriers to Education." Gansu Survey of Children and Family Papers, University of Pennsylvania, 2008.

Hanson, Stephen E. *Post-Imperial Democracies: Ideology and Party Formation in Third Republic France, Weimar Germany, and Post-Soviet Russia*. New York: Cambridge University Press, 2010.

Harding, Harry. *China's Second Revolution: Reform after Mao*. Washington, DC: Brookings, 1987.

Hardy, Julia. "Afterlife and Salvation." Patheos Religious Library, June 11, 2012. Online. www.patheos.com

Harmel, Robert, and Yao-Yuan Yeh. "Corruption and Government Satisfaction in Authoritarian Regimes: The Case of China." Paper presented at the Annual Meeting of the American Political Science Association, Seattle, September 1–4, 2011.

Harrell, Stevan, and Jonathan N. Lipman, eds. *Violence in China*. Albany: State University of New York Press, 1990.

He Qinglian. "The Relationship between Chinese Peasants' Right to Subsistence and China's Social Stability." Trans. J. Latourelle. *Human Rights in China*. April 1, 2009. Online.

Heidenheimer, Arnold J. "Perspectives on the Perception of Corruption." In Arnold J. Heidenheimer, Michael Johnston, and Victor T. Levine, eds. *Political Corruption: A Handbook*. New Brunswick: Transaction, 1990.

Heidenheimer, Arnold J., Michael Johnston, and Victor T. Levine, eds. *Political Corruption: A Handbook*. New Brunswick: Transaction, 1990.

Henochowicz, Anne. "Machine Guns: Not Just for Soldiers Anymore." *China Digital Times*, June 28, 2012.

Hershatter, Gail. *The Gender of Memory: Rural Women and China's Collective Past.*
    Berkeley: University of California Press, 2011.
    "State of the Field: Women in China's Long Twentieth Century." *Journal of Asian
    Studies*, Vol. 63, No. 4, November 2004.
Hess, Henner. *Mafia and Mafiosi: The Structure of Power.* Trans. Ewald Osers. Lexing-
    ton, MA: Lexington Books, 1973.
Hillman, Ben. "Factions and Spoils: Examining Political Behavior within the Local State
    in China." *The China Journal*, No. 64, July 2010.
Hilton, Rodney. *Bond Men Made Free.* New York: Viking, 1973.
Hinnebusch, Raymon. "Syria: From 'Authoritarian Upgrading' to Revolution." *Inter-
    national Affairs*, Vol. 88, 2012.
Hobsbawm, E. J. *Primitive Rebels.* Manchester: Manchester University Press, 1959.
Holbig, Heike, and Bruce Gilley. "Reclaiming Legitimacy in China." *Politics and Policy*,
    Vol. 38, No. 3, 2010.
Hornsby, Robert. *Protest, Reform, and Repression in the Soviet Union.* New York:
    Cambridge University Press, 2013.
Howell, Jude, ed. *Governance in China.* Lanham, MD: Rowman and Littlefield, 2004.
Hu Jintao. "Corruption Could Be 'Fatal' to Party." *China Digital Times*, 11/11, 2012.
    "Corruption Could Be 'Fatal' to Party." *China Digital Times*, 11/11, 2012.
Huang, Philip C.C. *The Peasant Economy and Social Change in North China.* Stanford,
    CA: Stanford University Press, 1985.
Huang, Wenguang. *The Little Red Guard: A Family Memoir.* New York: Riverhead/
    Penguin, 2012.
Huang, Yasheng. *Capitalism with Chinese Characteristics.* New York: Cambridge
    University Press, 2008.
Hudson, Eric. "The Poppy vs. the Pension: Treatment and Remembrance in Interwar
    Germany and Britain." *Primary Source: The Indiana University Undergraduate
    Journal of History*, Vol. 2, Issue 1, Fall 2011; 27–32.
Hung, Ho-fung. *Protest with Chinese Characteristics: Demonstrations, Riots, and Petitions
    in the Mid-Qing Dynasty.* New York: Columbia University Press, 2011.
Hurst, William. "Mass Frames and Worker Protest." In *Popular Protest in China*, ed. Kevin
    J. O'Brien. Cambridge, MA: Harvard Contemporary China Series, 15, 2008.
Jacques, Martin. *When China Rules the World: The End of the Western World and the
    Birth of a New Global Order*, 2nd ed. New York: Penguin, 2012.
James, Aaron. *Assholes: A Theory.* New York: Random House, 2012.
Jing, Jun. *The Temple of Memories: Power and Morality in a Chinese Village.* Stanford,
    CA: Stanford University Press, 1996.
Johnson, Chalmers. *Peasant Nationalist and Communist Power: The Emergence of
    Revolutionary China.* Stanford, CA: Stanford University Press, 1962.
Johnson, Ian. *Wild Grass: Three Stories of Change in Modern China.* New York:
    Pantheon, 2004.
Johnson, Kay Ann. "The Politics of Infant Abandonment." Unpublished manuscript,
    2011–2012.
Karklins, Ramsa. "Anti-Corruption Incentives and Constituencies in the Post-
    Communist Region." Paper for Workshop I: Creating a Trustworthy State,
    Collegium Budapest, craft, September 2001.
    "Typology of Post-Communist Corruption." *Problems of Post-Communism*, Vol. 49,
    No. 4, July–August, 2002.
Kelliher, Daniel. *Peasant Power in China*, New Haven, CT: Yale University Press, 1992.

Kennedy, John James. "The Face of 'Grassroots Democracy' in Rural China: Real versus Cosmetic Elections." *Asian Survey*, Vol. 42, No. 3, May–June 2002.

"Rural China: Reform and Resistance." In *Politics in China*, ed. William A. Joseph. Oxford: Oxford University Press, 2010.

Key, V. O. "Techniques of Political Graft." In *Political Corruption: A Handbook*, ed. Arnold J. Heidenheimer, Michael Johnston, and Victor T. Levine. New Brunswick, NJ: Transaction, 1990.

King, David. "Book review." (Eric Schickler, *Disjointed Pluralism*), *American Political Science Review. September*, 2002.

Kipnis, Andrew, and Shanfeng Li. "Is Chinese Education Underfunded?" *China Quarterly*, Vol. 202, June 2010.

Kleinman, Arthur. *Deep China: The Moral Life of the Person – What Anthropology and Psychology Tell Us about China Today*. Berkeley: University of California Press, 2011.

"How Bodies Remember: Social Memory and Bodily Experiences of Criticism, Resistance, and Delegitimization Following China's Cultural Revolution." *New Literary History*, Vol. 25, Summer 1994.

Kleinman, Arthur, and Joan Kleinman. "The Appeal of Experience." Daedalus, Vol. 125, No. 1, Social Suffering, Winter 1996.

Kleinman, Arthur, Veena Das, and Margaret M. Lock. *Social Suffering*. Berkeley: University of California Press, 1997.

Klitgaard, Robert. *Controlling Corruption*. Berkeley: University of California Press, 1987.

Knight, John, Terry Sicular, and Xue Ximing. "Educational Inequality in China: The Intergenerational Dimension." November 10, 2010. Online.

Kopstein, Jeffrey. "Chipping Away at the State: Workers' Resistance and the Demise of East Germany." *World Politics*, Vol. 48, 1996.

Ku, Hok Bun. *Moral Politics in a South Chinese Village: Responsibility, Reciprocity, and Resistance*. New York: Rowman and Littlefield, 2003.

Kuhn, Anthony. "Beijing Wary of Rising Tide of Veterans' Discontent." NPR, July 29, 2010.

Kuhn, Philip. *Origins of the Modern Chinese State*. Stanford, CA: Stanford University Press, 2002.

Kwong, Julia. *Chinese Education in Transition: Prelude to the Cultural Revolution*. Montreal: McGill-Queens University Press, 1979.

The Political Economy of Corruption in China. Armonk, NY: M.E. Sharpe, 1997.

Laliberté, André, and Marc Lanteigne, eds. *The Chinese Party-State in the 21st Century: Adaptation and the Reinvention of Legitimacy*. London and New York: Routledge, 2008.

Lande, Carl. *Leaders, Factions, and Parties: The Structure of Philippine Politics*. New Haven, CT: Yale University Press, 1965.

Landry, Pierre F. *Decentralized Authoritarianism in China: The Communist Party's Control of Local Elites in the Post-Mao Era*. Cambridge: Cambridge University Press, 2008.

Lane, Robert E. *Political Thinking and Political Consciousness*. New Haven, CT: Markham, 1969.

Lardy, Nicholas. *Agriculture in China's Modern Economic Development*. New York: Cambridge University Press, 1983.

Lary, Diana. *Chinese Migrations: The Movement of People, Goods, and Ideas over Four Millennia*. Lanham, MD.: Rowman and Littlefield, 2012.

LeDoux, Joseph. "Emotion, Memory, and the Brain." *Scientific American*, Vol. 270, June 1994.

The Emotional Brain: The Mysterious Underpinnings of Emotional Life. New York: Simon and Schuster, 1996.

The Synaptic Self: How Our Brains Become Who We Are. New York: Viking, 2002.

Lee, Ching Kwan. *Against the Law: Labor Protest in China's Rustbelt and Sunbelt*. (Berkeley: University of California Press), 2007.

Lee, Lily Hsiao Hung, and A. D. Stefanowska, eds. *Biographical Dictionary of Chinese Women: The Twentieth Century, 1912–2000*. New York: M.E. Sharpe, 2003.

Lee Sing and Arthur Kleinman. "Suicide as Resistance in Chinese Society." In *Chinese Society: Change, Conflict and Resistance*, ed. Elizabeth J. Perry and Mark Selden. New York: Routledge, 2000.

Lemos, Gerard. *The End of the Chinese Dream: Why Chinese People Fear the Future*. New Haven: Yale University Press, 2012.

Levitsky, Steven, and Lucan A. Way. *Competitive Authoritarianism: Hybird Regimes after the Cold War*. New York: Cambridge University Press, 2010.

"The Rise of Competitive Authoritarianism." *Journal of Democracy*, Vol. 13, No. 2, April 2002.

Levy, Richard. "Corruption in Popular Culture." In Perry Link, Richard Madsen, and Paul Pickowicz, eds., *Popular Culture: Unofficial Culture in a Globalizing Society*. Lanham, MD: Rowman and Littlefield, 2002.

Lewis, John Wilson. "Memory, Opportunity, and Strategy in Peasant Revolutions: The Case of North China." Paper presented at the Research Conference on Communist Revolutions, Carleton Beach Hotel, St. Croix, V.I., January 24–28, 1973.

Lewis, Mark Edward. *Writing and Authority in Early China*. Albany: State University of New York Press, 1999.

Li, Cheng. "The End of the CCP's Resilient Authoritarianism? A Tripartite Assessment of Shifting Power in China." *China Quarterly*, Vol. 211, September 2012.

Li, Lianjiang. "Elections and Popular Resistance in Rural China." *China Information*, Vol. 15, No. 2, 2001.

"The Magnitude and Resilience of Trust in the Center: Evidence from Interviews with Petitioners in Beijing and a Local Survey in Rural China." *Modern China: An International Quarterly*, Vol. 39, No. 1, 2013.

"Political Trust and Petitioning in the Chinese Countryside." *Comparative Politics*, Vol. 40, No. 2, 2008.

"Political Trust in Rural China." *Modern China: An International Quarterly*, Vol. 30, No. 2, 2004.

"Li Peng's Son Implicated in Massacre of Shengyou Farmers," AsianNews.it June 23, 2005.

Li Peng D. Confidential Harvard University source.

Liang, Jing. "From Ruling by Rhetoric to Ruling by Secret Police." Trans. David Kelly. *China Digital Times*, February 5, 2010.

Lieberthal, Kenneth G. "Introduction: The 'Fragmented Authoritarianism' Model and Its Limitations." In *Bureaucracy, Policy, and Decision Making in Post-Mao China*, ed. Kenneth G. Lieberthal and David M. Lampton. Berkeley: University of California Press, 1992.

Lieberthal, Kenneth, and Michel Oksenberg. *Policy Making in China: Leaders, Structures, and Processes.* Princeton, NJ: Princeton University Press, 1988.

Lim, Benjamin Kam. "China Veterans Stage 2,000-Strong Protest." *Reuters*, April 16, 2005. www.China Post.com.

"2,000 Retired Servicemen Stage Protests in Beijing." *The Seattle Times*, April 16, 2005.

Lim, Louisa. "China's New Leaders Inherit Country at Crossroads." National Public Radio, *All Things Considered*, October 30, 2012.

Lin, Justin Yifu. "Rural Reforms and Agricultural Growth in China." *American Economic Review*, Vol. 82, No. 1, 1992.

Lin, Justin Yifu, Tao Ran, Liu Mingxing, and Tang Qi. "The Problem of Taxing Peasants in China." Unpublished preliminary draft paper, June 2002.

Link, Perry. "China's Core Problem." 1990. Reprinted in *China in Transformation*, ed. Tu Wei-ming. Cambridge, MA: Harvard University Press, 1994.

"Popular Chinese Views of Official Corruption." August, 2007. aeipaper.doc.

Link, Perry, Richard Madsen, and Paul G. Pickowicz, ed., *Restless China*. Lanham, MD: Rowman and Littlefield, 2013.

Lippit, Victor D. "The Great Leap Forward Reconsidered." *Modern China: An International Quarterly*, Vol. 1, No. 1, January 1975.

Liu, Allen P. *Mass Politics in the People's Republic: State and Society in Contemporary China.* Boulder, CO: Westview, 1996.

"The Politics of Corruption in the People's Republic of China." In *Political Corruption: A Handbook*, ed. Arnold J. Heidenheimer, Michael Johnston, and Victor T. Levine. New Brunswick, NJ: Transaction, 1990.

Liu Bai. *The Wushan Governor's Murder.* Trans. Madeleine Ross and Fang Li. Probe International (online). January 1, 2010.

Liu, Denggao. "Suicide Rates Called Crisis for Rural Young People." *Beijing Xinhua Net*, November, 2003.

Liu Xin. *In One's Own Shadow: An Ethnographic Account of the Condition of Post-Reform Rural China.* Berkeley: University of California Press, 2000.

Liu Yawei. "Statement in Roundtable on Village Elections in China." Congressional Executive Commission on China, July 8, 2002.

Lorge, Peter. *Chinese Martial Arts: From Antiquity to the Twenty-First Century.* New York: Cambridge University Press, 2012.

Lu, Huilin. Lecture with film. Brandeis University, East Asian Colloquium, March 2012.

Lu, Huilin, and Pu Ngai. "Unfinished Proletarianization: Self, Anger, and Class Action among the Second Generation of Peasant Workers in Present-Day China." *Modern China: An International Quarterly*, Vol. 36, 2010.

Lu, Xiaobo. *Cadres and Corruption: The Organizational Involution of the Chinese Communist Party.* Stanford, CA: Stanford University Press, 2000.

Luehrmann, Laura M. "Facing Citizen Complaints in China, 1951–1996." *Asian Survey*, Vol. 43, No. 5, September–October 2003.

"Officials Face the Masses: Citizen Contacting in Modern China." PhD thesis, Department of Political Science, Ohio State University, 2000.

Lupo, Salvaore. *History of the Mafia.* Trans. Antony Shugaar. New York: Columbia University Press, 2009.

Mackinnon, Mark. "Is China Finally Confronting Its Dark History? *The Globe and Mail.* May 28, 2012.

MacFarquhar, Roderick. *The Origins of the Cultural Revolution*, vol. 2: *The Great Leap Forward.* New York: Columbia University Press, 1983.

Mallee, Hein. "Migration, Hukou and Resistance in Reform China." In *Chinese Society: Change, Conflict and Resistance*, ed. Elizabeth J. Perry and Mark Selden. New York: Routledge, 2000.

Manion, Melanie. *Corruption by Design: Building Clean Government in Mainland China and Hong Kong.* Cambridge, MA: Harvard University Press, 2004.

"Democracy, Community, Trust: The Impact of Elections in Rural China." *Comparative Political Studies*, Vol. 39, 2006.

"The Electoral Connection in the Chinese Countryside." *American Political Science Review*, Vol. 90, No. 4, December 1996.

"Issues in Corruption in Post-Mao China." *Issues and Studies*, Vol. 34, No. 9, 1998.

Mann, Michael. *The Sources of Social Power*, vol. 2: *The Rise of Classes and Nation-States, 1760–1914.* New York: Cambridge University Press, 1993.

Mao, Yushi. "Lessons from China's Great Famine." *The Cato Journal*, Vol. 34, No. 3, Fall 2014.

Markoff, John. *Waves of Democracy: Social Movements and Political Change.* Thousand Oaks, CA: Pine Forge Press, 1996.

Mauer, Mark, and Tracy Huling. "Young Black Americans and the Criminal Justice System: Five Years Later." *The Sentencing Project*, October 1995.

McLean, Stuart. *The Event and Its Terrors: Ireland, Famine, Modernity.* Stanford, CA: Stanford University Press, 2004.

Meisner, Maurice. *Mao's China and After: A History of the People's Republic*, 3rd ed. New York: Free Press, 1999.

Michelson, Ethan. "Climbing the Dispute Pagoda: Grievances and Appeals to the Official Justice System in Rural China." *American Sociological Review*, Vol. 72, June 2007.

Miles, James. *The Legacy of Tiananmen: China in Disarray.* Ann Arbor: University of Michigan Press, 1997.

Milwertz, Cecilila Nathansen. *Accepting Population Control: Urban Women and the One-Child Policy.* Richmond, UK: Curzon, 1997.

Minzner, Carl F. "Riots and Cover-Ups: Counterproductive Control of Local Agents in China." *The University of Pennsylvania Journal of Law*, Vol. 31, 2009.

"Social Instability in China: Causes, Consequences, and Implications." In *The China Balance Sheet in 2007 and Beyond.* Center for Strategic and International Studies, April, 2007. Accessed January 9, 2013. Online.

"Xinfang: An Alternative to Formal Chinese Legal Institutions." *Stanford Journal of International Law*, Vol. 103, 2006.

Moore, Barrington Jr. *Social Origins of Dictatorship and Democracy: Lord and Peasant in the Making of the Modern World.* Boston: Beacon, 1966.

Political Power and Social Theory. New York: Harper and Row, 1962.

Morash, Christopher. "Making Memories: The Literature of the Irish Famine." In *The Meaning of Famine*, ed. Patrick O'Sullivan. London: Leicester University Press, 1997.

Morris, Andrew D. *Marrow of the Nation: A History of Sport and Physical Culture.* Berkeley: University of California Press, 2004.

Morris, James P., Nancy K. Squires, Charles S. Taber, and Milton Lodge. "The Automatic Activation of Political Attitudes: A Psychophysiological Examination of the Hot Cognition Hypothesis." State University of New York at Stony Brook. ND. Online. Later published in *Political Psychology*, Vol. 24, No. 4, December 2003.

Motyl, Alexander J. "Deleting the Holodomor: Ukraine Unmakes Itself." *World Affairs Journal*, September/October 2010. Online.

Mulvenon, James. "So Crooked they Have to Screw their Pants On," *China Leadership Monitor*, No. 19, Fall, 2006. Online. www.hoover.org/.../so-crooked-they-have-screw-their

Nathan, Andrew J. "Authoritarian Resilience." *Journal of Democracy*, Vol. 14, No. 1, January 2003.

Chinese Democracy. Berkeley: University of California Press, 1985.

"Political Culture and Diffuse Regime Support in Asia." Working Paper Series No. 43, Asian Barometer Project Office, National Taiwan University and Academic Sinica, 2007 (and GLOBALBAROMETER).

Naughton, Barry. "The Assertive Center: Beijing Moves against Local Government Control of Land." *China Leadership Monitor*, No. 20, February 2007.

The Chinese Economy: Transitions and Growth. Cambridge: MIT Press, 2007.

"Claiming Profit for the State: SASAC and the Capital Management Budget." *China Leadership Monitor*, No. 18, Spring 2006.

Nee, Victor. "Peasant Household Individualism." In *Chinese Rural Development: The Great Transformation*, ed. William L. Parish. New York: M.E. Sharpe, 1985.

Netting, Robert McC. *Smallholders, Householders: Farm Families and the Ecology of Intensive, Sustainable Agriculture.* Stanford, CA: Stanford University Press, 1993.

Ngan, Tak-Hin Benjamin. "Crystallization of Cadres' Working Style." Unpublished paper, Politics 148, Brandeis University, Fall 2002.

Ni, Ching-Ching. "Mao's Utopia Made Real." *The Standard, Sing Tao Newspaper*, January 22–23, 2005.

North, Douglass C. "A Transaction Cost Theory of Politics." *Journal of Theoretical Politics*, Vol. 2, No. 4, 1990.

Institutions, Institutional Change, and Economic Performance. Cambridge: Cambridge University Press, 1990.

North, Douglass C., John J. Wallis, and Barry Weingast. *Violence and Social Orders: A Conceptual Framework for Interpreting Recorded Human History.* New York: Cambridge University Press, 2009.

O'Brien, Kevin J. "Implementing Political Reform in China's Villages." *Australian Journal of Chinese Affairs*, No. 32, July 1994.

"Neither Transgressive nor Contained: Boundary-Spanning Contention in China." In *State and Society in Twenty-First-Century China*, ed. Peter Hayes Gries and Stanley Rosen. New York: RoutledgeCurzon, 2004.

Popular Protest in China. Cambridge, MA.: Harvard University Press (Harvard Contemporary China Series, 15), 2008.

"Rightful Resistance." *World Politics*, Vol. 49, no. 1, October 1996.

O'Brien, Kevin J., and Lianjiang Li. "Accommodating 'Democracy' in a One-Party State: Introducing Village Elections in China." *China Quarterly*, Vol. 162, June 2000.

"Campaign Nostalgia in the Chinese Countryside." *Asian Survey*, Vol. 39, No. 3, May–June 1999.

"The Politics of Lodging Complaints in Rural China." *China Quarterly*, Vol. 143, September 1995.

Rightful Resistance in Rural China. Cambridge: Cambridge University Press, 2006.

"Villagers and Popular Resistance in Contemporary China." *Modern China: An International Quarterly*, Vol. 22, No. 1, January 1996; 28–61.

O'Brien, Kevin J., Lianjiang Li, and Mingxing Liu. "Petitioning Beijing: The High Tide of 2003–2006." *China Quarterly*, 2011.

O'Brien, Kevin J., and William Hurst. "China's Contentious Pensioners." *China Quarterly*, No. 70, June 2002.

Ogden, Suzanne. *Inklings of Democracy in China.* Cambridge, MA: Harvard University Asia Center, 2002.

Ó Gráda, Cormac. *Black '47 and Beyond: The Great Irish Famine in History, Economy, and Memory.* Princeton, NJ: Princeton University Press, 1999.

"Famine, Trauma and Memory." *Bealoideas*, Vol. 69, 2001.

Oi, Jean C. "Market Reforms and Corruption in Rural China." *Studies in Comparative Communism*, Vol. 22, Nos. 2–3, Summer 1989.

Rural China Takes Off: Institutional Foundations of Economic Reform. Berkeley: University of California Press, 1999.

State and Peasant in Contemporary China: The Political Economy of Village Government. Berkeley: University of California Press, 1989.

"Two Decades of Rural Reform in China: An Overview and Assessment." *China Quarterly*, Vol. 159 (1999).

"One Year of My Blood: Exploitation of Migrant Construction Workers in Beijing." *Human Rights Watch*, March 28, Vol. 20, No. 3, 2008.

Orlik, Tom. "Unrest Grows as Economy Booms." *The Wall Street Journal*, September 26, 2011. Online. www.wsj.com/.../sb10001424053119037036o...

Osnos, Evan. "Corruption Nation: Why Bo Xilai Matters." *The New Yorker*, April 16, 2013.

Oster, Shai. "President Xi's Anti-Corruption Campaign Biggest since Mao." *Bloomberg News*, March 4, 2014.

Pan Jiahua, Peng Wuyang, Li Men, et al. "Rural Electrification in China 1950–2004: Historical Processes and Key Driving Forces." Working Paper No. 60, Stanford Program on Energy and Sustainable Development, December 2006.

Pan, Philip P. "A Trip through China's Twilight Zone: One Woman's Quest for Truth in the Authoritarian Maze." *Washington Post Foreign Service*, December 18, 2004.

"Chinese Peasants Attacked in Land Dispute." *Washington Post Foreign Service*, June 15, 2004.

Pantsov, Alexander V., and Steven I. Levine. *Mao: The Untold Story.* New York: Simon and Schuster, 2013.

Parris, Kristen. "The Rise of Private Business Interests." In *The Paradox of Post-Mao Reforms*, ed. Merle Goldman and Roderick Macfarquhar. Cambridge, MA: Harvard University Press, 1999.

Pastor, Robert A. "The Centrality of Elections: A Global Overview." In "Elections after the End of History," special issue, *New Perspectives Quarterly*, Vol. 13, No. 4, Fall 1996.

Peh Shing Huei. "Corruption: 'Princelings' Rule China's Corporate World." *Straits Times*, July 25, 2009.

Pei, Minxin. "China's Governance Crisis." *Foreign Affairs*, September–October 2002.

    China's Trapped Transition: The Limits of Developmental Autocracy. Cambridge: Harvard University Press, 2006.

    "Corruption Threatens China's Future." *Carnegie Endowment Policy Brief* 55, October 2007.

    "Creeping Democratization in China." *Journal of Democracy*, Vol. 6, No. 4, October 1995.

    "The Long March against Graft." *Financial Times*, December 10, 2002.

    "The Myth of Chinese Meritocracy." *Project Syndicate*, May 14, 2012.

    "Rotten from Within: Decentralized Predation and Incapacitated State." In *The Nation State in Question*, ed. T.V. Paul, G. John Ikenberry, and John A. Halll. Princeton, NJ: Princeton University Press, 2003.

    Talk at Dartmouth College, Fall 2008.

Peng, Xizhe. "Demographic Consequences of the Great Leap Forward in China's Provinces." *Population and Development Review*, Vol. 13, No. 4, December 1987.

Perloff, James. "Holodomor: The Secret Holocaust in the Ukraine." *New American*, February 5, 2009. Online. www.thenewamerican.com/.../4656-holodomor-the-secret-holocaust

Perry, Elizabeth J. "Chinese Conceptions of 'Rights': From Mencius to Mao – and Now." *Perspectives on Politics*, Vol. 6, No. 1, March 2008.

    "Crime, Corruption, and Contention." In *The Paradox of China's Post-Mao Reforms*, ed. Merle Goldman and Roderick MacFarquhar. Cambridge, MA: Harvard University Press, 1999.

    "Cultural Governance in Contemporary China: 'Re-orienting' Party Propaganda." Harvard-Yengching Institute Working Paper Series, 2013.

    "From Mass Campaigns to Managed Campaigns." In *Mao's Invisible Hand: The Political Foundations of Adaptive Governance*, ed. Sebastian Heilmann and Elizabeth J. Perry. Cambridge, MA: Harvard University Press, 2011.

    "The Illiberal Challenge of Authoritarian China." *Taiwan Journal of Democracy*, Vol. 18, No. 2, December 2010.

    "Permanent Rebellion: Continuities and Discontinuities in Chinese Protest." In *Popular Protest in China*, ed. Kevin J. O'Brien. Cambridge, MA: Harvard University Press, 2008.

    Rebels and Revolutionaries in North China, 1845–1945. Stanford, CA: Stanford University Press, 1980.

    "Rural Collective Violence: The Fruits of Recent Reforms." In *The Political Economy of Reform in Post-Mao China*, ed. Elizabeth J. Perry and Christine Wong. Cambridge, MA: Harvard University Press, 1985.

    "Rural Violence in Socialist China." *China Quarterly*, No. 103, September 1985.

    "To Rebel Is Justified: Cultural Revolution Influences on Contemporary Chinese Protest." In *The Chinese Cultural Revolution Reconsidered: Beyond Purge and Holocaust*, ed. Kam Yee Law. New York: Palgrave-Macmillan, 2003.

"'To Rebel Is Justified': Maoist Influences on Popular Protest in Contemporary China." Paper presented at the Colloquium Series of the Yale University Program in Agrarian Studies, November 17, 1995.

Perry, Elizabeth J., and Mark Selden. "Introduction: Reform and Resistance in Contemporary China." In *Chinese Society: Change, Conflict, and Resistance*, ed. Elizabeth J. Perry and Mark Selden. London: Routledge, 2000.

  eds. *Chinese Society: Change, Conflict, and Resistance*. London: Routledge, 2000.

Peterson, Abby. *Contemporary Political Protest: Essays on Political Militancy*. Burlington, VT: Ashgate, 2001.

Peterson, Glen. *The Power of Words: Literacy and Revolution in South China, 1949–95*. Vancouver: University of British Columbia Press, 1997.

  "State Literacy Ideologies and the Transformation of Rural China." *Australian Journal of Chinese Affairs*, No. 32, July 1994.

Philipsen, Sanne, and Romie Frederic Littrell. "Manufacturing Quality and Cultural Values in China." *Asia Pacific Journal of Business Management*, Vol. 2, 2001.

Phillips, Michael R., Xianyun Li, and Yanping Zhang. "Suicide Rates in China, 1995–1999." *The Lancet*, Vol. 359, No. 9309, March 9, 2002.

Pianciola, Niccolo. "Kazakhstan and the Geography of the Soviet Famine of 1931–33: A Basis for Comparison." Paper presented at the conference on "Communism and Hunger," Holodomor Research and Education Consortium, CIUS, at the University of Toronto, September 26–27, 2014.

Pierson, Paul. *Politics in Time: History, Institutions, and Social Analysis*. Princeton, NJ: Princeton University Press, 2004.

Pitt-Rivers, Julian. *The People of the Sierra*. Chicago, IL: University of Chicago Press, 1969.

Pomeranz, Kenneth. *The Making of a Hinterland: State, Society and Economy in Inland North China, 1853–1937*. Berkeley: University of California Press, 1993.

Pu, Ngai, and Lu Huilin. "A Culture of Violence: The Labor Subcontracting System and Collective Action by Construction Workers in Post-Socialist China." *China Journal*, No. 64, July 2010.

Qian, Yangyi. "The Process of China's Market Transition, 1978–1998." In *China's Deep Reform*, ed. Lowell Dittmer and Guoli Liu. Lanham, MD.: Rowman and Littlefield, 2006.

Qin Hui. "China's Economic Miracle and the Threat of Future Shock." *Human Rights in China*, No. 4, 2005.

  "Tax and Fee Reform, Village Autonomy, and Central and Local Finance." In *Chinese Economy*, Vol. 38, No. 6, 2005.

Qin Shao. "Bridge under Water: The Dilemma of the Chinese Petition System." *China Currents*, Vol. 7, No. 1, Winter 2008.

Qiu, Jane. "China Faces Up to Groundwater Crisis." *Nature: International Weekly Journal of Science*, Vol. 466, No. 308. Published online July 13, 2010.

Qiu Xiaolong, *Death of a Red Heroine*. New York: Soho Press, 2000.

Qu, Lily. "New Army Regulations Underscore the Plight of the Chinese Army." *China-scope*, October 2005.

Reardon, David C. "Abortion Is Four Times Deadlier Than Childbirth." *Post-Abortion Review*, Vol. 8, No. 2, April–June 2000.

Reid, Donald. "Towards a Social History of Suffering: Dignity, Misery and Disrespect." Review article. *Social History*, Vol. 27, No. 3, 2002.

Richter, Melvin. "Tocqueville's Contributions to the Theory of Revolution." In *Revolution, Nomos VIII*, ed. Carl J. Friedrich. New York: Atherton Press, 1966.

Robben, Antonius C.G.M. "How Traumatized Societies Remember: The Aftermath of Argentina's Dirty War." *Cultural Critique*, Winter 2005.

Rocca, Jean-Louis. "Corruption and Its Shadow: An Anthropological View of Corruption in China." *China Quarterly*, No. 130, June 1992.

Rosen, Stanley. "The State of Youth/Youth and the State in Early Twenty-First-Century China: The Triumph of the Urban Rich?" In *State and Society in Twenty-First-Century China: Crisis, Contention, and Legitimation*, ed. Peter Hayes Gries and Stanley Rosen. New York: RoutledgeCurzon, 2004.

Ruf, Gregory. *Cadres and Kin: Making of a Socialist Village in West China, 1921–1991*. Stanford, CA: Stanford University Press, 1998.

Russell, Jenna. "A World of Misery Left by Bullying." *Boston Globe*, November 28, 2010.

Sabean, David Warren. *Power in the Blood: Popular Culture and Village Discourse in Modern Germany*. Cambridge: Cambridge University Press, 1984.

Saich, Tony. "Chinese Governance Seen through the People's Eyes." *East Asia Forum*, July 24, 2011.

"Citizen Perceptions of Governance in Rural and Urban China." *Journal of Chinese Political Science*, Vol. 12, No. 1, April 2007.

Sapio, Flora. *Sovereign Power and the Law in China*. Leiden: Brill, 2010.

Schacter, Daniel L. *The Seven Sins of Memory: How the Mind Forgets and Remembers*. New York: Houghton Mifflin, 2001.

Schiavenza, Matt. "Why Xi Jinping's Anti-Corruption Campaign Is Hollow, Unserious, and Ultimately Doomed." *The Atlantic Archive.com/china/archive*, March 7, 2013. Also see www.theatlantic.com/.../why-xi...anti-corruption-campaign-i...

Schickler, Eric. *Disjointed Pluarlism: Institutional Innovation and the Development of the U.S. Congress*. Princeton, NJ: Princeton University Press, 2001.

Schiller, Bill. "China's Public Enemy No. 1 Built a Cartel, Beat the System, and Moved to Canada." *Inside the Star.com*, November 29, 2009.

Scoggins, Suzanne E., and Kevin J. O'Brien. "China's Unhappy Police." Unpublished paper, Department of Political Science, University of California-Berkeley, December 8, 2014. Forthcoming in *Asian Survey*.

Scott, James C. *Comparative Political Corruption*. Englewood Cliffs, NJ: Prentice Hall, 1972.

Domination and the Arts of Resistance: Hidden Transcripts. New Haven, CT: Yale University Press, 1990.

"Hegemony and the Peasantry." *Politics and Society*, Vol. 7, No. 3, 1977.

"James Scott on Agriculture as Politics, the Dangers of Standardization and Not Being Governed." *Theory Talks*, no. 38, May 15, 2010. Online at www.theory-talks.org/2010/05/theory-talk-38.html.

"The Moral Economy as an Argument and as a Fight." In *Moral Economy and Popular Protest: Crowds, Conflict and Authority*, ed. Adrian Randall and Andrew Charlesworth. New York: St. Martin's Press, 2000.

The Moral Economy of the Peasant: Rebellion and Subsistence in Southeast Asia. New Haven, CT: Yale University Press, 1976.

"Patron-Client Politics and Political Change in Southeast Asia." *The American Political Science Review*, Vol. 66, No. 1, March 1972.

Seeing like a State: How Certain Schemes to Improve the Human Condition Have Failed. New Haven, CT: Yale University Press, 1998.

Weapons of the Weak. New Haven, CT: Yale University Press, 1985.

Sebag-Montefiore, Clarissa. "The Great Silence in China," *Latitude*, (in The New York Times, November 30, 2012).

Sen, Amartya. *Development as Freedom*. Oxford: Oxford University Press, 1999.

The Idea of Justice. Cambridge: Harvard University Press, 2009.

Sewell, William H., Jr. "Space in Contentious Politics." In *Silence and Voice in the Study of Contentious Politics*, ed. Ronald R. Aminzade. Cambridge: Cambridge University Press, 2001.

Shambaugh, David. "The Coming Chinese Crackup." *The Wall Street Journal*, March 6, 2015.

Shank, Megan. "China's Female Suicide Mystery." *The Daily Beast*, June 16, 2010. Online. www.thedailybeast.com/.../chinese-women-suicide-and-k...

Sharping, Thomas. *Birth Control in China, 1949–2000: Population Policy and Demographic Development*. London: RoutledgeCurzon, 2003.

Shelley, Louise I. *Policing Soviet Society: The Evolution of State Control*. London: Routledge, 1996.

Sheridan, Michael. "Review of Wild Grass." *Sunday-Times Books*, July 19, 2005.

Shi Nai'nan and Luo Guozhong. *All Men Are Brothers (Shuihuzhuan)*. Trans. Pearl S. Buck. Kingston, RI: Moyer Bell, 2006.

Shi, Tianjian. "Cultural Values and Political Trust: A Comparison of the People's Republic of China and Taiwan." *Comparative Politics*, Vol. 33, No. 4, 2001.

Shih, Chih-Yu. "The Decline of a Moral Regime: China's Great Leap Forward in Retrospect." *Comparative Political Studies*, Vol. 27, No. 2, 1994.

Shih, Victor, Christopher Adolph, and Mingxing Liu. "Getting Ahead in the Communist Party: Explaining Advancement of Central Committee Members in China." *American Political Science Review*, Vol. 106, No. 1, February 2012.

Shirk, Susan L. *China – Fragile Superpower: How China's Internal Politics Could Derail Its Peaceful Rise*. New York: Oxford University Press, 2008.

Shue, Vivienne. "Legitimacy Crisis in China?" In *State and Society in Twenty-First-Century China: Crisis, Contention and Legitimation*, ed. Peter Hayes Gries and Stanley Rosen. New York: RoutledgeCurzon, 2004.

The Reach of the State: Sketches of the Chinese Body Politic. Stanford, CA: Stanford University Press, 1988.

Shvarts, Alexander. "Rational Mafia: The Explanatory Power of Rational Choice Theory." *International Review of Modern Sociology*, Vol. 30, No. 1, Fall 2002.

Sicular, Terry, Xue Ximing, Bjorn A. Gustafsson, and Li Shi. "How Large Is China's Rural-Urban Income Gap?" In *One Country, Two Societies: Rural-Urban Inequality in Contemporary China*, ed. Martin King Whyte. Cambridge: Harvard University Press, 2010.

Sicular, Terry, Yue Xinming, Bjorn Gustafsson, and Li Shi. "The Urban-Rural Income Gap and Inequality in China." *The Review of Income and Wealth*, Vol. 53, Issue 1, March 2007 (published online February 28, 2007).

Skinner, G. William. "Chinese Peasants and the Closed Community: An Open and Shut Case." *Comparative Studies in Society and History*, Vol. 13, No. 3, 1971.

"Marketing and Social Structure in Rural China." *Journal of Asian Studies*, Vol. 24, Parts 1–3, 1964–1965.

Smil, V. "China's Food." *Scientific American*, Vol. 253, No. 6, 1985.

Snyder, Timothy. *Bloodlands: Europe between Hitler and Stalin*. New York: Basic Books, 2010.

Solinger, Dorothy J. "China's Floating Population." In *The Paradox of Post-Mao Reforms*, Merle Goldman and Roderick MacFarquhar. Cambridge, MA: Harvard University Press (Harvard Contemporary China Series 12), 1999.

Contesting Citizenship in Urban China. Berkeley: University of California Press, 1999.

"The New Crowd of the Dispossessed: The Shift of the Urban Proletariat from Master to Mendicant." In *State and Society in 21st-Century China: Crisis, Contention, and Legitimation*, ed. Peter Hays Gries and Stanley Rosen. New York: Routledge-Curzon, 2004.

Southwick, Steven, and Dennis S. Charney. *Resilience: The Science of Mastering Life's Greatest Challenges*. New York: Cambridge University Press, 2012.

Steinmueller, Hans. "Communities of Complicity: Notes on State Formation and Local Society in Rural China." *American Ethnologist*, Vol. 37, No. 3, 2010.

Stott, Rebecca. *Ghostwalk*. New York: Spiegel and Grau, 2007.

Su, Yang. *Collective Killings in Rural China during the Cultural Revolution*. New York: Cambridge University Press, 2011.

Su, Yang, and Xin He. "Street as Courtroom: State Accommodation of Labor Protest in South China." *The Law and Society Review*, Vol. 44, No. 1, 2010.

Subrahmanyan, Divya. "Feldman Examines Corruption and Political Legitimacy in China." March 11, 2013. Reporting on a February 6, 2013, talk by Harvard Law School Professor Noah Feldman, sponsored by the Harvard Law and International Development Society.

Sullivan, Lawrence R. "The Chinese Communist Party and the Beijing Massacre: The Crisis in Authority." In *China in the Nineties: Crisis Management and Beyond*, ed. David S. G. Goodman and Gerald Segal. New York: Oxford University Press, 1992.

Sun, Yan. *Corruption and Market in Contemporary China*. Ithaca, NY: Cornell University Press, 2004.

Swider, Sarah. "Behind Great Walls: Tolerated Illegal Migration and the Construction Industry." PhD thesis, Department of Sociology, University of Wisconsin-Madison, 2008.

"The Sydney Globalist Meets Kerry Brown." *Sydney Globalist*, April 3, 2013.

"Syria's Civil War Has Environmental Origins." *Global Risk Insights*, September 2013. Online. globalriskinsights.com/2013/...syrias-civil-war-has-environmental-origins...

Takeuchi, Hiroki. *Tax Reform in Rural China: Revenue, Resistance, and Authoritarian Rule*. New York: Cambridge University Press, 2014.

Tan, Ariel. "Anti-Corruption Sweep Targets Hundreds of Domestic Security Officials in China." *The Epoch Times*, February 17, 2013.

Tanner, Harold M. *Strike Hard! Anti-Crime Campaigns and Chinese Criminal Justice,*
1979–1985. Ithaca, NY: Cornell University Press, 1999.
Tanner, Murray Scot. "Campaign-Style Policing in China and Its Critics." In *Crime,*
Punishment, and Policing in China, ed. Borge Bakken. Lanham, MD: Rowman and
Littlefield, 2005.
  "State Coercion and the Balance of Awe: The 1983–1986 'Stern Blows' Anti-Crime
  Campaign." *The China Journal,* No. 44, July 2000.
  "Torture in China." Testimony to U.S.-Executive Commission on China, July 26, 2002.
Tarrow, Sidney. "The New Contentious Politics in China: Poor and Blank or Rich and
  Complex?" In *Popular Protest in China,* ed. Kevin J. O'Brien. Cambridge, MA:
  Harvard University Press, 2008.
Tatlow, Didi Kristen. "The Enduring Legacy of China's Great Famine." IHT *Rendez-*
vous, September 5, 2012.
Teng Bao. "A Hole to Bury You In." *The Wall Street Journal,* December 28, 2010.
Thaxton, Ralph A. Jr. *Catastrophe and Contention in Rural China: Mao's Great Leap*
Forward Famine and the Origins of Righteous Resistance in Da Fo Village.
  Cambridge: Cambridge University Press, 2008.
  "How the Great Leap Forward Ended in Rural China: 'Administrative Intervention'
  vs. Peasant Resistance." In *Eating Bitterness: New Perspectives on China's Great*
Leap Forward and Famine, ed. Kimberley Ens Manning and Felix Wemheuer.
  Vancouver: University of British Columbia Press, 2011.
  ISA Paper, 2002.
  Salt of the Earth: The Political Origins of Peasant Protest and Communist Revolution
in China. Berkeley: University of California Press, 1997.
Thelen, Kathleen. "How Institutions Evolve: Insights from Comparative Historical Analy-
  sis." In *Comparative Historical Analysis in the Social Sciences,* ed. James Mahoney and
  Dietrich Rueschemeyer. Cambridge: Cambridge University Press, 2003.
Thompson, Leonard M. *A History of South Africa.* New Haven, CT: Yale University
  Press, 2001.
Thompson, Paul. *The Voice of the Past: Oral History.* New York: Oxford University
  Press, 2000.
Thomson Reuters Foundation. *Factsheet on the World's Most Dangerous Countries for*
Women. Trustlaw, June 15, 2011. Online.
Thornton, Patricia. "Comrades and Collectives in Arms: Tax Resistance, Evasion and
  Avoidance Strategies in the Post-Mao Era." Paper prepared for the annual meeting
  of the Association for Asian Studies, 2002.
  "Comrades and Collectives in Arms: Tax Resistance, Evasion, and Avoidance Strat-
  egies in Post-Mao China." In *State and Society in 21st-Century China,* ed. Peter
  Hayes Gries and Stanley Rosen. New York: RoutledgeCurzon, 2004.
Thurow, Lester. "The Emergence of China and the Global Economy." Talk at the MIT
  Sloan School of Management, June 5, 2004. MIT-Tech TV, online. techTV.mit.edu/
  search?q///search...
Thurston, Anne F. *Enemies of the People.* New York: Alfred A. Knopf, 1987.
  Muddling toward Democracy: Political Change in Grassroots China. Washington,
  DC: U.S. Institute of Peace, 1998.
Tian, Qunjian. "Agrarian Crisis, WTO Entry, and Institutional Change in Rural
  China." *Issues and Studies,* Vol. 40, No. 2, June 2004.

Tilly, Charles. *The Contentious French*. Cambridge, MA: Harvard University Press, 1986.
 "Contentious Repertoires in Great Britain, 1758–1834." In *Repertoires and Cycles of Collective Action*, ed. Mark Traugott. Durham, NC: Duke University Press, 1995.
 From Mobilization to Revolution. Reading, MA: Addison-Wesley, 1978.
 Introduction to Block, *The Mafia of a Sicilian Village, 1860–1960*.
Tilly, Charles, and Sidney Tarrow. *Contentious Politics*. Boulder, CO: Paradigm, 2007.
Tomich, Dale. "The Order of Historical Time: Fernand Braudel and Italian Microstoria." In *The Longue Duree and World Systems Analysis*, ed. Richard F. Lee. Albany: SUNY Press, 2012.
Tong, Yanqi. *Transitions from State Socialism: Economic and Political Change in Hungary and China*. Lanham, MD: Rowman and Littlefield, 1997.
Traven, B. *Government*. Chicago, IL: Ivan R. Dee, 1971.
Treat, John Whittier. "Choosing to Collaborate: Yi Kwang-su and the Moral Subject in Colonial Korea." *Journal of Asian Studies*, Vol. 71, No. 1, February 2012.
Trevaskes, Susan. *Policing Serious Crime in China: From "Strike Hard" to "Kill Fewer."* London: Routledge, 2010.
 "Yanda 2001: Form and Strategy in a Chinese Anti-Crime Campaign." *The Australian and New Zealand Journal of Criminology*, Vol. 36, No. 3, 2003.
Tsang, Steve. "Consultative Leninism: China's New Political Framework." *Journal of Contemporary China*, Vol. 18, No. 62, November 10, 2009.
Tsou Tang. *The Cultural Revolution and the Post-Mao Reforms*. Chicago, IL: University of Chicago Press, 1986.
Tulving, Endel. "Episodic Memory: From Mind to Brain." *Annual Review of Psychology*, Vol. 53, 2002; 1–25.
Turner, Bryan S. *The Body and Society*. London: Sage, 1996.
Unger, Jonathan. "China's Conservative Middle Class." *Far Eastern Economic Review*, April 2006. Reprinted in *Capturing the Year 2006: Writings of the ANU College of Asia and the Pacific*, ed. Barbara Nelson and Robin Jeffrey. Canberra: Australia.
 "Review Article: State and Peasant in Post-Revolution China." *Journal of Peasant Studies*, Vol. 17, No. 1, October 1989.
 The Transformation of Rural China. Armonk, NY: M.E. Sharpe, 2002.
"Up to 2,000 Retired Soldiers Protest in Central Beijing." *Agence France Presse*, April 13, 2005.
Uslaner, Eric M., and Daniel Jordan Smith. "Critical Dialogue." *Perspectives on Politics*, Vol. 8, No. 4, December 2010.
Van Luyn, Floris-Jan. *A City of Floating Peasants: The Great Migration in Contemporary China*. Trans. Jeannette K. Ringold. New York: New Press, 2006.
Van Slyke, Lyman P. *Enemies and Friends: The United Front in Chinese Communist History*. Stanford, CA: Stanford University Press, 1987.
Van Wyk, Barry. "Survey of China's 24 Most Corrupt Officials." *Danwei*, January 29, 2013.
Vaughan, Mary Kay. *Cultural Politics in Revolution*. Tuscon, AZ.: University of Arizona Press, 1997.
"Veterans in Pension Protest Rounded Up–Police Break Up ex-Servicemen's Rally as PLA Marks is 78th Anniversary." *South China Morning Post*, August 2, 2005.
Vogel, Ezra F. *Deng Xiaoping and the Transformation of China*. Cambridge, MA: Belknap Press of Harvard University Press, 2011.
Volkov, Vadim. *Violent Entrepreneurs: The Use of Force in the Making of Russian Capitalism*. Ithaca, NY: Cornell University Press, 2002.
Wade, Rex A. *The Russian Revolution, 1917*. New York: Cambridge University Press, 2000.

Wang, Feiling. "Reformed Migration Control and New Targeted People: China's *Hukou* System in the 2000s." *China Quarterly*, Vol. 177, March 2004.

"Renovating the Great Flood Gate: The Reform of China's Hukou System." In *One Country, Two Societies: Rural-Urban Inequality in Contemporary China*, ed. Martin King Whyte. Cambridge: Harvard University Press, 2010.

Wang Feng. *Boundaries and Categories: Rising Inequality in Post-Socialist China.* Stanford, CA: Stanford University Press, 2008.

Wang Feng and Yang Su. "How Resilient China's Regime Is and Why: A State Capacity Perspective." Paper presented at the conference "1989: Twenty Years After," University of California-Irvine, November 5–8, 2009.

Wang, Feng, Yong Cai, and Bao Chang Gu. "Population, Policy and Politics: How Will History Judge China's One-Child Policy?" *Brookings Paper*, February 2013 (also in *Population and Development Review* (Supplement), 2012).

Wang Wei. "Call to Scrap 'Zero Petitions' Target." China.org.CN, March 16, 2009.

Wang Xiaoguang, and Angang Hu. *The Chinese Economy in Crisis: State Capacity and Tax Reform.* New York: M.E. Sharpe, 2001.

Wang Yanni. "An Introduction to the ABCs of Communization: A Case Study of Macheng County." In *Eating Bitterness: New Perspectives on China's Great Leap Forward and Famine*, ed. Kimberely Ens Manning and Felix Wemheuer. Vancouver: University of British Columbia Press, 2011.

Wasserstrom, Jeffrey N. "Reading China." *Boston Review*, February 16, 2005.

"Water: All Dried Up." *The Economist*, October 12, 2013.

Watson, James L. "Feeding the Revolution: Public Mess Halls and Coercive Commensality in Maoist China." In *Governance of Life in Chinese Moral Experience: The Quest for an Adequate Life*, ed. Everett Zhang, Arthur Kleinman, and Tu Weiming. New York: Routledge, 2011.

Wedeman, Andrew. *Double Paradox: Rapid Growth and Rising Corruption in China.* Ithaca, NY: Cornell University Press, 2012.

"Eight Questions: Andrew Wedeman, China's Corruption Paradox." *China Realtime*, March 26, 2013.

"Looters, Rent-Scrappers and Dividend-Collectors: Corruption and Growth in Zaire, South Korea, and the Philippines." *The Journal of Developing Areas*, Vol. 31, No. 4, 1997.

Weigelin-Schwiedrzik, Susanne. "Taking the Heat Out of a Problem: Party Historiography and Traumatic Experiences in Modern Chinese History." Paper presented at the Annual Meeting of the Association for Asian Studies, Boston, March 1999.

"Trauma and Memory: The Case of the Great Famine in the People's Republic of China, 1959–1961." *Historiography: East and West*, Vol. 1, No. 1, 2003.

Wemheuer, Felix. "Dealing with Responsibility for the Great Leap Famine." *The China Quarterly*, Vol. 201, March 16, 2010.

Famine Politics in Maoist China and the Soviet Union. New Haven, CT: Yale University Press, 2014.

"'The Grain Problem Is an Ideological Problem': Discourses of Hunger in the 1957 Socialist Education Campaign." In *Eating Bitterness: New Perspectives on China's Great Leap Forward and Famine*, ed. Kimberley Ens Manning and Felix Wemheuer. Vancouver: University of British Columbia Press, 2011.

"Stone Noodles: Rural Memories of the 'Great Leap Famine' in Henan Province (1958–61)." Paper presented at the annual meeting of the Association for Asian Studies, San Francisco, April 6–9, 2006.

White, Tyrene. *China's Longest Campaign: Birth Planning in the People's Republic of China, 1949–2005.* Ithaca, NY: Cornell University Press, 2006.

"Domination, Resistance and Accommodation in China's One-Child Campaign." In *Chinese Society: Change, Conflict and Resistance*, ed. Elizabeth J. Perry and Mark Selden. London: Routledge, 2000.

"Policy Case Study: Population." In *Politics in China: An Introduction*, ed. William A. Joseph. New York: Oxford University Press, 2010.

Presentation at the Brandeis University East Asian Studies Colloquium, April 30, 2004.

"Reforming the Countryside: Rebuilding Grassroots Institutions." *Current History*, Vol. 91, No. 566, September 1992.

"Village Elections: Democracy from the Bottom Up?" *Current History*, Vol. 97, September 1998.

Whiting, Susan. "The Cadre Evaluation System at the Grassroots: The Paradox of Party Rule." In *Holding China Together: Diversity and National Integration in the Post-Deng Era*, ed. Barry J. Naughton and Dali L. Yang. New York: Cambridge University Press, 2004.

Whyte, Martin King, Wang Feng, and Yong Cai. "Challenging Myths about China's One-Child Policy," *The China Journal*, No. 74, 2015.

Whyte, Martin King, ed. *One Country, Two Societies: Rural-Urban Inequality in Contemporary China*. Cambridge, MA.: Harvard University Press (Harvard Contemporary China Series, 16), 2010.

Myth of the Social Volcano: Perceptions of Inequality and Distributive Justice in Contemporary China. Stanford, CA: Stanford University Press, 2010.

"Views of Chinese Citizens on Current Inequalities: Rising Anger or General Acceptance?" Paper/talk given at Brandeis University, December 2007, and paper presented at the Third World Forum on China Studies, Shanghai, September 8–9, 2008.

Wirtschafter, Elise Kimerling. "Social Misfits: Veterans and Soldiers' Families in Servile Russia." *Journal of Military History*, Vol. 59, No. 2, April 1995; 215–235.

Wolf, Eric R. "Aspects of Group Relations in a Complex Society." In *Peasant Societies*, ed. Teodor Shanin. Baltimore, MD: Penguin, 1971.

"Kinship, Friendship, and Patron-Client Relations." In *The Social Anthropology of Complex Societies*, ed. Michael Banton. London: Tavistock, 1966.

Wolin, Sheldon S. *Politics and Vision: Continuity and Innovation in Western Political Thought*. Boston: Little, Brown, 1960.

Wong, R. Bin. *China Transformed: Historical China and the Limits of the European Experience*. Ithaca, NY: Cornell University Press, 1997.

"Taxing Transformations: Some Fiscal Features of Chinese States Past and Present." *Etudes Chinoises*, 2005. Online at www.afec-etudeschinoises.com.

Worden, Nigel. *The Making of Modern South Africa: Conquest, Segregation, and Apartheid*. Oxford, UK: Blackwell, 2000.

Wright, Daniel B. *The Promise of the Revolution: Stories of Fulfillment and Struggle in China's Hinterland*. Lanham, MD: Rowman and Littlefield, 2003.

Wright, Teresa. *Accepting Authoritarianism: State-Society Relations in China's Reform Era*. Stanford, CA: Stanford University Press, 2010.

Xi Chen. "Collective Petitioning and Institutional Conversion." In *Popular Protest in China*, ed. Kevin J. O'Brien. Cambridge, MA: Harvard University Press, 2008.

   Social Protest and Contentious Authoritarianism in China. New York: Cambridge University Press, 2012.

Xiang Biao. "Migration and Health in China: Problems, Obstacles and Solutions." *Asian Metacenter Research Paper Series*, No. 17, National University of Singapore, 2003.

Xiang, Lanxin. "The Bo Xilai Affair and China's Future." *Survival: Global Politics and Strategy*, Vol. 54, No. 3, June–July 2012.

Xiezhi Guo, *China's Security State: Philosophy, Evolution, and Politics*. New York: Cambridge University Press, 2012.

Xu Wang. *Mutual Empowerment of State and Peasantry: Village Self-Government in Rural China*. New York: Nova Science, 2003.

   "Review Article: Mutual Empowerment of State and Society: Its Nature, Conditions, Mechanisms, and Limits." *Comparative Politics*, Vol. 31, No. 2, January 1999.

Xu, Yi-Chong. "A Powerhouse Reform: Conversion from the Ministry of Electricity Power to the State Power Corporation." *Australian Journal of Political Science*, Vol. 36, No. 1, 2001.

Xu Youyu. "Erecting a Tombstone for 36 Million Famine Victims." *China Perspectives*, No. 1, 2009.

Yang, Dali. *Calamity and Reform in China: Rural Society and Institutional Change since the Great Leap Famine*. Stanford, CA: Stanford University Press, 1996.

   Remaking the Chinese Leviathan: Market Transition and the Politics of Governance. Stanford, CA: Stanford University Press, 2004.

Yang, Guobin. "China's Zhiqing Generation: Nostalgia, Identity, and Cultural Resistance in the 1990s." *Modern China*, Vol. 29, No. 3, 2003.

Yang Jisheng. *Tombstone: The Great Chinese Famine: 1958–1962*. New York: Farrar, Strauss and Giroux, 2012.

Yang Lian. "Dark Side of the Chinese Moon." *New Left Review*, Vol. 32, March–April 2005.

Yang, Min and Xieying, "Birth of the One Child Policy," *NewsChina Magazine*, December 10, 2010.

Yates, Francis A. *The Art of Memory*. Chicago, IL: University of Chicago Press, 1974.

Yeh, Emily T., and Jonna I. Lewis. "State Power and the Logic of Reform in China's Electricity Sector." *Pacific Affairs*, Vol. 77, No. 3, Fall 2004.

Yip, Winnie. "Disparities in Health Care and Health Status: The Rural-Urban Gap and Beyond," in Whyte, ed., *One Country, Two Societies: Rural-Urban Inequality in Comtemporary China*. Cambridge, MA.: Harvard University Press (Harvard Contemporary China Series, 16), 2010.

Yu, Jianrong. "Conflict in the Countryside: Emerging Political Awareness of the Peasants." *China Perspectives*, Vol. 3, 2007. Also in *Social Research*, Vol. 73, Spring 2006.

   "Maintaining a Baseline Social Stability" (Part 2). *China Digital Times*, March 8, 2010.

   "Social Conflict in Rural China." *WSI China Security*, Vol. 3, No. 2, Spring 2007.

Yu, Jianrong, and Minxin Pei. "Seeking Justice: Is China's Petition System Broken?" Presentation at the Carnegie Endowment for International Peace, April 5, 2006.

Yu, Verna. "Reform Unlikely Says China Expert Roderick MacFarquhar." *South China Morning Post*, October 31, 2012.

Zhai, Keith, and Minnie Chan. "Officials Go Undergound." *South China Morning Post*, March 27, 2013.

Zhan, Jing Vivian. "Decentralizing China: Analysis of Central Strategies in China's Fiscal Reforms." *Journal of Contemporary China*, Vol. 18, 2009.

Zhang, Everett, Arthur Kleinman, and Weiming Tu, eds. *Governance of Life in Chinese Moral Experience: The Quest for an Adequate Life.* New York: Routledge, 2011.

Zhao Ling. "Rural-Urban Labor Migration in Industralization and Urbanization – A Case Study of Hu Kou System and Nong Min Gong in China." Graduate School of International Development, Nagoya University. June 27, 2010. Online. www2 .gsid.nagoya-u.ac.jp/blog/anda/files/2010/06/27-zhao-ling.pdf

Zhao Shukai. "Report from the Field: Criminality and the Policing of Migrant Workers." Trans. Andrew Kipnis. *The China Journal*, Vol. 43, 2000.

Zhao, Xudong, and Duran Bell. "Destroying the Remembered and Recovering the Forgotten in *Chai*: Between Traditionalism and Modernity in Beijing." *China Information*, Vol. 19, No. 3.

Zhao, Zhong. "Rural Urban Migration in China: What We Know and What We Need to Know." Revised draft, July 2003. Online source.

Zhou, Kate Xiao. *How the Farmers Changed China: Power of the People.* Boulder, CO: Westview, 1996.

Zhou Xun. *Forgotten Voices of Mao's Great Famine, 1958–1962: An Oral History.* New Haven, CT: Yale University Press, 2013.

ed. *The Great Famine in China, 1958–1962.* New Haven, CT: Yale University Press, 2012.

Zhu Na, trans. "The New Must-Have Accessory for China's Corrupt Economic Elite." *Economic Observer*, February 20, 2013.

Zweig, David. *Freeing China's Farmers: Rural Restructuring in the Reform Era.* Armonk, NY: M.E. Sharpe, 1997.

Index

Books in the Series (*continued from p.iii*)